Autobiographies
by
Americans of Color
1995-2000

Autobiographies
by
Americans of Color
1995-2000:

An Annotated Bibliography

Deborah Stuhr Iwabuchi
&
Rebecca Stuhr

Library of Congress Control Number 2002106775

ISBN 0-87875-540-3

Printed in the United States of America

Dedication

To Manna and Hikari,
the two Americans of color at my house.
D. I.

To my children Helen and Martin,
and to my nieces and nephews,
Philip Jr., Manna, Julian, Hikari and Victoria.
I'm counting on you to make the world a better place!
R. S.

Contents

Acknowledgements

First and foremost, my thanks go to my co-author and sister, Rebecca, who invited me to participate in this project and gave me the opportunity to work with and learn from her professionally. Not only was it great to work with her so "closely" from such a distance, but it gave my life an entirely new facet. I would like to thank Amazon.com, Amazon.co.jp, my local broadband provider, and many other Internet sources. The advances in communications and on-line services were what made it possible for me to work on this book from Japan. Not all booksellers will ship overseas, and my thanks go to my parents for serving as the U.S. addressee and then sending the books on to me, after an initial preview. Our parents have always been our biggest supporters, and we look forward to (and depend on) seeing our various publications lovingly lined up on the coffee table on our visits home. I extend my appreciation to Barbara and Russell Tabbert who agreed to read through our manuscript on relatively short notice when we had loved it to the point where we couldn't edit it anymore, and Grinnell College which provided a grant for that purpose. I would also like to thank my husband, Ikuo, my daughters, and best friend Pamela who were involuntary but not unwilling participants in a project that the Japanese might describe as "endoresu (endless)."

D. I.
Maebashi, Japan

I too will begin my acknowledgements by thanking my co-author, Deborah. Deborah was a patient and careful editor of the first annotated bibliography (1980-1994) and was even more patient and careful as a co-author. Deborah moved to Japan while I was still in college. It was a wonderful experience for me to work so closely with her when we live so far apart. My heartfelt thanks go to Christopher McKee, the director of the Grinnell College Libraries for supporting me in this endeavor, and to my wonderful colleagues in the library for their interest in and support of my project. Special thanks go to Leslie Gardner, library assistant for interlibrary loan, who in fewer than three months fulfilled somewhere around 200 interlibrary loan requests for me (I wasn't counting but I did go over my limit!). I thank Grinnell College for my semester sabbatical during the fall of 2001 and for the generous grant from the college's Committee for the Support of Faculty Scholarship that allowed Deborah and me to take advantage of the exceptional editing skills of Barbara and Russell Tabbert of Grinnell, Iowa. I thank my mother and father, Barbara and Walter Stuhr, who have set an example for me both through what they have expressed and through their work and volunteer activities. In both small and large ways my parents have sought to bring about positive change to their community and the larger American society. I'd like to thank my friend Mark for listening to me describe many of the books as I read them, for showing continued interest in this project, proof reading excerpts, and for offering moral support whenever I needed it. Finally, I want to thank my children, Helen and Martin who are always a source of inspiration for me and who were patient and understanding at all of the right times. Helen deserves extra special thanks for carefully checking all of our bibliographic citations against OCLC's Worldcat database.

R. S.
Grinnell College
Grinnell, Iowa

Introduction to the 1980-1994 Volume

This introduction by Rebecca Stuhr was written for the first book in this series, Autobiographies by Americans of Color 1980-1994. *While the actual works cited in it are not in this particular book, the comments on methodology, ethnic/racial terms, and the significance of autobiographical work fully apply, and thus it is reprinted here. A new introduction on the characteristics of this current work is included following.*

The past twenty-five years have seen a steady increase in the writing of autobiography. The number of autobiographies included in this bibliography which were published during the first five years of the 1990s is exactly twice the number of autobiographies included which were published during the first five years of the 1980s (220 vs. 110). This growing number of personal stories made public encompasses a rich diversity of cultures, personalities, motivations, and, of course, experiences. There has been some scholarly discussion of what constitutes autobiography, and I believe the definition is wide open. Philippe Lejeune writes in "The Autobiographical Contract" that a work can be called an autobiography if the author of the work, the narrator, and the subject of the work all have the same name, and if the author claims to be telling the truth. He defines autobiography to be "a retrospective prose narrative produced by a real person concerning his own existence, focusing on his individual life, in particular on the development of his personality" (p. 193). Lynn Z. Bloom includes partial and full-length self portraits, dual portraits, group histories, diaries, letters, oral histories, collections of personal narratives, slave narratives, accounts of particular events, and blends of fiction, myth, and personal narrative (p. 171) among the kinds of literature that she would categorize as autobiography in her article "American Autobiography: The Changing Critical Canon." James Olney, in his book *Metaphors of Self,* includes poetry as a permissible genre for autobiography, and presents an extensive discussion of the autobiographical nature of T. S. Eliot's *Four Quartets.*

I have not applied a strict definition of autobiography in this compilation, and the term may seem to have been liberally applied in some instances. I did not include autobiographical fiction, but some works border on the fictional, such as Ray Young Bear's *Black Eagle Child,* Maxine Hong Kingston's *The Woman Warrior,* and Oscar Zeta Acosta's *Autobiography of a Brown Buffalo* and *Revolt of the Cockroach People.* Some of the books included are non-autobiographical collections of essays critiquing some aspect of society, but they nonetheless provide insight into the workings of the mind of the author. Some examples of this type of book are Richard Rodriguez' *Days of Obligation: An Argument With My Mexican Father,* Pat Mora's *Nepantla: Essays From the Land in the Middle,* Nikki Giovanni's *Racism 101,* and Patricia Williams' *The Alchemy of Race and Right.* A few of the works are family histories, focusing on parents, children, or siblings, but including the experiences, impressions, and feelings of the author. The works of internationally recognized writers and unknown individuals whose autobiographies may be their first and perhaps their only written work, oral testimonies instigated by the subject or by a third party, and "as told to" or "written with" works by celebrities or other socially prominent people are all included in this bibliography. I have excluded straight interviews, theses and dissertations, and unpublished materials such as typescripts. Also excluded are journal articles or isolated autobiographical chapters (the entries for Lucille Clifton and Haunani-Kay Trask might be considered exceptions to this policy). As one last detail, I will point out that there were 20 or so books that I was unable to locate, and these have been left unannotated.

Although this book aims at a comprehensive presentation of material published since 1980, I have, no doubt, overlooked some books. The autobiographies of sports stars and other high-profile celebrities, for example, may have been missed. Because of their renown, these individuals have transcended society's need (or perhaps merely that of the Library of Congress) to categorize citizens by race, and so their works are more difficult to track down. There are a number of idiosyncrasies in this compilation surrounding the limitation of dates. It is easy enough to select a cut off date (although it is tempting to include the autobiographies published during 1995), but it is difficult to define a clear starting date. The overall goal of this bibliography is to serve as a practical tool: it should establish the existence of this material and gather it together at one access point; it should also enable the reader to obtain as many of these books as possible either from book stores or libraries. A number of these autobiographies were written in the nineteenth century. Some were published at that time and only reprinted for the first time after 1980, whereas some were never published until after 1980. The peruser of this bibliography will find citations for books that were published in the decades preceding 1980, but which have been republished within the defined time frame, sometimes with new material or revisions. For the most part, however, I have not annotated this category of older books. Many of them will have been annotated in one of the several important bibliographies that should be consulted along with this one: Russell Brignano's *Black Americans in Autobiography*, David Brumble's *An Annotated Bibliography of American Indian and Eskimo Autobiographies*, Lynn Woods O'Brien's *Plains Indians Autobiographies*, and Briscoe, et al., *American Autobiography, 1945-1980.*

The entries are arranged alphabetically by author, except in one or two instances. Ethnic identification is provided by the index. Authors who are members of tribal groups are indexed by tribe and by the terms "Native American," or "Native Alaskan." "Chicano-Chicana" is used for American-born authors of Mexican descent. Writers born in Mexico are indexed under "Mexican American." In a few cases, because it seemed as though this is what the writer would wish, "Hispanic" has been used. Although it sounds awkward, and I apologize for this, writers from India have been indexed by the phrase "East Indian American" or "East Indian."

The appropriateness of autobiography as a genre for individuals who view themselves as, or are regarded as being, outside of the western European writing tradition has been explored by a number of theorists. David Brumble discusses this issue as it relates to the oral tradition of most Native American tribal groups in his book *American Indian Autobiography*. He examines specific examples of types of stories which he would describe as autobiographical in nature even if they do not conform to what is considered to be the western autobiographical tradition, and, therefore, finds that autobiography is a natural means of expression for Native Americans.

Frank Chin, in his provocative article, "This is Not an Autobiography," argues that autobiography is an inappropriate form for American writers of Chinese descent. He identifies autobiography with the Christian confessional tradition as exemplified by St. Augustine, and sees no place for Chinese American writers within this tradition.

Susanna Egan makes a powerful case for the power of autobiography as a survival tool for members of marginalized groups, including racial minorities, women, the working class, and gay and lesbian individuals. In her article, "The Changing Faces of Heroism," she describes the typical autobiography of an earlier era typified in the United States by the autobiographies of Ben Franklin, Henry Adams, and Henry David Thoreau. These men wrote toward the end of their lives when their reputations and value to society were already established. They were members of the ruling class. They assumed themselves to be the inheritors, as well as the conduits of a rich cultural heritage, a heritage which, without doubt, would be shared by their readers. In contrast, the new autobiographer, as described by Egan, does not come from the elite. According to Egan, "we now find literary talent and a strong autobiographical impulse emerging from all walks of life. . . . The palm has passed from white, middle class men of distinction to the . . . minorities of our culture who write precisely because of their lack of other kinds of power and their need to be heard" (p. 23). These authors write about rebellion and survival. Rather than looking back on a heroic journey, they are most likely writing in the midst of their lives. The end of the journey is yet to come, the problems they confront are still unresolved, their success or failure remains unevaluated. By writing, they establish their place in history, making their particular experiences, thoughts, and actions part of the permanent written record. Egan maintains that the very act of writing for "this modern crop of autobiographers . . . is not a matter of explanation, apology, or clarification of public record, but entirely a matter of survival" (p. 27).

This fight to affirm the value of self is clearly apparent in the autobiographies of the poet Jimmy Santiago Baca, who describes his prison ordeal; the journalist Jill Nelson, who writes about her experiences at the *Washington Post*; Melba Pattillo Beals, who survived a year-long fight to desegregate Central High School in Little Rock; the poet Louis Rodriguez, who opens his story with his fears for the spiritual and physical survival of his son; Sanyika Shakur, who writes from prison; Elaine Brown, the former Black Panther Leader, who ends her story with her escape from her former comrades; Assata Shakur, who was targeted by the FBI's COINTEL program; and Norma Marcere and Ruthie Bolton, who sought to re-establish a sense of personal value after having been victims of physical and emotional abuse.

By affixing their personal story onto the larger history of society, these autobiographers have also made it possible for those who share aspects of their recorded experiences to find a place for themselves in this society and in history. Many of the autobiographers included in this compilation relate their feelings upon first discovering their cultural heritage, either through books or from some knowledgeable mentor. Through writing, they gain an entirely new perspective of themselves in the world. These autobiographies, then, provide numerous opportunities for readers with similar experiences to find inspiration.

It is also important to share these stories with those individuals who believe they cannot relate to such narratives, or who would like to believe that they are untouched by the many struggles depicted within the stories. Johnetta Cole writes in her forward to Gloria Wade-Gayles's autobiography that "the recollections of one black woman become the mirror into which each of us can see how alike and how different we are. We can encounter the exquisite diversity and amazing similarity in the human condition" (p. viii). Julius Lester emphasizes the importance of understanding the experiences of others in his essay "Tied in a Single Garment." He writes that

> . . . to understand racism we must use our imaginations and enter the lives of others. Understanding racism requires us to know in the marrow of our beings that the way in which we experience the world is not how others always experience it, and more important, the way we experience the world is not the only way or even the best.   (p. 26)

The stories in these autobiographies show us that while our frames of reference and our individual circumstances cause each of us to have a unique outlook and a unique collection of experiences, we share the basic human need for love and acceptance, we share many of the same aspirations, hopes and fears, and we long for a certain spiritual fulfillment.

We are experiencing, in this decade of the nineties, a political backlash against, and an open hostility toward differences of race, socio-economic status, and issues of gender and sexual preference. We need more than ever to understand each other, to have insight into the experiences of all citizens of this country, to acknowledge that we are all, indeed, no matter what our ethnic background or number of years in residence, citizens of the United States. These life stories provide all readers with a broad, and perhaps truer sense of U.S. history than it is possible to obtain from a text book or scholarly journal. I consider it a privilege to have encountered each of these books. I have gained new perspective and a deepened understanding of many issues to which I might otherwise have remained oblivious. I hope that these stories will enlighten all of us to the variety of individuals living in this country, and to the myriad cultures which we are fortunate to share. We have all gained from each other, and our "American culture" changes each time a new person arrives. None of us is untouched by the other.

I prepared this bibliography in part for my own children, who are growing up in a small Midwestern town. Except for the racially-mixed nature of their own extended family, they lead a fairly homogenous existence. I hope that the knowledge I have gained in preparing this bibliography can be passed on to them, and that, when at some point they are able to read these life stories, they will develop an understanding of all that it means to be a citizen of this country.

Rebecca Stuhr (1997)

Works Cited

Bloom, Lynn Z. "American Autobiography: the Changing Critical Canon." *Auto/Biography Studies:A/B* 9.2 (Fall 1994): 167-180.

Brignano, Russell. *Black Americans in Autobiography: An Annotated Bibliography of Autobiographies and Autobiographical Books Written Since the Civil War.* Durham, North Carolina: Duke University Press, 1984.

Briscoe, Mary Louise, Lynn Z. Bloom and Barbara Tobias. *American Autobiography, 1945-1980: A Bibliography.* Madison: University of Wisconsin Press, 1982.

Brumble, H. David III. "A Supplement to an *An Annotated Bibliography of American Indian and Eskimo Autobiographies.*" *Western American Literature* 17 (1982): 243-260.

—. *American Indian Autobiography.* Berkeley: University of California Press, 1988.

—. *An Annotated Bibliography of American Indian and Eskimo Autobiographies.* Lincoln: University of Nebraska Press, 1981.

Chin, Frank. "This is Not an Autobiography." *Genre* 17 (June 1985): 109-130.

Egan, Susanna. "The Changing Faces of Heroism: Some Questions Raised by Contemporary Autobiography." *Biography* 10.1 (1987): 20-38.

Lejeune, Philippe. "The Autobiographical Contract" in *French Literary Theory Today.* Edited by Tvetan Todorov. New York: Cambridge University Press, 1982.

Lester, Julius. "Tied in a Single Garment." *Hungry Mind Review* 31 (September 1994).

O'Brien, Lynne Woods. *Plains Indian Autobiographies.* Western Writers Series. 10. Boise: Boise State College, 1973.

Olney, James. *Metaphors of Self: The Meaning of Autobiography.* Princeton: Princeton University Press, 1972.

Additional Reading

Bataille, Gretchen M. and Kathleen Mullen Sands. *American Indian Women, Telling Their Lives.* Lincoln: University of Nebraska Press, 1984.

Eakin, John Paul, ed. *American Autobiography: Retrospect and Prospect.* Wisconsin Studies in Autobiography. Madison: University of Wisconsin Press, 1991.

Holte, James C. "The Representative Voice: Autobiography and the Ethnic Voice." *MELUS: Society for the Study of the Multi-Ethnic Literature of the United States* 9.2 (June 1982): 25-46.

Kazin, Alfred. "Autobiography as Narrative." *Michigan Quarterly Review* 3 (September 1964): 210-216.

Krupat, Arnold. *For Those Who Come After: A Study of Native American Autobiography.* Berkeley: University of California Press, 1985.

Lidoff, Joan. "Autobiography in a Different Voice: Maxine Hong Kingston's *The Woman Warrior.*" *Auto/Biography Studies:A/B* 3.3 (Fall 1987): 29-35.

Nericcio, William Anthony. "Autobiographies at *La Frontera*: The Quest for Mexican-American Narrative." *The Americas Review* 16.3-4 (September 1988): 165-187.

Payne, James Robert, ed. *Multicultural Autobiography: American Lives.* Knoxville: University of Tennessee Press, 1992.

Rayson, Ann. "Beneath the Mask: Autobiographies of Japanese-American Women." *MELUS* 14 (March 1987): 43-57.

Saldivar, Ramon. "Ideologies of the Self: Chicano Autobiography." *Diacritics* (September 1985): 25-34.

Sanders, Mark A. "Theorizing the Collaborative Self: The Dynamics of Contour and Content in the Dictated Autobiography." *New Literary History* 25.2 (March 1994): 445-458.

Sands, Kathleen Mullen. "Telling 'A Good One': Creating a Papago Autobiography." *MELUS* 10 (1983): 55-65.

Stone, Albert, ed. *The American Autobiography: A Collection of Critical Essays.* Englewood Cliffs: Prentice-Hall, 1981.

Introduction to the 1995-2000 Volume

The most notable difference between this publication, covering a span of five years, and the 1997 volume, covering a span of fifteen years, is the length. The 1997 bibliography contains 499 entries, a significantly shorter work than the current bibliography, which contains 674 entries. Even after subtracting twenty-two cross-references, the number of autobiographies written during 1995-2000 is impressive, perhaps even startling. The 1997 bibliography took one person about a year-and-a-half to complete. This present volume took two people two-and-a-half years, and it is safe to say that when we undertook the project we gravely underestimated the amount of work involved. We made the false assumption that there would be fewer books to compile and read for a five year period of publication than for a fifteen year period. The American practice of generous interlibrary loan, and, of course, the United States publication of the books, made access to the autobiographies much easier for Rebecca than for me. We met three times over the course of the project, twice in the United States and once in Japan, but most of our communication was by email or telephone (often with one of us barely awake, and the other just falling asleep).

As with the 1997 volume, we relied initially on OCLC's WorldCat database, the closest thing to a world-wide online library catalog, to compile the bibliography. When using this database, one depends primarily on the Library of Congress subject headings for access to bibliographic records. The weaknesses inherent in these subject headings are described in the previous introduction. To supplement this database, we began to investigate other Internet resources available to anyone with a modem anywhere in the world. Amazon.com, for example, has a database of "biographies & memoirs: ethnic & national" that contains several thousand entries.

By sorting through this list by date of publication, autobiography or biography, and ethnicity, we were able to add many more books to the bibliography. Amazon.com's list includes autobiographies by celebrities and athletes, a category of autobiographies more difficult to identify in WorldCat and one less well represented in the 1980-1994 book.

Four hundred and thirty-five of the autobiographies in this bibliography were written by African Americans, compared to 247 for the previous fifteen years. Included in these 435 references is a selection of books written during the eighteenth and nineteenth centuries which have been digitized and are part of a growing collection called *Documenting the American South* created by the University of North Carolina at Chapel Hill, Academic Affairs Library (http://docsouth.unc.edu/). There are also several digitized books from the *Digital Schomburg Collection of African American Women Writers of the 19th Century* (http://digital.nypl.org/schomburg/writers_aa19/) presented by the New York Public Library's Schomburg Center for Research in Black Culture (http://www.nypl.org/research/sc/sc.html).

Among these 435 autobiographies are many by musicians, entertainers, and athletes. There is also a rich body of work documenting individual contributions to the fight to end segregation and exclusion dating back to the early decades of this century, and to the Civil Rights Movement of the 1950s and 1960s. Some books are by such prominent leaders as John Lewis, Fred Gray, Constance Baker Motley, and Andrew Young. There are also stories of the unsung heroes and heroines of the Civil Rights Movement, such as the people in the South who risked their lives and livelihoods to line up at the courthouses to register to vote and the people who had the courage to send their children to formerly all-white schools or to be named in anti-discrimination suits. Also collected here are the stories of teachers who were not allowed to attend colleges in their home states, but who went back to teach and give other African-American children an education, the stories of World War II veterans who risked their lives for democracy, and then returned home to treatment worse than that of the German POWs, and the stories of the children of sharecroppers who overcame seemingly insurmountable odds to pursue opportunities for a better life. Entertainers and athletes who lived and worked during the first two-thirds of the century contribute to the narrative of the Civil

Rights Movement as they tell of their struggle with lack of opportunity, discrimination, and unfair compensation practices. Many of
these well-known entertainers lent their names to activist causes or
pursued their own: Ossie and Ruby Davis, Sammy Davis, Jr., Dick
Gregory, Ruth Brown, and many more.

Along with the significant increase in autobiographies by
African Americans, I noticed three other categories that were either
new or better represented in this bibliography.

There is a small but significant number of books by Cuban
Americans, many of whom escaped from Cuba as children, during
the early 1960s. Cubans who received exit visas to the United States
were given no more than a few hours to leave their homes, and they
lost everything they owned. Those who were children grew up to
become Cuban Americans while many of their parents remained
exiles at heart. This younger generation, or "one-and-a-half" generation, as they call themselves, has just begun to write about their
lives and express their feelings about Cuba and Fidel Castro.

Japanese Americans incarcerated in camps during World
War II are beginning to tell of their experiences through their children and through oral history projects. Some of the books included
in this bibliography were written or recorded by third-generation
Japanese Americans (Sansei) who were born after the war, but who
have discovered that the World War II internment of their parents
and grandparents had an indirect but distinct impact on their own
lives. As with the Cuban Americans, the recording of history has
been left, for the most part, to the younger generation.

People of multiracial or multiethnic background are starting to record their struggle to come to terms with their complicated
identities. As an American who has lived her entire adult life in a
"foreign" country (Japan) and the mother of two multiracial daughters, I found the autobiographies of this group of people especially
interesting. (As a matter of fact, six of my parents' seven grandchildren are "Americans of color.") While the stories of this growing
segment of the population describe many of the problems of race
faced by their individual parents, they also present a new set of
dilemmas which are unique to the writers, and it is interesting to
note the similarities of their experiences and view points, no matter
what their racial or ethnic background. They most frequently note
their inability, or perceived inability, to fit into either or any of the
societies and cultures they represent.

The concept of feeling a sense of belonging to a particular society or culture brings me to my final point: the inherent value of reading the books we have annotated here. The walls between and surrounding cultures and the differences in experiences are daunting and as difficult to get across as a mine field. Working through each book in this collection meant spending time with each author. I felt as though I were sitting in the living room of the people whose stories I was reading, listening to them talk directly to me. Here was information I had been looking for most of my life: multicultural people who shared my problems, multiracial children who provided me with lessons on how to raise my daughters, people of other races and backgrounds who patiently sat down and explained their experiences to me. Although many of the explanations and lessons conflict with each other, each author's point of view is clear. After a few months of reading, it seemed to me that many of the barriers to peaceful human coexistence would dissolve if we all spent time reading about—in a sense listening to—each other. Rebecca and I are proud to present the following bibliography and hope that it will benefit you in both your personal and scholarly pursuits.

Deborah Stuhr Iwabuchi

A note about the bibliography:

As in the previous volume, we annotated all books that we were able to read. Those we were unable to purchase or borrow through interlibrary loan are included with full bibliographic information and indexed when possible, but have no annotation. Some autobiographies which were included in our first bibliography or predated that bibliography, have since been reissued in new editions. We included these in the present work, but did not annotate them. Finally, we did include, and, for the most part, annotate, works that should have appeared in the first bibliography but were missed.

The Bibliography

1. *Children of the Dream: Our Own Stories of Growing Up Black in America.* Edited by Laurel Holliday. New York, New York: Pocket Books, 1999. 431 pages; photographs; suggested reading. ISBN: 067100803X.

   Notes: Also published as "an abridged young readers edition" New York: Pocket Books, 2000. ISBN: 0671041274 (199 pages) and as an unabridged paperback New York: Washington Square Press, 2000. ISBN: 0671008064.

   Abstract: This is an anthology of thirty-eight essays by African Americans who have each written about a specific aspect of their childhood. Subjects include incidents of racial discrimination, discrimination within the black community, the matter of hair for black women, education, and many others. In the introduction, the editor describes the contributors: "Ranging in age from eleven to seventy-five and raised in twenty-two states, the writers in this volume provide a wide window on the experience of growing up black in the United States" (p. xi).

   Contents: Arline Lorraine Piper, "The Question." Amitiyah Elayne Hyman, "Sticks and Stones and Words and Bones." Staajabu, "255 Sycamore Street." Arthur B. Arnold, "Field of Beans." Bernestine Singley, "White Friends." Marion Coleman Brown, "My First Friend (My Blond-haired, Blue-eyed Linda)." Millicent Brown, "The Dippity-Do Revolution, or Grown-ups Don't Have a Clue." J. K. Dennis, "Silver Stars." Toni Pierce Webb, "Warmin' da Feet o' da Massa." Robert E. Penn, "War." Sarah Bracey White, "Freedom Summer." Kenneth Carroll, "Sunday Kinda Love." Ronald K. Fitten, "First Lesson in Rage; Fascination Turned to Hate in 1967 Detroit Riot." Tracy Price Thompson, "Bensonhurst: Black and Then Blue." Dianne E. Dixon, "The Lesson." Dawn D. Bennett-Alexander, "(R)Evolution of Black and

White." E. K. Daufin, "What I Dreaded." Yvonne "Princess" Jackson, "Runover." Anthony Ross, "Little Tigers Don't Roar." Tisa Bryant, "Zoo Kid." Aya de Leon, "Hitting Dante." Desiree Cooper, "Color My World." Antoine P. Reddick, "All the Black Children." Anita LaFrance Allen, "The Divided Cafeteria." Ben Bates, "Boomerism, or Doing Time in the Ivy League." LeVan D. Hawkins, "Fred." Crystal Ann Williams, "In the Belly of a Clothes Rack." Erica S. Turnipseed, "Hand Games." Touré, "Blackman-walkin." Charisse Nesbit, "Child of the Dream." Shilanda L. Woolridge, "Rite of Processes." Winston Eldridge, "Have a Nice Day!" Tess Alexandra Bennett Harrison, "'Mixed' Emotions." Mia Threlkeld, "A True Friend?" Anne Alexis Bennett Alexander, "The Black Experience. . . ?" Linnea Colette Ashley, "A Waste of Yellow: Growing Up Black in America." Caille Milner, "Black Codes: Behavior in the Post-Civil Rights Era." Jennifer Dawn Bennett Alexander, "Betrayal, in Black and White."

2.   *A Different Battle: Stories of Asian Pacific American Veterans.* Edited by Carina A. del Rosario. Historical essay by Ken Mochizuki and Carina del Rosario. Contemporary photographs by Dean Wong. Seattle, Washington: Wing Luke Asian Museum: University of Washington Press, 1999. 127 pages; photographs. ISBN: 0295979194.

Abstract: The Wing Luke Museum edited these fifty-one interviews which were originally conducted with Asian Pacific veterans by the Densho Japanese American Legacy Project, the Filipino American National Historical Society, and Seattle Sansei. In the preface, freelance writer Carina A. del Rosario states the purpose of the collection:

> We want to acknowledge and honor the thousands of people of Asian and Pacific Islander descent who fought in or with the United States Armed Forces, whose efforts have long been overlooked. We want people to see the faces of Asian Pacific Americans wearing U.S. military uniforms. . . . Beyond this recognition of military participation, however, is the desire to present the reality of war. We want to give people a look at war from the eyes of those who have experienced it.   (Preface)

Ethnic backgrounds of veterans include Chinese-American, Japanese-American, Filipino-American, Korean-American, Samoan-American, Guamian, and Chinese-Vietnamese-American.

The wars these veterans fought in include pre-World War II conflicts, World War II, the Korean War, the Vietnam Conflict,
Grenada, and the Persian Gulf War.

3.   *East to America: Korean American Life Stories.* Edited by Elaine
      H. Kim and Eui-Young Yu. New York, New York: New Press,
      1996. 386 pages; map. ISBN: 1565842979 : 1565843991.

Abstract: The editors decided to interview Korean Americans to
end the stereotypes of this ethnic group that grew out of the 1992
Los Angeles riots after the Rodney King incident.

> The two recurrent images most frequently
> [broadcast] by the commercial news media . . .
> were of Korean men on rooftops guarding their
> stores with guns . . . and of Korean merchants,
> mostly female, screaming hysterically or beg-
> ging and crying in front of their ruined stores.
> Korean American opinions were scarcely solicit-
> ed, except as they could be used in the already-
> constructed discourse on race relations, which
> for the most part blamed African Americans and
> Latinos for their poverty and scapegoated
> Korean Americans as robotic aliens who have no
> "real" right to be here in the first place, and there-
> fore deserve whatever happens to them.
>
> (p. xvi)

The editors conducted one hundred interviews with Korean
Americans, each between three and eighteen hours in length, and
published thirty-eight of them in this book. In choosing the interviews to be printed, the editors tried to maintain a balance
between immigrants, "1.5 generation," and second-generation
Korean Americans. They also looked for different types of occupations and experiences. The overall impression made by the subjects was also important:

> Because we could not offer the Korean-language
> interviews verbatim and because we recalled
> vividly how Korean immigrants were cast in the
> media as inarticulate aliens during the Los
> Angeles riots, we decided against using verba-
> tim transcript data. We edited and rearranged
> them, taking pains to follow people's words as
> closely as possible.   (p. xii)

The names of the interview subjects and the titles of their interviews are listed below. Each interview includes a brief sketch of the background of the subject:

> K. W. Lee, "Urban Impressionist." Stella Soon-Hi Koh, "Dirty Laundry." Dong Hwan Ku, "War Zone." Imjung Kwuon, "Launched." Tong Sun Lim, "Revitalizing America." Maeun Koch'u [sic], "Hot Pepper." Kyong-Ae Price, "Spiritual Tension." Dredge Kang, "Multiple-Box Person." Abbot Doh-An Kim, "Casual Connection." Eun Sik Yang, "Distorted History." Sung Yong Park, "Tasting America." Kyu [Min] Lee, "Chino." Kathy Kim, "Starting From Zero." Sean Suh, "Dragon." Brenda Paik Sunoo, "Tommy's Mother." Richard Chung, "Away From the Center." Kyung-Ja Lee, "A Humble Messenger." Youn Jae Kim, "A Seeker and a Fighter." Han Chol Hong, "Strong Determination." Hyun Yi Kang, "No Spokesperson." Y. Chang, "House of Haesun." Paul Kim, "Getting Real." Alexander Hull, "Cruise Control." Serena Choi, "Head of Household." Sandy Lee, "Non-traditional and Korean." Young Soon Han, "Second Homeland." Yanny Rhee, "Love Letter From a Stranger." James Ryu, "Hanging Onto My Dream." Nataly Kim, "One Chapter a Day." James Park, "Man of the House." Jay Kun Yoo, "Pilgrimage." Young Kim, "Born to Be a Soldier." Janine Bishop, "Adopted." Kook Kim Dean, "Black and Korean." Kun Soo Kang, "Year of the Sheep." Young Shin, "A Higher Ground." Sookhee Choe Kim, "Perpetually Marginal." Bong Hwan Kim, "As American as Possible."

4. *Flat-Footed Truths: Telling Black Women's Lives.* Edited by Patricia Bell-Scott with Juanita Johnson-Bailey. New York, New York: Henry Holt and Company, 1998. 230 pages; photographs. ISBN: 0805046283 : 0805046291.

> **Abstract:** In her introduction, editor Patricia Bell-Scott describes this collection,

>> This book is about the process of telling Black women's lives, with an eye toward what folks in my southern Black community called "flat-footed truths." To tell the flat-footed truth means to offer a story or statement that is straightforward, unshakable, and unembellished. This kind of truth-telling, especially by and about Black women, can be risky business because our lives are often devalued and our voices periodically

> silenced. . . . It is designed as an extended con-
> versation that covers four major themes. Part I
> discusses the challenge of telling one's own life;
> Part II, the adventure of claiming lives neglected
> or lost; Part III, the affirmation of lives of resist-
> ance; and Part IV, the optimism and healing of
> lives transformed.   (p. xix)

The anthology includes photographs, poetry and essays from the following contributors:

> Gilda Snowden, Ruth Forman, bell hooks, Patricia Bell-Scott, Juanita Johnson-Bailey, Marita Golden, Sojourner Truth, Brenda Faye Bell, Alice Walker, Pearl Cleage, Miriam DeCosta-Willis, Nell Irvin Painter, Akasha (Gloria) Hull, Robbie McCauley, Elaine Shelly, Audre Lorde, Anita F. Hull, Kate Rushin, Wini McQueen, Valerie Jean, and Becky Birtha.

5   *Growing Up Asian American: An Anthology.* Edited by Maria Hong. New York, New York: William Morrow & Company, 1993. 416 pages. ISBN: 0688112668.

Notes: Also published New York: Avon Books, 1993. ISBN: 0380724189.

Abstract: The editor explains in her introduction that the "essays, excerpts, and short stories in this anthology are all previously published works about growing up in the United States. They have all been written by authors identified as Asian American" (p. 13). The pieces were written throughout the twentieth century. Each story is preceded by a biographical sketch of the author.

Listed below are the authors, the titles of the pieces, the books they have been excerpted from if any, and his or her ethnic identification if not clear from the title:

> Sui Sin Far (*aka* Edith Eaton), "Pat and Pan" (Chinese American). Louise Leung Larson, "From Gee Sook to Beatty" (*Sweet Bamboo: Saga of a Chinese American Family*). Tooru J. Kanazawa, "Frontier Home" (*Sushi and Sourdough* [Japanese American]). Toshio Mori, "Through Anger and Love" (Japanese American). Wakako Yamauchi, "And the Soul Shall Dance" (Japanese American). Marie Hara, "Fourth Grade Ukus" (Japanese American). Gus Lee, "Toussaint" (*China Boy*). Lydia Minatoya, "Transformation" (*Talking to High Monks in the Snow: An Asian American Odyssey* [Japanese American]). Peter Bacho, from *Cebu* (Filipino American). Zia Jaffrey, "The Monkeyman" (East Indian American). Jeanne Wakatsuki

Houston and James D. Houston, from *Farewell to Manzanar* (Japanese American). Gene Oishi, from *In Search of Hiroshi* (Japanese American). Mary Paik Lee, edited by Sucheng Chan, from *Quiet Odyssey: A Pioneer Korean Woman in America*. Pardee Lowe, "Father Cures a Presidential Fever" (*Father and Glorious Descendant* [Chinese American]). Jade Snow Wong, "The Taste of Independence" (*Fifth Chinese Daughter* [Chinese American]). Frank Chin, "Railroad Standard Time" (Chinese American). Garrett Hongo, "Kubota" (Japanese American). Amy Tan, from *The Joy Luck Club* (Chinese American). David Mura, from *Turning Japanese: Memoirs of a Sansei*. Gish Jen, "What Means Switch" (Chinese American). Cynthia Kadohata, from *The Floating World* (Japanese American). Susan Ito, "Whatever Happened to Harry?" (Japanese American). Kartar Dhillon, "The Parrot's Beak" (East Indian American). Hisaye Yamamoto, "Seventeen Syllables" (Japanese American). Kim Ronyoung (*aka* Gloria Hahn) from *Clay Walls* (Korean American). Maxine Hong Kingston, from *The Woman Warrior: Memoirs of a Girlhood among Ghosts* (Chinese American). Shawn Wong from *Homebase* (Chinese American). Mavis Hara, "Carnival Queen" (Japanese American). Darrell H. Y. Lum, "Paint" (Chinese American). Sigrid Nunez, "Chang" (Panamanian Chinese German American). R. A. Sasaki, "First Love" (Japanese American). Indira Ganesan, from *The Journey* (East Indian American).

6. *Half and Half: Writers on Growing Up Biracial and Bicultural.* Edited by Claudine C. O'Hearn. New York, New York: Pantheon Books, 1998. 272 pages. ISBN: 0375400311 : 0375700110.

> **Abstract:** In the introduction, Claudine Chiawei O'Hearn, the child of an Irish American father and Chinese mother talks about growing up in Asia and the United States and about the racial stereotypes imposed upon her both by the cultures she has lived in and by her own family. She herself is at a loss to define her racial identity. O'Hearn writes, "These essays, exemplary of the legion of meanings of race and culture, are about inconstant categories and shifting skins. Skin color and place of birth aren't accurate signifiers of identity. . . . Cultural and racial amalgams create a third, wholly indistinguishable category where origin and home are indeterminate" (Introduction). Contributors, their ethnic background, and the titles of their essays are listed here:

Garrett Hongo (Japanese American), "Lost in Place." Danzy Senna (Caucasian Black Mexican), "The Mulatto Millennium." Roxane Farmanfarmaian (Caucasian Iranian American), "The Double Helix." lê thi diem thúy (Vietnamese American), "California Palms." Francisco Goldman (Jewish Spanish American), "Moro like Me." Bharati Mukherjee (East Indian American), "The Road from Bullygunge." David Mura (Japanese American), "Reflections on My Daughter." Meri Nana-Ama Danquah (Ghanaian American), "Life As an Alien." Malcolm Gladwell (Jamaican English American), "Lost in the Middle." Lisa See (Caucasian Chinese American), "The Funeral Banquet." Julia Alvarez (Dominican American), "A White Woman of Color." Philippe Wamba (Zairian [Congo] American), "A Middle Passage." Indira Ganesan (East Indian American), "Food and the Immigrant." James McBride (Jewish African American), "What Color is Jesus?" Lori Tsang (Chinese-American, Chinese-Jamaican), "Postcards from 'Home.'" Nina Mehta (East Indian Jewish American), "From Here to Poland." Rubén Martínez (Mexican Salvadoran American), "Technicolor." Gish Jen (Irish Chinese American), "An Ethnic Trump."

7. *Hawai'i Journeys in Nonviolence: Autobiographical Reflections.* Edited by Glenn D. Paige, Lou Ann Ha'aheo and George Simpson. Honolulu, Hawai'i: Center for Global Nonviolence Planning Project, Matsunaga Institute for Peace, University of Hawai'i, 1995. 152 pages; suggested readings; index. ISBN: 1880309106.

Abstract: This book, as described by the editors in the preface, is a "collection of eight autobiographical essays by persons whose life journeys have brought them to Hawai'i and nonviolence." The collection includes the following essays:

Lou Ann Ha'aheo Guanson, "Love Gives Life Within." Ho'oipo DeCambra, "Activism is Empowerment." Anna McAnany, "Swords into Ploughshares." James V. Albertini, "Journey to Malu'aina." Robert Aiken, "An Evolution of Views." Howard E. "Stretch" Johnson, "Evolution of Nonviolent Philosophy." Iraja Sivadas, "Insight." Johan Galtung, "On the Politics of Peace Action: Nonviolence and Creativity." George Simpson, "Afterword."

8.   *Here First: Autobiographical Essays by Native American Writers.*
     Edited by Arnold Krupat and Brian Swann. New York, New
     York: Modern Library, 2000. 422 pages. ISBN: 0375751386.

Abstract: This is a continuation of Krupat and Swann's first
anthology *I Tell You Now: Autobiographical Essays by Native
American Writers* (1987). Krupat and Swann's interests lie with
Native-American writers and autobiography, seeking to have
writers discuss their lives in relation to their art. Beyond being
informative, the essays in this collection represent "the extraordinary flowering of . . . writing by Native American people. We offer
these autobiographical reflections most of all for their power as literature" (p. xv). Krupat and Swann address the question of who
is or what qualifies one to claim Indian ancestry. At least one
writer refused to make a contribution to this anthology based on
his belief that many writers from the last anthology had questionable claims to Indian heritage. Krupat and Swann cite three
schools of thought on this matter, which they call the Nationalist,
the Indigenist, and the Cosmopolitan views. The Nationalist
school requires tribal enrollment to prove Indianess. The
Indigenist is more interested in whether or not the individual
reflects an "ecologically based philosophy or system of indigenist
values that define a global 'Fourth World'" (p. xii). Finally, the
Cosmopolitan viewpoint includes "anyone committed to the values of healing rather than stealing tribal cultures" (p. xii). Krupat
and Swann state that "[s]o far as we know, all those represented in
this book have legitimate, if on occasion complex claims to Native
American identity" (p. xiii). Authors and the titles of the essays
are listed below. The names of the tribe of each author is in paren-
theses:

Sherman Alexie (Spokane and Coeur d'Alene), "The
Unauthorized Autobiography of Me." Carroll Arnet (Gogisgi)
(Overhill Band, Cherokee), "Ayanvdadisdi: I Remember."
Betty Louise Bell (Cherokee), "Burying Paper." Duane
BigEagle (Osage), "In English I'm Called Duane BigEagle: An
Autobiographical Statement." Gloria Bird (Spokane),
"Autobiography as Spectacle: An Act of Liberation or the
Illusion of Liberation?" Kimberly M. Blaeser (Anishinaabe,
Minnesota Chippewa), "Rituals of Memory." Nora Marks
Dauenhauer (Tlingit), "Life Woven with Song." Charlotte
Declue (Kawashinsay) (Osage, Kiowa), "The Good Red Road."
Anita Endrezze (Yaqui), "A Journey to the Heart." Hanay
Geiogamah (Kiowa), "Self-Interview." Gordon Henry, Jr.
(White Earth Chippewa), "Entries into the Autobiographical
I." Patricia Penn Hilden (Nez Perce), "Displacements:

Performing Mestizaje." Roberta Hill (Oneida), "A Soul Like the Sun." Leanne Howe (Choctaw), "My Mothers, My Uncles, Myself." Rex Lee Jim (Navajo, Red House), "A Moment in My Life." Evelina Zuni Lucero (Isleto Pueblo, San Juan Pueblo), "On the Tip of My Tongue: An Autobiographical Essay." Louis Owens (Choctaw, Cherokee), "Motion of Fire and Form: Autobiographical Reflections." W. S. Penn, "In the Garden of the Gods." Greg Sarris (Miwok), "From a Place Called Santa Rosa." Vickie Sears (Cherokee), "Wind Circles." John E. Smelcer (Cherokee, Ahtna Athabaskan), "In the Past's Familiar Tongue." Luci Tapahonso (Navajo), "They Moved over the Mountain." Clifford E. Trafzer (Wyandot), "Red Echoes." Anna Lee Walters (Pawnee, Otoe), "The Buffalo Road." Elizabeth Woody (Confederated Tribes of the Reservation of Warm Springs), "The Child before Memory: Recognition of the 'Maker.'" Ofelia Zepeda (Tohono O'odham), "Autobiography."

9.   *Honor the Grandmothers: Dakota and Lakota Women Tell Their Stories.* Compiled and edited by Sarah Penman. St. Paul, Minnesota: Minnesota Historical Society Press. 147 pages; photographs. ISBN: 0873513842 : 0873513851.

Abstract: Penman has recorded and transcribed the stories of two Lakota and two Dakota grandmothers. She began this project after a chance meeting with Celane Not Help Him at Wounded Knee Cemetery during an event in recognition of the ninety-ninth anniversary of the Massacre at Wounded Knee. Celane Not Help Him, a Lakota woman, was born in 1928 on the Pine Ridge Indian reservation. She was raised by her grandfather, a survivor of Wounded Knee, and her grandmother. She retells the story of the massacre as it was told to her and recalls the harsh existence at the Indian boarding school that she was forced to attend. She describes the arts of beading and quilling which she learned from her grandmother. Stella Pretty Sounding Flute, born in 1924, is a Hahpekute-Hunkpati Dakota woman from the Crow Creek Reservation in South Dakota. She is a quilter and uses the star quilt design which she learned from her grandmother. She retells the legend behind the design and describes her early introduction to the art of quilting. Pretty Sounding Flute tells of the harsh conditions on the reservation, and the virulent racism she has encountered off of it. Cecilia Hernandez Montgomery is a member of the Oglala Sioux tribe of the Lakota Indians. She was born in 1910 on the Pine Ridge Reservation, where her father was a cattleman. Because of a lack of opportunity on the reservation, Montgomery moved to Rapid City where she met her husband, a Crow Indian from Montana. There Montgomery was active in many community programs to serve her people, including The Community Action Program, and Urban Renewal which worked to improve health care and living conditions for families and the elderly. She has also been active in teaching Indian history, stories, and dancing to young children. Iola Columbus was born in 1928 in Minnesota, a member of the Siseton-Wahpeton Dakota Indians, and raised on the Flandreau Reservation in South Dakota by her grandparents, who were traditionalists. Columbus's husband was from the Lower Sioux Community (Morton) in Minnesota. His reservation was influenced by the laws of the 1934 Indian Reorganization Act. By law, their traditional practices were suppressed, and the members of this community adapted to a white-American way of life. Columbus has since sought to reintroduce traditional spiritualism to the younger generation. She is active in tribal governance and was the first woman to be elected as a tribal chair in Minnesota.

10. *Las Mamis: Favorite Latino Authors Remember Their Mothers.* Edited by Esmeralda Santiago and Joie Davidow. New York, New York: Knopf, 2000.   189 pages; illustrations.   ISBN: 0375408797.

Abstract: Santiago and Davidow compiled this book to honor Latino mothers. Many of these women were immigrants who knew little or no English when coming to the United States, they were more often than not poor and had to struggle to raise their children. The editors found that many writers were unwilling to take up the challenge of writing about their mothers, and there were a few who intially agreed, but found the task too difficult and changed their minds. Davidow writes that children are "destined to exist in relation to their mothers. . . . Our achievements are their achievements. Our failures are their failures" (p. ix). Contributors include the following:

> Esmeralda Santiago, "First Born." María Amparo Escandón, "My Mother in the Nude." Mandalit del Barco, "'Hello dollinks': Letters from Mom." Alba Ambert, "Persephone's Quest at Waterloo: A Daughter's Tale." Piri Thomas, "Mami, a.k.a. Doña Lola." Gustava Pérez Firmat, "Mami's Boy." Liz Balmaseda, "Travels with Mami." Ilan Stavans, "September 19, 1985." Jaime Manrique, "A Mother Named Queen Solitude." Francisco Goldman, "¡Mamita Linda!" Dagoberto Gilb, "Mi Mommy." Junot Diaz, "How (in a Time

of Trouble) I Discovered My Mom and Learned to Live."
Gioconda Belli, "Just a Woman." Marjorie Agosín, "Frida,
Friduca, Mami."

11. *Lift Every Voice and Sing: St. Louis African Americans in the
     Twentieth Century.* Narratives collected by Doris A. Wesley.
     Photographs taken by Wiley Price. Edited by Ann Morris.
     Columbia, Missouri: University of Missouri Press, 1999. 219
     pages; photographs. ISBN: 0826212530.

Abstract: Doris Wesley, a reference specialist at the Western
Historical Manuscript Collection at the University of Missouri-St.
Louis, collected interviews from one hundred prominent African-
Americans who could talk about their own stories as well as integration and the Civil Rights Movement in St. Louis. Among them
are educators, businesspersons, musicians, doctors and nurses,
and politicians, including two mayors of the city. This project
evolved into a series of three exhibits at the Vaughn Cultural
Center at the Urban League of Metropolitan St. Louis, for which
Wiley Price took photographs of the interviewees. Ann Morris
edited the interviews, arranged them in a loose chronological
order, and prepared them for publication. In the introduction,
Morris gives a history of St. Louis which provides background for
the interviews. The black population began growing in 1904 when
African Americans traveled from the South for the St. Louis
World's Fair and found that desegregation was not as bad as they
thought and that there were opportunities for jobs there.
Although education was segregated, black schools, teaching col-
leges, and medical institutions provided their children with an
excellent education and a certain degree of upward mobility.
Black businesses flourished, the city was home to popular Negro
League baseball teams, and many musicians settled in St. Louis.
The black community was vocal, powerful, and fighting for equal
rights before most of the rest of the South. The original transcripts
and recordings of the interviews in this book are available at the
Western Historical Manuscript Collection at the University of
Missouri-St. Louis.

12. *MIS in the War against Japan: Personal Experiences Related at the 1993 MIS Capital Reunion, "The Nisei Veteran: An American Patriot."* Edited by Warren M. Tsuneishi and Stanley L. Falk. Vienna, Virginia: Japanese American Veterans Association of Washington, D.C., 1995. 142 pages; photographs. ISBN: none.

Abstract: The personal narratives collected in this work were originally presented at the 1993 Military Intelligence Service (MIS) reunion convened by the Japanese American Association of Washington, D.C. The stories, presented as part of a panel discussion, have undergone minimal editing, and the editors have provided brief biographical profiles to accompany each. Originally called the Fourth Army (Japanese Language) Intelligence School, the Military Intelligence Service Language School was founded in 1941 in San Francisco, and eventually moved to Minnesota. After the war, it was relocated to Monterey, California and renamed the Defense Language Institute. The goal of the 1993 reunion was to create a public record of the participants' war experiences as presented through panel discussions and documentation sessions. Of the twenty-three narratives, six are from non-Nisei participants. The contributors include the following:

Takashi Matsui, Toshio G. Tsukahira, Faubion Bowers, Allen H. Meyer, Dempster Dirks, Benjamin T. Obata, Richard M. Sakakida, Sunao Ishio, James Yukio Tanabe, George Oakley Totten III, Yoshito Iwamoto, Harvey Watanabe, Roy T. Uyehata, Nobuo Dick Kishiue, Benjamin H. Hazard, Nobuo Furuiye, Roy H. Hatsumoto, Hiro Nishimura, Arthur T. Morimitsu, Peter K. Okada, Ulrich Straus, Joseph Y. Kurata, Allen H. Meyer.

13. *Native Heritage: Personal Accounts by American Indians, 1790 to the Present.* Edited by Arlene B. Hirschfelder. Foreword by Jeffrey L. Hamley. New York, New York: Macmillan, 1995. 298 pages. ISBN: 0028604121.

Abstract: Hirschfelder compiled the stories in this work to share a fraction of the "rich and unique heritage of native peoples from the many regions of North America" (p. xix). Over half of the 120 excerpts from writers representing nearly seventy tribal nations are taken from "as-told-to" works or autobiographies, originally published as early as 1790 and as recently as the 1990s. Bibliographic information is provided so that the reader can continue with the full work from which the excerpt is taken. Hirschfield has grouped the excerpts into eight sections represent-

ing the themes of family, native languages, homeland, its flora and
fauna, spiritual and religious values and practices, Native educational practices, traditional stories, shared traditional practices,
and discrimination. There are many noted writers in this anthology including, Paula Gunn Allen, Simon Ortiz, N. Scott Momaday,
Anna Lee Walters, Leslie Marmon Silko, Wilma Mankiller, Sarah
Winnemucca Hopkins, and Luther Standing Bear.

14. *Once upon a Dream—The Vietnamese Experience.* Edited by De
Tran, Andrew Lam and Hai Dai Nguyen. Foreword by Stanley
Karnow. Kansas City, Missouri: Andrews & McMeel, 1995.
184 pages; photographs. ISBN: 0836205847.

Abstract: This collection of art work, poems, and stories—both
fiction and nonfiction—from thirty-nine young Vietnamese-
American writers is divided into four parts. The first section
includes work that chronicles the experiences of leaving Vietnam.
The second section presents pieces that portray the feelings of
exile and homesickness and nostalgia for Vietnam. Part three
explores Vietnamese identity, and part four describes reconnecting
with Vietnam.

15. *Souls Looking Back: Life Stories of Growing Up Black.* Edited by
Andrew Garrod, Janie Victoria Ward, Tracy L. Robinson and
Robert Kilkenny. Foreword by James P. Comer. New York,
New York: Routledge, 1999. 300 pages; index. ISBN:
0415920612 : 0415920620.

Abstract: Fifty black college and graduate-school students at
Dartmouth College in New Hampshire, Simmons College in
Boston, and McGill University in Montreal, Canada, were invited
to write about their experiences growing up in the United States,
Canada, and the West Indies. Of these, the editors chose sixteen
for publication. In the Preface, the editors, who worked closely
with the students, explain that one of the purposes of this project
was for the writers to achieve "greater self-understanding . . .
through reflection and articulation." The benefit to the reader is
that "we enrich our understanding of our own experience and of
the worldviews that this experience helps to construct. This book
tells the stories of unique . . . individuals from a broad diversity of
backgrounds who have tackled significant obstacles to achieve
degrees of self-understanding and success" (p. xv). The book is
divided into three thematic sections. Each section opens with a
theoretical overview by an African-American scholar. The author
outlines his or her particular focus. The introduction is then fol-

lowed by four to six personal narratives by students. Listed below
are the three sections, the titles of the introductions and their
authors, and the names of the narratives in each. Because the student writers are identified by their first names alone, only the titles
of the essays are included here:

> Section I: Social Class and Race. Peter C. Murrell, Jr.: "Class
> and Race in Negotiating Identity." "Born With a Veil." "What
> is Black Enough?" "Living Between the Lines." "I Reconcile
> the Irreconcilable."
> Section II: Identity. Jewell Taylor Gibbons: "The Social
> Construction of Race, Ethnicity, and Culture." Tracy L.
> Robinson, "The Intersections of Identity." "Color-blind."
> "Walking a Thin Line." "Becoming Myself." "Becoming
> Comfortable in My Skin." "Caught Between Two Cultures."
> "Lost in the Middle."
> Section III: Resilience and Resistance. Janie Victoria Ward:
> "Resilience and Resistance." "Gotta Keep Climbin' All de
> Time." "Finding Zion." "Feeling the Pressure to Succeed."
> "Running Hurdles." "Reflections on My Survival." "Quest for
> Peace."

16. *Speaking for the Generation: Native Writers on Writing.* Edited by
     Simon J. Ortiz. Sun Tracks, 35. Tucson, Arizona: University of
     Arizona Press, 1998.   228 pages.   ISBN: 0816518491 :
     0816518505.

Abstract: Acoma Pueblo writer Simon J. Ortiz is the editor and
provides an introduction in which he discusses the role of Native
writers in passing down their most basic philosophies:

> If anything is most vital, essential and absolute-
> ly important in Native cultural philosophy, it is
> this concept of interdependence: the fact that
> without land there is no life, and without a
> responsible social and cultural outlook by
> humans, no life-sustaining land is possible. . . .
> [W]e are living today because the generations
> before us—our ancestors—provided for us by
> the manner of their responsible living.
>
> (p. xii)

Authors, their tribes, and the titles of the essays are listed following:

> Leslie Marmon Silko (Laguna Pueblo), "Interior and Exterior
> Landscapes: The Pueblo Migration Stories." Gloria Bird

(Spokane Tribe), "Breaking the Silence: Writing as 'Witness.'"
Esther G. Belin (Navajo), "In the Cycle of the Whirl." Roberta
G. Hill (Oneida), "Immersed in Words." A. A. Hedge Coke
(Tsalagi, Huron), "Seeds." Daniel David Moses (Delaware),
"How My Ghosts Got Pale Faces." Elizabeth Woody (Yakama-
Warm Springs, Wasco-Navajo), "Voice of the Land: Giving the
Good Word." Jeannette C. Armstrong (Okanagan), "Land
Speaking." Victor D. Montejo (Maya), "The Stones Will Speak
Again, Dreams of an *Ah Tz'ib'* (Writer) in the Maya Land."

17. *Struggle for Ethnic Identity: Narratives by Asian American
Professionals.* Edited and with an introduction by Pyong Gap
Min and Rose Kim. Critical Perspectives on Asian Pacific
Americans Series, 4. Walnut Creek, California: AltaMira Press,
1999. 240 pages. ISBN: 0761990666 : 0761990674.

Abstract: In this collection of narratives, editors Min and Kim
seek to highlight the experiences of second-generation Asian
Americans. Twelve of the subjects either immigrated to the
United States at a very young age or were born in the United
States. Three of the subjects finished high school before moving to
the United States. Noting the impossibility of providing a cross
section of Asian-American experience with only fifteen narratives,
the editors chose to work with individuals who had finished college and were in the early stages of a professional career. Ten
women and five men, ranging in age from twenty-five to forty-
nine, were asked to address their experiences at home, school, and
work, relating to such topics as prejudice and discrimination; their
identification with their family's ethnic background or culture;
and friendships formed within and outside of their ethnicity. The
contents are as follows:

Pyong Gap Min and Rose Kim, "Introduction. About the
Book." Pyong Gap Min, "Ethnicity: Concepts, Theories, and
Trends." Rose Kim, "Ethnic Culture: an Identity in Conflict.
My Trek." Ruth Chung (Korean American), "Reflections on a
Korean American Journey." Alex Jeong (Korean American),
"A Handicapped Korean in America." Kavitha Mediratta
(East Indian American), "Building Coalitions: A Pan-Asian or
Non-white Identity? How Do You Say Your Name?" David
W. Wang (Chinese American), "Beyond the Golden Door."
Phuong Do (Vietnamese American), "A Girl Called Hoai."
Sayuri Mori-Quayle (Japanese American), "Living in Two
Worlds: A Bicultural Identity. Finding Myself." Monica Jahan
Bose (Bangladeshi American), "Multiple Identities." Shay

Sheth (East Indian American), "An Indian Boy in American Clothes." Eriberto P. Lozada, Jr. (Filipino American), "Blending in: Weak Attachments to the Ethnic Group. What Being Filipino American Means to Someone Called Fuji." Joel de la Fuente (Filipino American), "An (Asian American) Actor's Life." Jean Hotta (Filipino American), "My Own 'Family.'" Lakshmi Malroutu (East Indian American), "A New World: The First-Generation Experience. The Balancing Act." Margaret Yah-Min Kan (Chinese American), "Reaching the Glass Ceiling . . . at Home." Hoang Diem Hau (Vietnamese American), "An Unwilling Refugee." Pyong Gap Min and Rose Kim, "Coming to Terms: Forming One's Ethnic Identity."

18. *Sugar in the Raw: Voices of Young Black Girls in America.* Edited by Rebecca Carroll. Foreword by Ntozake Shange. New York, New York: Crown Trade Paperbacks, 1997. 144 pages. ISBN: 0517884976.

> **Notes:** Also published New York: Three Rivers Press, 1997. ISBN: 0517884976.

> **Abstract:** This book is a series of essays by young black women identified only by their first names, age, and city of residence. Rebecca Carroll collected fifty interviews with young black women throughout the United States, fifteen of which are included in the book. Carroll, an African-American teacher, was adopted by a white family and grew up in a predominantly white area. She was "drawn to interview black people because of the natural deprivation that I felt due to my circumstances growing up" (p. 15). The interviewees, aged eleven to twenty, who come from a variety of racial and socioeconomic circumstances, speak in matter-of-fact terms about their families, neighborhoods, friends, sexual orientation, personal attitudes and most important of all, dreams for the future. Carroll concludes the book by discussing black women's hair, comparing their preoccupation with it to the preoccupation of anorexics, usually young white women, with their bodies.

19. *Triumphs of Faith: Stories of Japanese-American Christians during World War II.* Edited by Victor N. Okada. Los Angeles, California: Japanese-American Internment Project, 1998. 173 pages. ISBN: none.

> **Abstract:** Fifty-two Christian Japanese-American men and women, Issei and Nisei, who were confined in the American con-

centration camps of World War II provide brief accounts of their experiences. Each narrator describes the hardships, and the fear and uncertainty that accompanied their stays in a variety of camps, including Manzanar, Tule Lake, Rohwer, and Jerome. Common experiences include the interruption of schooling, the loss of friendships, jobs, businesses, homes and property. Some of the narrators were already Christians when they entered the camps, and some were converted during their time of incarceration. All comment that their faith was important in helping them survive the war years. Editor Okada writes, "It is for the younger generations that these stories have been written. For Japanese Americans, recollections of the war years are often accompanied by pain and regret. These stories transcend the pain and regret and celebrate the triumphs of faith to which we are witness" (p. 173).

20. *Under Western Eyes: Personal Essays from Asian America.* Edited by Garrett Kaoru Hongo. New York, New York: Anchor Books, 1995. 334 pages. ISBN: 0385472390.

> **Abstract:** In his introduction, "Culture Wars in Asian America," Hongo writes about silences enforced upon minority group American writers by the cultural biases of the majority group, presumably white European Americans, and also about the silences enforced upon writers from within their ethnic communities. These are usually dictated by politics and cultural standards. In the case of Japanese Americans, silence is caused by a sense of shame over and a need for distance from their experience of internment camps. Hongo writes that he looked for essays which were "written against social silencing, but emerging from deep personal silences dedicated to reflecting upon moral, political, and identity issues. They are written against cultural conformism . . ." (p. 22). These essays have many themes in common, including that of language and the silences that arise when parents speak one language and children another, and the theme of belonging and home. Is home in the United States or across the Pacific or Atlantic? And what does it mean when neither your country of birth (the United States) nor the country of your parents and ancestors recognizes you as one of them? How do you fit in and at the same time hold on to your heritage? Included in this collection:
>
> > Peter Bacho, "The Second Room." Debra Kang Dean, "Telling Differences." Chitra Banerjee Divakaruni, "Lalita Mashi." Lillian Ho Wan, "Silence and the Graverobbers." Garrett

Hongo, "Kubota."   Jeanne Wakatsuki Houston, "Colors."
Geeta Kothari, "Where Are you From?" Geraldine Kudaka,
"Bad Blood."   Chang-Rae Lee, "The Faintest Echo of Our
Language." Li-Young Lee, "The Winged Seed." David Low,
"Winterblossom Garden."   David Mura, "The Internment of
Desire." Nguyen Qúi-Duc, "A Taste of Home." Amy Tan,
"Mother Tongue." John Yau, "A Little Memento from the
Boys."

21. *Voices of Vietnamese Boat People: Nineteen Narratives of Escape and
     Survival.* Edited by Mary Terrell Cargill and Jade Ngoc Quang
     Huynh. Jefferson, North Carolina: McFarland & Company,
     2000. 192 pages; photographs. ISBN: 0786407859.

Abstract: Of these nineteen narratives, three were written by the
narrators, and the others were transcribed and edited from interviews. Each narrative describes life in Vietnam following the fall
of Saigon, the dangerous escape, life in the refugee camps, and
then adjustment to a new home in the United States. Family members were often left behind, and many of the narrators have
worked hard to bring as many as possible to the United States.
This collection includes:

Ai-Van Do, "Simple Map, Small Compass, Three Flashlights."
Hung Lang, "The Miracle of the Whirlpool." Minh Nguyen,
"Stranger in the Rice Field, Whale in the Sea." Lan Nguyen,
"Gold Rings and Jeans."   Duyen Nguyen, "If I Die, Will
Anybody Know?" Ha Nguyen, "Our Lady of the Boat."
Suzanne Tran Cheang, "The Norwegian Protector."   Hung
Truong, "Drowning the Boat." Be Van Vo, "Out of San Diego
and into Saigon." Binh Le, "Vung Tau, Pulau Bidong, and
Bataan." Chau Nguyen, "Hainan, Hong Kong, and Tuen Mun
Camp." Phung Le, "Flight from Classification 13." Anton Yo,
"I'd Rather Die in the Sea." Hung Nguyen, "Coffee Shop from
Two Spoons." Nhan T. Le, "Coolie in America." Hien Trong
Nguyen, "To the Land of Snow." Nhut W. Huynh, "My Name
Is William, but Call Me Bill." Khon Luu, "Live Free or Die."
Jade Quang Huynh, "Return to Leam Sing Camp."

22. Abdul-Jabbar, Kareem. *A Season on the Reservation: My Sojourn with the White Mountain Apache.* Written with Stephen Singular. New York, New York: William Morrow & Company, 2000. 209 pages; photographs. ISBN: 0688170773.

Abstract: Professional basketball player, Kareem Abdul-Jabbar, looking for a new direction after the death of his mother and hoping to reconnect with basketball, decided to pursue coaching opportunities. A friend encouraged him to coach the tribal Alchesay High School basketball team, a group of athletes from the White Mountain Apache tribe. Following a brief negotiation with the superintendent of schools, Abdul-Jabbar agreed to coach for the fee of one dollar. He welcomed this opportunity for a number of reasons: he was anxious to return to the game, to get away from Los Angeles, and to research the connections between the African-American Buffalo soldiers and the Apache Scouts. His own ancestry included Native American heritage; his mother was part Cherokee and his father, a native of Trinidad, was descended from the Carib Indians. Abdul-Jabbar was interested in this part of his ethnic background and it seemed fortuitous to forge a stronger tie to this particular tribe with which he had already formed some bonds. Abdul-Jabbar started out by observing his team and quickly realized that there were many cultural issues manifested in how the boys played and that there were barriers to overcome before he could effectively communicate with them. It was also clear that basketball was important to the high school, the tribe, and the community. One of the coaches tells Abdul-Jabbar that the "basketball team are our warriors of the 1990s. When they play, they evoke the kind of things their ancestors did" (p. 20). Abdul-Jabbar was anxious to impart his knowledge of the basketball fundamentals, the skill and craft of basketball playing that he saw disappearing from professional basketball, but he discovered that team members did not like to be singled out for criticism or training. He writes, "Kids resisted change because, regardless of how difficult things might have been on the reservation, it remained, as people kept telling me, their home and comfort zone" (p. 86). Abdul-Jabbar hoped to expand that comfort zone. He struggled to reach the boys, and in the end, a mutual appreciation developed. He felt that the boys did learn and improve, and although they were not champions at the end of the season, they had grown as athletes and team players. Abdul-Jabbar became close to several of the boys and their families and learned about their culture and the social conditions of the White Mountain Apache people. "The closer you get to others," writes Abdul-Jabbar, "the more you see that everyone is similar, yet everyone holds a different piece of the gift and mystery of life. It's our differences that make us stronger, not weaker" (p. 208).

23. Abinader, Elmaz. *Children of the Roojme: A Family's Journey from Lebanon*. Madison, Wisconsin: University of Wisconsin Press, 1997. 303 pages; photographs; map. ISBN: 0299157342.

Notes: First published W .W. Norton & Company, 1991 as *Children of the Roojme: A Family's Journey*. ISBN: 0393029522.

Abstract: Abinader writes about the history of her family from about the time of World War I when her grandfather, a sheik, was trying to keep his family alive during the occupation of Lebanon by the Turks. Sheiks were often accused of crimes and killed, and many Lebanese were dying from famine and the Spanish flu. Her family left Lebanon, settling in Brazil for a time. Throughout the first half of the twentieth century, the family moved, little by little, to the United States. Abinader follows individual members of the family through their lives, rather than providing a purely chronological account. She also gives detailed descriptions of various locations, especially those in Lebanon and the United States.

24. Abu-Jamal, Mumia. *All Things Censored*. Edited by Noelle Hanrahan. Foreword by Alice Walker. New York: Seven Stories Press, 2000. 303 pages; photographs; compact disc sound recording. ISBN: 1583220224 : 1583220763.

Abstract: As in Abu-Jamal's work, *Death Blossoms*, this book is a collection of short essays. He provides the details surrounding his court cases fighting for his First Amendment rights of freedom of speech: to write, publish, and record. He describes the condition of life on Pennsylvania's death row. Abu-Jamal documents his participation in a demonstration against the presidential campaign of George Wallace during his early teen years and his subsequent beating by armed white men and a policeman. He gives his views on the Black Panthers and Huey Newton and he writes about self-censorship within the press and how that has effected his own fight for justice. Abu-Jamal also writes about his parents. A follower of the teachings of John Africa and a member of MOVE, Abu-Jamal writes about the group and explains why they consider themselves to be a religious movement. He describes the bombing and killing of eleven MOVE members and the arrest and illegal treatment of other members. Also included in this collection of essays are discussions of justice and a transcript of a conversation between editor Hanrahan and Abu-Jamal in 1995, minutes after he received his death warrant signed by the governor of Pennsylvania.

25. —. *Death Blossoms: Reflections from a Prisoner of Conscience.* Farmington, Pennsylvania: Plough Publishing House, 1997. 158 pages; photographs. ISBN: 0874860865.

> **Notes:** Also published [Farmington, Pennsylvania]: Litmus, 1996. ISBN: 0874860865 (153 pages).

> **Abstract:** In this series of essays, Mumia Abu-Jamal, born Wesley Cook, describes his beliefs and his history. As a young man, he searched for religion in various churches, synagogues, and mosques, finally finding what he was looking for in MOVE, a religious movement led by the late John Africa. He writes about his contempt for the sieges made on the MOVE community in 1978 and 1985 by the Philadelphia police and about the murders of community members. He discusses his youth, his membership in the Black Panther Party, his career in journalism, his arrest, the prison system, capital punishment, and conversations he has had with fellow prisoners.

26. —. *Live from Death Row.* Introduction by John Edgar Wideman. Reading, Massachusetts: Addison-Wesley Publishing Company, 1995. 215 pages. ISBN: 020148319X.

> **Notes:** Published in paperback New York: Avon Books, 1996. ISBN: 0380727668 (188 pages).

> **Abstract:** Mumia Abu-Jamal writes about life on death row in the Pennsylvania prison system. Abu-Jamal was a political activist from an early age. At seventeen, he and three friends heckled and were thrown out of a political rally for then-presidential candidate George Wallace, the governor of Alabama. They were then beaten up by whites as they prepared to take the subway back home. When they called for police help, a policeman came and kicked Abu-Jamal in the face. Later Abu-Jamal joined the Black Panther Party, but became disillusioned at the fighting between the factions of his two heroes, Eldridge Cleaver and Huey Newton. He went on to newspaper and radio journalism, reporting on events of particular interest to blacks. He became interested in the MOVE movement led by John Africa. His interest in this radical group on the fringes of society made him unpopular with employers, and he was forced to turn to taxi driving to make a living. One night in 1981, his brother's car was stopped by police. Abu-Jamal intervened and was shot by the policeman. The policeman himself was

also shot and killed, and Abu-Jamal was charged with the murder. The legality of the trial and his consequent conviction and death sentence have been in dispute ever since. When this book was written in 1995, his execution had been stayed pending an appeal for a new trial. The short essays that make up the book describe life on death row in Pennsylvania prisons. He talks about the preferential treatment received by white prisoners, the inordinate number of black prisoners, and the inhumane treatment of prisoners in supermaximum prisons throughout the United States, particularly non-contact visits with family and the denial of the use of typewriters or any educational materials. He calls into question the constitutionality of excusing potential jurors who object to capital punishment, death sentences for persons with mental handicaps, and the use of execution equipment which fails to kill efficiently. All of his assertions are backed up with court cases and the stories of men he has known on death row. The book concludes with details of his various trials written by his lawyer, Leonard I. Weinglass, and a list of resources for people interested in becoming involved in his cause.

27. Adams, Elizabeth Laura. *Dark Symphony, and Other Works*. Edited and with an introduction by Carla Kaplan. African-American Women Writers 1910-1940. New York, New York: G. K. Hall and Company, 1997. 282 pages. ISBN: 0783814291.

Abstract: Dark Symphony was written in 1942 when Elizabeth Laura Adams was in her thirties. She was raised in Los Angeles and Santa Barbara, California, the only child of a father who was a well-known head waiter in a Los Angeles hotel and a mother who was a painter. Her parents raised her to be infallibly obedient, polite, and well-behaved. She went to school with both white and black children and had many friends of both colors. There were times, however, when she was slighted for her race. Her parents forbade any form of aggression or revenge, teaching her instead to pray for the souls of those who had wronged her. Adams was always deeply interested in religion, especially Catholicism. She weighed the racial discrimination she incurred in the church against the enormity of her faith before she finally converted, after receiving her mother's permission, when she graduated from high school. Her father's early death and mother's frail health destroyed any hope of a college education, so she decided instead to enter a religious order. In the meantime, Adams wrote prose and poetry, a pastime she had taken up when recovering from a crippling bout of influenza. Her work was often received by publishers and editors with enthusiasm that would quickly dim when they found out she was black. During the Great Depression she was forced to go into domestic service to support her mother and herself. Adams writes of the depravity and cruelty of the white people she worked for, astonished that they had not had the same genteel breeding she had had. Discouraged with life, she became very ill again, and those around her encouraged her to join a religious order. The day before her departure, she found out her mother was going to separate from her second husband and would once again be dependent upon her. Fortunately, she was able to begin a new career in drama and literature, an opportunity offered her by a professor at UCLA. Adams concludes by discussing the depth of her faith and her thankfulness to priests, nuns, and various white people who befriended her and gave her new opportunities. She could not, however, forget the discrimination she had experienced in the church. "I learned that *knowledge* must accompany faith. I never enter a church without asking God to give me more faith in the Blessed Sacrament. I never kneel at an altar for Holy Communion without being fearful lest I be passed by. This will never change. . . . I am Colored" (p. 192).

28. Aguilera, Luis Gabriel. *Gabriel's Fire*. Chicago, Illinois: University of Chicago Press, 2000. 291 pages. ISBN: 0226010678.

Abstract: Aguilera's work covers the period of his life from age thirteen to his graduation from high school (1985-1991). Aguilera addresses adult role models and anti-models, gangs, the role of the church in leading and misleading youth, children forced into making adult decisions, and conflicting loyalties. He was born in Mexico and grew up with his mother, father, and two brothers on Chicago's South Side. He and his brothers were altar boys and attended the local Catholic school. At thirteen, Aguilera had an affair with one of his teachers, and he was the one forced by authorities to take responsibility for the situation. He writes about his working relationship with the parish priest, who was irresponsibly "hip" and blatantly bigoted. Aguilera suggests that this relationship bordered on the inappropriate, and again it was his responsibility to put a stop to it. His dedication to the church was further damaged when the two Catholic schools on the South Side were closed, and the students were forced to finish school in an all-white environment on the North Side. To Aguilera and the other children from the schools that were closed, this meant losing their safe haven and the support of the teachers with whom they had grown up. The closings were felt to be motivated by money, and biased in favor of white students. Aguilera describes the difficulty of avoiding gang-inspired violence. He became more and more angry at his betrayal by adults he trusted and at racist behavior of teachers and students at his new school. As his anger grew, so did his tendency to react violently when challenged. His own gang, the UPCs, were not "gang bangers" and had no interest in turf wars or other violence. As Aguilera was finishing high school, the UPCs disbanded because of the increasing threat of conflict, and Aguilera found himself being pulled into the cycle of violence. Aguilera had a scholarship to attend UCLA, but was ambivalent about the prospect. The book ends as he contemplates moving to Mexico to live with relatives in an attempt to escape what seems to be the inevitability of a violent and perhaps fatal confrontation.

29. Ahmed, Leila. *A Border Passage: From Cairo to America—A Woman's Journey.* New York, New York: Farrar, Straus, and Giroux, 1999. 307 pages. ISBN: 0374115184.

Notes: Published in paperback New York: Penguin books, 2000. ISBN: 0140291830.

Abstract: Leila Ahmed, the first professor of Women's Studies in Religion at Harvard Divinity School, grew up in Egypt during the 1940s and 1950s, which was a time of great change for that country. She was raised speaking the Arabic dialect spoken in Cairo and educated almost exclusively in English. She and her brothers and sisters all went to college in England. Ahmed attended Girton in Cambridge. Ahmed uses the story of her parents, her own childhood, and her British education to explore the general problem of identity for herself and other women of color and, in particular, that of Egyptians within the Arab and world communities. During years of soul-searching at Cambridge, she made a far-reaching study of Egypt and discovered how during the twentieth century the country had gone from being a multicultural, multireligious society which clearly supported Israel as a Jewish homeland, to an Arab-nationalistic culture whose identity seemed to hinge on its support of returning Palestine to the Palestinians. She discovered how little the change had to do with the will of Egyptians themselves and how each step in this transition was either carefully manipulated by Western powers or was a backlash to such manipulations. Ahmed concluded that the very definition of the word "Arab" as used by Egyptians and the rest of the Arab countries was based on Western bias. Ahmed's interests turned to feminism during a few years spent in Abu Dhabi, United Arab

Emirates, where she helped develop the educational system. She realized that Arabs from other countries, including herself, were using their own cultures intrusively to influence the education and advancement of women in a society that did not want it. At the same time, she couldn't leave things as they were because she found the traditional culture in Abu Dhabi much too prescribed for women. This new interest took her to the United States, where she became one of the pioneers in the field of women's studies.

30. Ailey, Alvin (1931-1989). *Revelations: The Autobiography of Alvin Ailey.* Written with A. Peter Bailey. Secaucus, New Jersey: Carol Publishing Group, 1995. 183 pages; photographs. ISBN: 155972255x.

Notes: Published in paperback, 1997. ISBN: 0806518618. Reprint published Bridgewater, New Jersey: Replica Books, 1999. ISBN: 0735100802.

Abstract: Dancer Alvin Ailey was born into a life of poverty. He never knew his father, and he and his mother made their home with a series of aunts. When he was eight, he and his mother moved from Texas to Los Angeles. He was introduced to dancing when he saw classmate and future dance partner Carmen de Lavallade dance at a school assembly. Ailey was afraid of what dance lessons would do to his reputation, but de Lavallade talked him into observing her dance classes at the Lester Horton studio. Ailey started attending off and on and quickly became devoted to the art. He and de Lavallade danced together with the Lester Horton dance troupe, which Ailey notes was one of only two dance companies that would accept black dancers, and later in New York until the early 1960s. Ailey founded his own dance troupe because the dance world was very European-oriented and actively excluded black dancers, always with the excuse that black dancers were not historically appropriate. Ailey sees this as ludicrous, writing, "What we're talking about here is dance. We're talking about fantasy, not reality. . . . It's the same as saying the Japanese dancers can't dance the blues—well they do in *my* company" (p. 128). Ailey's own troupe was integrated. He had complaints from the African-American dance community, which wanted it to stay entirely black. He also had complaints from the white dancers in the troupe, who felt he favored the African-American dancers in the company. Ailey says he reserved only one leading part, that in *Cry*, for a female African-American dancer because it is dedicated to his "mother and black women everywhere" (p. 129). Ailey writes about his work with many great African-American singers, musicians, actors, and dancers, including his collaboration with Duke Ellington. He describes his decline into cocaine use, alcoholism, and madness following the death of long-time friend and colleague Joyce Trisler. After hospitalization and a long, slow recovery, Ailey readjusted his working priorities to spend less time managing and more time creating. Many of Ailey's dances are autobiographical and require his dancers to act as well as dance. His most highly acclaimed works include *Revelations, Roots of the Blues, Memoria*, written after the death of Joyce Trisler, and *Phases*, the work written after his recovery. Ailey died in 1989, leaving behind two dance companies, The Alvin Ailey American Dance Center, which offers classes to 3,000 students a year, and a large repertory of ballets.

31. Aleckson, Sam (b. 1852). *Before the War and after the Union.* Chapel Hill, North Carolina: Academic Affairs Library, University of North Carolina at Chapel Hill, 2000.

    http://docsouth.unc.edu/neh/aleckson/menu.html

    Notes: Documenting the American South (Project).
    Available in paper Boston, Massachusetts: Gold Mind Publishing, 1990 (171 pages).

32. Allen, Marcus. *Marcus: The Autobiography of Marcus Allen.* Written with Carlton Stowers. New York, New York: St. Martin's Press, 1997. 313 pages; photographs. ISBN: 0312169248 : 0312966237.

    Abstract: Marcus Allen was born into a family of two parents and six sons. He credits his and his brothers' accomplishments to the support and encouragement they got from their parents. Allen and four of his brothers were accomplished athletes, including his brother Damon, who is a star in the Canadian Football League. After high school, Allen went to the University of Southern California to play for the Trojan football team, had an outstanding career there, and received the Heisman Trophy in his senior year. He was then drafted into the National Football League by the Los Angeles Raiders and started a promising professional career. Allen writes extensively about his eleven years with the Raiders. The owner, Al Davis, oversaw the day to day running of the entire organization and at some point developed a dislike for Allen. For years he refused to let the coaches play him, but also steadfastly refused to trade or otherwise release him. Finally in 1992, Allen taped an interview in which he spoke openly about his treatment by the Raiders' owner. The interview was broadcast during half time of a televised Raiders game, and Davis was finally forced to let him go. Allen was quickly approached by a number of other teams, and decided to join the Kansas City Chiefs. His career was rehabilitated, and he thrived on the open, friendly, and supportive atmosphere in the Chiefs organization and the unconditional support of Kansas City fans. He retired in 1997 to become a television sports commentator. Allen discusses his part in the controversy surrounding the O. J. Simpson criminal and civil trials. He also describes the employment conditions of football players, pointing out the disadvantages of the players in terms of ability to negotiate or take a degree of control over their own careers. As far as race is concerned, Allen says, "While the players are generally color-blind, management still has a long way to go" (p. 208), citing the small number of black head coaches as an example. Many talented black college coaches, he says, have refused to even look for a job in the NFL because of the marginal role they assume they would be given.

33. Allen, Richard (1760-1831) and Absalom Jones (1746-1818). *The Life, Experience, and Gospel Labours of the Rt. Rev. Richard Allen to Which Is Annexed the Rise and Progress of the African Methodist Episcopal Church in the United States of America: Containing a Narrative of the Yellow Fever in the Year of Our Lord 1793: With an Address to the People of Colour in the United States.* Chapel Hill, North Carolina: Academic Affairs Library, University of North Carolina at Chapel Hill, 2000.

     http://docsouth.unc.edu/neh/allen/allen.sgml
     http://docsouth.unc.edu/neh/allen/allen.html

     Notes: Documenting the American South (Project).
     Originally published Philadelphia: Martin & Boden, Printers, 1833 (60 pages).

34. Als, Hilton. *The Women.* New York, New York: Farrar, Straus, and Giroux, 1996. 145 pages. ISBN: 0374292051.

     Notes: Published in paperback New York: The Noonday Press, 1998. ISBN: 0374525293.

     Abstract: Hilton Als, writer and cultural critic, writes about his own life and identity as a homosexual, more specifically as a "Negress" or "auntie man" (the terms for homosexuals in his native Barbados), using stories of three women and a man. The first is his mother, a woman who lived in poverty with her children, refusing

to marry the rich man who had fathered most of them. His mother called herself a Negress, and this is the identity that Als has chosen for himself. He talks about being a "Negress" in terms of how
his mother saw herself and how society viewed her and other
black women. He thinks about the connection between his mother and himself as he watches her slowly die from physical causes
that he believes were triggered when his father left her for another woman. The next woman he writes about is Louise Little, the
mother of Malcolm X, who is remembered for nothing other than
that she was the target of her son's hatred. He uses the illustration
to show how many black women are known only in the context of
the men in their family. The third woman is Dorothy Dean, a highly educated and intelligent black woman who befriended white
homosexuals, acting as their escort in society. He focuses on the
hopelessness of her relationships with them. The one man he
writes about, Owen Dodson, was a writer during the Harlem
Renaissance. Als, then a teenager, met Dodson as an old, disabled
man, and they had a sexual relationship. Als scrutinizes the influence each of the above mentioned individuals have had on the
development and emergence of his own personality and identity.

35. Alvarez, Julia. *Something to Declare.* Chapel Hill, North
Carolina: Algonquin Books of Chapel Hill, 1998. 300 pages.
ISBN: 1565121937.

> **Notes:** Published in paperback New York: Plume, 1999. ISBN:
> 0452280672.

> **Abstract:** Poet, novelist, and teacher Alvarez has written a series
> of essays to answer the questions of readers "who want to know
> more than I have told you in my novels and poems. About my
> experience of immigration, about switching languages, about the
> writing life, the teaching life, the family life, about all those com-
> bined" (p. x). Born in the Dominican Republic, Alvarez's father
> was involved in the underground movement against the reigning
> dictator. Knowing that his and his family's lives would likely be
> threatened, the father obtained a student visa, and the family left
> for New York. While still in the Dominican Republic, Alvarez
> studied at a school where all subjects were taught in English, but
> it was still a shock to find herself surrounded by nothing but
> English when she arrived in the United States. When she started
> school, she finally began to understand the power and possibili-
> ties of language. Alvarez's new vision of language sent her solid-
> ly in the direction of writing. She has been inspired and influ-
> enced by many writers, but chiefly William Carlos Williams,

whose mother was Puerto Rican and spoke Spanish at home, and Maxine Hong Kingston, from whom she learned about dealing with "the duality of her experience" (p. 168). Alvarez writes from her experiences as a native-born Dominican and as a Latina in the United States. "By writing powerfully about our Latino culture, we are forging a tradition and creating a literature that will widen and enrich the existing canon" (p. 170). Alvarez has published several novels, including *How the Garcia Girls Lost Their Accent* (1992) and *In the Time of Butterflies* (1994), which is about the Mirabel Sisters of the Dominican Republic who were murdered during the Trujillo regime. She has also published several books of poetry. Alvarez taught at Middlebury College in Vermont but resigned her position to write full time.

36. Anderson, Thomas (b. 1785). *Interesting Account of Thomas Anderson, a Slave, Taken from His Own Lips.* Taken down by J. P. Clark. Chapel Hill, North Carolina: Academic Affairs Library, University of North Carolina at Chapel Hill, 2000.

   http://docsouth.unc.edu/neh/anderson/anderson.sgml
   http://docsouth.unc.edu/neh/anderson/anderson.html

   Notes: Documenting the American South (Project).

37. Angelou, Maya. *Even the Stars Look Lonesome.* New York, New York: Random House, 1997. 145 pages. ISBN: 0375500316.

   Notes: Published in paperback New York: Bantam Books, 1998. ISBN: 0553379720.

   Abstract: Noted poet, author, autobiographer, playwright, and screenplay writer Maya Angelou writes a series of short essays on her own life and commentaries on life in general. The themes of the essays range from the importance of the survival of African culture throughout the world to African art, African-American spirit, the strength of African-American women, the romanticizing of the history of slavery, her own changing views on aging, on having a house that is truly a home, her mother, and others. She includes the poetry of many African-American poets to illustrate her ideas, especially those about the importance and necessity of art as a part of life. She uses poems by Langston Hughes and Paul Laurence Dunbar in the essay "Art for the Sake of the Soul," in which she asserts that it is art that has made it possible for black Americans to persevere despite all hardships.

   > I have written of the black American experience,
   > which I know intimately. I am always talking

about the human condition in general and about
society in particular. What it is like to be human,
and American, what makes us weep, what
makes us fall and stumble and somehow rise
and go on from darkness into darkness that
darkness carpeted with figures of fear and the
hounds behind and hunters behind and one
more river to cross, and oh, my God, will I ever
reach that somewhere, that safe getting-up
morning. I submit to you that it is art that allows
us to stand erect.   (p. 130)

38. Arboleda, Teja. *In the Shadow of Race: Growing Up as a
Multiethnic, Multicultural, and "Multiracial" American.*
Mahwah, New Jersey: Erlbaum Publishers, 1998. 268 pages.
ISBN: 0805825746 : 0805825754.

Abstract: Arboleda is an actor, video artist, and writer. He travels
around the country performing his one man play Ethnic Man! (A
version of this play is available on video from Ethnic Diversity,
1997.) In one of his many conversations with the individuals he
comes into contact with while traveling and performing, he
described himself as follows: "Born in Brooklyn, grew up in
Germany, then New York, then Japan for 14 years. My father's
African-American/Native-American and Filipino-Chinese and
my mother's German/Danish" (p. 255). Arboleda's focus is his
diverse ethnic and cultural background. He testified before
Congress in support of adding a "multiracial" category to the 2000
census after having been pressured by previous census takers to
mark a box indicating his race. After three visits, Arboleda still
refused, so the census taker marked Hispanic. Arboleda's mother
was born in Germany, and his father was raised in the United
States and the Philippines. Arboleda's paternal grandfather left
the Philippines in his early teens and found that when he returned
to take over his family responsibilities with his part Gullah, part
Indian wife and children, he was not accepted by his Filipino family, nor was his wife ever welcomed in the community. Arboleda's
father found that he belonged with no community, neither African
American, white, nor Asian. He traveled in Germany, where he
met his wife-to-be. They also faced the problems of an interracial
marriage, both in Germany and in the United States. Arboleda
and his brother Miguel found as did their father, that they
belonged in no one's world. The Arboledas decided to move to
Japan, a possible neutral territory. Although Japan did not prove
to be a paradise, the children found a niche in their American

school, and their father was accepted and able to develop a rewarding career. Although Arboleda's father remained permanently in Japan, his mother left to live in the United States when Arboleda was in high school. When Arboleda returned to the United States to attend college, he endured continuous culture shock. Arboleda's life experiences and career have been shaped and colored by his multiracial and diverse cultural upbringing. His own desire to understand who he is has often run afoul of others trying to force their own definitions upon him. In his introduction, Arboleda writes,

> What I am is human. A high schooler might groan over that statement, but it is after all, the only truth. Everything else is political. . . . This is what the book is all about—my perceptions about who I am. Hopefully, this might encourage others to reflect on who they are outside of the limited categories of race, ethnicity, gender, religion, class, and all those other things that politically fragment what they are. After all, the basis of discrimination is sociopolitical—we, as humans, intellectualize our differences.   (p. ix)

39. Archuleta, Ruben E. (1945-). *I Came from El Valle: From the Fields to the Chief's Office.* Edited by Terry Freeman. Pueblo, Colorado: Shuster's Printing, 1999. 259 pages; photographs. ISBN: 0962974838.

Abstract: Law enforcement officer Ruben Archuleta begins his work with a description of the general area of his birth near Antonito, Colorado just north of the New Mexico border. His grandparents, who had a comfortable farm in the area, raised Archuleta and his sister while their parents did migrant farm work. Upon completing high school, Archuleta joined the Navy. He shipped to various locations in the Pacific and spent two years in action off the coast of Vietnam during the Vietnam Conflict. Following his six-year tour of duty, Archuleta returned to his parents' home in Pueblo, Colorado, and attended college. Settling on a career in law enforcement, Archuleta never looked back. He started out as a beat patrolman, was promoted to sergeant, attended the FBI National Academy, and was promoted to captain. Archuleta's responsibilities included working with the Russian inspection teams and the On Site Inspection Agency to monitor the Pueblo Depot Activity (PDA) in conjunction with the Intermediate-Range Nuclear Forces (INF) Treaty. He also provid-

ed security for high level visitors, including presidents, presidential hopefuls, and entertainers. Archuleta provides photographs
and recounts many of his adventures as a police officer in Pueblo.
He describes enduring several years of severe depression as he
struggled with a new police chief. Surviving this episode, he was
appointed as the next police chief. Strong willed and exhibiting
the utmost integrity, Archuleta found himself under pressure from
important political figures to compromise his beliefs and his professional standards. When he attempted to retire in the midst of
such pressure, an overwhelming flood of support from citizens,
coworkers, supervisees, youth, and community officials convinced him to stay on. Archuleta has a wife, to whom he is devoted, and three daughters. He is involved in a number of community activities, including the Special Olympics and the Latino
Chamber of Commerce.

40. Ariyoshi, Koji (1914-1976). *From Kona to Yenan: The Political
Memoirs of Koji Ariyoshi*. Edited by Alice M. Beechert and
Edward D. Beechert. Honolulu, Hawai'i: Published for the
Biographical Research Center by the University of Hawai'i
Press, 2000. 225 pages; photographs. ISBN: 0824823761.

Abstract: In 1951, Koji Ariyoshi was arrested along with six other
people under the Smith Act on charges of being a member of the
Communist Party and advocating the violent overthrow of the
U.S. Government. In the years that it took Ariyoshi's case to travel through the court system, he reflected on his life and the question of whether to plead guilty or not guilty. His reflections took
the form of a number of essays originally published in the
Honolulu Record, of which he was the editor. In his essays he
describes the events, observations, people, and experiences which
gave him his particular world view and path in life. Ariyoshi
grew up in poverty on his parents' small coffee farm, conditions he
later compared to poverty-stricken white tenant farmers in
Georgia and similar situations in India and China. He had completed his studies at the University of Georgia and was living in
California when the order was given to relocate all Japanese and
Japanese Americans from the West Coast during World War II. He
was sent to the Manzanar Relocation Center. Ariyoshi joined a
group of volunteers in the Idaho beet fields and later volunteered
for the army to work in military intelligence. His assignments
included a tour of duty in China, where he spent a significant
amount of his time in Yenan with the Communists. He had the
opportunity there to assess the differences between the
Communist Chinese under Mao Tse-tung and the Nationalists led

by Chiang Kai Shek. He left China strongly supporting the aims of the Communists, and his sympathies were with the laborer and the downtrodden. He had very little respect for what he viewed as the corrupt regime of Chiang. By the time his military tour of duty came to an end, U.S. politics began to take a serious shift to the right, and it was this political climate that eventually led to his arrest. He writes:

> I began opposing and fighting discrimination when I experienced bias toward me and my friends by other people because of color and ancestry. I saw the crime of intervention in foreign affairs from my China experience. All these made strong impacts upon me and helped shape my thinking. The conditions that I experienced developed me. A great many of these situations require improvement. No one disagrees on this point. I have directed my thoughts toward that end, and I have tried to find answers to the problems, just as many others likewise must have done and must be doing. In the eyes of the guardians of the status quo, to do so is a crime.
>
> (p. 197)

41. Arnett, Marvin V. *Pieces from the Crazy Quilt: The Childhood Memoirs of a Great-Grandmother.* Bloomington, Indiana: 1st. Books Library, 1997. 206 pages. ISBN: none.

Notes: Also published in a revised edition in 2000. ISBN: 1587210177; Lincoln: University of Nebraska Press, 2003. ISBN: 0803210647.

Abstract: Marvin V. Arnett was born in Detroit, Michigan, in 1928. She writes about the years of her childhood until 1943, when she finished junior high school. Each chapter describes a particular episode from her life, most of which have her parents at the center. Her father, William, was widely considered to be the wisest man in the neighborhood. He was looked to for solutions to particularly sticky problems and was the one who went down to the local grammar school to straighten out any injustices to the black students. Arnett's mother, Gracie, was viewed as a saint. She was a pillar of her church, an excellent cook and seamstress, and unfailingly kindhearted. Together, her parents looked after weaker members of the community, especially those considered for some reason to be inferior to the rest. At a time when mixed-race marriages were unthinkable, William encouraged the local Jewish fish-shop owner to marry his true love, a black mother who had been abandoned by her common-law husband. Arnett's mother befriended a woman who was scorned by the rest of the neighborhood because she was the mistress of a married man. She was also strong enough to face up to a well-liked and respected minister who she discovered had been sexually abusing young girls. Some of Arnett's stories are tragic, such as that of a handicapped child who was shot and killed by a policeman, the beating death of her godmother by her husband, and the race riots that broke out in Detroit in the summer of 1943. Arnett ends the book by describing how each character mentioned in the book taught her important lessons about life that she would like to see passed down to young people today.

42   Arteaga, Alfred (1950-). *House with the Blue Bed*. San Francisco, California: Mercury House, 1997. 114 pages. ISBN: 1562791060.

Abstract: Alfred Arteaga, Chicano poet and professor of literature at the University of California, Berkeley, offers a series of essays about places and events that seem at first to be unrelated. He writes about peaceful scenes, beaches in Ireland and Mexico, time spent in Paris, and various romantic encounters. He then links them to stories of violence, including traffic accidents he has witnessed, the rape of a neighbor, and a situation in which he comes home to find his daughter "in an assassination position, kneeling" (p. 57) while a policeman holds a gun to her head. He then uses irony to compare these scenes with even more extreme instances of cultural and partisan violence in the United States, especially in California, and in Ireland. For example, he attributes his success in calmly talking the policeman into letting his daughter go to a Chicano protest against the war in Vietnam in Los Angeles which he had witnessed many years before. The protest resulted in the violent deaths of journalist Ruben Salazar and others. He says he was able to give the policeman holding his daughter the images and words he could relate to,

> I did my best to speak my daughter out of insignificance and to move her image in his mind to an equivalency with that of a suburban Anglo girl of the bourgeoisie, the national icon he would be loathe to kill. . . . I think that had I not lost faith as a young man in East Los Angeles, I might have lost a daughter that day in San Jose.   (p. 58)

43. Asayesh, Gelareh. *Saffron Sky: A Life between Iran and America.* Boston, Massachusetts: Beacon Press, 1999. 222 pages. ISBN: 0807072109 : 0807072117.

> **Abstract:** Gelareh Asayesh, a newspaper reporter and writer, was born in Iran and went to the United States with her family for schooling in 1977 at the age of 15. Soon after they moved, the Shah was overthrown and the Islamic fundamentalists led by the Ayatollah Khomeini took over. Largely for this reason, neither she nor other family members went back to Iran until 1990. She writes about the happy reunion with her aunts, uncles, and cousins and how she reacquainted herself with Iranian life. Although she was encumbered by the new regulations for women as well as the increased importance of religious practices, she realized that she could still pursue many of the pleasures she remembered from her childhood. Interwoven with this story, Asayesh recounts the difficulties she had fitting into American life as a teenager and how she and her family did their best to assimilate. She also analyzes their reasons for staying in the United States despite the fact that they felt so much like outsiders and her parents' original determination that their family would eventually return to Iran. Following her initial trip home, she began to make trips as frequently as once a year. She writes about the birth of her daughter and their trips to Iran together. Now that Asayesh was spending more time in Iran, her next dilemma was how to maintain a balance of both cultures and assuage her homesickness and need for connection with her native culture. She spoke only Farsi to her daughter and demanded that her husband also study the language. They bought samovars, carpets, and other Iranian household articles, and did their best to keep up traditional Iranian celebrations. As the book ends, the family is getting ready to spend four months together living in Iran, and while she looks forward to going, she is already dreading the heartbreak of having to leave her home in the United States.

44. Ashby, William M. (1889-1991). *Tales without Hate.* Preface by Douglas Eldridge. Introduction by Clement Alexander Price. 2nd ed. Newark, New Jersey: Newark Preservation and Landmarks Committee/Upland Press, 1996. 221 pages; photographs; facsimile documents. ISBN: 0964291657.

> **Notes:** Originally published 1980. 2nd edition includes sixteen new chapters.

Abstract: In 136 vignettes, Mr. Ashby delineates his family history, provides a picture of his childhood and of his career as a social worker and director of the Urban League of Essex County, New Jersey, and Springfield, Illinois. One of ten surviving children, Ashby was born in 1899 to parents who, according to family lore, came from a long line of free, land-owning Negroes. Born and raised in Newport News, Virginia, Ashby moved to New Jersey with his mother and brother and then enrolled in Lincoln University in Pennsylvania, leaving home with the fifty-dollar tuition sewn into his shirt. Following graduation in 1911, Ashby, greatly influenced by Eugene Debs, was determined to find employment in some field that would allow him to aid his fellow human being. But few careers were open to him: only those of teacher, doctor, minister, and lawyer. Ashby found work as a waiter until he was financially able to return to school. He enrolled in the School of Religion at Yale University. One of sixteen African-American students enrolled in similar programs at Yale, Ashby recounts the racism he encountered from students and faculty alike. After finishing school, he returned to New Jersey, where he was eventually offered a position as the first director of the Essex County Urban League in 1917. Ashby remained deeply involved in this kind of work for most of his long career, not retiring until 1953. As an Urban League director, Ashby specialized in opening doors of employment for African Americans, especially the hundreds of thousands immigrating from the South during the first half of the twentieth century. Ashby's vignettes include stories of Marian Anderson, Paul Robeson, and the plight of African-American soldiers returning from World War II to find neither housing nor employment open to them. Thinking about retirement, Ashby writes,

> I was tired, dead tired physically. Moreover, for thirty-seven years, my mind and my emotions had been buffeted about from pillar to post as I tried to understand and assuage the hatreds of one man for another; as I tried to placate the wounds of men for whom justice was just a mockery; as I tried to give inspiration and aspiration to one who has peeped through the murk and seen a star, and set as his goal the reaching of that star. . . . I had not succeeded.
>
> (p. 202)

However he ends his book with a ray of hope. He tells about a small boy who comes up to the curb, takes his hand, and helps him across the street. Ashby decides from this that "mankind need not have fear that it will be blasted into oblivion tomorrow" (p. 213).

45. Awkward, Michael. *Scenes of Instruction: A Memoir*. Durham, North Carolina: Duke University Press, 1999. 208 pages; photographs; index. ISBN: 0822324024.

Abstract: Michael Awkward, a professor at the University of Pennsylvania, writes about his youth, using graduation from each level of schooling for his benchmarks: elementary school, junior high school, high school at a private prep school, college at Brandeis University, and graduate school at the University of Pennsylvania. Awkward states in his introduction:

> This book constitutes my risky attempt to circulate the major themes of my mother's narratives, and to demonstrate that I've absorbed their form and content well enough to contribute to feminism's efforts to challenge patriarchy's unabated rule. A record of events that have marked that still on-going search, it combines biographical recall, textual criticism, and institutional analysis in a form that . . . we might call "autocritography."   (p. 7)

Awkward was raised by his mother, an alcoholic, in South Philadelphia. His abusive father had left the home. Awkward excelled in school, but he always felt uncomfortable in the roles that black males were expected to have in terms of force and domination over females. He preferred mooning over the girl of his dreams and avoiding confrontation with anything sexually explicit or violent. He was so different from the men around him that his mother and sister finally asked him if he was gay. He became more confused about his identity when he went off to an elite prep school. The school was predominantly white, but he found himself forced into the Black Brotherhood, a group that demanded loyalty and kept itself segregated. He stayed with the group, feeling oppressed by it but also welcoming the familiarity. In college, he pursued his interest in feminism by attending a class, entitled "The Black Woman," in which he was treated with hostility by the professor. Awkward pursues these and other topics relating to his youth, linking them to his relationship with and feelings for his mother. He alternates narrative with criticism of black writers and intellectuals and discussions of various intellectual matters he has wrestled with as an adult to show how his early experiences have influenced his ideas and work.

46. Baek, Hongyong (1912-). *See* Lee, Helie.

47. Bagby, Rachel L. *Divine Daughters: Liberating the Power and Passion of Women's Voices.* San Francisco, California: HarperSanFrancisco, 1999. 279 pages. ISBN: 0062514261 : 006251427x.

> **Abstract:** Bagby writes about her efforts to exorcise the demons of racism, sexism, sexual abuse, and parental neglect by expressing her emotions through chanting, singing, dancing, and worship. She celebrates the feminine, affirming all that women represent, and seeks the divine in each woman. Bagby entered Stanford Law School in 1971. She was one of thirty-five women and seven black students out of a total class of 172. During this intense time, Bagby regularly turned to the mountains and forests for rejuvenation, and these natural forces have continued to sustain her during other times of recovery. After law school, Bagby was raped while attending a spiritual retreat. The wounds from the attack made it impossible for her to function in society, and she became destitute and homeless, sleeping in the San Francisco Airport. During this period, Bagby's self-hatred—especially for herself as an African American and as a woman—made her easy prey for sexual exploitation. To win herself back, she returned to her mother's house to learn her mother's stories and those of the other women of her family. She turned to intense spiritual experiences and celebrations, which included expressing herself through music and dance and which affirmed the divinity of women. Bagby tells her story because she believes that women must pass their stories on to their daughters—the bad with the good—so that their daughters can learn and be inspired and grow as part of a tradition or community of women. "I could not live without knowing and giving voice to how they had lived. Their stories were my breath and my birthright. They restored my soul" (p. 189). Inspirational chants and poetry are included throughout the book.

48. Bailey, Cornelia. *God, Dr. Buzzard, and the Bolito Man: A Saltwater Geechee Talks about Life on Sapelo Island.* Written with Christena Bledsoe. New York, New York: Doubleday, 2000. 334 pages; photographs; map. ISBN: 0385493762.

> **Notes:** Published in paperback New York: Anchor Books, 2001. ISBN: 0385493770.

> **Abstract:** The Geechee and Gullah people are believed to be directly descended from slaves brought from Sierra Leone specifi-

cally to grow rice on the Sea Islands off the coast of South Carolina and Georgia. The Geechee live predominantly on the islands along Georgia, and the Gullah, on the islands along South Carolina. Cornelia Bailey was born on Sapelo Island where her family has lived since slavery times. She spent the first part of her married life on nearby St. Simons Island, but soon returned with her husband to live in the community of Hog Hammock on Sapelo Island. It is one of the most isolated Sea Islands. In this work, Bailey describes life as it was on the island during her childhood. Because of the isolation, many religious beliefs and cultural and domestic practices of the early Geechee society remained intact. At the time of emancipation, many of the plantation owners left the island, but the freed slaves chose to remain. Although they were no longer slaves, the African-American islanders were still subject to the arbitrary whims of the local white landowners and employers. Bailey's father was cheated out of his family's land by his employer who forcefully moved families out of all but one area of the island. This destroyed the several distinct communities on the island, combining them all into one. In 1989, Bailey was part of a Gullah/Geechee delegation to Sierra Leone, where she noted a landscape and climate similar to Sapelo and recognized many objects, songs, practices, and food items. Bailey was overwhelmed by this evidence of her family's and community's direct connection to the people of Sierra Leone. Today Bailey continues to work to preserve Hog Hammock as a Geechee community. She concludes her work with the following:

> I want us always to have a community on this island. A community of people who enjoy quiet living, value the land, and want to raise children in a place that is still a paradise for kids. I want the state and people everywhere to be proud of us and to realize the distinct historic and cultural value we have as a people who've lived here ever since the time of slavery. . . . [W]e're about the last majority Geechee/Gullah population living on a major island unconnected to the mainland in the *entire string* of Sea Islands, from South Carolina to Florida.   (p. 333)

49. Baker, Terri. *I'm Not Dancing Anymore: O. J. Simpson's Niece Speaks Her Mind*. Written with Kenneth Ross and Mary Jane Ross. New York, New York: Kensington Books, 1997. 291 pages; photographs. ISBN: 1575662566.

> **Notes:** Also published New York: Pinnacle Books, 1998 as *I'm Not Dancing Anymore: O. J. Simpson's Niece Breaks the Silence*. ISBN: 0786005343 (303 pages).

> **Abstract:** Terri Baker is a niece of O. J. Simpson, the former professional football player who, in 1995, was tried and acquitted for the murder of his former wife, Nicole Brown, and an acquaintance of hers, Ron Goldman. Baker says that her family always maintained a great interest in Simpson, following his football and celebrity careers and treating him with deference. Simpson, however, was not attentive to his family, and chose instead to spend his time and money on his friends and lovers, most of whom were white. Baker always wondered about the situation, especially about the lack of attention given to her grandmother and mother, Simpson's mother and elder sister. When Simpson was accused and tried for the murder of his former wife, the family rallied around him. Baker was the only Simpson relative living in Southern California at the time and, along with making daily appearances at the Los Angeles courthouse (defense lawyers recommended a strong show of family support), she was given the tasks of shuttling San Francisco relatives to and from the airport, spending time at the jail with her uncle, and the enormous job of sorting through his mail. Because of the time away from work and stress of the trial, both she and her mother quit their jobs, and their personal lives were destroyed. After the trial, Simpson went back to his friends and, by this time, Baker had turned to drink. She finally sought help at a rehabilitation clinic where she received the treatment she needed. She was appalled that her family rarely visited her, even though they had given up everything for Simpson, with whom they had rarely had contact. She began venting the anger that had built up, and this venting caused a great deal of friction within her family, but she was able to move back into society and offer her support during the Simpson civil trial in 1996.

50. Baker, Vernon J. *Lasting Valor*. Columbus, Mississippi: Genesis Press, 1997. 294 pages; photographs. ISBN: 1885478526.

> **Notes:** Also published New York: Bantam Books, 1999. ISBN: 0553580620 (315 pages).

Abstract: Vernon J. Baker, the only living black veteran of World War II to receive the Medal of Honor, grew up in Cheyenne, Wyoming. As a young man, his best opportunity for employment was the United States Army. He describes the racial discrimination rampant in the military, and how the black soldiers, members of the Buffalo Soldier units, were not considered worthy of active service in World War II until white mothers began to complain that only their sons were dying. Baker was an officer in his unit, the 92nd Infantry Division, which served in Italy. Baker led his men during a battle to capture Castle Aghinolfi from the Germans. He lost nineteen of twenty-five men, but fought on, even after the white commander had fled, giving up the soldiers who remained for dead. Baker was decorated and promoted for his role in the battle, but he never knew that he had been nominated for the Medal of Honor. It was widely known that the U.S. Army refused to give its highest honors to black and Nisei soldiers who fought in World War II, even though they were widely lauded and given highest honors by the French and Italian governments. Baker stayed in the army for almost thirty years. He saw the army desegregate and was given command over white soldiers. He finally retired during the Vietnam War, discouraged and intimidated by the lack of morale among the troops and by rampant drug use. Fifty-two years after the end of World War II, in January 1997, Baker and six black soldiers who had died in battle were awarded the Medal of Honor by President Bill Clinton at the White House. The awards came about following a study commissioned by the Secretary of the Army to determine why no black World War II veterans had ever received this honor.

51.   Bandele, Asha. *The Prisoner's Wife: A Memoir*. New York, New York: Scribner, 1999. 219 pages. ISBN: 0684850737.

> **Notes:** Also published New York: Washington Square Press, 2000. (Includes WSP Readers Club guide.) ISBN: 0671021486.

> **Abstract:** Asha Bandele, a poet, writer and speaker, records the history of her relationship with Rashid, a Guyana-born prisoner in a New York correctional facility. As a college student, she volunteered to give poetry readings at prisons and met Rashid during this time. Two years later, they began a romantic relationship, first via letters and phone calls, and later through Bandele's frequent visits to the prison. Rashid was honest with her about the circumstances of his imprisonment. He had participated in a murder and was unable to even petition for parole for twenty years. She learned later that many wives and girlfriends had little informa-

tion on the crimes their men were convicted of, and while she appreciated Rashid more for his openness, she was also haunted by visions of the wife and child of the murdered man. When the two began examining the poverty and abuse of Rashid's child-hood in Guyana, she began to recall her own childhood and youth, remembering instances of sexual abuse she herself had suffered. Rashid helped her through this difficult period of coming to terms with her past, and this support enabled Bandele to complete col-lege and launch a career. Finally, they decided to marry, doing so inside the prison. They then became eligible for conjugal visits several times a year, and their relationship was consummated four months after the wedding. Bandele discusses the difficulties of making a success of a marriage to a prisoner. She has a career that takes her around the world, but finds herself running home to take a scheduled phone call or turning down opportunities because of prison visiting days. She describes the constant fear that prison authorities will revoke their visits, the devastating disappoint-ment of a rejected appeal, the agonizing decision to have an abor-tion, and the mind-numbing task of counting the days and months and years until her husband will be eligible to petition for parole. She also talks about how all of the unhappiness is constantly coun-tered by the joy of their relationship, and the support and love they give each other, and how, without each other, their individual stories could easily have been much more tragic.

52. Banks, William Venoid. *A Legacy of Dreams: The Life and Contributions of Dr. William Venoid Banks.* Edited by Sheila T. Gregory. Lanham, Maryland: University Press of America, 1999. 152 pages. ISBN: 0761812857.

Abstract: Dr. Banks began life in Geneva, Kentucky, the child of sharecropping farmers. His father was constantly in trouble because of his inability to bow to the petty and cruel demands made upon him and his family as a result of racial hierarchy and discrimination. One landlord, unhappy to hear that the Banks family was prospering, first insisted that Banks's mother also work on the farm. Then, when he found out that the mother had money in the bank, he rode over to insist that the children stop attending school and work on the farm as well. Banks's father's response sent the farmer running, but it also put the family's safe-ty in jeopardy, and they had to leave town as soon as their contract was up. The family moved frequently and often had difficulty finding work because of restrictions on hiring black men. Banks's mother saved enough money to send her sons to the private Lincoln Institute, where Venoid graduated from high school. He went on to Detroit, where he attended junior college and then the Detroit College of Law, earning his law degree and passing the bar exam in 1929. Banks found that the practice of law, whether in the north or south, ran under a system of racial discrimination. All of the judges were white and police and other officials could be bought. He found that he had to take criminal actions if he were to succeed at practicing criminal law. Banks discusses the inequities of law enforcement and the black community, the effects of segregation and vehement racial prejudice, and the need to learn how to operate within a racially stratified society to succeed. Banks founded, among other organizations, the International Free and Accepted Modern Masons, a Masonic organization for African Americans, and the WGPR radio and television stations in Detroit.

53. Barnes, Jim. *On Native Ground: Memoirs and Impressions.* American Indian Literature and Critical Studies Series, 23. Norman, Oklahoma: University of Oklahoma Press, 1997. 279 pages. ISBN: 0806128984.

Abstract: Born in 1933, Barnes was the fifth child in his family. He is one-eighth Choctaw because he had a grandmother who was one-half Choctaw. He grew up in Indian Territory in Oklahoma in the vicinity of the Fourch Maline River and Holson Creek, and his childhood was shaped by the landforms and wildlife there. When Barnes thinks back over his life, and especially his childhood, it is the landscape that he recalls most prominently. In 1995 he returned with his wife to Oklahoma for a funeral. "Everywhere I look are images that bring the past up to now and signal the future. No matter how different I may have wanted my life to be, what remains is the fact that I am tied to this place, this blood, and the ethic that continues to emanate from my native ground" (p. 278). In *Native Ground*, Barnes combines prose and poetry to evoke the past. In terms of being a writer, however, regionalism or ethnicity is a characteristic of secondary importance, he says. He identifies himself as writer first and foremost. Barnes contemplates his inspirations and his life-long love of words and reading. Barnes attended college, majoring in French, English, and drama. His academic experiences "opened up the world" for him because of the "unlimited access to thousands of volumes of books and magazines" (p. 138). Barnes began his writing career as a short story writer. After writing what he thought to be his first good work, he spent ten years finding a publisher for it, and during that time, he turned more and more to poetry writing. His writing secured him several fellowships to study, translate, and write in

Europe. He has also traveled and taught in Japan, Korea, and Guam. Along with his childhood experiences in Oklahoma, his visits to these countries have a strong presence in his writing.

54. Battle, Leroy A. *Easier Said: The Autobiography of Leroy A. Battle*. Annapolis, Maryland: Annapolis Publishing Company, 1995. 198 pages; photographs; facsimile documents.   ISBN: 1884878040.

Abstract: Accomplished musician and former Tuskegee Airman Leroy A. Battle was born in 1921 in New York. He spent his earliest years in Harlem and, in the fifth grade, moved with his family to an integrated neighborhood in Brooklyn. Not every business establishment was integrated, however, and after he and his friends were refused service at a new ice cream parlor, they made a point of stopping by each day to heckle the owner. The owner eventually sold out, and the new management served any and all who chose to enter. Battle's early instinct to resist discriminatory treatment followed him into his early career as a musician, through his military experience, and back into the professional music world. A percussionist, he had learned jazz at the elbows of the noted musicians of the day and excelled as a parade concert percussionist as well. Battle was inducted into the service in 1943, just as his musical career was taking off. Initial tests qualified him for the Tuskegee program, and he became an air cadet. He graduated from his training as a lieutenant and was sent to Freeman Field in Seymore, Indiana. There, Battle and one hundred other officers protested the whites-only officers' club by attempting to enter. When they refused to leave the club, the officers were all arrested and eventually released with a reprimand (which, much later, was rescinded altogether). They had made their point and were able to move official United States policy to integrate the armed forces that much closer to realization. Battle's training was completed as the war ended, and he took the first opportunity to be discharged and resume his musical career. He entered Morgan State University in Maryland and was then paid by the state of Maryland to attend graduate school in another state at a school that would accept African Americans and allow him to get his teaching credential. Battle returned to teach in the Maryland public school system at Douglass High School, where he took a fledgling music program and led it to national honors. He continued to resist racist stereotyping, language, labeling, and policies. He supported the movement to desegregate schools and did what he could to encourage students who suffered from white opposition. All the while, Battle continued his own performing career, which included a thirty-year association with the jazz combo, the Altones.

55. Baxter, Freddie Mae. *The Seventh Child: A Lucky Life*. Edited by Gloria Bley Miller. New York, New York: Knopf, 1999. 223 pages. ISBN: 0375406204.

> **Notes:** Published in paperback New York: Vintage Books, 2000. ISBN: 0375705937.

> **Abstract:** In this narrative, Freddie Mae Baxter, a seventy-five-year-old retired housekeeper, starts out with her history. She was the seventh of eight children, a number she believes gave her luck. Born in Denmark, South Carolina, she has no recollection of her father and has always resented him for leaving their mother to raise them single-handedly. Baxter has great admiration for her mother, who managed to raise her children with love, attention, and firm discipline while working as a housecleaner. She has many good memories of closeness with her brothers and sisters, but the family was extremely poor, and Baxter clearly recalls being left out and ignored by other children. These experiences have led her to be kinder and more considerate of others. As a young woman she was a professional musician, playing saxophone in various bands. She also worked in other jobs, quitting when she decided demands were unreasonable. Later she worked as a housekeeper and helped to raise other people's children. Baxter talks about her lifestyle and her philosophy on life. Even now, living in Harlem, Baxter is not well off. She speaks wistfully of one day winning the Lotto, and concludes that she doesn't have anything material to give to other people. She tells them instead, "All I got to give you is I'll be there if you need me" (p. 60). She enjoys gambling in Atlantic City, but carefully restricts the amount she spends and always pays her bills at the beginning of the month. She maintains a careful regimen, which includes keeping house for herself, staying in contact with numerous friends and relatives who depend on her comradeship and support, and walking for her health. She also insists on the need to enjoy oneself. She watches soap operas several hours a day, something she could never do when she had to work, dances whenever the opportunity arises, and tells jokes and funny stories.

56. Baye, Betty Winston. *Blackbird*. Newport News, Virginia: August Press, 2000. 140 pages. ISBN: 0963572032.

> **Abstract:** Betty Baye is an editorial writer and columnist for the *Louisville Courier-Journal* in Louisville, Kentucky. She was born

and raised in New York City and attended Hunter College and Columbia University Graduate School of Journalism. She has her own television show with Insight Cable Television and WYCS-TV 24. *Blackbird* is a collection of Baye's newspaper columns. In them she discusses black womanhood, interviews Afeni Shakur, the mother of slain musician Tupac Shakur, assesses personal direct action to achieve personal goals, and presents her thoughts on public speaking. She writes about her time in Ghana and a visit to Cuba with the William Monroe Trotter Group. Baye also discusses her own family. She describes her love for her mother and lists her words of wisdom. Baye remembers her father and his struggle with cancer. As she goes through menopause, Baye recalls how she dismissed the symptoms of her mother and aunts. Baye also reflects on her return to New York City after twelve years in Louisville, Kentucky, saying that despite having carved a place for herself in a new city, she is still a New Yorker at heart.

57. Beals, Melba Pattillo. *White Is a State of Mind: A Memoir.* New York, New York: G. P. Putnam's Sons, 1999. 337 pages. ISBN: 0399144641.

Notes: Published in paperback New York: Berkley Books. ISBN: 0425172694.

Abstract: Melba Pattillo Beals, one of the nine black high school students (known as the Little Rock Nine) who first integrated Central High School in Little Rock, Arkansas in 1957, begins her story where her first autobiography, *Warriors Don't Cry: A Searing Memoir of the Battle to Integrate Little Rock's Central High* (1994), ended. During the summer of 1958, she and the other Little Rock Nine were feted as heroes as they toured the United States to talk about their year at Central High School. Beals came back to Little Rock to find her family under siege by the white community, which still vehemently opposed integration, and the black community, which was suffering the rage and economic vengeance of the whites. In the fall of 1959, the five remaining black students at Central High discovered that the Ku Klux Klan was offering money for their capture and murder. Their families decided to send them out of the state to safe houses in the North. Melba was sent to Santa Rosa, California, where she was placed in a white family, the McCabes, and attended a white high school. After eighteen years in Arkansas, the shock was enormous. She could only assume that the family would treat her as a servant, and she was terrified to ask for any help from white teachers or students at Montgomery High School. After a while she learned to trust her new family and was able to look whites straight in the eye without fearing for her life. She was still, however, overwhelmed by the differences between life in Santa Rosa and Little Rock:

> In my Little Rock world, the primary focus had been on survival. In this Santa Rosa world the focus seemed to be on having fun. They must have already learned how to survive. . . . Much of my time had been spent listening to Grandma India and Mother Lois worry out loud about two things: how to squeeze money out of turnips and . . . keep us housed and fed; and second, how to keep the white folks' feet off our necks—how to live day to day without breaking the rules of segregation and getting trounced or hanged.
>
> (p. 105)

These differences, aggravated by her eviction from Santa Rosa's public swimming pool, caused Beals to suffer a nervous breakdown. When the McCabes sent her home to Little Rock for rest, Beals discovered that she was more unwelcome there than ever. She was also terrified that she would forget to follow the rules of being a submissive black in the South. Beals later returned to Santa Rosa, and the McCabes helped to enroll her at San Francisco State College. Beals continued to struggle, but also learned to open up and express herself. She married a white military policeman and quit school when she became pregnant. Six years later, they were divorced and Beals went on welfare to support herself and her daughter. She finished college, was accepted into graduate school at Columbia University, and was hired as a newscaster at the NBC affiliate in San Francisco. The book ends with Beals, age fifty-six, the adoptive mother of twin boys, ready to start on a new adventure in life.

58. Beamon, Bob. *The Man Who Could Fly: The Bob Beamon Story.* Written with Milana Walter Beamon. Columbus, Mississippi: Genesis Press, 2000.   175 pages; photographs.   ISBN: 1885478895.

Abstract: Born in 1946, Bob Beamon was raised with little attention from his grandmother, father, or stepmother. He grew up feeling alone and craving love and affection, which led to difficulties at school in New York City, where he drifted easily into gang life. After attacking a teacher, Beamon was sent to an alternative high school, P.S. 600. Somehow the admonitions of the judge and the expectations of his teachers helped to turn him around, and he

began to excel in sports and music. Beamon was allowed to transfer to the mainstream Jamaica High School and began competing
in track. His athletic prowess led to many college scholarship
offers. He accepted an offer from the University of Texas at El
Paso (UTEP). It was a newly integrated school where staff were
just beginning to work with black male athletes. The athletes
themselves, however, actively pursued civil rights, and Beamon
was one of many athletes who lost their scholarships when they
refused to compete against Brigham Young University because of
its support for the Mormon doctrine that African Americans are
inferior to whites. Several UTEP professors and staff raised
money to help the disenfranchised athletes remain in school. At
this same time, Beamon was training fiercely for the Mexico City
Olympics of 1968. The Olympic trials were postponed to observe
the funeral of Robert Kennedy, and then thrown into further turmoil when sociologist Harry Edwards called for an Olympic boycott to protest the treatment of black athletes. Beamon made up
his mind to go ahead and compete in the Olympics. He won the
gold medal in the long jump, breaking the world and Olympic
records by two feet. His record held for twenty-three years. After
the Olympics, Beamon returned to UTEP to complete his studies,
but was frustrated because of a lack of money and because of his
track and field performance. When he was offered a scholarship
to Adelphi University in New York with no strings attached, he
transferred there and graduated with a B.A. in cultural anthropol-
ogy at the age of twenty-six. Beamon's life has not been easy. He
has been married five times, and it was difficult for him to learn
how to navigate the professional world of agents and promoters.
On the positive side, he has worked successfully with youth, pursued both musical and artistic activities, and is an accomplished
public speaker, businessman, and a father and husband.

59. Bell, Geneva E. (1929-). *My Rose: An African American Mother's
     Story of AIDS*. Foreword by Jeremiah A. Wright. Cleveland,
     Ohio: Pilgrim Press, 1997. 86 pages. ISBN: 0829811605.

Abstract: Geneva Bell, the mother of an adult homosexual son
with AIDS, writes about her experience caring for him. She
laments the lack of support from the African-American community in general and from her home church in particular. She cared
for her son and her aging father, fielded complaints from other
family members, and battled a constant flow of crises. She did all
of this in relative solitude, because she could not bring herself to
confide in either her family, friends at church, or colleagues at
work for fear that they would condemn her son for his sexual ori-

entation. Following the death of her son, also a church member, her church, Trinity United Church of Christ in Chicago, established an active HIV/AIDS ministry. The book is written with questions at the end of each section intended to further consideration and discussion of issues such as homosexuality, AIDS, the loss of loved ones, stress, and Christian community response.

60. Benavidez, Roy P. *Medal of Honor: A Vietnam Warrior's Story.* Written with John R. Craig. Foreword by H. Ross Perot. Washington, D.C. (Dulles, Virginia): Brassey's, 1995. 211 pages; photographs; illustrations. ISBN: 0028810988.

> **Notes:** Also published in paperback as *Medal of Honor: One Man's Journey from Poverty and Prejudice.* Washington, D.C. [Dulles, Virginia]: Brassey's, 1999. ISBN: 1574882031.

> **Abstract:** Benavidez was born in 1935. His parents, a Yaqui Indian mother and Mexican-American father, both had died of tuberculosis by the time he was seven. After his mother died, Benavidez and his brother were taken to live with their paternal uncle, his wife, and eight cousins. Benavidez's temper frequently got him into fights, and he dropped out of school at age fifteen. He joined the National Guard, and eventually volunteered for the U.S. Army. His early days in the army were plagued by his temper and sense of pride, and he lost rank more than once because of fights or insubordination. However, Benavidez succeeded in moving into his military area of choice, starting out in the infantry and moving from the military police to air borne and, finally, to special forces. He served during the Korean War and had two tours of duty in Vietnam. Struck by an exploding land mine in Vietnam, Benavidez was sent home and faced the possibility of never walking again. He was determined to recuperate, however, and in six months was back on his feet. He eventually became part of the Special Forces, and was sent back to Vietnam as a Green Beret. In May of 1968, Benavidez volunteered for a deadly rescue mission. He was almost immediately wounded, but continued to move other wounded and dead soldiers to rescue helicopters. Benavidez came so close to death that he was being placed in a body bag when one of his friends recognized him and double checked for a heart beat. It was for his valor in this rescue operation that Benavidez was awarded the Medal of Honor in 1981. In his book, Benavidez reflects on the human losses of the Vietnam Conflict, the role and duty of soldiers, and mistakes that may have been made at the cost of the lives of nearly sixty thousand American soldiers and over two million South Vietnamese. While

writing this book, Benavidez was working with the youth advocacy organization LifeSupport, Inc. of Houston, Texas. He also took part in the Fifth Special Forces Group, which received the Civic Action Medal from the Republic of Vietnam for carrying out tens of thousands of reconstruction projects in Vietnam.

61. Benton, Corrine. *The Return to the Promised Land*. Pittsburgh, Pennsylvania: Dorrance Publishing Company, 1995. 25 pages. ISBN: 0805936378.

Abstract: Benton uncovered the story of her family through genealogical research. Her great great grandmother Mary was raised in a Scottish mission in Barbados. She was sent to Louisiana and then Arkansas as an indentured servant and was assured that she would inherit land when her servitude was over. Because she had learned to read and write at the mission, Mary was able to teach and preach to the slaves associated with her household. Her owner, who was also the father of her two daughters, built a church for Mary so that she could hold services with the slaves. Mary's two daughters were each given land by their father. The darker of the two was given land in what Benton calls the wilds of Arkansas where she could live in safety with her husband and children. The lighter daughter moved with her family to the city. Benton writes that the members of this family passed for Arabs and other lighter-skinned ethnicities and stayed away from the extended family. Benton's grandmother Cora was the daughter of Mary's daughter who had remained in rural Arkansas. Benton tells stories of the hardship and poverty endured by the family and of the migration of aunts and uncles away from Arkansas to cities in the North, East, and West. These relatives then chose to send their own children back to Arkansas to spend the summers with their grandmother and to experience the rural life that they had left behind. Benton writes that knowledge of the hardships endured by her ancestors because of poverty and discrimination has been important to the younger generations of the family, inspiring them to pursue an education, to work hard, and to set their goals high.

62. Berry, Bertice. *I'm on My Way but Your Foot Is on My Head: A Black Woman's Story of Getting over Life's Hurdles*. New York, New York: Fireside Books, 1997. 255 pages. ISBN: 0684831406.

Notes: Originally published as *Bertice: The World According to Me*. New York: Scribner, 1996. ISBN: 0684814579.

Abstract: Scholar and television talk show host Bertice Berry talks about her life and how she achieved success and happiness. Born into a large family and raised by an alcoholic mother, Berry took every opportunity available and all the resources she had within to pull herself out of a cycle of abuse and self-destruction that had controlled the women in her family for many generations. Some high school teachers derided her efforts to get into college, but others encouraged and supported her. She went to Jacksonville College in Florida, where she had a patron who paid whatever educational expenses she could not afford. She graduated with honors and received the President's Cup for outstanding student in her class. She decided to go on to graduate school in sociology and was accepted at Kent State in Ohio. Both as an undergraduate and graduate student she was a member of a small black community that struggled with discrimination and ignorance, and she used her spirit and sense of humor to maintain her mental balance. In graduate school she taught undergraduate classes, using humor to keep students interested and engaged, and found that the motivation resulted in higher grades. Used to doing whatever work was available, she began doing stand-up comedy to help pay her school expenses. She earned her Ph.D., successfully defending her dissertation on color discrimination in black society. As her fame in comedy spread, Berry was approached about hosting a talk show. It was broadcast for a year. Berry still works in television and is raising three children, the biological children of one of her sisters. Berry uses the story of her life and her many successes to encourage others with similar backgrounds to depend on Christian faith, stay determined, endure hardships, make careful choices about relationships, and keep an open mind in order to achieve their goals and happiness in life.

63. Bettelyoun, Susan Bordeaux (1857-1945). *With My Own Eyes: A Lakota Woman Tells Her People's History.* Written with Josephine Waggoner. Edited and introduced by Emily Levine. Lincoln, Nebraska: University of Nebraska Press, 1998. 187 pages; photographs; maps. ISBN: 0803212801.

Abstract: Bettelyoun decided to write the story of her life and her tribal family because of the many inaccurate histories that were being written and taught about the Plains Indians. Bettelyoun's father was a white fur trader and her mother was a member of the Brulé Band of the Lakota Sioux of the northern plains. Bettelyoun was born and grew up in the vicinity of Laramie, Wyoming, at her father's trading post along the North Platte River. Her family was one of many mixed-blood families, the fathers of which were often traders, trappers, or guides, who lived on or near reservations or in close contact with their Indian family bands. Bettelyoun witnessed the mass migration of white settlers crossing the plains, the escalation of hostile actions by the U.S. soldiers against Indian tribes, and the resistance of Indians against the invading emigrants, soldiers, and traders. She recounts the epidemics of cholera, small pox, and measles that devastated Plains Indian tribes. Bettelyoun writes that no matter how far the individual bands would go into the mountains or even into Canada, they were unable to escape the diseases and often spread them as they traveled. Bettelyoun recalls the punishment of innocent Indians by U.S. military personnel and unprovoked attacks on Indians who were hunting or just passing through. Bettelyoun told her story to Josephine Waggoner, who was herself the daughter of a white father and an Indian mother from the Hunkpapa Band of Lakota Sioux. Waggoner, a generation younger than Bettelyoun, was a teacher and interpreter. She, too, was anxious to record as many of the stories and as much of the history of her people as possible. She and Bettelyoun negotiated with the Nebraska State Historical Society for years, literally until their deaths, in an attempt to publish their manuscript. Levine, the editor who has finally brought the manuscript to publication, writes that traditionally publishers have wanted to verify facts and events and have been troubled by the nonchronological structure of most Indian narratives. Bettelyoun had good reason to distrust the "corrections" being made to her manuscript by white editors and historians. They sought to verify her narrative with military and government records, the very records that Bettelyoun had been hoping to correct. Levine writes that the scholarly and publishing climate has changed, and publishers are now willing to accept narratives as they receive them. Thus, Bettelyoun's story is finally part of the published record.

64. Bibb, Henry. *The Life and Adventures of Henry Bibb: An American Slave.* Introduction by Charles J. Heglar. Wisconsin Studies in Autobiography. Madison, Wisconsin: University of Wisconsin Press, 2000. 237 pages. ISBN: 0299168905 : 0299168948.

   Notes: Originally published New York: H. Bibb, 1849.

65. Birchfield, D. L. *The Oklahoma Basic Intelligence Test: New and Collected Elementary, Epistolary, Autobiographical, and Oratorical Choctologies.* Frank Waters Memorial Series, 2. New York, New York: Greenfield Review Press, 1998. 184 pages. ISBN: 0912678976.

> **Abstract:** D. L. Birchfield is a member of the Choctaw Nation of Oklahoma, a writer, and a teacher of American Studies at Cornell University. In this collection of essays, he describes his personal background, explores subjects such as hunting with his brother, eulogizes his grandmother, examines his development as a writer, and discusses the general treatment of Native-American history in the United States. The title piece is a tongue-in-cheek quiz about facts as viewed by Oklahoma natives, and several other pieces include bits of humor from the quiz. Many of the essays are about inaccuracies in U.S. history as written by non-Natives. He asks writers to carefully research facts:
>
> > Consider this entry for "Choctaw Indians" from the *Basic Everyday Encyclopedia*: "After the Revolution, settlers poured into the Gulf area, and in 1831-32, the C moved to a reservation on the Red R in SE Oklahoma, where they set up a US-style government." Sounds like they just decided to pick up and go, doesn't it? And it sounds like there was already a place called Oklahoma and that the good people of that place made room for the Choctaws by letting them have a reservation in the southeastern part of it. ... Such an entry ... has a point of view, in this case to pretty up two events, one of which was one of the most inhumane, genocidal, and mean-spirited episodes in U.S. history, the forced march of the Choctaws, from their ancestral homeland east of the Mississippi River, ill-provisioned and in the dead of winter, and the other is to cover up the betrayal of the Choctaws by the United States after their removal.   (p. 24)
>
> He suggests two sources that provide the necessary facts: *And the Still Waters* by Angie Debo and *Chief Pushmataha American Patriot: The Story of the Choctaws' Struggle for Survival* by Choctaw historian Anna Lewis.

66. Black, Leonard. *The Life and Sufferings of Leonard Black: A Fugitive from Slavery.* Chapel Hill, North Carolina: Academic Affairs Library, University of North Carolina at Chapel Hill, 2000.

> http://docsouth.unc.edu/neh/black/black.sgml
> http://docsouth.unc.edu/neh/black/black.html
>
> **Notes:** Documenting the American South (Project).
> Originally published New Bedford: B. Lindsey, 1847.

67. Blackwell, Clester Lanier. *Revival: Memories of the Backwoods.* St. Louis, Missouri: Hardbound, 1999.   127 pages; photographs. ISBN: none.

> **Abstract:** Blackwell writes nostalgically of her childhood in a closely knit family in rural Western Tennessee in Gibson and Crockett Counties. Her family moved from farm to farm, working as tenant farmers or sharecroppers. Their many moves were always motivated by the hope of finding better land and better terms with a more generous land owner who would allow their children to stay in school. The family had very little, but Blackwell recalls the few good harvests that meant new clothes or a bicycle. Happy times were spent with family on Saturdays in town, at the various town fairs that came at cotton-picking time, and especially at church revival events, when families would come from out of town, children played, and plenty of food was available. She writes that this was a time for community building and neighborly love. Blackwell tells the story of her grandfather who, under threat of losing his farm during the Great Depression due to bank foreclosure, wrote to President Roosevelt to inform him of his situation and ask for help. The family was astonished when Roosevelt responded and the bank extended her grandfather's loan. She also remembers the story of her father's brush with a lynching mob, his escape, and the attack by the mob at his family home. Education was important to Blackwell's parents, both of whom attended school to the eighth grade. Determined that their children would go to high school and college, the family celebrated when two of the children finished elementary school and were ready to attend the boarding school in another town. As the preparations to attend were being made, however, the family home, with all of their belongings, burnt to the ground. Blackwell recalls that the family got into their car, drove to the next town, and started over.

68. Blakey, Durocher Lon (1909-). *Sharing Divine Life: The Story of My Life & My Teaching Ministry in Zion Methodism.* [United States]: A T. Odukoya, 1997. 139 pages; photographs. ISBN: 1575025515.

> **Notes:** Also published Kearney, Nebraska: Morris Publishing, 1997. ISBN: 1575025515.

> **Abstract:** Durocher Blakey writes that he received the call to the ministry three times. The first time when he was nine years old and began to question the meaning of his Sunday school lessons. The second time he was sixteen, and had a vision of himself as a minister. At the time, however, he could not quit work to attend school, and continued to set the call aside. At the age of thirty-one, Blakey received his third call, and finally decided to study for the ministry. Between 1944 and 1947, he attended Livingstone College and Johnson C. Smith University, both in North Carolina. He later attended Hood Theological Seminary, and was the first African American to graduate from this predominantly white institution. Besides his ministerial degree, Blakey received training in pastoral care and counseling, attended Duke Divinity School, Queens College for business and accounting and culminated his education with a doctorate from Chicago Theological Seminary in 1982. Between the years 1943 and 1995, Blakey was affiliated with churches in Alabama, North Carolina, Georgia, Arkansas, and Michigan. In this book, he discusses his understanding of his vocation within the African Methodist Episcopal Zion church; his convictions and warrants of faith. He also discusses church governance, A.M.E. Zion doctrine, pluralism in beliefs and worship practices, and various kinds of stewardship.

69. Blockson, Charles L. *Damn Rare: The Memoirs of an African-American Bibliophile.* Edited by Barbara Hope. Tracy, California: Quantum Leap Publisher, Inc., 1998. 334 pages; photographs; index. ISBN: 1892697009.

> **Abstract:** Charles Blockson is world-renowned as a bibliophile and African-American historian. Ever since his fourth grade teacher declared that "Negroes have no history," he has searched the world over for artifacts, books, and people who could tell him more about the history of black Americans. A graduate of Pennsylvania State University, Blockson was a talented athlete as a young man, playing football and throwing the discus. His love, however, has always been collecting books. While serving in the military during the Korean War, he collected books on his leaves.

After leaving the service, Blockson traveled the world, spending time in used bookstores in Europe, Asia, the Caribbean islands, and in Africa. The story of his life is interspersed with the history of blacks, as he tells how he researched through hundreds of years of history looking for his ancestors. This study led him to write *Black Genealogy* (1977, 1991), which is an important reference work for blacks putting together their family trees. Blockson also received accolades for an article he wrote for the *National Geographic Magazine* in 1984, "Escape From Slavery—The Underground Railroad." Some of the books he has written are, *Pennsylvania Black History* (1975, updated in 1994), *The Underground Railroad in Pennsylvania* (1981), *The Underground Railroad: First-Person Narratives of Escape to Freedom in the North* (1987), and *Hippocrene Guide to the Underground Railroad* (1994). While doing his research, Blockson was often invited to other countries to give lectures, and during these travels, he assembled a collection of twenty thousand items related to African-American history. He decided that he would donate the collection to Temple University in Philadelphia, located in the heart of the black community. Temple accepted his conditions that he serve as the curator of the collection, acknowledged to be the largest private collection related to black culture ever assembled, and that he have a budget for aquiring additional items. The book includes information on the work of black authors, poets, and historians, as well as past and present black bibliophiles.

70. Blue, Tabitha Lewis. *A Walk Back in Time.* Edited by Hsanni Wade. Dayton, Ohio: Mrs. T's Enterprises, 1996. 81 pages; photographs. ISBN: 0965536904.

Abstract: Tabitha Blue was raised at Peacock Farm in Bladenboro, North Carolina. Her family moved to Baltimore for a time and lived with an aunt and five cousins. They eventually returned to the farm in North Carolina. She writes that "no movies, drive-in theaters, bowling alleys, or nice eating establishments [were] available for blacks until the late '50s and early '60s" (p. 25). Blue recalls going downtown with her friends for fast food, but refusing to eat at establishments where she was forced to buy her food through a window. Her family enjoyed vacations at Atlanta Beach, where, although the beach was segregated, the black section had black-owned establishments, making it a comfortable and relaxed atmosphere for the family. Blue moved to Trenton, New Jersey, at the age of nineteen, but what seemed like a positive opportunity turned into a nightmare. She was threatened sexually by her cousin and later raped by two of his acquaintances. Blue became pregnant and subsequently suicidal. Through the supportive influence of her mother and aunt, however, she recovered from her emotional trauma and gave birth to a healthy baby boy. Blue married her childhood sweetheart who left for Vietnam shortly following their honeymoon. He returned from the war wounded. He did recover and the family began to enjoy financial success. When it was clear, however, that her husband was addicted to drugs, Blue decided to separate, although her hope is to repair the damage and someday reunite.

71. Boen, William. *Anecdotes and Memoirs of William Boen, a Coloured Man, Who Lived and Died near Mount Holly, New Jersey: To Which Is Added, the Testimony of Friends of Mount Holly Monthly Meeting Concerning Him.* Chapel Hill, North Carolina: Academic Affairs Library, University of North Carolina at Chapel Hill, 2000.

http://docsouth.unc.edu/neh/boen/boen.sgml
http://docsouth.unc.edu/neh/boen/boen.html

Notes: Documenting the American South (Project).

72. Boggs, Grace Lee. *Living for Change: An Autobiography.* Foreword by Ossie Davis. Minneapolis, Minnesota: University of Minnesota Press, 1998. 301 pages; photographs. ISBN: 0816629544 : 0816629552.

Abstract: Activist Grace Lee Boggs grew up in New York City, the daughter of Chinese immigrants. She graduated from Barnard College in 1935 and earned her Ph.D. in philosophy from Bryn Mawr in 1940. After graduate school, she went straight into political activism, getting involved in a Chicago tenant's organization, the Socialist Workers Party, and the budding Civil Rights Movement. She worked closely with C. L. R. James until their ideological split in 1962. In 1951, Boggs, with her brother and brother-in-law, began publishing the newspaper *Correspondence* for their split-off branch of the Socialist Workers Party. Boggs had broken with the main party over a number of issues, including whether or not to go underground during the McCarthy-era Communist purges. Boggs and her group chose not to go underground, but to continue to openly organize rank-and-file workers, blacks, women, and youth—the four groups that they identified as the "revolutionary social forces" (p. 67). Grace Lee Boggs met the African-American union and socialist activist Jimmy Boggs in 1952. They married and worked together on *Correspondence* and were involved in many causes until 1968, when they slowly moved out of frontline leadership positions as the political climate changed. They were responsible for organizing many groups, including the National Organization for American Revolution and the Asian Political Alliance. They were central to the development of the Detroit Summer in 1992, which was a move to revitalize the city. The James and Grace Lee Boggs Community Foundation and the James and Grace Lee Boggs Center to Nurture Community Leadership provides funding and training to develop community leadership. Jimmy Boggs died in 1992, and Grace Lee Boggs, in her eighties, has continued to act as a resource person and networker for activist causes. She writes, "I am glad that I am still around not only as a participant but as a griot to pass on the story of how we got to this place—because, to paraphrase Kierkegaard, if the future is to be lived, the past must be understood" (p. 272).

73. Boggs, James. *See* Boggs, Grace Lee.

74. Bond, Horace Mann and Julia W. Bond. *The Star Creek Papers.* Edited by Adam Fairclough. Foreword by Julian Bond. Athens, Georgia: University of Georgia Press, 1997. 160 pages; photographs; index. ISBN: 082031904X.

> **Abstract:** Horace Mann Bond, father of Civil Rights activist and politician Julian Bond, was a scholar and writer who did the bulk of his work in the 1930s. This book contains three of his works, "Portrait of Washington Parish," "Star Creek Diary," and "Forty Acres and a Mule," as well as an account by his wife, Julia Bond, of a lynching which figures largely in each of the other pieces. Adam Fairclough, who did the research behind and editing of this work wrote an introduction and epilogue which gives historical background on the work of the Bonds. Horace and Julia Bond moved to Star Creek District in Washington Parish in southeast Louisiana. Their job was to visit the Rosenwald Schools, schools which were built and operated partially by funds provided by a white philanthropist of the same name. The Bonds discovered that an entire black community was involved in additional fundraising for and maintenance of each school and noted that the school, and not the churches, was the center of the community. In his diary, Bond describes life in Star Creek and nearby towns. He describes how black community leaders calculated how much white backing they could get for their schools and how they refused to kowtow to whites, maintaining their dignity as they made their requests. Another subject Bond treats is the racial

make-up of the area. He found white and black families with the same last names and learned that they were all related. He first assumed that the links went back to the days of slavery, but was told that the intermingling still continued in a fairly open way, with many black landowners getting their property with the assistance of white relatives. "Portrait of Washington Parish" tells the story of a lynching and also describes the black and white communities that serve as background to it. Two brothers, John and Jerome Wilson, were involved in a minor argument over a mule that led to the shooting death of a sheriff's deputy. John was mortally wounded, and Jerome was tried by a white jury, found guilty of shooting the deputy, and subsequently lynched. This lynching left the local blacks in fear for their lives and livelihood. The Bonds were encouraged to leave Washington Parish for their own safety, which they did. "Forty Acres and a Mule" was written after the lynching with the idea that any royalties from it could be given to the Wilson family. In the piece, Bond gives the history of black farmers after the end of slavery, using the history of three generations of the Wilsons and Magees of Washington Parish as its basis, and culminating with the story of the lynching. "Forty Acres and a Mule" was never published because the Wilson family left Louisiana and moved to Chicago, and Bond abandoned the project. Horace Mann Bond died in 1974, but sixty years after he first wrote the piece, it was published as a result of Adam Fairclough's extensive research with the cooperation of Julia Bond.

75.   Bowens, Richmond (1908-). *Will-o'-the-Wisp: Mr. Bowens' Days along the Ashley.* As told to Thelma Hughes Gillam. Mount Pleasant, South Carolina: Marsh Wind Press, 1995. 58 pages. ISBN: 1575020548.

Abstract: Richmond Bowens's family came from Barbados in the early eighteenth century with the Drayton family. Drayton Hall was built in 1732, and Bowens's family has been associated with it ever since. His great grandfather was born into slavery and stayed at the plantation after emancipation. Bowens's father preached, worked in the phosphate mines, and cut hair. Bowens, born in 1908, worked at Drayton Hall until leaving for Chicago during the Great Depression. He missed his Southern home and wondered at all of the people who left everything behind to make a go of it in the North. Bowens himself stayed in Chicago for thirty years. In 1977, he returned to South Carolina and Drayton Hall, where he worked as a gatekeeper and historic interpreter at the plantation.

76. Bowley, Freeman S. (b. 1846). *A Boy Lieutenant: Memoirs of Freeman S. Bowley, 30th United States Colored Troops Officer.* Edited by Pia Seija Seagrave. Introduction by Ronald Roy Seagrave. Fredericksburg, Virginia: Sergeant Kirkland's Museum and Historical Society, 1997. 124 pages; illustrations; maps. ISBN: 1887901019.

    Notes: Originally published Philadelphia: H. Altemus Company, 1906.

77. Boyd, Robert D. *The Power of the Mind: An Autobiography.* Detroit, Michigan: Harlo, 1997. 111 pages; photographs. ISBN: 0818703105.

78. Boza, Maria del Carmen. *Scattering the Ashes.* Tempe, Arizona: Bilingual Review/Press, 1998. 387 pages; photographs. ISBN: 0927534754.

    Abstract: Maria del Carmen Boza, who was born in Cuba and came to Miami, Florida, with her family at about the age of ten, writes primarily of the suicide of her father and its aftermath. Boza's father, Ramiro Boza, was a well-respected elder statesman of the Cuban exiles in Miami. He committed suicide on May 19, 1989, the same date as the death of Jose Marti, a journalist and poet who founded the Partido Revolucionario Cubano and inspired the last Cuban War of Independence. Speaking from the point of view of the Cuban exiles, she explains how having to live as an exile and his treatment by the U.S. government gradually drove her father mad. As background for her father's act and the story of how her family came to be in the United States, Boza reviews the history of the Communist takeover of Cuba and the subsequent interaction between the U.S. government, the CIA, and the Cuban exiles. Boza discusses how the CIA and then-President John Kennedy used anti-Castro forces to invade Cuba at the Bay of Pigs in 1961. The CIA orchestrated the entire affair, sending several thousand Cubans to death or imprisonment in antiquated, shabby ships and airplanes under the promise of protection by U.S. forces that never arrived and were never meant to arrive. The next betrayal by Kennedy came during the Cuban Missile Crisis in 1962. The exiles wanted the United States to use the Soviet missiles based in Cuba as an excuse to invade the island and depose Castro. On this one point, however, Boza looks back and decides to differ from her father. Although Kennedy's promise never to invade Cuba crushed the last hopes of exiles for a return to their homeland, Boza decides that such an invasion would have meant the annihilation of the island and perhaps the entire Northern Hemisphere.

79. Bragg, Janet Harmon (1907-1993). *Soaring above Setbacks: The Autobiography of Janet Harmon Bragg, African American Aviator.* As told to Marjorie M. Kriz. Foreword by Johnetta B. Cole. Smithsonian History of Aviation Series. Washington, D.C.: Smithsonian Institution Press, 1996. 120 pages; photographs; index. ISBN: 1560984589.

Notes: Paperback published Washington, D.C.: Smithsonian Institution Press, 1997. ISBN: 1560987553.

Abstract: Aviator Janet Harmon Bragg was born and raised in Griffin, Georgia, in a family of seven children. She credits her father's motto as the driving force behind all of her accomplishments: "He always said, 'If Jack can do it, so can Jill.' That meant there was no time wasted, that I was part of a family that cared, and that I could do whatever I set my sights on" (p. 2). Bragg trained at Spelman College to be a nurse, one of the few professions open to women at the time. While working in Chicago as a nurse for an insurance company, she noticed a billboard advertising an aviation school and soon began attending a class open to blacks. She discusses her teachers, training, and the camaraderie between instructors and students. Together, they formed the Challenger Aero Club, which became the Challenger Air Pilots' Association, and built their own airport in an all-black community south of Chicago. Bragg bought an airplane, the first for the airport. Disappointed when, in 1939, the U.S. government announced that the new Civilian Pilot Training Program (CPTP) would be open only to whites, she and her group formed the National Airmen's Association of America "to further stimulate interest in aviation and to bring a better understanding in the entire field of aeronautics" (p. 36). They put all of their financial assets into their efforts to promote flying by blacks and eventually convinced President Roosevelt to open the CTPT to all citizens, although on a limited basis. In 1943, after many setbacks due to racial discrimination, Bragg became the first African-American woman in the United States to receive her commercial pilots' license after training at the CPTP at the Tuskegee Institute. Flying, however, remained an avocation. Bragg was a nurse during her entire working career, and she and her second husband, Sumner Bragg, eventually opened and operated several nursing homes in Chicago. One of her flying instructors, John Robinson, went to

Ethiopia after World War II at the invitation of Emperor Haile Selassie. When Robinson met students there bound for college in the United States, he had them look up Bragg upon their arrival. Thus began her career as a second mother to many African students in the United States. In 1970, historians began studying the first black aviators. In 1982, the National Air and Space Museum opened a traveling exhibit entitled "Black Wings: The American Black in Aviation." Bragg was involved in many of the events surrounding the exhibit, and subsequently received many awards and honors for her role in the field.

80. Brent, William Lee. *Long Time Gone: A Black Panther's True-Life Story of His Hijacking and Twenty-Five Years in Cuba.* New York, New York: Times Books, 1996. 276 pages; photographs. ISBN: 081292486x.

Notes: Also published San Jose: toExcel, 2000. ISBN: 0595002889.

Abstract: William Lee Brent was born in Louisiana in 1930 and spent most of his youth in Oakland, California. After a brief stint in the U.S. Army, he sold drugs, stole cars, and broke into houses, and consequently served two jail terms. When Brent got out of prison, he became interested in the Black Panthers, which originated in Oakland in the 1960s, and became a member in 1967. Brent worked in security patrols at public gatherings, conducted classes, and did anything else he was asked to do. He writes about leaders Huey Newton, Eldridge Cleaver, Bobby Seale, and Bobby Hutton. In time, he became discouraged with the group because of the inside struggles and the duplicity of the leadership. In November 1968, Brent was involved in a Panther-police shootout in San Francisco and was publicly disclaimed by his colleagues. Knowing he would end up back in jail, Brent, with the encouragement of his remaining friends, decided to hijack an airliner to Cuba. In June 1969, he managed an uneventful hijacking and landed at Jose Marti Airport in Havana. He was immediately taken into custody and spent almost two years in a Cuban jail cell. Upon release, he was sent to live in a house of non-Cubans, many of whom had hijacked their way to the island. Brent found work in a factory. He later entered the University of Havana and graduated in 1981 with a bachelor's degree in Hispanic languages. With this degree he was able to teach English in the public school system. Brent still lives in Cuba. He has witnessed changes in government policy that he sees as detrimental to the revolution and against the best interests of the people there. He is anxious about what changes will mean for him, an exile who is unable and unwilling to return to his own country.

81. Brewer Family. *See* Benton, Corrine.

82. Bridges, Ruby. *Through My Eyes*. Articles and interviews com-
    piled by Margo Lundell. New York, New York: Scholastic
    Books, 1999. 63 pages; photographs. ISBN: 0590189239.

    Notes: Also published New York: Scholastic Books, 2000. ISBN:
    0590546309; New York: Scholastic Books, 2001. ISBN: 0439362210.

    Abstract: Ruby Bridges tells the story of the year she was the first
    black student to attend the all-white William Frantz School in New
    Orleans. In 1960, Bridges was one of four children chosen from
    the kindergartens in New Orleans to start the court-ordered school
    desegregation. Three of the girls would attend McDonogh
    Elementary School, and Bridges alone would attend William
    Frantz. On the first day of school, segregationists formed a mob
    around the school, and Bridges and her mother were escorted by
    four U.S. marshals to the entrance. Bridges was the only child in
    the school on that first day. She and her mother spent the entire
    day in the principal's office. The next day she was taken to her
    classroom and introduced to Mrs. Henry, a teacher from Boston.
    Bridges was the only child in the class. U.S. marshals remained
    posted outside her classroom door and even escorted her to the
    bathroom. Other first graders, when they eventually came to
    school, were taken to other classrooms. Bridges wasn't even
    allowed to eat in the cafeteria with them. Seeing nobody else dur-
    ing the school day, Bridges became very attached to Mrs. Henry.
    She imitated her speech patterns, which were not southern, and
    her mannerisms. Because Bridges was involved with school
    desegregation, her father lost his job. The family's house was
    guarded at all times by the neighborhood patrol. White families
    who attempted to take their children to school were also victims of
    violence. One family gave up and left New Orleans and the South
    altogether. Throughout this difficult time, Bridges's family
    received letters of support, money, and gifts from around the
    country and from overseas. She remembers that her mother was
    especially pleased with the letter they received from Eleanor
    Roosevelt. The following year, Mrs. Henry was gone, and Bridges
    attended second grade with the white children. The protection
    from federal officials, and support from NAACP representatives
    and others also disappeared. She recalls thinking that the teacher
    was mean to her and made fun of her adopted northern accent,
    and she felt that she was on her own trying to make sense of what
    was happening to her. Dr. Robert Coles, who met with her and
    other children who were actively involved in desegregation, wrote

a children's book about Bridges that was published in 1995. Bridges founded the Ruby Bridges Foundation, which put profits from the book into programs at the William Frantz School, which ironically had become a poor, inner-city school attended primarily by black students. Through the publication of the book she was reunited with her first grade teacher, Mrs. Henry. Bridges makes frequent public appearances and has received two honorary degrees.

83. Brookins, Naomi A. *Naomi's Story: You Don't Have to Be Broken.* Baltimore, Maryland: American Literary Press, 1997. 55 pages. ISBN: 1561673595.

Abstract: Brookins grew up in what she calls an upside down world. The family farmed under a sharecropping arrangement and her father gave away to others what little money they made. Brookins's family lived on cornmeal mush and cornbread made, according to their father's restrictions, without eggs or lard. Once a year, Mr. Brookins held a big celebration for the community. He raised funds to send someone from the family church to the local high school, but he would not allow his children to attend school, nor did he provide money for them to buy clothes or shoes. Brookins concluded that her father hated her mother and his children. When she was eleven, her grandmother explained to her that at the age of seventeen, her father had witnessed the murder of his father, Rev. Milligan Newsome, by a group of white men. The white men resented the Newsome family's prosperity and had been pressuring Rev. Newsome to give up most of his property; he owned a sizeable amount of land and supported a church and a school. Newsome refused to sell off his land and advised others in the community to do the same. After he was murdered, all of the land was taken from his survivors. Brookins's father's reaction to this horrific experience was to refuse ever to own land and to forbid his children either an education or a career. Brookins, however, was determined to finish school and to teach. She left home to do so and paid her way through high school and college. She married after earning her B.S. degree in education. Fifteen years later, after raising four children, she returned to school, earning a teaching certificate and two masters degrees. She taught for twenty-five years, becoming "a positive force in an upside down world" (p. 55).

84. Brown, Eric B. *God Ordained My Steps*. Chicago, Illinois: Pulpit Ministry, 1997. 50 pages. ISBN: 0965831507.

85. Brown, James. *James Brown: The Godfather of Soul*. Written with Bruce Tucker. Introduction by Dave Marsh. New York, New York: MacMillan, 1986. 336 pages; photographs; discography. ISBN: 0025174304.

> **Notes:** Also published New York: Thunders Mouth Press, 1990. ISBN: 0938410970; New York: Thunders Mouth Press, 1997. ISBN: 1560251158 (352 pages).
>
> **Abstract:** James Brown's mother abandoned him when he was just four years old, and his father abandoned him a few years later, leaving him with his aunts in Augusta, Georgia. Brown grew up without playmates, living with his aunts in a house of gambling, drinking, and prostitution. As a teenager he became involved in crime, committing a steady stream of burglaries. He was arrested when he was sixteen and sentenced to eight-to-sixteen years at the Georgia Juvenile Training Institute. Finally ready to turn himself around, Brown boxed, played baseball, played piano, and formed a gospel quartet while in prison. His hope was to become a gospel singer after he was released. After three years, he was offered release on parole if he was able to find a job. That accomplished, Brown moved to Toccoa, Georgia. He sought out musical opportunities and formed The Flames, a singing group. They later changed their name to the Famous Flames and began touring and recording. Brown describes the ups and downs of the group through 1957, when their recording company, Universal, decided that the band should change its name to James Brown and the Famous Flames. The rest of the group quit, and Brown was on the road touring alone. He continued to record and formed a new group of Flames. Brown moved out of the South as soon as he began earning money. He had a successful series of concerts at the Apollo Theater in New York, where he recorded his pioneering album, *Live at the Apollo*. Brown became involved in politics, lent his reputation to the Civil Rights Movement, performed for troops on active duty in Vietnam, and sponsored the "Don't Drop-Out" campaign. After difficulties with the IRS, contract woes with record companies, and controversies sparked by his endorsement of Richard Nixon and his songs "America is My Home" and "Black and Proud," Brown made a successful comeback with appearances in the movies *The Blues Brothers* and *Rocky IV*. In 1986 he was among the first musicians to be inducted into the Rock and Roll Hall of Fame.

86. Brown, James R. (1918-). *My Journey through Life.* New York, New York: Vantage Press, 2000.   258 pages; photographs. ISBN: 0533131340.

Abstract: James R. Brown is a retired military man and a recovered alcoholic. His mother died when he was five years old, and he was left in the care of his grandfather, who, soon after Brown's arrival, gave up farming to work on the railroads. James then went to live with an aunt, but was never accepted as one of the family. He never got enough food, was not given a bed to sleep in, and was beaten severely without provocation. He left for good at the age of sixteen and was fortunate to be taken in by another family who took good care of him. Brown worked at a variety of positions, but alcohol abuse made it difficult for him to keep a job or to stay in one place for any length of time. He tells of work, liaisons with a number of women, and homelessness. He was saved from a nearly vagrant lifestyle in Cincinnati when he was drafted into the army in 1942. Brown was sent to North Africa and Europe, where his undisciplined behavior got him into a variety of scrapes, one of which resulted in a court marshal and four months in the stockade. After his release, Brown found that he had been separated from his unit. He spent several weeks taking trains to various locations, before finally being sent home on his own. He reenlisted for another three years and was sent to Germany. Brown returned to Cincinnati following his discharge and soon connected with a young woman whom he married. His marriage quickly deteriorated, but having been abandoned by his own father, Brown was determined to stay with his wife and be a father to their child. The couple eventually had four children, and despite marital ups and downs, they remained together. Brown studied to get a license to work with high pressure boilers and eventually became the chief engineer at Longview State Hospital. His road to success was not smooth, however, because of continued problems with alcohol. Brown feels that although he was given many chances in life, he regrets his lack of a formal education. He was a self-taught man, taking many opportunities while in the military to study and read. "I . . . learned that if you read a lot you can teach yourself a lot about everything and people in general. . . . I educated myself" (p. 243). Brown is proud of his children and has been pleased to be responsible for caring for his grandchildren and great grandchildren. After a lifetime struggle with alcohol, he was able to give it up totally at the age of sixty-seven.

87. Brown, Ruth. *Miss Rhythm: The Autobiography of Ruth Brown. Rhythm and Blues Legend.* Written with Andrew Yule. New York: D. I. Fine Books, 1996. 360 pages; photographs; index; discography. ISBN: 1556114869.

> **Notes:** Also published New York: Da Capo Press, 1999. ISBN: 0306808889.

> **Abstract:** Ruth Brown was one of the most popular rhythm and blues singers in the 1950s. She got her start as a singer for a band, and was discovered by Blanche Calloway, sister of the legendary Cab Calloway, who then introduced her to Atlantic Records, a recording company that was just getting started. She writes about the life of black singers during the late 1940s and 1950s. Along with the records they made, singers had to take tours into the Deep South in order to make a living. They were often harassed by the local police and arrested and frequently had their cars confiscated. Even when they managed to arrive for a performance, they often ended up having to sing from the back of trucks for their poor black audiences. Another problem was the common practice of "covering." A black singer would rise to the top of the rhythm and blues charts with a song that would then be "covered" (that is, recorded) by a white singer, who would then make substantial money off of it, taking it to the top of mainstream charts. Atlantic Records used Ruth Brown and her wildly popular records for all of its advertising, but when it came to paying royalties, she and other singers were always informed that they were still in debt for recording-studio charges, and they never received more than a few hundred dollars in advances. Because of the lack of income and the effects of several unsuccessful and abusive marriages, Brown found herself almost indigent. She took jobs driving school buses and working as a teacher's aid to provide a living for herself and her son. Because she had so many fans, however, she managed to stage several comebacks. She played the role of Motormouth Maybelle in the film *Hairspray*, won a Tony award for her role in the Broadway production *Black and Blue*, and was inducted into the Rock and Roll Hall of Fame. For twenty years, in the 1970s and 1980s, Brown fought to get royalties she felt were owed her by Atlantic Records. In 1983, she met Howell Begle, an attorney and long-time fan who was flabbergasted to learn that her total record earnings over the years had come to $785 and that Atlantic claimed she still owed them money. The two spent the next six years relentlessly chipping away at the record company. In 1989, Atlantic paid Brown and seven other artists a total of $250,000 and promised to start audits on behalf of twenty-eight

others. Brown received $30,000 of this and now is paid royalties that accumulate each year. She and Begle also got Atlantic to pay $1.5 million into the Rhythm and Blues Foundation, a fund that the two set up to honor and compensate other singers who have never been paid for a lifetime of work.

88. Brown, William Wells (1815-1884). *The American Fugitive in Europe. Sketches of Places and People Abroad.* Chapel Hill, North Carolina: Academic Affairs Library, University of North Carolina at Chapel Hill, 2000.

> http://docsouth.unc.edu/neh/brown55/brown55.sgml
> http://docsouth.unc.edu/neh/brown55/brown55.html

> **Notes:** Documenting the American South (Project).
> This is an enlarged American edition of the British edition published under the title: *Three Years in Europe, or Places I Have Seen and People I Have Met.*
> Orginally published Boston: J. P. Jewett, 1855 (320 pages).

89. —. *Three Years in Europe, or, Places I Have Seen and People I Have Met.* Chapel Hill, North Carolina: Academic Affairs Library, University of North Carolina at Chapel Hill, 2000.

> http://docsouth.unc.edu/neh/brown52/brown52.sgml
> http://docsouth.unc.edu/neh/brown52/brown52.html

> **Notes:** Documenting the American South (Project).

90. Browne, Martha Griffith. *Autobiography of a Female Slave.* Banner Books. Jackson, Mississippi: University Press of Mississippi, 1998. 418 pages. ISBN: 157806046X : 1578060478.

> http://metalab.unc.edu/docsouth/browne/browne.sgml
> http://metalab.unc.edu/docsouth/browne/browne.html

> **Notes:** Originally published New York: Redfield, 1857 (407 pages). Also available electronically from Academic Affairs Library, University of North Carolina, Chapel Hill. Documenting the South (Project).

91. Bruce, Henry Clay (1836-1902). *The New Man: Twenty-Nine Years a Slave, Twenty-Nine Years a Free Man: Recollections of H. C. Bruce.* Introduction by Willard B. Gatewood. Blacks in the American West. Lincoln, Nebraska: University of Nebraska Press, 1996. 176 pages; illustrations. ISBN: 0803261322.

   Notes: Originally published York, Pennsylvania: P. Anstadt, 1895.

92. Bryant, Thelma Harper. *The Memoirs of the Harper Family, 1865-1995.* New York, New York: Vantage Press, 1997. 163 pages; photographs. ISBN: 0533119669.

93. Bullock, Clarence C. *Bullock, the Artist.* London: Minerva Press, 1998. 58 pages; photographs; reproductions. ISBN: 0754102866.

   Notes: Originally published as *Bullock: The Autobiography of an Artist.* New York: Vantage Press, 1984.

94. Bulosan, Carlos. *On Becoming Filipino: Selected Writings of Carlos Bulosan.* Edited with an introduction by E. San Juan, Jr. Philadelphia, Pennsylvania: Temple University Press, 1995. 221 pages; photographs. ISBN: 1566393094 : 1566393108.

   Abstract: Editor San Juan, a Bulosan scholar, has put together a collection of short stories, poetry, essays and a brief autobiographical essay by the writer. San Juan's introduction provides historical context for Bulosan's life and writings. He has also included a list of works by Bulosan and a bibliography of criticism and commentary. Carlos Bulosan, 1911-1956, lived with his father in the remote mountain village of Mangusmana, part of the town of Binalonan in the province of Pangasinan. His father fed a family of nine by farming one hectare of land, and his mother sold salted fish in the markets. She lived in Binalonan with Bulosan's four brothers and two sisters. Bulosan attended school sporadically, and only went to three semesters of high school, but before leaving for the United States in 1930, he had absorbed the lore and legends of his homeland from local elders and storytellers. Once in the United States, he writes, "I lived violent years of unemployment, prolonged illnesses, and heart-rending labor union work on the farms of California" (p. 16). He refused to be disillusioned by his experiences and believed in the fabled promises of hope and equal opportunity in the United States. Bulosan spent two years in the Los Angeles County Hospital suffering from tuberculosis.

He read voraciously the whole time and formulated his "grand dream for a better society." It took him five years following his release from the hospital to begin writing and then he was unstoppable. He wrote about his

> grand dream of equality among men and freedom for all. To give literate voice to the voiceless one hundred thousand Filipinos in the United States, Hawaii, and Alaska. Above all and ultimately, to translate the desires and aspirations of the whole Filipino people in the Philippines and abroad in terms relevant to contemporary history.   (p. 216)

Bulosan read Whitman, Dreiser, Faulkner, Hemingway, and many other American writers, analyzing their point of view and their representations of America. He learned from these readings that he should write from his own experience and his own knowledge of Filipino history, culture, and lore. He felt that "the duty of the [expatriate] artist is to trace the origins of the disease that was festering American life" (p. 26). Bulosan's writings were published in *Harper's, The New Yorker, The Saturday Evening Post* as well as other magazines in the U.S. and abroad. His novels, poetry, and essays were published by Harcourt, Brace & Company, Coward-McCann, and others. His full length autobiography, *America Is in the Heart*, was published in 1946 by Harcourt, Brace and Company. It was reprinted in 1973 by the University of Washington Press.

95. Burkes, Major Lee. *In the Shadow of Austin*. Austin, Texas: L. Star Publishing, 2000. 225 pages; photographs. ISBN: none.

96. Burton, Thomas William (b. 1860). *What Experience Has Taught Me: An Autobiography of Thomas William Burton*. Chapel Hill, North Carolina: Academic Affairs Library, University of North Carolina at Chapel Hill, 1998.

http://metalab.unc.edu/docsouth/burtont/burton.sgml
http://metalab.unc.edu/docsouth/burtont/burton.html.

Notes: Documenting the American South (Project).
Originally published Cincinnati: Press of Jennings Graham, 1910 (126 pages).

97. Burton, Wiley M. *Divided We Stand*. San Bernadino, California: Brown's Publishing Company, 1996. 234 pages; photographs. ISBN: 0962594431.

Abstract: Wiley Burton considers important elements of his life and discusses racism and the importance of language in promoting racist attitudes. He provides detailed historical and statistical evidence of wrongful thinking, misguided policies, and racist events. Burton grew up in Pittsburgh, Pennsylvania, but family gatherings took place in Virginia at the farm of his grandparents. It was on visits to Virginia that Burton experienced the worst displays of racism. At the age of twelve, he was returning to Pittsburgh with his father and uncle when they drove past two African-American men who had been hung and stripped naked near the roadside. On another visit, he witnessed the tar-and-feathering of an African-American male at a county fair. Burton, whose grandparents were both African American and Native American, is extremely light skinned. On various occasions, he has taken the opportunity to experience the world from both sides of the color line. As an adult, Burton took a trip to observe and listen to white people as a white person. He was shocked by the intensity of the racist attitudes he heard and the blindly hypocritical behavior he observed. Burton notes that many white people are perplexed with the changes in terminology used by African Americans to refer to themselves. "A name is important to all concerned. Whatever we call a people, a race, is a great influence to their perception of the world, their perception of each other, and other's perceptions of them" (pp. 23-24). Burton includes examples of graphic material used over the centuries to present demeaning images of African Americans. He has also collected written material—both popular and scholarly in nature—that gives a similarly insulting representation of African Americans.

> If all that was taught about a "race" of people was projected improperly for generations, it's no wonder that it's going to be a difficult task to eliminate "racism." I don't even like to use the words "race" and "racism," they make it sound competitive, this "race" against that "race."
>
> (p. 24)

Burton also discusses the Clarence Thomas hearings, the O. J. Simpson trial, and the Rodney King beating, trial, and riots. He describes his life as a basketball player at Los Angeles City College and his co-ownership of a night club. He also writes about his brief romance and marriage to Martha Reeves of the Vandellas, his friendship with Florence Ballard of the Supremes, and his courtship of and marriage to singer Nancy Wilson.

98. Butler, Jerry. *Only the Strong Survive: Memoirs of a Soul Survivor.* Written with Earl Smith. Black Music and Expressive Culture Series. Bloomington, Indiana: Indiana University Press, 2000. 266 pages; photographs; discography; index.   ISBN: 0253337968.

Abstract: Soul singer Jerry Butler was born in Mississippi in 1939. His parents decided to move to Chicago in the 1950s when conditions in the South became more and more difficult for blacks. He began singing in the church and first traveled as a singer with the Traveling Souls Spiritualist Church. Just before his fourteenth birthday, his father died and Butler became the man of the house. He was a leader in high school, got good grades, and was studying to be a cook. Butler and three friends, one of whom was future star Curtis Mayfield, formed a group which they called the Roosters. They were highly successful performers and were eventually picked up by an agent who convinced them to change their name to The Impressions. The group recorded "For Your Precious Love" for the new VeeJay recording company. The thrill of making their first record was soon replaced by the chagrin of discovering that it had been released under the group name of Jerry Butler and The Impressions. The group continued to perform and record together, but it wasn't long before tension among the members led Butler to decide to break off and become a solo act. He continued to record through the 1970s and continues to perform to full houses of enthusiastic fans to the present day. Along with the story of his life, Butler talks about his family, friends, and associates in the entertainment business, including Curtis Mayfield, Sam Cooke, Otis Redding, Patti LaBelle, Bill Cosby, and many others. The book also serves as a history of the recording companies that have been recording soul music since the late 1950s.

99. Cadet, Jean-Robert. *Restavec: From Haitian Slave Child to Middle-Class American.* Austin, Texas: University of Texas Press, 1998. 182 pages. ISBN: 0292712030 : 0292712022.

Abstract: Jean-Robert Cadet's mother, a black Haitian, died before he was a year old, apparently poisoned by jealous friends. His father, Blanc Philippe, was a wealthy and prominent white man, and although he contributed some money to Cadet's welfare, he did not want Cadet around to embarrass him. Blanc Philippe chose another woman, a former lover, to care for Cadet, but this woman treated him as a restavec, or child slave. Restavecs were victims of physical and sexual abuse. They might attend school, but generally could not participate in activities. They were not allowed to smile, laugh, or ask questions of or speak to their owners. They lived with very little, slept on the floors, and cooked their own food. Cadet was sent out to other families as well. He always had hopes that his father would acknowledge him, and when he escaped his last family to place himself before his father, his father gave him to another woman until he could arrange to send him to New York, where his first "mother" had gone. When Cadet arrived in New York, he was treated a little better but was still the servant in the family. He had no idea how to act as a member of a family. He was eventually thrown out of this household and struggled with homelessness while trying to attend high school. With some help and tireless persistence, Cadet graduated from high school and immediately joined the army. There he did well as a soldier, but fit in with no one, and he never had the courage to tell people that he had no family and no home. Finally, lonely and desperate, he began writing letters to himself. He concocted a mother and two girlfriends. He would read his letters out loud to his barracks mates. Cadet joined the Rangers, an elite unit within the army, where his race seemed to be far less important than the esprit d'corps of the group. He thrived as a member of this unit, but found himself once again homeless and friendless after he was discharged. He attended college on the GI Bill and graduated from the University of South Florida where he first began seeing a psychiatrist. Despite this treatment, Cadet found it difficult to participate in social occasions or to be part of a family. Finally, Cadet became a teacher and, while student teaching, met the woman who became his wife. When they married, he became a stepfather and the couple had a child together. Cadet writes that his soul began to heal when he became a father. He concludes his autobiography with a plea that the practice of child slavery be stopped:

> Restavec slavery is wrong. It is the worst crime imaginable, because the victims are incapable of resisting their adult predators. It is a crime against nature as well, because the child's very rights to life—to belong, to grow, to smile, to love, to feel, to learn, and to be a child—are denied, by those whose ancestors were slaves themselves   (p. 183)

100. Caldwell, Erskine. *In Search of Bisco.* Foreword by Wayne Mixon. Athens, Georgia: University of Georgia Press, 1995. 219 pages. ISBN: 0820317845.

> **Notes:** Originally published by Farrar, Straus, and Giroux, 1965. This edition reprinted with a new introduction and foreword by Wayne Mixon.

101. Campbell, James L. (1908-). *From Slavery to the 21st Century As Seen through the Eyes of a Grandson.* Mooresville, North Carolina: Performance Business Services, 2000. 44 pages; photographs. ISBN: none.

102. Campo, Rafael. *The Poetry of Healing: A Doctor's Education in Empathy, Identity, and Desire.* New York, New York: W. W. Norton & Company, 1997. 270 pages. ISBN: 0393040097.

> **Notes:** Originally published New York: W. W. Norton & Company. *The Desire to Heal,* 1998. ISBN: 0393317714.

> **Abstract:** In this collection of essays, Campo, a doctor, writes about his struggle to accept himself as a gay man within the context of his family and the medical profession and as a poet. His resistance to his homosexuality had often expressed itself in his inability to empathize, even sympathize with his seriously, often terminally ill patients. After coming to grips with his own identity, Campo was a resident at the University of California at San Francisco Hospitals, where many of his patients were HIV-AIDS patients. Campo, with his long-term male partner, were members of the gay community in San Francisco. He alternately embraced and rejected the more open life style of his friends and acquaintances. Campo found the atmosphere of homophobia in which he worked a threatening environment, making it difficult for him to come out among his coworkers. Campo describes the lessons he learned from his experiences with patients and how the emotional release and the healing he gained through the writing of poetry led him to be a more humane and compassionate doctor.

103. Cantu, Norma Elia. *Canicula: Snapshots of a Girlhood en la Frontera.* Albuquerque, New Mexico: University of New Mexico Press, 1995. 132 pages; photographs; map. ISBN: 0826315925.

> **Abstract:** This is the second book in a trilogy that goes from the 1800s to the 1900s. The first, *Papeles de Mujer* (written entirely in

Spanish), and the third, *Cabanuelas,* make up a chronological, fic-
tionalized, history of her family. The present book is a collection
of vignettes based on family photographs. Cantu says that some
of the events are based on truth and others are completely fictional. She goes on to explain,

> But then again, as Pat Mora claims, life en la
> frontera is raw truth, and stories of such life, fic-
> titious as they may be, are even truer than true. I
> was calling the work fictional autobiography,
> until a friend suggested that they really are
> ethnographic and so if it must fit a genre, I guess
> it is fictional autobioethnography.   (p. xi)

Some of the subjects covered in the vignettes reflect tragic events
in a family's life, such as the death of a brother in Vietnam, losing
a newborn baby, natural disasters, etc. But most are small events
which describe the life of Mexican Americans living on the border.
Examples are confusion over the American custom of Halloween
trick-or-treating, meal preparations, visiting relatives in Mexico
and having them visit in Texas, relationships between siblings,
and being treated for head lice.

104. Cardona-Hine, Alvaro. *A History of Light: A Memoir.* Santa Fe,
New Mexico: Sherman Asher Publishing, 1997.   56 pages.
ISBN: 1890932019 : 1890932000.

> **Abstract:** Cardona-Hine was born in Costa Rica in 1926. He came
> to the United States when he was thirteen. He lives in Santa Fe,
> where he works as an artist, composer, and writer. This book con-
> tains the memories of his love at the age of twelve for the little
> German girl who lived next door to him. The friendship ended
> when she was sent back to Germany to attend school.

105. Carlson, Peggie (1951-).   *The Girls Are Coming.*   Midwest
Reflections. St. Paul, Minnesota: Minnesota Historical Society
Press, 1999. 203 pages. ISBN: 0873513754 : 0873513762.

> **Abstract:** Peggie Carlson decided to find employment at one of
> the Big Three employers in the Saint Paul area after hearing about
> the good pay and the new opportunities for women following the
> passage of the Equal Employment Act of 1972. The Big Three
> included Bell Telephone, Minnegasco, and Northern States Power.
> Carlson was one of the first women hired at Minnegasco. She
> gives a humorous account of the not-always-humorous events
> surrounding her entry into the men's world she found there. One

of her superiors proudly announced to her that there were no women working at Minnegasco, not even "girl clerks, except for downtown where people expect that kind of thing" (p. 11). Carlson found her co-workers to be curious, hostile, and threatening, but she also found acceptance, and at least two crew leaders who were happy to work with her and train her. She was first assigned, along with several other women, to read meters, but quit after only a few days when she was threatened with a knife by an elderly woman who was terrified at the prospect of having an African American in her house. Carlson was then transferred to the buildings and grounds crew, where she began training as a pipe fitter. She was soon joined by one other woman, the wise and easygoing Sonny, who saw Carlson through the worst of her introductory period at Minnegasco. She and Sonny together were inducted into the union, and Carlson earned the coveted pipefitters' license. Because the pay was good, she stayed at the company and began to lose interest in attending college. Over the years, she observed a change in attitude among the employees. When her first mentor retired, he had his wife clean up his treasured engineer's cap and he gave it to Carlson, a sign that he considered her to be an equal: "You gotta have a cap" (p. 199).

106. Carr, Johnnie Rebecca. *Johnnie: The Life of Johnnie Rebecca Carr, with Her Friends Rosa Parks, E. D. Nixon, Martin Luther King, Jr., and Others in the Montgomery Civil Rights Struggle.* As told to Randall Williams. Illustrations by Jeffrey Hurst. Montgomery, Alabama: Black Belt Press, 1996. 56 pages; illustrations. ISBN: 1881320537.

Abstract: Told in the third person and intended for younger readers, this work tells the story of Johnnie Rebecca Carr, Rosa Parks, and the Civil Rights Movement in Montgomery, Alabama. Born in 1911 in Montgomery, Carr grew up on the family farm. She attended Miss White's School, a private school established to teach young African-American girls academic and domestic skills. At Miss White's School, Carr and Rosa (McCauley) Parks were classmates. The school closed when Carr was in seventh grade, and by then her mother was supporting the family through domestic work and could not afford to continue her children's education. Carr married at sixteen and had two children. After several years, she left her husband and went back to school. She became a nurse and later began selling insurance. While living and working in Montgomery, Carr joined the NAACP, where she and Rosa Parks rekindled their friendship. She became active in voter registration activities and later played a supporting role in the Montgomery Bus Boycott. In 1964, Carr, her second husband, and their son Arlam decided that they would challenge the segregated school system, and were named in a suit (*Carr v. Montgomery City Board of Education*) that would go to the U.S. Supreme Court. Even though the case went unsettled for almost thirty years, Arlam graduated from once all-white Sidney Lanier High School. Carr became president of the Montgomery Improvement Association in 1967. She and her husband continue to serve as poll officials.

107. Carroll, Rebecca Evans (1917-). *Snapshots from the Life of an African-American Woman*. Baltimore, Maryland: C. H. Fairfax Company, 1997. 397 pages; photographs. ISBN: none.

Abstract: Dr. Rebecca Evans Carroll retired as the deputy superintendent of the Baltimore Public Schools, following a career in which she taught in both segregated and desegregated schools in that city. A native of Baltimore, Carroll attended schools during a time of strict segregation. State law prohibited her from attending graduate school at the University of Maryland. Instead, the state provided all expenses, including transportation, for African-American students to attend graduate school anywhere but in Maryland. Carroll chose to attend the University of Chicago. At the time, she notes, African-American women had essentially two career options: nursing or teaching. Having always loved school and having excelled in academics, she chose to teach and returned to pursue her career in the still segregated schools of Baltimore. While teaching, Carroll completed a B.S. degree and earned masters and doctoral degrees in education. Seeing both the good and the bad in the post-*Brown v. Board of Education* world of southern schools, Carroll writes

> Desegregation, the law of the land, was a forward step for the nation; however, implicit were hundreds of unarticulated relationship problems that were spawned by the racism that, in many instances, was and is still with us. I wonder how much self-esteem of blacks and how many self-concepts and how much achievement were placed on the altar of sacrifice during the early days of desegregation.... And what about the curriculum geared primarily to middle-class Caucasians? How terribly the black students were being short-changed emotionally as well as academically. (p. 59)

108. Carson, Ben. *The Big Picture: Getting Perspective on What's Really Important in Life.* Written with Gregg Lewis. Grand Rapids, Michigan: Zondervan Publishing House, 1999. 271 pages; photographs. ISBN: 0310225833.

> **Notes:** Also published in paperback Zondervan Publication House, 2000. ISBN: 031023834x.

> **Abstract:** Renowned African-American surgeon Ben Carson writes about his three experiences surgically separating craniopagus Siamese twins, or twins joined at the head, particularly his second and third cases, both conducted in South Africa. In the second case, the surgical team discovered after nineteen hours in surgery that the two girls were dependent upon one another for life-sustaining functions and could not survive separated. Carson realized only later, when confronted with the third case, that although the efforts to save the two little girls were doomed from the start, preparing for their surgery brought much-needed medical equipment to the black medical school at Medunsa where the surgery was performed, and gave him invaluable experience which helped make his third case a success. Carson writes that this experience helped him to develop his philosophy of looking at the "big picture" and convinced him of how important this is for a successful life. Carson tells the story of his mother, who was married at thirteen, and after having two children (Carson and his brother) discovered that her husband was a bigamist and had a second family. The boys' father's departure left them destitute, but their mother was able to make their money stretch. Despite her own inability to read, she took the boys' education in hand, insisting that they stop watching television and begin reading at least two books a week. Carson went from failing grades to all A's, and proceeded on his chosen course to medical school. He gives examples of how his mother taught him to set priorities and to make carefully considered decisions. He discusses what he learned from his early life of hardship and how he has applied those lessons. As an adult, Carson was inducted into the Horatio Alger Society, an organization of individuals who have risen from the lowest socio-economic rungs to become the most successful practitioners in their fields. Carson describes several inspiring Alger members. He also writes about the importance of being "nice," learning that the world does not revolve around us, and learning to see from the other person's perspective. He writes about the issue of political correctness, the value of racial diversity, and the mistake of denying the existence of racial prejudice. Carson gives his views on racial profiling, affirmative action, the importance of

education, and the problems of health care and managed health. He sees that one of the major problems of managed health organizations is that the care of the patient is not the first priority, and he outlines his own vision of a successful health insurance program. He writes about how his Christian faith figures in his life as a professional and as a family man, and he illustrates his experiences with the healing power of prayer.

109. —. *Gifted Hands.* Written with Cecil B. Murphey. Grand Rapids, Michigan: Zondervan Publishing House, 1990. 232 pages; photographs. ISBN: 0310546508.

> **Notes:** Also published Zondervan Publishing House, 1996. ISBN: 0310214696; New York: HarperPaperbacks, 1993. ISBN: 0061042536. These editions published with the title *Gifted Hands: The Ben Carson Story.*
>
> **Abstract:** This is the first book by Ben Carson. He writes about his childhood and education, his early career as a surgeon, and how he became a pioneer in the hemispherectomy, a surgical procedure that involves removal of half of the patient's brain. It is used to alleviate symptoms in the most severe cases of epilepsy and allows the patient to lead a normal life. (See Carson, Ben. *The Big Picture: Getting Perspective on What's Really Important in Life* for further autobiographical details.)

110. Casanova, Ronald. *Each One Teach One: Up and out of Poverty, Memoirs of a Street Activist.* As told to Stephen Blackburn. Willimantic, Connecticut: Curbstone Press, 1996. 260 pages. ISBN: 1880684373.

> **Abstract:** Ron Casanova was raised in an orphanage in Staten Island, New York. He began escaping from the orphanage to find his brothers and sisters at about the age of eight. He finally located his brother and learned that his mother had died leaving eleven children, and that his father was an alcoholic. For the rest of his youth Casanova was in and out of the orphanage, jail and mental institutions, and the homes of his siblings. In between, he would often sleep on stair landings or other places. "I liked my independence, however poor that may have been. To me it was preferable to the risk of closeness that comes from living in a family" (p. 27). As an adult, he had no place to live, and he was again in and out of prison over a period of fourteen years. After he was released, he went to the La Guardia Shelter in New York and worked for various mission groups, developing new ideas for

ways to serve the homeless. He eventually decided that such organizations could not provide the help the homeless required.

> In my experience, all institutions tend to want you to remain dependent on them. That's the welfare system, that's the AFDC, that's Christianity. It is great to go out and feed people, but it is more important to help people learn to feed themselves. . . . As long as you depend on someone else, you are in their control. You are not your own person if you are on Aid to Families with Dependent Children all the time, or on the dole from the church.   (p. 118)

From that point, in 1988, Casanova began to organize homeless people in the Tompkins Square Park area in New York City. He spent the next years working for the autonomy of displaced persons, even meeting with Jack Kemp, Secretary of Housing and Urban Development, during a march on Washington D.C. At that meeting, Kemp made promises that were never kept. Casanova continues to organize the homeless in other cities, such as Los Angeles and Kansas City. He is disappointed that even when adequate housing is provided, people are unable to maintain their homes properly. His conclusion is that he and others must continue to be there to offer food and housing and wait for people to make the decision to take control of their own lives. Casanova continues his activities despite the fact that he is suffering from AIDS.

111. Cepeda, Orlando. *Baby Bull: From Hardball to Hard Time and Back*. Written with Herb Fagen. Dallas, Texas: Taylor Publishing Company, 1998. 238 pages; photographs. ISBN: 087833212x.

Abstract: Orlando Cepeda was born in Ponce, Puerto Rico in 1937. He was the son of baseball player Perucho Cepeda. As a boy, his family moved from town to town following Perucho's baseball career. Negro League players were often in Puerto Rico playing during the winter months, and so Cepeda had, besides his father, many of the great Negro League players to look to for inspiration. At fifteen, Cepeda began playing with an amateur team and from there was picked up by the professional Santurce Crabbers. The owner of the Crabbers, Pete Zorilla, had connections with the New York Giants, and he sent Cepeda to try out for the team in Miami, Florida. Cepeda was sent to a low level team in Virginia where he was depressed both by his inability to communicate in English and the conditions of segregation he found there. He slowly moved up through team levels until he was signed by the San Francisco Giants in 1958. Cepeda believes that it was racism toward black players, especially Latin black players, that impeded his progress to the major leagues. Cepeda proved himself his first year, however, when he was named National League Rookie of the Year as well as the Giant's Most Valuable Player. His fortunes faltered when the Giants hired Alvin Dark to manage. Dark was openly racist, divided the team along racial lines, and abused the black and Latin players. Cepeda found himself in contract disputes and was accused of faking a knee injury. Although he was crushed when he was traded to the St. Louis Cardinals, it turned out to be a good move for him. He was named National League Most Valuable Player during the 1967 season, a year the Cardinals won the World Series. Cepeda was traded in 1969 to the Atlanta Braves, and then to the Oakland A's in 1972. By then, because of another knee injury, his career was over, and Cepeda stayed with the A's only three months, although he played another year with the Boston Red Sox as their first designated hitter. Following retirement, Cepeda went into an emotional decline and hit rock bottom when he was arrested and convicted for possession of marijuana. Following his release from prison, Cepeda began practicing Buddhism, which helped to turn his life around. He was able to get back into baseball when San Francisco Giants owner Peter Magowan hired him for public relations and community outreach, and he became active in youth and community services in northern California. Cepeda came within seven votes of being inducted into the Baseball Hall of Fame. He devotes one chapter of his book to remembering and noting important Latin baseball players and their legacy to American professional baseball.

112. Cervantez, Ernesto E. (1941-). *Once upon the 1950s*. Bethel, Connecticut: Rutledge Books, 1997. 111 pages. ISBN: 1887750657.

Abstract: Cervantez grew up in a closely knit family in a small mining town in New Mexico. He has a passion for the rock and roll music of the 1950s. He describes his high school years, and recalls the songs that he listened to while spending time with friends and falling in love. Cervantez's fondest memories surround baseball, football, and his first serious love. He writes that these were the "happiest days of our lives, because we were a group of kids that stuck together in almost everything we did and in the way we walked, talked, and dressed" (p. 56). Following graduation, Cervantez and his older brother, unsuccessful in finding work, joined the United States Air Force. Early on, his brother received a medical discharge, returned home, and married his high-school sweetheart. A younger brother also married his high-school sweetheart, but Cervantez, still in the Air Force, received a Dear John letter. He is still full of regret when he thinks of his lost high-school romance. Despite this disappointment, he considers his friends from high school to be his friends for life.

113. Ch'i, Shouhua. *See* Qi, Shouhua.

114. Chacón, Rafael (1833-1925). *Legacy of Honor: The Life of Rafael Chacón, a Nineteenth-Century New Mexican.* Edited by Jacqueline Dorgan Meketa. Las Cruces, New Mexico: Yucca Tree Press, 2000. 439 pages; photographs; maps. ISBN: 1881325245.

Notes: Originally published Albuquerque: University of New Mexico Press, 1986. ISBN: 0826308864 : 0826308872.

Abstract: Rafael Chacón was born in 1833 and died in 1925 having seen New Mexico go from a Spanish and Mexican territory, to a U.S. Territory, to an official state of the Union. Chacón describes the Rebellion of the Cantón of La Cañada of 1837 and its successful suppression by General Armijo. For this event, as well as for others scattered throughout the text, Chacón elucidates his own writing with the decimas and cunadas, ballads and poems, from his native New Mexico. These poems are presented in English in the main body of the text, but included in their original Spanish in an appendix. At 11 years old, Chacón left home as a cadet in the Mexican army. He suffered hardship and neglect but was taken in by a friendly and nurturing Captain Gómez. He witnessed, at home with his family, the American invasion of New Mexico, and recalls with regret the days before American hegemony, the "sane and sober" (p. 74) times when neighbor helped neighbor and all, Pueblo Indians and Mexicans, celebrated the feast days together. Chacón also describes in some detail many customs, practices, occupations, and celebrations of his region of New Mexico. A great deal of Chacón's autobiography is devoted to his days as a commissioned officer in the volunteer army of the United States during the years of the Civil War. The initial purpose in forming an army from the New Mexican territory was to prevent an invasion from Texas. Chacón was also responsible for "pacifying the hostiles," primarily, the Navajo and Apache of present day New Mexico, Arizona, and Colorado. Honorably discharged in 1864,

Chacón returned to his family in New Mexico, eventually uproot-
ing and taking them by wagon to what is now Trinity, Colorado, a
new territory at the time. There he made and lost a fortune
through sheep herding and land acquisition. Throughout his life,
Chacón had many occupations, including buffalo hunter, Indian
trader, farmer, shopkeeper, tailor, clerk, territorial senator (in
Colorado), officer in the army, justice of the peace (in New
Mexico), and rancher. Chacón and his wife Juanita had eleven
children, seven of whom died in infancy. Author Meketa provides
historical detail and context for Chacón's work, filling out the
details of his life and the times in which he lived.

115. Chambers, Veronica. *Mama's Girl*. New York, New York:
Riverhead Books, 1996. 194 pages. ISBN: 1573220302 :
1573225991.

Abstract: Chambers, a young writer and *Glamour* magazine editor, tells the story of her childhood in New York. Her parents, both
born in the Caribbean, were divorced when she and her brother
were quite young. Her brother eventually went to live with their
father, and she stayed with her mother. She continually tried to
impress her mother and get her attention with good grades and
other achievements. Her mother, however, seemed to be more
concerned about her brother and generally preoccupied with
other aspects of her life. After her mother remarried, Chambers
found living at home to be more and more difficult and moved in
with her father. During the years with her negligent father and
abusive stepmother, Chambers still managed to maintain a brilliant academic record and was able to move away from home
when she was accepted at age sixteen to Simon's Rock College.
Chamber's story of her struggles and achievements is mixed with
description of her overwhelming desire to evoke a spark of emotion or affection in her mother. The two of them were finally par-
tially reconciled when she begged her mother for financial help to
get through college, and her mother responded with consistency
and generosity. As Chambers worked her way through college,
she got a job that kept her in close proximity to her mother, and
she finally began to understand the difficult job her mother had to
provide for her family. One night, she was finally able to ask her
mother for the emotional support she needed, and the two
reached a much fuller understanding.

116. Chang, Leslie. *Beyond the Narrow Gate: The Journey of Four Chinese Women from the Middle Kingdom to Middle America*. New York, New York: Dutton, 1999. 288 pages. ISBN: 0525942572.

> **Notes:** Published in paperback New York: Plume, 2000. ISBN: 0452277612.

> **Abstract:** Leslie Chang, a young writer, describes her childhood as well as that of her mother and three of her mother's childhood friends and their children. The four women in the elder generation were born in China and fled to Taiwan during the revolution. In Taiwan they were classmates at the same school for girls, and eventually all emigrated to the United States. Chang explores the families and other circumstances of the women, follows them to middle age, and their children into adulthood. She compares their situations. Chang's mother lost her parents at an early age and had to look after herself and her younger siblings. She got a scholarship to study in the United States and stayed there. She was one of the few Chinese women of her generation who managed to enter mainstream U.S. society, becoming an aggressive real estate agent and desegregating the local swimming pool. Chang herself grew up in a predominantly white community and went to white schools, but she lived by the expectations of her Chinese parents. Chang managed to avoid the academic career in the sciences that her parents had planned for her, and instead became a writer. As she interviewed and studied the lives of her mother and her mother's friends, Chang made important discoveries about herself, and eventually concluded that, although she is Chinese by heritage, she and the children of her mother's friends now have their own lives to lead. On the final page she writes:

> > I wish for a moment that we could all be here making dumplings together, like our mothers used to do in Taipei. I know it will never happen. We each of us have struck out on our own paths, as different from one another as the lives that our mothers have made for themselves in America.   (p. 286)

117. Chang, Pang-Mei Natasha (1965-). *Bound Feet and Western Dress*. New York, New York: Doubleday, 1996. 215 pages. ISBN: 0385479638 : 0385479646.

> **Notes:** 1st Anchor Books edition, 1997.

> **Abstract:** Chang, an American, writes the story of her childhood as part of a family of Chinese immigrants. She tried to blend in with white society, but at the same time felt a bond with China and

her great-aunt, a woman who lived an unusual life during a period of change in China. Her great-aunt Yu-i was born into a large
family of eight boys and four girls. Her elder sister had bound
feet, but when Yu-i's turn came to have her feet bound at the age
of three, her constant screams so distressed her brother that he
promised to care for her even if no one would marry her and he
demanded that the binding stop. This effectively ended the custom in her family. She married a man who barely acknowledged
her presence for years, until he demanded a divorce when the couple was living in England. Yu-i divorced her husband and moved
in with a brother in Germany. After several years, she moved back
to China and settled in Shanghai with her young son. She taught
German at a university and became the president of the Shanghai
Women's Savings Bank. She cared for her former husband's parents for the rest of their lives, and even took over the responsibilities for burying the ex-husband himself when he died in a plane
crash. She left China twenty years later during the Chinese civil
war and went to live in Hong Kong. In 1972, she immigrated to
the United States to be with her son and his family.

118. Chapman, Serle. *Of Earth and Elders: Visions and Voices from
Native America.* Introduction by Dennis J. Banks. Photographs
by Serle Chapman. Postscript by Bruce Ellison. Missoula,
Montana: Bear Print, 1998. 218 pages; photographs; illustrations. ISBN: 0952860740.

Abstract: Serle Chapman, an Anglo-European, has compiled this
work in the name of justice, equality, and human rights. He, and
all contributors, wish to paint a picture of Native America today.
Clearly, there is no monolithic Native culture. Disparate nations
traded with each other across many miles. Changes were occur-
ring before the Europeans arrived and continue to this day.
Chapman writes that the people who contributed to this book
point out historic events and bring to light little-acknowledged
facts to illustrate the condition of Native people today. This book
is "a collection of thoughts, explanations, opinions, prose, and
individual perspectives" (p. xiii). In his introduction, Dennis
Banks writes similarly that "crucial issues standing before Native
people are explained from individual insight and personal experience, each choosing to say how it really is as opposed to what
might be comfortable for others to imagine" (p. 5). Chapman con-
tributes many photographs, an initial chapter, and introductory
pages for seven interviews. Contributors include the following:
Chief Arvol Looking Horse, Vine Deloria, Jr., Ron Valasco, Gregg
Bourland, Ronnie Lupe, Robert Mirabal, N. Scott Momaday, Joy

Harjo, Avis Little Eagle, Maryann Andreas, Bernice Kaigelak, Keith Secola, Joe Camarillo, Tim Giago, Chief Wilma Mankiller, J. Carlos Peinado (J. C. White Shirt), Chief Oliver Red Cloud, Mario Gonzalez, Marley Shebala, Joanne Shenandoah, and Tim Lame Woman. The following individuals are interviewed: Floyd Red Crow Westerman, Apesanahkwat, Steve Reevis, Fern Mathias, Sonny Skyhawk, Arigon Starr, and Larry Sellers.

119. Charlton, Lewis. *Sketch of the Life of Mr. Lewis Charlton and Reminiscences of Slavery.* Transcribed by Edward Everett Brown. Chapel Hill, North Carolina: Academic Affairs Library, University of North Carolina at Chapel Hill, 2000.

> http://docsouth.unc.edu/neh/charlton/charlton.sgml
> http://docsouth.unc.edu/neh/charlton/charlton.html

> **Notes:** Documenting the American South (Project).

120. Charr, Easurk Emsen. *The Golden Mountain: The Autobiography of a Korean Immigrant, 1895-1960.* Wayne Patterson. 2nd ed. The Asian American Experience. Urbana, Illinois: University of Illinois Press, 1995. 315 pages; photographs. ISBN: 0252022173 : 0252065131.

> **Notes:** Originally published Boston: Forum, 1961 (302 pages).

> **Abstract:** Easurk Emsen Charr emigrated from his native Korea to the United States in 1904. He writes about his childhood in Korea and his life after coming to the United States. Charr and his family lived in the city of Pyeng Yang. The entire family had been converted to Christianity, and Charr was sent to a mission school where he developed strong ties with American missionaries. This alliance served him well when he went to the United States. He and his cousin sailed to Hawai'i, and then went on to the U.S. mainland. He moved around the country looking for work and schooling. Although laws were often not in favor of Asian immigrants, he always found people, both Korean and white Americans, who would help him out. He was encouraged to enter Park College in Parkville, Missouri, a school that did not charge tuition or room and board, but let students work their way through school. While still studying at Park to get into medical school, Charr joined the U.S. Army during World War I and was allowed to join the medical corps. After the war, the United States passed a law allowing all war veterans to become naturalized U.S. citizens. It turned out, however, that this did not include Koreans, Chinese, or Japanese, and it was not until much later, in 1935, that

Charr got citizenship through the lobbying efforts of the American Legion. He made several unsuccessful attempts to get into medical school and finally went to Chicago, where he became a draftsman with the Rand McNally Company. It was there that he met his wife, Elaine Kim, or Lotus Flower, who was on a student visa from Korea. Charr lost his job during the Great Depression, and he and Lotus Flower moved with their family to San Francisco. After he gained U.S. citizenship, he joined the U.S. Civil Service, which took him to Nevada and Oregon. He worked with both the Soil Conservation Commission and the Indian Service. Charr was never able to return to Korea, nor did he ever see his parents after leaving in 1904. Despite the many difficulties and the discrimination that he encountered, he was devoted to his new country and writes in his preface, "Indeed this is the New Promised Land that I found flowing with milk of wisdom and honey of freedom. I am exceedingly glad that I came to America, and I am humbly proud that I am an American citizen. May God bless America, my country, my home!"

121. Che, Sunny (1929-). *Forever Alien: A Korean Memoir, 1930-1951.* Jefferson, North Carolina: McFarland & Company, 2000. 253 pages; photographs; maps. ISBN: 0786406852.

Abstract: Che was born to a farming family in Pohang, South Korea. Her father left for Japan soon after she was born. He traveled from Kyushu to Hokkaido looking for work and a place to move his family. He finally settled in Fukui on the coast of the Sea of Japan. No sooner had the family joined him there than Che's father was sent back to Korea because he had developed tuberculosis. He was in Korea for five years, where he studied acupuncture and continued his work as a Chinese herbalist. He returned to Japan and gained his medical license to practice acupuncture. Within a year of his return, Che's mother died. The children were happy when their father remarried because it meant fewer household chores, but they were soon to regret their father's choice. Che and her four siblings were at constant odds with their stepmother, who clearly favored her own daughter. As war escalated in Europe and Asia, the family moved to Nagoya and then back to Korea. Following the defeat of Japan and the liberation of Korea, there was a serious shortage of food, heating fuel, and work. Che chronicles her remaining years in Korea, during which she and her oldest brother attempted to escape and return to Japan. After her brother attempted suicide, Che devoted herself to caring for him and saw him through to recovery. She eventually left to go to school and earn a living in Seoul. Christian missionaries helped her to attend the Methodist Mission School and then the school's seminary. Admission to the seminary meant an unheard-of three meals a day. A job with the U.S. military also meant that Che had money to send to her landlord to help him with the cost of caring for his family. When North Korea invaded South Korea, Che was once again on her own, and she became a refugee, traveling from place to place to find safety, shelter, and food. She traveled to Pusan with a Red Cross ambulance, which she describes as "the most liberating and joyous moment I had experienced since leaving Seoul" (p. 231). Again with the help of the Christian missionaries, Che managed to receive a passport to the United States. In 1952, with no word of anyone in her family, with little money and no possessions, Che set sail for San Francisco on the *Sea Serpent* with the "soaring joy of liberation" (p. 248).

122. Chin, Duncan. *Growing Up on Grove Street, 1931-1946: Sketches and Memories of a Chinese-American Boyhood.* Foreward and afterword by Sandy Lydon. Capitola, California: Capitola Book Company, 1995. 110 pages; illustrations. ISBN: 0932319033.

Abstract: Duncan Chin accompanies his pencil sketches with short memories of his childhood in Watsonville in the Pajaro Valley of California. Watsonville was an agricultural town that was home to dust bowl migrants as well as immigrants from Mexico, Europe, and Asia during the Great Depression. Chin portrays family members and friends. His drawings depict scenes of communal meals, of laborers in the family apple orchard, of school days, and of workers in the fields. In text and drawings, Chin portrays the activities of harvesting and drying apples, the businesses along Lower Main Street, soldiers on leave from nearby Monterey, hobos cooking under a railroad bridge, and the adventure of rescuing his dog from the local dog pound. Chin's memories are mostly happy ones, but they also show the darker side of Watsonville, including police raids at the local brothel and violence against African Americans and Japanese Americans. A historical essay about Chin's family, the Watsonville area, and the Chinese community there concludes the work.

123. Chin, Justin (1969-). *Mongrel: Essays, Diatribes, and Pranks.* New York, New York: St. Martin's Press, 1999. 178 pages. ISBN: 0312195133.

> **Abstract:** Justin Chin is a gay, Chinese immigrant from Singapore. He first acknowledged his sexual orientation at the age of seventeen as a junior-college student in Singapore, and it was at that point that he began to live an openly gay lifestyle. At the age of eighteen, he immigrated to the United States, to San Francisco, where he became a writer of prose and poetry and a solo performer. In the essays that make up the book, Chin discusses a variety of topics, most of them related to gay living and culture. The essay "Saved" discusses a "web of Christian ministries attempting to lead gays and lesbians out of 'the life.'" The main problem with these, Chin decides, is that gays and lesbians come to these groups out of a profound guilt over their lifestyles, and when they are unable to change after several years of "rehabilitation," the guilt grows even stronger. "Smile" delves into the sex industry in Thailand and particularly that part of it aimed at gay clientele. The article was originally written for *Progressive*, a gay magazine, which then decided not to publish it. The topic, he states, is "thorny" because "many different issues collude on this one issue, not the least of which are consent, individual autonomy, and labor relations" (p. 159). Other topics include gay perceptions of gay society, gay society's perceptions of its Asian members, a reflection of the Castro—the famous gay neighborhood in San Francisco, commentary on a Mr. Asian beauty contest, the culture of food in Singapore, the popularization of Buddhism, and a cross-country book tour.

124. Chin, Soo-Young. *See* Kim, Dora Yum.

125. Chin, Tung Pok (d. 1988). *Paper Son: One Man's Story.* Written with Winifred C. Chin. Asian American History & Culture. Philadelphia, Pennsylvania: Temple University Press, 2000. 147 pages; photographs. ISBN: 1566398002 : 1566398010.

> **Abstract:** Tung Pok Chin immigrated from China to the United States in 1934 at the age of nineteen. Chin immigrated as a "paper son," which entailed paying for the paperwork that would prove he was the child of a U.S. citizen and memorizing all of the false facts necessary to pass the quizzing by immigration officials when entering the country. Chin had a wife and family in China, but because he entered the United States proclaiming to be a single man, he was unable to send for them. He ultimately divorced his

wife after he found out that she had had a child by another man.
Chin was educated in the United States and served in the Navy
during World War II. After the war, he went back to his pre-war
employment of running a hand laundry. Chin received financial
assistance from the Chinese Hand Laundry Alliance (CHLA) in
New York. Chin wrote poetry and had hundreds of poems published by the *China Daily News* under his real name, Lai Bing Chan.
Because he was a competent speaker of English, he served as interpreter at the True Light Lutheran Church for twenty years. Since
he was legally single in the United States, Chin was able to marry
a woman from Hong Kong with whom he had two children.
Trouble cropped up in the early 1950s during the years of
McCarthyism. Chin was associated with a known Communist,
wrote for the Chinese newspaper with the strongest Communist
leanings, wrote under an assumed name, and had dealings with
the CHLA, which was also suspected of Communist sympathies.
Throughout the 1950s, he was followed and frequently visited by
FBI agents, who questioned his loyalty to his adopted country.
Afraid of the consequences, he burned all of his poetry and
stopped writing for several years. He started again in 1959 and
began composing his memoirs in 1986 after retiring in 1978. His
daughter, Winifred Chin, edited the manuscript and prepared it
for publication after Chin's death in 1988.

126. Chinn, Florence J. (1927-). *A Tree Growing in Gold Mountain: A
Journal of the Chinn Family of Sacramento, California.* Honolulu,
Hawai'i: F. J. Chinn, 1997. 126 pages; photographs; maps.
ISBN: none.

127. Chiplin, Charles K. *Roads from the Bottom: A Survival Journal for
America's Black Community.* Brandon, Mississippi: Quail Ridge
Press, 1996. 183 pages. ISBN: 0937552739.

> **Abstract:** Chiplin assesses the disintegration of African-American
> communities. He compares present day communities to his own
> experience growing up in small town Mississippi during the Jim
> Crow era and the emergence of the Civil Rights Movement.
> Chiplin himself was aware of the indignities of Jim Crow from an
> early age. He experimented with entering a whites-only restau-
> rant and, shortly before the Montgomery Bus Boycott triggered by
> Rosa Parks, conducted a one-boy protest by refusing to sit in the
> back of a bus. Chiplin's father understood his son's motivation,
> but asked him to hold back on his activities because he feared los-
> ing his job. His father was fired after all, however, when he signed

a petition demanding equal education for his children. After serving in the Vietnam War, Chiplin's brother was arrested for attending a whites-only Catholic Church. All of these events led to Chiplin's and his father's committed involvement in the Civil Rights Movement. They became active in voters' rights, opening a freedom school, and working with the publication of the Vicksburg *Citizen's Appeal*. Later, when the freedom school was completely destroyed in a bomb blast, the Chiplin family offered freedom school classes on their back porch, after which the family grocery store was also bombed. The father refused to submit to terrorism and opened his store the next morning, selling salvageable goods from amidst the ruins of his business. The bombings succeeded in bringing the black community together, and Chiplin was able to see slow, positive changes taking place. Chiplin attended Alcorn and Jackson State Colleges. He continued his work with civil rights into the 1970s while teaching at Jackson State College and working with the "Second Chance" program in his county's prison system. Chiplin is a poet, a musician, and a minister. In the book, he presents ten "roads for present day America, particularly Young America" (p. 161). He hopes that if parents will give these "roads" a try, there will be a turn around in the conditions of the family and community.

128. Chu, Rosemary (1929-). *Rosemary: A Journey from East to West*. As told to Lou Ann Locke. Arkadelphia, Arkansas: The Pete Parks Center for Regional Studies, Ouachita Baptist University, 1999. 219 pages; illustrations; photographs. ISBN: none.

Abstract: Rosemary Chu was born in the village of Tai Tou in the province of Shan Tung in China. Before her birth, her grandmother had become a Christian. The whole family followed her example and converted. Chu's father was a Lutheran minister and Chu and her sisters were educated at a private Catholic school. In 1949, when the Communists took over China, Rosemary was about to graduate from high school. Her family, not optimistic about their chances of survival, decided that she was the only family member they could smuggle out of the country. Chu traveled by train for eight days, miraculously avoiding detection of her undocumented status, and making it over the border to Hong Kong. From there, she was able to get a scholarship from the Lutheran Church to study in the United States. Chu attended Wittenberg College in Springfield, Ohio. After graduation, she went to work for the Moody Bible Institute in Chicago and married Finley Chu, a young man from the same part of China as herself. Finley had completed his doctoral studies and was soon hired by Oklahoma Baptist University in Shawnee, Oklahoma, where their only child, Jane, was born. After seven years, in 1963, Finley was recruited to head the Business and Economics Department at Ouachita Baptist University in Arkadelphia, Arkansas, and the family soon felt at home there. Finley, however, became ill, and died of cancer in 1967. Chu was immediately offered the responsibility of running a residence hall at the university, and she has been there ever since, looking after two generations of young women and participating actively in college and church life. In 1973, after twenty-three years of total separation from her family, she received a letter from one of her sisters. Finally, in the 1980s, Chu participated in a tour to China, subsidized by her friends and supporters at Ouachita. During the tour, she was reunited with her brothers and sisters. Her parents had died before she was able to make the trip.

129. Chuck D. *Fight the Power: Rap, Race, and Reality*. Written with Yusuf Jah. New York, New York: Delacorte Press, 1997. 274 pages; photographs. ISBN: 0385318685.

Notes: Published in paperback New York: Dell Publishing, 1998. ISBN: 0385318731.

Abstract: Leader of the rap group Public Enemy, Chuck D is concerned about the health of black youth, the black community, and black culture. His music provides him with a means of communicating to a broad audience. "Once I realized that I'm a voice that people listen to, I realized I had to fill my voice with something of substance" (p. 5). His songs prominently address racial issues and controversies. In his book, Chuck D also delivers messages concerning alcohol and drugs, gratuitous materialism, support of the African-American community by African Americans, and getting ahead. History is important to him. He believes, that if young, rising entertainers would pay attention to older, experienced musicians they would avoid many business, legal, and artistic pitfalls. Chuck D hopes to "expose to the reader the beauty and depth of Rap and Hip-Hop. . . . This book damn sure ain't a passive introduction to this world, nor is it an autobiography. . . . *Fight the Power* will ruffle" (p. xiii). Chuck D describes his entry into the music world. He began as a deejay and emcee, and then became a singer, songwriter, and performer. He writes about Public Enemy's recording history, their touring experiences, their collaborations with other performers, and the controversies the rap group has inspired. Chuck D examines his career within the context of rap and hip-hop music in America. He discusses his experiences with the recording industry and touring. He addresses some of the questions that have arisen regarding his song lyrics and videos. He shares his views on black culture and education and comments on Public Enemy Griff's comments concerning Jews, the diamond industry, and slavery. Today Chuck D is involved in many community outreach projects including, REACH (Rappers Educating All Curriculum Through Hip-Hop), and MusicCares.

130. Chung, Donald K. *Remembrances of the Forgotten War: A Korean American War Veteran's Journeys for Freedom.* Introduction by William C. Westmoreland. Pacifica, California: Pacifica Press, 1995. 185 pages; photographs. ISBN: 093555310x.

Abstract: Chung describes the process of writing and publishing *The Three Day Promise*, which began when he went to North Korea in 1983 and reunited with his three sisters and their families for the first time in thirty-three years. After returning to his home and medical practice in Long Beach, California, Chung began writing articles for the *New Korea Times* and giving presentations about his trip. Careful to protect the welfare of his family, Chung did not criticize North Korea. This displeased the South Korean government and even provoked a visit from the FBI. After a second trip to North Korea, Chung began writing his memoirs and had them published privately. He arranged an initial printing of two thousand copies and planned to donate all proceeds to the Korean War Veterans Memorial Fund. Chung was advised to send the book to "Dear Abby," who had publicly supported fundraising for the memorial. Abby decided to highlight the book in one of her columns and met with Mr. and Mrs. Chung to help them prepare for the consequences. Despite Abby's advice, they were woefully unprepared when six thousand requests arrived three days after the column appeared. In all, Chung raised more than $400,000 from sales of the book worldwide. He prepared a Korean translation that was sold in U.S. Korean communities and in South Korea. South Korean television created a fifty-episode television series based on the book which aired in 1991 in South Korea and on Korean television in the United States. Following the success of his book and television series, Chung found that he was no longer viewed favorably in North Korea, but was well-loved in South Korea. He writes, "I am neither pro-North Korea nor anti-North Korea, nor pro-South Korea, nor anti-South Korea. I remain a proud and grateful American, and I am, and always have been, a supporter of Korea, my *one* native country" (p. 120). Chung received many phone calls, letters, and photographs from readers of the book and viewers of the television series. He writes that many aged Korean refugees made appointments at his cardiology clinic to talk to him and share their own experiences, essentially turning his medical practice into "Chung's Refugee Counseling Clinic" (p. 126). He concludes his book with a selection of letters and photos he received from those who responded to the "Dear Abby" column and his book. Many were veterans and families of members of the military who were killed in action in Korea.

131. —. *The Three Day Promise: A Korean Soldier's Memoir.* Tallahassee, Florida: Loiry Publishing House, 1988. 406 pages; photographs. 0933703910.

Notes: Also published Tallahassee, Florida: Father and Son Publishing, 1989, 1990. ISBN: 0942407067.

Abstract: In his memoir, Chung describes his years growing up in North Korea and Manchuria under the Japanese occupation. Born in the far northern Korean village of Taehyang in 1932, Chung moved with his family to Harbin, Manchuria, where his father worked with the Japanese government. Chung could speak and write Korean, but his first language was Japanese. In Manchuria, he was given a Japanese name and attended Japanese schools. During World War II, Chung was in the hospital recovering from a burst appendix when the United States dropped the atomic bomb on Nagasaki and Hiroshima. The Japanese began a quick retreat from Manchuria, and Soviet occupying troops began flooding into the area. Before the family's repatriation to Korea, however, Chung witnessed many horrific events, including the gang rape of his sister by Soviet troops. When the family returned to Korea, they found a home near their native village. Chung attended a medical high school and college with the intention of becoming a doctor. By his second year, medical students were being encouraged to join the North Korean Army. Soon the college closed and all the students were drafted. Chung escaped, at his mother's insistence, by hiding inside a large clay pot. He remained in hiding for seven weeks until the advance of the South Korean Army put the Chung family within allied territory. Their town's liberation was brief, however, and soon the South Korean Army was retreating as North Korea advanced with the aid of the Chinese. Chung escaped south with the South Korean Army, promising his mother that he would return in three days. Unfortunately, he was not able to return to his family for another thirty-three years, four years after the death of his mother. After arriving in the South, Chung was immediately inducted into the

South Korean army. Following the war, he entered Soo-do Medical College in Seoul and graduated in 1960. In 1962 Chung was accepted into residency at Missouri Baptist Hospital in St. Louis. He became certified as a cardiologist, married a young South Korean woman, fathered two children, and eventually became a U.S. citizen.

132. Clement, Samuel Spottford (b. 1861). *Memoirs of Samuel Spottford Clement: Relating Interesting Experiences in Days of Slavery and Freedom.* Chapel Hill, North Carolina: Academic Affairs Library, University of North Carolina at Chapel Hill, 2000.

http://docsouth.unc.edu/neh/clement/menu.html

Notes: Documenting the American South (Project).

133. Clement, Thomas Park. *The Unforgotten War: Dust of the Streets.* Bloomington, Indiana: Truepeny Publishing Company, 1998. 139 pages; photographs; poetry. ISBN: 0966795202.

Notes: Also published [United States]: T. P. Clement.

Abstract: Clement was born out of wedlock to his Korean mother during the height of the Korean War. He assumes that his father was an American GI. One day when he was four or five years old, his mother abandoned him on the street in the middle of a city. He lived on the streets for a year or two, staying with a gang, begging, scavenging, and stealing food. Clement was picked up by a Methodist Missionary, and taken to an orphanage. The orphanage had advantages over the street, but conditions were not good. The children received one meal a day, and physical abuse was an everyday occurrence. Clement was lucky to be one of the children chosen for adoption after the United States passed a law allowing Korean adoptees to come into the country. His parents were June and Richard Clement, who lived in North Carolina with their three children. The home atmosphere was loving and supportive, but everything about his new life was different to him. Clement was baffled by his sudden inability to communicate. He thought the electric lights were fire and that each visit his mother made to the grocery store was a prelude to Christmas. Very insecure, he lived in fear that his family would leave or that he would be sent back to the orphanage. He found that he was constantly reminded of his differences and took the designation of "Alien" on his birth certificate to heart. Clement was very slow to learn English and so had a difficult time in school. In high school, he excelled in electronics, which gave him some self-confidence and direction. He went on to college and graduate school in electrical engineering and worked in research and development for a urological medical device company before starting his own successful business. Clement met other Korean adoptees for the first time when he attended a conference designed especially for that purpose. In his book, he gives some advice to adoptive parents of international children and to adoptees hoping to find their birth parents. He has chosen not to look for his birth mother, although he hopes one day to return to visit Korea.

134. Cleveland, Edward Earl (1921-). *Let the Church Roll On: An Autobiography.* Boise, Idaho: Pacific Press Publishing Associates, 1997. 125 pages. ISBN: 0816313830.

Notes: Originally published by the author in 1974.

Abstract: Cleveland's father was a devout member of the Church of Seventh Day Adventists. He joined the medical corps branch of the military during World War I as a conscientious objector and risked court martial and even death to uphold his beliefs and the requirements of the church. Cleveland shared his father's zeal and pursued his education with the intent of becoming a minister. Cleveland attended Oakwood College in Huntsville, Alabama, during a time when all Seventh Day Adventist institutions were segregated by race, including schools, hospitals, and cemeteries. Cleveland's dedication for finding lost souls was matched by his determination to break down segregation. As an evangelist, he never held segregated tent meetings, even when he traveled throughout the southern United States, and he refused to observe "whites only" restrictions in South Africa. In 1950, he became the first black man to teach white students in his denomination. He was a founding member of the first Seventh Day Adventist Human Rights Committee and was part of the "flying squad" that investigated injustice throughout North America. From 1954 to 1977, Cleveland held the position of associate secretary of the Ministerial Association of the General Conference. He was considered twice for promotion to vice president, but did not want to discontinue his missionary work. He preached in sixty-seven countries on six continents. He is the author of fourteen books, including *Middle Wall* (1969) and *Free at Last* (1970). When questioned about the apparent segregation of churches within his denomination, Cleveland explains that all churches and conferences are integrated, but that the majority of Blacks have no appetite for the White cultural worship style. So the Black church, born in slavery, will not go away. It is now, and has been, a refuge from the withering winds of social, economic, political, and spiritual alienation in our society. An organization can only remove exclusion and foster inclusion. The worship preference must be left to the individual. (p. 100)

135. Cole, Natalie. *Angel on My Shoulder: An Autobiography.* Written with Digby Diehl. New York, New York: Warner Books, 2000. 353 pages; photographs; discography; index. ISBN: 0446527467.

Notes: Also published in a large print edition Rockland, Massachusetts: Wheeler Publishing, 2000. ISBN: 1568959915 (448 pages).

Abstract: Natalie Cole is the eldest daughter of Nat King Cole, a black singer who was wildly popular in the 1950s and 1960s. She tells the story of her childhood, her career, and her relationship to her family. Raised in Hancock Park, one of the most exclusive neighborhoods in the Los Angeles area, Natalie Cole had a comfortable childhood, but her parents were often away from home for long stretches of time. She began singing at an early age, accompanying her father on an album or two as a child. Nat King Cole died in February 1965, when Cole was still in high school. She recalls this as the time her family began to fall apart. Cole began singing professionally after graduating from the University of Massachusetts. Her first album, in 1975, contained two number-one hits, "Inseparable" and "This Will Be." Cole won a Grammy award for "This Will Be." She has continued to record regularly ever since. Success, however, was not able to keep her away from drugs. She and her first husband, Marvin Yancy, were both involved in dealing and other illegal activities to maintain their heroin and crack habits, and Cole was jailed for drug possession a number of times in the United States and Canada. In 1984, she admitted herself into Hazelden, a drug and alcohol rehabilitation center in Minnesota. After a six-month stay, she was able to return home to her son, Robbie and her career. She has remained drug-free ever since. In 1991, she released the album *Unforgettable . . . With Love*, a collection of songs that her father had sung. It included a "duet" by Nat and Natalie Cole of "Unforgettable," with her voice recorded to blend in with a recording of his. This labor of love became a hit throughout the world, and the album sold millions of copies, relaunching Cole's career and creating renewed interest in the work of her father. The most important result of the album, however, was that she was able to start resolving the pain she had felt ever since her father's death. Cole also began to over- come her lifelong inferiority complex, pulling herself mentally out of the shadow of her famous father. In the concluding chapters, Cole discusses the split between the Cole siblings and their moth- er over their father's fortune and details of her second marriage.

136. Connerly, Ward. *Creating Equal: My Fight against Race Preferences*. San Francisco, California: Encounter Books, 2000. 286 pages; photographs; index. ISBN: 189355404x.

Abstract: Ward Connerly became famous for his role, as University of California (UC) regent, in ending affirmative action practices within the UC system. He explains his position by describing his childhood. He lost his mother and was abandoned by his father, but was raised with love and discipline by an aunt, uncle, and grandmother. His uncle, especially, instilled pride in hard work and being able to provide for one's family. At about the age of thirteen, his grandmother claimed welfare benefits for him, and he chafed against his feelings of shame over this. Just before he turned fifteen, he declared that he would never accept another welfare check, and he went to work, earning twenty dollars more a week than welfare had provided. Based on this background, Connerly has always believed that hard work is the way to attain goals and that they must be attained in the same way by everyone. Connerly went to junior college and college, where he was fortu- nate to have mentors who encouraged him to excel. Pete Wilson, then a California State Senator, shared Connerly's views, and he asked him to serve on the California assembly's Housing and Urban Affairs Committee. After Wilson was elected governor, he appointed Connerly to the University of California Board of Regents. It was in this capacity that Connerly became aware of the effects of affirmative action, what he calls "race preference." He uncovered the admissions formulas that favored minorities, par- ticularly blacks, and that, he believed, were biased against whites and Asians. Amid enormous publicity and hostile opposition, Connerly persuaded the regents that the system was not fair, and, in 1995, affirmative action was banned in the UC schools. Following this victory, Connerly set his goal to end affirmative action in all fifty states. The passing of Proposition 209 accom- plished this in California in 1996. The next battlefields were Texas in 1997, where Measure A was defeated, and in Washington, where Initiative 200 was passed in 1999. Connerly is now involved in stopping the practice of affirmative action in Florida. He finishes his book by describing academic programs that tutor and support underprivileged and underachieving children with the goal of bringing them up to a level necessary to successfully enter and complete college.

137. Cook-Lynn, Elizabeth. *Why I Can't Read Wallace Stegner and Other Essays: A Tribal Voice.* Madison, Wisconsin: University of Wisconsin Press, 1996. 158 pages. ISBN: 0299151409 : 0299151441.

Abstract: When Elizabeth Cook-Lynn was a high school teacher, she was recruited, as an enrolled member of the Sioux Nation with an undergraduate degree, to enroll in a master's program especially developed for American Indians at the University of South Dakota. The program was funded by the U.S. government to qualify American Indians to work in educational institutions. Although attitudes toward such affirmative action became hostile and the programs evaporated, Cook-Lynn felt "the affirmative action years gave me a brief vision of grace, the hope of a transcendent time when people like myself would be welcomed as *American Indians* into America's modern debates concerning society and knowledge which raged then and continue to rage today" (p. xi). After nineteen years (1971 to 1991) teaching and doing research at Eastern Washington University, she resigned because she felt she had lost the institutional support she needed to do her work. This book is divided into five sections. The first is a collection of her reviews of works on American Indian topics published in the last decade. Most of these reviews were controversial because she wrote against publications which were largely well-received, but which Cook-Lynn found to have factual and ethical problems. The second section includes two essays, including "Why I Can't Read Wallace Stegner." Stegner, and many other authors of European ancestry, write about Indians, their lands, and their culture as though they were virtually extinct. They conclude that the American Indians reached their end in 1890 after the massacre of hundreds of Minneconjous at Wounded Knee, South Dakota. Although this tragic event further dispossessed Native Americans, Cook-Lynn states that the massacre was "the beginning of hard times," not the end of the culture. The third section is chiefly about a novel, *Hanta Yo*, published in 1979, which contains many dubious facts about Indians. Part four contains two essays on the role of American Indian women historically and today. They deal with the differences in the way American Indian women are perceived within their communities and by the larger American society. In the final section, "The Last Word," Cook-Lynn raises a few last additional points and questions.

138. Cool J, LL. *See* LL Cool J.

139. Cooper, Cynthia. *She Got Game: My Personal Odyssey.* Written with Russ Pate. New York, New York: Warner Books, 1999. 229 pages; photographs; index.   ISBN: 0446525669 : 0446608394.

Abstract: Cynthia Cooper was the fourth of her mother's eight children.   The children were raised in the Watts area of Los Angeles, one of the poorest and most crime-ridden urban areas in the country. Cooper watched her mother work several jobs at once to buy a house and give them all a better life, and Cynthia was determined to do what she could to improve herself. In high school, she played basketball and did well. She was recruited by the University of Southern California, where she played for the Lady Trojans. Although the team won the NCAA championship and was invited to the White House to meet then-President Reagan, her years in college were overshadowed by the death of her favorite brother, her mother's struggles to make ends meet, and her own inability to keep up with her studies. She quit college to work and help support her family and then went back because of her strong desire to play basketball. In 1986, still short of graduation, she received an offer to play for a professional team in Spain and left to play basketball in Europe. For ten years she was one of the top players there, first in Spain and then in Italy. She loved life in Italy, where she was well known and loved, and she learned to speak the language. Cooper has played on two Olympic teams; in 1988, she was on the U.S. women's basketball team that won the gold medal in Seoul. In 1992, the team was upset in Barcelona, but, with the participation that year of the men's so-called Dream Team, the National Basketball Association finally took a serious look at women's basketball and set the wheels in motion for professional women's basketball in the United States. Cooper was one of the sixteen original stars chosen to be distributed evenly throughout the original eight WNBA teams. She was sent to the Houston Comets, and starting at the age of 34, she was able to lead the Comets to the national championship three years in a row. As the book ends, Cooper describes her elation at belated recognition, her plans to continue playing basketball, and her hopes and dreams for her nieces and nephews, seven of whom she is raising herself. She continues to speak out publicly to encourage girls, especially those from underprivileged backgrounds, to set ambitious goals for themselves.

140. Coppin, Fanny Jackson. *Reminiscences of School Life, and Hints on Teaching.* Introduction by Shelley P. Haley. African American Women Writers, 1910-1940. New York, New York: G. K. Hall and Company, 1995. 191 pages; photographs. ISBN: 0816116334 : 0783813961.

> **Notes:** Originally published Philadelphia: A.M.E. Book Concern, 1913.

> **Abstract:** Fanny Jackson Coppin's grandfather bought his own freedom and that of four of his daughters, but for some reason, perhaps because his fifth daughter had a child, did not buy Fanny's mother's freedom. Coppin herself was freed by her aunt, Sarah Orr Clark, "who, working at six dollars a month saved one hundred and twenty-five dollars, and bought my freedom" (dedication page). Coppin went to work as soon as she received her freedom. She attended school except on washing day, ironing day, and cleaning day. Despite the difficulty of gaining an education, she was able to enroll in the Rhode Island State Normal School and later to attend Oberlin College, the only college in the United States at that time to enroll African-American students. Upon graduating, she taught in Philadelphia, where schools and services were segregated and employment options for African Americans were few. Coppin, along with the other teachers at the Friends Institute for Colored Youth, worked to add an industrial institute to the school so that African Americans would have the opportunity to learn a trade. In response to the general refrain of "we do not employ colored people," Mrs. Coppin reflects,

> > Thank heaven, we are not obliged to do and die, having the preference to do or die, we naturally prefer to do. But we can not help wondering if some ignorant or faithless steward of God's work and God's money hasn't blundered. It seems necessary that we should make known to the good men and women who are so solicitous about our souls and our minds that we haven't quite got rid of our bodies yet, and until we do we must feed and clothe them. (pp. 36-37)

> After successfully raising money for the industrial institute, Coppin worked for the *Christian Recorder*, a newspaper published

by African Americans, to raise money to pay off their debt. She traveled to England in 1888 as a delegate of the Women's Home Missionary Society of the A.M.E. Church, and also to South Africa in 1900 as a missionary with her husband, Bishop L. J. Coppin. A large portion of her work is dedicated to a discourse on elementary education teaching methods.

141. Cox, Suzy. *Diary of a Secretary: Humility and Pain.* Capitol Heights, Maryland: Suzy Cox & Company, 1997. 166 pages. ISBN: 0964504219.

142. Cross, Dolores E. *Breaking through the Wall: A Marathoner's Story.* Chicago, Illinois: Third World Press, 2000. 242 pages; photographs. ISBN: 0883781654: 0883781662.

Abstract: Dolores Cross, a prominent African-American educator, was an insecure child who stuttered. Her mother was often too ill to care for her children. Cross was encouraged to go to college by a co-worker of her mother's, and in 1954, she entered Seton Hall University. She married a fellow student at age nineteen and focused on getting her husband through school. Cross graduated eight years after she began college, by which time she had two children. She describes the difficulty black students had in college in those days because of the lack of support or mentorship from their schools. Cross earned her Ph.D. at the University of Michigan in 1971 and was hired by Northwestern University as assistant professor in education and director at the School of Education's master of arts in teaching program. She moved to California when she was appointed Director of Teacher Education by the Claremont Graduate School. After four years there, at the age of forty, the City University of New York chose her as its first black female vice chancellor. Based on her achievements in this position, she was appointed by the governor of New York to serve as president of the New York State Higher Education Services Corporation. In this capacity, she worked to provide financial assistance to struggling college students. In 1988, Cross went on to the University of Minnesota and then was chosen to serve as president of Chicago State University (CSU), a struggling school on Chicago's South Side with a student body that was ninety-percent black. During her eight years at CSU, Cross did much to turn the school around, including increasing retention, improving its financial situation, and building facilities. At age fifty, she ran her first long-distance race, the New York City Marathon. Running was a physical discipline that helped her center herself and keep herself calm and under control. After retiring from CSU and having a hard time finding work she wanted to do as she turned sixty, Cross used running as a form of therapy, keeping up her practice schedule as far as she was physically and mentally capable. In 1998, she was recruited as president of Morris Brown College, one of the six traditionally black colleges in Atlanta, Georgia. She feels it was her running that helped her make the transition to life in the South, where she has found a new home and satisfying work.

143. Cuffe, Paul (1759-1817). *Captain Paul Cuffe's Logs and Letters, 1808-1817: A Black Quaker's "Voice from Within the Veil."* Edited by Rosalind Cobb Wiggins. Introduction by Rhett S. Jones. Washington, D.C.: Howard University Press, 1996. 529 pages; illustrations; maps; index; facsimiles. ISBN: 088258183X.

> **Notes:** Cuffe's memoir was originally published York, England: C. Peacock, 1811. It is available in microform. The original is held in the Schomburg Collection, New York Public Library.

> **Abstract:** Cuffe was born in Massachusetts in the middle of the eighteenth century. His father was a freed slave born in Ghana and his mother was a Wampanoag Indian from Martha's Vineyard. Cuffe's father, who was self-taught, managed to purchase property and run a successful business. Because Cuffe's father had been bought by Quakers, the family was familiar and sympathetic with Quaker teachings. Cuffe himself was heavily involved with the Society of Friends, both as a religious faith and through trading relationships. Like his father, Cuffe was a diligent entrepreneur. As an adult, he broke all prevailing stereotypes of African Americans because he was a wealthy landowner and literate. He was active as a social reformer, and he opened a school on his own property known as Cuff's [sic] School, which was open to all children in the village, regardless of race. Cuffe worked in the shipping industry. With his brother-in-law as a partner, he built and sailed his own ships. His crews included extended family and were generally all black. He traded, fished, and whaled up and down the East Coast. Traveling south required great care, because Cuffe or any of his crew could be kidnapped and pressed into slavery due to the Fugitive Slave Law, which required only the word of a white man as proof of ownership. Cuffe sought to create a new climate of trade with West Africa, which would benefit both Africans and African Americans by creating a healthy trade in goods rather than in humans. To do this, Cuffe sailed to Sierra Leone, setting up the Friendly Society in Freetown and a companion entity, African Institutions, in the United States. He

sought support from businessmen and philanthropists in the
United States and England, primarily among Quaker acquaintances and colleagues, to set up markets and connections. Cuffe
died in 1817, probably from heart disease. Cuffe's letters and logs
cover his financial and business dealings, his voyages to England
and Sierra Leone, and his trips to Washington, D.C., to meet with
the House of Representatives and to speak with President
Madison. Editor Wiggins provides two historical and interpretive
essays: "Introducing Captain Paul Cuffe, Friend," and
"Preparations for a Voyage." Rhett S. Jones provides an extensive
historical introduction, "The African Diaspora in British North
America in the Time of Paul Cuffe."

144. Curtis, Florence Hargrave (1935-). *Daughter, Be Somebody.*
Buffalo, New York: Cupelo Press, 1997. 281 pages; photographs; maps. ISBN: none.

145. D, Chuck. *See* Chuck D.

146. Daly, James A. *Black Prisoner of War: A Conscientious Objector's
Vietnam Memoir.* Lawrence, Kansas: University of Kansas
Press, 2000. 267 pages. ISBN: 0700610596 : 070061060x.

Notes: Originally titled *A Hero's Welcome.* Indianapolis, Indiana:
Bobbs-Merrill, 1975. ISBN: 0672520303.

147. Dandridge, Dorothy. *Everything and Nothing: The Dorothy
Dandridge Tragedy.* Written with Earl Conrad. New York, New
York: HarperCollins, 2000. 240 pages; photographs. ISBN:
0060956755.

Notes: Also available in paperback from Harper Perennial (229
pages); originally published New York: Abelard-Schuman, 1970.
ISBN: 0200716905 (215 pages).

148. Danquah, Meri Nana-Ama. *Willow Weep for Me: A Black
Woman's Journey through Depression, a Memoir.* New York, New
York: W. W. Norton & Company, 1998. 272 pages. ISBN:
0393045676.

Notes: Also published in paperback New York: One World, 1999.
ISBN: 0345432134.

Abstract: Meri Nana-Ama Danquah immigrated to the United States from Ghana with her family as a child. As a young adult she began to experience serious bouts of clinical depression. In her book, Danquah explores the possible causes of her illness: childhood trauma, foreign roots, life as a minority female, childbirth, failed relationships, and genetic predisposition. She traces her struggle with depression through many years until she is able to acknowledge it and seek help. Her belief that depression was a "white disease" created an obstacle to Danquah seeking help. She found that people were dismissive when she mentioned she was depressed and that there was a pervasive stereotype of black women as towers of strength and positive thinking, able to withstand any hardship. *A Washington Post* article on depression in the black community opened her eyes to its pervasiveness. She realized, "We are the walking wounded. And we suffer alone because we don't know that there are others like us" (p. 184). She made many attempts to seek professional help, finally deciding that even though she required the assistance of doctors and therapists, she must take control of her situation herself.

> I was sick and tired of waiting for miracles, waiting for approval, waiting for happiness. For years I had been waiting, asking over and over and over and over, "Why me?" and I never found the answer so I figured what the hell, and decided to try asking, "Why not me?"　　(p. 230)

She was motivated to not give up on life because of her desire to succeed as a writer, the impact her disease could have on her young daughter, and the fact that her younger sister was also struggling with depression.

149. Darkins, Claudia M. *A Name I Can't Read: The Rocky Road to Literacy: A Mother's Story.* Houston, Texas: Cane Publishing, 1998. 197 pages; photographs. ISBN: 0964815400.

Abstract: Darkins writes about the school careers of her two sons. The abilities of both boys were constantly underestimated by their teachers, and they were left to languish scholastically despite their expressed desire to learn. The eldest, Gregory, was earmarked for special help as soon as he began school, even though there was no proof of any special needs, and he was generally discriminated against by his teacher. The younger, Chris, a precocious child, was consistently assigned work that was below grade level, despite test results which showed him several years ahead. By the time Gregory was in high school, he was so discouraged that he was unable to complete his education. Several years later, he achieved a GED and started his own business. Chris managed to struggle through and entered college. While in college, he excelled scholastically and athletically and was drafted by the Green Bay Packers football team. Darkins explains her purpose in writing the book:

> My hope is that every person who reads this story will take a demonstrative interest in correcting the problems that cause our children to fail. Correcting problems of this nature is the responsibility of entire communities because the problem is bigger than those directly affected.
>
> (p. 191)

150. Davenport, R. J., III. *Memoirs of a Regular Guy*. San Jose, California: Writers Club Press, 1999. 99 pages. ISBN: 0595088759.

Abstract: R. J. Davenport's most significant memories start when he was twelve years old. He lived with his mother and siblings in Germantown, Pennsylvania. Most of his friends were from his block, so it was difficult for him socially when his African-American family moved to an apartment complex inhabited primarily by white senior citizens. He became obsessed with graffiti and started to skip school and to shoplift. He failed ninth grade. The family moved back to Germantown, and Davenport was able to get back on course with school work. He went on to college, and now works as a computer consultant and writer.

151. Davis, Eric. *Born to Play: The Eric Davis Story: Life Lessons in Overcoming Adversity on and off the Field*. Written with Ralph Wiley. New York, New York: Viking, 1999. 278 pages; photographs. ISBN: 0670885118.

Notes: Also published New York: Signet Books, 2000. ISBN: 0451201043 (324 pages).

Abstract: Eric Davis was raised in Los Angeles, the son of a homemaker and a man who worked two jobs for many years to support his family. Davis credits his father's work ethic for keeping him motivated throughout a brilliant but difficult professional baseball career. A natural athlete as a child, Davis was drafted by the Cincinnati Reds after he graduated from high school in 1980. He never missed practice or games, but was constantly getting injured in the outfield, running into walls to catch balls. He was criticized for his time on the injured list by the Cincinnati media, but managed to hit and field well when he played. In 1990, Davis was one of the strongest players on the Reds team that beat the Oakland A's in the World Series, but in the last game of their four-game sweep, Davis dived for a ball and fell, destroying one of his kidneys. He recovered from the near-fatal injury, but was deeply disappointed to discover that his team had left him in Oakland in a hospital intensive care unit, and gone back to Cincinnati to celebrate their victory without him. After playing with the Los Angeles Dodgers and Detroit Tigers he retired in 1994 at the age of thirty-two after his seventh surgery in eight years. He and his wife and daughters enjoyed retirement, but in 1996, he went back to the sport, playing with the Reds again and then the Baltimore Orioles. After a few months with the Orioles, Davis was diagnosed with colon cancer and underwent surgery to remove the tumor. While still undergoing a course of chemotherapy, he resumed the season and went on to have a spectacular year with the Orioles, hitting in thirty straight games. The next year, he was offered a better salary with the St. Louis Cardinals, and the book ends as he looks forward to the 1999 season. Davis appreciates the love and upbringing he received from his parents and the guidance given him by older baseball players. He tries to return the favor by looking after new players. He participates in various organizations aimed at helping and encouraging underprivileged young people, and he serves as a national spokesperson for the National Cancer Society.

152. Davis, Flora P. *Don't Cry.* Written with Lauree G. Lane. Atlanta, Georgia: Naja Press, 1995. 159 pages; photographs. ISBN: 096494670x.

> Abstract: Davis grew up with seven brothers and sisters on the farm given to her grandfather by his former owner. Davis provides the history of her family and describes social and religious life in Mt. Olive, North Carolina. Her family prospered on what they could grow and raise on their farm. Davis explains the preparation of food, the methods used for growing and preserving produce and raising and butchering livestock. Davis's parents believed that education was paramount. They sent their children to school, instructing them to return home and teach their parents what they had learned. Six of the eight children went to college and two, including Davis, earned Ph.D.s. Davis earned her B.A. at Hampton Institute, her master's degree from Columbia University, and her Ph.D. from Walden University. She did post-graduate work in foods and nutrition at several U.S. universities, and also studied in France, England, and Italy. Davis provides a detailed

account of the educational accomplishments of her siblings and of the two brothers that remained at home to run the farm. She writes of the emotion she feels when she thinks of the progress her family has made in just one generation.

153. Davis, Noah (b. 1903). *A Narrative of the Life of Rev. Noah Davis a Colored Man: Written by Himself, at the Age of Fifty-Four.* Chapel Hill, North Carolina: Academic Affairs Library, University of North Carolina at Chapel Hill, 1999.

> http://metalab.unc.edu/docsouth/neh/davisn/sgml
> http://metalab.unc.edu/docsouth/neh/davisn/html

> **Notes:** Documenting the American South (Project).

154. Davis, Ossie and Ruby Dee. *With Ossie and Ruby: In This Life Together.* New York, New York: William Morrow & Company, 1998. 476 pages; photographs; index; acting credits. ISBN: 0688153968.

> **Notes:** Published in paperback, New York: Quill, 2000. ISBN: 0688175821.

> **Abstract:** Actors Ossie Davis and Ruby Dee tell how they began their careers and how they met each other and married. Davis was a student at Howard University when Marian Anderson sang on the steps of the Lincoln Memorial in 1939. The event "sealed" his calling, and he and a friend went to New York City to pursue acting. Dee grew up in New York and began acting while still a student at Hunter College. She acted in many film and stage productions, often starring opposite Sidney Poitier. She had a successful run performing a one-woman show she wrote called *My One Good Nerve*. Davis had a successful career as an actor and film director. His dream of writing a play of his own was realized with *Purlie Victorious* in the 1960s. Together they appeared in many screen and stage productions, hosted a syndicated radio show, *The Ossie Davis and Ruby Dee Story Hour*, and ran their own production company for several years. The couple has three children, all of whom work in the entertainment industry. The book discusses their philosophy of child-rearing and family. Social activists as well as entertainers, the couple has been involved in the Civil Rights Movement, politics, and many humanitarian activities.

155. Davis, Sammy, Jr. (1925-1990). *Sammy: An Autobiography. [With Material Newly Revised from Yes I Can and Why Me?].* Written with Burt Boyar and Jane Boyar. New York, New York: Farrar, Straus, and Giroux, 2000. 533 pages; photographs. ISBN: 0374293554.

Abstract: This autobiography of Sammy Davis, Jr. was published ten years after his death in 1990. Cowriter Burt Boyar who, with his wife, collaborated on Davis's previous memoirs, *Yes, I Can: The Story of Sammy Davis, Jr.* in 1966 and *Why Me?: The Autobiography of Sammy Davis, Jr.* in 1989, revised the material from these two books, incorporated unpublished material, and added a new introduction and epilogue. Davis was born in the 1920s and began traveling at the age of three with his father and his father's partner, who were in vaudeville. Soon after, they began featuring Davis in their act, the Will Mastin Trio. Davis never went to school. During his younger years, he was at the mercy of nationwide segregationist practices: when he was hired to perform at a hotel, he had to find a place to room elsewhere; in Las Vegas, he could not gamble in the casinos. Many popular performers, most notably Frank Sinatra, took him under their wing and helped promote his career. Davis was still subjected to constant snubs and blatant discrimination by whites, while, ironically, black society had little appreciation for him and considered him to be a sell-out to white audiences. For example, he campaigned for the Kennedy brothers at their request, but was slighted by them when having a black man around became a political liability. Under President Nixon, he served on committees looking into problems prevalent in black society. He also went to Vietnam to study the drug abuse problems in the U.S. Army, managing to create rapport with black troops and bringing their demands back to the president. The more he was appreciated by the Republicans, however, the more he was despised by the Democrats and mainstream blacks. Eventually, bitterness became the driving force behind everything he did. When he became famous, he spent more money than he had in an effort to prove to himself that he was as good as anyone. Davis got his greatest gratification from his associations with the rich and famous and from frequenting clubs and hotels which had never before admitted blacks. Davis liked to surround himself with his friends and expensive possessions to create a cocoon of security in his own home. He married Swedish model May Britt, but found it impossible to focus on his family, rather than on himself and his lifestyle. Britt left him after several years. Later he married Altovise, a woman who shared his bon vivant attitudes and agreed to an open marriage. Davis was constantly in demand at hotels and night clubs, playing to packed houses his entire career. By his late fifties, however, Davis's lifestyle caught up with him. He was diagnosed with liver problems and suffered a general breakdown of health. He managed to change his habits, however, and went back to performing. In 1988 and 1989, until a few months before his death, Davis, Frank Sinatra, and Dean Martin staged a tour which played to packed halls and stadiums throughout the country.

156. Davis, Terrell. *TD: Dreams in Motion*. Written with Adam Schefter. New York, New York: HarperCollins, 1998. 204 pages; photographs. ISBN: 0060192828 : 0061098825.

Notes: 1999 paperback edition includes a new chapter (296 pages).

Abstract: National Football League player Terrell Davis writes about his life, with the focus on the two Super Bowl wins by his team the Denver Broncos; first in 1998 (XXXII) against the Green Bay Packers, for which he was named Super Bowl Most Valuable Player, and then in 1999 (XXXIII) against the Atlanta Falcons. In 1998, Davis became one of a handful of players to ever rush for over 2000 yards in a single season, and he was named the NFL's Most Valuable Player that year. Davis was born the youngest of six boys and had a turbulent home life. He talks about how he learned important lessons that kept him away from drinking, cigarettes, and drugs and how a night spent in jail after a botched robbery convinced him never to do anything that would cause him to return. All his life, Davis has been plagued by migraine headaches, a condition that left him incapacitated for days at a time throughout his youth. Despite disadvantages and health problems, Davis participated in sports and did exceptionally well in football. Although he played in high school, he was not actively recruited but managed to get a football scholarship to the University of Georgia. As a senior, he was drafted into the NFL by the Denver Broncos in the final round, a position informally known as Mr. Irrelevant. Sheer determination and hard work during training sessions brought him to the attention of Bronco coaches, and he started his rookie year on the first team. Davis talks about his family, the support of his mother, and the importance of hard work, determination and taking care of one's health. He discusses other young men who he feels were more talented than he, but who were not successful because they did not have the drive to make something of themselves.

157. Dawson-Batts, Ruth. *Ruth Jeanette Dawson-Batts: Reflective Years, Reflective Moments: My Memoirs.* Waco, Texas: R. Dawson-Batts, 1996. 316 pages; photographs; facsimiles. ISBN: none.

> **Abstract:** Ruth Dawson-Batts has put together a collection of photographs of her extended family: grandparents, parents, siblings, grandchildren, nieces, nephews, and in-laws. Along with the photographs, she has included family trees and documentation of achievements and events such as weddings, awards, and retirements. Dawson-Batts has written a brief biography of each of her siblings, herself, her parents and grandparents. Born in Rocky Branch, Texas, Dawson-Batts attended school there and in Wortham, Texas. She attended Huston-Tillotson and Prairie View A&M University, majoring in home economics and science. She also earned a master's degree in elementary education. Dawson-Batts and her husband, Fred Jr., were both teachers and school principals. She has been a member of many organizations, including the Huston-Tillotson Alumni Association and the YWCA and has participated in educational programs such as Crossover Program for Successful Integration and the Texas Association for Childhood Education. She and her husband have been active in many community service organizations in the city of Waco.

158. Dawson, George. *Life Is So Good.* Written with Richard Glaubman. New York, New York: Random House, 2000. 260 pages. ISBN: 037550396x.

> **Notes:** Also published in a large print edition New York: Random House, 2000. ISBN: 0739408585 (477 pages); New York: Penguin, 2001. ISBN: 0141001682; large print edition Rockland, Massachusetts: Compass Press, 2000. ISBN: 1568959370 (364 pages).

> **Abstract:** George Dawson, born in 1898, first made the news when he began taking adult basic education classes near his home at the age of ninety-eight. Richard Glaubman, a schoolteacher from the state of Washington, took an interest in Dawson's story and began setting it down as narrated to him. George Dawson was born and raised in Marshall, Texas. The eldest of five children in a poor family, he never had the opportunity to attend school because he had to help his parents make a living. As a child, Dawson was carefully trained to avoid causing trouble with white people, and at age twelve, he was hired out to a white family in return for room, board, and a weekly salary. He worked harder

than anyone and was unfailingly polite in all of his dealings with whites. On his twenty-first birthday, his father pronounced him an independent man, and he left home to see the world. Dawson traveled through the South, living and working in Tennessee and New Orleans, and he traveled to Cincinnati and Canada. He also went to Mexico, where he was astounded to be treated as an equal by people of all colors. He was tempted to stay there, but felt drawn back to his family. Dawson eventually settled in Texas, married, and raised seven children. He worked at a dairy and, because he couldn't read, taught himself how to operate and repair complicated machinery by taking it apart to see how it worked. He helped his children with their homework every night, asking them to read their assignments aloud and never revealing his lack of education. All of his children graduated from both high school and college. Dawson outlived four wives. At age ninety-eight, after ten years of living alone in retirement, he decided to join an adult education program, thus beginning his career as a full-time student. He learned to read and, at age 101, was still attending school each day. As Glaubman researched the book, he asked Dawson about many of the most important historical events in the twentieth century, such as World War I and II, the Great Depression, the spread of the automobile, the Scopes trial, and the Civil Rights Movement. Dawson talks about these events in the context of his own life.

159. De Ferrari, Gabriella. *Gringa Latina: A Woman of Two Worlds*. Boston, Massachusetts: Houghton Mifflin, 1995.   176 pages. ISBN: 0395709342.

Notes: Also published New York: Kodansha International, 1996. ISBN: 1568361459.

Abstract: Gabriella de Ferrari was born and raised in Tacna, a small city in Peru. Her parents were Italians who immigrated to South America. Her family was one of the wealthiest in town; her father was well-known for his wisdom and generosity and her mother was famous for her garden and her cooking. The Italian Day that her parents held in their home every June was one of the major social events of the city. De Ferrari had a difficult time in school because the other children and many of the teachers treated the wealthy students differently from the rest, and indeed the well-to-do families themselves made sure that their children did not mix too thoroughly with the locals. She was sent to England for a year of schooling, and upon her return she went on a hunger fast until her parents agreed to send her to the United States for college to a small Catholic school in St. Louis. In Peru, de Ferrari was known as a gringa or white woman. At college, she became famous as the only Latina at her school. Life in the eastern U.S. and her marriage to a man in a "proper" New England family in which emotional displays were firmly discouraged further emphasized the Latin side of her upbringing. After years in the United States, she began to put together her own identity and to accept the many different cultures that she embodies. As the book ends, she is flying back to her home and family in New York after her mother's funeral in Peru. She looks forward to going home, "to my friends, who have accepted me so unquestioningly; to being an adult; to living my life as my own version of a gringa Latina" (p. 159).

160. Dee, Ruby. *My One Good Nerve*. Introduction by Ossie Davis. New York, New York: John Wiley & Sons, 1999. 178 pages; photographs. ISBN: 0471317047.

> **Notes:** Originally published by Third World Press as *My One Good Nerve: Rhythms, Rhymes, Reasons*, 1986. ISBN: 088378114X : 0883781158 (124 pages).

> **Abstract:** This book is a collection of poetry and essays written by renowned actress Ruby Dee and used in her one-woman show *My One Good Nerve*. The pieces are divided up into sections, with an introduction to each by the author. The sections include remembrances about her childhood and family, a tribute to her husband, Ossie Davis, and their fifty-year marriage, social commentary on young black artists, and tributes to people who have influenced her and others and whom she describes as "unorthodox." Dee also writes about her children and provides social commentary.

161. Deernose, Agnes Yellowtail. *See* Voget, Eric.

162. Delaney, Samuel R. *Heavenly Breakfast: An Essay on the Winter of Love*. Flint, Michigan: Bamberger Books, 1997. 115 pages. ISBN: 0917453336.

> **Notes:** Originally published New York: Bantam Books, 1979.

163. Delany, Sarah Louise (1889-). *On My Own at 107: Reflections on Life without Bessie.* Written with Amy Hill Hearth. Illustrations by Brian M. Kotzky. San Francisco, California: HarperSanFrancisco, 1997. 151 pages; illustrations; photographs. ISBN: 0062514857 : 0062514865.

Abstract: In 1993, when Sara (Sadie) and Annie Elizabeth (Bessie) Delany were 104 and 102 respectively, they were catapulted to fame with their best-selling book *Having Our Say: The Delany Sisters' First 100 Years.* In 1994, they published their second book, *The Delany Sisters' Book of Everyday Wisdom.* The first book was adapted as a Broadway production and is in the process of becoming a motion picture. The two sisters were born into an elite African-American family of ten children, many of whom became well known in black society in New York. Both sisters were educated professionals. Sadie was a teacher, the first black woman to teach domestic science on the high-school level in New York City. She retired at the age of 70. Bessie was only the second black woman licensed to practice dentistry in New York, and she had a successful practice for many years. Both forewent marriage so they could continue their careers, and they lived together their entire lives. Bessie died on September 25, 1995, leaving Sadie as the last surviving Delany sibling. On her own for the first time in her life, Sadie writes a series of reflections on the life of her sister and their relationship. She talks about Bessie's funeral and the reaction of people to her death, the state of Bessie's beloved garden, and how she, Sadie, is learning to deal with her solitary life. Sadie celebrated her 107th birthday almost exactly a year after her sister died, and the book ends with her birthday party and her decision to make the most of her remaining years. The book is illustrated with paintings of many of Bessie's favorite flowers, and of the Delany Sisters Rose, a rose of two colors, red and ivory, that was developed by a man in Maryland, J. Benjamin Williams, and presented to Sadie as a birthday present.

164. Derricotte, Toi. *The Black Notebooks: An Interior Journey.* New York, New York: W. W. Norton & Company, 1997. 205 pages. ISBN: 0393045447 : 0393319016.

Notes: Published in paperback in 1999.

Abstract: Poet Toi Derricotte wrote this book using material from journals she kept over a twenty-year period. She explains her motivation for writing the book,

> My writing was an expiation, a penance. It was
> a way I gained distance and control. It was
> finally a way to transform what I hated and
> denied into something beautiful and true.
> Ironically, it became the way I took on, publicly
> and irrevocably, the very identity I was
> ambivalent about. (p. 15)

The book uses many of Derricotte's own experiences as a very light-skinned black woman, including house-hunting in a white neighborhood, not being allowed to join the whites-only Tall Oaks Country Club, having to endure racist comments from unsuspecting white people and then agonize over whether to reveal her race to them, struggles to resolve her relationship with her mother, and the inability to save her marriage. Along with her own comments, she presents the opinions and reactions of her friends, colleagues, family, and the schoolchildren and graduate students she has taught over the years, white and black, light-skinned and dark. The discussion is both an emotional and intellectual one which does not seek a right or wrong answer but which examines the reasons behind the reactions that different people can have to the same people and events. She concludes:

> Later, someone asked me if writing *The Black
> Notebooks* had helped me to get better, and I
> talked about writing it in the middle of a terrible
> depression, being overwhelmed by feelings of
> shame. I said that by writing *The Black Notebooks*,
> I have come to realize that we negotiate a very
> complicated reality, and that we do the best we
> can, and that there is no perfect past to go back
> to. It is at this point of understanding that I
> think we develop compassion for ourselves and
> each other. (p. 202)

165. Dickerson, Debra J. (1959-). *An American Story*. New York, New York: Pantheon Books, 2000. 285 pages. ISBN: 037542069x.

Notes: Published in paperback New York: Anchor Books, 2001. ISBN: 0385720289.

Abstract: Debra Dickerson grew up in a poor but hard-working family in North St. Louis. She attended an elementary school for gifted children where she developed a love of language and reading. This, and her devotion to her studies, isolated her from others in her family and neighborhood and offered her a means of escape from a harsh existence. Dickerson was recruited by many elite colleges, but because of her father's attitude that women were of secondary importance to men, she had no confidence in herself.

> I wouldn't last a week at a university before I'd be found out as the unworthy upstart I was and thrown out. I saw no connection between my intellectual yearnings, my grades, and a college education. . . . No one had to tell me I couldn't go to college because I was poor and black.
>
> (p. 70)

Dickerson found a place for herself in the Air Force where she was rewarded for her hard work and her desire to achieve and learn. She also developed very conservative beliefs that distanced her even more from her family and neighborhood and made it difficult for her to identify with other African Americans. She went from the Air Force on to college and then to Harvard Law School. Gradually, she found herself becoming more and more politically engaged. She realized that there were social forces that worked against individuals and that African Americans were not responsible for all of the difficulties they encountered. "In 1983, I hated to come home because their 'choices' so infuriated me. By 1986 I hated to come because I was so infuriated *for* them. Was a life of simple dignity, whatever your aspirations or status, too much to ask?" (p. 188). Dickerson always struggled with fitting in no matter where she was or what she was engaged in. She said she was the

> Harvard trained, world-traveled, neurotic attorney turned writer with a Gold Card . . . who would rather have eaten cornbread and collards than sushi, rather have listened to gospel than hip-hop . . . [b]ut whose favorite food, next to fried chicken and mustard greens is Vietnamese. Who loves classical music and opera as well as the blues."
>
> (p. 278)

Dickerson is a senior fellow at the New America Foundation, where she writes about poverty and race. She also writes for a number of prominent news magazines both print-based and electronic.

166. Dickerson, Mahala Ashley (b. 1912). *Delayed Justice for Sale: An Autobiography*. Anchorage, Alaska: Al-Acres, 1998. 263 pages; photographs. ISBN: 0966562100.

Abstract: Born in 1912 in Montgomery, Alabama, Mahala Dickerson became the first black female attorney in the state of Alabama. She attended Miss White's School, a school dedicated to the education of young black girls, where Rosa (McCauley) Parks was one of her classmates and a long-time friend. Dickerson received her B.A. from Fisk and her law degree from Howard University. Because Phi Beta Kappa was not allowed on black campuses at the time she graduated, Dickerson received her key fifty-one years later. She practiced law in Alabama, Indiana, and Alaska. In her work, Dickerson always championed the underdog. In Alabama, she was one of the few lawyers to whom black people could turn to challenge the vicious injustice of a system driven by racism. She wrote that she began to feel settled in her life and with her career despite the "injustice which my practice was unearthing being even deeper than what I thought it was as a lay person" (p. 62). When she moved to Alaska, it took her a year, rather than the customary ninety days, to get her license to practice law there. She faced both gender and race discrimination from other attorneys and from the courts. She became embroiled in a wide-ranging suit stemming from false charges brought against her by the district attorney's office. When Dickerson was finally cleared of the charges, she reflected that the reason God intended her to be a lawyer was so "I would be able to represent myself in the many travails I would have trying to protect the rights of the underdogs, who are not the favorites of society or of the courts" (pp. 99-98). Despite the difficulties Dickerson encountered in setting up practice in Alaska, she loves the state and has enjoyed a successful career dedicated to pursuing justice and preserving civil rights for those who call upon her services no matter what their gender or color. Dickerson describes many of her cases, discusses her associates and colleagues, and tells about the accomplishments and contributions of the members of her family. She was elected the first black president of the National Association of Women Lawyers. In 1998, Dickerson was still practicing law as a trial attorney at the age of eighty-six. She concludes her book with a separate epilogue for the years 1991 to 1998, giving her thoughts on world events and her own activities for each year.

167. Dirie, Waris. *Desert Flower: The Extraordinary Journey of a Desert Nomad*. Written with Cathleen Miller. New York, New York: William Morrow & Company, 1998. 228 pages; photographs. ISBN: 0688158234.

Notes: Published in paperback New York: Quill, 1999. ISBN: 0688172377.

Abstract: Waris Dirie grew up in Somalia, the daughter of nomads. She suffered female circumcision, now known as female genital mutilation, at about the age of five and was promised in marriage to an elderly man when she was just fourteen. Dirie writes of how she escaped from her home to avoid the marriage, running away to Mogadishu, the capital of Somalia. When she found out that one of her uncles had been designated Somalian ambassador to Britain and was moving to London, Dirie begged to be taken on as a servant. She spent the next four years hostage to her aunt in their London home, obliged to take care of her cousins and keep house. At the end of her uncle's term, Dirie managed to stay on in London by herself, living with people who would take her in, and pursued a career as a model. After she appeared in a James Bond movie, her career took off, but Dirie soon found that there was a limit to what a black model could earn in London and that a lack of a legal status kept her from leaving the country to look for more lucrative work. Her first marriage was to an Irishman and her second to an Englishman. Dirie married both men for the legal status they could provide. The circumstances of her second marriage finally made it possible for her to get a British passport and go to work in New York. It was not until early on in her modeling career that Dirie became aware that not all women had suffered genital mutilation and that the constant pain she suffered during her menstrual periods and when urinating was not the norm. It took several years before she got up the courage to have surgery to make these bodily functions easier, and she also realized what she had sacrificed in terms of ability to achieve sexual gratification. As Dirie became better known in the fashion world, she began speaking out against female mutilation. Dirie's first breakthrough was an interview with Laura Ziv published in the magazine *Marie Claire* entitled "The Tragedy Of Female Circumcision." Readers were horrified by the situation and overwhelmingly supportive of Dirie's courage to speak out. She was also featured in a segment on the TV program *20/20* entitled "A Healing Journey." After the program aired, the United Nations invited her to be a special ambassador in its fight to stop female mutilation.

168. Dixon, Joe Robert. *Hard Times: Memoirs of a Southern Black Boy Raised during the Depression.* Indianapolis, Indiana: 1st Out Publishing Company, 1996. 96 pages; photographs. ISBN: none.

Abstract: Joe Robert Dixon was born in Savannah, Tennessee, during the 1920s. His father was a cook working at a café and on the steamships on the Tennessee River. Members of the family, including Dixon, also worked as farm laborers, chopping cotton and corn and picking berries. As a field hand, Dixon was paid fifty cents a day. The family had a large garden which provided them with vegetables all summer and black-eyed peas, butter beans and pinto beans to dry for the winter. Dixon also earned money stoking the furnaces for his school. He would get up at 5:00 a.m., walk to school to stoke the furnaces, return home at 7:00 a.m. for breakfast and then walk back to attend school at 8:00 a.m. Dixon describes supplementing the family food supply through hunting. He and his father and uncles would hunt blackbirds, rabbit, possum, and raccoon. According to Dixon, his family was the poorest in the South, but members of the family each did what he or she could and always had food and shelter. Dixon left school to work at a Civilian Conservation Corps camp. When he returned, he worked a variety of jobs, including as a bus boy at a hospital and railroad work. He was drafted in 1942 and sent to North Africa, Italy, and the Philippines. Upon his return, he married his high-school sweetheart. They eventually moved to Indianapolis, where he worked and raised his family of three children, retiring from the National Starch Company in 1987. Dixon describes his religious convictions and his experiences as a member of the Holiness Church. He gives his advice for raising children and maintaining a strong marriage (he and his wife celebrated their fiftieth anniversary in 1996) and he extols the merits of hard work

169. Dogg, Snoop. *See* Snoop Dogg.

170. Dorr, David F. *A Colored Man Round the World.* Edited by Malini Johar Schueller. Ann Arbor, Michigan: University of Michigan Press, 1999. 195 pages. ISBN: 047209694x : 0472066943.

Notes: Originally published Cleveland, Ohio: The Author, 1858.

Abstract: David Dorr was the slave of Cornelius Fellowes, a businessman in New Orleans. In 1851, Dorr accompanied Fellowes on a three-year journey throughout Europe and the Middle East. They traveled to London, France, Germany, Belgium, Italy, Turkey, Syria, and Egypt. They spent their winters in France and were there for the coup d'etat of Napoleon II in December 1851. Dorr clearly enjoyed the attention he received as an American traveler and the obsequious service he received in hotels, restaurants, trains, and carriages around the world. In the Netherlands he had dinner with a king, the father of the current Queen of the Netherlands, the "old King of Wurtemburg." He writes, "He is going out—he bows to me" (p. 60). Dorr notes that Fellowes did not receive the same gesture of respect from the king. Dorr describes the points of interest that he saw on his wide travels, he elaborates on his own tastes, and describes the many fine people he met. His sense of humor permeates his narrative. Apparently Col. Fellowes had promised Dorr his freedom upon their return to the United States, but "as he refused me on old bachelor principles, I fled from him and his princely promises, westward, where the 'star of empire takes its way,' reflecting on the moral liberties of the legal freedom of England, France and our New England states . . ." (p. 12). Dorr made his way to Cleveland, Ohio where he wrote and published his narrative.

171. Drumgoold, Kate. *A Slave Girl's Story: Being an Autobiography of Kate Drumgoold.* Chapel Hill, North Carolina: Academic Affairs Library, University of North Carolina at Chapel Hill, 2000.

> http://docsouth.unc.edu/neh/drumgoold/drumgoold.sgml
> http://docsouth.unc.edu/neh/drumgoold/drumgoold.html
>
> **Notes:** Documenting the American South (Project).

172. Dryden, Charles W. *A-Train: Memoirs of a Tuskegee Airman.* Tuscaloosa, Alabama: University of Alabama Press, 1997. 421 pages; photographs. ISBN: 0817308563.

> **Abstract:** Lieutenant Colonel Charles W. Dryden joined the Army Air Corps in August 1941. He was in the second class of African-American cadets after the Army started training African Americans as pilots in what was called the Tuskegee Experiment. Dryden first wanted to fly when he was four years old. He trained as a civilian while in college and joined the army soon after reading a notice announcing the change in U.S. Army policy. Shortly after Dryden graduated from his cadet training, one of only three of the original class of eleven, the United States entered World War

II. Dryden was eventually sent to fight in North Africa and Italy. He provides several accounts of triumphant and tragic battles. Dryden also writes that he was struck by what it meant to be a black serviceman fighting for the United States while back home his fallen comrades were being refused burial in cemeteries in their home towns. "What do we expect to gain if we succeed in helping to defeat foreign enemies, overseas? We expect to help defeat domestic enemies back home: Jim Crow attitudes and practices' in government, schools, jobs, churches—everywhere!" (p. 139). In fact, the German POWs had more access to services than the black Army Air Corps men. Dryden and his company did not take this passively, but set off on a massive letter-writing campaign. He writes that perhaps it was this constant chipping away at segregationist policy and unequal treatment that eventually led to Truman's decree to desegregate the army. Surviving the war unwounded, Dryden continued his tour of duty in the States as a flight instructor. He married Irma Pete Cameron, a lieutenant in the Army Nurse Corps. Dryden's long career in the military included a tour of duty in Korea. He earned several college degrees, including a masters degree in public law and government from Columbia University. He also attended Air Force schooling in communications. He had assignments in Germany and Washington, D.C. and taught Air Science at Howard University. Following a postponement after the construction of the Berlin Wall, Dryden retired with the rank of Lieutenant Colonel. He concludes his memoir with a chapter remembering his comrades from the Army Air Corps and Air Force.

173. Duncan, C. W. (1934-). *Sprinting Backwards to God*. Hopkinton, Massachusetts: Two Canoes Press, 2000. 217 pages. ISBN: 1929590040.

Abstract: Sings-Alone combines his Coyote teaching tales with the poetry of his wife and the stories of his own life. A Cherokee Indian of mixed heritage, Sings-Alone, born C. W. Duncan, grew up in a Christian, "Anglo-assimilated" family. His father was a minister, and Sings-Alone also chose this path for himself, attending seminary and becoming an ordained minister in the Disciples of Christ church. He found himself in conflict with the leaders of the church as he became more involved with the spirit world through the Spiritual Frontiers Fellowship. He eventually left the church to study counseling psychology. By the time he had earned his doctorate, his seventeen-year marriage had dissolved. After two years he left clinical practice and a teaching position to work on the Mohave Indian reservation in Arizona. There he sought to

become closer to his Indian heritage, studying Native American
spirituality with Rolling Thunder at Metatanay in Carlin, Nevada.
He found it more difficult than he had expected to be accepted by
the Native American communities with which he was working:

> Arriving in Arizona, I had expected to be ac-
> cepted as a mixed-blood Cherokee wanting to
> find himself. The whole notion amused my
> hosts. . . . They cared not a whit about my blood
> quantum or my quest. . . . Wanting to be just like
> the people, I immediately discovered that
> Indianess could not be donned like a coat. I
> could only be myself and evolve into whatever I
> would become. Besides there was no typical
> *them* to emulate.   (p. 104)

Sings-Alone moved to Maryland and eventually worked with
spiritual leader White Wolf. During his seven-year sojourn with
White Wolf, he became accepted as a part of the Indian community. He founded and, for a time, was national chief of the Free
Cherokees, a nationwide tribal organization with which many
bands have affiliated. Throughout his stories, Sings-Alone
addresses issues of alcoholism, learning through listening and
observing, and close communication with God.

174. Eagle Elk, Joseph (1931-). *The Price of a Gift: A Lakota Healer's
Story*. Written with Gerald Vincent Mohatt. Lincoln, Nebraska:
University of Nebraska Press, 2000. 226 pages; photographs.
ISBN: 0803232047.

Abstract: Joseph Eagle Elk was born in 1931 and raised by his
grandparents after the divorce of his parents. His grandfather was
a medicine man, and he and Eagle Elk's grandmother were often
away leading ceremonies that involved the use of the illegal hal-
lucinogen peyote. Both were careful that Eagle Elk did not
become involved with these ceremonies, but after he started
school, it was reported that he was involved with peyote, and he
was asked to leave. This ended Eagle Elk's formal education, and
he never learned to read or write. Illiteracy severely limited the
occupations open to him. After he was rejected from the army, he
began to travel and work on ranches. His ability to work was further reduced by depression and a growing problem with alcohol.
All of this changed after he began to work on the ranch of Henry
Griswold. Griswold liked Eagle Elk and helped him through his
roughest times, standing by him when he was arrested. Griswold
encouraged Eagle Elk to come back to live and work at the ranch

while staying away from alcohol. Despite Eagle Elk's one or two relapses, Griswold continued to support him and urged him to spend his final three-year probation period exclusively on the ranch.   Eagle Elk stayed on the Griswold ranch until after Griswold's death. After leaving the ranch, Eagle Elk returned to the reservation, where his father, like his grandfather, was a medicine man. Eagle Elk began to learn about Lakota medicine and ceremonies, eventually becoming a healer according to Lakota precepts. He describes the various ceremonies that he performs and their purposes, the people who became close to him, and the people whom he helped. He also tells about his trips to Europe and Alaska. Mohatt, who interviewed Eagle Elk for this autobiography, concludes the book with the transcript of a conversation with people who were connected to him.

175. Edelman, Marian Wright.   *Lanterns: A Memoir of Mentors.* Boston, Massachusetts: Beacon Press, 1999. 180 pages; photographs. ISBN: 0807072141.

Notes: Published in paperback New York: Perennial, 2000. ISBN: 0060958596.

Abstract: Marian Edelman, a civil rights lawyer and children's advocate (president of the Children's Defense Fund), writes about her experience with the many mentors who helped nurture her as a child, guided her through her youth, education, and career choice, and served as leaders in the Civil Rights Movement. She also includes many African-American historical figures, all of whom influenced her and who, through their accomplishments, opened up new doors and created new opportunities for those who followed. Her initial mentors were her parents and people in her church community, especially older women, who cared for her and raised her to see her role in life as helping others. At Spelman College she was greatly influenced by Morehouse College president Benjamin Elijah Mays, who taught students they were God's instruments for transforming the world; Howard Zinn, a white professor who introduced her to the Civil Rights Movement; and Charles E. Merrill, son of the founder of the Merrill Lynch brokerage house, who served on the Morehouse board of trustees and sponsored scholarships for Morehouse and Spelman students, including Edelman, to study abroad. Her mentors during the Civil Rights Movement included leaders such as Bob Moses and Martin Luther King, Jr., as well as uneducated, poor blacks who insisted on their rights while risking their lives, such as Fannie Lou Hamer, Mae Bertha Carter, and Unita Blackwell. In the latter half of the book, Edelman discusses the needs of all children for mentors and involved parents and the responsibilities of all adults for the next generation. She gives detailed guidelines on how to meet the specific needs of children.

176. Edwards, David Honeyboy. *The World Don't Owe Me Nothing: The Life and Times of Delta Bluesman Honeyboy Edwards.* As told to Janis Martinson and Michael Robert Frank. Chicago, Illinois: Chicago Review Press, 1997. 287 pages; photographs. ISBN: 1556522754 : 1556523688.

Abstract: Musician David Honeyboy Edwards was born June 28, 1915. His father was part Creek Indian and part Mollyglasper, which a note in the book defines as a descendent of the Malagasy, a tribe from the island Madagascar. Edwards's mother was from Kentucky and also part Indian. His father, a sharecropper, could read and write, which was fairly unusual for the time. As was common among sharecroppers, Edwards's family moved from plantation to plantation, trying to find a better contract. Edwards describes life in the south working on plantations. The bosses had control over your finances, personal life, and working life. Edwards writes, "They treated us like we was property. Come all through slavery time and they still wanted us to be slaves" (p. 49). Edwards's mother died at the age of thirty-two when Edwards was twelve. It was after this that he learned to play guitar from his father and soon music became a driving passion for him. Once Edwards left the farm, he kept on the move: "[O]nly thing I carried with me was my guitar and harp and those dice in my pocket" (p. 87). Edwards played with many of the great blues men, most of whom were working their way from tavern to tavern and town to town. Edwards first met his wife-to-be, Bessie, in 1947. They married in 1952 and were together until her death in 1972. The two traveled to Louisiana, Mississippi, Texas, Florida, Tennessee, and Arkansas, working and playing music until they settled permanently in Chicago in the early 1960s. Edwards made his first recording for Alan Lomax and the Library of Congress in 1942, for which he earned a room and board for a night or two, plus twenty dollars. In the 1950s he made some recordings and played some engagements for musical impresario Lola Anne Colum of ARC. It was not until later in his music career, as white interest in blues increased, that Edwards began making significant money performing. He traveled to Austria, Belgium, Germany, Holland, Scotland, Ireland, Japan, and Argentina. At the time Edwards was writing his autobiography he was still performing around the world. About the blues he writes,

The blues might change but it's going to stay around. Young people now play a different style of blues, hard and fast, but it's still the blues. When I was a child coming up, it was mostly ragtime stuff. Then it grew, that big road blues, country blues, then the shuffle and the low-down-and-dirty blues. It just keeps on changing. The blues are always going to stand.

(p. 206)

177. Egami, Hatsuye (1902-). *The Evacuation Diary of Hatsuye Egami.* Edited and with an introduction by Claire Gorfinkel. Pasadena, California: Intentional Productions, 1995. 103 pages; photographs; drawings. ISBN: 0964804212.

Abstract: Egami's diary begins May 12, 1942, the day she, her husband, and four children were ordered to leave on a train to an unknown destination. Egami writes, "Since yesterday, we Pasadena Japanese have ceased to be human beings—we are now simply numbers or things" (p. 20). She records her feelings upon arriving at the bleak Tulare Assembly Center, entering this prison setting with no idea how or when they would leave. She tells her children that life will be "largely primitive and naked here. . . . It may be that in a naked life there is poetry and truth. I think that from this bare life we can weave something creative and interesting" (pp. 27-28). She begins to realize, too, that having grown up with a different code than the Issei, the first generation of Japanese immigrants to this country, the youth in the camps would have a more difficult time maintaining a moral center and sense of purpose. The older Japanese all seek to find a place and a purpose within the camp. The diary covers four months at the center. Most of the 5,000 inhabitants were moved to other camps in August. Throughout, Egami seeks to maintain a positive outlook. She writes about her motivation for keeping this diary: "The contribution of Japanese over a period of fifty years toward building a better civilization on this coast was over-night turned into oblivion. I deeply felt my responsibility as an individual and as a Japanese to record this historic upheaval" (p. 64).

178. Elders, M. Joycelyn. *Joycelyn Elders, M.D.: From Sharecropper's Daughter to Surgeon General of the United States*. Written with David Chanoff. New York, New York: William Morrow & Company, 1996. 355 pages; photographs; index. ISBN: 0688147224.

>   **Notes:** Also published in a large print edition Thorndike, Maine: Thorndike Press, 1997. ISBN: 0786209585; published in paperback New York: Avon Books, 1997. ISBN: 0380786486.

>   **Abstract:** Joycelyn Elders was born Minnie Lee Jones in the town of Schaal, Arkansas, population ninety-eight, and raised in a farming family. She excelled in school, graduated from high school as valedictorian at the age of sixteen, and was awarded a full scholarship by Philander Smith College in Little Rock. It was there that she changed her name to Joycelyn, the name of a peppermint candy she liked. While at Smith, Elders was inspired to become a doctor after hearing a talk given by Dr. Edith Irby Jones. Not having the money to go to medical school, Elders joined the United States Army Women's Specialists Medical Corps so that she could get college training, attain the rank of second lieutenant, and take advantage of G.I. Bill funds after her tour of duty. She finished her military service as a licensed physical therapist, applied for medical school, and was accepted at the University of Colorado, Meharry Medical School, and the University of Arkansas. She chose Arkansas because it was closest to home. Elders was one of three black medical students in the entering class of 1956. She describes her medical education, internship, and residency. She was awarded the position of Chief Resident at the University of Arkansas Medical School, unheard of for a woman, let alone a black woman. She considered going into private practice, but was persuaded by her mentor, Edward Hughes, to join the faculty at the medical school. Elder, a pediatric surgeon, developed specialties in diabetes and treatment of children with ambiguous sexuality. After twenty-five years at the medical school, Elders was tapped by Governor Clinton to be the director of the Arkansas Department of Health. She accepted this position reluctantly, but, shocked at what she learned about the state of children's health in Arkansas, became a crusader for health education and readily available clinics for children and teenagers as a means to slow the rate of teenage pregnancy. It was her advocacy of school-based clinics which would, among other things, make condoms available to high school students under certain circumstances, that put her in the middle of a raging controversy. President Clinton appointed her to the position of Surgeon General of the United

States, but she was still unwilling to give up her priorities for the sake of political acceptability. Elders was asked to resign after only eighteen months because of a remark she made during an informal discussion about ways to address teenage sexual activity and the threat of HIV/AIDS. Elders returned to the faculty at the University of Arkansas Medical School following her resignation. As a pediatric surgeon, she says, her first and foremost concern is for children and their well-being.

> I feel absolutely committed to the issues I have always been about: comprehensive health education, prevention of teenage pregnancy, early-childhood education, school-based clinics to make health care available for all children, a preventive approach to health care for everyone.
> (p. 336)

> If I could keep [the children] well, keep them from having children while they were still children themselves, and give them some hope they could go to college, that's what I wanted. That was my idea of affirmative action. After they got past that, they could take care of themselves. . . . I want us—you and I—to think of all those kids as our children. That's what I really want.
> (p. 343)

179. Eldridge, Elleanor (1784-1845) and Frances H. Green (1805-1878). *The Memoirs of Elleanor Eldridge.* Chapel Hill, North Carolina: Academic Affairs Library, University of North Carolina at Chapel Hill, 2000.

   http://docsouth.unc.edu/neh/eldridge/menu.html

   Notes: Documenting the American South (Project).

180. Elijah Muhammad. *The True History of Elijah Muhammad, Messenger of Allah.* Compiled and edited by Nasir Makr Hakim. Atlanta, Georgia: M.E.M.P.S., 1997. 307 pages. ISBN: 1884855113.

   Notes: "Autobiographically Authoritative."

   Abstract: This collection of sermons focuses more on Elijah Muhammad's message to the faithful than on details of his life. He does include some autobiographical details. Elijah Muhammad was born in Georgia and lived there until he was twenty-five. He

left for Detroit in 1923 and worked for the Southern Railroad
Company as a tramroad foreman and builder. He was converted
to Islam in the early 1930s after hearing Mr. Wallace Fard speak.
He was convinced after his first meeting with Fard that he was the
Son of God or the Second Coming of Jesus. Fard encouraged
Elijah Muhammad to begin teaching this. For three years he stud-
ied Biblical scripture and Islam with Fard, "day and night" (p. 39).
It was Fard, who became Fard Muhammad, who gave Elijah
Muhammad his name, first Elijah Karriem, and then Elijah
Muhammad. In 1942, Elijah Muhammad was arrested by the FBI
for preaching against African-American participation in World
War II. He was imprisoned until 1946. Elijah Muhammad writes
briefly about his son's, grandson's, and brother's rejection of him
as the Last Messenger of Allah. He also touches on his feelings
about Malcolm X and Martin Luther King, Jr. In his sermon,
"Ignorance and Opposition," he writes that black leaders are making a mistake working with the white man. He would like to see
African Americans come together under the teachings of Allah,
and work for "one and the same common cause: elevating our people into the knowledge of self and others and create the unity or
purpose that we might be able to acquire some of this land that we
can call our own for our 22 or more million people here" (p. 87).
Elijah Muhammad wrote many of the sermons and messages in
this volume after forty years spent preaching across the United
States.

181. Elizondo, Virgilio P. *The Future Is Mestizo: Life Where Cultures
Meet.* Boulder, Colorado: University Press of Colorado, 2000
ISBN: 0870815768.

> **Notes:** Translation of *L'Avenir est au Metissage*, Paris: Nouvelles
> Editions Mame, 1987. Also published New York: Crossroad, 1992.
> Oak Park, Illinois: Meyer-Stone Books, 1988.

> **Abstract:** This revised edition includes a new foreword by poet
> Sandra Cisneros and an introduction by Davíd Carrasco.

182. Elliott, Duong Van Mai. *The Sacred Willow: Four Generations in
the Life of a Vietnamese Family.* New York, New York: Oxford
University Press, 1999. 506 pages; photographs. ISBN:
0195124340 : 0195137876.

> **Abstract:** Duong Van Mai Elliott's family was descended from a
> long line of important and revered scholars. Until the influence of
> Western culture under the French, scholarship, not wealth, was

honored in traditional Vietnamese society: it was better to live modestly and to serve the country and your fellow citizens than to exploit them for personal wealth. As French influence strengthened under colonization, this scholarly tradition waned and was overtaken by Western values including that of capitalism. Western theories of education replaced the traditional Confucian values inherited from the Chinese. Elliott's father was among the last generation of Vietnamese to earn the status of mandarin and to have his scholarly accomplishments qualify him for government service. It is from the perspective of a family tied to government service that Elliott recounts the history of Vietnam under French colonial rule and U.S. intervention. She writes that, like many Vietnamese families, hers was divided during the long civil war. She traces the history of the French in Vietnam beginning in 1863, the rebellion begun by Ho Chi Minh in 1930, and her own family's involvement as supporters both of Ho Chi Minh and of the established Vietnamese government supported by the French. Her father, a loyal and dedicated administrator, felt great ambivalence toward the French. Like many middle-class Vietnamese, however, he distrusted the Communist movement of Ho Chi Minh. Elliott's account represents both her father's point of view of the civil conflict and her own experience as a child sharing the shifting fortunes of her family and South Vietnam under a series of French-sanctioned governments. Her narrative includes the story of the Viet Minh as she understands it from her older sister's twenty-year involvement in resisting first the French and then the United States. Elliott left Vietnam with her American husband several years before the withdrawal of American troops and the fall of Saigon. She describes the evacuation of most of her large family, the story of those family members that were left behind, and the reunion of almost all the members of the family who survived the war and its aftermath.

183. Elmore, James Mack (1924-). *The Autobiography of Mr. James Mack Elmore.* Bowling Green, Kentucky: J. M. Elmore, 2000. 41 pages. ISBN: none.

184. Enoch, Carlton. *"Eye See Me": A True Life Story.* Toledo, Ohio: C. Enoch, 2000. 62 pages. ISBN: 0970156200.

185. Equiano, Olaudah. *The African: The Interesting Narrative of the Life of Olaudah Equiano.* London, England: Black Classics, 1998. 217 pages. ISBN: 187450962x.

> **Notes:** Also published New York, New York: W. W. Norton & Company, 2001. ISBN: 0393974944. First published London: The Author, 1794.

186. Ervin-Watson, Bessie P. *Southern Heritage: Growing Up in the Mississippi Delta.* St. Louis, Missouri: B. P. Ervin-Watson, 1996. 207 pages; photographs.

187. Espiritu, Yen Le. *Filipino American Lives. Asian American History and Culture.* Philadelphia, Pennsylvania: Temple University Press, 1995. 216 pages; photographs. ISBN: 1566393167 : 1566393175.

> **Abstract:** Yen Le Espiritu is a Vietnamese immigrant to the United States whose husband is Filipino American. She has collected interviews with Filipino Americans to serve as a resource to the younger generation. Espiritu notes that it was important to those interviewed to have their words edited and refined for publication. As an immigrant herself she was careful to oblige that request. Espiritu's introduction gives a history of Filipino immigration to the United States. The interviews are ordered by age of the interviewee. The following are included in the collection:
>
> > A. B. Santos and Juanita Santos, "We Have to Show the Americans that We Can be as Good as Anybody." Ruth Abad, "I Was Used to the American Way of Life." Connie Tirona, "Sometimes I Am Not Sure What it Means to Be American." Luz Latus, "My Dream is to Be Able to Give Something Back to My Country and My People." Paz Jensen, "My Experience is Atypical." Leo Sicat, "I Sacrificed My Five-Year Education to Become a Steward." Nemesia Cortez, "I Only Finished First Grade." Edgar Gamboa, "International Medical Graduates Are Tested Every Step of the Way." Anamaria Labao Cabato, "PASACAT Became My Whole Life." Daniel Grutas, "I Knew That I Wanted to Be a Naval Officer." Dario Villa, "I Offended Many Filipinos Because I Was an FOB." Joey Laguda, "I Could Not Cope with Life." Lisa Graham, "Everybody Seemed to Be Either White or Black, a Full Race."

188. Estes, Simon. *In His Own Voice: An Autobiography.* Written with Mary L. Swanson. Cumming, Iowa: LMP, 1999. 143 pages; CD sound disc; photographs; discography. ISBN: 1890621013 : 189062103x.

Abstract: Opera singer Simon Estes was born in Centerville, Iowa. His father, the son of slaves, was a coal miner in the then-thriving Iowa coal mines. He also did odd jobs to keep the family fed, clothed, and sheltered. Estes's mother stayed home to raise their five children. During Estes's youth, African Americans accounted for less than one percent of the population in Iowa. Segregation, perhaps not as virulent as in the South, existed in the form of white-only cafés, and racism and discrimination were commonplace. Estes's sister Patty and his mother were both talented singers. Patty was a member of a professional choir that was invited to sing in several southern churches, but church officials asked the group not to bring "the colored girl." Devastated, Patty became severely depressed and committed suicide at the age of twenty-five. Estes himself was rejected when he auditioned for the 240-voice University of Iowa chorus. When he auditioned for the Old Gold Singers, a small ensemble of about twenty singers, the conductor liked him, but stipulated that he could join the ensemble only if the other singers would agree to sing with an African American. More interested in Estes's singing ability than his skin color, the group took him in without much debate. It was at the University of Iowa that Estes began studying with the new vocal instructor Charles Kellis. Warned not to waste his time on Estes, Kellis ignored detractors and worked enthusiastically with the young singer, becoming his advisor and mentor and giving him daily lessons at no charge. He gave Estes the background and confidence he needed to win a full academic scholarship to the Julliard School of Music. Estes spent only one year at Julliard before beginning his career in the opera houses of Germany. In his first year, he won the Munich Competition and took third place in the Tchaikovsky Competition, a showing sufficient to begin building a reputation for himself in the United States. Estes gives the highlights, low points, and some humorous episodes of his prestigious career. Deeply religious, Estes has been eager to give back to society the many rewards he has reaped through his successful career. He has raised money for many organizations, especially those that help children. Some of his foundations include the Simon Estes Fund at the University of Iowa, the Simon Estes Educational Foundation, Iowa Arts Council Scholarship for the Arts, the Simon and Westella Estes Scholarship Fund, and the Simon Estes International Foundation for Children. Estes has three daughters to whom he is devoted and calls daily from wherever he is in the world. He writes, "I hope to be remembered as a man who cared, who wanted to share, and who loved. My fondest wish is that people feel my life and my music have made a difference" (p. 143).

189. Evers, Charles (1922-). *Have No Fear: The Charles Evers Story.* Written with Andrew Szanton. New York, New York: John Wiley & Sons, 1997. 333 pages; photographs; index. ISBN: 0471122513.

Abstract: Charles Evers, the older brother of slain civil rights activist Medgar Evers, gives the story of his life intertwined with a history of the Civil Rights Movement and national politics through the administration of the elder George Bush. He also describes his relationships with many activists, politicians, and U.S. presidents. Charles and his brother Medgar served in World War II, the former in the Pacific and the latter in Europe. The people in these areas did not discriminate against them because of their race, and this made them determined to fight for rights in their own country. In 1946, after returning to Mississippi, the brothers registered to vote, but were not able to vote because of white resistance. They joined the NAACP in 1948. In 1953, Charles Evers became voter registration chairman for the NAACP of Mississippi. He appreciated the NAACP structure and the way it helped people in need, but felt that more efforts should be made to help blacks learn to advance themselves economically. By 1955, he was running the family funeral parlor, selling burial insurance, bootlegging, running a "Negro café" and a taxi service. He also started a radio program that he used to urge blacks to vote. He was eventually run out of town because he was so successful. He fled to Chicago and used his income from business dealings there to finance his brother's civil rights activities. He kept in close touch with his brother, speaking to him only two days before he was fatally shot. After Medgar's death, Charles took over the leadership of the Mississippi NAACP. He successfully pressured small towns, such as Natchez, to give civil rights to its black citizens. He was a witness to President Johnson's signing of the Civil Rights Act of 1964, traveled with Robert Kennedy during his U.S. Senate campaign, and was with him the day he was assassinated. Evers was devoted to Kennedy and appreciated how he dealt with the poor and underprivileged. Evers fought blacks who did not cooperate with NAACP activities and even picketed Alcorn A&M, his alma mater, for persecuting professors and students involved in the movement. Evers ran for public office unsuccessfully a number of times, but did serve five terms as mayor of Fayette, Mississippi, during which he improved the town infrastructure and health care services. He also served on the Democratic National Executive Committee in several presidential elections.

190. Evers-Williams, Myrlie. *Watch Me Fly: What I Learned on the Way to Becoming the Woman I Was Meant to Be.* Written with Melinda Blau. Boston, Massachusetts: Little, Brown and Company, 1999. 324 pages; photographs; index. ISBN: 0316255203.

Abstract: Myrlie Evers-Williams has been known most of her adult life as the widow of slain civil rights activist Medgar Evers. She was born and raised in Jackson, Mississippi, by her grand-mother and aunt. She made her first venture into the world when she entered Alcorn College, the only college in Mississippi that offered a music major for black students. There she met Medgar Evers, and they were married when she was only eighteen. After her sophomore year, they moved to Mound Bayou, Mississippi, an all-black township, where Medgar became deeply involved in the Civil Rights Movement. They were constantly aware of the threat to his life, and although his assassination in 1963 was traumatic to his wife and three children, they were prepared for it. Evers-Williams decided to leave Mississippi and make a new life for her family in California. She moved to Claremont and enrolled in the Claremont Colleges to complete her education. She made a living travelling and speaking for the NAACP, which continued to pay her Medgar's salary. Evers-Williams graduated in 1968 and was immediately hired at the school as assistant director of planning and development. In 1976, she began working as director of con-sumer affairs for ARCO. In 1987 she made an unsuccessful bid for a city council seat in Los Angeles, but was appointed by Mayor Tom Bradley as commissioner of public works. After that, she moved to Bend, Oregon, with her second husband, Walter Edward Williams, for retirement, but she was called to serve as chairman of the NAACP after accusations of corruption rocked its founda-tions. Evers-Williams writes about her life with Medgar Evers, but focuses more on what she was able to achieve following his death. She shares what she has learned about raising children, running a household, managing finances, and promoting a career. She expresses appreciation to her children, who have always been her staunchest supporters, and her second husband, who lived in her shadow as well as that of her first husband, but throughout remained her "Rock of Gibraltar." Evers-William writes in detail about the struggle to bring Byron De la Beckwith to justice for the murder of Medgar (he was convicted in 1994) and the heartbreak of the death of her second husband from cancer in 1995.

191. Ezell, Nora McKeown. *My Quilts and Me: The Diary of an American Quilter*. Montgomery, Alabama: Black Belt Press, 1999. 191 pages; photographs. ISBN: 1881320219.

Abstract: Nora Ezell was born in Mississippi in 1917. Her family moved to Birmingham, Alabama, in 1925. She married in 1936 and moved to Aliceville in 1938. There she was introduced to quilting by her aunt. Ezell decided to learn quilting, but she didn't want to follow the patterns her aunt used; she wanted to design something that no one else had done. At the age of seventy-seven, she was still helping support her family by chopping cotton, but had also succeeded in making nearly three hundred quilts. When she isn't quilting, she sews, knits, crotchets, embroiders, and tats and does crewel work, petit-point, macramé and cross-stitch. In her book, Ezell describes the art of her craft and the stories behind her quilts. The text is accompanied with detailed color photographs of many of her quilts.

192. Fernandez-Barrios, Flor. *Blessed by Thunder: Memoir of a Cuban Girlhood*. Seattle, Washington: Seal Press, 1999. 244 pages. ISBN: 1580050212 : 1580050425.

Abstract: Flor Fernandez-Barrios, known to her family as Teresa, was born in Cuba during a thunderstorm. Her grandmother said she had been "blessed by thunder" and received spiritual powers. Fernandez-Barrios had an idyllic childhood, with a home in the city and two sets of grandparents with farms in the country. She was privy to the healing powers of her paternal grandmother, who was preparing Fernandez-Barrios to follow in her footsteps. Their comfortable family life, however, was destroyed by political upheaval in the country. Her father's work and the prosperity of his family meant that he was constantly under suspicion as an anti-Castro sympathizer. In 1959, the family fled their home in town when Castro forces took over the government. At the same time, her grandparents' farms were confiscated, and the entire country was plunged into poverty. Food was rationed when available, and clothing, shoes and other necessities were rarely available at all. At the age of ten, Fernandez-Barrios and all of the other children at her school were dispatched to farm tobacco for forty-five days. They lived in filthy conditions and had very little food to eat. She hated the forced labor and the Communist indoctrination. The forty-five days stretched into two years. During that time, her father was also sent to a forced-labor camp because he had applied to leave the country. Finally, her family received permission to leave Cuba and live in the United States. The family was turned out of their home within a few hours of the notice and left the country within a few days. They settled in Los Angeles, and although they had clothing and food, life was not easy for them. Fernandez-Barrios graduated from UCLA and began to work. She found that the longer she was in the United States, the more difficult it was to maintain her Cuban heritage. A visit by her grandmother emphasized this conflict even more. After the death of her grandmother, however, she realized the importance of using the spiritual powers she had received at birth and passing on the teachings and practices of her grandparents. Fernandez-Barrios was able to go back to some of the Cuban practices she had given up and create a harmony between the two cultures she embodied.

193. Fielder, Walter Beatty. *Dreamer beneath the Wings: Northeast and South of Chehaw, Alabama.* St. Louis, Missouri: Howard Butler Press, 1995. 153 pages; photographs. ISBN: none.

Abstract: Walter Beatty Fielder's brief history of the civilian corps of the 309th Sub-Depot, part of the "Black Experiment" of the United States Air Corps, takes the form of a series of brief biographies and interviews. Public Law 18, passed in 1939, required civilian schools to offer primary flight training for the military. The law also required that at least one school train African-American pilots. Schools that offered the civilian training to African Americans included Tuskegee Institute, Hampton Institute, Delaware State, North Carolina A&T, Lincoln University in Missouri, and Harlem Airport in Chicago. Following the establishment of this law, the Army decided to train a company of African-American pilots as an experiment at the Tuskegee Institute, which became the 99th, 332nd, and 447th companies. The 309th Sub-Depot provided the ground support for these pilots. Fielder believed that while the stories of the pilots of the 99th, 332nd, and 447th "will live in infinity," the contributions of the 309th Sub-Depot Support Group will disappear "like vapor" (p. xiii). To remedy this, Fielder provides an account of his own entry into the experiment. He went from being an $800-a-month employee at Fort Sam Houston in Texas to a $2,200-a-month aircraft painter at the Tuskegee Institute. Along with some commentary and supplementary descriptions of his colleagues, Fielder includes reproductions of several pages from *The Commentator* and the *Hawks Eye*, newspapers of the 309th Sub-Depot. Included are interviews

with twenty-nine men and four women who made contributions
to the 309th.

194. Fisher, Ada Lois Sipuel. *A Matter of Black and White: The
Autobiography of Ada Lois Sipuel Fisher.* Written with Danney
Goble. Foreword by Robert Henry. Norman, Oklahoma:
University of Oklahoma Press, 1996. 204 pages; photographs;
index. ISBN: 0806128194.

Abstract: In 1946, Ada Lois Fisher was chosen to be the plaintiff
in a case aimed at desegregating the law school at the University
of Oklahoma (UO). The state of Oklahoma had established
Langston University to serve as the separate-but-equal college for
black students, but the school remained unaccredited because of
poor facilities, an absence of a law school or many of the other
graduate departments available at the University of Oklahoma.
The NAACP and civil rights lawyer Thurgood Marshall chose
Fisher, a recent college graduate with an excellent academic
record, to be their test case. Compared to schools in many
Southern states, the atmosphere at UO was not as hostile, and
many students supported opening the school to blacks. The state
government and the college board, however, were against it and
passed a resolution rejecting a change in policy. The case went
through the Oklahoma courts and on to the U.S. Supreme Court.
In 1948, the Supreme Court reversed the decisions of the
Oklahoma Supreme Court and remanded the case back to it. The
college regents, however, opened a slapdash law school at
Langston University and announced that it now had separate but
equal facilities available. In the midst of Oklahoma's controversy,
the University of Arkansas became the first public all-white university in the South to admit blacks. Meanwhile in Oklahoma, further suits were filed, and the Langston Law School closed for lack
of funds in the summer of 1949. The next day, the UO president,
granted Fisher admission to the law school and let several other
blacks into other graduate schools, maintaining separation in the
classroom seating arrangements. In the summer of 1951, Fisher
graduated from law school. By this time integration of the university had ceased to be a major issue and her graduation was a
quiet event. Fisher, who was married and had a daughter, accepted a position as a professor of law at Langston University after
failing to earn an income as a lawyer. In 1991, Fisher received an
honorary degree from UO, and in 1992 she was appointed a regent
of the school.

195. Flipper, Henry Ossian (1856-1940). *Black Frontiersman: The Memoirs of Henry O. Flipper, the First Black Graduate of West Point.* Compiled and edited by Theodore D. Harris. Fort Worth, Texas: Texas Christian University Press, 1997. 190 pages; photographs. ISBN: 0875651712.

Abstract: Henry Ossian Flipper wrote his memoirs in 1916 for a long-time friend. They cover his years in the American Southwest and Northern Mexico during the years 1878-1916, while he was a second lieutenant with the cavalry. In 1877 he was the first black graduate of the U.S. Military Academy at West Point and the only black officer in the U.S. Cavalry. Flipper was born a slave in Georgia in 1856 and grew up in Atlanta. During his years with the army he was stationed at various forts in the Southwest. His duties called upon his skills as surveyor, map maker, and engineer. Racism and jealousy led several fellow soldiers to frame him for embezzling, and this resulted in Flipper's dishonorable discharge from the army: "I was warned by civilians and never did a man walk the path of uprightness straighter than I did, but the trap was cunningly laid and I was sacrificed, effective June 30, 1882" (p. 37). Despite this setback, Flipper had a successful career as a private agent and as a U.S. Department of Justice field investigator of mine, mineral, and land claims. A scholar, Flipper also wrote and published several articles on Southwest and Spanish American history and folklore. In 1896 he published a small tract, reprinted in the present work, entitled, "Did a Negro Discover Arizona and New Mexico." This tract presented Flipper's research and translations of documents related to the activities of the slave Steven of the Marcos de Niza expedition. Flipper was accepted by many influential people, and his skills, knowledge, and reliability were acknowledged. At the same time, he was often subjected to racist actions, and he usually found effective ways to retaliate. Once a doctor refused to attend a celebratory dinner honoring Flipper because he didn't want to sit at the same table as a black man. Flipper writes, "Sometime afterwards there was an election for school trustee and this doctor ran against another Democrat. I got out and worked for the other fellow and beat this Negro-hating doctor by a good majority" (p. 49). The present edition of Flipper's memoir includes a lengthy introduction, Flipper's letters, a discussion of the false rumor spread about Flipper's connections with Pancho Villa (including the rumor that he may have been Pancho Villa), and the 1896 tract.

196. Foreman, George (1949-). *By George: The Autobiography of George Foreman.* Written with Joel Engel. New York, New York: Villard Books, 1995. 262 pages; photographs. ISBN: 0679443940.

Notes: Also published New York: Simon & Schuster, 2000. ISBN 0743201124.

Abstract: George Foreman was born and raised in the Fifth Ward, a poor section of Houston, Texas. He was the fifth of seven children raised in poverty by his mother, who worked numerous jobs to keep food on the table. Foreman was a large young man who was constantly looking for a fight. He dropped out of high school, and eventually joined Job Corps, a program that was part of President Lyndon Johnson's War on Poverty. In the Job Corps he got the schooling that allowed him to pass his GED and he also learned practical skills. In the process, he met trainers who got him started in boxing. Although he had many disagreements with his trainers, coaches and managers, he was a successful boxer who moved quickly to the top ranks. As an amateur, he won the gold medal for boxing at the heavyweight rank in the 1968 Olympics in Mexico City. After this success, he turned pro, beating the legendary Joe Frazier in Kingston, Jamaica, in 1972, heavyweight champion Joe Roman in Tokyo, Japan, in 1973, and Kenny Norton in Caracas, Venezuela, in 1974. In 1974, he fought Muhammad Ali for the championship in Kinshasa, Zaire. After a fight with Jimmy Young in San Juan, Puerto Rico in 1977, Foreman had a conversion experience. He quit boxing, sought to soften his volatile personality, and became a preacher. For the next ten years he spent most of his time preaching, raising his seven children from multiple marriages, and looking for a woman who would love and nurture his children. He married Joan, his present wife, and opened the George Foreman Youth and Community Center in Houston. After several years, his money from boxing began to run out. In 1987, he went back to the sport to raise money to keep his center in operation. He enjoyed great success and was widely popular among boxing fans. On November 5, 1994 in Las Vegas, Nevada, at the age of forty-five, Foreman beat Michael Moorer to become the heavyweight champion of the world.

197. Foster, Henry W. (1933-). *Make a Difference: The Founder of the I Have a Future Program Shares His Vision for Young America.* Written with Alice Greenwood. Foreword by Senator Edward Kennedy. New York, New York: Scribner, 1997. 192 pages; index. ISBN: 0684826852.

Abstract: Henry Foster, M.D., was born and raised in Pine Bluff, Arkansas. Both of his parents were teachers, and his father had a very strict work ethic. During World War II, when he was only thirteen, he and his father ran a business selling chickens and eggs. Along with school and work, he also learned how to fly and got his pilot's license at the age of nineteen. Always ambitious, Foster decided early on to become a doctor and he was one of two blacks in his class at the University of Arkansas Medical School. He decided to go into obstetrics and gynecology and was accepted at Meharry Medical College for his residency. This involved working for six months in Tuskegee, Alabama, at John A. Andrew Memorial Hospital, a hospital that treated some of the poorest people in the country. Before his residency was over, he was offered the position of chief of ob/gyn at the hospital, and he soon realized that improving medical care for the poor meant adding to the medical staff and changing the living conditions and the attitudes of most of his patients. His work in the hospital and the area became a model for regionalized perinatal care. Foster personally treated countless patients and delivered thousands of babies. In the 1970s, he was chosen to head a multimillion dollar program aimed at improving health services for teenagers and young people. This led to a special interest in teen pregnancy as he realized the devastating impact it had on the lives of both mothers and their children. From this sprang his "I Have a Future" program in Nashville, Tennessee. The goal of the program is to encourage low-income teenagers to stay in school, to keep from getting pregnant, and to convince them to stay away from drugs, alcohol, and crime. Foster sought to increase the students' self-esteem and get them focused on what they could do for their futures. With all of his work in public health, Foster was a natural choice for Surgeon General of the United States when the position opened in 1994 during the Clinton administration. Senate confirmation hearings, however, focused on his participation in a handful of abortions during his long career and unfounded rumors that he had been involved in the infamous syphilis study carried out by the U.S. Public Health Service at Tuskegee Institute. His nomination was rejected. Foster saw this disappointment as no more than one door closing. He continues to be on the forefront of U.S. health care issues.

198. Fowler, Wyatt Camblyn. *Whites Did, Blacks Do*. Durham, North Carolina: Fowler Publications, 1999. 166 pages; photographs. ISBN: 2548248663.

Abstract: "Our Business Foundation" founder Fowler, begins his book by talking about the nature of black self-hatred caused by slavery. He describes his eighteen-year career in the U.S. Navy, which he joined in 1941 at the age of sixteen, when the U.S. armed services were still segregated. Fowler was in a supply division and a cook at a base in Hawai'i. At the war's end, he and his company observed the celebrations of the white soldiers, uneasy about how they would fit into civilian society and what kind of conditions they would be returning to. Fowler re-enlisted and was initially quite successful, moving up from E-4 to E-5. His initial sense of accomplishment was short lived, however, and he did not fare as well as he moved to other bases throughout the world. Fowler's youth and sense of discouragement led him to make many poor decisions. He drank too much, was prone to violence, and during a particularly bad assignment, went AWOL, became homeless, and attempted suicide. Having survived this ordeal, Fowler returned to his ship and worked to get a discharge with honor, which he succeeded in doing. In civilian life, Fowler enrolled in a barber college, made a good marriage, became a father, and eventually ran a number of profitable businesses. He and his wife set up the "Our Business Foundation," which provided a learning center for children and adults and classes aimed at helping adults start their own businesses. Fowler ends his books with advice and a series of steps to lead readers to self-esteem, healthy living, and success.

199. Franklin, Aretha. *Aretha: From These Roots*. Written with David Ritz. New York, New York: Villard Books, 1999. 254 pages; photographs; discography. ISBN: 0375500332.

Abstract: Soul singer Aretha Franklin was born in 1941 in Memphis, Tennessee. When she was six, her parents divorced, and she and her four sisters and brothers moved with her father, C. L. Franklin, to Detroit, where he was a well-known and highly respected minister. Her mother moved to Buffalo, New York, to live with her own parents. She maintained contact with her children and they spent their summers in Buffalo, but she died when Franklin was only ten. This was also the age at which Franklin began singing in her church. At age fifteen, Franklin was traveling with her father who preached throughout the East. Before she was twenty, Franklin signed a contract with Columbia Records and began her own career. She lived in New York and visited her family in Detroit as often as she could. Both of her sisters sang and wrote songs, and her brother was her manager until he died in 1989. Franklin always had strong crossover appeal with fans of all tastes. She was featured in the popular movie *The Blues Brothers* in 1979, which gave her an even wider audience. In 1993, Franklin's career hit new heights when it turned out that newly-elected President Bill Clinton and his wife Hillary were her fans. They invited her to sing at two inaugural balls and for the inaugural telecast. Franklin writes in the book about her relationships with her parents, her brothers and sisters, her four children, her two husbands, and her many lovers. She describes the circumstances under which many of her hits were written and recorded, and about the people she has worked with.

200. Franklin, Buck Colbert (1879-1960). *My Life and an Era: The Autobiography of Buck Colbert Franklin*. Edited by John Hope Franklin and John Whittington Franklin. Baton Rouge, Louisiana: Louisiana State University Press, 1997. 288 pages; photographs. ISBN: 0807122130.

Notes: Published in paperback Baton Rouge: Louisiana State University Press, 2000. ISBN: 0807125997.

Abstract: According to John Hope Franklin, the author's son, Buck Colbert Franklin began work on his autobiography after a debilitating stroke. He worked on it until his death, hoping that he would see it published. John Hope Franklin kept the manuscript with him, working on it sporadically, and it was finally published nearly forty years after his father's death. Franklin believed that,

> he had a destiny to fulfill. The high standards he maintained in the practice of law, his numerous efforts to serve, in a variety of ways, the communities in which he lived and worked, and his strong belief in a Power greater than any that he could behold drove him to pursue the highest and noblest goals to which he could aspire.
>
> (p. ix)

Buck Colbert Franklin was born in 1879 in the Chickasaw Nation of Indian Territory. His grandfather was the property of a Chickasaw Indian. He bought his own freedom as well as that of his wife and ten children. Buck Franklin was the first in the Franklin family to attend college. He attended Roger Williams

College in Nashville and also Atlanta Baptist College (now Morehouse College), where his mentor John Hope was president. He returned to Indian Territory during the rush to get on official tribal membership rolls in order to claim land. Tribal enrollment entitled an individual to an allotment of land. As freedmen with land, and because their mother was one-quarter Choctaw, the Franklin children all had allotments in Indian Territory. During this time Franklin acquired a license to represent those making land claims. He chose to represent a woman who was a Choctaw of mixed descent. By the time the case was resolved, Franklin was determined to practice law. He passed the Oklahoma bar exam with the second-highest scores and was admitted to the bar in 1908. Franklin recounts his and his family's experiences living in the all-black town of Rentiesville, Oklahoma, and the many controversies he created due to his nonconformist political and social views. He describes his reaction to the passage of pivotal racist laws, including those established by *Plessy v. Ferguson* and the Dred Scott case, and their long-term and ongoing effects. Similarly, Franklin describes the precipitous degradation of life as the new state of Oklahoma implemented Jim Crow laws and other discriminatory legislation.

201. Franklin, Kirk. *Church Boy*. Written with Jim Nelson Black. Nashville, Tennessee: Word Publishing, 1998. 131 pages. ISBN: 0849940508.

Abstract: As a child, Kirk Franklin was a gifted piano player and musician. While this made him popular with adults, it did not help his image with his peer group. He spent a miserable childhood and emerged as a rebellious teenager. At sixteen, he received a scholarship to Professional Youth Conservatory at Texas Wesleyan University in Fort Worth, a private music school for gifted young people. He thrived in the atmosphere, made many friends, and became a born-again Christian. Before graduation, however, he was thrown out for verbally abusing a teacher who he felt had belittled him. Back at home and out of school, he was hired to lead music programs in a number of churches and started his own gospel group called the Humble Hearts. Franklin finally gained a name for himself when he was discovered by Milton Biggham, a preeminent figure in gospel music, who hired him to help with the mass choirs in Dallas/Fort Worth and Washington, D.C. Finally, Kirk began his own group, Kirk Franklin & The Family. They signed a contract with GospoCentric Records and produced a record, "Why We Sing." This song went to the top of the gospel charts, selling over a million records, as it crossed over

to the rhythm & blues category. As his success grew, Franklin was
in constant turmoil over his promiscuous lifestyle, and he spent
many years trying to change. In 1996, he married Tammy and set
up a household with his son and her daughter. Two years later,
their daughter Kennedy was born. With the stability and satisfaction that his family has given him along with a miraculous recovery from a near-fatal accident, Franklin feels that he has finally
matured. His gospel group continues to be popular, and he uses
their concert tours and television appearances to teach about the
faith that changed his life.

202. Franks, Gary (1953-). *Searching for the Promised Land: An
African American's Optimistic Odyssey*. New York, New York:
Regan Books, 1996. 207 pages; photographs. ISBN:
0060391561.

Abstract: Gary Franks, one of the only African-American
Republicans in the U.S. Congress, was born and raised in
Waterbury, Connecticut. His parents sent him to a private
Catholic school to give him educational advantages. Franks was
the star of the basketball team, served as class president, and did
well academically. He was accepted at Yale University, where he
studied hard and played basketball. When a career in professional basketball did not pan out, Franks went into private industry,
working for several Fortune 500 companies over the next ten
years. Some of his work was in affirmative action, and he helped
cut down on cronyism and actively expanded the pool of prospective employees for his companies. This meant going into inner
city areas and looking for talent among different racial and economic groups. In 1984, Franks was recruited to run for alderman
in Waterbury and was elected by a narrow margin. In 1986, he ran
for the U.S. Congress. The main challenge confronting him was
that his district was ninety percent white. Franks campaigned
aggressively, outworking and outsmarting his complacent oppo-
nent, and won the office, which he held until 1996. On arriving in
Washington, D.C., he joined the Congressional Black Caucus
(CBC) and discovered that he was both the only Republican and
only conservative. He was at odds with other members on almost
every issue and became a pariah, with CBC constantly struggling
to keep him out of their discussions. Franks fought district gerry-
mandering to create concentrations of voters of a certain race.
Although the supposed purpose of this practice was to increase
the number of nonwhite congressmen and women, it served to
further polarize constituencies. Franks has always contended that
the right person will be elected no matter what, and pointed to his

support among voters of all races in his district. He was against the Million Man March on Washington, D.C., in 1995 because of the racist views of Louis Farrakhan, one of the leaders. Franks felt that a march that excluded so many (only black men were encouraged to attend) could not have a positive effect. He has also fought for welfare reform, supporting changes that would encourage people to better themselves, make an independent living, and strengthen their families.

203. Frazier, Joe. *Smokin' Joe: The Autobiography of a Heavyweight Champion of the World, Smokin' Joe Frazier*. Written with Phil Berger. New York, New York: Macmillan, 1996. 213 pages; photographs. ISBN: 002860847x.

Abstract: Boxing champion Joe Frazier was born in Laurel Bay, Beaufort County, South Carolina. He was the twelfth child and the baby of the family. His parents owned ten acres of land and hired out to white farmers. Frazier developed an interest in boxing at a young age and worked out regularly one hour a day with a homemade heavy bag. His uncle predicted that he would be the heavyweight champion of the world, a prediction that Frazier expected to fulfill, but which most others laughed off. At fifteen, in 1959, Frazier left South Carolina for New York and then Philadelphia, where he worked at a slaughterhouse. He discovered the Police Athletic League Gym and soon began training for a boxing career in earnest. During the early 1960s, Frazier began winning amateur meets and training for the 1964 Olympics. He was an alternate and sparring partner to Buster Mathis. When Mathis developed an injury, Frazier stepped into the competition, and won the gold medal with a judges' vote of three-to-two against Germany's Hans Huber. Olympic gold did not translate into a boxing career or financial security at home. Having injured his hand in the championship round, Frazier was laid off temporarily from his slaughterhouse job, and his family found it difficult making ends meet on his wife's salary. A Philadelphia sports writer wrote an article for the local newspaper describing the financial woes of the Frazier family, and members of the community began sending money, food, and gifts. The family survived their hard times, Frazier's hand healed, and he began a professional career. By 1970, Frazier had earned the world heavyweight title. He achieved this, however, while Muhammad Ali was in prison for resisting the draft, and when Ali was released, their rivalry commenced along with a series of multimillion dollar challenge fights. Frazier won the first fight, earning 2.5 million dollars and the undisputed heavyweight title. He later lost his title to

George Foreman, and then two further challenges to Ali. Frazier
found it difficult to hang up his gloves even after another loss to
Foreman, but finally retired with a record of thirty-two wins in
thirty-six fights. After retiring, Frazier coached upcoming boxers,
including his two sons Marvis and Hector. He pursued a singing
career and was inducted into the Boxing Hall of Fame.

204. French, Albert. *Patches of Fire: A Story of War and Redemption.*
New York, New York: Anchor Books, 1997. 241 pages. ISBN:
0385483635 : 038548366x.

Abstract: African American Albert French writes about his experience fighting with the U.S. Marines in the Vietnam Conflict and
about his life after leaving the service. French was a twenty-one-
year-old corporal in the Marines in the summer of 1965 when he
was sent to Vietnam to serve in the infantry. He describes the constant fear and tension the troops were under, the conversations he
and his fellow servicemen had, and details of their daily routine.
He writes about his emotions when he killed a Vietnamese for the
first time and the overwhelming and constant desire to leave it all
behind him and go home. In early December, the squad he lead
was caught in a battle at Chu Lai that left him badly wounded and
most of the others dead. In shock from his own wounds and the
death of his friends, he was immediately sent back to the United
States, still wearing his battle fatigues. The first part of the book
ends as he is reunited with his family in Philadelphia for
Christmas. Part II begins in 1987, when he had been working as a
newspaper photographer for thirteen years. He had started his
own magazine, which, despite a successful beginning, failed. The
ensuing depression and sense of helplessness took him to the
Vietnam Veterans' Center, where he received counseling and participated in a support group of veterans. He discovered that he
was not the only one with feelings of trauma and guilt that were
still fresh many years after the war had ended. A business failure,
however, sent him back into despair. He began writing about his
war experiences as a way to deal with his depression. The resulting work became Part I of this book. While waiting for a literary
agent to sell it, French feverishly wrote two novels, *Billy* and *Holly*,
within the space of a few months. When these novels were published (in 1993 and 1995 respectively), their success in the United
States and England brought French a respectable income. For the
first time in almost thirty years, French found himself to be a func-
tioning member of society, experiencing normal, human emotions
and even falling in love.

205. Frost, David (1917-). *Witness to Injustice*. Edited by Louise Hutchings Westling. Introduction by Charles Reagan Wilson. Jackson, Mississippi: University Press of Mississippi, 1995. 110 pages; index. ISBN: 0878058206 : 0878058435.

Abstract: In his narrative, Frost, an Alabama native, tells about his early childhood. He describes two things that had a strong influence on his life: "(1) Watching my parents make moonshine in our back yard in a washpot . . . and (2) listening to my parents tell the story of how the Peterson boy had been lynched here in Eufaula" (p. 5). In speaking of his early years, Frost focuses on the lynchings and the fear of white people that he developed because of these lynchings. He describes a beating he himself got during an early run-in with the law. As a young man, he began to make moonshine, and this was his main occupation for many years. Once when he was caught, he chose a three-month prison term in Kilby Prison rather than pay to be let out of jail. He was proud later to learn that this was the way Martin Luther King, Jr. and Malcolm X had handled their own incarcerations. In 1948, he joined the NAACP, registered to vote, and, subsequently, faced the wrath of the local white population. This and his continued moonshine production kept him in constant trouble with the law. (He notes that when George Wallace, the future governor of Alabama, was judge in Balfour County, he was fair to black men and suggests that the racist attitudes Wallace demonstrated later as a politician were something he devised to maintain his popularity.) While involved in activities to improve schools for blacks and get a fair price for land, Frost was arrested a final time for operating a still, and this time served a three-year prison term. The sentence was set by George Wallace's brother, also a judge: "I was looking for him to give me a year and a day, like he had been giving all the other people for making moonshine. But Judge Wallace gave me three years. Then I realized that the one year was for the moonshine and the two years were for my civil rights activities" (p. 85). Frost notes the changes in black-white relations and the gains in civil rights for African Americans since his childhood.

206. Fulwood, Sam. *Waking from the Dream: My Life in the Black Middle Class*. New York, New York: Anchor Books, 1996. 247 pages. ISBN: 0385478224.

Abstract: Sam Fulwood III, a correspondent for the *Los Angeles Times*, writes about his life as a middle-class African American and how economic and career success does not mean acceptance in society as a whole. Fulwood was born into a middle-class family in Charlotte, North Carolina. His father was a well-respected Presbyterian minister and his mother was an elementary school teacher. He grew up in a cocooned society in which his parents did what they could to keep him from having to leave home and deal with white society. He ventured out of this sanctuary when he was chosen to integrate a junior high school and later when he attended the University of North Carolina, Chapel Hill (UNC), where black and white students were clearly divided. Fulwood managed to move among both groups of students by working on the otherwise all-white staff of the school newspaper, the *Daily Tar Heel*, and helping found UNC's chapter of Alpha Phi Alpha, the oldest black fraternity in the United States. After graduation, he began working for a series of major newspapers. Fulwood always tried to be accepted for who he was and what he was capable of doing, but never failed to uncover a reason related to race for every promotion or lack of one. At the *Charlotte Observer*, he was transferred from the sports section to the business section in what he suspected was a gesture to appease the black business community in Charlotte. After being hired by the *Baltimore Sun*, he was assigned to work one summer in South Africa, and he realized there that "Nothing I shall ever accomplish or discover or earn or inherit or buy or sell or give away nothing I can ever do will outweigh the fact of my race in determining my destiny" (p. 164). This made him angrier and more disillusioned than ever. Upon his return, he found out that he was on a "black headhunting list" that newspapers referred to when they found themselves in need of a token black employee. Fulwood had great expectations for a move to Atlanta, Georgia, the black mecca, but found the same situation there. Finally, in 1989, he was hired by the *Los Angeles Times* to work in its Washington, D.C. bureau. He has covered Clarence Thomas's confirmation to the U.S. Supreme Court, the emergence of Colin Powell as a public figure, and the Los Angeles riots following the Rodney King affair. Fulwood thought that the Thomas appointment forced African-American views into the public eye, "ripping away a façade of unity." About the Rodney King riots, Fulwood notes that black journalists were on the streets in Los Angeles getting the story, and white writers were getting the bylines.

207. Galindo, Rudy. *Icebreaker: The Autobiography of Rudy Galindo.*
Written with Eric Marcus. New York, New York: Pocket Books,
1997. 255 pages; photographs. ISBN: 0671003909 : 0671003917.

Abstract: In 1996, Rudy Galindo was the first Mexican-American
ice skater ever to win the U.S. National Championships. A native
of San Jose, California, Galindo was raised in a trailer park by a
mother with a mental illness and a father who was often away
from home. Although the family had little money to spare, his
father managed to pay for private ice skating lessons for Galindo
and his sister after they exhibited great talent for the sport. His
sister eventually dropped out of skating when it became apparent
that there was not enough money to pay for the two of them.
Eventually Galindo teamed up with Kristi Yamaguchi, and the
two skated in pairs competitions for six and a half years.
Yamaguchi's family took him in and he lived with them during
most of the time they worked together. In 1990, however,
Yamaguchi decided to concentrate on her promising singles
career, and Galindo was left alone. He looked for a coach and
scrambled to get back into singles competition. During this period of his life, Galindo also had to deal with the declining health
and deaths of his father and his brother, the latter of whom had
AIDS. After two of his coaches also died of AIDS during these
years, Galindo was forced to recognize and come to terms with his
own homosexuality. Galindo often found it difficult to both keep
up his social life and the grueling practice sessions. To stay alert,
he began taking cocaine. By the time he qualified for the U.S.
National Championships, he had given up drugs, fired coaches
who were too demanding, and hired his sister as his coach. Under
the tutelage of his sister, Laura, Galindo was able to achieve his
potential and win the Championships in 1996. His consequent
fame meant he had money for the first time in his life, but it also
meant constant public attention, as well as expectations from the
gay community to serve as a spokesperson. At the end of 1996,
Galindo decided to retire from competition to become a professional skater.

208. Gao, Qian (1981-). *West to East: A Young Girl's Journey to China.*
San Francisco, California: China Books and Periodicals, 1996.
179 pages; photographs. ISBN: 0835125491.

Abstract: Qian Gao lived in Fuzhou, China until she was five. She
and her parents immigrated to the United States, where her father
had a job at Texas A&M University. When Gao was eleven, her
parents made their first trip back to China, and this book is based

on her diary of that trip. Beginning in Hong Kong, the family went on to visit friends in Guanghzhou, Beijing, Shanghai, and finally their extended families in Fuzhou. Because she was so young when she left China, Gao remembered almost nothing; everything was new to her. She describes the Forbidden City in Beijing, their trip to the Great Wall, Tiananmen Square, and many other places. She also talks about the thrill of trying to ride a bicycle in crowds of bicyclists, the smells of the trains and the stations, the almost-forgotten taste of her favorite foods, the excitement of open markets, and so on. After a long visit with her beloved grandmother and various aunts, uncles and cousins, Gao found it difficult to return to her life in Texas after rediscovering her "home" in China.

209. Gardner, LeRoy (1924-). *Prophet without Honor*. St. Paul, Minnesota: The Author, 1996. 178 pages; photographs. ISBN: none.

> **Notes:** Also published St. Paul: Neo Life Publications, 1991. ISBN: none, (173 pages).

> **Abstract:** Gardner was born in segregated Kansas and moved, while still a young child, with his parents to St. Paul, Minnesota. He writes that he escaped segregation but not the "broad tentacles of the 'white supremacy ethic'" (p. 31). Time after time throughout his life he was confronted with ignorance, racist attitudes, and racist epithets. He became a lifeguard at a public pool only after having to wrestle and subdue the mock victim, who had purposely nearly drowned the previous African-American applicant for the position. He was sent to a reform school at the age of fifteen after defending himself against five white boys who attacked him on the street. It was after this incident that he knew that he would have to follow a different set of rules if he was to survive. He learned to control his anger and his reactions, to make a point politely, and to decide when to let something pass. Gardner graduated from high school and became a Christian while at the reform school. He planned to attend seminary, but had to work for several years to earn tuition. After earning the requisite tuition money, Gardner decided to go to Bethel Seminary in St. Paul. When he arrived, however, he was told that he couldn't register because they didn't accept African Americans. He was admitted only after signing a contract stating that he would set an example for the race and that if he were to be found offensive in any manner he would be expelled and no other African Americans would ever be admitted. "I learned that the profession of Christianity was often divorced from its practice in regard to persons of color"

(p. 58). In 1957, after working at various other jobs, Gardner organized the North Central Baptist Church. He maintained a barbershop and was an unpaid pastor to the mission church. Gardner describes the progress of the church and his work as an evangelist and pastor. Although the North Central Baptist Church struggled financially it nonetheless ran a construction training program and a drug abuse counseling service. Church members, seeking to help low income families buy houses, raised money to build nineteen houses and created a fund for down payments.

210. Garrison, Zina. *Zina: My Life in Women's Tennis*. Written with Doug Smith. Berkeley, California: Frog Limited, 2000. 211 pages; photographs. ISBN: 1583949146.

Abstract: Zina Garrison began playing tennis at the age of ten. While a senior in high school, Garrison won the Wimbledon, U.S. Open, and JAL junior cup competitions. She decided to turn professional directly out of high school. In her book, she alternates chapters on her life and game strategy with chapters describing each of her games at the 1990 Wimbledon. At that competition, Garrison beat Monica Seles and Steffi Graf, but lost to Martina Navratilova in the finals. Garrison's role models were Wimbledon champions Arthur Ashe and Althea Gibson, and she trained briefly with Gibson at her tennis camp as a junior competitor. Garrison's career had many ups and downs. She describes how her mother and siblings all pitched in to make it possible for her to travel around the world on the junior competition circuit; the dissolution of her friendship and working relationship with teammate and childhood friend Lori McNeil; the demise of her marriage; her ongoing struggle with bulimia; the complex and often less-than-honest world of professional agents and management companies; and life after the professional tour. Garrison retired in 1996, after achieving a career-high ranking of number-four in the world and completing fourteen years on the professional circuit. She sees herself working with children and encouraging more African Americans to take an interest in tennis. She writes about the physical and emotional dangers of young girls turning pro while in their early teens and gives several examples of young stars who burnt out quickly. Garrison is clear about what one must give up to be a professional, but despite personal losses, she has few regrets.

211. Gebramariam, Medina.   *Castaway Pearls: Claiming Our Inheritance.* Virginia Beach, Virginia: Cornerstone Publishing, 1995. ISBN: 1882185293.

> **Abstract:** Medina Gebramariam was born in a small village in Ethiopia, one of nine children. Her mother died when she was six. Gebramarian was devastated and left her father's house to stay with her oldest sister. Unfortunately, she was beaten by her sister, and returned to her father after six months. By this time her father had remarried a woman with three children of her own. Her father and stepmother were not happy at Gebramariam's return, and they gave her away to a family in a distant city. This was the beginning of years of travel from city to city, house to house, and job to job for her. Gebramariam worked for a number of different families in conditions that ranged from tolerable to horrific. At the age of ten, she was kidnapped and raped, and then sold into prostitution. She experienced serious illness, mental depression bordering on insanity, and continuous poverty. As war in Ethiopia escalated, Gebramariam traveled on foot for seven months to escape to Sudan. From there she went to Saudia Arabia, where she was hired by the royal family. She traveled to Europe as a maid to one of the princesses. She fell out of favor with the princess, however, because she was a Christian, and was sent back to Sudan. Through various schemes, Gebramariam made it onto a list of refugees bound for the United States and was sent to Baltimore. She was stunned to find poverty and homelessness in the United States, but was happy to have a second chance at life. After serious hardship and a difficult adjustment period, Gebramariam settled in Virginia. She believes that only Christian faith allowed her to survive her many brushes with death. She hopes to return to her native village in Ethiopia to help children there who may be hungry or sick. She feels that "God has providentially blessed America, not because Americans are good, but because in God's scheme of things, God is using America to provide refuge to all refugees from around the world. Red, yellow, black and white— are people all precious in God's sight" (p. 88).

212. Gibbs, Mifflin Wistar. *Shadow and Light: An Autobiography with Reminiscences of the Last and Present Century.* Introduction by Booker T. Washington. Lincoln, Nebraska: University of Nebraska Press, 1995. 372 pages; photographs. ISBN: 080327050x.

> **Notes:** Originally published Washington, D.C.: M. W. Gibbs, 1902.

213. Gibson, Aliona L. *Nappy: Growing Up Black and Female in America*. New York, New York: Harlem River Press, 1995. 165 pages; photographs. ISBN: 086316322x.

Abstract: Aliona Gibson, a native of Oakland, California, writes about her life in the East Bay area. The first part of the book discusses images of beauty and self-appreciation. She describes the problem of hair for black women, the amount of time and energy that goes into hairstyles, and the number of ways they can go wrong. Gibson herself has hair that is especially difficult to style:

> From years of pressing and chemicals, my hair was ruined. It had died a second death. Ironically enough, I was writing my thesis on American standards of beauty and their effect on women of color. My section on black people and our hair, coupled with my experience, was enough to convince me to cut mine off.   (p. 5)

Her subsequent delight with her extremely short hair was tempered by the generally negative reaction of other blacks, and for her, the battle with hair continues. Another aspect of self-image that Gibson writes about is the matter of different shades of color and the importance of that in society in general as well as in black culture. She was shocked to find out that a woman with whom she was friendly, considered Gibson too dark for her sons. Other subjects covered in the book are Gibson's experiences in education as a child and later as a college student in both predominantly white and predominantly black schools in the San Francisco East Bay, a trip she made to Africa after graduating from high school, her decision not to rush into child rearing (she was the only childless woman in her family over the age of twenty-two), and the differences in black culture on the East (New York City) and West (Northern California) coasts. Gibson devotes her final pages to several women who have served as mentors and "second mothers" to her, guiding her through many lifestyle decisions and into adulthood.

214. Glancy, Diane. *The Cold-and-Hunger Dance*. Lincoln, Nebraska: University of Nebraska Press, 1998. 109 pages; photographs. ISBN: 0803221738.

Abstract: Glancy was born the child of a Cherokee man and an English and German mother. She never felt accepted by either of the cultures. She married, had two children, and divorced after nineteen years. She now teaches Native American literature and creative writing at Macalester College in St. Paul, Minnesota. She enjoys writing in many different styles. Her subjects include the art of writing, her Native-American culture and its religions, and Christianity. Along with several autobiographical sections, Glancy's book includes a number of essays and poems, many of a religious nature:

> "The Autobiography of My Life with Jesus," "Sun Dance" (about Lakota and Dakota ceremonies she attended), "The House of Him Who Hath His Shoe Loosed," "Photography" (a poem), "The Bible and Black Elk Speaks" (a comparison of Christianity and Native-American religion), "nahna adulvdi gesvi (of that wanting which is)" (a poem), "Headwind" (about a visit to China, and thoughts on Christianity), "On Boards and Broken Pieces of the Ship" (a contemplation of God and Lakota religion), "Why Nations War" (thoughts on rage and weakness based on the noise caused by the bakery in front of her house), "North Shore Portrait" (on writing), "A Ute Sun Dance Story" (a Ute legend), "She-ro-ism" (about writing), "A Fieldbook of Textual Migrations" (comments on the Cherokee language), "Newmerica" (a poem), and "Eggs" (contemplation of her mixed culture).

215. Glover, Savion. *Savion! My Life in Tap*. Written with Bruce Weber. Foreword by Gregory Hines. New York, New York: William Morrow & Company, 2000. 79 pages; photographs. ISBN: 0688156290.

Abstract: Glover was born in 1973 and raised with his two brothers by his mother in Newark, New Jersey. He came from a musical family: his father was a dancer, and his mother and grandparents were musical. His mother recognized his special talents and started his Suzuki training and drum lessons at the age of four-and-a-half. At seven, Glover began playing in a band with several other young boys. He began dance lessons in 1982, after he was introduced to several famous tap dancers when his band played at the Broadway Dance Center. Once he started dancing, it was all he wanted to do. Glover's career quickly took off. In 1984, he was given the lead role in the Broadway production of *The Tap Dance Kid*, the third child to take the lead in this long-running musical. In 1988, he went to Paris to perform in *Black and Blue*, which later moved to New York. Glover writes, ". . . during "Black and Blue" was when I started realizing I could create my own kind of dance. Up to that point all I was doing was dancing" (p. 58). Tap dancer Gregory Hines saw Glover in *Black and Blue* in Paris, and created a part for him in the musical review *Jelly's Last Jam*. Glover developed a close working relationship with Hines, who became an important mentor and father figure to him. Glover's career continued to prosper with the production of his own musical, *Bring in 'da Noise, Bring in 'da Funk*, in 1995. Glover notes the influence of all of the dancers who came before him, and the importance of respecting tradition and following professional rules.

216. Gomez, Cecil (1923-). *Mama and Papa's Twelve Children and the "Y."* Wyandotte, Oklahoma: Gregath Publishing, 1997. 341 pages; photographs. ISBN: none.

217. Gooden, Dwight. *Heat: My Life on and off the Diamond*. Written with Bob Klapisch. New York, New York: William Morrow & Company, 1999. 242 pages. ISBN: 0688163394.

Abstract: 1984 Rookie of the Year and 1985 Cy Young-winning pitcher Dwight Gooden was a professional baseball player from 1983 to 1998. He played the first twelve years with the New York Mets and was a member of the 1986 team that won the World Series. He had a promising career ahead of him, but managed to get caught up in alcoholism and drug abuse. He was suspended from playing in order to get help for his addictions, and this was followed by a stretch of seven years when he neither drank nor used cocaine. In 1994, he went back to drugs and was suspended and subsequently released from the Mets. Once more, he fought to get over his addiction and was hired by George Steinbrenner for the New York Yankees. He pitched well, but was not assigned to the regular pitching rotation. After the 1997 season, the Yankees decided not to pick up the option on his contract and he became a free agent. He spent his final season with the Cleveland Indians and decided to retire because of his health. Gooden talks about many of the other players he worked with during his career, especially Darryl Strawberry, a good friend who had similar problems. Gooden expresses his appreciation to George Steinbrenner for taking a chance on him with the Yankees. A major portion of the book is devoted to a no-hitter game he pitched for the Yankees on May 14, 1996, an evening when his father was having open-heart surgery. Rather than going to his bedside in Florida, Gooden opted to stay in New York and pitch, dedicating the game to his father.

218. Gordon, Taylor (1893-1971). *Born to Be.* Introduction by Muriel Draper. Foreword by Carl Van Vechten. Introduction to this edition by Thadious M. Davis. Lincoln, Nebraska: University of Nebraska Press, 1995. 236 pages. ISBN: 0803270526.

   Notes: Originally published New York: Friede Civici, 1929.

219. Graham, Stedman. *You Can Make It Happen: A Nine Step Plan for Success.* Foreword by Stephen R. Covey. New York, New York: Simon & Schuster, 1997. 270 pages. ISBN: 068481448x : 0684838664.

   Abstract: Stedman Graham, a successful businessman, weaves the story of his life into a self-help book on achieving success. Graham was born and raised in Whitesboro, New Jersey. He discusses the stigma attached to the town ("nothing good comes out of Whitesboro") and the one attached to his family because he had two younger brothers with intellectual handicaps. Graham was tall and good at basketball, and his athletic talents took him through college. He had always assumed that he was headed for a career in professional basketball, but when this failed to materialize, he joined the U.S. Army, where he played basketball for the military as well as for a European professional team. After earning a master's degree in education, Graham joined the federal department of corrections and worked his way up to the director of education at the U.S. Metropolitan Correctional Center in Chicago. Presently a successful independent businessman who is best-known for his romantic relationship with talk show host Oprah Winfrey, Graham is the founder of Athletes Against Drugs, a national organization that provides role models for young people. Graham also serves on the board of several organizations, including National Junior Achievement, a group that helps young people learn how to succeed. He describes his own nine-step plan for success, using many methods that he has followed to overcome obstacles, learn to work with people, and achieve his potential.

220. Gray, Fred D. *Bus Ride to Justice: Changing the System by the System: The Life and Works of Fred D. Gray, Preacher, Attorney, Politician.* Montgomery, Alabama: Black Belt Press, 1995. 400 pages; photographs. ISBN: 1881320235.

   Abstract: Civil Rights lawyer Fred Gray was born and raised in Montgomery, Alabama. Because of his race he was unable to attend the University of Alabama Law School, and went instead to

Case Western Reserve University in Cleveland, Ohio. Following graduation in 1954, he passed the Alabama bar exam and began a practice in his hometown with the goal of "destroying everything segregated I could find" (p. 19). He soon found himself in the thick of the Civil Rights Movement when he represented Rosa Parks after she refused to give up her seat on a bus to a white person, thus instigating the Montgomery Bus Boycott, on December 1, 1955. Gray was subsequently involved in trying many famous civil rights cases throughout Alabama. His first case before the U.S. Supreme Court was to argue against the disenfranchisement of black voters in Tuskegee, which took place after the local government redrew the city map. On the first day, he presented a map that dramatically portrayed Tuskegee boundaries before and after they were changed. The map showed that the Tuskegee Institute was no longer a part of the city. This shocked Supreme Court Justice Frankfurter and cleared the way for Gray's court victory. Gray also successfully represented Dr. Martin Luther King, Jr., who was tried for tax evasion. Gray worked for the NAACP, represented protest marchers, and handled cases aimed at desegregating schools and protecting the property of black owners. In 1970, he was elected to the Alabama Legislature and held office for four years. He left politics without regret, however, feeling that he was more effective as a lawyer. In 1979, he was nominated for United States District Judge for the Middle District of Alabama. The confirmation, however, did not go smoothly. Gray assumed that his controversial work in civil rights was behind this, but he never learned what the real problem was. He finally withdrew his candidacy when promised that another African American would be nominated and quickly confirmed. Despite lingering regrets over losing the position, Gray continued his highly successful legal career. Since 1980, his personal practice has boomed and he has received many citations and awards for his civil rights work. Looking back over the years, Gray notes,

> Power has been utilized in the Movement to change society from total segregation to one which is becoming ever more just. . . . I believe that the success of the legal cases that I have been involved in speaks well for democracy and for the Constitution. It shows that one can use the system, abide by its rules and regulations, and change society. . . . However, one of the most disheartening observations I have made over the years is that most of the persons who made up what we called the white power structure have

never gone beyond doing exactly what the
courts ordered.   (p. 355)

221. Green, Al. *Take Me to the River*. Written with Davin Seay. New
York, New York: HarperEnterntainment, 2000. 343 pages; photographs. ISBN: 0380976226.

Abstract: Singer Al Green, born Albert Greene, grew up in a family of five boys and five girls in rural Jacknash, Arkansas. When
the family moved to Grand Rapids, Michigan, the transition was
traumatic for him. Bullied at school, lost in the streets, and lonely
for the natural environment and sounds of his rural childhood, he
began to fail in school. Music was always a highlight for him,
however, both through the music available at school and at home
singing with his brothers. Green was in love with the popular
sounds of the day, but his father forbade him from playing the hit
tunes in the house. He kicked Green out when he refused to com-
ply. Thus, on his own at an early age, Green lived with friends
while trying to earn money and form a band. He formed the
Creations and they cut a couple of singles with the short-lived
Zodiac studio. The group evolved into Al Greene and the Soul
Mates. They self-produced the hit record "Back Up Train." This
was to be the Soul Mates's only hit. After reaching nationwide
popularity and performing nine encores at New York's Apollo
Theater, the group went their separate ways. Green dropped the
"e" from his name and set out to establish himself in a solo career.
While touring, he connected with Willie Mitchell, who took charge
of Green's career. This partnership developed into a major business enterprise. Green's first big hits were "Can't Get Next to You"
and "Tired of Being Alone." "After a lifetime of work, I'd become
an overnight sensation, and in little more than two short years, I'd
racked up five million-selling singles. . ." (p. 287). During a tour in
California, Green had a life-changing religious experience. Three
albums later he broke with Mitchell, and started his own production company. Green then bought the Full Gospel Tabernacle in
Memphis, Tennessee, and studied to become an ordained minister.
He moved from pop and R&B music to gospel music, and, for this
later phase of his singing career, he has received three Grammy
awards. Green devotes himself to church activities and continues
to perform and record.

222. Green, Dennis. *No Room for Crybabies*. Written with Gene
McGivern. Champaign, Illinois: Sagamore Publishing. 224
pages; photographs. ISBN: 1571671757.

Abstract: Dennis Green, the second African American hired as a
head coach in professional football, grew up in Harrisburg,
Pennsylvania, where he started playing football in junior high.
His parents died when he was fourteen, but he had older brothers
and neighbors to look to for support. Green, like many of his
classmates, aspired to have a professional career in sports and
worked hard to accomplish his goal. He received a scholarship to
attend the University of Iowa and was one of fifteen African
Americans on the football team. Green felt that although the
school was in many ways open to its increasing African-American
student body, it was not fully prepared, and tension between the
players and administration continued throughout his time there.
Because of injuries, Green was not NFL material following his
graduation. He volunteered as a coach with the Iowa Hawkeyes,
was offered a position at the University of Dayton, and then
returned to Iowa as a paid member of the coaching staff. From
Iowa, Green joined Stanford's coaching staff and then went with
the head coach to the San Francisco 49ers. He had his first opportunity to head up a coaching staff at Northwestern University,
becoming the first African-American head coach in an NCAA
Division I-A school. Green returned to the 49ers in 1986 as Bill
Walsh's chief of staff, and then to Stanford as head coach in 1989.
In his work with Stanford, the 49ers and Northwestern, Green was
successful in turning around teams that had fallen on hard times.
It was this experience that led to a coaching offer from the
Minnesota Vikings. His transition to Minnesota was not easy. His
initial press conference was thorny, and his poor relationship with
the Minnesota media continued through the writing of this autobiography. He feels that racism is clearly a factor in the poor
chemistry, citing his good rapport with the media while with
Northwestern, San Francisco, and Stanford. Green realizes that
you cannot change a person's prejudices, but you can fight discriminatory actions. "I will fight these actions whenever I can. I
also will never accept the fact that I was, will be, or could be
denied an opportunity on the grounds that I'm the descendant of
African-American and Native-American grandparents" (p. 164).
Green writes that he is

baffled by America's inability to deal with equal
rights. Are you trying to tell me that the color of
someone's skin or their religious beliefs are supposed to determine how we should interact and

treat each other? You have to be kidding me.
People are people. There is only one mankind
that inhabits this one earth, and we better start
thinking like one people.   (p. 164)

223. Green, Wanda Jean (1929-). *And They Called It Public School Education: The Cleveland Public Schools.* Cleveland, Ohio: Educational Academy for a Competitive Edge, 2000. 94 pages; photographs. ISBN: none.

Abstract: Dr. Wanda Jean Green writes of her thirty-eight-year career in the Cleveland Public School District and her adversarial relationships with a succession of school superintendents. She began her teaching career at Rawlings Junior High School, a black school, and was promptly informed that she would be teaching "thugs and hoodlums." When the school superintendent tried to move her to a predominantly white high school because it was a "waste" to have her teaching at Rawlings, Green held her ground and refused to move. She felt that this was an outrageous insult to black students, to her school, and to all black teachers. She describes the innumerable inequities between black schools and white schools in the school district. For example, black schools did not teach algebra and were so overcrowded that children were reduced to three-hour school days. There were no such problems at the white schools, and she watched as the school board shifted school boundaries to effectively maintain this racial separation. Green went on to earn credentials to become a guidance counselor and was later assigned to head the new Adult Education Center that had as many as two thousand students attending. She kept it open from 8:00 a.m. to 10:00 p.m., and graduated one hundred students three times a year. Green was also consultant to the Head Start program for seventeen years. School superintendents saw her as a threat to their efforts to consolidate political power and tried to obstruct her efforts by moving her around and dismantling her departments. But they never managed to get rid of her or defy the court-mandated desegregation plans which were still being implemented well into the 1980s. Green was never satisfied:

How could well-trained educators view children
as worthless thugs and 'Non-learners'? How
could good teachers and educators take away
from children challenging educational opportunities? I was talking education, like reading programs, expansion of algebra, test preparation,
etc. Their thoughts were on politics, race con-
tainment, money. . . .   (p. 33)

224. Green, William. *Narrative of Events in the Life of William Green (Formerly a Slave): Written by Himself.* Chapel Hill, North Carolina: Academic Affairs Library, University of North Carolina at Chapel Hill, 2000.

> http://docsouth.unc.edu/neh/greenw/greenw.sgml
> http://docsouth.unc.edu/neh/greenw/greenw.html
>
> **Notes:** Documenting the American South (Project).

225. Greene, Lorenzo J. *Selling Black History for Carter G. Woodson.* Edited with an introduction by Arvarh E. Strickland. Columbia, Missouri: University of Missouri Press, 1996. 428 pages; illustrations. ISBN: 0826210686 : 0826210694.

> **Abstract:** Lorenzo J. Greene was a protégé of Carter G. Woodson, professor and scholar at Howard University and founder of the Association for the Study of Negro Life and History. An earlier selection of diary entries for 1928-1930 appeared as *Working With Carter G. Woodson, the Father of Black History: A Diary, 1928-1930* (Baton Rouge: Louisiana State University Press, 1989). The present diary focuses on Greene's campaign to sell the books published by the Association throughout the North and Southeast United States over a two-year period. Among the books he was selling were *The Negro in Our History, Negro Makers of History, African Myths,* all by Woodson, and *Negroes of Africa* by Maurice Delafosse. While on his campaign, Greene's own book, *The Negro Wage Earner,* was published by the Association, and he began to take orders for this title as well. Greene's diaries are full of his observations on black employment, the communities he visits, the various churches and people he meets, talks with, and visits. During his two years spent on the road, Greene came into his own as an established scholar in the field of black history. He was a ladies' man, and in his diary Greene comments on his long and short term relationships with a number of young women. He discusses his relationship with Woodson. Greene was dedicated to the cause of Negro history and was in many ways supported and mentored by Woodson, but Greene believed that Woodson took undue credit for Greene's accomplishments. He felt that more young men might be inspired to enter the field and take a serious scholarly interest in the work of the Association if Woodson were of a different temperament.

226. Gregory, Dick. *Callus on My Soul: A Memoir.* Written with Shelia P. Moses. Atlanta, Georgia: Longstreet Press, 2000. 301 pages; photographs. ISBN: 1563525542.

Abstract: Dick Gregory was born into poverty in St. Louis, Missouri, in 1932. He and his numerous siblings were raised by his mother, who worked as a domestic. As a high school student, he joined the track team because he wanted to be able to use the showers. He became one of the fastest runners in the country, and Gregory's coach used his connections to help get Gregory into college. His mother died at the age of forty-eight while Gregory was in college. When his coach left the school, he left, too. He began to work as an emcee at night clubs and gradually gained a reputation as a comic. In 1959, he married his wife Lillian; his first daughter was born soon after. They lived in poverty for a while, but their fortunes changed as Gregory got more lucrative work. About this time, the Civil Rights Movement was gaining steam, and Gregory went to Mississippi to help distribute food and register blacks to vote. From that time on he was deeply involved in nonviolent activities and was especially close to activist Medgar Evers. In 1967, Gregory ran against Richard Daley in the Chicago mayoral race. His nonviolent convictions also lead him to an interest in animal rights, and he subsequently became a vegetarian. During his years as an activist, Gregory suspected that he was being harassed by the FBI and other government agencies: for example making sure he was denied visas. He also suspected such interference in the Civil Rights Movement. The Gregory family grew larger; he and his wife had eleven children. They moved from Chicago to a farmhouse in Plymouth, Massachusetts. In 1976, Gregory ran for president of the United States. When Carter won, Gregory proclaimed himself "president-in-exile," and held inaugural balls in Washington D.C. He continued his activism, visiting the Ayatollah Khomeini after the U.S. embassy in Tehran was seized in 1979, and making several cross-country runs and holding fasts to bring attention to world hunger. Gregory also became concerned with diet and health. He developed a successful health drink called Formula X, and he has helped extremely obese people lose weight. As the book ends, Gregory discusses many important social issues and his stand on them. His philosophy of fasting and "Dick Gregory's Weight Loss System" are included as an appendix.

227. Grier, Barnett John Wesley (1915-). *Trek to Equality: An Autobiography*. Riverside, California: Riverside Museum Press, 1996. 248 pages; photographs; tables. ISBN: 0935661239.

Abstract: In his book, Grier focuses on his work as a member of the NAACP, the Black Parent Committee, and the Naval Weapon's Systems Laboratory's Equal Opportunity Advisory Committee and as a realtor furthering the goals of Riverside, California's black community. A physicist with a master's degree in mathematics and work toward a Ph.D. in theoretical physics, Grier went to Riverside in the early 1950s to help open the Missile Division of the National Bureau of Standards on the West Coast. He describes Riverside as a microcosm of racist attitudes and practices and discusses his and his wife's work, as well as the work of others, to enact change. Besides his work in civil rights, Grier helped to start a credit union, an investment group, and a co-op grocery store. He was active in politics, served on the Riverside Coalition on World Hunger, and organized the Riverside affiliate of Habitat for Humanity. Looking back, Grier feels that conditions for African Americans have deteriorated since the gains of the 1960s: "Discrimination and racial bias are more sophisticated now, more difficult to prosecute in the courts and to prove" (p. 135). He believes that blacks are victimized by inflation, income erosion, fiscal conservatism, lack of health care, and the dissolution of affirmative action programs. Despite this bleak view, Grier has hope for the future: "I must and you must continue to have short-term goals, long-term goals and Dreams. . . . We must encourage our children to do likewise" (p. 234). His book also includes the story of his parents, who were born slaves, his own childhood, and a mention of some of the major events in the United States, especially those that have affected the lives of African Americans.

228. Griffey, Ken, Jr. *Junior: Griffey on Griffey*. Written with Walter Iooss. New York, New York: Collins, 1997. 112 pages; photographs. ISBN: 0002252198 : 0006491545.

Abstract: This is a coffee table book full of photographs of, and text by, Seattle Mariner Ken Griffey, Jr. In this book, Griffey describes his feelings at being drafted into the major leagues at the age of seventeen, his philosophy of baseball, the difficulty of being well-known and dealing fairly with the public, and his relationships with teammates. He also discusses the importance of his family (wife Melissa, son Trey, and daughter Taryn) and how he was taught by his father, professional baseball player Ken Griffey,

Sr., to always put his family first. He writes about the pleasure of playing professional baseball with his father, playing golf, his interest in architecture and his contributions to designing his house.

229. Grillo, Evelio. *Black Cuban, Black American: A Memoir.* Introduction by Kenya Dworkin Mendez. Houston, Texas: Arte Público Press, 2000. 134 pages; photographs. ISBN: 155885293x.

Abstract: Evelio Grillo was born into a black Cuban family that had immigrated to the United States in the early twentieth century to work in the cigar-making industry. While the best cigar tobacco came from Cuba, much of the manufacturing was based in Tampa, Florida. Grillo grew up in Ybor City, a Latin community within the city of Tampa. He discusses the differences in the lives of white Cubans and black Cubans and those of black Cubans and black Americans. Public schools and black colleges, he says, were what brought all blacks together. Grillo himself did very well in school, and one day one of his school teachers announced that he would be taking him to Washington, D.C., the next day so that he could more actively pursue his education. Grillo attended Dunbar High School in Washington, D.C., an elite public school for blacks, and thrived under the mentorship of the African-American community there. After high school, his mentors sent him to New Orleans to go to college at Xavier University, where they felt he would benefit from the familiarity of Catholicism and the warmer climate. The nuns who ran Xavier gave him plenty of attention and saw that he had work and scholarships sufficient to see him through his four years there. He felt, however, that they probably regretted the penchant he had for speaking out on issues of racial discrimination. During World War II, he served in the U.S. Army, and was appalled by the rampant discrimination he and all other African-American soldiers encountered. Throughout his military career, he was viewed by his superiors as both a troublemaker and a good leader. Based in the jungles of India, he took the lead in making life for black soldiers more pleasant, organizing basketball leagues and publishing newspapers. After the war, Grillo went to graduate school and was hired by the city of Oakland, California, to work in a community of poor blacks and Mexican Americans. He stayed in the Bay Area for the rest of his career, involved in many aspects of social welfare and politics. The pinnacle of his career came during the Carter administration, when Arabella Martinez, Assistant Secretary for Human Development Services at the Department of

Health, Education and Welfare, appointed him to serve as Executive Assistant for Policy Development.

230. Guillermo, Emil. *Amok: Essays from an Asian American Perspective.* San Francisco, California: AsianWeek Books, 1999. 230 pages. ISBN: 0966502019.

Abstract: This book is a collection of the columns written since 1995 by Emil Guillermo for AsianWeek magazine. A native San Franciscan of Filipino descent, Guillermo graduated from Harvard in 1977. Graduating the same year Bill Gates would have had he not quit, Guillermo writes that "I admire the hell out of Bill Gates. . . . Now I don't have to make all the money in the world. Bill has it. I can just call Bill every now and then to make sure it's all safe. And then I can spend the rest of my time pursuing the things money can't buy" (p. 3). In order to pursue his writing career and put aside more worldly aspirations, Guillermo claims that he had to first summon the strength to reject Harvard's established definition of success. When he looks back over the two decades since his graduation, Guillermo has no regrets. His columns cover current issues and events that deal closely and directly with being an Asian American in the United States. He writes about the condition of immigrants in this country, stating that the degree of public disfavor they endure varies with the fortunes of the American economy. He examines the laws that affect immigrants and the varying degrees to which these laws are enforced. Guillermo recalls an instance when he was once called a foreigner and told to go home by an Asian Indian who had immigrated to the United States and become a naturalized citizen. He believes that as the country's minority population grows, racism will not be limited to white Americans. He discusses the Clinton fund-raising scandal and the racism of the *National Review*. He examines the good and bad side of affirmative action, as well as its current fall from grace. He discusses the growth of intermarriage and the resulting multiracial children, their ethnic labels, and the Tiger Woods phenomenon. Guillermo also writes about animal rights, vegetarianism, and the fresh kill butchering practices prevalent in Chinatowns across the country. Finally, Guillermo writes about the dearth of Asian legislators and the general unsavoriness of U.S. politics in the 1990s.

231. Guinier, Lani. *Lift Every Voice: Turning a Civil Rights Setback into a Strong New Vision of Social Justice.* New York, New York: Simon & Schuster, 1998. 336 pages; index. ISBN: 0684811456.

Abstract: On April 29, 1993, Lani Guinier, a veteran civil rights lawyer and faculty member at the law school of the University of Pennsylvania, was nominated by President Clinton for the position of Assistant Attorney General for Civil Rights. She was immediately attacked in the press by a columnist who dubbed her the "Quota Queen." This label spread quickly throughout the media, along with out-of-context quotations and misinterpretations of her writings. None of these accounts of her law review articles or her experience as a civil rights attorney were ever publicly refuted, nor was she ever publicly supported by President Clinton or his staff. At the end, she was allowed to go on the television news program *Nightline*, her first opportunity to speak about her views and the unmitigated bad press she had received. Shortly thereafter, on June 6, 1993, the nomination was withdrawn, even before a confirmation hearing was convened. Guinier uses this book to speak for herself and to review her career as a civil rights lawyer working with the NAACP Legal Defense Fund to defend the spirit of the Voting Rights Act of 1967 and individuals, primarily African Americans, who are effectively left out of the process of American politics and governance. Guinier concludes by advocating conversations on race beyond study circles and the classroom. The goals would be "to rebuild communities, to reconnect concerned citizens, and ultimately to provide laboratories for social justice. They would seek to rekindle the sense of struggle and the concept of participatory democracy that was at the heart of the civil rights mass movement (p. 310)." Conversations would give a voice to disparate constituencies. By

returning to the lessons I learned from the real civil rights clients I had represented, I ultimately survived my own personal tutorial in the politics of racial justice. . . . I had mostly represented black people who had been intimidated into silent suffering, and who were released from silence by the legal process and by their own actions. I had watched them fight the system, trying to coax it into allowing them to participate, not just by voting but by having a say in the decisions that affected their lives.   (p. 310)

232. Gutiérrez, Jose Angel. *The Making of a Chicano Militant: Lessons From Cristal.* Wisconsin Studies in Autobiography. Madison, Wisconsin: University of Wisconsin Press, 1998. ISBN: 0299159809 : 0299159841.

Abstract: Jose Gutiérrez worked to build Chicano and Hispanic organizations throughout Texas, the Pacific Northwest, and cities and counties throughout the country. His focus was on the town of Cristal, or Crystal City, Texas, his hometown, where Chicanos lived on one side of the railroad track and whites on the other. Gutiérrez began his political activities after graduating from high school the year that the Political Association of Spanish Speaking Organizations (PASO) formed in Cristal. PASO ran five Chicano candidates for city council and mayor. All the candidates were successful and the city offices were now run by members of the Chicano Community. As a student at Texas A&I (the present-day Texas A&M University), Gutiérrez formed a student PASO, which sought equal representation for Chicano students on campus. He founded the Mexican American Youth Organization (MAYO), was involved with Ciudadanos Unidos (CU), and was instrumental in founding the La Raza Unida Party. One of his major activities with MAYO, and later in Cristal, was to organize school boycotts, that, if successful, would lead to Chicanos becoming teachers and school administrators and serving on school boards. Although it was initially successful in electing slates of candidates at the local level, several factions developed within La Raza Unida, and forces attacked it from without. As the party began to disintegrate and Gutiérrez's position within the party and as a force in Texas politics withered, he decided to leave Texas with his wife and four children. The family moved to Portland, Oregon, where Gutiérrez taught at Western Oregon State College. He also worked for United Way and founded the Oregon Council for Hispanic Advancement (OCHA). Gutiérrez returned to Texas in 1986 and rejoined Chicano political activities. At that time he pursued a law degree and graduated from Bates College of Law in 1989. Along with his own story, Gutiérrez provides a brief historical context for Chicanos in Southwest Texas. He also traces the history of the term *Chicano*, differentiating it from *Hispanic* and *Latino*. Gutiérrez concludes by speaking to the importance of passing on the fundamentals of activism to the next generation: "These fundamentals are commitment to our cause: the right of our people to exist in dignity, safety, and well being; the right to our homeland; the right to have our culture; and the right to a future" (p. 304).

233. Haizlip, Shirlee Taylor and Harold C. Haizlip. *In the Garden of Our Dreams: Memoirs of a Marriage.* New York, New York: Kodansha International, 1998. 306 pages; photographs. ISBN: 1568362544.

> **Notes:** Also published New York: Anchor Books, 2000. ISBN: 0385497598.

> **Abstract:** Shirlee Taylor and Harold Haizlip write alternately about their life together, beginning with their courtship in the late 1950s when Haizlip was an Amherst College graduate studying at the Harvard Graduate School and Taylor Haizlip was an undergraduate at Wellesley. It was love at first sight for both of them. They married right after she graduated. Taylor Haizlip went to work as an editor for a medical journal, while Haizlip began teaching at private schools. In the 1960s, the Haizlips were in demand as companies were seeking qualified African Americans to serve in professional capacities. Intelligent, articulate, well-dressed and attractive, they also found themselves on lists of socially acceptable blacks to be invited to parties and other society events. Both enjoyed living "as if we were rich," but felt uneasy about their role as representatives of their race. While headmaster at the innovative New Lincoln School in New York, Haizlip was recruited by the governor of the U.S. Virgin Islands to serve as his commissioner of education. In the 1970s, the Haizlips and their two daughters spent eight years on the island of St. Thomas. Haizlip served as commissioner of education until the government was ousted from power, and Taylor Haizlip went to work for the local television station. By the late 1970s, when they decided to return to the mainland, neither was able to find a job because hiring blacks for high-profile positions had gone out of vogue, and their prospects were bleak. When Taylor Haizlip was offered a job in Los Angeles, the couple decided to relocate there, despite having to leave their family on the East Coast. They remain in Southern California to this day. Haizlip is actively involved in community work dealing with young people, especially in the wake of the riots following the Rodney King incident. Taylor Haizlip wrote the book *The Sweeter the Juice* (Simon & Schuster, 1994), a project aimed at finding the white side of her mother's family, relatives from whom her mother, who was on the black side, had been separated her entire life. She succeeded in reuniting her mother with her sister and expanding an already large, loving family.

234. Halbert, Willie Holton. *Precious Treasures*. Rochester, Illinois: We Write Corporation, 1998. 192 pages. ISBN: 1576350231.

Abstract: Willie Holton Halbert works as the Assistant Supervisor for the Illinois Department of Corrections in the Community Services Division. She has worked as a counselor and caseworker at the medium security Logan Correctional Center and the maximum security Pontiac Correctional Center. Besides her official work, Halbert has also volunteered her time to direct theater productions in both correctional centers. Halbert describes her calling to prison work and the twists and turns that led her to this career. Besides her work, Halbert writes about her family and friends in Texas and Illinois and tells the story of her daughter's successful fight with cancer. Halbert and her husband both attended Illinois State University in Normal, Illinois, and continue to live in Bloomington, where they are active in the Baptist Church and have worked with church youth. Halbert is a member of the National Association of Blacks in Criminal Justice and has served as the Human Relations Commissioner for the City of Bloomington. She is active with Cultural Festival, Inc., which organizes an annual multicultural arts festival each year and with the "Not in Our Town" organization, which was formed to fight racism and hate crimes in the Bloomington/Normal area. Looking back on her life, she considers each of her memories to be treasures and writes, "Everyone has precious treasures more valuable than money—more impressionable on the soul than power or fame. Everyone has a story to tell" (Foreword). Halbert stresses that it is important to recall and tell others about our important and positive memories to counteract the stories we hear about societal and world problems.

235. Hall, Bruce Edward. *Tea That Burns: A Family Memoir of Chinatown*. New York, New York: Free Press, 1998. 308 pages; photographs; index. ISBN: 068483989x.

Abstract: Writer Bruce Hall is a fourth-generation Chinese American. His mother was a white woman from Oklahoma and his father a third-generation Chinese American. As a child, Hall's family moved whenever his father was promoted and, eventually, Hall lost almost all connection to his mother's family.

> Chinatown was the only constant in my life, it seemed, the only spot to which I could always return to familiar surroundings and see the thumbprint of generations that had died before living memory. . . . It was a place with tradition,

> with customs, with old people who knew my
> father and would call him by baby names I never
> heard anywhere else. It was a place that
> America hadn't homogenized out of existence,
> and there one could smell the village where the
> Ancestors had lived for perhaps a thousand
> years before.   (p. 2)

Hall traces his family history from the time his great-grandfather left his village in China in 1873 to come to the United States. The history of his family coincides in large part with that of Chinese immigration to the United States and so he combines the history of his family with a history of New York City's Chinatown. Hall used books, newspapers, and other reference material to help fill in the blanks of memories, letters, and family stories. The book gives an account of daily life in early Chinatown, the dismal ratio of men to women, the effect of various immigration laws on the population, and the people and organizations that were active in supporting the residents of Chinatown. Hall provides background on such elements of Chinatown as the Tong wars and sweat shops. He describes how his schoolmates focused on his Chinese ancestry and the various ways his blonde mother dealt with confusion caused by the appearance of her children. He recounts the many aspects of his Chinese background that have given him connection and ethnic roots.

236. Hammad, Suheir. *Drops of This Story*. New York, New York: Writers & Readers / Harlem River Press, 1996. 93 pages. ISBN: 0863162436.

> **Abstract:** Poet Suheir Hammad was born in a Palestinian refugee camp in Jordan. Her family lived in Beirut during the civil war in Lebanon. Later, they moved to Brooklyn, New York, where her father ran a butcher shop. Hammad found it difficult to relate to her parents' traditional, Palestinian lifestyle. She felt more comfortable with the culture of her black neighbors and classmates than to that of her parents. But with family still in the Middle East, and an uncle killed by Israeli soldiers, Hammad has developed an attachment to her Palestinian heritage. She writes that she is "[a] Palestinian woman speaking for herself, without some sympathetic anthropologist talking for her. A poor kid who grew up to tell the stories she lived. The want of my feet for Palestinian soil and Brooklyn concrete. The itch of fingers for a hand to hold. Burn of heart for a lover. The tear of my eye for some peace" (p. 89).

237. Hankins, Anthony Mark. *Fabric of Dreams: Designing My Own Success.* Written with Debbie Markley. New York, New York: Dutton Books, 1998. 288 pages. ISBN: 0525943293.

Abstract: Anthony Mark Hankins was born in Elizabeth, New Jersey, the youngest of seven children. He was interested in fashion and design at an extremely young age, and at age seven, he sewed a suit for his mother which she proudly wore to a wedding. His natural curiosity, exuberance, and seemingly unending energy led him to do well in school. After high school, Hankins was accepted at Pratt Institute, where he served as an intern to Homer Layne, a well-known but unassuming designer. Hankins worked for Layne, continued to make clothes for people around him, and still managed to keep up with his assignments, including a "Hula-Hoop dress" which caused a sensation at the school. Hankins ultimate goal was to go to Paris and work for designer Yves San Laurent. He managed to schedule an interview at Ecole de la Chambre Syndicale de la Couture Parisienne in Paris, but had no money to get there. He used his connections to publicize his plight on television, and the result was a ticket to Paris from an anonymous donor, tuition paid by Yves Saint Laurent, and eventually a job at Laurent's world-renowned fashion house. Returning home, Hankins found himself out of work. Small jobs earned him some degree of fame, and he was eventually hired at J. C. Penney headquarters in Dallas, Texas. He designed an attractive, affordable line of clothing which he created with his mother and her friends in mind. The company agreed to produce the line, but never fully supported it despite its successful sales. After two years he decided to leave J. C. Penney and start his own company with the help of Bruce Ackerman, a Penney's veteran who saw promise in Hankins. His company remains located in Dallas, and at the time of publication, Hankins was selling his designs at department stores throughout the country, over Black Entertainment Television, and on the Home Shopping Network. He was also about to launch a new clothing line for Sears. In 1997, Hankins was recognized as a Young Star at the Trumpet Awards, an annual awards ceremony established to recognize African-American accomplishments.

238. Hargrove, Gloria. *Mission in Life: The Journey to Find My Dream.* New York, New York: Vantage Press, 1998. 131 pages. ISBN: 0533123208.

Abstract: Hargrove's book is divided into three sections: the first describes her life and the events that brought her to the ministry;

the second contains a selection of her sermons; the final is a case study. Hargrove was born in Brooklyn, New York, in 1953. At age five, she was raped by a man who lived in her building. She was never able to talk about it because the man threatened to kill her. She suffered from nightmares and became very fearful. As a young woman, Hargrove and her friends got work with a modeling agency, and at the age of fifteen, she started her own modeling business. She and her friends were quite successful, but they were working in an environment where there was a ready supply of drugs, and many of the girls were in abusive relationships. At one point, Hargrove attempted suicide, taking an overdose of pills. She was rescued and taken to the hospital. As she was recovering, she knew intuitively that her grandmother and mother were praying for her, and this motivated her to look for a less destructive path to follow. Years later, after Hargrove had married, borne children, and left New York for Florida, she learned that her younger sister was in the final stages of AIDS, and she went back to New York to be with her. Hargrove promised her sister that she would organize a big gospel concert in her honor and invite a famous evangelist to speak. Organizing the concert was an enormous job, but she was able to carry it off. Part of Hargrove's work entailed forming and training a children's choir, comprised largely of at-risk children from her neighborhood in Florida. It was while working on this concert that Hargrove began her work as a minister in the Pentecostal church.

239. Haro, Juan. *The Ultimate Betrayal: An Autobiography.* Pittsburgh, Pennsylvania: Dorrance Publishing Company, 1998. 173 pages. ISBN: 080594379x.

240. Harris, Eddy L. *Mississippi Solo: A River Quest.* New York, New York: N. Lyons Books, 1988. 250 pages. ISBN: 1558210016.

Notes: Also published New York: Henry Holt and Company, 1998. ISBN: 0805059032; New York: Perennial Library, 1989. ISBN: 0060972475.

Abstract: Harris decided to take an October canoe trip down the Mississippi River. He started at Lake Itasca in Minnesota and continued down to New Orleans. Harris's first steps were to secure a canoe and moral support from his friends. Armed with some supplies and determination, Harris began his trip, developing his canoeing skills along the way. Except for one encounter with two unfriendly white men and another with a pack of wild dogs, most of Harris's trip was pleasant though back breaking. The people

Harris met along the way were interested in his trip, chatted with him, shared a meal with him, or gave him rides. Although there were a number of times Harris was ready to give up, he success-fully completed his voyage, maneuvering through lakes and locks and dams and sharing the water way with tugs, tow boats, barges, and tankers.

241. —. *Native Stranger: A Blackamerican's Journey into the Heart of Africa*. New York, New York: Simon & Schuster, 1992. 315 pages. ISBN: 0671748971.

Notes: Also published New York: Vintage Books, 1993. ISBN: 0679742328.

Abstract: Harris traveled to Africa to learn about a continent he felt drawn to, but not a part of. A travel writer, Harris has previ-ously described his travels through the American South, along the Eastern seaboard of the United States, and in Harlem. He travels to discover aspects of himself, his heritage, and the larger context of being an American or "Blackamerican." Harris prepared for his African journey in Paris. There he met with immigrants from Senegal, Ivory Coast, and Algeria. From Paris, Harris traveled to Tunis, Algeria, Morocco, Western Sahara, Mauritania, Senegal, Gambia, Guinea-Bissau, Mali, Ivory Coast, Liberia, Burkina Faso, Togo, Benin, Nigeria, Cameroon, Central African Republic, Zaire, Rwanda, Burundi, Zambia, and Zimbabwe. He concluded his travels in South Africa. Harris writes,

> So how does a Blackamerican travel to Africa? Certainly not as an African, for that I am not. Nor as a cultural European, for I am more than merely that. And more, too, than hybrid. Another race, perhaps, newborn and distinct, forged in the blast furnace of slavery, tempered and tested in the foundry of survival.
>
> (pp. 28-29)

At the end of his journey, Harris considered the many aspects of Africa that he found troubling and unacceptable. He felt that he did not get to know the continent sufficiently, and he describes his experiences as "full of dullness and pain," "interesting and agoniz-ing" (p. 313). Harris's year in Africa left him with questions about his own cultural identity unanswered.

242. —. *South of Haunted Dreams: A Ride through Slavery's Old Backyard.* New York, New York: Simon & Schuster, 1993. 254 pages. ISBN: 0671748963.

Notes: Also published New York: Henry Holt and Company, 1997 as *South of Haunted Dreams: A Memoir.* ISBN: 0805055746.

Abstract: Harris learned from his experiences touring through Africa that his roots were not in Africa, but in the American South. Harris was raised in St. Louis, but his father was from the South and had been forced to leave his hometown after angering a group of white men. Harris was raised on such stories about his father, as well as stories of school integration, lynchings, bombings, and burning crosses. He set out from St. Louis on motorcycle to tour the South with a preconceived notion of what race relations would be like, how he would be treated, and what he would find. Harris writes, "I travel to the South to confront the source of my anger. I am half hoping to hurt someone. At the same time I am longing to find a new South, a new America, hoping with heart and soul that all is not hopelessness and despair" (p. 22). Although he found remnants of the old South he had heard about from his father, Harris also found kindness, hospitality, generosity, interest, and change. He talked with the white and black people whom he came across sitting on porches, eating in cafes, or working in gas stations. His book describes the thoughts, encounters, and impressions which he gathered as he traveled through the states of Georgia, Kentucky, Louisiana, Arkansas, Alabama, Tennessee, North Carolina, and Mississippi.

243. —. *Still Life in Harlem: A Memoir.* New York, New York: Henry Holt and Company, 1996. 276 pages. ISBN: 0805048510 : 0805048529.

Abstract: For Harris, "Harlem" is not only a geographical designation but a metaphor for "the world of black folk." Harris decided to move to Harlem after a period of time living a more cosmopolitan life style. He had chosen at an early age to be "a man," rather than "a black man," and had hopes of not being defined by his skin color. He decided it was time, however, to rejoin the black community. Harris invokes images of the Harlem of history and, for many, of legend. Upon his arrival, however, he found a Harlem that contrasted starkly with his expectation: rats and trash, burnt out buildings and cars, many people without prospects or hope. In this book, Harris seeks to come to terms with what it means to be black and what his role might be in the black community, either in or outside of Harlem. He views leaving Harlem as a surrender, but he also suggests that coming back to it is a kind of surrender as well. He feels that it constitutes giving in to white expectations for failure and white desire for separateness. Harris describes the people he meets: those who are part of the criminal drug element; those who found that they had to leave Harlem to prosper; and those who left but came back. Harris finds the single most devastating factor for people trapped in poverty in Harlem to be the loss of hope. He sees a need for positive role models within the community who could provide examples of a way of life that leads to economic success and who could prove that there are reasons to care about the future. Despite the innumerable obstacles to change within Harlem, Harris ends his book with a note of optimism. He says that there is indeed reason to believe that there can be a reversal of the hopelessness and despair that permeate life on the streets of Harlem and the souls of many of its residents.

244. Harris, LaDonna. *LaDonna Harris: A Comanche Life.* Edited by H. Henrietta Stockel. Lincoln, Nebraska: University of Nebraska Press, 2000. 147 pages; photographs. ISBN: 080322396x.

Abstract: A member of the Comanche Indian tribe, activist, and former U.S. vice-presidential candidate, LaDonna Harris grew up in Southern Oklahoma and was raised primarily by her grandparents. Her mother was the first in her family to marry a white man, and she lived and worked away from the family farm in Walters, Oklahoma. Harris was in a variety of activities in high school and graduated, despite the high Indian dropout rate and the fact that she was dyslexic. She met her husband Fred while in high school and they married right before graduation. Harris changed quickly from a farm girl with a high school education to an independent social and political activist. Fred, who began his political career with the Oklahoma State Legislature, went on to the United States Senate and ran for U.S. President twice. Harris was always a partner in his campaigns. It was highly unusual, even shocking, for a candidate's wife to be on the campaign trail during their early political days in Oklahoma, but both Fred and LaDonna ignored their detractors and became a winning team. LaDonna describes her many local and national activities which focused on better opportunities for African Americans and tribal people in Oklahoma and elsewhere and on mental health issues. Her earliest community activities, however, were close to home. She was active with the Honcho Group, which worked to integrate public places in Lawton, Oklahoma. Their first effort was to integrate the restaurants. They succeeded through quiet peer pressure and by asking the owners "respectfully to integrate their establishments" (p. 55). The group moved on to integrate housing, jobs, and the public swimming pool. Harris helped found the Oklahomans for Indian Opportunity. Through this organization, she got state agencies involved in Indian education issues and tribal living conditions. Harris also surveyed mental health institutions in Oklahoma and made a report which Fred used to enact state legislation to implement improvements. When Fred went to Washington, D.C., as a senator, Lyndon Johnson appointed Harris to the Mental Health Commission to work as an advisor to the War on Poverty campaign and to the National Indian Opportunities Council. After leaving Washington, D.C., Harris founded the Americans for Indian Opportunity and continues to be actively involved. She writes, "AIO has grown beyond my wildest dreams and today has a long list of accomplishments" (p. 117). One of AIO's major goals is to work tribal governments into the federal system and to solidify their sovereignty and independence. In 1980, Harris was the vice-presidential candidate for the Citizens' Party, running with presidential candidate Barry Commoner.

245. Harris, Lynne Gray. *Finally Me!* Foreword by D. Marilyn Fullard. Tracy, California: The Pallen Company, 1997. 143 pages. ISBN: 0965787206.

Abstract: Lynne Harris was a single mother with a two-year-old son when she met William "Bubba" Paris, left tackle for the San Francisco 49ers football team. She had goals and ambition and was just taking her first steps in a promising career with Digital Equipment Corporation when Paris asked her to marry him. After accepting his proposal, he informed her that he did not want his wife to hold a job. Although she tried to convince him that it would be important to her and useful to them both for her to continue to work, she finally agreed to quit. After that, she gave in to every demand Paris made, including his insistence that she not use birth control. Harris consequently had five children within as many years. Harris describes her ten-year marriage to an abusive man, her mother's death, her attempts to change her husband, and finally her determination to divorce him. When the divorce was finally settled, Harris moved with her children to Tracy, California. She later reunited with the father of her first child, and entered into a balanced relationship in which the interests of both husband and wife were taken into consideration.

246. Harrison, Alvin and Calvin Harrison. *Go to Your Destiny.* Foreword by André Farr. New York, New York: Hyperion, 2000. 157 pages; photographs. ISBN: 0786867884.

Abstract: Runners Alvin and Calvin Harrison are identical twins who have shared almost all aspects of their tumultuous lives. They were first raised by their grandmother in a poor neighborhood in Orlando, Florida, and, at age eight, they moved to Salinas, California, to live with their father in a more affluent and stable environment. In high school, both brothers excelled at track and field, winning in national and international competitions. Their stable life, however, was disrupted when they moved back to Florida with their father. By this time, they considered Salinas their home and convinced their father to let them return. The next two years, however, found them scrambling for a place to live and food to eat. They received track scholarships to the local community college, but finances finally forced them to go back to Orlando where they found that most of their friends were selling drugs and involved with gangs. Determined to resist this lifestyle, the brothers returned to Salinas to train for the 1996 Olympic trials. Alvin made the Olympic team and gained sponsorship, but Calvin lost his heat by seven-thousandths of a second. In Atlanta, Alvin won a gold medal in the four-by-four hundred meter men's relay. His Nike endorsement allowed both brothers to continue to train and compete on the international circuit, but they were plagued by severe injuries and, worse, the murder of their sister and the death of their grandmother. They were able to recuperate mentally and physically to attend the trials for the 2000 Olympics in Sydney, Australia. This time they both made the team and, together with Michael Johnson and Antonio Pettigrew, won the gold medal in the the four-by-four hundred meter relay. Full of optimism, they see nothing but opportunity for themselves in the world of track and field.

247. Hart, Elva Treviño. *Barefoot Heart: Stories of a Migrant Child.* Tempe, Arizona: Bilingual Press/Editorial Bilingüe, 1999. 236 pages. ISBN: 0927534819.

Abstract: Elva Treviño Hart writes in anecdotal form about her life as a poor Mexican-American child in a family of migrant workers. Born the sixth child seven years after her closest brother in a family of otherwise-closely spaced children, she had a somewhat lonely childhood. The family lived in Pearsall, Texas, in an almost-entirely Mexican environment, and they spent many summers toiling in the beet fields of Minnesota. Hart spent these summer days in the family car feeling left out and waiting to be signaled to bring water at break time because she was too young to work. Her father insisted that all of his children graduate from high school, and as the siblings grew up and moved out, they sent for Elva to spend her vacations with them in Minnesota, Wisconsin, and New York. She excelled at her studies, even though she only qualified for the award of "High Point Mexican Girl" and her mother considered her love of reading suspicious. Hart became the first person in her family to go to college. She got a job with IBM, complete with a high salary and corporate jet at her disposal. After years of therapy in which she dealt with her belief that she was a "useless child," she began to write down stories of her past and came to terms with her father before he died. She concludes: "I saw how much power there is in embracing exactly who you are. For me it is being a Mexican American writer. I am no longer alone; I have found my pack" (p. 236).

248. Haskins, Clem. *Clem Haskins: Breaking Barriers*. Written with Marc Ryan. Champaign, Illinois: Ports Publishing, Inc., 1997. 238 pages; photographs. ISBN: 1571671439.

Abstract: Clem Haskins is a man who has quietly accomplished many firsts. He was born in 1943 into a farming family in Kentucky, the fifth of eleven children. He describes his mother as the glue in the family and his father as the hero. He showed promise as a basketball player early in junior high school, and his coach urged him to attend Taylor County High School. This meant breaking the color line. It took him twenty-eight days to get up the nerve to even enter the school building. When he finally got through the doors, however, he found he had very little trouble with the students or the majority of teachers. He found his teammates exceptionally supportive and still counts some of them among his friends. Haskins went on to be one of the two first African Americans to attend Western Kentucky University. Although he found his classmates and most of his professors to be supportive, the town was not, and the fans of the visiting teams were viciously abusive. Haskins dreamed of a professional basketball career, but he was taken by surprise when he was the first round pick of the Chicago Bulls. Haskins's career also took him to Phoenix to play with the Suns, and then to Washington to finish his nine years as a professional with the Bullets. After retirement, Haskins pursued a coaching career. When he became Western Kentucky's first African-American head basketball coach, he also became Kentucky's first black head coach at a Division I school. His coaching career took him to the University of Minnesota to become the head coach of its struggling basketball team. Haskins took the team to the NCAA championship finals. The Gophers were designated the number one seeded team that year after having been left out of the competition of sixty-four schools all together during the previous two years. Haskins has much to say about collegiate and professional basketball and basketball players. He also writes about the importance of family and his dedication to his wife and children.

249. Havens, Richie. *They Can't Hide Us Anymore*. Written with Steve Davidowitz. Foreword by James Earl Jones. New York, New York: Spike, 1999. 331 pages; photographs; drawings. ISBN: 0380977184.

Abstract: Richie Havens grew up in the Bedford-Stuyvesant neighborhood of Brooklyn, New York. An artist and poet as well as a singer, Havens started his work career as a street portrait artist in Greenwich Village. He began visiting various clubs and cafes there, reading his poetry and listening to the poetry of others. As the poetry scene drifted into the folk scene, Havens taught himself guitar, using his own unique system, which he describes in the book, and began singing. Folk music attracted a large audience, and Havens was "discovered" and signed to a recording contract. He remembers significant events in his career, such as being the opening act at the original Woodstock Festival, performing in Israel live for both Israeli and Egyptian television at the invitation of both countries, meeting Paul McCartney and John Lennon, and singing one of Bob Dylan's songs (thinking it was written by someone else) with Dylan in the audience. Havens talks about the difficulties of fame, the ins and outs of the recording business, and the dark side of the entertainment industry. An unfailingly positive person who is passionately involved with music and art, Havens also found time to participate in the founding of two important environmental organizations aimed at teaching young people about their world: the Natural Guard, centered in New Haven, Connecticut, and the North Wind Undersea Institute, located in the Bronx in New York City.

250. Hawaii Nikkei History Editorial Board. *Japanese Eyes, American Heart: Personal Reflections of Hawaii's World War II Nisei Soldiers*. Honolulu, Hawai'i: Tendai Educational Foundation, 1998. 448 pages; photographs. ISBN: 0824821629 : 0824821440.

Abstract: This book was inspired by the success of a similar book commissioned by Bishop Reverend Ryokan Ara and published in

Japanese by the Japanese publisher Heibonsha. The translated title of the book is *Hawaii's Japanese American Soldiers: For What Did We Fight?* The purpose of the Japanese-language book was to help the Japanese people have a better understanding of the United States and its people, especially U.S. citizens of Japanese ancestry. The present work consists of sixty-two essays in thirteen sections by fifty-two second-generation Japanese Americans who served in the U.S. military during World War II. Each essay is accompanied by one current and one war-time photograph of the author. The essays provide insight into what Hawai'i's Japanese American veterans felt about their war-time experiences and the fight for equality that they faced upon their return home. The subjects also provide a few details about their families and childhoods. The first chapters in this book describe each of the four divisions in the U.S. military to which the Japanese-American soldiers were assigned. It concludes with a list of the members of those divisions, both Japanese American and otherwise, who died during the conflict. The thirteen sections are as follows:

> "Hawaii's Nisei Soldiers: Who Were They?" "December 7, 1941: A Morning that Changed Our Lives Forever," "Boys to Men," "Our Place in the Sun," "Oya no ai: The Love of a Parent," "An Ocean Away," "From the Front Lines," "We Are Our Brothers' Keeper," "Coming to Terms," "Taking Ownership," "Building Bridges," "Let There Be Peace on Earth," "Epilogue."

251. Hawkins, Tiny. *Strong Family Ties: The Tiny Hawkins Story.* As told to Debra L. Winegarten and Ruthe Winegarten. Austin, Texas: SocialSights Press, 1998. 98 pages; photographs. ISBN: 0961034092.

> **Abstract:** Tiny Hawkins grew up in a rural Texas community. Her grandmother was born a slave and lived to be 104. Her father was a minister. When he died, he gave Tiny, the ninth of twelve children, the responsibility of keeping the family together; a charge she took to heart. Tiny writes, "over the period of some 40-odd years since his death, I have tried to keep them together—the aunts and uncles, the brothers and sisters and nieces and nephews, the kids and the grandkids. I've tried to keep a strong family relationship" (p. 15). Tiny did not like picking cotton on the family farm, and this hardened her resolve to attend school and work in some other occupation. She went to beauty school and eventually opened her own beauty shop in her kitchen. While working as a beautician and cleaning houses, she attended college

night classes for fifteen years before earning her B.A. degree. As her own children began school, Tiny worked as a substitute teacher. She also worked part time as the activity director at a nursing home, where her hard work led to a series of promotions. She finally bought the nursing home, and became the first African American to own and operate a nursing home in Texas. Tiny continued her schooling and received a Doctorate of Business Administration from Pacific Western University in Los Angeles in 1988. She then attended the Southern Baptist Bible Institute from 1992 to 1995. She has received many honors throughout her life, including the Negro Achievement Award from the *National Negro Magazine* in 1952 and the "Mother of the Year" award from her children's high school in 1963. She helped found, and was the third president of, the Oak Cliff Branch of the National Council of Negro Women, receiving that organization's "Salute to Black Women Who Make It Happen" award in 1985. Tiny Hawkins never accepted discriminatory treatment, never took "no" for an answer if she judged it out of order, and accomplished whatever she set out to do. The book also includes contributions from Tiny's siblings, children, pastors, and associates.

252. Hayes, Diana L. *Trouble Don't Last Always: Soul Prayers.* A Liturgical Press Book. Collegeville, Minnesota: The Liturgical Press, 1995. 72 pages. ISBN: 0814622976.

Abstract: Diana L. Hayes was Assistant Professor of Theology at Georgetown University at the time she published this book. Hayes practiced law in Albany, New York for a number of years. Her life changed dramatically when she converted to Roman Catholicism. She completed the pontifical program in theology as well as a Ph.D. in religious studies at the Catholic University of America and a Doctor of Sacred Theology degree from the Catholic University of Louvain, Belgium. As she neared the completion of her studies, Hayes was stricken with chondromallatia, or rheumatoid arthritis. Her book delineates her struggle with pain and illness and her sudden transformation from an athletic and physically active person to a bedridden invalid. She feels that her battle with chronic illness has helped her to identify more closely with all oppressed people, especially those oppressed by poverty, racism, and sexism. In her introduction, Hayes writes,

> I believe I have learned, because of my own
> struggles, how to see, hear, and feel the struggles
> of others voiced and unvoiced. . . . I firmly
> believe that I have been sent to be of service to

> those, who unlike myself, have not yet found
> their voices and been awakened to the graced
> but burdensome knowledge that, as children of a
> loving God, they are sent not to suffer, but to live
> a life free from oppression.   (p. 6)

Hayes presents a collection of short inspirational meditations that focus on her struggle and the faith that helps her to continue her work and activities.

253. Hayre, Ruth Wright (1910-). *Tell Them We Are Rising: A Memoir of Faith in Education*. Written with Alexis Moore. Foreword by Ed Bradley. New York, New York: John Wiley & Sons. 206 pages; photographs; index. ISBN: 0471126799 : 0471327220.

Abstract: Ruth Wright Hayre, a retired educator, is the grand-daughter of Richard Robert Wright. He was born into slavery, freed as a young boy, and went to school in a so-called freedom school in an abandoned boxcar. When a patron of the school, General Oliver Otis Howard, a Union army officer for whom Howard University was named, visited the school, he asked the students "Now, what message shall I take back North?" (p. 9). Wright responded, "Sir, tell them we are rising" (p. 9). The general took the message North where the poet John Greenleaf Whittier included it in his poem "General O. O. Howard at Atlanta." Hayre received her Ph.D. from the University of Philadelphia. She was an educator her entire working career, becoming the first black senior high school principal in Philadelphia in 1956. After her retirement and the death of her husband from Alzheimer's disease, she conceived the idea of the "Tell Them We Are Rising Program," a plan to follow two classes of sixth grade graduates through middle school and high school and then pay their tuition for up to four years of college education. The program was launched in 1988, when Hayre was seventy-seven. The two classes of black children, from two Philadelphia inner-city elementary schools, numbered 116 students. In the following six years, Hayre and a group of over 100 mentors followed the students, befriending and counseling them, always encouraging them to graduate from high school and go on to college. Hayre talks about the program, its activities, the numerous difficulties faced by the children, known collectively as Risers, in terms of their economic background, parental circumstances, peer pressure, and motivation. She also tells the stories of several of the individual students, both the successes and failures. One major problem was unplanned pregnancy. Twenty-two of 56 girls had babies between seventh

and twelfth grades. Thirty-nine of the original 116 finished high
school in 1994, with another 20 or so due to graduate the next year.
In summary, Hayre finds it difficult to explain why some students
were able to succeed and others were not, but states emphatically
that the effort was worth it to her and to all other parties involved.

254. Heard, William H. (1850-1937). *From Slavery to the Bishopric in
the A.M.E. Church: An Autobiography*. Chapel Hill, North
Carolina: Academic Affairs Library, University of North
Carolina at Chapel Hill, 2000.

> http://docsouth.unc.edu/neh/heard/heard.sgml
> http://docsouth.unc.edu/neh/heard/heard.html

> **Notes:** Documenting the American South (Project).
> Includes the poem: "The Life of William H. Heard" by Ephraim D.
> Taylor.

255. Heath, Gordon. *Deep Are the Roots: Memoirs of a Black
Expatriate*. Introduction by Doris Abramson. Amherst, Massachusetts: University of Massachusetts Press, 1992. 200 pages;
illustrations; photographs; maps. ISBN: 0870237780.

> **Abstract:** Multitalented Gordon Heath was born in New York in
> 1918. His father was from Barbados and his mother was "a sec-
> ond-generation American with African and Indian bloodlines" (p.
> 10). Heath's mother was devoted to him, an only child. His father
> had many faults as a husband and was very strict, but he provid-
> ed a stable and secure home life. Both gay and African American,
> Heath describes instances of discrimination and violence during a
> mostly peaceful youth. He grew up with a sense of self-esteem
> and self-assurance. His acquaintance with Owen Dodson inspired
> Heath to go into theater. Dodson became a celebrated director and
> playwright as well as a mentor and life-long friend to Heath.
> Heath describes how he was encouraged by his high school librar-
> ian to read the great works of theater, his employment with the
> National Youth Administration during the Great Depression, and
> his work with several small college and off-Broadway theater
> groups. In 1945 he appeared in *Deep Are the Roots*, by James Gow
> and Arnold D'Usseau and directed by Elia Kazan. This play, about
> an African-American soldier returning to the South after serving
> in World War II, featured both black and white actors and actress-
> es. It opened in the United States and played successfully on
> Broadway. Heath's career as an actor was set when he stayed with
> the play upon its move to London. Heath briefly returned to the

United States following his success in England, but shortly thereafter moved to Paris, where he lived the rest of his life. In Paris,
Heath opened a small club with his life partner and fellow actor
and singer, Lee Payant. He continued to act in Paris and London.
Once he played Othello for BBC National Television. He occasionally returned to act in the United States as well. Heath talks
about his friends and mentors. He discusses the theater in the
United States and abroad. Heath died in 1991. In his final para-
graph, "Doxology," he writes, "I'm sorry I have no public image for
this generation to rub this memoir up against—like sandpaper
used for wrapping. I am not so deep as a well and I haven't flown
so high. What I was and what I did that I cannot recollect will be
interred with my bones. . . . I have loved life: it's been—interesting" (p. 169).

256. Henri, Alex W. *Ain't No Mountain Too High.* Philadelphia,
Pennsylvania: Xlibris. 310 pages. ISBN: 0738833312 :
0738833320.

257. Henry, Aaron. *Aaron Henry: The Fire Ever Burning.* Written
with Constance Curry. Introduction by John Dittmer.
Margaret Walker Alexander Series in African American
Studies. Jackson, Mississippi: University of Mississippi Press,
2000. 263 pages; photographs. ISBN: 1578062128.

Abstract: Aaron Henry grew up in Clarksdale, Mississippi on the
Flowers brothers' plantation. He was orphaned at the age of five
and taken in by his maternal uncle and aunt, whom he considered
to be his mother and father. He describes the life of sharecroppers,
his utter distaste for picking cotton, and the futility of sharecroppers improving their conditions. Henry writes, "The owners were
dealing with people whom they felt were subhuman, and they felt
no moral obligation for fairness in the treatment of their tenants"
(p. 9). Henry's family finally left the plantation and moved into
town. In 1941, following his graduation from high school, Henry
became night manager and bell boy at a local white-run motel.
This is where he first began to make friends and enemies among
white people. Henry returned to school and earned a degree and
became a licensed pharmacist. He entered partnership with a
white drugstore owner and simultaneously became active in the
NAACP. He protested murders and unjust arrests by the police
and began to pursue voters' rights. Henry was active in the
Regional Council of Negro Leadership (RCNL) which was formed
to press for African-American economic development. They later

formed a committee to campaign for the "equal" clause in the "separate but equal" law which had grown out of the 1896 *Plessy v.
Ferguson* U.S. Supreme Court decision. RCNL also worked on
issues related to voter registration. Following the 1954 *Brown v.
Board of Education* decision, Henry took part in the growing movement to dismantle the institution of segregation. He worked with
the Congress of Racial Equality, Student Nonviolent Coordinating
Committee, NAACP, and Southern Christian Leadership
Conference. He was instrumental in establishing the Council of
Federated Organizations. Henry was arrested a number of times
under false pretences, suffered through the murder of and attacks
on many of his coactivists, and had his home fire-bombed. He
concludes his story with his account of the formation of the
Mississippi Freedom Democratic Party and its attempt to represent Mississippi on the floor of the 1964 Democratic convention.
Constance Curry, who assisted Henry in writing his autobiography, includes anecdotes about him provided by fellow civil rights
workers, colleagues, and family members.

258. Henry, George (b. 1819). *Life of George Henry Together with a
Brief History of the Colored People in America.* Chapel Hill, North
Carolina: Academic Affairs Library, University of North
Carolina at Chapel Hill, 2000.

> http://docsouth.unc.edu/neh/henryg/henryg.sgml
> http://docsouth.unc.edu/neh/henryg/henryg.html

> **Notes:** Documenting the American South (Project).

259. Henry, Nathaniel J. *Never Anything Too Easy: N.A.T.E.: An
Autobiography.* Chicago, Illinois: NNSJA Publishing, 2000. 110
pages; photographs. ISBN: 0967058457.

> **Abstract:** Henry was born in 1970. His mother died when he was
> five years old, leaving his father distraught. He sent the children
> to live temporarily with their maternal grandparents and eventu-
> ally lost custody of them altogether. The children were split up,
> and Henry was sent to Chicago's Department of Children and
> Family Services (DCFS) to become a ward of the court. Henry
> lived in group homes until he was twelve, when his father was
> able to regain custody. In less than a year, however, Henry was
> returned to DCFS after being sexually abused by an uncle. He
> describes a program that did not encourage or nurture children,
> instead keeping them depressed and isolated. Henry was allowed
> to attend Kenwood Academy High School for two years. During

that time he tried to hold down a job, maintain a good grade point average, and run track. Despite the fact that he was managing well enough, he was removed from the school by DCFS and sent to Lawrence Hall, a reform school. There, completely despondent, Henry heard his first words of encouragement from a DCFS staff member. This was enough to motivate him to pursue his interests and goals, and he was soon allowed to take part in the Independent Living Program. After graduating, Henry was finally on his own. In the next phase of his life, he married a fifteen-year-old girl, and the couple had five children over the next eight years. While raising a family, Henry and his wife both graduated from junior college and transferred to universities. Henry attended Northeastern Illinois University, where he majored in psychology and communications and played basketball. He admits to making mistakes as a father and husband, but he was devoted to his family and was taken off guard when his wife suddenly left him, taking all five children. It was months before Henry was able to visit or spend any time with his children. He got a job in child care at the Lydia Children's Home, where he was gratified to participate in a program in which children were able to have positive, nurturing experiences. His goal is to earn a master's degree in speech as well as in social work. He works as a motivational speaker and has established the publishing company, NNSJA.

260. Henson, Father Josiah (1789-1883). *The Life of Josiah Henson, Formerly a Slave, Now an Inhabitant of Canada.* Chapel Hill, North Carolina: Academic Affairs Library, University of North Carolina at Chapel Hill, 2000.

> http://docsouth.unc.edu/neh/henson58/henson58.sgml
> http://docsouth.unc.edu/neh/henson58/henson58.html
>
> **Notes:** Documenting the American South (Project).

261. Henson, Matthew Alexander (1866-1955). *A Negro Explorer at the North Pole.* Introduction by Robert Cummings. Original foreword by Robert E. Peary. Original introduction by Booker T. Washington. Heritage Series, 6. Grand Rapids, Michigan: Candace Press, 1996. 147 pages; illustrations; photographs. ISBN: 1889073091.

> **Notes:** Originally published New York: Frederick A. Stokes, 1912; Lincoln, Nebraska: University of Nebraska Press, 1989. ISBN: 0803272456.

262. Hernández, Roberto. *Why We Are Still Here*. Miami, Florida: Editorial Interamericana Publishing, Inc., 1997. 88 pages; map. ISBN: 0964150662.

Abstract: The Hernández family arrived in the United States from Cuba as political refugees in 1967. Because the Cuban government confiscates all property and belongings when anyone leaves the country, the family arrived penniless. They were sponsored by the Broadway Methodist Church in Salem, New Jersey, and church members helped them get settled, find jobs and an apartment, and establish credit. From Salem, the family moved to Vineland, New Jersey. Roberto Hernández was a worker in a glass factory, a teacher and guidance counselor, and finally an ordained Presbyterian Minister. Mary Hernández, his wife, has worked as a teacher and a vice principal in the public schools. Hernández points out that even though Cuban immigrants arrive with nothing, the Cuban community is among the most prosperous in the United States. He contrasts the upward progress of the Cuban Americans with stories of what Cuba was like before and after Castro. He also discusses his youth in Cuba. In 1959, Hernández had been an ardent Castro supporter. He traveled to the United States to speak at different youth camps about the revolution. By the time he returned to Cuba everything had begun to change, and it was becoming clear that Castro would put together a Communist government. Hernández discusses the reasons why the United States may have chosen not to invade Cuba to overthrow the Communist government and his feelings about that lost possibility.

263. Herrera, Juan Felipe. *Mayan Drifter: Chicano Poet in the Lowlands of America*. Philadelphia, Pennsylvania: Temple University Press, 1997. 272 pages; photographs; glossary. ISBN: 1566394813 : 1566394821.

Notes: This work includes the play *Jaguar Hotel* and the long poem "Anahuak Vortex (Mexico City 1995)."

Abstract: Poet Juan Felipe Herrera felt driven to investigate his history in 1986 after the death of his mother from pneumonia. Having visited the land of his ancestors, the Lacandón Mayan village of Nahá in Chiapas, Mexico, in 1970, he chose to revisit the area in 1992 to gain a deeper understanding of the people, the culture, the changes they had faced in the intervening twenty-three years, and the future they were likely to confront. Herrera intended to take notes and pictures and record stories, legends, and the language, but he abandoned these plans after reaching the village, realizing the perhaps well-intentioned motivation of foreign anthropologists and ethnographers have lead to the despoliation of the Mayan environment and their way of life. Herrera, clearly an outsider, leaves offerings from Western civilization and takes away with him more questions and fewer answers than he might have hoped for when he set out.

264. Hilden, Patricia Penn. *When Nickels Were Indians: An Urban Mixed-Blood Story.* Illustrated by Anne-Marie Hamilton. Smithsonian Series of Studies in Native American Literatures. Washington, D.C.: Smithsonian Institution Press, 1995. 259 pages; photographs; drawings. ISBN: 1560986018.

Abstract: Patricia Hilden provides an interpretation of Indian history as presented by anthropologists, historians, and popular culture. She combines scholarly analysis with personal reaction and her own experiences as a fair-skinned, blue-eyed, mixed-blood Indian. Descended from the Nez Perce tribe, Wallowa Band, and possibly from the Osage tribe as well, Hilden's closest connection to Native American culture was her paternal grandfather. Hilden's mother, of European descent, was careful to instill in her children an awareness and appreciation of their Nez Perce background, more so than their father. Hilden became active in Indian issues while attending college. She spent close to eighteen years working with the War on Poverty and the Equal Opportunity Program. She also taught in the public school system, at the University of California at Davis, and in Davis's Upward Bound Program. Hilden discusses her own internal conflict and discomfort with claiming her Indian background and fits this into a discussion of "identity police," blood quantum debates, "wannabes," fakes, and true and faux Indian spirituality. She ends her book with a long letter to a friend who, like Hilden, is a mixed-blood Indian, but unlike Hilden, "looks" Indian. She compares his advantages of visually fitting into the Indian community, with hers of being able to be in both the white and the Indian world, but in neither comfortably or fully. Hilden also discusses issues of gender within the context of race and ethnicity and traditional Native cultures.

265. Hill, Anderson C. *In Search of the Truth: A Real Life Story about What an Attorney Should "NOT" Do!* Orlando, Florida: Prime Time Publishers, 1997.   310 pages; photographs; facsimiles. ISBN: 0965862879.

Abstract: Anderson C. Hill was a lawyer involved in illegal activities. He was a chronic user of cocaine and alcohol, and he was addicted to money, expensive cars, and an expensive lifestyle. Hill had humble beginnings in Little Rock, Arkansas. Interested only in sports and partying, he did not intend to go to college. His mother and older sister, however, forced him to. He first enrolled at Langston University, then the University of Oklahoma, and subsequently Clark College in Atlanta. He majored in accounting and eventually began working at Bethune-Cook College. Earning a law degree, he worked his way to the top administrative levels at the college. By this time, Hill had, in addition to his work at the college, a number of financial ventures and a private law practice. When a major investment began to fail, he realized that he was in financial trouble. Trying to recoup his losses, he became involved with a dishonest developer, and, although he did not realize the extent of the developer's dealings, he voluntarily participated in unethical behavior, such as kickbacks, fraudulent loans, and conflicts of interest. He involved not only himself but forged signatures which assigned financial responsibility to the college for some of the loans. Facing bankruptcy and finally removed from his position at the college, Hill began backing out of his questionable business relationships. Nonetheless, he was guilty of a variety of serious crimes and began cooperating with the FBI in their investigation of his former business partner, the developer. In exchange, he received some immunity and reduced charges. At the end of it all, Hill was convicted of a felony and sentenced to ten months in federal prison. He describes his time in prison and his determination to reform. His family stood by him through everything, and, as he writes this book, he is attempting to be readmitted to the Florida bar.

266. Hill, Grant. *Change the Game: One Athlete's Thoughts on Sports, Dreams, and Growing Up.* New York, New York: Warner Books, 1996. 134 pages; photographs. ISBN: 0446520411 : 0446672629.

Abstract: In this book, 1994-1995 NBA Rookie of the Year Grant Hill writes about his upbringing and how he views his life after his first year as a professional basketball player with the Detroit Pistons. Hill was born into an upper-class black family, the only child of Janet and Calvin Hill. His mother was a Wellesley College graduate from a well-to-do family and his father was a professional football player. Grant writes about his mother's strictness, about how he felt as a child having a famous father, and about his youth and adolescence. Colleges began recruiting him when he was still a high school freshman, and he eventually decided to go to Duke University, where he excelled as a student and athlete. After graduation he was drafted by the Detroit Pistons. Although he was chosen as co-Rookie of the Year and as a member of the All Star team, Hill's team had a disastrous season, and the book ends as he looks forward to a better record in 1995-1996. Hill writes about the necessity of having attainable goals as well as dreams. He is honest about the slim chances of making it as a professional athlete. He encourages young people to always have a back-up plan. He also discusses how sex and substance abuse can put a quick end to any sort of dream. He talks about what it feels like to be well known and about how he wants to use his celebrity to have a positive influence on society.

> Potentially I can be a leader, and I would like to be someone that kids can look to as a man of principle and example: a public figure. I look at it like, "Who wouldn't want that?" Not everyone gets this opportunity. There is responsibility, and pressure, but there's also a power to change or improve people's lives. I want that burden.
>
> (p. 109)

267. Hill, Oliver W. (1907-). *The Big Bang: Brown vs. Board of Education and Beyond: The Autobiography of Oliver W. Hill, Sr.* Edited by Jonathan K. Stubbs. Winter Park, Florida: Four-G Publishers, 2000. 376 pages; photographs. ISBN: 1885066791 : 1885066627.

Abstract: Civil rights lawyer and Presidential Medal of Freedom recipient Oliver Hill, Sr. describes the social, recreational, and institutional aspects of growing up in Richmond, Virginia, at the beginning of the twentieth century. Hill writes that segregation was stringent and that he had few contacts with white people as a child: "I was fortunate in that respect. At an early point in my development I concluded that for white people to get a job at anything that brought them into contact with the public, a major prerequisite was to have a nasty attitude towards Negroes" (p. 1). Hill began working when he was nine years old. As an adult, he worked as a waiter. His parents and most of the adults he knew had jobs in service, and they all encouraged him to pursue his education so he could go into another line of work. Hill attended Howard University and then entered its law school, which at the time was a part-time evening program. By the time he graduated in 1933, however, it had developed into a full-time day program and received full accreditation. Howard's mission to train African-American lawyers to "properly prepare cases and develop adequate records for achieving success in the Supreme Court" (p. 76) matched Hill's goals perfectly. He passed the Virginia bar exam in 1934 and started his law practice in Richmond. Hill was well versed in the legal treatment of African Americans, particularly the difficulty in obtaining fair trials and the arbitrary behavior to which law-enforcement officials subjected them. His detailed knowledge of both the constitutions of Virginia and the United States served him well in challenging illegal and unfair courtroom procedure. Hill started out by representing defendants in rape trials, later taking on an African-American teacher salary equity case, issues of school equality, and the segregated public transportation system. Hill was on the legal team that took *Brown v. Board of Education* to the Supreme Court. He describes his legal work, including his contributions in challenging the constitutionality of the "separate but equal" doctrine and the even more difficult task of enforcing the Supreme Court decision in *Brown*. Hill worked in voter registration and equal employment opportunity issues. He was an active politician at the local level and ran for the House of Delegates as well as city council. He provides his views of the presidents he has observed and worked under, describing their varying contributions to matters of civil rights. Hill sees human relationships and the advancement of African Americans as an evolutionary process. His advice to those who fight to preserve racial segregation or gender inequity is to see that change is coming and inevitable: "It doesn't make any difference what you do, creation is still evolving. Therefore, we have to constantly look at all institutions that affect the human being and try to see how we can improve conditions for the commonweal" (p. 340).

268. Him, Chanrithy. *When Broken Glass Floats: Growing Up under the Khmer Rouge: A Memoir.* New York, New York: W. W. Norton & Company, 2000. 330 pages; photographs; map. ISBN: 0393048632.

Abstract: At the time the Khmer Rouge gained control of Cambodia, Chanrithy Him's family numbered eleven. By the time the Khmer Rouge lost power to the invading Vietnamese, there were only five. Him's once-prosperous family avoided the early years of civil conflict by escaping to Phnom Penh, but when the

Khmer Rouge seized the city, all citizens were forced to evacuate. The family returned to their father's native village, but soon the father and his brothers were taken away and killed. The rest of Him's family survived due to timely advice given to their mother. Throughout the years of Khmer Rouge rule, the family was scattered among a number of work camps. Despite the chaos, they managed to keep track of each other, and the children would periodically make it back to their mother and youngest brother. For the most part, the family existed in a state of starvation and over work. There was no medicine for the many bouts of malaria, infection and dysentery to which three siblings and their mother eventually succumbed. Informers in camps kept careful watch of all activities, but there were also kind persons who provided food, water, and medicine or who permitted leave from one work camp to visit a sick sibling or mother in another. Kindness was offered with the knowledge that if discovered it would lead to punishment and perhaps death. The surviving members of the family were liberated when the Vietnamese advanced far enough into the country to free the work camps. Him describes their travels to and time in a series of refugee camps, the discovery of an uncle living in Portland, Oregon, and the endless paperwork preparing for their departure for the United States. She ends her story as the five surviving family members and an older sister's husband and adopted daughter leave the Philippines for the United States.

269. Himes, Chester B. (b. 1909). *The Quality of Hurt: The Autobiography of Chester Himes*. New York, New York: Thunder's Mouth Press, 1998. 351 pages. ISBN: 1560250933.

> **Notes:** Originally published Garden City, New York: Doubleday, 1972 in two volumes: *The Quality of Hurt* and *My Life of Absurdity*.

270. Hinojosa, Maria. *Raising Raul: Adventures Raising Myself and My Son*. New York, New York: Viking, 1999. 240 pages. ISBN: 0670884456.

> **Notes:** Also published in paperback New York: Penguin, 2000. ISBN: 0140296360.

> **Abstract:** Maria Hinojosa, an urban affairs associate for CNN, tells the story of her marriage and her difficulties conceiving a child. Using a mixture of English and Spanish, she discusses two miscarriages, her eventual successful pregnancy, her son's birth, and the decisions about working and motherhood that she faced. As a part of her story, she describes the elements of the different

cultures from which she sought answers. Hinojosa also writes about her mother, a traditional Mexican wife, who emigrated with her doctor husband to the United States. Hinojosa grew up as a Mexican child in Chicago, though the family made frequent visits to Mexico. She and her family always felt more at home in Mexico, but also sensed the way their ideas of raising children, keeping house, growing up, working, etc., were creating a distance between themselves and their relatives. Conflicts about the notion of what a Mexican wife and mother should be have followed Hinojosa throughout adulthood and have affected all of her decisions. Her husband, German, is an "Afro-Taino" from the Dominican Republic. The two lived in New York City and faced the decision of whether to stay in their ethnically diverse neighborhood or move somewhere safer. Extended trips to her husband's homeland also added to Hinajosa's questions about life and child-rearing. The greatest challenge Hinojosa eventually faced was that her job as a television correspondent kept her away from home, sometimes for days at a time. She found that her son, Raul Ariel, was becoming closer to his father than to her. Hinajosa's vision of being the perfect Mexican mother has continually conflicted with her desire to succeed in her chosen profession.

271. Holdsclaw, Chamique. *Chamique on Family, Focus, and Basketball.* Written with Jennifer Frey. New York, New York: Scribner, 2000. 189 pages; photographs. ISBN: 0743202201.

Notes: Published in paperback New York: Simon & Schuster, 2001. ISBN: 0743212703.

Abstract: Chamique Holdsclaw, a member of the Washington Mystics basketball team, writes about her life. Because both of her parents had serious problems, including excessive drinking, Holdsclaw took responsibility for raising her younger brother. After her father started a fire in their New York apartment and her mother came home drunk, she and her brother were placed in the custody of her grandmother. Although her brother eventually returned to their mother, her grandmother refused to relinquish custody of Holdsclaw, and enrolled her in a private grammar school to assure that she got the discipline and structure her life required. In the Astoria housing project, Holdsclaw played basketball on the public courts with the boys, always doing at least as well and usually better than they did. Her school basketball coach contacted the coach at Christ the King High School, which had a championship basketball team. The coach came to watch her play and recognized her talent immediately. Christ the King emphasized academics as well as sports, and Holdsclaw thrived there, taking her team to national championships. Actively recruited by over 150 colleges and universities, she chose the University of Tennessee at Knoxville and led the team to three consecutive NCAA championships. After graduation from college, she was drafted by the Washington Mystics, a team in the Women's National Basketball League. During her first year, the team was not successful, and at the end of the book Holdsclaw is anticipating her second year, and participation in the 2000 Olympic Games in Sydney. She discusses what being famous means in terms of her personal life, her relationships with friends, family, and coaches who have supported her, and the amount of hard work and determination required to have achieved what she has.

272. Holland, Endesha Ida Mae (1944-). *From the Mississippi Delta: A Memoir.* New York, New York: Simon & Schuster, 1997. 318 pages; photographs. ISBN: 0684810115.

Notes: Also published Chicago: Lawrence Hill Books, 1999. ISBN: 1556523416.

Abstract: Endesha Ida Mae Holland, a professor at the University of Southern California's School of Theatre as well as the Program of the Study of Women and Men in Society, writes about her upbringing in the 1950s and 1960s in the town of Greenwood, Mississippi. Holland describes life in the Delta town and tells her own story: She was raped by a white man at the age of eleven, was a chronic truant from school, and became a part-time prostitute, a circus performer, and a striptease dancer. Her life changed when she participated in the Civil Rights Movement of the 1960s, helping to enroll black voters in her town. Activists from the North were impressed with her abilities, and she became determined to continue her education. She writes about the initial affects of the Civil Rights Movement, in particular the Freedom Riders and the Student Nonviolent Coordinating Committee (SNCC), on the black populace of the Deep South. Because some blacks felt that a segregated society was the only way they would be left in peace by whites, they were initially opposed to change. They knew that any attempt at adjusting the balance between the races would only draw white wrath, which was much more concrete to blacks than the seemingly absurd notion of equal rights and voting privileges. They also believed that the Freedom Riders from the North would not stay to protect them if white retribution began in earnest. A shift in attitude began when local whites stopped distributing surplus food from the U.S. government to blacks, who were then forced to line up at SNCC headquarters to receive food. In the rush to distribute food and register people to vote, Holland was hired to work in the SNCC office because she could read and write. This was when her own participation in the movement began in earnest. Later, as a Ph.D. candidate at the University of Minnesota, she took a class in acting and wrote two plays about her mother, *Second Doctor Lady* and *The Reconstruction of Dossie Ree Hemphill*. The latter received the National Lorraine Hansberry Award in 1981.

273. Holliday, Laurel. *See* entry at *Children of the Dream*.

274. Holly, Ellen. *One Life: the Autobiography of an African American Actress*. New York, New York: Kodansha International, 1996. 274 pages. ISBN: 1568361580.

Notes: Published in paperback in 1998. ISBN: 1568361971.

Abstract: Ellen Holly was raised in a middle-class black family. She is descended from one of the first black female physicians in the United States. Her mother was a housewife and her father was a chemical engineer. As a college student, Holly became interested in theater and began her career as an actress in the 1950s. No matter how well she was received by reviewers and audiences, she never earned the success predicted for her, primarily due to the limited number of roles for African Americans in the television and film industry. When the occasional role came along, Holly was usually rejected for being too light-skinned. She played in New York Shakespeare Festival productions for many years and acted in a number of Broadway and Off-Broadway plays. None of these, however, had lengthy runs, and she would be out of work again in short order. Holly found a niche for herself in daytime television; for seventeen years she acted the part of Carla Benari in the daytime drama *One Life to Live*. The original story included several ethnic families and quickly drew a large African-American following. During her years on the show, however, she discovered that ABC knew the dearth of jobs available to African Americans and paid its African-American actors at a level far below that of its white actors. Holly had hoped that "the soaps" would be a step to greater success and recognition, but she was not able to go on to better-paying and more visible roles in either television or films. In 1985, she was summarily fired from the program and the roles for African-Americans and other ethnic groups were completely eliminated from the story line. Holly writes further of the discrimination she uncovered and the ways she tried to fight back.

She also describes her personal life, her fight with alcoholism, her sadness at never having children, and her lifelong passion for Harry Belafonte.

275. Holmes, Larry. *Larry Holmes: Against the Odds.* Written with Phil Berger. New York, New York: St. Martin's Press, 1998. 282 pages; photographs. ISBN: 031218736x.

Abstract: Boxer Larry Holmes was born in Georgia in 1950. His family moved to Philadelphia when he was six, and his father abandoned them shortly after, leaving his mother to raise twelve children alone in impoverished conditions. Holmes describes himself as an indifferent student. He dropped out of high school and was already on his own at sixteen when he moved in with an older woman and became the father of two children in a short period of time. Holmes was about nineteen when he started to take an interest in boxing. He began competing at age twenty, and turned professional when he did not make the cut for the 1976 Olympics. In describing his career, Holmes documents a professional world where the boxer is a pawn for the promoter. Millions of dollars exchange hands, but only a few lucky boxers get any major financial rewards. Holmes worked hard to be taken on by the notorious promoter Don King, whom he describes as the "ultimate user/abuser": "It was on the likelihood of his making me a player in this game that I had signed with one of Don's corporations, Sportsville, only to discover much later how the contract was full of three-year options that tied me to King for damn near ever" (p. 45). Holmes goes on to recite a litany of talented boxers who missed their chance through bad luck, bad management, serious injury, and alcohol or drug abuse. "Boxing had always been a business where rascals running things took advantage of the fighters. Short changed them, sometimes worse—sometimes forced them to participate in fixed fights" (p. 178). Holmes fought his way to become the heavyweight champion of the world and hung on to his title for over five years. He found it difficult to get out of the sport, hanging up his gloves temporarily, but still fighting and winning matches into the late 1990s as he neared the age of fifty. Holmes was strongly influenced by the poverty of his childhood and was always careful to make good use of his earnings. He bought a house for his mother with his first big win. Raised without a father, Holmes has also made it a point to take his family duties seriously. Throughout his career, he has remained in his hometown of Easton, Pennsylvania. He has contributed to youth programs and holds annual fundraising events to support their work.

276. Holsey, Lucius Henry Bp. (1842-1920). *Autobiography, Sermons, Addresses, and Essays of Bishop L. H. Holsey, D. D.* Chapel Hill, North Carolina: Academic Affairs Library, University of North Carolina at Chapel Hill, 1999.

> http://metalab.unc.edu/docsouth/holsey/holsey.sgml
> http://metalab.unc.edu/docsouth/holsey/holsey.html

> **Notes:** Documenting the American South (Project).

277. Hom, Ken. *Easy Family Recipes from a Chinese-American Childhood.* New York, New York: Knopf, 1997. 319 pages; photographs; illustrations. ISBN: 0394587588.

> **Abstract:** Ken Hom was born in Tucson, Arizona. He and his mother moved to Chicago's Chinatown after his father died in 1950. He describes the important role of food in his childhood and in Chinese culture. His mother was an avid cook, and his uncle owned a restaurant to which Hom was apprenticed at the age of eleven. Even Hom's next door neighbor, a professional gambler, was "lovingly and deliciously involved with food" (p. 4). He writes of his experiences and his memories of Chinese food shops, neighborhood gardens, and important family celebrations.

>> I have discovered that my experiences in growing up are quite similar to those of almost every other Chinese-American I know. Social isolation tempered by extended-family ties, the tenacity of tradition, the central importance of traditional foods and family gatherings—these are part of the common ground shared by all Chinese in America.   (p. 13)

> Although Hom was inculcated with his mother's belief that Chinese food and cooking and the Chinese attitude toward food were superior to any other, he found that he enjoyed his schoolmates' sandwiches as much as his own home-packed lunch. Hom describes the closeness of the Chinese communities, the history behind Chinese-American immigration, and the reasons, both imposed and chosen, for the development of Chinatowns. In describing the history of the Chinese restaurant in America and its adoption by both Chinese Americans and whites, Hom regrets that more people do not attempt Chinese cooking at home. He presents the methods, tools, ingredients, and recipes that he grew up with in hopes of remedying this situation. He accompanies each recipe with a related childhood memory. Hom has published at least thirteen cookbooks and has been featured in several BBC

television series. He lives in Berkeley, California and Paris when he is not traveling around the world as a chef and restaurant consultant.

278. Hongo, Garrett Kaoru. *Volcano: A Memoir of Hawai'i.* New York, New York: Knopf, 1995. 339 pages. ISBN: 0394571673 : 0679767487.

Abstract: This book by poet Hongo, is a long, slow exploration of place, family, and self. Of Japanese ancestry, both Hongo and his parents were born in Hawai'i. He was raised speaking Japanese and the Pidgin English spoken by non-white Hawai'ians. He was five when his family moved to the Los Angeles area in California, leaving behind most of their extended family. Once there, Hongo's mother insisted that he learn to speak mainland English. His father, who had a hearing problem, never mastered standard English. Hongo is certain that this, combined with his father's discomfort in the new environment, relegated him to a position of outsider, and he was never well accepted outside of the household. The death of Hongo's father so far away from his homeland filled Hongo with the desire to return to his birthplace and ultimately to write this autobiography. This book documents Hongo's first trip back to Hawai'i and Volcano, the village of his birth, and his many subsequent trips back with his wife and child. In Volcano, he explores both his family history and the natural history of Hawai'i. He examines how forced internment during World War II defined the consciousness of the Nisei and Sansei. Hongo examines his own feeling of being a native of Hawai'i and the Japanese community there while at the same time having been forever changed by growing up on the mainland. As he begins to come to terms with his place in the Japanese Hawai'ian community as a returning native son, Hongo writes:

> I don't have to live in the past, as the past was lived . . . I am not locked in to the opinion of the community here, not enclosed and defined by its gossip, not subject to all of its mores. Yet, full of nostalgia and retrospect, I catch my self wanting to be. I feel a bit ashamed that I, a man, can make sushi the way they made it in Kahuku village a generation ago . . . and I won't be howled down for it at Volcano's Saturday Market or at the Fourth of July fair. What will be noticed and with amusement, by the old-timers I care about . . . is that a man made the sushi, and not

his wife or mother, or his daughters. Or it will
have been made by his haole wife. I see that if
the ethnic past is to be transmitted, it will be
through this ungendered and interracial jumble
like the dark core of vinegared vegetables and
pink shrimp powder at the center of a roll of
sweetened rice. . . . I belong nowhere, I tell
myself. And, I belong in Volcano.   (p. 332)

279. hooks, bell. *Bone Black: Memories of Girlhood*. New York, New
York: Henry Holt and Company, 1996. 183 pages. ISBN:
080504146x : 0805055126.

Abstract: hooks, Distinguished Professor of English at City
College of New York and a prolific writer, wrote this book about
her childhood years. It is anecdotal in form and deals with events
and people who had a great influence on her. Born into a poor
black family in the South, hooks was raised in a family of six girls
and one boy. She was the black sheep of the family, someone who
had her own interpretation of life, one that did not match any of
the rest of the family. In their tiny house, she was eventually given
her own room because her sisters could not bear to share a room
with her. She describes her siblings, parents and grandparents,
and many of the people around her, especially older people with
whom she felt an affinity and thought of as "right-hand men of
God" (p. 86). "There is much to celebrate about being old. I want
to be old as soon as possible for I see the way the old ones live free.
They are free to be differentuniquedistinct from one another" (p.
88). Other than these older people, hooks found herself at odds
with just about everyone. She read constantly, an activity her family found bewildering. She became involved with Christianity, but
not the church of her family. She wanted to have her hair ironed
even though it was straight. She did not want to follow the accepted path of a woman because she saw the way her father abused
her mother and how her personality changed when her father was
not around. The book ends when a Catholic priest gives hooks a
copy of Rilke's *Letters to a Young Poet* to read. She finally discovers
writing: "In my journal I write to belong in this place of words.
This is my home. This dark, bone black inner cave where I am
making a world for myself" (p. 183).

280. —. *Remembered Rapture: The Writer at Work.* New York, New York: Henry Holt and Company, 1999. 237 pages. ISBN: 0805059091 : 0805059105.

Abstract: Gloria Watkins changed her name to bell hooks to honor her mother and grandmother and to establish an identity for herself which "Gloria" did not provide. hooks began writing as a child and has never stopped. An avid journal writer, she believes that the exercise and discipline of daily entries helped her not only to maintain her well being, but to develop an autonomous voice. Her early inspiration came from Rilke's *Letters to a Young Poet*, the poetry of Emily Dickinson, and an anthology of African-American poetry which she checked out from her school library and kept with her as much as possible. She finished her first book *Ain't I a Woman: Black Women and Feminism* (1991) at the age of nineteen, but it was ten years before it was published. The third in a series of autobiographical writings, hooks began *Remembered Rapture* as an answer to readers who wanted to know "how the work came to be what it is and other less gentle interrogators who found my engagement with writing suspect" (p. xi). hooks attempts to answer her critics who claim that she writes too much, is too radical or is not radical enough, doesn't promote herself or promotes herself too much. She talks of the hurdles faced by black women writing and of the capitalistic culture of publishing and its accompanying marketing and hype. She writes about autobiography and its combination of truth and fiction, its confessional nature, its therapeutic effects, and its current marketability. hooks believes that African-American writers, coming out of a different set of cultural values and familial expectations, have more difficulty with the confessional and revelatory side of autobiography than those coming from privileged, and often white, backgrounds. She explores these differences and her own experiences with them. hooks concludes the book with chapters devoted to each of the following writers:

Zora Neale Hurston, Emily Dickinson, Ann Petry, Lorraine Hansberry, Toni Morrison, and Toni Cade Bambara.

281. —. *Wounds of Passion: A Writing Life.* New York, New York: Henry Holt and Company, 1997. 260 pages. ISBN: 080504146x : 0805057226.

Abstract: *Wounds of Passion* is the second of three memoirs written by bell hooks. In this volume, hooks writes of her development as a writer from about the age of nineteen, when she began work on *Ain't I a Woman: Black Women and Feminism* (Boston:

South End Press, 1991) through the completion of her Ph.D. from the University of California at Santa Cruz and her appointment as assistant professor at Yale University. During this period, hooks was in a committed relationship with "Mack," a graduate student whom she met at a Gary Snyder poetry reading. This tumultuous relationship with the scholar, writer, and poet provided hooks with inspiration and discipline to pursue her own career as a writer. She was committed to her relationship with Mack, but his support and caring was coupled with a detrimental sense of rivalry and often abusive behavior, so that when hooks left for her position at Yale, she also left the relationship. hooks traces her shift from being a reader and writer of poetry to becoming a writer of political essays. She considers the difficulties of being a woman who is a serious writer involved in a committed relationship. She also touches on her work of viewing feminism from a black, female perspective.

282. Hopper, Isaac T. (1771-1852). *Narrative of the Life of Thomas Cooper*. Chapel Hill, North Carolina: Academic Affairs Library, University of North Carolina at Chapel Hill, 1999.

http://metalab.unc.edu/docsouth/hopper/hopper.html

Notes: Documenting the American South (Project).

283. Horn, Gabriel (1947-). *Contemplations of a Primal Mind*. Foreword by Anne Wilson Shaef. Novato, California: New World Library, 1996. 166 pages. ISBN: 1880032554.

Notes: Also published Gainsville, Florida: University Press of Florida, 2000. ISBN: 0813017548.

Abstract: Gabriel Horn served as one of the original teachers in the American Indian Movement (AIM), and helped establish the AIM Survival Schools in the 1970s. He has received recognition for his teaching as well as for his work to promote and preserve the traditions and beliefs of Native Americans. His book consists of six essays. "Civilized and Primal Thought" discusses the distinction between what is considered "primitive" and what is "civilized." He shows how what he calls primitive thought indicates a closeness to nature and the powers of nature as well as a person's true purpose in life and place in the grand scheme of nature. The second chapter, "Original Instructions" considers the behavior each living entity in nature was programmed to have. He illustrates the idea with a visit to the Dolphin Research Center in the Florida Keys, where he comes into contact with dolphins which he feels are still true to their own "original instructions." "Paints Her Dreams" talks about spiritual connections to the past and describes the Native American custom of Peace Day. "Ancestors Among the Stars" considers connections with the Star People and life on another planet. Chapter five, "Old Ways," is a mystical story about his mother-in-law and a possible explanation of why some males in her family are born with six fingers on one hand. In the final chapter, "The Cord," Horn talks about how his people and family survive despite the efforts of the civilized world to destroy them. Throughout the book he talks about his relationship with his three children and how he has taught them about their primal origins, his two great-uncles who taught him much about culture and spirituality, and especially about the love he still has for his wife, a member of the Ojibway tribe, whom he lost to cancer.

284. Horne, Esther Burnett (1909-). *Essie's Story: The Life and Legacy of a Shoshone Teacher*. Written with Sally McBeth. American Indian Lives. Lincoln, Nebraska: University of Nebraska Press, 1998. 215 pages; photographs; map. ISBN: 0803223862.

Notes: Published Lincoln: University Press of Nebraska Bison Books edition, 1999. ISBN: 080327324x.

Abstract: Esther Burnett Horne is the great-great-granddaughter of the famous American Indian, Sacajawea. Stories of her ancestor were passed on to her from her earliest years and are an important part of her sense of self. Her mother's family was descended from Sacajawea's adopted son and nephew, and her paternal grandfather, Fincelious Burnett, the agricultural agent for the Wind River Shoshone Reservation, knew her. A good portion of Horne's story is devoted to the stories of Sacajawea, as well as a carefully researched account of the debate surrounding the year and place of Sacajawea's death. Horne's father was born and raised on the reservation along with his Shoshone wife-to-be, Mildred Large. After they married, they left the reservation to homestead in Idaho. Both Horne's mother and father raised the children to feel pride in their Indian heritage. After her father died in 1922, her mother was unable to care for her children and make a living, so the Burnett family, Horne's paternal grandparents, arranged for the four older children to enroll in the Haskell Indian Institute in Lawrence, Kansas. Although terribly homesick, Horne found the institute to be a secure and nurturing environment. The official policy was to Americanize the Indian students, but the students from many tribes learned about Indian culture from each other. Horne trained to become a teacher and taught at the Eufaula

Boarding School, a Creek girls institute, in Oklahoma. After marrying her Haskell high school sweetheart, Hoopa Indian Robert Horne, Horne joined her husband and began teaching at the Wahpeton Indian School in North Dakota, where they stayed until their retirement. During her long teaching career, Horne saw official priority shift during the years 1933-1945 from the goal of Americanizing the students to helping them maintain their Indian identities. Horne, like her own Indian teachers, always taught her students to have pride in their heritage. She learned Indian dances, about tribal clothing, and Indian arts to aid her in teaching her students about their traditions. After her retirement, Horne continued her work with children by participating in programs aimed at at-risk Indian youth.

285. Hosokawa, Bill. *Out of the Frying Pan: Reflections of a Japanese American.* Niwot, Colorado: University Press of Colorado, 1998. 192 pages. ISBN: 0870815008 : 087081513x.

Abstract: When journalist Bill Hosokawa went to kindergarten in pre-World War II Seattle he spoke no English, because only Japanese was spoken in his home. His second-class status as a Japanese American was apparent to him in most aspects of his life. His parents, born in Japan, were forbidden by U.S. law from becoming naturalized citizens and owning property. His mother attended naturalization classes nonetheless and ironically, tutored immigrants from Europe to help them pass the required tests. His father grew tired of, as Hosokawa put it, helping other people buy their houses through his rent payments and finally bought a house in the name of his youngest son. After high school, Hosokawa attended the University of Washington, where he majored in journalism. He was advised not to go into this field because, he was told, no paper would hire a "Japanese boy," and he was the only student who was not assigned an internship. Hosokawa's first positions were with an English-language Japanese paper in Singapore and then in Shanghai. Following his year in Shanghai, Hosokawa joined his wife and child in Portland, a few months before the Japanese attack on Pearl Harbor. Because of his work with the Japanese newspapers, Hosokawa was called before a federal grand jury. Although the charges brought against him were dropped, suspicion followed him and his family into their first relocation camp in Puyallup, and they were sent from there to the Heart Mountain camp in Wyoming. Hosokawa describes the conditions and daily life of the camps, the opportunities for self-governance, efforts by the camp inmates to better their conditions, forms of protest, and the good and the bad of government management. Hosokawa started a camp newspaper, *The Sentinel*, which provided a way for camp inmates to express their opinions. For instance, *The Sentinel* took on the *Denver Post* after the notoriously conservative newspaper published a series of anti-Japanese articles. After the war, Hosokawa, surprisingly, was offered a position with the *Des Moines Register*. He found the newspaper a welcoming place to work and Iowa a good place for his family. However, when he was offered a position with the *Denver Post*, which was under a new and more liberal management, his family was anxious to move westward, and so he took the position. Hosokawa worked there until his retirement at the age of sixty-eight. Hosokawa was also a long-time columnist for the *Pacific Citizen*, a publication of the Japanese American Citizens League, and he includes a sampling of his columns from that newspaper.

286. Houston, Cissy. *How Sweet the Sound: My Life with God and Gospel*. Written with Jonathan Singer. New York, New York: Doubleday, 1998. 282 pages; photographs. ISBN: 0385490100 : 0385490101.

Abstract: Cissy Houston, mother of popular singer Whitney Houston, has had and continues to have a significant musical career. Cissy Houston begins her autobiography with a description of her family's hometown in Early County, Georgia. She writes of the hostile conditions for African Americans and the special hate of white people reserved for land-owning African Americans. Her family, the Drinkards, owned land, but it was taken from her grandparents on the grounds of unpaid taxes. Houston was born in Newark, New Jersey, where many members of the extended Drinkard family relocated. Her mother died of a cerebral hemorrhage at the age of thirty-nine, when Houston was only eight, and she was raised by her eldest sister, Reebie. The family were all devout Christians. Music was a central part of worship services, and the children sang together as the Drinkard Singers. The group gave them a reason to stay together, and their father kept them on a rigid schedule of chores, school, rehearsals, performances, and church. They performed in large venues and recorded with RCA-Victor, but their father never allowed them to tour or experiment with popular music. Houston married John Houston, and he began to manage a singing group made up of her nieces and some of their friends. Although the younger generation was allowed to work in popular music, Houston's family disapproved of her doing so. After doing one session as a substitute singer, however, Houston was suddenly in continuous demand. She performed with her nieces and later with her own group, the

Sweet Inspirations. They made recordings of their own and backed up major singers, including Houston's niece Dionne Warwick, Aretha Franklin, the Drifters, and Elvis Presley. Before taking a pause in her musical career to spend more time with her children, Houston also recorded a solo album. She writes about the many singers, composers, and arrangers she has worked with. She also describes her family and especially the growth of her daughter Whitney's career. Houston had many ups and downs in her life, most significantly, the deaths of her parents and her divorce from John Houston. In 1995, she received the Pioneer Award from the Rhythm and Blues Foundation and honorary degrees from Kean College and Essex County College, both of New Jersey. In 1996 she fulfilled her dream of releasing a gospel album, *Face to Face*, for which she won the Grammy Award in the Traditional Soul Gospel category. Today Houston continues to record and write songs and to find solace and strength from her Christian faith.

287. Houston, Jeanne Wakatsuki and James D. Houston. *Farewell to Manzanar: A True Story of Japanese American Experience during and after the World War II Internment.* New York, New York: Bantam Books, 1995. ISBN: 0553272586.

> **Notes:** Originally published Bantam Books, 1973. ISBN: 0553272586.

288. Hubbard, Philip G. (1921-). *My Iowa Journey: The Life and Story of the University of Iowa's First African American Professor.* Singular Lives. Iowa City, Iowa: University of Iowa Press, 1999. 193 pages; photographs. ISBN: 0877456720.

> **Abstract:** Hubbard spent most of his childhood and youth in Des Moines. Living on the edge of the black neighborhoods, he was often the only black child in his classrooms. Hubbard recalls that school was a place where race was rarely an issue for him, but outside the school system, there was an established system of unofficial segregation. Many restaurants only allowed blacks to use take-out service; movie theaters and swimming pools were segregated. In considering his career options, Hubbard did not want to rely on racially biased corporations for employment and he wanted something that would be an intellectual challenge. He settled on engineering and entered the University of Iowa (UI) with plans for a chemical engineering degree. Before he graduated, however, he was drafted into World War II and directed by the armed services into electrical engineering. Following the victory in Europe,

the dean of the engineering school at UI helped Hubbard get a discharge so that he could return to school to conduct research. Hubbard completed a master's degree in 1949, and his Ph.D. in 1954. During this time he married and started a family, which would include five children. Although Hubbard had a number of other employment prospects, he chose to remain at the University of Iowa with respected colleagues and in an open community. In 1956, he was the first African American to receive tenure at the University of Iowa. He was promoted to full professor in 1959. Hubbard was recognized for his teaching and scholarship, served on many boards and committees, and was made Dean of Academic Affairs in 1965. Throughout his career he made a point of seeking out minority students and encouraging women and minorities within the department of engineering. He writes, "My guiding star has been the welfare of humankind collectively *and individually*; actions in pursuit of a global goal or on behalf of people at a distance should not jeopardize the welfare of those close at hand" (pp. 87-88). Hubbard writes about his involvement in the community on such issues as civil rights and open housing. He was involved with the program known as "Opportunity at Iowa" which sought to increase minority enrollment at the university, and by 1994, the university had achieved a nine percent minority enrollment. Hubbard has remained active in his church, the community, and at the university following his retirement.

289. Hughes, Dorothy Pitman. *Wake Up and Smell the Dollars! Whose Inner-City Is This Anyway!: One Woman's Struggle against Sexism, Classism, Racism, Gentrification, and the Empowerment Zone.* Phoenix, Arizona: Amber Books, 2000. 214 pages; photographs. ISBN: 0965506479.

Abstract: Dorothy Pitman Hughes has been a community activist since she was unable to find acceptable child care for her first child. Born in Charles Junction near Lumpkin, Georgia, Hughes was the third of six children. Her church and her community were important influences in her development. In 1957, she moved to New York City, where she worked as a domestic during the day and sang at nightclubs during the evening. She later quit her domestic work to operate a laundry out of her home. Unable to find suitable childcare, Hughes had to give up her singing career. She decided to set up her own drop-in day care operation in her apartment and, at the same time, became a child-care advocate and community activist. Hughes's day care expanded and grew into a three-story building, complete with kitchen, laundry, and office space. Never complacent, Hughes served on citywide and national committees in pursuit of children's rights, decent family housing, and day care. One of her targets was New York City's notorious rat-infested welfare hotels. Hughes found that for each occupant, $2,000 a month in public funds went straight to the landlords of these neglected buildings. She showed that for the same cost she could put up a family for a month in the luxurious Waldorf Astoria Hotel. As Hughes's reputation as a social and political activist grew, she was asked to teach courses at Columbia University, College of New Rochelle, and City College. She also accompanied Gloria Steinem on a three-year speaking engagement. With successful business experience behind her, Hughes sought to encourage black entrepreneurship. She believed it was important for African Americans to own their own businesses and to claim ownership by buying stock in publicly held American corporations, thus creating a foundation for increased African-American influence and power. Hughes was especially interested in encouraging Harlem residents to spend their money in their own neighborhood and to create an environment that would encourage African Americans to start up businesses there. To further her vision for such a black-business renaissance, Hughes arranged for her own business, Harlem Office Supply, to go public. She sold shares for one dollar, with the goal of enrolling as many children as possible, providing them with the experience of pride of ownership.

290. Huntley, Bobby R. *Italy and Back: A Black Man's Odyssey.* [S.l.]: B. R. Huntley, 1997. 136 pages. ISBN: 0967233909.

Abstract: In 1978, Bobby Huntley was the first member of his family to graduate from high school. He was proud of his accomplishment and expected to reap benefits from it. Unable to find meaningful work, however, his brother and cousin convinced him to sign up for the Marine Corps. Huntley expected that his hard work, dedication, and determination would be rewarded on the same basis as all other Marines. He found, however, that in case after case "his skin was his sin." Racism was prevalent within the ranks and in the command structure. He was denied opportunities for advancement, unjustly arrested, questioned, set up, and abused. There were instances of cross burnings and fights, discrimination in promotions and assignments, and inconsistent punishment. Huntley was eventually promoted to the rank of sergeant, but not without having to plead his case and go over the heads of his immediate superiors. When Huntley's military career took him to Italy, he and another African-American Marine were the subject of false accusations, attacks, and court martials for four

years. Both Marines were active in the Black American Cultural
Organization (BACO) set up by the Marine Corps to provide positive, morale-boosting activities and learning opportunities for
black Marine families. Huntley was the president of this organization, and this apparently factored into much of the abusive
treatment he received. Huntley was not recommended for reen-
listment by his commanding officer in Italy, and he received an
honorable discharge. Although none of the charges or accusations
brought against him were ever substantiated and the commanding officer who refused to recommend him was under investigation for misconduct, Huntley was unsuccessful in his attempt to
remain in the Corps. Huntley's story tells of his hard work in the
Marine Corps and his determination to stand up for what was
right. He wrote this book to call attention to the flagrant misuse
of authority within the Marine Corps, but found the writing
process to be a healing experience. Huntley harbors no bitterness
and remains loyal to the men and women with whom he served.

291. Hutchinson, Earl. *A Colored Man's Journey through 20th Century
Segregated America*. Written with Earl Ofari Hutchinson. Los
Angeles, California: Middle Passage Press, 2000. 150 pages;
photographs. ISBN: 1881032175.

Abstract: At the age of ninety-seven, Earl Hutchinson records his
"personal recollections and impressions of the people, places, and
events that shaped and influenced my life and that of millions of
other Negroes in 20th Century segregated America" (p. 9). Born in
1903, Hutchinson was a native of Clarksville, Tennessee. His family moved to St. Louis when he was ten. By this time, he notes,
over one thousand African Americans had been lynched at the
hands of white mobs. Hutchinson parallels the events of his life
with the slow progress for the African American in the United
States. As an adult, Hutchinson moved to Chicago expecting to
find improved conditions, but found segregated neighborhoods
and limited job opportunities. As a postal worker, he was not
allowed to work in any position that involved handling money or
directly serving white patrons. Hutchinson describes the elabo-
rate process he and his wife had to follow to buy an apartment
building in an all-white neighborhood. When violence and other
tactics failed to drive them from the area, white families began to
move away until the entire neighborhood was occupied by
African-American families. Hutchinson points out that the pre-
dictability of white flight was a bonanza for real estate agents who
bought out home owners cheaply and then sold to incoming
African Americans at inflated prices. After retirement from the

postal service in 1960, Hutchinson, his wife, and children moved to Los Angeles. He found that the Los Angeles area had the same restrictive housing codes and "red lining" practices that he had left behind. (Red lining was a way for banks and other financial institutions to restrict the availability of real estate purchases by neighborhood.) Hutchinson went into the real estate business and worked with several organizations to change discriminatory housing practices. He concludes by writing:

> [M]y great hope is that just as colored persons fought hard to end my journey through 20th Century segregated America, others will continue to fight to make sure colored men and women will not have to repeat that same journey through 21st Century America. I pray that God fulfills that hope.   (p. 96)

292. Hyman, Rick and Ronda Hyman. *My Texas Family: An Uncommon Journey to Prosperity [Featuring Photographs from 1912 to 1927].* Charleston, South Carolina: Tempus, 2000. 128 pages; photographs. ISBN: 0738501816.

> **Notes:** Also published with the imprint Arcadia Publishing.

> **Abstract:** Hyman presents many photos and stories to tell the history of his mother's family, the Martins of Round Top, Texas. An artist, Hyman is in the process of interpreting the family photo collection into a series of paintings, some of which are included in the book. He interviews several cousins to provide background to the Martin family history from their days as slaves in Virginia to their move by covered wagon to Texas in 1863. Henry Martin, Hyman's great-great-grandfather, was the patriarch of the family. He owned a considerable tract of land on which oil would later be discovered. Hyman presents several stories about his great-great-grandfather, his role in the African-American community of Round Top, his resistance to Texas style racism, and the prosperity he helped his family to achieve.

293. Hytche, William Percy. *Step by Step to the Top: The Saga of a President of a Historically Black University.* Winter Park, Florida: Four-G Publishers, 1999. 345 pages; photographs. ISBN: 1885066538.

> **Abstract:** Retired president of the University of Maryland, Eastern Shore (UMES), Hytche was motivated to write his story in the hopes that "my account gives hope and encouragement to

everybody no matter what his or her roots in life are, whether rich or poor, old or young, educated or street smart, White or Black" (p. xiii). Hytche was unable to attend college because he could not pay tuition and fees. A cousin convinced him to try Langston University in Oklahoma where he was given employment, which allowed him to pay his way. He graduated in 1950 with two teaching offers, but was inducted into the army, and rose to the rank of first sergeant. Following his tour of duty, Hytche taught mathematics at Ponca City, Oklahoma. During this time, he bought the Blue Moon restaurant. He immediately made it the first integrated restaurant in the county by bringing in black people and paying for their meals. In 1960, after a profitable sale of the Blue Moon, Hytche was invited to teach math at UMES, then called Maryland State College, a historically black college in Princess Anne, Maryland. While teaching, Hytche purchased another soon-to-be successful restaurant, was promoted to a deanship, and eventually became college president. Hytche's path was not always smooth, and he describes many instances of discrimination and racism. He attended Tullahasse School, an all black school which was left unfinished by the WPA and had no water or electricity. This was his "indoctrination to an unfair world because of one's race" (p. 47). Hytche recalls many incidents in the army, including those below him in rank refusing to take his orders, and incidents with policemen and bus drivers in the towns in which he was stationed. Hytche never accepted the status quo, and sought to desegregate businesses and community organizations. After years of struggling to receive appropriate funding and support for his college, Hytche was able to say that, during his final years as president, he received compliments for his work and spent less time having to plead for money and defend the role that UMES played within the University of Maryland system. He describes sweeping changes to the physical plant and in the size and diversity of the student body, faculty, and staff (at all levels). Hytche and his wife Deloris are world travelers who have been received as guests of honor in Taiwan, People's Republic of China, Cameroon, Zambia, Kenya, Egypt, Israel, South Africa, and Mexico.

294. Hyun, Peter. *In the New World: The Making of a Korean American.* Honolulu, Hawai'i: University of Hawai'i Press, 1995. 290 pages; photographs. ISBN: 082481648x.

Abstract: This sequel to Hyun's *Man Sei!* (1986) begins in 1924 as he, age seventeen, arrives in Honolulu via Shanghai where his family had fled to escape the Japanese occupation of Korea. Hyun lived a remarkable and colorful life. He graduated from high school struggling with English and trying to adapt to U.S. customs and mannerisms, all of which contrasted sharply with those of Korea. He attended college for two years at DePauw in Indiana, leaving to study theater in New York under the direction of Eva LeGalliane. Unfortunately, his work in the theater was tarnished by a pervasive racism. He writes that "a live Asian working on the stage of a New York theatre was unheard of, not to mention as a stage manager. It wasn't only that I was a foreigner; I was an 'Oriental,' a 'chinaman,' an inferior" (p. 94). Racism eventually drove Hyun out of his job. He successfully formed his own company, The Studio Players, and directed with the Workers' Lab Theatre/Theatre of Action. When Hyun was directing *The Revolt of the Beavers* for the New York Federal Theatre, the announcement from the producer that the play would go to Broadway was followed by the cast refusing to go with a "chinaman" director. Hyun left the production and directing for good. "I shuddered at the thought of spending the rest of my life fighting and struggling against the unseen phantom. . . . I had to refuse to be mired in the filth of racial prejudice" (p. 157). His next job was surveying for the United States Army in Hawai'i. He joined the armed forces after the United States entered World War II, and became a Japanese language specialist. He was sent to be liaison to a group of "Japanese" prisoners of war who turned out to be Koreans who had been pressed into slave labor by the Japanese army. He was later promoted to major and sent to U.S.-occupied South Korea following the war. Hyun comments on the totalitarian nature of the U.S. occupation of South Korea and notes that the Koreans were perceived as inferior and that while the Americans were well-fed and groomed, the Koreans were either "sick or dying" (p. 217). While in Korea, Hyun was arrested, presumably for his contact with Communists, expelled from Korea and discharged from the army. Later, due to his work with national peace organizations, Hyun was called before the House Committee on Un-American Activities, where one witness accused him of being Mao's number one agent in the United States. Despite the discrimination he faced, Hyun clings to his "faith that the human race is endowed with the potential to construct a world of peace and tolerance that our own sons and daughters will inherit" (p. 279).

295. Ice T. *The Ice Opinion: Who Gives a Fuck?* As told to Heidi Siegmund. New York, New York: St. Martin's Press, 1994. 199 pages; photographs. ISBN: 0312104863.

Abstract: Rapper Ice T grew up in a New Jersey ghetto before moving to South Central Los Angeles. He got into film and rap music after four years in the military, time spent working in a low-paid government job, and making the decision not to take up a criminal career. His first single was "Six in the Morning." A number of years later, he signed with Warner Brothers and released three gold albums in a row. He formed the rock group Body Count, which released an album with the controversial single, "Cop Killer." This plunged Ice T and Warner Brothers into the middle of a censorship battle. Ice T eventually left Warner Brothers feeling that, although they had supported him through the controversy, it was his battle to fight, and not theirs. He writes that "35,000 black police officers said they would not join in with any boycott of Ice T or Time Warner because they knew I was saying the truth. Since July, hundreds of cops have come up to me saying, 'Ice, I know what the record is about, I'm not dumb'" (p. 175). Ice T also presents his point of view on a variety of other contemporary issues with the goal of inspiring conversation. They include the condition of people living in the ghetto, gang life and culture, and the prison experience and inmate culture. Ice T debunks the myths about the "good old days" and "traditional values." He questions any meaning these phrases could possibly hold for African Americans. Ice T speaks to school-age children all over the country. He encourages them to identify the skills they have to live in the streets, skills that could also help them be successful off the street and in jobs. He believes children from the ghetto should be given the opportunity for college so that they have the opportunity to get out: "You don't choose the ghetto. Everybody would like to be surrounded by beauty and would like to feel safe in their homes. I want to explain to people that when they do get over the wall, *leave*, but come back and pick up your friends. Give them a chance to make a better life for themselves, too" (p. 20). Ice T seeks success to set an example for youth still in the ghetto to demonstrate that it is possible to leave and accomplish your goals: "I love the notion that my kid might have the chance to die of old age" (p. 21).

296. Ichihashi, Yamato. *Morning Glory, Evening Shadow: Yamato Ichihashi and His Internment Writings, 1942-1945*. Annotated and with a biographical essay by Gordon H. Chang. Asian America. Stanford, California: Stanford University Press, 1997. 552 pages; illustrations; photographs. ISBN: 0804727333.

Abstract: Gordon Chang has collected Ichihashi's diary entries, letters to friends, and research-oriented essays, as well as the letters of Mrs. Ichihashi, all originating from their three years in three relocation camps during World War II. A historian and professor in the history department at Stanford University, Ichihashi carefully observed and recorded conditions, self-government activities, and community developments. In his letters to his friends at Stanford he seeks to give a detailed account of life in the camps. Others depict the severe emotional and physical strain most of the inmates suffered due to the demoralizing conditions and requirements. His wife Kei's letters cover day-to-day emotions and necessities. In May 1942, the Ichihashis were initially sent to the Santa Anita Center in Arcadia, California where they were assigned to wooden sheds with no ceilings, no furniture, and no privacy. Rules were set and changed arbitrarily. Ichihashi tried to make himself useful to both the camp inmates and members of the administration, but he was viewed with suspicion by both sides. In August, the Ichihashis were relocated to Tule Lake, a camp with somewhat better conditions. Shortly after their arrival there, Ichihashi was arrested by the FBI and taken to a camp near San Francisco. He writes about the crisis for camp inmates caused by the infamous loyalty questions 27 and 28. All men and women, Issei and Nisei, were required to answer yes or no to two questions that asked if they were willing to serve in the armed forces and whether they would pledge allegiance to the United States and renounce all allegiance to Japan. They were then segregated by loyalty as judged by their responses. Those deemed "disloyal" stayed at Tule Lake, while the "loyal" inmates were transferred to other camps. The Ichihashis were sent to Amache Relocation Camp in Granada, Colorado. As the years passed and younger people were encouraged to go to school or find work in nonrestricted areas of the country, only older people and children remained in the camps, and many of the older people felt unable to face a future that meant starting over from nothing. The documents end with a letter in May 1945 from Ichihashi to one of his co-internees describing his and Kei's homecoming to Palo Alto. The Ichihashis were lucky to have had friends who watched out for their property and belongings, and who greeted them warmly upon their return. All the same, homecoming and readjustment were difficult and life did not resume where it left off for them.

297. Jackson, Eugene W. (1916-). *Eugene "Pineapple" Jackson: His Own Story*. Written with Gwendolyn Sides St. Julian. Foreword by Zaiid Leflore. Jefferson, North Carolina: McFarland & Company, 1999. 223 pages; photographs. ISBN: 0786405333.

Abstract: Eugene W. Jackson began his acting career at the age of seven. A talented tap dancer, Jackson had become a regular winner of a local amateur talent contest when the directors of the contest urged Jackson's mother to take him to the movie studios to get into film. He quickly became a favorite and received a number of small parts. In 1924, at age nine, Jackson was hired into the "Our Gang" series, and played the character "Pineapple," a name that has stayed with him through his entire acting and entertaining career. After a year with "Our Gang," Jackson struck out on his own and was featured in a number of comedy series. Besides acting, Jackson starred in a vaudeville duo with his brother, Freddie Baker. They were managed by their mother, Lillie Baker, who signed their contracts and collected their pay—not always an easy task. Jackson was also an all-around musician, and played saxophone and clarinet. With his brother on drums and Virgil Johnson on piano, Jackson formed the Jackson Trio. His musical career was interrupted by induction into the army, but he joined the military band. Jackson is still active in the entertainment field as a musician, dancer, and actor. He has loved his work and is proud of his contributions to the film industry. Jackson urges the public to understand and respect the early African-American actors and actresses for their many accomplishments and for leading the way for future generations of African Americans into the film industry: "I believe that the old-time black actors are sometimes ridiculed for the roles we played, but I must say that we did not control Hollywood . . . (p. 86). Please be proud of our roles and hard work. We did contribute. We did make a difference" (p. 88).

298. James, Etta (1938-). *Rage to Survive: The Etta James Story*. Written with David Ritz. New York, New York: Villard Books, 1995. 304 pages; discography; photographs; index. ISBN: 0679423281.

Notes: Also published New York: Da Capo Press, 1998. ISBN: 0306808129 : 030680784x.

Abstract: Etta James was born Jamesetta Hawkins in Los Angeles, California. She began singing in church as a child, and in 1953, at age fourteen, she was offered a job on the road. She forged the signature of her mother, who was in jail at the time, quit school, and began her career as a solo singer. Her first recording was "Roll With Me, Henry," and it became a hit. Etta James's life followed a single path for the next thirty years. She remained enormously popular. All of her records sold well, and enthusiastic crowds greeted her live performances. At the same time, she was attracted to abusive men and almost continuously addicted to heroine. James participated in numerous rehabilitation programs which restored her to health long enough so that she could become readdicted, and she was arrested repeatedly for drugs, writing bad checks, and skipping parole. Through all this, she still managed to hang onto her career. Finally, in the 1980s, she found herself without a manager or work. James refused to give up and began booking her own appearances. A turning point in her life came when she was asked to sing at the opening ceremony of the 1984 Olympics in Los Angeles. With her career revived, she checked herself into the Betty Ford Clinic in Palm Springs and was finally able to cure her addictions permanently. She continues to sing and record. In 1994, James won her first Grammy award, in the Best Jazz Vocal category, for her *Mystery Lady* album: "After forty years of singing R&B and blues, it was funny to finally win as a jazz singer. No matter, I was glad. I accepted the mystery" (p. 264). She was inducted into the Rock and Roll Hall of Fame in 1992. "Honors are nice," she says, "[b]ut the truth is that I'm of two minds about these things. Part of me is thrilled to be recognized, but another part resents the lily-white institution that sends down its proclamations from on high. *They* decide who is rock and roll and who isn't; *they* decide who was important and who wasn't" (p. 256). Etta James currently lives in California with her husband, Artis Mills, and her two sons, Donto and Sametto.

299. James, Rev. Thomas (1804-1891). *Life of Rev. Thomas James by Himself.* Chapel Hill, North Carolina: Academic Affairs Library, University of North Carolina at Chapel Hill, 2000.

> http://docsouth.unc.edu/neh/jamesth/jamesth.sgml
> http://docsouth.unc.edu/neh/jamesth/jamesth.html

> **Notes:** Documenting the American South (Project).

300. James, Walter (1964-). *From the Carolinas to Immortality: The Autobiography of Walter James III.* Chapel Hill, North Carolina: Chapel Hill Press, 1997. 132 pages. ISBN: none.

301. Jamison, M. F. (1848-1918). *Autobiography and Work of Bishop M. F. Jamison, D.D. ("Uncle Joe"), Editor, Publisher, and Church Extension Secretary: A Narration of His Whole Career from the Cradle to the Bishopric of the Colored M. E. Church in America.* Chapel Hill, North Carolina: Academic Affairs Library, University of North Carolina at Chapel Hill, 2000.

    http://docsouth.unc.edu/neh/jamison/jamison.sgml
    http://docsouth.unc.edu/neh/jamison/jamison.html

302. Japanese American Historical Society of Southern California. *Nanka Nikkei Voices: Resettlement Years, 1945-1955.* [S.l.]: Japanese American Historical Society of Southern California, 1998. 109 pages; photographs; maps. ISBN: none.

    Abstract: Many changes took place after the release of the Japanese-American community from internment camps where they were incarcerated during World War II. Before the war, most of the community had been concentrated along the West Coast in rural areas. After the war, the War Relocation Authority (WRA) attempted to break up this concentration and move Japanese-Americans away from the Pacific Coast by convincing families to settle in other areas, such as Denver, Chicago, and Minneapolis. No matter where they went, however, they faced housing and employment discrimination. Families who chose to return to their homes in California faced the loss of property and belongings, as well as discrimination and violence. This collection of narratives focuses on this period of resettlement following the war. Contributions are from both professional and first-time writers, teenagers and children ("Sansei and Yonsei Views"), and military veterans. The stories cover postwar Los Angeles, employment and unemployment, the reestablishment of religious communities, and the conditions of transience experienced by many Japanese Americans.

303. Jaramillo, Cleofas M. *Romance of a Little Village Girl.* Pasó Por Aquí. Albuquerque, New Mexico: University of New Mexico Press, 2000. 200 pages; photographs. ISBN: 0826322867.

    Notes: Originally published San Antonio: The Naylor Company, 1955.

Abstract: Cleofas M. Jaramillo was born into an old Spanish family in the Spanish territory of New Mexico. This territory became part of Mexico, and was later taken over by the United States. Her memoir serves as a sequel to her work on New Mexican life *Shadows of the Past* (Santa Fe: Seton Village Press, 1941) and provides the details of her life as well as a picture of life in the territory during the early part of the twentieth century. Jaramillo's family farmed, ranched, and operated a store. She met her husband when she was eighteen, and they were married two years later, in 1898. Her husband was from a wealthy Spanish family which was unhappy with the match. However, she and her husband were devoted to each other and remained so throughout their life together. Jaramillo describes her courtship, wedding, and adjustment to marriage. She and her husband traveled together visiting at different times California, New York, Washington, D.C., where they attended the presidential inauguration, St. Louis for the World's Fair, and Mexico to visit family. Jaramillo conceived their first child ten years into their marriage and the baby died five days after birth. Their second child lived only fifteen months. Their third child survived, only to be murdered at age eighteen, and Jaramillo's husband died when this daughter was four. After the death of her husband, Jaramillo was left to handle all of the vast properties that he had accumulated. She discovered that her financial situation was precarious and spent the next decade attempting to clear up debt. During this hectic time, her daughter was growing up in a different social climate than Jaramillo had experienced in her youth. She looks back wondering if she was too strict or too cold with her daughter. In her later years, Jaramillo became concerned with preserving the culture in which she was raised. She founded the Spanish Folklore Society, published a book of Spanish fairy tales, a cook book, and other works documenting the early New Mexican Spanish society and traditions.

304. Jin, Sarunna. *My First American Friend*. Written with Shirley V. Beckes. Boston, Massachussetts: Houghton Mifflin, 1996. 30 pages. ISBN: 0395731682.

305. Johnson, Dwayne. *See* The Rock.

306. Johnson, James Weldon. *Along This Way: The Autobiography of James Weldon Johnson*. Introduction by Sondra Kathryn Wilson. New York, New York: Da Capo Press, 2000. 418 pages. ISBN: 030680929x.

   Notes: Also published New York: Penguin, 1990. ISBN: 0140184015; originally published New York: Viking, 1933.

307. Johnson, Kevin R. *How Did You Get to Be Mexican?: A White/Brown Man's Search for Identity*. Philadelphia, Penn- sylvania: Temple University Press, 1999. 245 pages; photographs. ISBN: 1566396506 : 1566396514.

   Abstract: Kevin R. Johnson, a graduate of Harvard Law School and professor of law at the University of California at Davis, paints a clear picture of the difficult path the minority scholar must follow to find a place within academia. He begins by describing the confusion he experienced growing up the son of a Mexican-American mother, who attempted to deny her ethnic background, and a white, Swedish-American father, who encouraged Johnson to embrace his Mexican heritage. Johnson's parents divorced when he and his brother were still quite young. Initially, they lived with their mother in the racially mixed neighborhood of Azusa, California, but when their living situation deteriorated the boys left to live with their father in a white neighborhood in Torrence, California. Neither Johnson nor his brother were clearly identifiable as Mexican American by look or by name, and so, although he considered himself Mexican American, he never felt like he fit into this group. Once in college at U.C. Berkeley, Johnson found that studying with professors such as sociologist Harry Edwards and Chicano Studies professors Mario Barrera and David Montejano "opened my eyes to many things and built on the racial sensitivity that my father had taught me" (p. 96). Johnson writes, "My education provided me with a better understanding of my racial identity" (p. 97). He describes the kind of discrimination rampant in academia from students, administrators, and faculty alike. Minorities are often suspected of achieving only because of affirmative action; one's motivations are often considered suspect when supporting other minority faculty members and students; a minority scholar is often questioned by minority students and colleagues if he or she is not considered radical enough; and the minority scholar is often questioned by white faculty and students if he or she is even slightly proactive in matters of race and ethnic politics.

308. Johnson, Keyshawn. *Just Give Me the Damn Ball: The Fast Times of an NFL Rookie.* Written with Shelley Smith. New York, New York: Warner Books, 1997. 223 pages; photographs. ISBN: 0446521450.

Abstract: Keyshawn Johnson writes about his first year with the New York Jets as the number-one pick of the NFL draft. He talks about his frustration while his agents and the Jets labored over the contract negotiations past the start of the rookie reporting date. He gives a full account of the Jets' one-win fifteen-loss season and his season-long frustration at not getting the ball. Johnson recounts his early teen years scalping tickets, selling drugs, and participating in burglaries. He was arrested several times, always for ticket scalping, and served a number of months in a juvenile detention center. Johnson became friends with probation officer Murphy Ruffin, who urged him to clean up his act and to stay out of prison. Johnson was heavily influenced by Ruffin and determined to make a go of it. He made it through high school, played football with several junior colleges, and was accepted to the University of Southern California. Johnson had a high regard for the coaching staff there and for the support they gave him. He remembers with appreciation all of those who stood by him and saw him through to his professional career. He is pleased to give help in return. At the end of the book, Johnson looks forward to a new season with the Jets and to playing with a new coach.

309. Johnson, Nellie Stone. *Nellie Stone Johnson: The Life of an Activist.* As told to David Brauer. Saint Paul, Minnesota: Ruminator Books, 2000. 234 pages. ISBN: 1886913358.

Abstract: African-American social activist Nellie Johnson grew up on her family's farm in Lakeville and Pine County, Minnesota. Her father, who was active in the Nonpartisan League, organizing the local dairy farmers to get fair prices for their milk, introduced her to labor organizing. To this day, she shares his motto of "Equal opportunity, good education, and good health" (p. 31). By the time she finished high school, Johnson was already deeply involved in the labor movement. As an activist, she helped to organize Local 665 of the Hotel and Restaurant Workers, and she always held that the betterment of working people could only be achieved through unions. As a young woman, Johnson was a member of the Young Communists. She was called before a grand jury to name other Communist Party members but refused to. Later, she was active in both the Democratic-Farmer-Labor Party in Minnesota and the Progressive Party. She campaigned for platforms rather than individuals, although she was closely associated with Hubert Humphrey up until he began to publicly support the Vietnam War. Johnson later publicly resigned from both the Progressive Party and the Young Communists because her memberships hurt her ability to campaign and organize. Johnson has remained active into her nineties. She had the ear of Minnesota Governor Rudy Perpich, helped to found the Fair Employment and Housing Commission, and campaigned for the Fair Employment and Housing Act. Johnson was also on a committee to assure that affirmative action would be utilized in the construction of the Mall of America. She writes, "You don't have to be a Superman or Superwoman to accomplish things. You can be a regular person just like anyone else" (p. 3).

310. Johnson, Rafer. *The Best That I Can Be: An Autobiography.* Written with Philip Goldberg. Introduction by Tom Brokaw. New York, New York: Doubleday, 1998. 270 pages; photographs. ISBN: 0385487606.

> **Notes:** Also published New York: Galilee, 1999. ISBN: 0385487614.

> **Abstract:** Rafer Johnson was one of the best-known athletes in the United States in the late 1950s and early 1960s. He was born in Texas, but raised in the largely white town of Kingsburg, California, in the San Juaquin Valley. The Johnsons were one of the few black families, and Rafer was the only African American in his high school class. Kingsburg, however, was fairly free of racial discrimination. Johnson's coaches groomed him for athletic fame in the decathlon from an early age, and throughout his athletic career, the Kingsburg population supported him, celebrating his victories and homecomings. He has remained their favorite son. In the early 1990s, long after the end of his athletic career, eighty-one percent of the town voted to name a new school Rafer Johnson Junior High School. Johnson claims that the life he had in Kingsburg gave him his optimistic attitude and values. While in college at UCLA, he won the decathlon at the 1955 Pan American Games in Mexico City and qualified for the 1956 Olympics in Melbourne, Australia where he won the silver medal. Throughout his years as a decathlete, he broke the world record a number of times. For the 1960 Olympics, he and Taiwan athlete C. K. Yang both trained with the same coach and formed a fast friendship. Johnson won the gold, and Yang was close behind with the silver, both breaking the world record. After the Olympics, Johnson retired from athletic competition. He had brief careers in film and

television broadcasting and worked for People to People International, an international goodwill program, Continental Telephone, and numerous social organizations. During the 1960s, he became friends with Robert Kennedy and was with him when he was murdered. Johnson managed to twist the gun out of the assassin's hand and, with Rosie Grier, subdued him until police arrived. His relationship with the Kennedy family also led him to involvement in the Special Olympics, run by Kennedy's sister Eunice Shriver, still one of his favorite causes. Johnson, who is married and has two children, remains active in social and athletic activities and, along with many other honors, was chosen to light the Olympic torch in Los Angeles at the 1984 Olympics.

311. Johnson, Ralph W. *David Played a Harp: An Autobiography.* Davidson, North Carolina: Blackwell Ink, Inc., 2000. 452 pages; photographs. ISBN: 0970271301.

Abstract: Ralph Johnson lived in Davidson, North Carolina, a town that had no public education for black children. A school behind the church offered education to African-American children through the seventh grade. Acknowledging Johnson's strong desire to learn and his love of reading, his widowed mother sent him to a private high school, but he soon had to quit to earn money to support the family. At the age of sixteen, his formal education was over and his fifty-year effort to rebuild the family barbershop business had begun. In North Carolina, as in many other southern states, the barbershop business was strictly segregated by law. You either cut the hair of white people or black people. Johnson was in the business of cutting the hair of white people. He found that he was expected to work hard, but not prosper or advance. This attitude was held by African Americans in the community as well as whites. Still a student at heart, Johnson studied constantly, both in the evening after leaving work and during slow times in his shop. He took high-school education correspondence courses to complete his high school education and studied commercial art and law. Again, this was something that was frowned upon by blacks and whites alike, and Johnson became the target of the anger of both races. One night, the home that he had built and nearly paid for was destroyed in an arson attack, although the family escaped without harm. In 1968, students at all-white Davidson College decided to picket and boycott Johnson's whites-only barbershop. No one ever approached Johnson about changing his policy, nor was the state law requiring segregated barbershops taken into consideration. Johnson felt that he was being held responsible for the conditions of segregation that he himself had had to fight and endure.

> I wonder if these bright young men had consid-
> ered whether it was unfair, unjust and immoral
> for them to secretly arrange an attack upon me
> and my business for a condition that had been
> imposed upon me by their elders and had been
> severely maintained by all the pressures of a
> white-controlled society. It was indeed a strange
> morality that excused them from culpability in a
> sneak attack upon an innocent victim of the very
> wrongs that they, in an extremely odd quirk of
> reasoning now accused me of perpetrating on
> Negro people.   (pp. 365-366)

Johnson did desegregate his shop, but business deteriorated, and, in 1971, he decided to close his business. Johnson retired with extreme bitterness. He finished writing this book in 1973 and decided to call it *Horn of Trouble*. It was not published for another twenty-seven years. In the meantime, he renamed it *David Played His Harp* as an indication that conditions had indeed improved over time.

312. Johnson, Shirley E. Oglesby Smith. *Touch My Soul—I Are Fine.* Kansas City, Missouri: Oglesby Communications, 1998. 155 pages. ISBN: none.

Abstract: Johnson writes about growing up in Pine Bluff, Arkansas. She was the oldest of thirteen children, several of whom were born after she left home. Her father was very strict, and her mother allowed the children to develop their own interests and personalities. Her parents' marriage was fiery, and Johnson found school to be a safe haven. Johnson excelled in her studies and participated in every available extra-curricular activity. She and her siblings attended a segregated high school, but Johnson writes that they had good opportunities and fine facilities. Johnson's English teacher taught the students both the rules of Black English and of Standard English and the appropriate uses for both and she urged the students to respect those who spoke Black English. Johnson attended AM&N College, a traditionally black school, now the University of Arkansas, Pine Bluff. She majored in business administration and planned to become a lawyer. She moved to Flint, Michigan, after college and then to Kansas City, Missouri, after she married Clinton M. Johnson. She earned her master's degree at the University of Kansas City Missouri (UMKC) and became a teacher. Comparing her experiences at UMKC and AM&N, Johnson writes that the faculty and staff of black colleges gave students the support they needed, while predominantly white schools, such as UMKC, set artificial blocks in the way of African-American students. Johnson gives her views on marriage and describes her own, as well as some of the positive and negative marital experiences of her siblings. Johnson tells how the family came together after the death of their father to care for their mother, who was suffering from Alzheimer's disease.

313. Jones, Bill T. *Last Night on Earth.* Written with Peggy Gillespie. New York, New York: Pantheon Books, 1995. 286 pages; photographs. ISBN: 0679439269.

Abstract: Dancer Bill T. Jones began life in Bunnell, Florida. His large family consisted of four children from his mother's previous marriage and the eight his parents had together. Jones remembers his father gathering the children all around and telling them stories of his childhood and family and how they, according to family lore, came to the United States from the Andes or possibly the Indies. These stories and the tradition of storytelling later became an important part of Jones's work as a dancer. The family moved to Binghamton, New York, where he was raised with traditional southern African-American culture even while living in a predominantly white area of the city. He was drawn to the arts and became aware of his gay sexual orientation at a fairly young age. Both his southern background and sexual identity have figured strongly in his dancing and choreographic work. He met his partner of seventeen years, Arnie Lane, while still a freshman at SUNY Binghamton. Lane and Jones followed several paths together before they founded the Bill T. Jones/Arnie Lane Dance Company and danced as partners. They were referred to as "the same-sex choreographic duo" and described as "tall and black, short and white" (p. 203). Lane died in 1988 after contracting HIV/AIDS in the early 1980s. Jones describes his dancing career, his inspirations and the details of his many dances and the stories behind them. He sees his personal history within the context of the nation's, providing a chronology that begins in the sixteenth century as Europeans "penetrated the Dark Continent," and ending December 30, 1994 at 9:00 p.m. as he and his current companion, Bjorn Amelan, settle down to a quiet evening at home after having been stopped in their car by the police, who mistakenly suspected that Jones was wanted for armed robbery.

314. Jones, James Earl. *James Earl Jones: Voices and Silences.* Written with Penelope Niven. New York, New York: Scribner, 1993. 394 pages; photographs. ISBN: 0684195135.

> **Notes:** Also published New York : Simon & Schuster, 1994. ISBN: 0671899457.
>
> **Abstract:** Actor James Earl Jones's boyhood memories include the warm light of a coal lamp at the moment of his birth, discussions about slavery, issues of skin color, the difficulty of attending school, and the absence of his father. His mother was generally away working and Jones lived with his grandparents, aunts, uncles, and a cousin. His father was an actor and a boxer, both occupations were frowned upon by his grandparents. Jones was kept from him as a child. Jones began stuttering at about the age of six and rarely spoke until he was fourteen. When urged by an English teacher to read a poem he had written, Jones discovered that he could read out loud without a stutter. This event threw him into the world of poetry and literature. At the age of twenty-one, he renewed his relationship with his actor father, Robert Earl Jones, and they became quite close, working together on a number of occasions. Jones and his cousin Randy were determined to attend college and became the first of their family to do so. Jones started out studying medicine, but soon decided to switch to Drama and English. A member of ROTC, Jones expected to be sent to Korea, but the truce came, and he left the service to study on the GI Bill at the American Wing Theatre. Jones describes his education in theater and acting, his many theatrical associates, and what it was like working with his father. He also gives a detailed account of many of the plays in which he has performed, paying particular attention to his role as Othello and to his controversial one-man production of the life of Paul Robeson.

315. Jones, LeAlan and Lloyd Newman. *Our America: Life and Death on the South Side of Chicago.* Written with David Isay. Photographs by John Brooks. New York, New York: Scribner, 1997. 203 pages; photographs. ISBN: 0684836165.

> **Notes:** Published in paperback New York : Pocket Books, 1998. ISBN: 0671004646.
> Based on recorded interviews by LeAlan Jones and Lloyd Newman between 1993 and 1996. Originally produced for radio by David Isay of Sound Portraits and National Public Radio. Photographs by John Brooks, teenage resident of the Ida B. Wells housing project in Chicago.

Abstract: In 1993 LeAlan Jones and Lloyd Newman, both teenagers, were selected by David Isay to create a recorded diary of one. week in their lives at the Ida B. Wells housing project in Chicago. They recorded their own activities and thoughts; they talked to members of their families, the principal of their elementary school, and local business people. Jones interviewed his grandmother who has custody of Jones and his siblings due to his mother's mental illness. He does not know who is father is. He also interviewed his seventeen-year-old sister, who, already the mother of a two-year-old, has dropped out of school. Jones asks her if any of her friends have been killed and she responds that probably thirty to forty of her close friends are dead. Newman interviewed his father, a chronic alcoholic who does not live at home, and his two teenage sisters, who have raised the younger children since their mother died of cirrhosis of the liver at the age of thirty-five. Jones and Newman give a vivid depiction of a life lived in the midst of frequent shootings and killings, and vacant, crumbling housing. They write of the difficulty of connecting to school when one is hungry and scared and when expectations for a future beyond high school are nonexistent. Two years after completing this first project, Newman and Jones contacted Isay about another project. They wanted to cover the story of Eric Morse, a five-year-old boy who was thrown from a fourteenth story apartment in the project by two boys, ages ten and eleven. An entire hour was devoted to their presentation on NPR's *All Things Considered*. Altogether, Isay produced six hundred pages of transcript from Jones's and Newman's recordings. Isay worked with both young men in preparing the manuscript of *Our America*, which includes "Life 1993," taken from the transcripts resulting from "Ghetto Life 101"; "Death 1995," taken from the transcripts from "Remorse: The 14 Stories of Eric Morse"; and "Life 1996," a follow-up on how Jones and Newman have done and where they are heading, how their families are doing, and what changes have taken place in the Ida B. Wells projects. Jones finished high school and went on to attend Florida State University. At the time the book was being completed, Newman had a year of high school left. Jones provides the concluding chapter to the book in which he describes two Americas. In the African American's America, children

> make day-to-day decisions about whether to go
> to school or to go on the corner and sell drugs.
> As children, they know that there may not be a
> tomorrow. Why are African-American children
> faced with this dilemma at such an early age?

> Why must they look down the road to a future
> that they might never see? . . . I live in a com-
> munity that waves a white flag because we have
> almost given up. I live in a community where on
> the walls are the names of fallen comrades of
> war. I live in a second America. I live here not
> because I chose to, but because I have to. . . . This
> is LeAlan Jones on November 19, 1996. I hope I
> survive. I hope I survive. I hope I survive.
> Signing off. Peace.   (pp. 199-200)

316. Jones, Richard O. (1946-). *When Mama's Gone: A True and
     Inspiring Story of a Single Father overcoming All Odds to Become a
     Positive Role Model*. Los Angeles, California: Milligan Books,
     1998. 274 pages. ISBN: 1881524167.

> **Abstract:** Richard Jones was raised in an abusive household, mak-
> ing money from a paper route to help his family get by. As an
> adult, he had a hard time holding on to a job, and it was just after
> he was fired from a bank that he met his wife. They had a turbu-
> lent marriage, with Jones making a living on ingenious scams of
> all kinds. When his wife died in a car accident, he was left with
> four daughters to raise. He sent them to live with his mother and
> sisters and their families in Mississippi, while he continued to con-
> duct scams, alone and with his female friends. It was not until the
> girls were in their teens and twenties that Jones began to give up
> his life of crime and was able to bring all of his children back to
> Los Angeles to live together. He began to write columns for LA
> newspapers and wrote a book describing his criminal activities
> entitled *Tips Against Crime, Written From Prison*. Jones was conse-
> quently featured on television programs that reenacted some of
> his scams, and he made an appearance on the *Oprah Winfrey Show*.
> He became involved in a writer's group, and has published sever-
> al volumes of poetry.

317. Jones, Star. *You Have to Stand for Something, or You'll Fall for
     Anything*. Written with Daniel Paisner. New York, New York:
     Bantam Books, 1998.   235 pages.   ISBN: 0553108549 :
     0553580345.

> **Abstract:** Jones, a lawyer turned TV personality, writes about her
> life and her philosophy of life. She describes her childhood,
> enfolded in the bosom of enormous extended families on both
> sides. She writes about how she wanted to become a lawyer as a
> child, and managed to achieve this dream with the support of her

mother and the rest of her family. Jones talks about her Christian faith and what it means to her. She recounts her early years in the district attorney's office and describes some of the moral decisions she had to make in court cases. After several years practicing law, Jones was recruited to provide commentary for *Court TV* when it first began. Eventually she was noticed by James Blue, who worked for the NBC *Today Show*. NBC News quickly hired her as its legal correspondent. She is now featured on *The View* along with Barbara Walters. Jones presents her views on many aspects of life, including race, religion, sex, the role of women, personal appearance and grooming, and social responsibility in journalism, politics and law.

318. Jones, Syl (1951-). *Rescuing Little Roundhead: A Childhood in Stories.* Minneapolis, Minnesota: Milkweed Editions, 1996. 202 pages. ISBN: 1571312153.

Abstract: Writer Syl Jones, or Little Roundhead as he refers to himself in this book, was born in Cincinnati, Ohio in 1951. He uses anecdotes from his childhood to tell his story. Many are sad, but he intersperses them with the humorous observations of a child. Jones was doted on by his mother and grandparents, but raised strictly by his father. The entire extended family lived together for a number of years before his parents bought their own home in a different part of the city. Their new home was infested with rats and cockroaches, which were immune to poison, and the neighborhood was full of colorful and dangerous characters whom Jones describes in humorous detail. Little Roundhead did well in school, and he was blessed with many teachers who did their best to encourage him and offer him opportunities for enrichment. At age eight, Jones was sexually molested, and the experience caused permanent damage to his relationship with his father, who blamed him for the attack. To make matters worse, everyone knew what happened and it gave him a bad reputation as a sissy and a tattler. At the end of junior high school, Jones was accepted into Auburn Hills High School, an elite public school in Cincinnati. For the first time he had friends who thought like him, and he thrived in the competitive but eclectic and creative atmosphere. Jones had sold newspapers for years and years, and at age fifteen, he finally decided that he could write better than the reporters. He submitted samples of his work from the school newspaper to the editor of the *Call and Post*. The editor was impressed and sent him out to cover a college basketball game for the paper. His story was accepted for publication, and he was paid twenty-five dollars. In the ensuing years, Jones continued to write for the newspaper, and

his work helped to finance his college education and to get him
started in his writing career.

319. Jordan, June. *Soldier: A Poet's Childhood*. New York, New York:
Basic Civitas Books, 2000.   261 pages.   ISBN: 0465036813 :
0465036821.

Abstract: Writer June Jordan's father expected and wanted a boy.
He raised his daughter to be a man, teaching her to defend herself,
fish, do carpentry and plumbing, withstand harsh conditions and
a certain amount of brutality, and above all, to excel in academics.
Jordan was reading Shakespeare, Dunbar, McKay, Zane Grey, and
other writers at the age of six. She was able to read anything, but
her comprehension level was low. She was, however, required to
memorize and explicate her reading for her father, and if she did-
n't understand something, she was sent back to her room to work
on it some more. Some of the daughter-father camaraderie that
came with being "the boy" in the family was positive. Jordan
recalls the exciting annual event of putting up the clothes line,
which required her to lean out of an upper story window to check
the operations. But she also had to watch her father pour boiling
water on squalling cats, go deep-sea fishing, which she hated, and
prepare for his sneak attacks. Although Jordan's mother did not
support her husband's desire to make a man out of their daughter,
she suffered her own share of abuse, and had very little opportunity to influence Jordan's upbringing. Jordan's unusual childhood
perhaps contributed to her developing a wild temper. Her love of
Zane Grey made her fanatical about the wild West, and she recalls
wanting a gun more than anything. She also developed an intense
love of words. In the memoir, Jordan, an accomplished writer
with more than ten volumes of poetry as well as plays, children's
books, and political essays to her credit, expresses her memories in
both prose and poetry.

320. Jordan, Michael. *For the Love of the Game: My Story*. Edited by
Mark Vancil. New York, New York: Crown Publishers, 1998.
156 pages. ISBN: 0609602063.

Notes: Also published in a two volume edition: New York: Crown
Publishers, 1998. ISBN: 0609602063 (160 pages); and in paperback
New York: Crown Publishers, 1998. ISBN: 1892866064 (112 pages).

Abstract: Michael Jordan tells the story of his professional basketball career as a member of the Chicago Bulls from 1984 until he
retired for the second time at the end of the 1997-1998 season.
During those thirteen seasons, Jordan's team won the NBA cham-

pionship six times. Jordan himself was named Most Valuable Player during each of the championship finals. In addition to telling his story as a professional basketball player, Jordan comments on his time on the University of North Carolina team which won a collegiate national championship, his participation on two U.S. Olympic Gold Medal teams (known as the Dream Teams), his brief career as a professional baseball player during his first retirement, his gambling habit, his lucrative contract with the Nike shoe company, and his close relationship with his father, which ended with his father's murder. Jordan claims that, unlike many of his contemporaries, his career was driven by "the love of the game" and not by a desire for money or celebrity status.

321. Joseph-Gaudet, Frances (1861-1934). *"He Leadeth Me."* Introduction by Chanta M. Haywood. African American Women Writers 1910-1940. New York, New York: G. K. Hall and Company, 1996. 144 pages; photographs. ISBN: 0816116296.

Notes: Originally published 1913.

Abstract: Frances Joseph-Gaudet's work begins with letters and excerpts from newspaper stories attesting to her work with prisoners, especially incarcerated juveniles. Joseph-Gaudet felt spiritually called to go into New Orleans prisons to spread the Christian faith, preaching and singing hymns to save both the condemned and those who would return to the world outside the prisons. Joseph-Gaudet also sought to improve conditions for women, who were often the victims of male prison guards, and she begged clothing on the street for prisoners who were in need. For those who convinced her of their innocence, she collected evidence, taking it to court to aid in their defense. She sought releases for the old and sickly, sometimes finding them shelter outside the prison and other times finding them transportation to return to their homes outside New Orleans. Joseph-Gaudet had particular concern for African-American prisoners and children and was instrumental in founding the Colored Industrial School for homeless children. However, she worked for anyone in need, rarely receiving any compensation for her efforts. Remarkably, Joseph-Gaudet had the respect of the white mayors of New Orleans, police chiefs, sheriffs, and other officials with whom she worked, and sometimes fought, to change conditions and to aid those in need. This was in the years following reconstruction during a time when laws became more restrictive for African Americans, and many doors as well as minds were tightly closed. As a delegate of the Women's Christian Temperance Union, Joseph-Gaudet traveled to Scotland, Ireland, London, and France where she spoke and preached. This edition of her memoir is accompanied by an extensive historical introduction.

322. Joyner-Kersee, Jacqueline. *A Kind of Grace: The Autobiography of the World's Greatest Female Athlete.* Written with Sonja Steptoe. New York, New York: Warner Books, 1997. 310 pages; photographs. ISBN: 0446522481.

Abstract: Jackie Joyner-Kersee, an African American, was born in 1962. She lived with her mother and father, two sisters and brother in East St. Louis, Illinois. The construction of the Mary E. Brown Community Center down the street from her home was a life-changing event for her. She took advantage of everything the center had to offer and usually spent her entire day there. It was at the center that Joyner-Kersee was introduced first to dance and then basketball and track. In school, she became an athletic cheerleader and learned a variety of jumps, such as jumping up in the air, touching her toes, and landing in a splits position. These gave her the strong legs and stamina that helped her on her way to becoming a champion heptathlete and long-jumper. A well-known athlete by the time she graduated from high school, Joyner-Kersee was recruited by many colleges. After careful consideration and refusal of all bribes offered, Joyner-Kersee chose UCLA. There she excelled academically and athletically, playing basketball and running track. Her two areas of competition were the heptathlon and long jump. It was also at UCLA that she met her coach and husband-to-be, Bobby Kersee. Joyner-Kersee describes the major competitions in her life, including her first Olympics in 1984, at which she won the silver medal for the heptathlon event. In the 1988 Olympics she won gold medals for both the long jump and the heptathlon. After this spectacular performance, however, she was suspected of taking steroids. For months after, she was questioned and tested over and over. Since her childhood in inner-city East St. Louis, Joyner-Kersee has had a strong aversion to drugs of any kind, and no test she took ever showed any signs of steroids. In 1992, Joyner-Kersee again won the gold medal in the heptathlon and the bronze medal in the long jump. In her farewell Olympics in 1996, Joyner-Kersee won the bronze medal in the long jump after having to withdraw from the heptathlon because of injuries.

323. Kamdar, Mira. *Motiba's Tattoos: A Granddaughter's Journey into Her Indian Family's Past.* New York, New York: Public Affairs, 2000. 289 pages; photographs; Gujarati and Hindi glossaries. ISBN: 1891620584.

> **Notes:** Published in paperback New York: Plume, 2001. ISBN: 0452282691.
>
> **Abstract:** Mira Kamdar is the daughter of an East Indian man and white American woman. In this book, she talks about the life of the Indian side of her family, beginning with her great-grandfather. Her grandmother, Motiba, was raised in Rangoon, Burma, where her father had a successful business. Motiba was married to a man, a Jain, who had decided that he would follow Gandhi. He finally gave up his desire to be a celibate disciple of the Mohatma at the urging of his family and by Gandhi himself. The couple eventually went back to Burma, where Kamdar's grandfather, Bapuji, also had a successful business. The family fled when Burma was invaded by Japan in 1942, but Bapuji continued to go back and forth. In 1962, however, a military coup in Burma ended in the banishment of all Indians and the confiscation of all of their assets in the country. Kamdar's father finished high school in Bombay and went to the United States to study at a time when most Indians still aspired to study in England. While a graduate student at Oregon State College, he met Kamdar's mother, a girl from an Oregon farm. When Kamdar and her sister were children, they and their mother spent extended periods of time in Bombay with their grandparents, where they became familiar with Indian culture. Her mother learned how to cook the vegetarian dishes that her husband had been raised on, and they comprised the family's main diet upon their return to the United States. Kamdar discusses both the difficulties and benefits of being from a bicultural family during the 1960s and points out how different the situation is now for children of immigrants from Asia. As an adult, she went back to India and to Rangoon to trace the history of her family and to better understand her father and his parents.

324. Kanafani, Fay Afaf. *Nadia Captive of Hope: Memoir of an Arab Woman.* Armonk, New York: M. E. Sharpe, 1999. 346 pages; photographs. ISBN: 076560311X : 0765603128.

> **Abstract:** Kanafani was born in 1918 in Lebanon during the French mandate. After she married, she moved in with her husband's family in Palestine, where she stayed until the war, caused by the creation of the Israeli state, made it too dangerous to remain there. She and her in-laws returned to Lebanon. This respite from

war soon ended when Lebanon's strife with Israel began, and various warring religious factions took over. Kanafani provides the reader with the Arab perspective on the changes that occurred as Jewish settlers arrived from Europe, and Palestine was gradually transformed into Israel. More personally, Kanafani focuses on the traditional treatment of women in her culture, and particularly its effect on her own life. She was abused both physically and emotionally by her father. She was angry with her mother for not intervening, but she later experienced her own sense of powerlessness as her first husband abused their children. Mothers did not have legal custody of their children, and thus, after the death of her first husband, Kanafani struggled to pursue an education, career, and independence and still maintain her tenuous ties with her three children. Because of her resistance to the status quo for women in her culture, Kanafani was viewed as irrationally rebellious by the other women in her family and the few female friends she mentions. Kanafani settled in the United States in 1985, and her story ends with the death of her second husband. An afterword by the editor describes Kanafani's current activities in San Francisco, where she eventually settled.

325. Kang, K. Connie. *Home Was the Land of Morning Calm: A Saga of a Korean-American Family.* Reading, Massachusetts: Addison-Wesley Publishing Company, 1995. 307 pages; photographs. ISBN: 0201626845.

Abstract: Journalist Connie Kang tells the story of her family. Her parents were young children when the Japanese first occupied Korea, and both were forced to learn Japanese and follow Japanese customs. Kang gives a vivid account of the international diplomatic games played at Korea's and the Koreans' expense. Following World War II and the liberation from Japan, Kang's father left for a special assignment in the United States. This trip, which was meant to last four months, turned into an absence of several years. While he was in the United States, the Korean War broke out, and Kang, her mother, grandmother, and uncle's family were among the flood of refugees escaping from the North to the South. They ended up in Pusan. Her father made his way to Tokyo, and Kang and her mother eventually escaped to Japan. Initially arrested for entering the country illegally, the two were finally reunited with Kang's father and settled in Tokyo and then Okinawa. Following high school, Kang traveled to the United States to attend college at the University of Missouri. Upon graduation, she pursued graduate work at Northwestern University and received an internship with a Rochester, New York, newspa-

per. Kang left the newspaper to pursue a doctoral degree, but realizing that her heart was not in her studies, returned to South
Korea, where her parents now lived, to work. Although happy to
be back, Kang discovered that she no longer met all of her parents
expectations and had been influenced enough by her stay in the
United States to no longer fit in comfortably. She returned to the
United States with her American husband, but believed that she
was shirking her responsibility to her family. Eventually, she
divorced her husband, began pursuing a journalism career in San
Francisco, and was joined there by her brother and parents. Kang
describes her desire to be independent, but also to take responsibility for her parents. Kang never severed her emotional ties to
Korea, but after a lengthy assignment there for the *San Francisco
Examiner*, she was ready to say that the United States was her
home. Kang now lives in Los Angeles where she writes about
Asians, Koreans in particular, from an Asian and Korean point of
view.

326. Keckley, Elizabeth (1818-1907). *Behind the Scenes, or, Thirty
Years a Slave and Four Years in the White House*. Edited by
Frances Smith Foster. The Lakeside Classics, 96. Chicago,
Illinois: R. R. Donnelley & Sons, 1998. 319 pages. ISBN: none.

Notes: Originally published New York: G. W. Carleton &
Company, 1868 (371 pages). Also published Urbana, Illinois:
University of Illinois Press, 2000. ISBN: 0252070208.

327. Kenny, Maurice. *Backward to Forward: Prose Pieces*. Fredonia,
New York: White Pine Press, 1997. 170 pages. ISBN:
1877727695.

Abstract: The majority of the essays in this collection are histori-
cal in nature, however, the final three are autobiographical. In
"Waiting at the Edge," Kenny describes himself as a word hunter.
He writes that he has "hunted not only words and images,
metaphors, but, to my mother's relish, also song" (p. 125). Kenny
is a Mohawk Indian who grew up in the foothills of the
Adirondacks. His father, an accomplished hunter, passed on to
Kenny a love and respect for nature and wildlife. Although
Kenny's father never traveled far from home, he imagined the
beauty of other places. Kenny himself has traveled widely, and
this has led him to contemplate the meaning of place and home.
While invoking all that he considers elements of home, Kenny also
laments the toll that agricultural chemicals and acid rain have
taken on humanity, especially farm workers, and the natural

world. In other essays, Kenny relives the trials and fortunes of the touring poet. He also recalls his decision to leave the amenities of city life and return to the simpler, more natural setting of northern New York.

328. Kidd, Mae Street. *Passing for Black: The Life and Careers of Mae Street Kidd.* Lexington, Kentucky: University Press of Kentucky, 1997. 193 pages; photographs. ISBN: 0813119960.

Abstract: Mae Street Kidd was born in Millersburg, Kentucky, in 1904. She and her brother and sister all shared the same white father, although they never met him. Nearly six feet tall, blonde, and light-skinned, Kidd never attempted to pass for white. She writes that if she had tried to live as a white person she would have been rejecting her mother, something she never could have done. Growing up in the South, Kidd lived by the rules of segregation, but refused to be defined by those rules or by the society's expectations for whites and blacks. She began her professional career at age eighteen when she began selling insurance for the black-owned insurance company Mammoth. Kidd met her first husband at Mammoth, and they married in 1930. In 1937, her husband bought a house in his name only. Kidd gave him two weeks to put her name on the deed "and if you don't, not only will I not live in that house with you, but I'll not live with you anywhere" (p. 73). When her husband died in 1942, she decided to pursue an opportunity with the American Red Cross. She trained in Washington, D.C., obtained the rank of captain, and was stationed in England, where she served as assistant director of a Red Cross service club for black soldiers. Following her tour of duty, Kidd found that she was not ready to pick up her old life in Louisville, and so she worked briefly in Portland, Maine with the United Seaman's Service. While there, she developed public relations skills which she took back with her to the Mammoth Insurance Company. Kidd persuaded the company to allow her to pioneer a public relations office, which she managed for eighteen years. In 1968, Kidd was persuaded to run for the Kentucky legislature. During her twelve-year political career, she sponsored a bill that established a housing corporation to provide mortgage loans to low-income people and another that provided for the screening and prevention of lead poisoning. Kidd was also responsible for organizing the first Urban League Guild outside of New York. She is proud of her life-long independence and extensive professional life and considers herself to be a role model for young women.

329. Kilby, James M. *The Forever Fight*. Pittsburgh, Pennsylvania: Dorrance Publishing Company, 1998. 55 pages; photographs. ISBN: 0805941703.

Abstract: James Kilby was one of nineteen students to desegregate Front Royal, Virginia's Warren County High School in 1959. Although he started high school at out-of-town institutions that would take African Americans, when it came time for his sister to enter high school, his father decided that young girls should be allowed to stay in town. He filed a suit against the county demanding that his children be allowed to attend the local whites-only high school. As a result, James Kilby was one of the first two African-American students to graduate from Warren County High School in 1961, an accomplishment of which he is proud. The accomplishment however came with a high price—daily abuse at school and nightly visits at home intended to terrorize the family. Following graduation, Kilby's parents spirited him out of Front Royal to Washington, D.C., because he had been convicted of throwing rocks at white boys and received a one-year suspended sentence. In Washington, D.C., Kilby applied for work with the CIA and was assigned to work as a messenger at the White House. In the early 1990s, Kilby began TEAR (Treat Every American Right), an award to recognize people who did the right thing with no thought of how they could benefit from it. His first TEAR award went to Frank Wells, the security guard who discovered the Watergate burglars in the Nixon-era scandal. When Kilby returned to live in Front Royal, thirty-four years after leaving, he was disappointed to see that not much had changed from his youth. There were racial slurs spray-painted on the walls of the high school, Klan literature was being distributed, and the black section of town had been abandoned. "I have concluded that changing racial attitudes and behaviors will continue to be an uphill battle—a forever fight. . . . Maybe that's why I try to speak out; I like to see people treated well. I'm not a trouble maker or a revolutionary, just somebody who cares" (p. 54). Kilby was awarded the Dallas G. Pace, Sr. Humanitarian Award from the Anne Arundel County Human Relations Commission of Annapolis, Maryland.

330. Kilgore, Thomas (1913-1998). *A Servant's Journey: The Life and Work of Thomas Kilgore*. Written with Jini Kilgore Ross. Valley Forge, Pennsylvania: Judson Press, 1998. 253 pages; photographs; index; sermons; speeches. ISBN: 0817012974.

Abstract: Rev. Thomas Kilgore was born in South Carolina in

1913. His parents were tenant farmers who had a rare opportunity to farm 150 acres of leased land with a fair contract. They were successful farmers until the bottom fell out of the cotton market. The family was forced to leave the farm and eventually settled in Brevard, North Carolina. Following graduation from high school, Kilgore worked for fifteen months as a butler in order to earn his tuition, room, and board to Morehouse College. Trained for the ministry, Kilgore first served his home congregation in Brevard and then moved to Winston-Salem, North Carolina, with his wife Jeannetta. While in North Carolina, Kilgore was active in the community. His church ran a voter registration school in 1942, and he personally escorted the graduates to the government office to see that they were successfully registered. Kilgore and family moved to Harlem, where he served a church for fifteen years. In New York, he was also director of the New York Southern Christian Leadership office and active in the NAACP and YMCA. In 1963, Kilgore became pastor of the Second Baptist Church in Los Angeles. He continued to be active in community and in global outreach programs. Kilgore was responsible for founding the Gathering, a religious interracial and ecumenical movement to deal with social problems in the Los Angeles Area. He also devised the Black Agenda, which focused on economic development and housing issues for the black community. Kilgore was elected president of the American Baptist Convention for 1969-1970. He was the first African American to be so named. He was considered a militant, but he referred to himself as a militant of love. Kilgore and his wife retired in 1986. A selection of his speeches, sermons, and writings are included in this publication.

331. Kim, Dora Yum. *Doing What Had to Be Done: The Life Narrative of Dora Yum Kim.* Written with Soo-Young Chin. Asian American History & Culture. Philadelphia, Pennsylvania: Temple University Press, 1999. 229 pages; photographs. ISBN: 156639693x : 1566396948.

Abstract: Dora Yum Kim was born in Manteca, California, in 1921 during a time when United States and California law did not allow Asian immigration, and neither foreign nationals nor their U.S.-born children were allowed to own land. Soon after her birth, her family moved to Chinatown in San Francisco, the only part of the city in which they were allowed to rent. They operated a variety of businesses, including a cigar stand, a restaurant and pool hall, and a grocery. Later they owned rental property, purchased in their lawyer's name. Despite the small number of Koreans in the area, her parents maintained most of the traditions of their native country. Kim writes about the Korean manner of arranging marriages. Her father told her mother that he would kill Kim if she married outside the Korean culture, and then he would kill himself. Thus, Kim never considered marrying anyone who was not Korean. She notes that none of her children or grandchildren have felt a need to do so. Her mother encouraged her to go into a profession, so Kim became a real estate agent. The San Francisco Real Estate Board, however, refused to let her join, despite the fact that she had passed the required test and received her license. She tried nursing, but it was not to her liking. She eventually found her way into social work and was employed by the State Department of Employment to act as a liaison for newly arrived immigrants. While working for the state in what she felt was essentially a dead-end position, she cofounded the Korean Community Service Center and received grant money to start a hot meal program. After retiring from her state position, Kim worked full time at the Community Center, focusing her efforts on the Senior Meals program. She arranged for a Korean cook and justified food items such as kimchi to the state nutritionist. Through her work, Kim became aware of the differences in the various waves of Korean immigrants and concerned that their stories were being recorded and interpreted without sufficient input from the subjects themselves. Kim was designated a Living Treasure by the California Assembly for lifetime achievements in the Asian-American Community and received a Certificate of Honor from the San Francisco Board of Supervisors for public service. Soo-Young Chin, a native of Seoul, Korea, who attended school in the United States, met Kim while she was working at the Korean Community Service Center. Chin spent five years interviewing Kim and writing her narrative. Chin weaves in her own observations, and compares her life story as an immigrant to that of Kim's life as a native-born Californian.

332. Kim, Elizabeth. *Ten Thousand Sorrows: The Extraordinary Journey of a Korean War Orphan.* New York, New York: Doubleday, 2000. 228 pages. ISBN: 0385496338.

Abstract: Kim was born to a Korean woman and an American GI in Korea during the Korean War. After her father returned to the United States, her mother went back to her rural village, where the family rejected her and eventually killed her because she refused to sell her multiracial daughter into servitude. Kim's life was spared due to the intervention of an aunt, and she was placed in a Christian orphanage. Kim was never given a birth date, and no record remained of the identities of her mother and father. She was adopted by a Christian missionary couple from the Los Angeles area. They were very strict with Kim, demanding that she do the housekeeping, play piano, and proselytize other children. They gave her very little affection in return. Kim learned to speak English and follow the instructions of her parents, but their endless restrictions meant that she never fit in with her peer group and had almost no friends. Longing for affection and love, she allowed herself to be coerced into marriage directly out of high school to a young man of her parents choosing. Unfortunately, her husband was controlling and severely abusive. The need to protect her daughter from becoming either a victim of or witness to abuse finally motivated Kim to leave. She describes her first taste of freedom living alone with her daughter, her continued emotional struggles, her string of unhealthy relationships with men, the repair of her ties with her mother and father, her work as a reporter, and the development of her daughter into a healthy and happy young woman.

333. Kim, Richard E. (1932-). *Lost Names: Scenes From a Korean Boyhood*. Berkeley, California: University of California Press, 1998. 198 pages. ISBN: 0520214242.

> **Notes:** Originally published London: Deutsch, 1970. ISBN: 0233963049; New York: Universe Books, 1988. ISBN: 0876636784.

334. Kincaid, Jamaica. *My Brother*. New York, New York: Farrar, Straus, and Giroux, 1997. 197 pages. ISBN: 0374216819.

> **Notes:** Published in paperback Noonday Press, 1998. ISBN: 0374525625.

> **Abstract:** American writer Jamaica Kincaid writes about her brother who died of AIDS at age thirty-three in their native Antigua. The story serves as the backdrop for an in-depth look at the relationship of the author with her family, especially her mother, father, and brother, and her struggles with her feelings for them in adulthood after her devastating childhood. Her life was changed when her brother was born. His arrival into the family meant that her father could no longer support them and resulted in her being sent away at the age of sixteen to earn money for the family. Kincaid gives a vivid, lyrical description of life and deprivation on the West Indies island. She also explores the attitudes of Antiguans to life in general and AIDS in particular.

335. King, B. B. *Blues All around Me: The Autobiography of B. B. King.*
Written with David Ritz. New York, New York: Avon, 1996.
336 pages; photographs; discography.   ISBN: 0380973189 :
0380787814.

Notes: Also published New York: Spike, 1999. ISBN: 0380807602.

Abstract: Blues singer B. B. King was born Riley B. King. His parents were separated and his mother died when he was still young. He lived off and on with his father, working on farms, driving tractors and picking cotton. He was married at seventeen and joined the army at eighteen, in 1943. After basic training, farm workers were called back home to work at farming, so-called "vital jobs," and he took the opportunity to go back to his wife. Anxious to get out of sharecropping, however, he left the farm in the Mississippi Delta region to go to Memphis, Tennessee, with one eye towards a career in music. During the 1940s, B. B. King developed his blues style, influenced by many other musicians. His first job was hosting a ten-minute radio show during which he sang, talked, and played a jingle he wrote for a tonic drink. This led to appearances at a night spot and then to more jobs. He eventually began recording at Sun Records. In the ensuing years, King had his own band that traveled with him. Despite his success, King had trouble managing his finances and schedules and was constantly in trouble over taxes with the IRS. He also found it difficult to move ahead in his career. In 1968, he was introduced to Sid Seidenberg, an accountant who agreed to manage his career. Seidenberg straightened out King's accounts, got his taxes in order, and began scheduling him to play in more prominent venues, bringing him to the attention of a broader and whiter audience. King began recording with large record companies, and in 1970 he released his most popular hit, "The Thrill is Gone." Eventually, he reached international prominence, performing in countries around the world and selling as many records abroad as in the United States. Although he has over forty albums to his name, he has always made his main living from live appearances, and he still routinely performs over three hundred days a year. He credits his father, who claimed that a man could never work too much, with his dedication to and love of his work. Along with describing his career, adventures, musical influences, and his guitar, which he calls "Lucille," King also talks about his other passions in life, women and sex. He has had two brief marriages, fifteen children by fifteen different women, and incalculable numbers of other lovers everywhere he performs.

336. King, Martin Luther, Jr. *The Autobiography of Martin Luther King, Jr.* Edited by Clayborne Carson. New York, New York: Intellectual Properties Management, 1998. 400 pages; photographs. ISBN: 0446524123.

Notes: Also published New York: Intellectual Properties Management/Warner Books, 2001. ISBN: 0446676500.

Abstract: Although Martin Luther King, Jr. never wrote a comprehensive autobiography, many of his writings included autobiographical material. Editor Clayborne Carson is director of the King Papers Project. To construct this autobiography, he incorporated hundreds of documents and recordings. He used material from the following works by King: *Stride Toward Freedom: The Montgomery Story* (1958); *Why We Can't Wait* (1964); *Where Do We Go from Here: Chaos or Community?* (1967); and numerous articles, speeches, sermons, public statements, interviews, letters, and other documents. The autobiography traces King's spiritual and political journey. Becoming a minister was almost inevitable in King's family; his father, grandfather, great grandfather, and brother were all ministers. His family was politically active as well, and his parents attempted to prepare their children for the realities of segregation. King's mother told him to "feel a sense of 'somebodiness' . . ." even though they would "face a system that stared [them] in the face every day saying you are 'less than' you are 'not equal to'" (p. 3). King, Sr. was the president of the Atlanta, Georgia, branch of the NAACP. He played a role in equalizing teacher salaries in Atlanta and doing away with Jim Crow elevators in the courthouse. King, Sr. also refused to take the segregated city buses. King had his first experience of life without Jim Crow during a summer working in Connecticut. This, combined with his family's activism, his religious faith, and his boyhood experiences with racism, led him to his leadership role in the Civil Rights Movement. King entered Morehouse College at fifteen. He read Henry David Thoreau's "On Civil Disobedience," and began formulating his ideas about nonviolent resistance. After graduation, he attended Crozer Seminary in Pennsylvania. There, under the influence of Walter Rauschenbusch's *Christianity and the Social Crisis,* and with an introduction to Karl Marx and Gandhi, King began his "serious quest to eliminate evil" (p. 17). Following Crozer Seminary, King attended the Boston University School of Theology. His mentors at Boston were Edgar S. Brightman and L. Harold DeWolf. The autobiography covers all of the well known events in King's life: the Montgomery Bus Boycott, receiving the Nobel Peace Prize, leadership in the Selma to Montgomery March in pursuit of voting rights, the Poor People's Campaign, protest of the Vietnam War, and his jail sentences. The work also sheds light on the crumbling of the nonviolent resistance movement with the growing prominence of the competing philosophies of Malcolm X and Stokely Carmichael and the Black Power movement. The work ends with the complete text of King's final speech on April 3, 1968, given in Memphis in support of the sanitation workers' strike, the day before his assassination.

337. King, Robert H. (1922-). *Pastor Jenkins Said, "Hang on to Matthew 6:33": Autobiography of Robert H. King, Ph.D.* St. Louis, Missouri: Concordia Publishing House, 1999. 190 pages; photographs. ISBN: 0570053943.

Abstract: King was born in 1922 in Sunny South, Alabama. There were no public schools for black children in the area in which King and his family lived. He attended a Baptist-sponsored school several miles from home for one year until it closed, and then another school twelve miles away until the family car broke down. After a year with no school options, King began attending a Lutheran school in Selma, Alabama. He graduated with much financial difficulty, having already decided that he wanted to be a pastor. When he was drafted into the army in 1942, he asked that he not be put into a combat situation, and so was assigned to the medical corps. After leaving the army, King attended Immanuel Lutheran College and Seminary in Greensboro, North Carolina. He was sent to churches in Chicago and Youngstown, Ohio, for his internship training. At Peace Lutheran Church in Youngstown the membership consisted of five children and four adults. King later transferred to St. Phillips in Chicago, and pursued graduate work at Garrett Theological Seminary and Lutheran School of Theology. King describes obstacles and triumphs, his oldest daughter's serious illness and recovery, his wife's teaching career and work with him in the church. Both he and his wife earned Ph.D.s from the University of Indiana. His work was in adult education and Jean King's degree was in counseling psychology. King taught at Concordia College in River Falls, Illinois, and also at Lincoln University in Jefferson City, Missouri. Mrs. King taught at Lincoln University and at Drury College. While teaching at Lincoln, King also served as pastor at Pilgrim Lutheran Church. At the time of his retirement from Pilgrim, he had been appointed as second vice president of the Lutheran Church, Missouri Synod. The book concludes with a chapter by Mrs. King describing her own childhood, education, marriage, and career.

338. Kingston, Maxine Hong. *Hawai'i One Summer*. A Latitude 20 Book. Honolulu, Hawai'i: University of Hawai'i Press, 1998. 72 pages; photographs. ISBN: 0824818873.

> **Notes:** Originally published San Francisco, California: Meadow Press, 1987. Designed and created by Leigh McClellan. 150 copies printed.

> **Abstract:** The much honored writer, Maxine Hong Kingston, presents a collection of essays which originally appeared as *Her*, a series of columns in the *New York Times* during the 1970s. Kingston, with her husband and son, moved to Hawai'i from Berkeley in 1968 to "escape" the Vietnam War. They chose to live off of their savings for a period of time, making use of found objects and discarded grocery store food to avoid feeding the war economy. The first essay describes her mixed feelings when they gave up renting and bought their first home, with all the implications of owning property. In another essay, Kingston describes her thoughts as she prepares to attend her twentieth high school reunion. In an essay on dishwashing, she contemplates its few pleasures and abundant displeasures. In her introduction she comments that she now enjoys dishwashing, although in her essay she is only able to acknowledge that washing dishes is a part of what makes up daily life. In writing about the third annual Asian American Writers' Conference, held in Hawai'i, Kingston describes the division among male and female Chinese-American writers and the need to protect one's own personal poetic rhythms when surrounded by the rhythms of others. In another essay, Kingston describes her fear and wonder at the surfing addiction of many of the young boys she teaches, including her own son. In noting that surfing is a silent endeavor, she encourages her son and students to put what they see and feel into words. And finally, she writes a tribute to poet Lew Welch, who disappeared during the spring of 1971.

339. Kitt, Eartha. *I'm Still Here: Confessions of a Sex Kitten*. New York, New York: Barricade Books, 1991. 280 pages; photographs. ISBN: 094263733X : 0942637798.

> **Notes:** Originally published, 1989 as *I'm Still Here* and in 1991 as *Confessions of a Sex Kitten*.

> **Abstract:** Eartha Kitt, the popular singer, was born into the most impoverished of circumstances. Her earliest memory is of sleeping in a forest in the Deep South with her mother and baby sister. No one would take them in because she was of mixed (presum-

ably white and black) parentage. When she was a small child, an aunt in New York cared for her and sent her to school for the first time. She went on to enter, but not complete, the New York School of Performing Arts. She ran away from her aunt, joined the Katherine Dunham Company, and began to sing and dance, touring the world. She became successful as a solo artist in Paris, but constantly struggled for recognition in her own country. Her career appeared to go into a free-fall for several years after she publicly challenged Lyndon and Lady Bird Johnson at an official luncheon. The book describes her friendships with many celebrities, such as James Dean, Harry Belafonte, and Sammy Davis, Jr.; her many love affairs; the heads of state she has met in her trips abroad; and her work for equality for all minorities. She was married briefly to Bill McDonald and bore a daughter, Kitt. The story ends with Kitt's marriage and Eartha's complex feelings about a loss of intimacy in the only close family she has ever had.

340. Kiyama, Henry Yoshitaka. *The Four Immigrants Manga: A Japanese Experience in San Francisco, 1904-1924.* Translated with an introduction and notes by Frederik L. Schodt. Berkeley, California: Stone Bridge Press, 1999. 152 pages; comic book. ISBN: 1880656337.

Abstract: This book, originally published by the author and printed in Japan, was written in a combination of Japanese and English and entitled *Manga Yonin Shosei* (The Four Students Comic). In his introduction, which gives a background on Kiyama and on the situation of Japanese immigrants of the same period, Schodt explains the importance of this work.

> Tragically, there are relatively few books in English of any sort on the first-generation Japanese Americans, the issei. Part of this is due to language problems, but it is due also to the human disaster of World War II and the effects of the incarceration of Japanese Americans in concentration camps. Many important documents were destroyed and lost; the issei were demoralized and confused; and the experience of the camps . . . was so overwhelming that it has dominated subsequent writing on Japanese Americans. Yet the history of Japanese Americans today cannot be fully understood without understanding the issei and the experiences of people like Henry Kiyama.
>
> (Introduction)

The book, which is actually a comic book, includes historical events such as the San Francisco earthquake, racial discrimination, and exclusionary laws. It also describes experiences of Kiyama and his friends, some of whom held down jobs as "schoolboy" servants, took art classes, lost money in investments, tried their hand at farming, and married Japanese women, so-called mail-order brides. Despite the tragic nature of much of the content, the book remains a comic book with a punch line at the end of each episode.

341. Kiyota, Minoru. *Beyond Loyalty: The Story of a Kibei.* Translated by Linda Klepinger Keenan. Honolulu, Hawai'i: University of Hawai'i Press, 1997. 252 pages; photographs; documents. ISBN: 0824818865 : 082481939x.

Abstract: Kiyota writes, "The history of racist oppression and maltreatment is the backdrop to my own story as an American teenager of Japanese ancestry who was incarcerated in internment camps for four long years by his own government" (p. 66). During World War II, Kiyota, age nineteen, was evacuated with his mother to the Topaz Relocation Center in Utah. From the start, Kiyota was viewed with suspicion because of his four years of schooling in Japan. When he applied for release from Topaz to attend college, he was interrogated by the FBI. He was called a "dirty Jap" and accused of being an agent for the Japanese. This attack cemented his bitterness at his imprisonment and treatment at the hands of his own country and influenced his decision to answer "no" to the infamous question 28 which asked whether he would declare his loyalty to the United States and renounce Japan: "I began to see the loyalty question as my only opportunity to take a stand against oppressive government authority" (p. 101). As a result, Kiyota was separated from his mother and sent to the Tule Lake Segregation Center for dangerous inmates. There he was intimidated and beaten by both the camp guards and by the violent pro-Japanese groups within the camp. He was unable to eat, suffered from hives, and experienced nightmares. Under the extreme conditions of the camp, Kiyota renounced his citizenship when the United States government "offered" him this option. He later regretted this decision and tried unsuccessfully to revoke it. It was not until the Renunciation Act was declared null and void in the courts that Kiyota would regain his citizenship. In the meantime, he was fortunate to find a community of Christian pacifist workers in the camp who took charge of nursing him to health and provided him with a community. When he was released in March of 1946, Kiyota attended College of the Ozarks in Arkansas. There he witnessed, for the first time, extreme Southern racism and segregation. Again, his inability to conform made him a target for physical attack, and he left Arkansas to finish his studies at the University of California at Berkeley. Kiyota worked as a civilian with the United States Air Force in Japan and Korea during the Korean War. Following the war, he returned to Japan to fulfill his dream of studying both Western and Eastern philosophy. He completed a master's degree and a Ph.D. before he returned to the United States to teach philosophy at the University of Wisconsin-Madison. Kiyota hopes to demonstrate through this book

> how extreme and unreasonable government demands designed to ensure the absolute and unquestioning loyalty of citizens causes tremendous anguish and suffering for many people. In every nation, the individual is vulnerable to the power of the state, and any government—democratic or otherwise—that would abrogate the human rights of its own citizens is guilty of oppression.   (p. 248)

342. Kline, Johnny. *Never Lose: From Globetrotter to Addict to Ph.D.: An Autobiography.* Detroit, Michigan: Papa Joe's Book Company, 1996. 295 pages; photographs. ISBN: 0965213099.

Abstract: John Kline was raised by his mother and aunt in a hardworking family in Detroit, Michigan. He writes that "[F]amily values, sense of community, trust and mutual support gave me a wonderful childhood" (p. 16). Successful in school, Kline was in student government and an avid athlete. He ran track and played softball and basketball. Kline attended Wayne State University beginning in 1950, one of the first African Americans to be admitted to that school. Kline was on the track and basketball teams. His commitments multiplied when he married in 1951. He held down two jobs to support his new family and help out his aunt and mother. By 1953, he had lost his athletic eligibility because of poor academic standing. Kline received no encouragement from his coaches, and he left the university. He began his professional basketball career with the Harlem Globetrotters that same year. Kline describes his five years and more than one thousand games with the team. While traveling throughout the United States and in many countries around the world, Kline experienced racism and had ample opportunity to become involved with women, drugs, and drinking. Kline left the Globetrotters in 1959, separated from his wife, moved to New York to play with the Eastern Pro League, and became involved with the Nation of Islam. He describes attending a meeting to hear the Honorable Elijah Muhammad speak and admiring all of the "neat, clean, upright black men and women surging in the streets to do something positive" (p. 112). He felt that the Nation of Islam, and especially the words of Malcolm X, provided him with a "tremendous opportunity to express his manhood" (p. 115). During the following decade, Kline struggled with heroine and cocaine addiction and turned to criminal activities to support his habit. He was arrested on a variety of charges and finally given a warning by a judge who felt that Kline still had something to offer the Detroit community. Kline cured himself of his addictions in 1969. In 1970 he was back in school, and living with his former wife and eight children. He got work as a drug counselor in a methodone program and began working with the state Department of Mental Health. Kline continued his education and sought to help his community through counseling, rehabilitation programs, positive thinking programs, and healthy living seminars. He worked in drug counseling and patient's rights for the state, and the city, and the Detroit public schools. Klein also formed his own consulting company. He earned a Ph.D. from Wayne State College of Education and made several trips to Ghana. Kline sees a general deterioration in the black communities in large cities and in American culture generally. He would like to see a resurgence in black pride, and he encourages a healthy and holistic life free from drugs, alcohol, and other chemicals.

343. Knight, Gladys. *Between Each Line of Pain and Glory: My Life Story.* New York, New York: Hyperion, 1997. 280 pages; photographs. ISBN: 0786863269.

   Notes: Also published in large print. Thorndike, Maine: G. K. Hall and Company, 1998. ISBN: 0783883943 (353 pages).

   Abstract: Gladys Knight first took the stage to sing at the age of four. In those early days, she was already a belter. Her mother told her that she was an old soul with a grownup's voice. At seven, her mother took her to New York to audition for the *Ted Mack Amateur Hour.* She made it through nine competitions and won the finals at Madison Square Garden. Knight remarks that she felt many of the white competitors were chagrined to lose to a little black girl with a missing tooth. At age nine, Knight, her brother, sister, and two cousins formed a singing group that they called the Pips. They won talent shows and earned regular engagements in Atlanta, their hometown, before Gladys's mother arranged for the children to work with voice coach Maurice King.

By the time Knight was twelve, the Pips were on the Supersonic Attractions Tour. The group stayed together and toured throughout Knight's school years. When she was seventeen, the Pips began recording and released their first hit, "Every Beat of My Heart." Shortly after high school graduation, Knight became pregnant and married her high school sweetheart. She lost the first baby, but had two more children before her marriage fell apart. Meanwhile, the Pips continued to prosper under the management of the flamboyant Marghuerite Mays. She managed their clothing, taught the Pips to dance, and guided them in the development of the style that would be their hallmark. The group eventually signed a seven-year contract with Motown, but was never one of their priority groups. Nonetheless, the Pips had several hits before leaving Motown for Buddha Records, with whom they recorded "Midnight Train." That same year, the Pips won Grammies in both the pop and rhythm and blues categories. Knight describes the hard life of a touring performer, in which there are no guarantees for the future, despite your previous successes. She writes of her unsuccessful second and third marriages, her addiction to gambling, and her recovery. Knight describes the many positive experiences she has had working with other singers, but also of the lack of unity and support within the business. She also describes the inherent racism in the recording and broadcasting industry. Black singers are almost always classified as rhythm and blues, a category that is not included on the play list of many radio stations. White singers, even if they are singing soul, are considered pop or rock and roll and receive nationwide radio play. "I simply wish that there did not have to be barriers and that it could be about the music, not about race, as too many things in our society are" (p. 318). Still, in spite of the many hardships and disappointments she has experienced, Knight writes that she is a "glutton for life" (p. 333). After fifty years in music, she is still performing.

344. Krall, Yung. *A Thousand Tears Falling: The True Story of a Vietnamese Family Torn Apart by War, Communism, and the CIA.* Foreword by Griffin B. Bell. Afterword by Quinlan J. Shea, Jr. Atlanta, Georgia: Longstreet Press, 1995. 412 pages; photographs. ISBN: 1563522314.

Abstract: Yung Krall's story begins in 1954 with the defeat of the French at Dien Bien Phu, Vietnam. Her father fought with the Viet Minh. He and his oldest son went to Hanoi to work with Ho Chi Minh. Krall, her younger siblings, and her mother went to live with their grandparents in Long Thanh, part of South Vietnam, where their aunt and cousins were actively assisting the Viet Cong. Krall's family's existence was complicated by its connections with prominent and active supporters of the north and by its location in the south, with both forces exerting pressure on Krall's mother to take a more active part. Krall herself became vehemently anti-Communist. Although she was not sympathetic with the American presence in Vietnam, Krall took a job at the American military installation. There she met her husband, Lieutenant John Krall and went with him to live in the United States. As the fall of Saigon became imminent, Krall and her husband began to arrange for her mother's and sisters' evacuation. In order to facilitate this, Krall agreed to provide any information she could to the American government. Soon Krall was operating as a double agent for the CIA and the Socialist Republic of Vietnam (SRV; North Vietnam). During this time, Krall had several reunions with her father, who was now the SRV ambassador to the Soviet Union. When the Justice Department decided to arrest one of Krall's SRV contacts, she was asked to testify, and Krall describes the chaos into which this turn of events threw her. She was worried about the safety of her father and brother in Vietnam. Both she and her extended family were threatened. In her last visit with her father, she angered both her parents by trying to convince him to leave the country. Eventually daughter and father agreed to accept each other's political affiliations. Krall ends her story as she prepares to testify.

345. Kwan, Michelle (1980-). *Michelle Kwan, Heart of a Champion: An Autobiography*. As told to Laura M. James. New York, New York: Scholastic Books, 1997. 151 pages; photographs. ISBN: 0590763407.

> **Notes:** Revised edition published New York: Scholastic Books, 1998. ISBN: 0590763563 (166 pages).

> **Abstract:** Michelle and Karen Kwan began ice skating while quite young. Michelle was just five years old. They practiced every day, had lessons four to five days a week, and advanced steadily through the ranks. This required enormous sacrifices on the part of the family. Their parents drove them long distances to skating rinks, and ended up selling their house to pay off bills. In 1992, Michelle and Karen had both advanced to the junior level of the United States Figure Skating Association (USFSA) and Michelle had made it to Nationals. They were noticed by Linda Fratianne, who arranged for them to audition for coach Frank Carroll. They passed the audition, were accepted to skate on the private rink at

Ice Castle in Lake Arrowhead, and began year-round residency there. Mr. Kwan commuted two hundred miles round trip to work each day so that he could stay at Ice Castle with the girls. Mrs. Kwan remained at the family residence in Torrance so that their son could finish high school at home. Michelle always saw herself as a champion. She describes what it takes to be a champion skater and the importance of maintaining a positive attitude and of envisioning your success rather than your failures. In 1996, Michelle won the gold medal at both the National and World Championships. After a disastrous 1997 Nationals competition, she won the silver medal at the World Championships. As she finished this book, Michelle, at the age of sixteen, was setting her sights on the 1998 Olympics.

346. LaBelle, Patti. *Don't Block the Blessings: Revelations of a Lifetime.* Written with Laura B. Randolph. New York, New York: Riverhead Books, 1996. 305 pages; photographs. ISBN: 1573220396.

Notes: Also published New York: Boulevard Books, 1997. ISBN: 1572973242; New York: Berkeley Boulevard Books, 1997. ISBN: 0425169987. Published as a large print edition Thorndike, Maine: G. K. Hall and Company, 1997. ISBN: 0783880693 (397 pages).

Abstract: Patti LaBelle was born Patricia Holte. Her parents divorced when she was small, and she was raised by her mother but remained close to her father. LaBelle was shy as a child, but found her calling when she began singing at her church. When she was eighteen, she and a few of her friends put together a group that debuted as the Ordettes. The other members of the group gradually quit and were replaced. The group was finally reborn as the Bluebelles, with LaBelle, Cindy Birdsong, Nona Hendryx, and Sarah Dash. The group was extremely well-received and had concerts every night. However, they never seemed to make very much money and lived hand to mouth, wearing the same costumes every night. One of the high points of the Bluebells' career was a six-week tour playing with the Rolling Stones. A new manager convinced them to change their group's name to LaBelle and to give up love songs and close harmony for a social tone that matched the atmosphere of the 1960s. She got them out of their matching dresses and into something rougher. By 1972, the designer Larry LaGaspi asked to design some costumes for them, and thus was born their trademark look: "silver, the cabling, the breastplates, the feathers, the platforms, the space suites, the helmets . . ." (p. 172). Soon, fans were being invited to wear their own costumes to concerts. LaBelle's wild popularity peaked about the time of their only number-one hit, "Lady Marmalade," in 1975. By this time, Patti LaBelle was married and had a child. The rest of the group remained single, and she was torn between performing and being with her family. The group broke up in 1976, and LaBelle began a solo career. Although she has never had a definitive hit, she has always done well and had a large following. She has recorded many albums and done some acting. The great tragedy of her life has been the loss of so many members of her family. When she was in her thirties, she lost her mother to diabetes, and all three of her sisters died of cancer when they were in their early forties. LaBelle alone has lived to see her fiftieth birthday. She feels blessed to have met and married Armstead Edwards, the man who remains her husband to this day. The couple has a son, Zuri.

347. Lacy, Sam (b. 1903). *Fighting for Fairness: The Life Story of Hall of Fame Sportswriter Sam Lacy.* Written with Moses J. Newson. Centreville, Maryland: Tidewater Publishers, 1998. 262 pages; photographs. ISBN: 087033512x.

Abstract: A reporter and journalist, Sam Lacy has written more than three thousand columns in a sixty-year career. He has spent most of his career with the Baltimore *Afro American,* but he has also written for the *Chicago Sun,* the *Washington Tribune,* and others. Lacy is a sports writer who used his columns and his influence to address issues of race and gender, including discriminatory practices, lack of opportunity, segregated teams, and segregated accommodations for athletes. Lacy was born in 1903 in Connecticut. He and his parents moved to Washington, D.C., when he was two. Despite his family's limited means, Lacy attended school with the African-American elite. He began working at the age of eight and was playing semi professional baseball before he graduated from high school. After high school, he played both baseball and football and also worked as a coach and referee. Lacy's journalism career began when he became sports editor for the *Washington Tribune* in 1934. In 1937, Lacy made his first trip to a group of major league baseball team owners to discuss the hiring of African-American players, and in 1945, he was a member of a committee formed by major league baseball to address integrating the teams. In his book, Lacy describes the events leading up to the hiring of Jackie Robinson and the problems faced afterwards, such as segregated accommodations for baseball and football players. Lacy talks about the professional teams that refused to hire black players and the success of other teams when they did so. Lacy addresses the present-day lack of leadership positions for African Americans in professional and collegiate sports, including the dearth of black quarterbacks, and the reluctance of owners to hire blacks as coaches. Lacy writes about issues of race and the Baseball Hall of Fame, the 1961 AAU decision to send an all-white team to South Africa, the questionable sport of boxing, segregated golf courses, and the media-enforced invisibility of black golfers. Lacy documents the progress that he has seen for African Americans in professional sports in the United States, but also points out changes that still need to be made.

348. Lane, Isaac (1834-1937). *Autobiography of Bishop Isaac Lane, L.L.D. With a Short History of the C.M.E. Church in America and of Methodism.* Chapel Hill, North Carolina: Academic Affairs Library, University of North Carolina at Chapel Hill, 1997.

http://sunsite.unc.edu/docsouth/lane/lane.html

Notes: Documenting the American South (Project).

349. Latifah, Queen. *Ladies First: Revelations of a Strong Woman.* Written with Karen Hunter. Foreword by Rita Owens. New York, New York: William Morrow & Company, 1999. 173 pages; photographs. ISBN: 0688156231.

Notes: Also published in paperback New York: Quill, 2000. ISBN: 068817583x.

Abstract: Rap singer Queen Latifah, born Dana E. Owens, writes about her life, hoping to inspire other women through examples of how she overcame difficulties. Latifah explains:

> I'm writing this book to let every woman know that she, too—no matter what her status or her place in life—is royalty. This is particularly important for African-American women to know. . . . For so long in this society, we have been given and have allowed ourselves to take the role of slave, concubine, mammy, second-class citizen. . . . Many of us have been so hurt and so dogged out by society—and by men and by life—that we can't even wrap our brains around the notion that we deserve better, that we are queens.   (p. 2)

She recounts trials she has been through and the difficulties she has overcome, encouraging others to follow her example. Subjects covered include the strength of her mother, the problems presented by her parents' divorce, how her father's adultery and other vices affected her feelings about men in general, how she broke into the music business and learned to differentiate between friends and colleagues who would have a positive effect on her life and those who would not, avoiding drugs, getting through the pain of her brother's death, learning how to say no to sexual relationships with men, and how to ignore hurtful gossip. Latifah also discusses the necessity of appreciating one's body, no matter what the size or shape, and the importance of developing one's own style.

350. Latta, Rev. M. L. (b. 1853). *The History of My Life and Work: Autobiography by Rev. M. L. Latta, A.M., D.D.* Chapel Hill, North Carolina: Academic Affairs Library, University of North Carolina at Chapel Hill, 2000.

http://docsouth.unc.edu/neh/latta/latta.sgml
http://docsouth.unc.edu/neh/latta/latta.html

Notes: Documenting the American South (Project).

351. Lawrence-Lightfoot, Sara. *I've Known Rivers: Lives of Loss and Liberation.* Reading, Massachusetts: Addison-Wesley Publishing Company, 1994. 654 pages. ISBN: 0201581205.

Notes: Published in paperback New York: Penguin Books, 1995. ISBN: 0140249702.

Abstract: Lawrence-Lightfoot remembers the special family time at the diningroom table with family members telling stories and narrating the events of their day. Her parents also used the time to fill gaps in their children's education by steeping them in the poetry of black poets and expanding on neglectful or wrong-headed teaching on African Americans and other cultures outside the European tradition. Lawrence-Lightfoot was introduced to the writing of E. Franklin Frazier when his book *Black Bourgeoisie* (1957) was discussed by her parents and their friends at the dinner table. Reading it again as a graduate student, Lawrence-Lightfoot was mesmerized by this book about her own experience in the black middle class. She felt both pleasure and disappointment in it. While Frazier took a refreshing approach to the study of African Americans, demonstrating the diversity of the community, he also accused the "black bourgeoisie" of having forsaken their cultural roots. Lawrence-Lightfoot responds to what she believes is Frazier's two-dimensional description of black middle class life by presenting the stories of three men and three women from the black professional middle-class, all in their forties and fifties. Lawrence-Lightfoot spent a year "in deep conversation with each one. Our conversations were intense, exhausting, exhilarating, and often painful. All six were willing to appear here under their own names" (p. 11). They describe the losses that have accompanied their social privileges. Kate Cannon is a philosopher, theologian, and ordained Presbyterian minister. She teaches at the Episcopal Divinity School in Cambridge, Massachusetts. She was born in Kannapolis, North Carolina. Charles Ogletree teaches at Harvard Law School. He is a criminal defense lawyer and political activist. He grew up near Merced, California. M. Antoinette Schiesler, a native of Chicago, became a nun and a chemist. After leaving her religious order, she married and studied to be ordained as an Episcopal priest. Felton Earls is an epidemiologist and psychiatrist at the Harvard School of Public Health. He was raised in New Orleans. Cheryle Wills owns radio and television stations across the United States. She was born in Jefferson, Missouri and settled in Cleveland. Orlando Bagwell lived in Baltimore until moving to New Hampshire with his family in his teens. He is a documentary filmmaker.

352. Lebrón, Lolita (1919-). *See* Vilar, Irene (1969-).

353. Lee, Bill. *Chinese Playground: A Memoir.* San Francisco, California: Rhapsody Press, 1999. 277 pages. ISBN: 0967002303.

Abstract: Bill Lee writes of his experiences with organized crime and gang warfare in San Francisco's Chinatown. His parents were both born in the Guangdong (Canton) province of China and immigrated to the United States. Although Lee was born in the United States, in 1954, he identified more closely with the foreign-born Chinese, since he grew up speaking three dialects of Cantonese and no English until he began school. Lee describes the cultural conflicts of growing up in a traditional Chinese household within an American-influenced culture. Life at home and in the streets was harsh. His father had strong ties with one of the Tong organizations, participating in activities somewhere between legal and illegal. Tong loyalties fed directly into gang loyalties and rivalries. Lee's involvement with gang life changed as he grew up. He distanced himself from it and concentrated on his studies while in high school, but found himself once more involved as a college student. Gang violence escalated throughout the first half of the 1970s and peaked with the Golden Dragon massacre of 1977. Lee describes the massacre and the counter attacks, arrests, court trials, and imprisonments. Lee once again drew away from gang life. Perhaps because of his own troubled childhood and youth, Lee was interested in psychology and a counseling career, and he found work in human resources in Silicon Valley industries. He worked as a recruiter for International Circuit Devices (ICD). He found in Silicon Valley corporate culture, as in Chinatown, intrigue, duplicity, and rivalry, with a murky line between legal and illegal activities. Lee left ICD to begin his own consulting firm. He took a six-month leave of absence from his consulting work to take an assignment for Electromagnetic Systems Laboratories (ESL). Although reluctant to leave his own successful enterprise, Lee sensed that he had a mission at ESL. This mission was revealed the day an unhappy former employee entered ESL loaded with weaponry, shooting everyone in his path. Lee was able to safely clear out employees in his own department, and to utilize his crisis-intervention skills throughout the five-and-a-half hour siege. Lee credits his ability to stay calm and level-headed to the numbness he developed to the violence of Chinatown. Although happy to have served an important role in working with victims and families of victims during and following the ESL crisis, Lee sees himself as part of the overall problem. He writes that he was "still entrenched on the dark side, continuing to lie, cheat and hustle, in all areas of my life" (p. 275). Lee began a healing process which included examining his past and learning to "trust and find decency" in himself (p. 277). As he finished this memoir, he had taken a break from the high tech industry and was working on his recovery. He is committed to serving as a good role model for his college-aged son.

354. Lee, Gaylen D. *Walking Where We Lived: Memoirs of a Mono Indian Family.* Norman, Oklahoma: University of Oklahoma Press, 1998. 208 pages; photographs; maps; index. ISBN: 0806130873 : 0806130863.

Abstract: Gaylen Lee, who was raised in a traditional Mono, or Nim, Indian lifestyle, has acted as a family historian his entire life. This book describes how American whites ran the Indians from their lands in California, the story of his own family, spanning six generations, and the documentation of the folk stories his grandparents told him as he grew up. California Indians were first endangered when gold was discovered in the Sacramento area. Miners wanted to get Indians off the lands so that they could claim it and mine for gold. They were assisted by Christian missionaries who wanted to change the lifestyles of the Indians and make them more open to their religion and way of life. The U.S. government forced the Indians out of their homelands and destroyed their livelihood over the span of a few generations. Lee, who spoke only the Nim language before he began school, writes about how his ancestors lived and how his mother and grandmother maintain the traditional lifestyle in which he himself was raised. He describes how babies in his family are raised in baby baskets that keep them secure and happy during the first years of their life. Such baskets, as well as those for storing and cooking food and carrying possessions, are still made by women. Acorns are a dietary staple. They are collected, ground into flour, and made into traditional dishes. Lee learned how to fish in local rivers using bait and spears, and grabbing fish by hand. He describes the hunting methods of Indians and how his grandfather could creep up behind animals without the animals knowing it. Lee also describes some of the religious ceremonies that he grew up with and the long tradition of mysticism among Indians.

355. Lee, Helie. *Still Life with Rice: A Young American Woman Discovers the Life and Legacy of Her Korean Grandmother*. New York, New York: Scribner, 1996. 320 pages. ISBN: 0684802708.

> **Notes:** Also published New York: Simon & Schuster Touchstone Edition, 1997. ISBN: 0684827115.

> **Abstract:** Helie Lee, a woman born in South Korea and raised in the United States, took a trip to Korea and China to discover the places where her mother grew up. Upon her return from the trip she decided to record the life of her maternal grandmother, who lived in California. Her grandmother, Hongyong, was born in 1912 and raised in Pyongyang, North Korea, in a wealthy family. After she married, she and her husband left Korea and fled to China to avoid Japanese oppression. During their years in China, her grandmother made her family's fortune by selling opium and running a restaurant. Just before Japan surrendered at the end of World War II, the family, now numbering five children, left China to go back to North Korea, where they bought a large plot of land only to have it confiscated by the new Communist regime. In the confusion prior to the closing of the border between the two Koreas at the 38th parallel on January 4, 1951, the family managed to slip across to South Korea. Hongyong and the children managed to make it to the port of Pusan, where they were reunited with her husband. The escape, however, permanently separated her from her eldest son. Penniless, the family made their home

with Hongyong's younger sisters and their families. She was eventually able to make a living practicing ch'iryo, a form of healing that involves pinching and slapping the body to improve blood circulation. Hongyong's eldest daughter married a soldier, and the two emigrated to Canada with their two daughters. (The younger, Helie, is the author of this book.) Hongyong joined them in Southern California in the 1970s when ch'iryo became illegal in South Korea. She and her sisters resumed their practice in Los Angeles. The book ends in 1991, as Helie returns from Korea and China to learn about her grandmother's story, and, miraculously, they receive news that Hongyong's eldest son is alive in North Korea.

356. Lee, Joann Faung Jean (1950-). *Asian American Actors: Oral Histories From Stage, Screen, and Television.* Jefferson, North Carolina: McFarland & Company, 2000. 226 pages; photographs. ISBN: 0786407301.

> **Abstract:** Lee reviews the state of acting for Asian Americans. Not much, she claims, has changed from the time when lead roles featuring Asian characters were played by white actors to today, when Asian actors are confined largely to "race roles." Lee looks at why this might be, observing not only an entrenched racism in the film, television, and stage industries, but a conscious or subconscious tendency for film and television to reinforce a white homogenous view of American society. Lee interviews actors in New York, San Francisco, and Los Angeles. She seeks to find out how and why Asian American actors persevere in a field of such narrow opportunity and what drives them to take roles that can be stereotypical and demeaning. Lee also asks the subjects to talk about why they entered acting, their individual experiences as actors, the goals they have set for themselves, and what opportunities they see for their future and for Asian actors in general. Lee notes the healthy state of Asian-American theater and the enhanced experience and opportunities for both actors and for audiences. She divides her subjects into aspiring and veteran actors as follows:
>
> > Aspiring New York actors: Raymond Moy, Billy Chang, Mel Gionson, Karen Tsen Lee, Lia Chang, Fay Ann Lee; Veteran New York actors: Jadin Wong, Tisa Chang, Peter Kwong, Pat Suzuki; Aspiring California actors: Greg Watanabe, Sharon Omi, Ken Narasaki, Linda Chuan, Joanne Takahashi, Sharon Iwai, Karen Lee; and veteran California actors: Lane Nishikawa, Cherylene Lee, Nancy Kwan.

357. Lee, Li-Young. *The Winged Seed: A Remembrance.* New York, New York: Simon & Schuster, 1995.   205 pages.   ISBN: 0671707086.

> **Notes:** Also Published St. Paul, Minnesota: Hungry Mind, 1999. ISBN: 1886913285.

> **Abstract:** Lee tells his story both through a straightforward series of memories and impressions, and through metaphorical tales and dreams. He was born in 1958 in Jakarta. A year later, his father was arrested on charges of sedition and imprisoned for nineteen months. The Lee children were cared for by their older sister, who was only nine, while their mother spent each day at the prison hoping to see her husband. Following his father's release from prison, the family was spirited away to Hong Kong where his father pursued his ministry. From Hong Kong they went to Japan and then to Pennsylvania. Lee writes of visiting the sick and elderly with his father during their time in Pennsylvania, caring for his father as he approached death, and dreaming of him after he died. Lee expresses confusion over the angry father who demanded absolute obedience and the minister who cared so lovingly for his parishioners, over his family's harsh daily existence, and the miracle-enacting God of his father's beliefs and preachings.

358. Lee, Patrick J. *The Yellow Kid: Comics.* Time's Up, 6. Burbank, California: Airik Lee Productions, 1997. ISBN: none.

359. Lee, Spike. *Best Seat in the House: A Basketball Memoir.* Written with Ralph Wiley. New York, New York: Crown, 1997. 327 pages; photographs. ISBN: 060960029x.

> **Abstract:** Spike Lee, famous as a front-row-season-ticket-holding fan of the New York Knicks basketball team, chronicles the fortunes of the team over thirty years. In the process of analyzing the good and bad times of the Knicks, looking in detail at the team's players and at many of their important games, Lee divulges some of the details of his own life, not all directly related to basketball. Lee grew up one of four children. His mother was a high-school English teacher and his father a professional jazz bass player. Lee believed that growing up in Brooklyn meant being an avid sports fan. He and his friends played every kind of ball and followed the local teams with enthusiasm. Lee began attending basketball games at an early age. He was given a ticket to the seventh game of the Knicks' 1969-1970 championship bid, but was forced to

make a choice between the game and a concert his father was playing in. The game won out despite the fact that the rest of the family attended the concert. Lee graduated from high school in 1975 and attended Morehouse College in Atlanta, as did many members of his family spanning several generations. It was during his first summer vacation from college that Lee picked up a Super 8 camera, whetting his appetite for filmmaking and setting the stage for his prestigious film career. Following college, Lee attended New York University, where his final film project won the Students' Academy award. Several years later, Lee made the film *She's Gotta Have It*, and two important things happened: he bought his first Knicks season tickets and, based on his use of Air Jordan tennis shoes in the film, Nike asked Lee to direct a series of commercials featuring Michael Jordan and a character in his film who wore Nikes. Thus began a long relationship between Lee and Jordan. On other subjects, Lee considers the potential power of African-American athletes in a sports industry that is owned by white Americans, and he looks forward to the day when franchises will be owned by African Americans. He discusses and provides several examples of the inherent racism in sports reporting and tallies the handful of black reporters working for television, magazines, and newspapers.

360. Leguizamo, John.   *Freak: A Semi-Demi-Quasi-Pseudo Auto-biography*. Written with David Bar Katz. New York, New York: Riverhead Books, 1997.   125 pages; photographs.   ISBN: 1573220922.

> **Abstract:** John Leguizamo is an actor and comedian who is known for the one-man shows *Mambo Mouth* and *Spic-O-Rama*. He has also starred in a television series and been featured in a number of motion pictures. *Freak* is the name of another dramatic comedy production of his, and this work is the contents of the show rendered in book form. The story in *Freak* was originally meant to be a humorous break from the work Leguizamo and cowriter David Bar Katz were engaged in, but they ended up taking a hard look at the dark aspects of Leguizamo's childhood. According to the writers, the book is "100% kind-of-true" (p. xiii), with all of the scenes based on composites of his experiences and written as satire. According to the story, Leguizamo was loved by his mother, whom he calls Lala, and grandmothers, but simultaneously belittled by them at every turn. His father, dubbed Fausto, was a brutal man who was psychologically beaten by his experiences as an immigrant to the United States and who took out his frustrations on his children, especially the author.

Leguizamo is constantly waiting for the occasion when his father will voice his affection for him. Other scenes include Leguizamo's first love, how he lost his virginity at a Kentucky Fried Chicken Restaurant, how his parents separated, and his beginnings as an actor playing stereotypical Hispanic roles.

361. Lei-lanilau, Carolyn. *Ono Ono Girl's Hula.* Madison, Wisconsin: University of Wisconsin Press, 1997. 180 pages. ISBN: 0299156303 : 0299156346.

Abstract: Lei-lanilau's essays explore ethnicity and what it means to be Hawai'ian. Lei-lanilau's heritage includes Hawai'ian, Chinese, Hakka, and Portuguese. She refers to herself alternately as Chinese Hawai'ian, Chinese Hawai'ian Portuguese, and Native Hawai'ian, but the labels are not as important as her own sense of who she is. Language has always been an important element of her identity. Lei-lanilau's parents required their children to speak dictionary (first pronunciation) English in the household. Although her father spoke Hawai'ian outside of the house, they were never allowed to speak it inside and were not taught it. Her maternal aunt and grandmother spoke Hakka, but while her parents discouraged Lei-lanilau from learning it, she was encouraged to learn the language by her aunt. Studying languages is a passion for Lei-lanilau, and she has learned Mandarin and Cantonese Chinese, Hawai'ian, French, Latin, and Hakka. The subtleties of language and the cultural oppression or expression that use of a particular language signifies runs as a theme throughout the book. Lei-lanilau includes information about her family, her children, her husbands, and her full-tilt approach to life into and around her discussion of language.

> That's why me and my husband like have these mental orgasms when we "translate" English or Chinese or American or Hawaiian or behavior or situations from language to language. He did proudly acknowledge that he was **marginal**. Me too, me too! When your vocab and life experiences take you beyond language, movies, adventures, Little Pleasure, you have reached multicultural multi-ethnic crack-up. If you can still drive a car and arrive to work on time and even contribute, you deserve a long hug and sloppy Hawaiian wet kiss!   (p. 54)

362. Lemon, Ralph. *Geography: Art, Race, Exile.* Written with Tracie Morris. Afterword by Ann Daly. Hanover, New Hampshire: Wesleyan University Press, 2000. 202 pages; drawings; paintings; photographs; maps; journal entries. ISBN: 0819564435.

Abstract: This work represents journal entries, letters, art work, and text that describe the creation of the dance work *Geography*. Beginning in 1995, Lemon traveled in Australia, Haiti, and West Africa to prepare for the creation and production of this work. He was born in Cincinnatti, Ohio, although his family origins were in South Carolina and in Georgia. His mother's family was very light-skinned with ancestral origins in Ireland, France, West Africa, and Cherokee Indian. Lemon had the darkest skin color in his family and felt that this bothered his family. They claim, however, that he has consciously taken on the role of outsider. Lemon remembers, however, being treated "like a prince" by his paternal grandmother, who was "very, very dark" (p. 37). Lemon was happy to leave Cincinnati and move with his family to Minneapolis, where he had both white and black friends, most of whom he lost track of when he began attending the University of Minnesota. His mentors in the art world were white women Nancy Hauser and Meredith Monk. In New York, he worked with a small community of black artists, but when he formed his own dance company, all of his dancers were white. He found that his work and his company were questioned because of his company's racial make up and that he was both artistically and personally rejected by the black dance world. "I was never invited to any of the black dance conferences that meet annually. . . . I suppose I am not considered a 'black dance artist.' This is not painful; mostly it's hearsay. Much of the conflict part I've probably made up, but I do feel slightly insulted" (p. 35). After ten years, Lemon disbanded his dance company and dedicated his enterprise, Cross Performance, to the creation of new performance forms and presentations. He describes *Geography* as "in part a performance, but it was equally an anthropological collaboration about being American, African, brown, black, blue black, male, and artist" (p. 8).

363. Lester, Joe N. *I Am Not Afraid to Dream.* Conyers, Georgia: Joewolf Publishing, 1999. 193 pages. ISBN: 0967134404.

Abstract: Although Joe Lester and his siblings grew up with a legacy of domestic violence, they were raised to never fight except in self-defense. This teaching paid off, and the appearance of violent tempers did not carry over into their generation. Lester's parents started out as sharecroppers and were able to eventually buy their own land. His father was disappointed that none of the children remained to take on the farm responsibilities, but all ten children graduated from college, and most of them earned graduate degrees. Although Lester was an average student, he made up his mind in high school to be a dentist and was accepted into Meharry Medical College. After struggling through the initial coursework, Lester discovered that he was good at working with patients, his kind and patient manner quickly winning their confidence and trust. He graduated from Meharry in the top ten percent of his class and received several awards. Anxious to give something back to the black community, Lester, his wife Kim, and their two children moved to Fort Valley, Georgia, to set up practice, borrowing a large sum of money to do so. The patients he saw could not pay for dental work, and they usually bartered with food. In an attempt to make some money and maintain his own practice, Lester sought part-time work in a Plains, Georgia, clinic. He was the first black doctor to work there, and staff were concerned that he would not be accepted by the white clientele. Again, however, Lester's exceptional manner with patients overcame any prejudices they may have brought with them to the dentist's chair. Lester later worked as a dentist in the Georgia prison system and became dental director of the Georgia Department of Corrections.

364. Lewis, John. *Walking with the Wind: A Memoir of the Movement.* Written with Michael D'Orso. New York, New York: Simon & Schuster, 1998.   496 pages; photographs; index.   ISBN: 0684810654.

> **Notes:**   Also published San Diego: Harcourt Brace, 1999 (1st Harvest Edition). ISBN: 0156007088 (526 pages).

> **Abstract:**   John Lewis, chairman of the Student Nonviolent Coordinating Committee (SNCC) from 1963 to 1966, tells the story of his life and gives a history of the Civil Rights Movement. Born in the poor farming town of Carter's Quarters in Pike County, Alabama, Lewis questioned the lives his parents and neighbors led as sharecroppers, never able to get ahead after paying rent to landowners. He also questioned the differences for white and black children in the schools. When the landmark Supreme Court decision in *Brown v. Board of Education* in 1954 failed to bring any change in his own education, Lewis was bitterly disappointed. In 1955, he was inspired when he heard Dr. Martin Luther King, Jr. speak over the radio about the Montgomery bus boycott. Upon

high school graduation, Lewis was financially unable to attend college, and he enrolled instead in the American Baptist Theological Seminary in Nashville, Tennessee, which required no tuition payments. All of the students worked on campus for their room and board. As a sophomore, Lewis became more and more involved with the Civil Rights Movement. He joined SNCC and studied nonviolent resistance, something he continues to believe in as the most effective tool for change. Training sessions led to the lunch counter sit-ins in Nashville and civil rights activities over the entire South. Lewis worked and came into regular contact with all of the major figures in the movement, including Dr. King and the other leaders of the Southern Christian Leadership Conference (SCLC), the NAACP, and the Congress of Racial Equality (CORE), along with participants in SNCC, such as Stokely Carmichael and Julian Bond. He met with presidents Kennedy and Johnson and worked for the Carter administration. He participated in peaceful resistance activities during the 1950s and 1960s, such as the Freedom Riders, black passengers riding in the front of Greyhound and Trailways buses, sitting beside their white comrades as they traveled through the Deep South. Their lives were constantly in danger, but the action eventually drew so much attention throughout the United States that a reluctant federal government was forced to take steps. Lewis describes in detail the struggle to get the Voting Rights Act signed into law, the spirit and courage of the local people in the Southern towns where he registered voters, the strength of women who were kept out of leadership positions in the movement, and his distress at the growing disillusionment of the black leadership in the ability to achieve change through nonviolent resistance. He writes first hand of the tragedies of the four young girls who were killed in the bombing of the Sixteenth Street Baptist Church in Birmingham, Alabama, in 1963, the violent attack by Alabama state troopers on the peaceful marchers who were planning to walk from Selma to Montgomery in March 1965, the assassination of Dr. King, and the assassination of Robert Kennedy, for whose presidential campaign he was working. In 1986, John Lewis was elected to the United States Congress as the representative of the Fifth District of Georgia, defeating his close friend, Julian Bond. He remains in that seat at present.

365. Lewis, Reginald (1942-1993). *Why Should White Guys Have All the Fun? How Reginald Lewis Created a Billion-Dollar Business Empire.* Written with Blair Walker. New York, New York: John Wiley & Sons, 1995.   318 pages; photographs.   ISBN: 0471042277.

Notes: Paperback edition published in 1997. ISBN: 0471176893.

Abstract: This work is a combination of autobiographical excerpts and biography. Developed from interviews with Lewis, his family, and work colleagues, Blair Walker describes, with Lewis's verbatim excerpts sprinkled throughout, Lewis's childhood, education, and growth into the head of the multinational, billion-dollar enterprise, TLC Beatrice International Holdings, Inc.   Born in Baltimore, Maryland in 1942, Lewis attended Dunbar High School in Washington, D.C., where he excelled in sports.   He worked summers at a private country club where he proved to himself and others that he could work harder and get further than anyone else. He attended Virginia State University and played football during his freshman year.   He quit the next year to devote himself to academics.   Lewis decided to attend law school and took advantage of a special summer program Harvard was offering to a select number of African-American students.   Lewis was accepted into the law school immediately after completing the summer program.   Following graduation, Lewis went to work at the law firm of Paul, Weiss, Rifkind, Wharton & Garrison in New York.   He spent two years in the corporate law division before setting up practice for himself while working for the New York Urban Coalition.   Lewis worked for the Coalition by day and courted business clients by night.   Lewis and Walker chart Lewis's growing success in private practice, and his dynamic entry into the business world orchestrating larger and larger acquisitions, including McCall Patterns and TLC Beatrice.   Walker describes Lewis's hard-driving and sometimes controversial business style, his round-the-clock work practices and his devotion to his family. Not only interested in billion-dollar business deals, Lewis worked to improve conditions and opportunities for African Americans. In the 1970s, Lewis defended Benjamin Chavis under the auspices of the Commission for Racial Justice.   He was a strong campaigner for and contributor to Jesse Jackson's presidential campaign. Lewis was also a generous contributor to a variety of causes, both as a private citizen and through the Lewis Foundation.   Lewis made the largest ever one-time contribution, three million dollars, to the Harvard Law School, and the Reginald F. Lewis International Law Center at Harvard was dedicated in 1993. Lewis died of brain cancer the same year.

366. Lewis, Richard. *Black Cop: The Real Deal: The True Story of New York City's Most Decorated Cop.* Shippensburg, Pennsylvania: Destiny Image, 1996. 244 pages; photographs. ISBN: 1560435836.

Abstract: Retired law-enforcement officer Richard Lewis was born in 1943 in Brooklyn, New York. He grew up in the Red Hook housing project and joined the United States Air Force in 1962. In 1968, he joined the New York City Housing Authority Police Department after initially being rejected by the New York Police Department. He served as a patrol officer, an undercover plainclothes police officer, and then as a detective. Lewis was awarded seventy medals throughout his twenty-year career, including two Medals of Honor, the only officer ever to achieve two such awards. In his book, Lewis focuses on the racism and corruption at all levels of the New York Police Department. He describes the early efforts to keep black applicants from getting into the police force (he himself was rejected as having been a quarter of an inch too short), the reluctance to promote black officers, and the problem of white police officers shooting black plainclothes police officers ("black men with guns"). Lewis also observed that white police officers were far more likely to shoot at a suspect without taking time to investigate. In his experience, black police officers took time to assess the situation before shooting. During his career, Lewis filed complaints against the police department, but nothing ever came of them. His advice to other black police officers when faced with discrimination and prejudicial hiring and promotion practices is to work even harder. He says that when someone tries to discredit you, your record will speak for itself. The one haven from racism Lewis found in the police department was Police Officers for Christ. Since retirement in 1988, Lewis travels as a missionary and speaks regularly at schools in New York City.

367. Liacuris, Basilio. *Latino-Go Home!: The Saga of a Latin American Immigrant in the United States for over 40 Years.* Washington, D.C.: B. Liacuris, 1997. 182 pages; photographs. ISBN: none.

Notes: English and Spanish text on facing pages.

Abstract: Liacuris was born in Argentina. His mother died when he and his siblings were young children, and they were raised by their Greek father. A businessman, Liacuris's father moved continuously in hopes of finding expanded opportunity. He moved the family from Argentina to Chile, Venezuela, and Panama, never living anywhere more than three or four years. When his father decided that his children should attend college in the United States, Liacuris prepared to attend the University of Maryland. He had grown up speaking Greek and Spanish and had studied French and Italian in school, but he knew no English. To remedy this, he spent six months in an American high school and learned English through immersion. Liacuris graduated from college with a degree in business administration and international trade. Following a tour of duty in the army, he joined the Peace Corps and served in the Ecuadorian Andes. He entered the world of international trade as vice president at the Pan American Development Foundation in Washington, D.C., and later pioneered the field of international trade consultant. As a consultant, Liacuris helped U.S. companies enter new markets overseas. In his book, he discusses the causes of and problems related to illegal immigration to the United States and suggests some ways to address these issues. He comments on the difficulties presented by the debt load carried by many Latin American countries and the social and economic consequences of the resumption of U.S. arms sales to Latin America. Liacuris has retired to Ecuador, where he works to provide opportunities for Latin American corporations in the United States. He feels that cooperation through trade and cultural exchange are important elements in reducing poverty, lowering illegal immigration, and developing a healthy society.

368. Lim, Shirley Goek-Lin. *Among the White Moon Faces: An Asian American Memoir of Homelands.* New York, New York: Feminist Press at the City University of New York, 1996. 348 pages; photographs. ISBN: 1558611444 : 1558611797.

Abstract: In this book, for which she won a 1996 American Book Award, Shirley Geok-Lin Lim writes about her childhood in Malacca, Malaysia, where she was born to Chinese parents. She describes the poverty of the family, the difficulty of being the only girl in a large family of boys, how she and her brothers were abandoned by their mother, and how she was able to excel academically and advance from a convent school to a public high school and then to the University of Malaya in Kuala Lumpur. She then received a Fulbright Scholarship to study at Brandeis University and moved to Boston. The issues that Lim dealt with in the United States included a lack of validation of her work and ability, the difficulty of making and maintaining interpersonal relationships, and her own confusion over her role in society as a woman and as someone not born and raised in the United States. She was discouraged when her professors refused to take her poetry or literary studies seriously. This was ironic because Lim was never educated in the Malay languages and had always communicated almost exclusively in English. Her education in Malaysia, a British colony at the time, was entirely within the British school system. She taught literature and composition at several colleges, but found a glass ceiling at a junior college where she was not promoted despite her successful teaching, the honors she received for her work within the British Commonwealth, and her many invitations to more prestigious institutions to give lectures and readings. Her searching and dissatisfaction eventually softened when Lim married, had a son, and took U.S. citizenship so that her child would become grounded as a U.S. citizen. Perhaps the decisive factor in establishing herself as an American was being hired by the University of California at Santa Barbara.

> The job description asked for a creative writer who was also working on Asian-American literature and on feminist issues. It could have been written for me. I knew then that . . . I would choose to live and work in California, a state geographically bound to the islands of Southeast Asia. . . . California is perhaps the closest thing possible to moving home for Asian-Americans, whose identity, as any Japanese, Korean, or Chinese national will tell you, is peculiarly American, forged in U.S. history.   (p. 228)

She believes this move is finally heading her in a direction she can call "home."

369. Lindsay, Savon. *My Naked Soul: A Startling Autobiography of a Black Recovering Addict.* Portland, Oregon: We Do Recover Publications: Copper Sylk Company, 2000. 168 pages; photographs. ISBN: 1893879747.

> **Abstract:** Writer and recovered drug addict Savon Lindsay describes his family as caring, loving, and hardworking. As a child he required a lot of attention because he suffered from a number of ailments, including tuberculosis and adolescent arthritis. He writes that no matter how much attention he got, he craved more and would do whatever he needed to get it. His first exposure to alcohol came when he was seven. Even at that young age, he was overwhelmed with the sensation and immediately began to look for another opportunity to drink. By his teen years, he spent most of his time on the streets, drinking and working as a pimp. Lindsay led a bleak, violent, and destructive life. He was in

and out of prison, robbed, ran prostitutes, and sold and used drugs. Although Lindsay made many promises to quit drugs and went to countless detox centers and twelve-step meetings, he was unsuccessful until 1995, when his latest drug source was sent to prison and all of the storekeepers in the area recognized him and treated him like a thief. He made up his mind one more time to free himself of his addictions and went immediately to a twelve-step meeting. Lindsay told his story, found a sponsor, and began attending meetings several times a day. He made up his mind to do everything that was suggested to him by those already in recovery. Lindsay describes the struggle of trying to cure an addiction, the many obstacles to remaining on the path to recovery, the moments that changed his life, and the people who stayed with him in his final effort to become drug and alcohol free. A poet and writer, Lindsay has two other books: *The Soul of an Addict* and *Tired of Being Sick and Tired* (1998).

370. Lindsey, Cordell. *Step-by-Step Across the Pond*. Pittsburgh, Pennsylvania: Dorrance Publishing Company, 1996. 111 pages. ISBN: 0805938486.

Abstract: In 1950, eighteen-year-old high-school senior Cordell Lindsey decided to drop out of school and join the army to fight in the Korean War. He did so with two other friends. They were three of the four African Americans in their basic training platoon at Ford Ord in California. Although military life in general seemed to agree with Lindsey, his experiences were peppered with racial slurs and racially motivated confrontations. After basic training, Lindsey was sent to Camp Roberts for orientation in preparation for his assignment in Korea. He describes the sea voyage during which he spent seven days in the brig for hitting a sergeant; his time in combat, again, as one of just a few African-American soldiers, and his happiness at returning home. While in Korea, Lindsey stunned his fellow U.S. soldiers and impressed a troop of Korean soldiers by singing the Korean national anthem. After returning to the United States, Lindsey served as a driver and clerk and was promoted to staff sergeant before ending his tour of duty.

371. Little Coyote, Bertha and Virginia Giglio. *Leaving Everything Behind: The Songs and Memories of a Cheyenne Woman.* Norman, Oklahoma: University of Oklahoma Press, 1997. 166 pages; photographs; song transcriptions. ISBN: 0806129840 : 0806129867.

> **Notes:** Includes CD. Book and CD set, ISBN: 0806129875.

> **Abstract:** Born in 1912, Bertha Little Coyote began attending school at the Cantonment Boarding School in Oklahoma at the age of seven, the year of the 1919 flu epidemic. She and two male employees were the only ones not stricken, and Little Coyote remembers that the men would cook up a broth and carry it upstairs. From there she would carry bowls of soup and hard tack to any that were able to eat. The school was primarily made up of Arapaho and Cheyenne children, but when Otoe and Ponca children also began attending, all Indian language was banned because there was not a shared language among the children. Little Coyote says that despite the ban and their introduction to many elements of white culture, including Christianity, they maintained their own languages, games, and other aspects of their cultures. After sixth grade, Little Coyote went to public school, but did not pass because "I was too busy fighting the white kids" (p. 21). She returned to government school for eighth and ninth grade. Because she suffered from tuberculosis, however, she was unable to go on to Haskell Indian Institute as she had hoped, and thus her formal schooling ended. Little Coyote's first marriage was an unhappy one lasting only six years. She had her first and only child in 1931. Her second marriage was healthier, although she left several times because of her husband's drinking. After her husband was drafted during World War II, Little Coyote and he married a second time at a courthouse because the U.S. government no longer recognized Indian marriages for the purposes of veterans' benefits. Her husband, Horace Little Coyote, died in 1955 in a construction accident. Little Coyote was famous regionally for her singing, and in 1969 made a recording, *Seventeen Southern Cheyenne Songs*, for Indian Records, Inc. The record, still available on CD, includes Round Dance Songs, War Dance Songs, Scalp Dance Songs, and what Little Coyote calls Forty-Nine songs. She describes the nature of each type of song and the dance that accompanies the songs. Little Coyote notes that music and words just come to Indians when they are singing. Writing the song down is for white people. Little Coyote discusses her participation in the Mennonite Church, the health of the Cheyenne language, the use of the shawl in dancing, and many other details of Cheyenne life, and of her life.

372. Liu, Eric. *The Accidental Asian: Notes of a Native Speaker.* New York, New York: Random House, 1998. 206 pages. ISBN: 0679448624.

> **Notes:** Published in paperback, New York: Vintage Books, 1999. ISBN: 0375704868.

> **Abstract:** In this collection of essays, Eric Liu examines his own sense of ethnicity to discern what it has meant for him to be Chinese, in particular Chinese American, growing up in a predominantly white society. A native-born American, he compares himself to his parents, who were Chinese emigrants to the United States. Liu has been a radio broadcaster, an essayist for the e-journal *Slate*, a founder of the journal *The Next Progressive* (Washington, D.C., 1991-), a speech writer for President Clinton, as well as an aid to U.S. Senator David Boren. From his position in the center of U.S. politics, Liu examines the racism inherent in U.S. society as exemplified by the media presentation and political exploitation of the "Asian money scandal" of the 1996 presidential campaign. In other essays, Liu discusses the nomenclature of ethnicity, in particular "Asian American," "Chinese American," and "Chinese-American." He examines the concept of assimilation, describing it as a two-way process, "an act of creation as much as destruction" (p. 56). He writes further that "America is White no longer, and it will never be White again" (p. 56). Finally, Liu considers the personal and social implications of his interracial marriage and the sense of identity his children will eventually develop.

373. LL Cool J. *I Make My Own Rules.* Written with Karen Hunter. New York, New York: St. Martin's Press, 1997. 234 pages; photographs. ISBN: 0312171099 : 0312967861 ("All Audiences edition").

> **Notes:** Also published by St. Martin's Press in a "parental advisory edition." ISBN: 0312171102 : 0312967314.

> **Abstract:** LL Cool J was born James Todd Smith in 1968 in Long Island, New York. He chose the name LL Cool J, which stands for Ladies Love Cool James, when he was fourteen. He had a bad start in life that included abusive and even violent relationships with his father and stepfather. His grandfather, a jazz musician, helped him turn his life around with a collection of stereo equipment that started him on his way to becoming a rap musician. It took a while for LL Cool J to get his career started, however, and his first demo tape was soundly rejected by everyone he sent it to.

He finally got the attention of producer Rick Rubin, who helped get him started and arranged for him to perform, to appear in some films, and, to sign with Def Jam Records. LL Cool J talks about his difficulties with relationships and the wrong turns his career has taken due to poor management and incompetent financial advice. He also describes high points in his life such as earning his G.E.D., marrying Simone, the mother of his three children, and winning two Grammies. LL Cool J has achieved a string of platinum records and has appeared in films and hosted a television show. He believes that it is important for American children to have positive role models, and he also feels that it is important for him to include positive messages in his songs: "I want to make music that is real and honest, that has integrity" (p. 195). He describes his political activities, including campaigning for Bill Clinton and speaking on behalf of Rock the Vote and Americorps. LL Cool J has also been an honorary chairman for Youth Enterprises, founded by Charles Fisher. He emphasizes the importance of having a supportive and close family and of maintaining faith in God. Through his book, LL Cool J hopes to speak to "racist human beings who look at other human beings as subhuman animals . . . [to] children who feel unwanted . . . [and to] young people who are confused and struggling" (p. 11). He hopes to show the multidimensionality of rap music, to support the hip hop community, and to show what it is like to be African American in the United States.

374. Locklear, John Paul. *My Journey.* New York, New York: Vantage Press, 1995. 198 pages; photographs. ISBN: 0533111749.

Abstract: Paul Locklear was born October 28, 1929. As a child, he knew little about his ancestry, except that he was an Indian. Growing up in the South meant he had to abide by the strict limitations imposed by Jim Crow segregation laws. Of Cherokee and Scottish heritage, Locklear grew up in a family with nine children that moved from farm to farm, usually under conditions of extreme poverty. His father was angry, abusive, and violent. He beat his wife, Locklear's mother, relentlessly, and was killed in a shoot-out with the police when she finally turned him in to the sheriff. Locklear and his siblings despised their father and did their best to protect their mother, even threatening her second husband with death if he ever mistreated her. As Locklear grew older, however, he began to understand that discriminatory treatment and hurtful episodes he experienced were because he was Native American. He gradually came to understand at least some of the roots of his father's anger. Locklear felt that, were it not for his loyalty to his family, he could just as easily have become a bitter and angry man. Locklear joined the military before graduating from the eighth grade in an attempt to ease family financial problems. He reached a turning point in his life while stationed in Alaska. In a small Baptist church in Anchorage, Locklear became a Christian. He then dedicated the rest of his life to church work and eventually to the ministry. Much of Locklear's book is devoted to anecdotes of his and his wife's work with the various churches in which he served. He also expresses his bewilderment and indignation at the treatment of Native Americans as well as the poor in the United States at the hands of the powerful and rich.

375. Logan, John A. Turk, Jr. *The Reality of a Fantasy*. Dayton, Ohio: Logan Communications, Inc., 1997. 216 pages; photographs. ISBN: 0967650003.

Abstract: John Logan grew up in and around Dayton, Ohio. He attended a private Catholic school until his father's sudden death at age thirty-four. His mother, who was an alcoholic, was unable to keep up with house or school payments, and Logan became the only African-American student at the local public high school. After graduation, Logan had several jobs, including a good position with Frigidaire. He was soon drafted into the army, however, and then discharged on medical grounds. Logan returned to Frigidaire and began attending the International Broadcasting College. After completing his studies there, he got a sales position at WDAO Radio. Although he was not particularly successful as a salesman, he was able to land a part-time engineering position which led to an opportunity to announce over the air, and this was a first step in fulfilling his dream to work as a disc jockey. Logan gradually advanced to more prominent hours, then to music director, and finally to program director. Logan expanded public service programming and developed contests to encourage students to stay in school and earn good grades. Despite a few violent situations and law suits from contest losers, Logan has been successful in his work and has received several awards for community service. He is also recognized for his work in highlighting and providing air play for Ohio musicians. Logan's goal is to own his own radio station.

376. Lopez, Jack (1950-). *Cholos & Surfers: A Latino Family Album.* Santa Barbara, California: Capra Press, 1998. 204 pages. ISBN: 0884964299.

Abstract: Writer and professor of English Jack Lopez writes a series of essays about his childhood, his family, and his thoughts about race in the United States. He was born and raised in Southern California to a lower-middle-class family. His father, whom he credits with giving him his values and his outlook on life, always instructed him to refer to himself as "an American of Mexican descent" rather than Latino or Chicano. The important point was that he was, first and foremost, American. Lopez writes about being caught shoplifting as a child, the summer he spent surfing in Hawai'i after graduating from high school, his experiences skiing and sailing, going to college to avoid the draft, being accepted into graduate school, his adventures in academia, and raising his son. In each episode, Lopez discusses the matter of race in the United States. He believes that Americans of Mexican descent, despite their number in the population, have been largely ignored. He says that Americans are not racist, but race aware. He claims that everyone knows what being a certain race or color means in the racial hierarchy. Lopez has had enormous difficulty getting his work published because, he is told, there is a lack of demand for Latino work. He and a fellow writer have started the Chicano Surfing Association, a joke that refers to the dearth of both Chicano surfers and writers.

377. López-Stafford, Gloria (1937-). *A Place in El Paso: A Mexican-American Childhood.* Albuquerque, New Mexico: University of New Mexico Press, 1996. 212 pages; photographs. ISBN: 0826316875.

Abstract: López-Stafford tells the story of her childhood, first in the Segundo Barrio of El Paso, Texas, and then the Five Points neighborhood, where she lived with her godparents. López-Stafford's mother died when she was five years old, and has no memories of her except stories told her by her godmother. Her father, a white man from South Texas, was sixty-five when he married her much-younger mother, leaving another family and career behind to do so. The couple had three children, the youngest of whom was Gloria. After her mother's death, López-Stafford's father did his best to look after her, leaving her with a string of caretakers. Finally, her brother arranged for her to live with her godparents, who eventually adopted her. When her father died, López-Stafford was twelve. At that time, she began to understand, for the first time, that she was Mexican and that to some this meant she was not American and, in fact, inferior to "true" Americans. When an adored classmate told López-Stafford that she could not play with her because her mother didn't like Mexicans, López-Stafford became confused about her identity and what it meant to have a white father and a Mexican mother. After a period of confusion, López-Stafford began to realize that who she was had to do with the people who had loved and cared for her, and she learned to embrace her heritage.

378. Love, Darlene. *My Name Is Love: The Darlene Love Story.* Written with Rob Hoerburger. New York, New York: William Morrow & Company, 1998. 303 pages; photographs; discography; index. ISBN: 0688156576.

Abstract: Darlene Love's story encompasses a forty-year singing career. Love's father was a Pentecostal pastor, and her parents and their congregation viewed pop music as inherently evil. Nonetheless, Love began singing with a group called the Blossoms, also known as the Ronnettes, the Hushabyes, and the Rebelettes, while she was still in high school. They were primarily backup singers, but they did make a number of recordings on their own. During the early 1960s, Love worked with producer Phil Spector, who used her as a backup singer and soloist, but rarely gave her any credits or royalties for her chart-topping work. Some of her big hits, such as "He's a Rebel" and "He's Sure the Boy I Love," were credited to the Crystals, and her work with Bobby Darin was recorded under the name Bob B. Soxx and the Blue Jeans. Love would later win a suit against Spector for his ongoing use of her name and voice as well as back royalties for his use of her songs on several soundtracks and in the million-selling compilation *Back to Mono.* Love also worked with producer Lou Adler and sang backup for the Kinks, the Rolling Stones, Tom Jones, Elvis Presley, Peggy Clifton, Marvin Gaye, Dionne Warwick, and many others. Her wish to have a successful solo career, however, was never realized. Love describes the many wrong turns her career took because of her own naiveté, as well as poor management, unfavorable contracts, and bad-faith promises. She writes about her three failed marriages, her attempts to have both a family and a career, and her current happy marriage. Although Love never considered herself a rhythm-and-blues singer, she was awarded the Rhythm and Blues Foundation's Pioneer Award in 1995. She has had several small but successful roles in movies, on television, and on Broadway, including a part in the *Lethal Weapon* film series, the Bottomline Café production of her life story,

Portrait of a Singer, and Broadway productions of *Leader of the Pack* and *Grease*.

379. Love, Preston. *A Thousand Honey Creeks Later: My Life in Music from Basie to Motown—and Beyond*. Introduction by George Lipsitz. Hanover, New Hampshire: Wesleyan University Press, 1997. 270 pages; photographs. ISBN: 0819563188 : 081956320x.

Abstract: Born in Omaha in 1921, musician Preston Love was one of nine children in a single-parent household. He and his siblings were supported by his mother and their older brother who worked as a porter in a local hotel. One evening, his brother, Tommy (Dude) Love, came home with an alto saxophone. He later brought home a trumpet and tenor saxophone. Tommy mastered the alto saxophone and left town to pursue a career in music. Preston Love began playing the tenor saxophone that had been left behind, and eventually bought himself an alto. By 1941, Love was pursuing his own career in music. He was a big fan of Earle Warren, who was first alto saxophone with the Count Basie Orchestra. Love copied his playing style and sat in the front row of all the Count Basie performances in Omaha. One day, Warren asked Love to stand in for him while he took a medical leave from the orchestra. All Love's dreams came true as he toured and recorded with the Count Basie Orchestra until Warren's return. In 1948, Love decided to set out on his own and develop his own orchestra. He started touring about 1950, and the band began to take off in 1951. Love describes the grueling touring schedule, the low pay, and the budget-busting bus that the band drove from concert to concert. After disbanding for a period of time to recover from his debts, Love reorganized with a more economical bus and a successful set of touring dates. In 1962, he packed up his family and moved to Los Angeles, where he worked primarily as a recording-session and back-up artist. He toured with the Ray Charles Orchestra and played in back-up bands for Motown artists such as the Temptations, Aretha Franklin, Martha and the Vandellas, Marvin Gaye, and Smokey Robinson. Love and his family returned to Omaha in 1971. In 1983 he went on a Count Basie European reunion tour with some of the earliest members of that orchestra. In his book, Love talks about his views of music and jazz. He discusses the issue of race in the jazz world and mourns the disappearance of African Americans from the mainstream jazz scene.

380. Love, Robert Earl. *The Bob Love Story: If It's Gonna Be It's up to Me*. Written with Mel Watkins. Foreword by Michael Jordan. Chicago, Illinois: Contemporary Books, 2000. 208 pages; photographs. ISBN: 0809225972.

Abstract: Robert Earl Love was born on the O'Neill plantation in Delhi, Louisiana, in 1942. Except for a brief time spent with his mother and an abusive stepfather, he spent his childhood with his grandparents and his mother's twelve siblings. Love was happy in this environment, but he developed a serious stutter that stayed with him well into his adult years. In school, his teachers were supportive, but he endured endless teasing from his classmates because of his stutter. This changed when Love became active in sports, playing football and basketball in high school. He played basketball at Southern University, and by his senior year he had participated in the Olympic trials, was a member of the National Basketball Team, and the first black player to make the All-South team. Love graduated from Southern University with a degree in food and nutrition and was drafted into the National Basketball Association as a fourth-round pick of the Cincinnati Royals. He was subsequently traded to Milwaukee and then to Chicago. Although Love was one of only a few players who could play both defense and offense and was one of the top scorers in the league, he had difficulty communicating, especially under stress, and he never earned much media attention or the respect of his coaches. Love's basketball career ended in 1977 after a season with the Seattle Supersonics in which he sustained serious back injuries that made it difficult for him to walk. After retirement, he looked for work coaching and in the food industry, but was unsuccessful. Because of his stutter, people refused to take him seriously and he was generally viewed as unintelligent. During this period, Love's wife left him, but he remained determined to support his six children. He took a job as a bus boy at a Nordstrom department store cafeteria and within a few months advanced to cashier. The owners of the department store offered to help him advance within the company if he would get speech therapy for which they would pay. Love threw himself into his therapy and made enormous progress in a short time. He began making public speeches and moved up the ladder at Nordstrom, eventually becoming the company spokesman. Love returned to basketball when he was asked back to Chicago to become the Bull's spokesman. The team retired his jersey in 1994. Love writes that he has a "genuine concern and respect for the people I meet, and the joy of knowing I've faced the toughest challenge in my life and come out a better person. And it's all because I refused to play the victim. I didn't give up on my dreams" (p. 201).

381. Luttery, Kevin. *A Stranger in My Bed*. Orange, New Jersey: Bryant & Dillon Publishers, 1997. 214 pages. ISBN: 1889408034.

Abstract: Kevin Luttery writes about his experiences with two women, Jackie, an African American, and Chris, a white woman. Issues of race were always present in his relationship with Chris. He not only felt guilty and self-conscious about her being white, but she seemed to be unable to believe or accept his experiences with discrimination or the significance of race in his everyday life. Comparing the two relationships, Luttery draws some conclusions on how black women and white women differ based on their upbringing and the nature of their experiences. Luttery describes the painful process of breaking up with Chris and his pursuit of a writing career.

382. Lynne, Gloria. *I Wish You Love*. Written with Karen Chilton. New York, New York: Tom Doherty Associates, 2000. 288 pages; photographs. ISBN: 0312870310 : 0312870299.

Abstract: Gloria Lynne, born Gloria Wilson, was born in Harlem in 1931. She was raised in New York and made her debut as a singer at Amateur Night at the Apollo Theater when she was fourteen years old. She won first prize and soon began getting performance dates at local clubs. At nineteen, she was married and had a son who she left in the care of her mother as her singing career took off. Lynne sang in a number of groups before deciding to go solo. In 1957, she recorded her first album, *Miss Gloria Lynne*. She got her first hit, "I Wish You Love," in 1963. By this time, Lynne was in great demand, but no matter how many albums she made and no matter how many appearances she had, she could barely make a living. It was not long before she discovered that recording companies rarely if ever paid their artists. Years could go by and millions of records be sold, and the companies continued to report to artists that they were still paying off the original costs of making the recordings. Lynne found herself in and out of prosperous times. At one point she, her mother, and her son lived in a mansion in a wealthy neighborhood. At other times, they shared a one-room apartment. In the 1970s, she left New York to pursue her career in California. She did well for a number of years, but once again became broke and homeless. Back in New York in 1986, Lynne performed a number of reunion concerts with other jazz performers, and was sponsored by a couple she met who paid her rent and gave her living expenses so that she could sing and write. Lynne regrets that music today seems to require little talent from its performers and that music videos are focused on showing as much of the singer's skin as possible. She is confident, however, that good music by talented artists will endure and that young people will discover and learn to love her work. In 1997, she received the Pioneer Award from the Rhythm & Blues Foundation, an organization founded by singer Ruth Brown and supported by contributions from record companies to pay tribute and provide monetary awards to rhythm and blues artists who were never properly paid for their recordings.

383. Mabry, Marcus (1967-). *White Bucks and Black-Eyed Peas: Coming of Age Black in White America.* New York, New York: Scribner, 1995. 303 pages. ISBN: 0684196697.

Abstract: Journalist Mabry tells his story and discusses race relationships and the prospects for improvements from his perspective as a black man living in a "largely white world" (p. 301). Born in 1968, Mabry grew up in his grandmother's house in New Jersey, with his mother and brother, several uncles, and an aunt. He attributes his success to the hard work and determination of his mother and grandmother. Despite this, he describes the early years of his childhood as unstable and surrounded by domestic turmoil. At sixteen he applied for entrance to Lawrenceville, a prestigious residential prep school, and received a full scholarship. Always a bookworm, Mabry easily adapted to the difficult curriculum, but as time went on he felt more and more an outsider. Although he always had friends and always excelled, racism was an ever-present cloud. Mabry admits that he sometimes saw racism where it probably wasn't the motivating factor, but the reality was that it did permeate society. Expecting to win the fourth-form prize, Mabry was told that he didn't because the masters felt that he did what he did to prove that black people were able to do things as well as white people and that "that was not in the spirit of the prize." Mabry writes, "I realized that when blacks performed below par we risked being tarred as affirmative action candidates, but I had no idea that if we were good, we'd be painted as racial zealots, out to prove we were better than whites. . . . All my accomplishments had been reduced to fodder in a war of the races" (p. 142). However, Mabry left Lawrenceville appreciative of his experiences there. He went on to receive undergraduate and graduate degrees in French, English, and International Relations from Stanford University. Following Stanford and a sojourn in Paris, he began working as a correspondent for Newsweek. Mabry writes of meeting his father, a judge in Florida, for the first time, and of his struggle to reconcile his father's life-long absence and neglect of Mabry and his mother with his desire to be loved and approved of by him. He also writes of his brother's early fatherhood, and the hard work and minimum wage jobs he took to help care for his daughter.

384. Mah, Adeline Yen. *Falling Leaves: The True Story of an Unwanted Chinese Daughter*. New York, New York: John Wiley & Sons, 1998. 278 pages; photographs; index. ISBN: 0471247421 : 0965693015.

> **Notes:** Also published as *Chinese Cinderella: The True Story of an Unwanted Daughter*. New York, New York: Delacorte, 1999. ISBN: 0385327072; *Falling Leaves: The True Story of an Unwanted Chinese Daughter*. New York, New York: Broadway Books, 1999. ISBN: 0767903579; New York: Dell-Laureleaf, 2001. ISBN: 0440228654 (205 pages). Originally published London: Michael Joseph. *Falling Leaves Return to Their Roots: The True Story of an Unwanted Chinese Daughter*, 1997. Large print edition published Thorndike, Maine: Thorndike Press, 1999. ISBN: 0786219149 (437 pages).

> **Abstract:** Adeline Mah was born in Tianjin, China, the fifth child of wealthy parents. Her mother died soon after her birth, entrusting Mah to her husband's sister. Her father remarried within a few years and all five children were relegated to second-class citizen status in the household. Mah's elder sister was favored as a way of undermining the other children and her three brothers were given decent treatment because they were boys. Mah was singularly despised as the fifth child and a girl. Her aunt did everything she could for her, encouraging her to excel in her studies as a way of becoming independent. Throughout World War II and the Chinese revolution, Mah was sent to boarding schools cum orphanages as the rest of the family fled to Hong Kong. She was only pulled out of China and taken to Hong Kong when her stepmother's sister happened to remember she was still in the country. Her father eventually took an interest in her academics because she always did well and agreed to send her with her brothers to medical school in London. Mah became a doctor and found work in Hong Kong. Back in Hong Kong, her parents took control of her life, dictating her every move, but leaving her in a state of emotional and material neglect. To escape, she wrote to the Medical Education Department at the Presbyterian Hospital in Philadelphia, which hired her as an intern and loaned her the money for a plane ticket to the United States. Soon after her arrival, Mah married a man who abused her for years. She and her daughter finally left him and went to California, where she

had a successful practice as an anesthesiologist. She later married a man who cared deeply for her and her daughter, but she was unable to escape the manipulation of her parents and the equivocal treatment by her brothers and sisters, many of whom she and her husband supported and cared for. After both of her parents were dead, Mah found out that she alone had been cut out of any inheritance. Her only comfort was being able to go back to Tianjin and nurse her aunt in her final days, the aunt who raised her and gave her the only love and encouragement Mah ever received from her family.

385. Majozo, Estella Conwill. *Come out the Wilderness: Memoir of a Black Woman Artist*. The Cross-Cultural Memoir Series. New York, New York: Feminist Press at the City University of New York, 1999. 241 pages; photographs. ISBN: 1558612068 : 1558612076.

Abstract: Estella Conwill Majozo was born in Louisville, Kentucky. Both her mother and grandmother had mystical powers and deep Catholic faith. These two women became the mainstays in Majozo's life. Following marriage, birth of a daughter, and divorce, she went back to school, wading through white-centered curriculums, until she finally found a professor who opened the door to women's literature and, with it, black women's literature. She got a teaching job at the University of Louisville and self-published a book of poetry. She and her daughter then moved to Iowa, where she took Afro-American Studies at the University of Iowa. It was during this time that *Roots*, based on the book of the same name by Alex Haley, was broadcast on television. It was a major event for her and the entire black community, and she realized the need to communicate the stories of lives, especially black lives. The need for a black community took Majozo and her daughter back to Louisville, where they found a floundering artistic community. Majozo, who created her own last name in honor of three Black American heroines, Mary McLeod Bethune, Josephine Baker, and Zora Neale Hurston, bought a building to use as a center for black culture, which she called "Blackaleidoscope." The center taught dance, music, martial arts, storytelling, etc. and tutored children in their school work. After a second brief marriage and a second child, Majozo was offered a job at Hunter College. While teaching, she and her brother, Houston, put together a team of artists that made a pilgrimage to many cities around the United States where they created pieces of public art, one of which was "Revelations," a peace memorial in honor of Martin Luther King, Jr. at Yerba Buena Gardens in San

Francisco. Her book *Libation: A Pilgrimage through the African American Soul* (Harlem River Press, 1995) is the story of this project, which originated with a poem communicated to Majozo in a dream.

386. Majumdar, Debu. *From the Ganges to the Snake River: An East Indian in the American West.* Photographs by Robert Bower. Caldwell, Idaho: Caxton Press, 2000. 224 pages; photographs. ISBN: 0870043978.

Notes: Most of the essays in this book were originally published in *Rendevous: Journal of Arts and Letters* (Vol. 33, no. 1). Also published Pocatello, Idaho: Idaho State University Press, 1999. ISBN: 0937834653 (132 pages).

Abstract: Majumdar has written a series of essays in which he reflects on his adult life in Idaho and his childhood and youth in Calcutta. Majumdar first arrived in the United States to attend university in Philadelphia. He eventually earned a Ph.D. in physics and began work with a federal lab program which took him, his wife, and two sons to Idaho Falls, Idaho. In his new home, he found that even though he had lived in the United States for some time, he still had much to learn and many adjustments to make. Majumdar's essays reveal his reaction to the significant snowfall of Idaho, the new experiences of fishing and hunting, and the local love of horses. In one essay he compares the Snake River with Calcutta's Ganges. He examines the experience of being a life-long foreigner and compares his own situation to that of the few African Americans living in the state. Majumdar attempts to find out about the Shoshone and Bannock tribes of Idaho and compares the colonization of the Americas with that of India. He also includes a detailed account of his life as a young boy in Calcutta.

387. Malvin, John. *North into Freedom: The Autobiography of John Malvin, Free Negro, 1795-1880.* Edited and with an introduction by Allan Peskin. Cleveland, Ohio: Western Reserve Historical Society, 1996. 93 pages. ISBN: 0911704485.

Notes: Originally published: *Autobiography of John Malvin.* Cleveland: Leader Print Company, 1879.

388. Manigault, Sandra. *Fragments of a Woman's Life: A Memoir*. Art work by Donald Manigault. Stafford, Virginia: Godosan Publications, 2000. 96 pages; illustrations. ISBN: 0965854116.

Abstract: Sandra Manigault is a writer, teacher, artist, motivational speaker, and conference facilitator. She has degrees from Long Island University and Pennsylvania State University. She has taught mathematics at the high school and community-college levels in New York and Virginia. Currently she works with her husband at his Manigault Institute, which offers preparation courses for the SAT and educational workshops for students, teachers, and parents. They also present motivational sessions together. In her book, Manigault writes brief profiles of her parents, children, and husband. She reflects on her work as a teacher of mathematics and on what makes a worthwhile life. Manigault describes the writing life and her experiences while on sabbatical. She includes memories of church, traveling through North Carolina with her mother, and attending various artistic events featuring her son or daughter. She also explores different ways to reach an understanding of mathematics, including through music and art. Another book by Manigault is *The Book for Math Empowerment: Rethinking the Subject of Mathematics* (Godosan Publications, Inc.).

389. Mar, M. Elaine (1966-). *Paper Daughter: A Memoir*. New York, New York: HarperCollins, 1999. 292 pages. ISBN: 0060182938.

Notes: Published in paperback New York: Harper Perennial, 2000. ISBN: 0060930527.

Abstract: M. (Man Yee) Elaine Mar writes about her childhood, from her birth in Hong Kong to her graduation from Harvard. She spent her first years living with her parents in a Hong Kong apartment along with four other families. When she was about four, her father immigrated to Denver, Colorado to live with relatives and work in a Chinese restaurant. She and her mother followed two years later, in 1972. The family made their home in the basement of the house of a relative to whom they were constantly beholden. Mar lived a nightmare at school, where she was constantly taunted and teased and treated as an outsider. Her parents, to whom hard work and self-sacrifice were only natural, had a difficult time understanding her problems. She writes about the Chinese restaurant in which the entire family worked, about being temporarily forced out of the business, and about their further descent into poverty. As a teenager, she discovered some comfort and refuge in writing. She was accepted into the Telluride

Association Summer Program, a scholarship-only seminar for high school students at Cornell University in Ithaca, New York. That summer, spent with young people to whom she could relate, gave her a first look at the world outside her school, family, their restaurant, and Denver. The following year she was accepted at Harvard and made an almost complete break from her family.

390. MarDock, Julian (1918-). *The First of Many: The Story of a Pioneering Chinese Family Who Lived in Texas for One Hundred Years.* Austin, Texas: Nortex Press, 1998. 166 pages; photographs; facsimiles. ISBN: 1571689230.

Abstract: In *The First of Many*, Julian MarDock tells his story as well as that of his father, Sam MarDock. His father was born Mar Yum Eh and emigrated from China in 1875 at the age of thirteen. Sam arrived in California with his uncle and worked on ranches, with the railroad as a cook, and as a translator. He moved to Tyler, Texas, with a cousin in hopes of owning property and becoming a citizen. Together, and with the help of the local business community, MarDock and his cousin opened a café. Their business was prosperous and MarDock returned to China to arrange his marriage. His wife, aged sixteen at the time, did not come over to the United States for another fifteen years. Once settled in Tyler, MarDock and his wife, Wong, had three children, Julian, Lucille, and Sam Jr. Julian MarDock describes his childhood in the ethnically diverse railroad town of Tyler. His father was a respected member of the community. During his most prosperous times, he was generous with his land, provided work for unemployed railroad men, and fed the hungry. Because of U.S. immigration laws, however, Sam was never able to become a citizen. Julian and his siblings felt at home and comfortable in Tyler. Their first real experiences with discrimination came from outside. When competing in out-of-town sports events, they were often jeered by the home team, and when they first looked for work, many businesses refused to allow them to apply. MarDock attended Tyler Junior College and the University of Texas at Austin. He and his older brother both joined the aviation cadet program during World War II. After recovering from serious injuries sustained in a plane crash, Julian was sent to England. After being discharged from the Air Force, he attended medical school at Cornell University. He and his wife had five children together. In 1955, the family sought to make their mother, Wong, a U.S. citizen, but her application was denied. Cut off from any connection to her native land, at eighty-two, she traveled with Julian and his family to San Francisco in an unsuccessful effort to find family or members of her village. Both

Sam and Wong, however, felt at home and content in Texas. Julian MarDock writes, "We look back to the past with respect and love. We look forward to the future with faith, hope, and love" (p. 162).

391. Mariano, Eleodoro Barawed (1907-1995). *Papant's Diaries: The Diaries of Eleodoro Mariano (1907-1995)*. [Compiled and Edited by Joseph Mariano]. Flushing, New York: Joseph Mariano, 1997. 216 pages. ISBN: none.

392. Mars, James (b. 1790). *Life of James Mars: A Slave Born and Sold in Connecticut: Written by Himself*. Chapel Hill, North Carolina: Academic Affairs Library, University of North Carolina at Chapel Hill, 2000.

   http://docsouth.unc.edu/neh/mars/mars.sgml
   http://docsouth.unc.edu/neh/mars/mars.html

   Notes: Documenting the American South (Project).

393. Marshall, Joseph, Jr. *Street Soldier: One Man's Struggle to Save a Generation, One Life at a Time*. Written with Lonnie Wheeler. New York, New York: Delacorte Press, 1996. 305 pages. ISBN: 0385314302.

   Notes: Also published New York: Delta Trade Paperbacks, 1997. ISBN: 0385317069.

   Abstract: Joseph Marshall grew up in South Central Los Angeles. He describes his family as loving and supportive and he was encouraged by both his parents and grandparents to lead a life of learning. In 1964, he enrolled at the University of San Francisco under the mistaken impression that it had a large black enrollment. It was there, however, that he became interested in African-American history after reading a book on Malcolm X, and he set out to educate himself about African-American achievements and history. After graduation, Marshall was hired as a full-time teacher and assigned to the San Francisco School District's Guidance Service Center, which he directed for five years. There, he worked with many abandoned children and quickly developed a sense of the immensity of the problems facing teenagers. Next Marshall became a math teacher at Potrero Hill Middle School. There he met Jack Jacqua, who worked with the counseling department. Jacqua was absolutely committed to helping children who were at risk. Marshall describes the many discussions he and Jacqua had about individual children from the school, the fate of graduates, and the crisis situation for teenagers on the street. These conversations formed the basis for a close working relationship, and together they formed the Omega Boys Club. This club, intended for African-American students, focused on academics, staying away from drug use and out of gang culture, and learning African-American history and culture. Thirty students attended the first meeting of the club, and the program quickly developed and expanded to include college preparation classes, peer counseling, counseling at juvenile homes and prisons, and a radio program called *Street Soldier*. *Street Soldiers* provided an avenue for teenagers in trouble, often affiliated with gangs, to talk about their problems and aspirations, to seek advice and support, and to start new lives. Marshall describes some of the success stories, some of the more ambiguous achievements, and letters and testimony from club members. Eventually, Marshall was able to introduce some of his programs to young people in South Central Los Angeles. He found a station to broadcast *Street Soldiers*, and he worked with members of the Bloods and Crips gangs to seek a remedy to the relentless pattern of killing and revenge. Marshall and his colleagues also started the Omega Institute to train individuals to start up programs similar to the Omega Boys Club. In 1994, Marshall received an Essense award, a Children's Defense Fund Leadership award, and a MacArthur Fellowship.

394. Mason, Betty Hopkins. *Closed Chapter: An African American Educator's Memoir*. New York, New York: Vantage Press, 2000. 179 pages; photographs; index. ISBN: none.

Abstract: Mason was born in 1928 in Tulsa, Oklahoma. She writes that Tulsa was rigidly segregated and that it was not unusual for an African-American child to reach adulthood without having had any significant contact with white people. Mason's father, who worked for a tire company, died when she was twelve. Her mother worked as a domestic. When she was urged to break up her family after her husband died, she refused. She was determined to not only raise all of her children but to realize her and her husband's dream of sending them all to college. Mason graduated from Bishop College in Texas, married, and moved to Dallas. Unable to find work as a teacher in Dallas, Mason got a job as a newspaper editor and worked on the voter registration drive for the NAACP. After divorcing her husband, Mason and her daughter decided to move to California, where Mason's brothers were already living. They settled in Oakland, and Mason began working for the Berkeley school district. She moved steadily up the ladder, starting as a teacher and receiving a quick succession of

promotions, including director of Title I schools, assistant principal, and director of pre-kindergarten and elementary instruction.
Mason returned to Oklahoma to be director of high schools in
Oklahoma City. While there, she earned her doctorate in educational administration. By the time she left for the position of
superintendent of the Gary, Indiana school district, Mason had
been promoted to assistant superintendent in Oklahoma City.
Mason started out in a strong position in Gary by helping the
school district avert a teacher's strike, but the school board was in
a period of transition, and Mason soon realized that she was at
odds with the majority of its members. After two years of having
all of her proposals rejected by the board, she returned to
Oklahoma City, where she was reinstated as assistant superintendent of the school district. She soon became acting superintendent and then superintendent. Mason was the first African-
American woman to hold the position of school district superintendent in the state. She retired in 1995 after thirty-two years in
public education.

395. Mason, Gilbert R. *Beaches, Blood & Ballots: A Black Doctor's Civil
Rights Struggle*. Written with James Patterson Smith. Margaret
Walker Alexander Series in African American Studies.
Jackson, Mississippi: University Press of Mississippi, 2000. 227
pages; photographs. ISBN: 1578062780.

Abstract: A native Mississippian, Mason grew up with Jim Crow
and segregation, but also with a father who "talked freedom." He
attended Tennessee State University and graduated with distinction in 1949 with a double major in biology and chemistry. Mason
was accepted into the Howard University medical school and was
the first African-American extern at St. Elizabeth's Hospital in
Washington, D.C. He chose to return to Mississippi with his wife,
Natalie, and son, Gilbert Jr., to set up practice in Biloxi in 1955.
The town had a twenty-six-mile stretch of beach that had always
been whites only. Mason wanted to challenge that restriction and
organized a wade-in in 1959. Nine people participated in the
wade-in, including Mason and his young son, and all were arrested. In a subsequent wade-in in 1960, Mason organized a larger
number of protestors, but as local police and FBI agents looked on,
participants were brutally attacked by whites, and two men were
killed. Mason writes, "Jim Crowism was a wild, mad-dog system
in its effects. How else could you explain how the simple desire
of 125 people to use a few yards of a twenty-six-mile long beach
could trigger such rage, mayhem, and murder?" (p. 78). Mason
continued to press for access to the beach, and in 1968, the U.S.

Supreme Court upheld an appeals court ruling in favor of opening it up to African Americans. Mason describes his work in desegregating the school system with his son as the lead plaintiff. Biloxi children first began attending desegregated schools in 1964, with full integration finally achieved in 1970. Mason, a vice president for the Mississippi Conference of the NAACP for thirty-three years, stresses the importance of local motivation and participation in all of the protest movements in Biloxi and elsewhere in Mississippi. He writes that although they took advantage of NAACP advice and legal assistance, all desegregation and voting rights efforts were locally initiated. Mason continued to work for the rights of African Americans in Biloxi on issues such as hunger and discriminatory treatment. He concludes with his wish that "[W]e affirm the children, and so give them unconquerable spirits and the faith and determination to keep climbing" (p. 206).

396. Massaquoi, Hans J. *Destined to Witness: Growing Up Black in Nazi Germany.* New York, New York: William Morrow & Company, 1999. 443 pages; photographs. ISBN: 0688171559.

Notes: Published in paperback New York: Perennial, 2001. ISBN: 0060959614.

Abstract: Massaquoi was born in Germany to a white mother, Bertha, and Al-Haj, the son of the General Consul to Germany from Liberia. The three lived together, but the couple never married, and when the Massaquoi family went back to Liberia, mother and child remained behind. In 1932, when Massaquoi began attending school, the Nazi Party was coming to power and Nazi hysteria was taking over the country and the school system. Taken in by the propaganda along with everyone else, it took years for Massaquoi, one of a very few blacks in the country, to associate the treatment he received with Hitler and the Nazis. As political conditions deteriorated in Germany, Bertha was fired from her job for being politically unreliable, and mother and child began to make do on what she could earn at menial jobs. Not fit for college because he was officially non-Aryan, Massaquoi apprenticed as a machinist. Although he came close to being arrested on a number of occasions, he and his mother survived the war. Massaquoi's skin color became an asset during the Allied occupation, both because of the sense of solidarity Massaquoi shared with the African-American soldiers and because it was often assumed that he must be an American. Not eligible for refugee aid, Massaquoi spent several years surviving as a musician and black market trader. After an unsuccessful reunion with

his father in Liberia, he received a student visa to the United States
and went to live with maternal relatives in Illinois. After settling
with an aunt and uncle who farmed in Illinois, Massaquoi was
drafted into the U.S. Army and was slated to fight in Korea. He
notes that he was not ready to give his life to a country to which
he had such a tenuous connection and managed to stall until the
situation in Korea had begun to stabilize. Both his experiences in
Illinois and in the army exposed him to American-style racism and
this deadened any ideas he had of an idyllic life in the United
States. After serving in the military, Massaquoi was able to bring
his mother over from Germany. Now a journalist, he has made
return trips to Liberia and Hamburg, Germany, on a regular basis.
He is the general manager of *Ebony Magazine*.

397. Masumoto, David Mas. *Epitaph for a Peach: Four Seasons on My
Family Farm*. San Francisco, California: HarperSanFrancisco,
1995. 223 pages; photographs. ISBN: 006251024x : 0062510258.

Abstract: A third-generation Japanese-American farmer in the
San Juaquin Valley of California, David Masumoto writes about
farming and his philosophy of life in general. In August 1987,
Masumoto wrote an article for the *Los Angeles Times* on a variety of
peach, the Sun Crest, with superior flavor and texture which he
was going to give up because the color and short shelf life made it
difficult to sell. Reaction to the article was overwhelmingly in
favor of keeping the orchard. "The day the bulldozer arrived, I
met it out in the fields and stopped it from entering my Sun Crest
orchard. I decided to keep those trees for one more harvest" (p. 3).
The book then goes through the next year, describing the year-
long process of preparing a field, caring for a crop, harvesting and
selling it, and then taking account of the crop after costs and sales.
While discussing his work, Masumoto also talks about his move
into organic and more natural farming methods, the influence
farming has had on his marriage and the way he raises his children, and the connection it has helped him to maintain with his
extended family, surrounding farmers, and the Japanese-
American community. In the end, Masumoto succeeded in his
farming enterprise because a company specializing in organic
baby food bought the entire crop, and the yield from his peaches
balanced losses from his poor raisin crop. The baby food company, however, would only buy the single crop, and Masumoto was
again left looking for a buyer for the next year.

398. —. *Harvest Son: Planting Roots in American Soil.* New York, New York: W. W. Norton & Company, 1998. 302 pages; photographs. ISBN: 0393046737 : 0393319741.

Abstract: David Mas Masumoto is a third-generation Japanese American (Sansei) who chose to come home to Del Rey, California, after graduation from University of California at Berkeley. He returned to work on the family farm begun by his father and grandfather following their release from internment camps at the end of World War II. The family raises peaches, especially the Sun Crest variety which they sell under the Masumoto Family Farm name, and grapes, which are used exclusively for raisins. Masumoto writes about life on the farm, all of the work involved in caring for the peach trees and vineyards and the countless risks involved in farming. He describes the aspects of his life and work that he is especially fond of, such as planting wildflowers for groundcover, finding treasures in the family junk pile, having short but meaningful exchanges with his father, and teaching his daughter to operate a tractor. He also writes about the Japanese-American community in Del Rey: how the elders survived the long years in internment camps and then found new homes on farms in California, first renting and then buying the land. Now the community is shrinking, as Issei (first-generation) and Nisei (second-generation) farmers die out, and the Sansei make their homes and occupations elsewhere. In many ways, Masumoto has led the life of an obedient Japanese-American son and in others he has made his own mark. He is trying to farm using more sustainable, environmentally friendly methods than those normally used. His wife is the only Caucasian in the Japanese-American community, and they have the first interracial children. His wife, despite her different cultural background, participates in all community activities and, he acknowledges, her job in town makes it possible for the farm to stay afloat in uncertain times.

399. McBride, James. *The Color of Water: A Black Man's Tribute to His White Mother.* New York: Riverhead Books, 1996. 228 pages; photographs. ISBN: 1573220221.

Notes: Published in paperback in 1997. ISBN: 1573225789.

Abstract: James McBride alternates the story of his mother with his own story. His mother, born Ruth Shilsky, emigrated from Poland with her family in 1921 and grew up in Suffolk, Virginia where her father was the local rabbi and eventually a shopkeeper. A lack of attention and affection eventually drove her from her home and to New York, where she met and married Andrew D.

McBride, a young man (half black and half Native American) who, with her, started a church in their living room. She and Andrew had seven children together, and she was pregnant with their eighth when Andrew died of lung cancer. She remarried a black man, Hunter Jordan, with whom she had four more children. When explaining to her son why she never left the African-American community, she talks about how her own family turned her away when she was widowed and destitute, and how the members of their church, the housing project they lived in, and her first husband's family came to her aid, and how they encouraged her to marry Hunter Jordan. "That's how black folks thought back then. That's why I never veered from the black side. I would have never even thought of marrying a white man" (p. 193). McBride grew up in a world that revolved around his enormous family, especially his mother. He describes in detail his home life, which while it appeared to border on dysfunction and anarchy, was actually in the iron grip of his mother, who decreed that nothing mattered as long as you stayed in school and went to church. He had a rough youth, including involvement with drugs and crime that was triggered by the death of his stepfather when he was fourteen. While McBride finally recovered, thanks especially to a stepsister, finished high school, went on to college and a promising career in music and journalism, he continued to search for his own identity. Race was not a subject his mother would discuss. This book was the culmination of his lifetime of struggle. It is a sorting out of his own life that he was able to do as his mother very gradually told him hers. His conclusion about himself and his siblings, all twelve of whom are successful professionals who maintain close contact with each other, is that they are their mother's "own nation, a rainbow coalition . . . a rainbow coalition . . ." (p. 217).

400. McCall, Nathan. *What's Going on: Personal Essays*. New York, New York: Random House, 1997. 217 pages; index. ISBN: 0679455892.

Notes: Also published New York: Vintage Books, 1999. ISBN: 0375701508.

Abstract: After writing *Makes Me Wanna Holler* (Random House, 1994) and experiencing the reactions of people to it and their approaches to him to help with their own searching, McCall felt compelled to write this book as a follow up. In it McCall recounts not only his personal experiences, but his "*perceptions* about some of the issues that divide people and keep us racially polarized." He feels that there are many situations in which blacks and whites have deeply rooted assumptions that prevent blacks from excelling in all fields. In exploring these perceptions, McCall discusses   professional sports, in which, he says, both black and white competitors believe that "blacks are more gifted as athletes than whites but that God somehow shortchanged brothers on brains." In the chapter, "Airing Dirty Laundry," which McCall "respectfully requests that white people abstain from reading," he criticizes the unwritten rule against blacks criticizing people of their own race in a public arena. In yet another chapter, McCall speaks of the need for whites to have true spiritual leadership: "Blacks can't look to white folks to save them. White folks can't even save themselves."

401. McCline, John (1852-1948). *Slavery in the Clover Bottoms: John McCline's Narrative of His Life during Slavery and the Civil War.* Edited by Jan Furman. Voices of the Civil War. Knoxville, Tennessee: University of Tennessee Press, 1998. 155 pages. ISBN: 1572330074.

Abstract: This manuscript, given by John McCline to his employer, H. J. Hagerman, in 1932, begins around 1858. It covers McCline's years as a slave on the Hoggett Plantation in Middle Tennessee and his service with the Union Army. McCline provides a vivid description of the Hoggett Plantation and its surroundings. The plantation itself covered one thousand cultivated acres plus pasture and was maintained by one hundred slaves. McCline remembers that everyone feared the appearance of Mrs. Hoggett. "She was never without her whip, in fact it was always in evidence and as much a part of her being as her pink sun bonnet" (p. 19). He also recalls the brutality of Phillips, the overseer, and the outright murder of an adult slave who refused to be intimidated. McCline writes of the excitement among the slaves as rumors of war began to circulate. Word of John Brown's activities motivated all the enslaved men in the area to find guns, and the announcement of the election of Lincoln was cause for rejoicing. McCline witnessed both the Confederate and Union armies marching through the plantation, with the latter camping and headquartering there for a number of weeks. He remembers that the soldiers were friendly to the slaves, paying some of them for work and encouraging them to follow the army to freedom. McCline left his plantation mule by the side of the road one day and followed the Thirteenth Infantry Regiment from Michigan, staying with the company as a muleteer until the end of the war. McCline witnessed the battle of Lookout Mountain and marched through Atlanta with Sherman's army. As the regiment made its way to North Carolina and Virginia, it was followed by thousands of fugitive slaves: "[T]here were times when many of them were on the point of starvation, and at such times many of them were told they would have to shift for themselves. How they managed to get anything at all, was a mystery to all of us" (p. 99). After the war, McCline went with his regiment to Washington, D.C. and was released from service in St. Louis. He made his way to Michigan, working there, in Chicago, and then St. Louis before heading to Colorado and the Southwest, where he spent the rest of his life.

402. McCray, Billy Quincy (1927-). *Between These Walls: Working for the People*. Written with Jon Roe. Newton, Kansas: Mennonite Press, 2000. 179 pages; photographs. ISBN: 0967709210.

Abstract: In 1966, reapportionment created a new seventy-seventh district in Wichita, Kansas. Residents of that district convinced Boeing photographer Billy Q. McCray to run for the newly established seat in the Kansas House. He ran a very personal, low budget, door-to-door campaign and won by a respectable margin. As a new legislator, McCray set out "on a self-appointed mission to make life appreciably better . . . for the 80,000 people of my race throughout the state and to make life more fair and just for everyone" (p. 42). His work in the Kansas House included passage of fair-housing legislation and instituting African-American history as part of the Kansas public school curriculum. With other black house members, McCray formed the Minority Caucus with the aim of creating a statewide coalition to maximize the combined influence of all minorities. In 1972, McCray ran for the state senate and won. He was the only black senator at that time. Feeling comfortable with his constituency, McCray acted as an independent Democrat, and voted as he saw appropriate rather than according to party wishes. He addressed bussing issues and established the Kansas Food Bank and the Black Historical Society. In 1982, McCray lost his bid for Kansas secretary of state. He knew the race would be difficult and his campaign funds were minimal, but he felt that it was important for an African American to run for state office. After this, McCray was appointed director of the state's Division of Minority Business. In this position, he focused on training the minority business community to go through the state bidding process and encouraging banks to make loans more accessible to them. In his tenure as director, state contracts with these businesses quintupled. McCray once again ran for office in 1986, this time for a seat on the Sedgwick County Commission. He won his race and served nearly two terms. He resigned in 1993 to spend time with his wife, who was suffering from a serious heart problem. Before his wife died in 1995, McCray worked with her to establish a community newspaper which they called *Community Voice*.

403. McCray, Carrie Allen. *Freedom's Child: The Life of a Confederate General's Black Daughter*. Chapel Hill, North Carolina: Algonquin Books of Chapel Hill, 1998. 269 pages. ISBN: 1565121864.

> **Notes:** Also published as *Freedom's Child: The Story of My Mother, a Confederate General's Black Daughter*. New York: Penguin Books, 1999. ISBN: 0140282521.

> **Abstract:** Carrie Allen McCray, born in 1913, was her mother's ninth child. McCray was seventy-three, a retired social worker and teacher, when she became a writer and began researching her mother's life and putting together her own memories of her. McCray's mother, Mary Magdalene Rice, was the daughter of former slave Malinda Rice and her employer, Brigadier General John Robert Jones, CSA, Ret. Mary's relationship with her father after her mother's death is not clear, but while she was alive, he doted on her, taking her many places Negroes were not allowed. Mary went to Hartshorn Memorial College and excelled scholastically. Her education was cut short, however, when she married Gregory Willis Hayes, the thirty-two-year-old president of Virginia Seminary. The two had seven children together and were known as a devoted couple. Mary learned about fighting for equality from her first husband. McCray notes: "Gregory gave her the courage to fight not only racism but sexism and any other unfairness wherever she saw it. All through our young lives, we watched Mama going out the front door in that red felt cloche hat, on her way to fight for 'full freedom'" (p. 85). Ahead of the times her entire life, Mary served as interim president of the college for two years after Hayes's untimely death. She remarried William Patterson Allen, a black lawyer, one of the first turn-of-the-century blacks to graduate from the University of Michigan Law School. They had three daughters, including the author. The family moved to Montclair, New Jersey, where Allen was able to earn a good living as lawyer to blacks and other minorities. Mary never stopped fighting for civil rights. She was gentle but persistent as she led her local branch of the NAACP, raised money for blacks in danger of losing their land, fought for equality in education, persuaded many local businesses to serve blacks, and went door to door urging women to vote. Just as persistently as she dealt with

major civic matters, she took on local projects. She befriended and housed many poor and displaced persons, and her home served as a Thursday gathering place for black people to get together on their day off. The family also hosted many black artists who were a part of the Harlem Renaissance. McCray found a large number of the letters her mother had written in support of her causes in the NAACP files housed in the Library of Congress. This was how she discovered that her mother continued to work on civil rights activities almost until the day she died at the age of sixty after an extended period of ill health.

404. McDonald, Janet. *Project Girl.* New York, New York: Farrar, Straus, and Giroux, 1999. 231 pages; photographs. ISBN: 0374237573.

Notes: Also published University of California Press, 2000. ISBN: 0520223454.

Abstract: Lawyer Janet McDonald grew up in what she called the traditional American family, with a father, mother, and seven children, in the housing projects of Brooklyn. She was a high achiever in school and was skipped through several grades. She was accepted into and attended the mostly white Erasmus Hall High School. As she was more interested in fitting in than in academic achievement, she ended up taking make-up classes at night and during the summer before earning her diploma. She knew that she was smart enough to succeed academically, but lacked the self-confidence and guidance she needed to pursue college admission. She attended classes at Harlem Preparatory School, where she received the support she needed. From there she was accepted to Vassar College. At college she was again plagued by insecurity, and began taking heroin. McDonald graduated from Vassar, majoring in French, and spent two years studying and working in Paris. She was accepted at Cornell University Law School and was raped during her first year there. The trauma of the trial and lack of support left her suicidal and dependent on drugs and alcohol. After a leave of absence, she transferred to New York University, where she began setting fires in the dormitory. McDonald was emotionally depleted, angry, seriously depressed, and terrified. Her rapist had been sent to prison, but was released after three years. He threatened to sue the district attorney's office for false imprisonment. In the midst of her personal struggles, McDonald began attending Columbia School of Journalism, graduated, and was readmitted to New York University. She graduated at the age of thirty-two, and was hired to work at a prestigious white law firm. Never comfortable with her environment and still struggling to recover from the rape, McDonald left New York and moved to a new law firm in Seattle. Required to testify against her rapist once more, ten years after the crime, McDonald felt strong enough and understood the legal tactics well enough to withstand the defense attorney's attacks on her. The rapist was returned to prison. McDonald pursued and succeeded in fulfilling her dream of returning to Paris. There she works as an international corporate lawyer.

405. McDowell, Deborah E. *Leaving Pipe Shop: Memories of Kin.* New York, New York: Scribner, 1996. 285 pages; photographs. ISBN: 0684814498.

> **Notes:** Also published New York: W. W. Norton & Company, 1998. ISBN: 0393318435.

> **Abstract:** McDowell's father, uncle, and grandfather all worked at the U.S. Pipe and Foundry, the "Pipe Shop," in Bessemer, Alabama. Her grandfather worked there for forty-four years starting at the age of sixteen, and her father for thirty years. Employment practices at Pipe Shop had the white workers on one track that allowed for advancement and the African-American workers on another track that kept them at a single level their entire working career. The work her father did was menial and dangerous, and employees could barely live on their wages. When investigating her father's work at Pipe Shop, McDowell found that he had started at just over $1.00 an hour, and thirty years later was receiving just over $4.00 an hour. Twenty years after his death, McDowell's aunt encouraged her to file a claim for asbestos poisoning for her father. She was doubtful about whether she could do this, but went back to Pipe Shop to see the places in question and to look into her father's records. During the investigation of her father's working career, McDowell re-examines her childhood and family. She was born in 1951 and was raised as much by her grandmothers as her parents. She learned to read at the age of four-and-a-half by reading the Bible with her Great Grandmother Edie. Her extended family was large and close, despite conflicts and anger, and there was a structure of care and a set of rules for the children to abide by, primarily enforced by the network of grandparents and great grandparents. McDowell remembers that as the grandparents began to sicken and die, the fibers that held the family together began to disintegrate. In 1956, she began attending Pipe Shop Elementary, which remained a fully segregated school even after the *Brown v. Board of Education* desegregation ruling. It was not

until fifteen years later that the first signs of desegregation began to appear in Pipe Shop. McDowell went to college at the Tuskegee Institute and received her Ph.D. from Purdue University.

406. McElroy, Colleen J. *A Long Way from St. Louie: Travel Memoirs.* Minneapolis, Minnesota: Coffee House Press, 1997. 241 pages. ISBN: 1566890594.

Abstract: Poet and college professor Colleen J. McElroy writes about her world travels. She is constantly drawn to travel, and her motto is "There is something out there beckoning me. I don't know what; I don't know where. But I can hardly wait for my ticket to get there" (p. 241). She visits different countries, always with specific travel goals in mind, and she writes not only about what she has seen, but what she has to go through to meet each of these goals. In addition, she finds herself an anomaly—a black woman traveling alone in a foreign country—and many of her experiences are related to local reactions to her color. On her trip to Egypt, she takes a trip down the Nile.

> "Nubian," the boatman said, pointing to me. "Nubian," he said, pointing to himself. I was tempted to correct him, but on second glance, one of the women . . . looked somewhat like my cousin Loveta, the same complexion and high cheekbones, the same pout of lower lip. I thought, if I could be mistaken for Ethiopian in Italy, Tuareg in Morocco, and Garifuna in Belize, I could certainly be Nubian in Egypt.   (p. 219)

McElroy uses her travels to try to learn about the people in each country, their cultures and sensibilities, and she does her best to conform to both. When told that Ayers Rock in Australia is a sacred place for the Aboriginal people and that they do not approve of tourists climbing it, she instead takes a hike around it. When her friends at home ask her if she climbed it, her response is, "No, but I didn't climb Notre Dame, either" (p. 227). In similar ways she travels in Mexico, through the Yucatan forest, Peru, Malaysia, Japan, and Fiji. Extended stays in Germany and Yugoslavia offer intimate observations of those cultures. Although McElroy participates in tours when this is the most expedient way to get a foothold in a new place, she avoids them as much as possible, and gives her reasons for this attitude, writing with humor about tours, tour guides and her fellow tourists.

407. McGill, Nicole. *Kindred Spirits: Family Legends & Childhood Memories*. Jacksonville, Florida: China Grove, 1997. 59 pages; photographs. ISBN: 1575025590.

Abstract: In this collection of columns for the *Florida Times-Union* of Jacksonville, Florida, journalist Nicole McGill remembers bits and pieces of her childhood, portrays her grandparents, and relates family history. She says that she writes because it is important for children to know the history of their family. McGill recalls her childhood summers in Kannapolis, North Carolina visiting her grandparents. On her first trip, she was amazed to discover that her grandmothers were black. In her mind, she'd always pictured the aged, gray-haired white grandmothers in her storybooks and it hadn't occurred to her that hers would look any different. McGill tells about ancestors who were slaves, her grandfather who learned to read at age seventy-three, her recollections of having her hair straightened, and more. McGill concludes by providing tips on researching family history.

408. McGown, Ruby. *The Real Ruby: Movin' on, Movin' on*. Fort Wayne, Indiana: Ivy and Ruby Guidance Inn, 1999. 71 pages; photographs. ISBN: 1883517133.

Abstract: Ruby McGown's memories go back to when she was six years old. She was unwanted and neglected. Although she worked in the fields, she attended school whenever possible and finished the ninth grade. At fourteen, McGown was pregnant. She left Mississippi with her baby and $30.00 and headed for Chicago and then Fort Wayne, Indiana, where she still lives. She had five more children, one of whom died at the age of twelve. She was always happy to be a mother and determined to let her children know that they were loved. McGown worked at a variety of jobs and attended Purdue University, where she studied Home Economics and Food and Nutrition. Working for the state extension, she visited unwed mothers, many of whom seemed unprepared to care for themselves or their children. In 1970, McGown bought a three-bedroom house and established the Ivy and Ruby Guidance Inn. Motivated by her own unhappy childhood, she worked to help other unfortunate girls become good mothers by providing them with a temporary shelter, basic education in caring for themselves and their children, and access to food, medical care, and permanent housing. The Guidance Inn was eventually moved to a ten-bedroom house, and McGown continues to work there full time and without pay. Many people have contributed to the success of the Inn, and McGown thanks the many teachers, doctors, lawyers, judges, electricians, grants writers, and pastors who have volunteered their services over the years.

409. McLin, C. J., Jr. (1921-1988). *Dad, I Served: The Autobiography of C. J. McLin, Jr.* As told to Mimmie Fells Johnson. Edited by Sarah Byrn Rickman and Lillie P. Howard. Dayton, Ohio: Wright State University, Office of Public Relations, 1998. 166 pages; photographs. ISBN: 0966164709.

Abstract: McLin was inspired by his father's service to the African-American community in the early stages of the Civil Rights Movement, leading pickets and boycotts as early as 1935. One of his earliest efforts led to the hiring of blacks at the Dayton Kroger Store. Although his family received threats because of his father's work, McLin writes that his time in the U.S. Army was even more harrowing than his childhood. Segregation was the norm, from eating and sleeping quarters to toilets and drinking fountains. McLin was not one to take discrimination or racism quietly, and he rebelled actively and loudly. He didn't regret his actions, even though it meant he was not promoted. "At least they knew I had arrived" (p. 44), he comments. The black soldiers were only allowed to take the bus into town on Saturdays, and McLin staged one of his more memorable protests when he and several others tried to take the bus on a different day. The soldiers formed a blockade to stop the bus from moving ahead, and when the bus driver refused to let them on, they rocked it and actually lifted it off the ground. In the end, the protesters were let aboard. McLin writes, "Lord, I just couldn't stay out of trouble. Racism just kept raising its ugly head and I felt compelled to stamp it out" (p. 48). After leaving the army, McLin joined the family mortuary business and soon decided to enter politics. Although he had a strong hatred for white people, he wanted to work within the system rather than just antagonize it. He vowed to help all people in need, not just African Americans, although this community was the focus of his formidable efforts. He was instrumental in forming the successful legislative caucus, Black Elected Democrats of Ohio, which demonstrated its strength in 1977, when its boycott of the state budget vote brought progress on its passage to a halt. McLin worked for the establishment and support of many important community institutions, and probably had his greatest impact on the development of the Wright State University School of Medicine and School of Professional Psychology. He was loyal to his constituency, built bridges as needed to meet his aims, and worked tirelessly until he died of cancer in 1988 at the age of sixty-seven. The closing section of the book includes several testimonials from colleagues and friends.

410. McMillan, James B. (1917-). *Fighting Back: A Life in the Struggle for Civil Rights*. Interview by Gary E. Elliott. Narrative interpretation by R. T. King. Reno, Nevada: University of Nevada Oral History Program, 1997. 181 pages; photographs. ISBN: 1564753743.

Abstract: McMillan was born in 1917 in Mississippi. His grandmother was born a slave in the West Indies, came to Mississippi, and was unofficially married to a white plantation owner. Her husband protected her and their children from white racists while he was alive. After his death, the family fled the South and the dangers of racism, eventually settling in Detroit, Michigan, during the Great Depression. McMillan graduated from high school in 1936 and received a full athletic scholarship to the University of Detroit, where he was one of only two black students and the only one on the football team. Following college, McMillan attended dental school at Meharry School of Dentistry. During World War II, he was drafted into the army and served as a dentist. He was eventually promoted to the rank of captain, but his experiences with segregation in the army marked him for life. He writes that he left the army an "angry young man and I stayed angry for a long time" (p. 61). After setting up practice in Las Vegas (one of only two black professionals in Nevada at the time) and tiring of the segregated conditions, McMillan joined and became president of the local branch of the NAACP. The organization led boycotts, ran and backed candidates, and confronted businesses. Finally, after failing to make progress with politicians, the group made deals with organized crime and managed to end segregation in hotels and discriminatory hiring practices. McMillan's confrontational style put him and his colleagues at risk, and his offer to resign as president was welcomed by the board members. McMillan assesses the record of the Democratic Party in supporting civil rights over a number of decades and provides insight into the work of U.S. presidents and various governors. He considers Lyndon B. Johnson to be one of the greatest presidents, "surely the greatest president that black people ever had" (p. 125). He decries the abandonment of the struggle for civil rights by many prominent African Americans who claim to have succeeded on their own.

We have these younger blacks that have gotten excellent educations, and they think that they

did it by themselves. Poor black people marched
and suffered and were beaten and jailed to make
things better, and these guys don't realize that
they should now contribute something back to
us. I just don't understand it.   (p. 142)

McMillan was a member of the Nevada State Board of Dental
Examiners for twelve years and an elected member of the school
board. An elementary school is named after him. He concludes
his history by considering the value of the work he has accomplished.

411. McNatt, Rosemary Bray. *Unafraid of the Dark: A Memoir*. New
     York, New York: Random House, 1998. 282 pages. ISBN:
     0679425551.

Notes: Paperback published New York: Anchor Books, 1998.
ISBN: 0385494750.

Abstract: In this story of her childhood on the South Side of
Chicago in the 1960s and 1970s, children's book author Rosemary
Bray McNatt uses the U.S. welfare system as one of her themes.
She writes in the preface, "I have written this book, in part, to
show the good that could happen—that did happen—under the
welfare system of the 1960s" (p. viii). It is her assertion that,
although her mother had to declare herself a single-parent household, despite the fact that McNatt's father was very much a member of the family, the income that welfare provided assured that
her mother was able to stay at home and devote herself to raising
her children, shielding them from a well-meaning but overbearing
father and encouraging them in their academics. McNatt's parents
had a tumultuous relationship, agreeing only on the importance of
education for their children. She writes of her intellectual awak-
ening and the comfort she took from a very early age from surrounding herself with her studies to keep away the more unpleas-
ant aspects of life. McNatt was accepted into the Francis W. Parker
School, an elite, predominantly white school on Chicago's North
Side. There she overcame her own insecurities arising from racial
and economic differences, flourished as a student, and was accepted by her peers. After graduation from Yale University, McNatt
went into publishing, beginning at a small newspaper in
Connecticut, then on to *Essence, Ms.*, and *The New York Times Book
Review*. McNatt writes of the efforts she and her husband made to
fit into and contribute to the renewal of the decaying African-
American community in Harlem and of their struggles with the
decision to move elsewhere. She finishes with an attack on recent

changes in the U.S. welfare system, wondering what would have become of her if her mother had been forced out of the home and into unskilled jobs and what will happen to the children of the country who are at the mercy of this system now.

412. McPherson, James Alan (1943-). *Crabcakes*. New York, New York: Simon & Schuster, 1998. 281 pages. ISBN: 0684834650 : 0684847965.

Abstract: Pultizer Prize winner James McPherson reflects deeply on a very few events in his life and how they are representative of the way people think and act, how he has acted, and the motivation behind his actions. The first part of the book centers on why he bought a house and his decision to sell it nearly twenty years later. He purchased a house in Baltimore, his hometown, so that the elderly couple living there would not be thrown out. He reflects on the validity of the act of buying it in the first place, the lives of the couple there, his relationship with them, and finally his decision to sell it after the elderly woman dies. He recalls his disillusionment with the state of Maryland stemming from the time he was arrested and badly intimidated by a police officer for failing to keep his car registration current. The latter half of the book is written as a letter to a Japanese teacher he had. He combines his own ideas about life learned through his experiences as an African American and a human being living in Iowa with what he has learned of Japanese philosophy.

413. McReynolds, Patricia Justiniani. *Almost Americans: A Quest for Dignity*. Santa Fe, New Mexico: Red Crane Books, 1997. 349 pages; photographs. ISBN: 1878610643.

Abstract: Patricia McReynolds's parents were both immigrants. Her mother, Ruth Kongsvold, came to the United States from Alesund, Norway, in 1920. McReynolds's father, José Justiniani, emigrated from the Philippines, the Island of Negros, in 1913. They met six months after Ruth's arrival. Although Ruth's plan was to visit the United States and return home, she never saw Norway or her family again. The Justinianis moved from New York to California, where they worked together as live-in domestics until Ruth became pregnant. After that, José worked on his own. The family kept a separate apartment, but, because her father often needed to be available to his employers around the clock, as McReynolds grew older she spent a considerable amount of time at work with him. Most of the Justinianis's friends were in mixed marriages as well, primarily Filipino husbands and white,

European wives. They were frowned upon by the society; many
states, including California, still maintained antimiscegenation
laws. Ruth found the discrimination in California especially
painful, often reminiscing about the more open society in New
York. McReynolds was a cherished only child. Her parents were
extremely protective. Despite the fact, or perhaps because they
themselves had left their homes and families never to return, they
expected McReynolds to stay close to home. McReynolds agreed
that this was what all Norwegian-Filipino children must do.
While in college at UCLA, she found it difficult to find a group of
students of which she could become a part. When asked by a
young man what kind of boy she would date, she responded that
she would only date a Norwegian-Filipino boy, of course. When
McReynolds did marry, she married a white man whose parents
were horrified at the prospect of his marriage to someone with an
Asian background. In 1948, the year of their marriage, California
law still forbade marriage between white individuals and individuals with "more than one-sixteenth amount of Black, Indian,
Mongolian, or Malay blood" (p. 288). And so, the couple traveled
to New Mexico to marry. McReynolds describes the difficulty she
experienced moving away from her parents and their disappointment over McReynolds's maturing children setting off on their
own to states not contiguous with California. She also writes
about her first marriage which ended with her husband's suicide
after a long struggle with alcoholism and depression.
McReynolds eventually remarried, an event which shocked her
parents. McReynold's parents died within eight months of each
other. She made pilgrimages to both the Philippines and Norway
to renew connections with her extended families. McReynolds
examines the state of immigration law in the United States and the
issue of families separated by miles and continents. She concludes
by considering the direct effect immigration and U.S. immigration
law have had on her own family.

> Photographs of a family reunion . . . capture the
> remarkable contradictions in our family clan.
> Brunette to blonde, round and almond eyed, tall
> and sleek, husky, petite, pale-faced and deeply
> tanned, we form a micro United Nations. . . . I
> look over this gathering of my clan; it is one of
> my joys to know that we are all Americans.
> (pp. 348-349)

414. Means, Russell (1939-). *Where White Men Fear to Tread: The Autobiography of Russell Means*. Written with Marvin J. Wolf. New York, New York: St. Martin's Press, 1995. 573 pages; photographs; maps. ISBN: 0312136218 : 0312147619.

Abstract: Russell Means was born in Greenwood, South Dakota, in 1939. His mother was raised on the Yankton Sioux Reservation and his father was from the Oglala band of the Lakota Nation. In his autobiography, Means reviews Lakota history, provides background on cultural practices, customs and beliefs, and tells the story of his development into a dedicated activist for the cause of Indian rights and sovereignty. During World War II, Means's family moved to Vallejo, California, where his father worked in the shipyards. His parents provided a base for Indians in the area, and Means and his brothers often returned to family in South Dakota for the summers. As a young man, Means lost interest in school and began to have a drinking problem. He tried to change his lifestyle and work within the structure of the Bureau of Indian Affairs (BIA), taking advantage of the relocation program which helped with housing and education, but he was constantly frustrated, bumping up against what appeared to be an obstructionist stance on the part of BIA employees. Means found direction and purpose in his life as he became active in the Indian rights movement. He established the Cleveland American Indian Center, and, having joined the American Indian Movement (AIM), he founded the Cleveland branch (CLAIM). Means became a central figure in the national AIM organization, and his political work put him into direct conflict with the BIA and the FBI. He gives a detailed account of the 1973 siege at Wounded Knee and the criminal charges against him that followed, including indictments for murder and for inciting the 1974 Sioux Falls courthouse riot. Means documents the prosecution's use of false witnesses. Despite a number of acquittals, Means was sent to prison for rioting to obstruct justice. After his release, Means continued to work with the AIM and organized the Black Hills Alliance and the Yellow Thunder Camp as a means of claiming the right to use the Black Hills area for sacred ceremonies. Means assesses the work that he accomplished or failed to accomplish through AIM, describes his feelings about the condition of Indians in the United States, and gives examples of how American Indians can help themselves collectively and individually. Means believes that it is vital to preserve the "indigenous world-view" (p. 536) and to "embrace the ideals of our ancestors" (p. 544).

415. Mei, Elizabeth. *Elizabeth.* Utica, New York: Mei Publishing, 1995. 267 pages; photographs. ISBN: 0964827700.

Abstract: Elizabeth Mei was born prematurely in the midst of a bombing raid in Chengtu, Szechuan Province, during the Japanese invasion of China. Her family moved from place to place in China and finally settled down in Hong Kong after the Communist takeover. Mei's father was an academic and had a position as an officer with the British Education Department. She remembers happy days of going to school, meeting her father on his way home from work, and playing with younger siblings. She was fifteen when her baby brother was born, and she quit school to take care of him and do the housework. When she finally decided to go back to school, she was demoted to the sixth grade. In 1963, Mei's father retired from his position with the British government to emigrate to the United States. In the United States, Mei took English classes and tried to go to school, but became very depressed when she did poorly. After a failed suicide attempt, she managed to graduate from high school and enroll in Fullerton Junior College. When things did not get easier for her, she attempted suicide again, lapsing into a coma that lasted six months. Mei writes about how her brother cared for her while she was unconscious, and the ten additional months she spent in the hospital regaining the ability to speak and use her arms and legs. As she gained strength and independence, her brother helped her to enroll at Chapman College. Mei describes her herculean efforts to live independently, attend classes, and to remain enrolled at Chapman over the seven-year period it took her to graduate.

416. Meketa, Jacquelin Dorgan. *See* Chacón, Rafael.

417. Melanson, Yvette D. *Looking for Lost Bird: A Jewish Woman Discovers Her Navajo Roots.* Written with Claire Safran. New York, New York: Avon Books, 1999. 233 pages. ISBN: 0380976013.

Notes: Also published New York: Bard Books, 1999. ISBN: 0380795531.

Abstract: In 1953, when Yvette Melanson was only a few days old, she and her twin brother were kidnapped from her parents, both Navajo Indians. They were kept in hiding for several years before they were adopted by white couples unable to adopt through conventional channels. She was raised as a Jew in New York and was a pampered child until her adoptive mother died when she was twelve. Her father and his second wife essentially abandoned her, and she spent her high-school years living in the homes of friends. Upon her graduation, her parents sent her to a kibbutz in Israel. When she came home after being wounded in armed conflict, they enlisted her in the U.S. Navy. She had a short-lived marriage while in the Navy, and gave birth to a son. After leaving the Navy she met and married a much older man. After their two daughters were born, Melanson began looking for her birth parents. A lead over the Internet led her to a Navajo reservation. This was the first inkling she had that she might be a Native American, and she fought against the idea. Indisputable proof, however, convinced Melanson that she had found her family. She was reunited with them, but it turned out that her mother had died a number of years before, still searching for her lost children. At about the age of forty, Melanson, her husband, and their two daughters decided to move from their home in Maine to the Tolani Lake Reservation in Arizona. Her Navajo family and everyone in the community welcomed the family warmly, but life on the reservation was hard. Her white husband had a difficult time fitting in, her daughters were bullied at school, their living conditions were poor, and Melanson's lifestyle habits, housekeeping and cooking abilities were constantly under the scrutiny of her sisters and other relatives. It was almost impossible to find work. Melanson describes the years the family spent looking for a way to make a living and to otherwise thrive in their new home. Melanson describes the spiritual practices and ceremonies of the Navajo. Her family used their spiritual powers to find her and continued to look for her twin brother. As the book ends, he is found and reunited with the family, and the twins, together, hold a ceremony, bringing them more completely into the fold of their Navajo tribe.

418. Melbourn, Julius (b. 1790). *The Life and Opinions of Julius Melbourn with Sketches of the Lives and Characters of Thomas Jefferson, John Quincy Adams, John Randolph, and Several Other Eminent American Statesmen.* Written with Jabez D. Hammond (1778-1855). Chapel Hill, North Carolina: Academic Affairs Library, University of North Carolina at Chapel Hill, 2000.

   http://docsouth.unc.edu/neh/hammond/menu.html

   Notes: Documenting the American South (Project).

419. Mendez, Gladys. *See* Vilar, Irene (1969-).

420. Mendoza, Tony (1941-). *Cuba: Going Back*. Austin, Texas: University of Texas Press, 1999.   153 pages; photographs. ISBN: 0292752326 : 0292752334.

Abstract: In 1960, Tony Mendoza, a Cuban native, was in Connecticut attending the Choate School when Fidel Castro came to power. His family immediately decided to leave Cuba for the United States. After college and graduate studies at Yale and Harvard, Mendoza decided to pursue a career as an artist. He moved to New York City, where he began his first relationship with a Cuban woman. To get closer to the Cuban-American community, the two moved to Miami. It did not prove to be a good environment for an artist, however, and they decided to leave when Mendoza was offered a position at Ohio State University. In 1996, Mendoza requested a sabbatical to return to Cuba to take photographs and keep a diary. This book presents his photos and the results of his interviews with two hundred people taken over a two-week period. Through these interviews, Mendoza seeks the popular view of the Cuban revolution. As he travels, he also observes general living conditions and the availability of food, goods, and services. He reports on his travels throughout the countryside beyond Havana, to his aunt's small ranch, and to the abandoned family beach house. Mendoza includes excerpts from a number of Castro's speeches.

421. Mfume, Kweisi. *No Free Ride: From the Mean Streets to the Mainstream*. Written with Ron Stodghill. New York, New York: One World, 1996.   373 pages; photographs. ISBN: 0345392205 : 0345413644.

Abstract: Kweisi Mfume, born Frizzell Gray, was born into poverty in Baltimore's inner city. A high-school drop-out, juvenile delinquent, and unmarried father of five, he became a Baltimore city councilman, member of the U.S. Congress, and CEO of the NAACP. Mfume was the eldest of four children. Their father was abusive and their mother died when Mfume was only sixteen. The siblings were separated, but Mfume spent most of his youth working to help support his three sisters, who lived with a grandmother on a limited income. When he began having girlfriends, they all became pregnant, and he became the father of five sons by four women over the course of two years. About 1970, he earned his high school equivalency certificate and got a job with WEBB, a radio station in Baltimore owned by singer James Brown. In 1972, he enrolled in the Community College of Baltimore, where he became involved with student activism. It was during this time that he changed his name to Kweisi Mfume, an African name which means conquering son of kings, to symbolize the new life he had embarked on. His popular radio programs became more and more political, earning the wrath of Brown, and Mfume had to move to a different station. In 1979, he took advantage of his popularity to run for Baltimore City Council. He won his election and served on the council until 1986, when he was elected to the U.S. Congress. This position gave him a platform from which to work for national and international causes, particularly the movement to end apartheid in South Africa. Mfume writes about how partisan politics complicate almost all issues brought before Congress and how he used his role as the chairman of the Congressional Black Caucus, representing a block of forty congressman, to further causes affecting black Americans. Mfume was on hand in South Africa when its first democratic elections were held, and he writes of his great admiration for and friendship with Nelson Mandela, the first black president. Based on his work for black causes throughout the United States and in South Africa and Haiti, Mfume was recruited in 1995 to serve as the CEO of the NAACP after a series of scandals and fears of encroaching irrelevancy shook the foundations of the association. The book closes as he prepares to begin this new stage of his life.

422. Miller, E. Ethelbert. *Fathering Words: The Making of an African-American Writer*. New York, New York: St. Martin's Press, 2000. 178 pages. ISBN: 0312241364.

> **Notes:** Published in paperback New York: Thomas Dunne Books, 2001. ISBN: 0312270135.

> **Abstract:** Writer E. Ethelbert Miller was introduced to black revolutionary philosophy, black history, black poetry, and the Black Arts Movement while at Howard University in Washington, D.C. Majoring in the new field of Afro-American History, Miller graduated dedicated to writing poetry and to working for African Americans at an African-American institution. He stayed on at Howard University, working in the Afro-American Reading Room, supported by the Afro-American Studies Department and the Institute for Arts and Humanities. Miller's mentors were Bob Stokes and Steven Henderson, both faculty members at Howard, and Ahmos Zu-Bolton, editor of *Hoo Doo Magazine*. Miller writes about his life as a poet, the poets and writers he worked and read with, his two marriages and two children, and his decision to leave Howard for the University of Nevada at Las Vegas. It was not until Miller had achieved a secure place in the publishing

world that his family began to understand his life as a writer, especially a writer dedicated to African-American culture. Miller remembers his older brother Richard, who had interests that were not supported by their father: a desire to dance and to read and a fervent Catholic faith that led him to join a Trappist monastery. Miller imagines that the family pressure to make other career choices which he himself felt must have been something like what his brother Richard faced giving up his life in the monastery for the family and, thus, never achieving his aspirations. Miller, in fact, seems to be the one child in the family who followed through on his dreams and did not succumb to familial pressure to lead a more traditional and conservative life. The untimely death of his brother and then his father's death two years later, lead Miller to write his memoir, to consider his relationships with his sister and mother, and to look closely at his own role as a father.

423. Miller, Reggie. *I Love Being the Enemy: A Season on the Court with the NBA's Best Shooter and Sharpest Tongue.* Written with Gene Wojciechowski. New York, New York: Simon & Schuster, 1995. 282 pages; photographs. ISBN: 0684813890.

Abstract: Reggie Miller kept a diary of his 1994-1995 season with the professional basketball team the Indiana Pacers. In that season the Pacers made it to the Eastern Conference Finals with the Orlando Magic, but lost their bid for the NBA championship. Interspersed with his description of the various games, players, and coaches, Miller describes coming into his own as a player, developing his style, individual player and team rivalries and camaraderie, and the advantages and disadvantages, including death threats and media pressure, of being a celebrity. Born in 1965, Miller came into the world with damaged hips and legs. He spent his childhood years in leg braces. He was always encouraged and supported by his family and developed into a top-rated athlete. Miller's family enjoyed spending time together shooting baskets, so basketball was a natural sport for the children to pursue. Miller's older sister Cheryl was on the 1984 gold-medal winning U.S. Olympic basketball team and is a member of the Basketball Hall of Fame. Miller recounts a post-game conversation with his sister: "I still remember the night I came home from a Poly Tech game after scoring thirty-nine points. I mean, I was feeling good about myself. Then Cheryl came home. 'Cheryl, I got 39.' 'Reggie, that's great.' 'Yeah, so how'd you do?' 'Uh, I got 105'" (p. 163). Miller eventually outgrew his sister and was able to beat her at one-on-one.

424. Minerbrook, Scott. *Divided to the Vein: A Journey into Race and Family*. New York, New York: Harcourt Brace, 1996. 259 pages; photographs. ISBN: 0151931070.

Abstract: *U.S. News & World Report* journalist Scott Minerbrook was born to a black father and a white mother. Both sides of his family have complicated issues of race and interpersonal relationships that Minerbrook has spent his entire life coming to grips with. His father was black, but the family was light-skinned and included many members who had passed as white. The Minerbrook family was proud and considered his father's marriage to a white woman below him, but they maintained ties with the couple and their children. Minerbrook's mother, on the other hand, was born into a poor white family in a small town in Missouri, and they cut her off completely when she married. As a young person, Minerbrook was constantly uncertain of interpersonal relationships and matters of race, and he did poorly in school. He decided to exert himself in high school and was accepted at Harvard, which presented an entirely new set of racial problems. His fellow students demanded that he take sides, either white or black, and his response was to try to look at matters from a nonracial viewpoint. He began to study African-American history and was frequently at odds with his professors, who demanded more of a pro-black anti-white stance. As an adult, Minerbrook made a happy marriage, and he and his wife had two children. Despite his improved family situation, however, he was still plagued by racial confusion and had a special hatred for the white side of his family. He made several attempts to contact them and finally went to Missouri to confront them face to face. They tried to explain to him the reasons why they could not accept him or anyone else in his family and the complexities of living in a small town with deep-seated racial prejudices. After much effort on Minerbrook's part, his relatives finally allowed him to establish a tentative form of contact with them, and this gives him hope.

425. Monroe, Lorraine. *Nothing's Impossible: Leadership Lessons from inside and outside the Classroom*. New York, New York: Times Books, 1997. 236 pages. ISBN: 0812929047.

Notes: Also published New York: PublicAffairs, 1999. ISBN: 1891620207 (223 pages).

Abstract: Lorraine Monroe helped found and was principal of the Frederick Douglass Academy in Harlem. A public school with a selective student body, the academy was eighty percent African American and twenty percent Latino. In 1997, as the school graduated its first class of twelfth graders, three-quarters of the senior class had been accepted into college, and the expectation was that nearly all of the rest of the class would receive acceptance letters as well. Monroe and her colleagues took a school with a poor reputation and a deteriorating building, renovated it, replaced some staff members, and opened with 150 students, a set of common goals, expectations, and non-negotiable rules. Monroe describes her own education, her growth as a teacher and school administrator, and the reasons why she gave up her international educational consulting career to return to working directly with students. In her book she describes her teaching and administrative methods and the importance of leadership to inspire and direct teachers.

426. Moore, Joanna P. (1832-1916). *"In Christ's Stead": Autobiographical Sketches.* Chapel Hill, North Carolina: Academic Affairs Library, University of North Carolina at Chapel Hill, 2000.

> http://docsouth.unc.edu/neh/church/moore/moore.sgml
> http://docsouth.unc.edu/neh/church/moore/moore.html

> **Notes:** Documenting the American South (Project).

427. Moore, Sam (1930-). *American by Choice: The Remarkable Fulfillment of an Immigrant's Dreams.* Nashville, Tennessee: Thomas Nelson Publishers, 1998. 216 pages; photographs. ISBN: 0785274537.

> **Abstract:** Sam Moore was born Salim Ziady in Beirut, Lebanon in 1930. His mother sent the children to Orthodox Christian schools. Following high school, Moore attended the Three Patriarchs College for three years, during which time he had a religious experience and converted to Christianity. After quitting school because of family financial difficulties, Moore and his three brothers went into business together and started a grocery store. Soon thereafter, Moore became convinced that he should go to school in the United States. He set out, with six hundred dollars in his pocket, for Columbia Bible College in South Carolina. During his first summer vacation, he went door-to-door selling Bibles and earned enough money to pay a year's tuition, buy a car, and a set of new clothes, and still put a little money in the bank. After two years, Moore transferred to the University of South Carolina. He later completed course work for a master's degree and, having decided to stay in the United States, became a U.S. citizen and changed his

name to Moore. Moore found that he made more money selling
Bibles than he had at any other occupation. He set up his own
book company, which he developed into the Royal Publishing
Company. Moore planned his first book to be a useful family
Bible. To accomplish this, he arranged for a variety of scholars to
contribute explanatory texts, and he included pictures, an index,
and a concordance. The Bible was called the *New Clarified
Reference Bible*. Moore describes the growth of Royal Publishing,
his purchase of Thomas Nelson Publishers, acquisitions of several
other book companies, and then near bankruptcy by 1984. As 1990
came to an end, the company was again profitable, and Thomas
Nelson was purchasing other companies. Moore describes the different Bibles he has published and his thoughts on leadership and
on being an American.

428. Mora, Pat. *House of Houses*. Boston, Massachussets: Beacon
Press, 1997. ISBN: 0807072001 : 080707201x.

Abstract: Writer Pat Mora writes about the history of her family
in a semi fictional format. The setting she uses is a "dream house
hovering near El Rio Grande between El Paso and Santa Fe" (p.
288). Six generations of her family, including both her mother's
and father's sides, herself, and her children share this imaginary
house and interact with each other as she tells the stories of the different family members. Her mother's family came to the United
States to escape Pancho Villa, a Mexican national hero, who, in the
process of liberating the poor of Mexico, killed everyone in his
path. Mora talks about the different grandparents and aunts and
uncles, and the relationship between her parents and their relationships with each other's families. She discusses her
Americanization and that of her brothers and sisters. Mora
describes how her children relate to Mexican family members,
both living and dead.

> Made up of earth as we are, this nested adobe
> house, its body is inherited and temporary, like
> ours, is protected by exterior walls we create and
> construct around the fertile interior, layers of
> vulnerable beauty. Within the body of the fam-
> ily dwell the homes of the next generation,
> another nesting, and within each of our bodies,
> all the selves we've been and are, held together
> by skin, fragile yet sturdy: a paradox, like the
> house that's yet green in the desert, visible yet
> private . . . private yet communal.   (p. 288)

429. Morales, Dionicio. *Dionicio Morales: A Life in Two Cultures: An Autobiography*. Houston, Texas: Piñata Books, 1997. 199 pages. ISBN: 1558852190 : 1558852115.

Abstract: Dionicio Morales's mother and father emigrated from Mexico during the Mexican Revolution, and Morales was born two weeks after his mother arrived in Yuma, Arizona. The family settled in Moorpark, California, where Morales's father worked on several ranches. Although the family bought property, they lived in a tent throughout Morales's childhood. Schools in Moorpark were segregated through the fourth grade. By the time Morales entered high school, many of his acquaintances had left California to return to Mexico. He had little encouragement from his teachers, despite his academic success, and was excluded from many activities, including college interviews, because the school principal didn't believe that Mexican Americans should leave the fields and attend college. Nonetheless, Morales left home with twenty dollars and encouragement from his parents to attend Santa Barbara State Teacher's College (later University of California, Santa Barbara). He majored in art under the mentorship of Professor Mary Croswell. She was particularly interested in Mexican art, and considered Morales a good investment of her efforts. She actively supported him, even while he was confined for eighteen months in a tuberculosis sanatorium. Back at home recuperating from the disease, Morales made his first foray into political action. Tired of the humiliation of the segregated movie theater in his hometown, he developed a plan that successfully integrated it. Next, Morales set out to improve conditions for Mexican laborers under the Bracero Program of World War II. Working through the Department of Agriculture, he enforced guidelines and conditions of the program. He later continued this work when the program was reinstated during the Korean War. Morales's major accomplishment was the founding of the Mexican American Opportunity Foundation (MAOF). With this foundation, Morales opened up employment opportunities for Mexican Americans in the corporate world, trained and employed the elderly, set up job training programs for prisoners and women, instituted subsidized day care for barrio children, and developed education programs to teach Mexican history and culture as a means of building self-esteem. In 1997, the MAOF had an annual budget of twenty million dollars, 322 full-time employees, twenty-five programs, and twenty-three outreach offices. He writes: "As I look back over eight decades of life in two cultures, I have concluded that our Mexican Heritage will neither disappear nor fade, but will flourish to illuminate the upward path of countless generations to come" (p. 199).

430. Morgan, Joan. *When Chickenheads Come Home to Roost: My Life As a Hip-Hop Feminist*. New York, New York: Simon & Schuster, 1999. 240 pages; index; reading group guide. ISBN: 0684822628.

> **Abstract:** Joan Morgan discusses feminism for black women and reactions to her involvement in this issue. A writer who began her career at *The Village Voice*, Morgan has written extensively about music and gender issues for the *New York Times*, *Ms.*, *Madison*, *Interview*, *Spin*, and numerous other publications. She starts this book by explaining that feminism is a volatile issue in the black community because it necessarily pits men against women and that taking sides with other women, often white women, means that black women appear to be in opposition to, rather than in support of, black men. She explains her task:
>
> > White girls don't call their men "brothers" and that made their struggle enviably simpler than mine. Racism and the will to survive it creates a sense of intra-racial loyalty that makes it impossible for black women to turn our backs on black men even in their ugliest and most sexist of moments. I needed a feminism that would allow us to continue loving ourselves and the brothers who hurt us without letting race loyalty buy us early tombstones.   (p. 36)
>
> Topics that Morgan discusses, laced with her own experiences and those of friends and family, include the degradation of women in rap and hip-hop lyrics, the destructive effect of the myth of the "STRONGBLACKWOMAN," how women tend to indulge but not respect the "ENDANGEREDBLACKMAN," and the need for black women to insist on certain standards before beginning a relationship with a man. She also deals with the question of why so many black women fall into the socioeconomic category of unwed mothers, how threatened otherwise-motivated black women are by the wiles of women (so-called "chickenheads") who are only interested in marriage and money, the matter of respecting masculine pride, and the importance of "sista's" supporting and empowering each other.

431. Mori, Kyoko. *The Dream of Water: A Memoir*. New York, New York: Henry Holt and Company, 1995. 275 pages. ISBN: 0805032606.

> **Notes:** Also New York: One World, 1996. ISBN: 0449910431.

Abstract: Kyoko Mori, a creative writing professor at St. Norbert's College in DePere, Wisconsin, was born in Kobe, Japan. She lived there until the age of twenty when she completely forsook Japan to live in the United States. Her mother committed suicide when Mori was twelve, and she was left in the care of her father and stepmother who forbade her and her brother to have any contact with her mother's side of the family and sabotaged their relationships with any other relatives. After her mother died, Mori's home life was punctuated by complaints from her stepmother and beatings from her father. Thirteen years after Mori left Japan to go to college, graduate school, and ultimately marry and begin a career in the United States, she made her first trip back to Japan. She went back with few feelings of connection, but with a desire to see her estranged relatives and old friends and, out of a sense of duty, to visit her father and stepmother. During her seven-week stay, and a few unhappy visits with her parents, Mori reexamined the way she was brought up following her mother's death and talked with her relatives about their view of how her father treated her. Eventually she was satisfied that her beloved aunts and uncles agreed that she had been mistreated, and she realized that, despite her warm reunions with other family members and old friends, her relationship to and ability to forgive her father would determine her feelings about Japan. At the airport, while on her way back to Green Bay, Wisconsin, Mori reflects that,

> Kobe seems such a long way off, already a foreign country. No matter how much I love its mountains and the sea, the downtown, the familiar neighborhoods and the streets, it is a place I left thirteen years ago to save my life. I will never spend a whole summer, a semester, or a year there. . . . How can I possibly spend more than a few weeks in the same city as my father?
> (p. 274)

432. —. *Polite Lies: On Being a Woman Caught between Cultures.* New York, New York: Henry Holt and Company, 1997. 258 pages. ISBN: 080504079x.

Notes: Also available in paperback New York: Ballantine/Fawcett, 1999. ISBN: 0449004287.

Abstract: Writer Kyoko Mori left Japan at the age of twenty to go to college in the United States. Almost twenty years later, she compares the two cultures and how they have affected her. She covers a variety of topics, beginning with language. She states that "having a conversation in Japanese is like driving without a headlight: every moment I am on the verge of hitting something and hurting myself or someone else, but I have no way of guessing where the dangers are" (p. 7). Other aspects of Japanese culture are also difficult for her to deal with, such as the reluctance of doctors to discuss a patient's condition with him or her, the obscurity of symbols used for communicating, the role of women, safety, and so on. Woven into the story of culture is Mori's own tragic childhood. Her mother committed suicide when she was twelve. Her father, apparently unable to show any affection to his children, remarried a women who consequently sabotaged the children's remaining relationships with extended family and friends, assuring that Mori grew up in a loveless household. In the United States, she settled in Green Bay, Wisconsin, where she continued to struggle with the meaning of her own life, trying to separate culture from emotional baggage.

> My mother spent most of her adult life trying to live a polite lie of a stable and harmonious marriage, trying, day after day, to make the lie become the truth somehow; her death meant a final rejection of that lie. If there was one thing she wanted me to do, it was to resist the polite lies and the silences of my childhood, to speak the truth. . . . All these years later, my conviction remains the same: I speak her words though I speak them in another language.   (p. 258)

433. Morris-Dotson, Cynthia E. *Tumbling Waters: A Historical and Autobiographical Novel.* Montgomery, Alabama: CeSalAlve, Ltd., 1998. 402 pages. ISBN: 096585082x.

Notes: Large print edition.

Abstract: In 1965, Cynthia Morris-Dotson and her two younger sisters were three of seventeen African-American students who integrated two formerly all-white schools in Wetumpka, Alabama. Morris-Dotson was in high school and her sisters were in the elementary school. Morris-Dotson depicts two-and-a-half years of name calling and serious physical abuse from both students and teachers. Each day she and her sisters waited for the school bus which never stopped to pick them up. When the bus driver was finally forced to stop for them, most white children stopped taking the bus. The girls were aware of what they were fighting for, and they received support from a number of civil rights activists. During these years, Morris-Dotson's family received death threats and were criticized by both black and white citizens of Wetumpka. Their house was set on fire and left to burn by the local fire department. Morris-Dotson left the all-white school after being raped. She became pregnant and was placed in "hiding" until the birth of her child. After giving birth, she left for Florida, where she finished eleventh grade, finally graduating from a high school in another town in Alabama. Following her graduation, Morris-Dotson joined the Air Force through the Air Force Reserves Officers' Training Corps (AFROTC) at the University of California at Berkeley. She served in Korea and became involved in the Tuskegee Airmen, Incorporated. Morris-Dotson was executive officer to the commander of the Headquarters, 549th Tactical Air Support Training Group at Patrick Air Force Base at the Kennedy Space Center, Cape Canaveral, at the time of the explosion of the space shuttle in 1986.

434. Morrison, George (b. 1919). *Turning the Feather Around: My Life in Art*. As told to Margot Fortunato Galt. Midwest Reflections. St. Paul, Minnesota: Minnesota Historical Society Press, 1998. 205 pages; photographs; art work. ISBN: 0873513592 : 0873513606.

Abstract: Artist George Morrison was born in 1919, in Chippewa City, Minnesota, on the shores of Lake Superior. He describes himself as five-eighths Indian. Morrison enjoyed drawing and art as a young child, and as he grew older he sold drawings and decorated objects to earn money. After finishing high school in 1938, he enrolled in the Minneapolis School of Art, graduating with highest honors and a scholarship to continue his schooling. Morrison moved to New York and began attending the Art Student's League. He describes his progress as an artist, showing his work in group shows, and then selling to collectors and museums. He writes about himself as an Indian and an artist, "I never played the role of being an Indian artist. I always just stated that I was a painter, and I happened to be Indian. I wasn't exploiting the idea of being an Indian at all, or using Indian themes" (p. 71). While his work was being exhibited at such prominent museums as the Whitney, museums featuring Indian art were not interested in it because it lacked an Indian theme. As Morrison developed his style, he moved from expressionism to abstract and later worked with wood and sculpture. He studied in Paris during the late 1950s on a Fulbright scholarship, has taught at the Minneapolis School of Art, the Rhode Island School of Design, and the University of Minnesota. As a teacher in American Indian Studies, Morrison and his second wife Hazel became active in the

American Indian Movement. Morrison describes his later paintings and exhibitions, his struggle with Castleman's disease and alcoholism, and his thoughts on Christian and Indian spirituality. He describes his artistic inspirations from nature, environments he has lived in, and both Indian and Western art traditions.

435. Morrow, Curtis. *Return of the African-American.* Huntington, New York: Kroshka Books, 2000. 148 pages. ISBN: 1560727179.

Notes: Originally published Chicago: C. Morrow, 1983.

436. —. *What's a Commie Ever Done to Black People? A Korean War Memoir of Fighting in the U.S. Army's Last All Negro Unit.* Jefferson, North Carolina: McFarland & Company, 1997. 138 pages; photographs. ISBN: 0786403330.

Abstract: Morrow joined the army in 1950 at the age of seventeen, anxious to volunteer to serve in Korea. He trained as a demolitions specialist and shipped out as part of the last segregated combat team in the army. Morrow describes his battlefront experiences and his growing disillusionment with what he was being asked to do in Korea. After nine months fighting on the front lines, he was knocked unconscious in a blast and woke up in a psychiatric ward in Pusan, Korea. After he recovered, he stayed to work at the hospital until being shipped back to the United States. He returned to his home in Michigan, proudly displaying his combat medals, but found that he was uncomfortable being showcased as a hero and role model. He felt incredible guilt for the killing that he had been involved in and left home before his leave was over to escape his conflicting feelings. Morrow was sent to Fort Leonard Wood in Missouri. The town in which the camp was located conducted business according to the Jim Crow system, and Morrow was discouraged and angry. He rebelled against what he thought were discriminatory practices and was confined to the stockade for three months. Following his release, Morrow was shipped to Japan for two years. He describes his work there, his training as a paratrooper, and his relationship with Keiko, a young Japanese woman. Morrow developed a love of the country, and appreciated the respect with which he was treated there.

437. Moss, Thylias. *Tale of a Sky-Blue Dress.* New York, New York: Bard, 1998. 259 pages. ISBN: 0380975505 : 0380793628.

Abstract: Thylias Moss, a professor of English at the University of Michigan and the author of six volumes of poetry and two children's books, was born to an African-American mother and "mixed blood" (Cherokee, French-American, African-American) father. She writes of a poor childhood, but one in which she was the much-loved only child. Her life changed when her parents decided to entrust her to a daughter of the family living next door, who then proceeded to abuse her several hours a day for the next several years. Moss never mentioned the abuse to her parents. Her low self-esteem, exacerbated by a school which insisted on seeing her as a below-average student before finally sending her on to "super-gifted studies," eventually resulted in abusive relationships with men, an unwanted pregnancy, and a second-trimester abortion. Looking back, the main dilemma of Moss's youth was her inability to cry out for help,

> I guess we cannot save ourselves. . . . We have to have some idea, however vague, of the assistance needed or we may not recognize nor take advantage of help. When we're in the quicksand, sometimes a rope is offered, a serpent is offered, but if we hang on to it, we might be extricated from a worse fate of total loss. Yes, we must let go of the serpent, but only after, though it's biting us, it has pulled us out of the quicksand to solid ground.   (p. 88)

Moss finally met a man who loved her and helped her get over her fears and insecurities. After they married, he continued to encourage her. Moss entered and graduated from Oberlin College and then went on to graduate school. She has developed her own celebratory style of poetry.

438. Motley, Constance Baker (1921-). *Equal Justice Under Law: An Autobiography*. New York, New York: Farrar, Straus, and Giroux, 1998. 282 pages; photographs; index. ISBN: 0374148651.

Notes: Published in paperback New York: Farrar, Straus, and Giroux, 1999. ISBN: 0374526184.

Abstract: Motley writes about her career as a black female lawyer and judge in an age when either was a rarity. She describes her family and its move to New Haven, Connecticut, from the tiny Caribbean island of Nevis. The bulk of her book, however, is devoted to the court cases which she feels had the greatest influence on the rights of black Americans during the twentieth century. The first was *Plessy v. Ferguson*, which determined that black and white facilities could be separate as long as they were equal.

As a result of *Plessy*, all of the Southern states, if
they had not already done so, set blacks aside in
separate schools, separate parks, separate cemeteries—anything that would keep the races apart
and allow for what the South called separate
development of people who are racially and cul-
turally different. We will never know what
twentieth-century America would have been
like in terms of race relations if the decision had
gone the other way in 1896.   (p. 94)

Motley asserts that the next century was spent undoing the harm
of *Plessy*. She worked on *Brown v. Board of Education* (1954) and
cases that attempted to force compliance to the desegregation ruling. She describes how the work of civil rights lawyers was affected by other aspects of the Civil Rights Movement, the Freedom
Riders, lunch counter sit-ins, and so on. Motley also discusses
how the original lawyers, including the late Supreme Court Justice
Thurgood Marshall, felt that most injustices based on racism
would be solved in major civil rights court victories, but instead
they led to ever-increasing litigation. She recalls her time as bor-
ough president of Manhattan, and in the New York State Senate,
and in the Federal District Court. Motley describes the discrimination against her, more because she was a woman than because
of her race. She closes by discussing affirmative action and the
detrimental effect that recent Supreme Court decisions have had.

439. Mura, David. *Where the Body Meets Memory: An Odyssey of Race,
Sexuality and Identity*. New York, New York: Anchor Books,
1995. 272 pages. ISBN: 0385471831 : 038547184x.

Abstract: Writer David Mura, a third-generation Japanese
American, describes the personal conflicts in his life, from childhood through to his middle adult years, and examines the possible causes. He goes back over his parents' lives beginning in the
internment camps during World War II. He looked for the anger
and the confusion that they either couldn't or wouldn't communicate to him, but which he felt must have been behind the way they
acted and raised their children. He is also confused about how
much of their behavior was based on traditional Japanese ways of
doing things. For Mura, confusion over race is mired in confusion
over sex, a problem he carried with him through high school, his
undergraduate career at Grinnell College, graduate school at the
University of Minnesota, and into marriage, where he was consistently unfaithful to a woman he loved. The fact that he was

attracted to and married a white woman only added to his questions. When his wife finally started taking steps to stop Mura's
infidelity and other abuse of her, he agreed to begin psychothera-
py in an effort to get to the root of his problems. One day, while
reading *Black Skin, White Masks* by Frantz Fanon, he had a revela-
tion:

> Here, I realized, was a truth that neither therapy
> nor my work on family systems nor addiction
> had ever addressed. None of that psychological
> thinking had ever considered very deeply the
> context of race.... I see a counterpart to my life-
> long perception of myself as a 'loser,' an outsider
> unable to make 'concrete contact with his fellow
> man.' [The main character's] wish to blame each
> flaw and defeat on skin color seems to echo my
> explanations of my sexual insecurity: I was a
> Japanese in a white world. It was as if I some-
> times could see no other cause for my neuroses,
> the flaws in my psyche.   (p. 232)

440. Murray, Albert. *South to a Very Old Place*. New York, New
York: Modern Library, 1995. 266 pages. ISBN: 0679601473.

   Notes: Originally published New York: Modern Library, 1971.

441. Murry, Terece. *A Measure of Time*. Baltimore, Maryland:
American Literary Press, 1999. ISBN: 1561674850.

442. Nall, Jasper Rastus (1861-1956). *Freeborn Slave: Diary of a Black
Man in the South*. Birmingham, Alabama: Crane Hill
Publishers, 1996. 106 pages; illustrations. ISBN: 1881548287.

   Abstract: Jasper Rastus Nall, was born in Alabama, probably in
   1861. He felt that it was important for his children to know something about their family history, and so he questioned both his
   mother and grandmother about their lives. He then told these stories to one of his three daughters, who wrote up a manuscript that
   has been kept in the family. Nall's grandmother Lucy was born
   the daughter of a slave owner and an Indian slave. She was sold
   as an infant under the condition that she would be freed at the age
   of twenty-one, but this promise was not kept, and she was a slave
   until the Emancipation. Her daughter, Nall's mother Ellen, was
   sold at the age of fourteen. She was three-quarters white and one-
   quarter Indian. Nall's father's side were slaves to the Nall family.

Nall's parents were on two separate estates at the time he was born, and he chose to take the name of his father's family. Although his mother's owner offered to educate him, his mother turned down the opportunity. He writes, "All I know I caught in the air. Yet in this way, I have gotten a practical education that I believe to be equivalent to a high school graduate" (p. 32). Nall had an entrepreneurial instinct. He describes the various jobs he held and the ingenious and careful way he went about earning and saving money. He worked as a mail carrier, in mining, and as a butcher. He also owned and operated a grocery store. He was active in politics, and formed the Colored Republican Party Club. The members of this group faced down the majority Democratic Party and went en masse to vote on election day. Nall was anxious that his children receive an education, and he had a special concern for the lack of opportunities for young African-American women. He spent years raising money and negotiating the building of a high school in Patton, Alabama. When it was completed, he was gratified:

> I feel that I reaped the benefits of all through the one 'master piece' of my life: my school building project! There are many men, now widely scattered over the United States, who were benefited by this school, but there is not another man besides me who had the pleasure of seeing all his children and his wife graduate from this school.
> (p. 96)

443. Nasdijj. *The Blood Runs Like a River through My Dreams: A Memoir*. Boston, Massachusetts: Houghton Mifflin, 2000. 216 pages. ISBN: 0618048928.

   Abstract: This memoir consists of twenty essays about the life of Nasdijj. Nasdijj's father was white and his mother was Navajo. As a child of migrant workers, as a Navajo, and especially as one of mixed heritage, Nasdijj was always conscious of being on the fringe of society, living on the edge of "White People Town" and on the edge of the reservation. His memories of his childhood are unhappy and dominated by his family's constant moving around. He writes that he never asked why; he knew there were no answers: "You had to find out your own answers, and the only place you were going to find them was in yourself" (pp. 35-36). Interested in writing since his adolescence, Nasdijj has attempted to make writing his sole means of employment. This meant that for a lengthy period he was homeless and moved with his dog and a tent back and forth between state parks. Nasdijj writes about his son Tommy Nothing Fancy, whom he and his first wife adopted as an infant. Tommy was diagnosed with fetal alcohol syndrome and died of seizures at the age of six. Nasdijj also suffers from a milder form of the syndrome, and his son's affliction brings back memories of his own mother's dependence on alcohol. Nasdijj describes his many years living on the Navajo reservation in New Mexico. Besides writing, he has worked as a teacher. Because he was not officially certified, he was arbitrarily assigned the children who couldn't succeed in a regular classroom. Nasdijj's story concludes as he leaves the reservation, after years of solitude and healing, with his new wife.

444. Navarrette, Ruben, Jr. *A Darker Shade of Crimson: Odyssey of a Harvard Chicano.* New York, New York: Bantam Books, 1993. 270 pages. ISBN: 0553089986.

Abstract: Ruben Navarrette writes about his experience at Harvard University as one of a handful of Mexican-American undergraduate students in the class of 1989. Raised in the San Juaquin Valley, Navarrette attended a high school that was nearly seventy percent Mexican American. Throughout his schooling he was an outstanding student. As a senior, he was valedictorian, had straight A grades, and high SAT scores. Yet, when his principal learned that he had applied only to U.C. Berkeley, Stanford, Princeton, Yale, and Harvard, he suggested that Navarrette also apply to the local state university. When Navarrette received his five acceptance letters they "beckoned a Mexican-American boy who knew nothing of racism. Of denial of privilege because of one's skin color" (p. 2). Nonetheless, his high school teachers and classmates clearly felt that Navarrette had gotten in because of his race and not because of his accomplishments. Navarrette explores the origins of this widely held belief that the minority student or job seeker rarely, if ever, deserves what they achieve. He examines the stereotypes of Mexican Americans in particular and how opportunities are shaped by the prevalence of these stereotypes among teachers, school administrators, and other professionals. Navarrette writes about how his own experiences were shaped by race, both his own attitude toward race, and that of his fellow students. He studies Richard Rodriguez's controversial book *Hunger of Memory* (Godine, 1982; Bantam, 1983), and tests Rodriguez's premise that language and mainstream and elite educational experiences distance the minority student from his home and family. Following Harvard, Navarrette entered a Ph.D. program in education at UCLA. He chose not to finish the degree, although he continues to seek a way, through writing and lecturing, to reform an educational system that strangles minority students from the outset of their time in school.

445. Neal, Lula Mae. *Little Colored Girl*. New York, New York: Vantage Press, 1998. ISBN: none.

446. Nelson, Jill (1952-). *Straight, No Chaser: How I Became a Grown-up Black Woman*. New York, New York: G. P. Putnam's Sons, 1997. 225 pages. ISBN: 0399142622.

> **Notes:** Also published New York: Penguin, 1999. ISBN: 0140277242.

> **Abstract:** Jill Nelson, a professional writer, also wrote the autobiographical work *Volunteer Slavery: My Authentic Negro Experience* (Noble Press, 1993). In *Straight No Chaser*, she discusses feminism and race. She believes women must claim a space for themselves and relinquish the idea that to proclaim oneself a feminist is to forsake the fight against racism. She asserts that black women in American society are socially invisible. They have been raised to believe that their physical appearance is inferior to white women; they are the victims of domestic abuse; they have been blamed for the ills of America in general and black men in particular. To illustrate her points, Nelson recalls the patriarchal nature of her own family, her own experience with domestic abuse, and the messages she received from childhood about what constitutes "good hair" and preferred skin color. She believes that black women have been asked to support black men, and yet there has been very little reciprocal support. She describes the many stereotypes by which black women have been constrained. Nelson calls on all black women to resist constraints and stereotypes. She lays out ten points for black women to follow to help themselves and other black women. Nelson concludes by asking women to "[i]magine how powerful we would be, what we could accomplish, if black women across the country were communicating and organizing. Reach out to black women where you find them" (p. 225).

447. Neville, Aaron, Charles Neville, Art Neville and Cyril Neville. *The Brothers*. Written with David Ritz. Boston, Massachusetts: Little, Brown & Company, 2000. 368 pages; photographs; index. ISBN: 0316730092.

> **Notes:** Also published Cambridge: Da Capo Press, 2001. ISBN: 0306810530.

Abstract: The Neville Brothers were born in New Orleans, in a rigidly segregated and intensely racist environment. Art was the oldest, followed in order by Charles, Aaron, and Cyril. In this book, each of the brothers tells his own story to make up a collective autobiography of this family of musicians. Art founded a singing group known as the Hawkettes, that was popular in New Orleans and other parts of the South. He also started up a group called the Meters, which had a successful career recording for Warner's Reprise label. The Meters traveled with and opened for both the Rolling Stones and the Grateful Dead. Charles was a saxophonist who married and went on the road at the age of fifteen. He saw crime as a way to get revenge on white society, so his musical and academic careers were interspersed with time spent in prison. Aaron made a chart-topping solo hit, "Tell It Like It Is," which he followed up with a tour managed by his brother Art. When he went to Los Angeles to pursue his career, he became addicted to heroin and involved in crime. Cyril, the youngest, admired his brothers from a distance, but had an inner rage that kept him in trouble with the law and sometimes at odds with his family. At one point, he and his brother Aaron formed a group called the Soul Machine that, while popular, never made any recordings. All four brothers finally came together with their Uncle Jolly to record an album with the Wild Tchoupitoulas. They were subsequently "discovered" by Bette Midler and began recording as the Neville Brothers for A&M records. One by one, the brothers were able to begin recoveries from their addictions, find some domestic peace, and enjoy long-deserved success as musicians. Famed rock promoter Bill Graham became the manager of the Neville Brothers and negotiated a successful recording contract for them with Rounder/EMI. Their story is not yet complete, but they look to their late parents and their Uncle Jolly for inspiration and hope to lead a life that has peace and harmony, both musical and spiritual.

448. Newton, Adolph W. (1925-). *Better Than Good: A Black Sailor's War, 1943-1945*. Written with Winston Eldridge. Annapolis, Maryland: Naval Institute Press, 1999. 182 pages; photographs. ISBN: 1557506493.

Abstract: Adolph Newton ran away to join the Navy when he was seventeen. He served from 1943 to 1946. He re-enlisted and served until 1948. Joining shortly after President Roosevelt ordered the Navy to accept African Americans into the Seaman-Fireman branch, Newton had the questionable fortune of participating in many Navy firsts. Although he trained as a diesel mechanic with an all-African-American group of enlistees at the Hampton Institute in Virginia, Newton worked in partnership with both white and black sailors once he shipped overseas. His primary working partner was white, and they developed a working relationship and close friendship. Following his discharge in 1946, Newton was unable to find work in his specialization. He was told at the employment office that no one would hire a Negro diesel mechanic, and this proved to be the case. After a period of idle unemployment, he re-enlisted in the Navy. Newton had experienced his share of racism during the war years, but after re-enlisting he was assigned to the engineering division of the ship, the *Donner*. Here he was the first black to work in engineering and the only one not working in a steward's capacity. Newton relates the many racism-related trials he underwent both at sea and on shore. Constantly in trouble, he almost received a bad conduct discharge, but the charges were dismissed after being reviewed in Washington, D.C. After leaving the Navy in 1948, Newton finally found civilian work as a diesel mechanic. He began working for General Motors in 1953 and became the first African-American supervisor working for General Motors south of the Mason-Dixon Line.

449. Nguyên, Dình-Hoà. *From the City inside the Red River: A Cultural Memoir of Mid-Century Vietnam*. Foreword by Graham Tucker. Jefferson, North Carolina: McFarland & Company, 1999. 217 pages. ISBN: 0786404981.

Abstract: Linguist Nguyên Dình-Hoà was born in Hanoi in 1924. He grew up with ten siblings, five boys and five girls, his father and his father's two wives. As was typical in Vietnam, Nguyên's mother brought her children up according to Confucian tenets: boys were encouraged to succeed at school and girls in the domestic arts. In school, Nguyên studied French, English, and Chinese as well as sciences and history. He writes that he gained his Western education from the French-Vietnamese system and learned "Oriental humanities" from his father, mother, aunt, and uncle. Following World War II, Nguyên worked for the United States vice consul in Hanoi and was recommended for study in the United States. At the age of twenty-four, he left home to attend Union College in Schenectady, New York. After graduating, he hitchhiked two thousand miles across the United States, brought his fiancé over from Vietnam, married her, and then moved to New York to attend graduate school at New York University School of Education. In 1955, Nguyên, his wife and two daughters returned to Vietnam. Nguyên began teaching at the University of

Saigon, where most of his extended family had moved. Nguyên continued to serve as dean of the Faculty of Letters and chair of the English Department. While teaching, he was made director of cultural affairs in the Ministry of National Education and also secretary general of the Vietnam National Commission for UNESCO. Through the latter position, Nguyên traveled to meetings in such places as Paris and Thailand. Nguyên and his family left Vietnam once again in 1965, eventually taking a teaching position in linguistics at the University of Southern Illinois. He did not return to Vietnam again until 1994. Nguyên describes his reunion with his sister and presents many details and descriptive anecdotes about the customs and practices of everyday life in Vietnam. His desire is to balance the many books about the war by presenting an accurate portrait of how the Vietnamese people conduct their lives.

450. Nguyen, Tuyet-Nga. *Fragrance of Flowers from the Old Garden.* New York, New York: Vantage Press, 1995. 75 pages; photographs. ISBN: 0533113628.

Abstract: Nguyen states that she wishes to portray the beautiful aspects of Vietnam and so says very little about her experiences during World War II or the Vietnam Conflict. She seeks to reveal "the fundamental Vietnamese culture, ways of life with inner values, the depth of sentiment, moral obligations, and conduct before the war, during the war, and beyond the war" (p. xi). Both Nguyen's parents were professionals, and so the three eldest children, including Nguyen, lived with their grandparents. Nguyen's grandfather had two wives and Nguyen had love and attention from both grandmothers and her grandfather. At the age of six, Nguyen returned to her parents, whom she hardly knew, so that she could attend school. Her father was affectionate, but her mother was strict and Nguyen was always frightened of her. She writes that her mother wanted her children "to be perfect in every way ..." (p. 45). Besides schoolwork, Nguyen's mother made sure that the girls learned all the skills they would need to run a household. Just after World War II, Nguyen, anxious to leave home, joined the revolutionary youth movement of Ho Chi Minh. At the age of thirteen, her job was to convert "illiterate peasants" to the Patriotic Movement. She was arrested by a rival revolutionary group and held as a prisoner for several months. In 1950 Nguyen married a journalist. He died in 1973, leaving her to support and raise their six children alone. Living in Saigon and working for a radio station sponsored by the U.S. embassy, Nguyen was among those taken out of Vietnam during the general evacuation at the fall of Saigon in 1975. She and her family, all except her third son who was living elsewhere, were shipped to Guam with nothing but their official papers. From there, they were sent to a refugee camp in Pennsylvania and finally to Washington, D.C. where Nguyen became a nurse. Ten years later, Nguyen was finally able to bring her third son and his family to the United States.

451. Nishimoto, Richard Shigeaki (1904-1956). *Inside an American Concentration Camp: Japanese American Resistance at Poston, Arizona.* Edited by Lane Ryo Hirabayashi. Tucson, Arizona: University of Arizona Press, 1995. 262 pages; photographs. ISBN: 0816514208 : 0816515638.

Abstract: Nishimoto was asked to take part in the Japanese American Evacuation and Resettlement Study (JERS) at the University of California at Berkeley beginning in 1943. He worked with the project following the war until 1948, acting as an observer, writing up reports and verifying facts and details. His observations and notes were used in a number of publications, including the three resulting publications of JERS. As part of his work for the project, Nishimoto wrote an autobiographical letter to Dr. Alexander M. Leighton of the Bureau of Sociological Research, dated November 1, 1942. He and his family were by then being held at the Colorado River Relocation Center, or Poston, near Parker, Arizona. In his letter, Nishimoto describes arriving in San Francisco in 1920 at the age of seventeen. After some months in the rice field of a distant relative in Colusa, California, Nishimoto returned to San Francisco and enrolled in high school. He spoke no English, but was taken under the wing of a schoolmate who taught him vocabulary and pronunciation. Following graduation, Nishimoto attended Stanford University, where he pursued an engineering degree. When it became clear that no U.S. corporation would hire an Asian engineer, Nishimoto moved to Los Angeles, where he became an insurance broker, a legal aide, and a court interpreter. In 1931, Nishimoto met and married a young Nisei woman from San Francisco. They had two daughters, born in 1932 and 1934. After his marriage and as the Great Depression took hold of the country, Nishimoto left the insurance business and ran a successful produce market "selling products of the Japanese to Caucasians" (p. 30). He kept close track of news both from Japan and the United States and predicted war with Japan as well as the incarceration of the Japanese population on the West Coast. Nishimoto ends his letter by describing a scene at his home with his family enjoying an evening together. A radio broadcast announces the order for the evacuation of all Japanese from the Pacific Coast. His youngest daughter remarks that she is an

American citizen and certainly will not have to go. Her mother states, "Yes, you are an American citizen, but your face is Japanese. Everyone with a Japanese face must go" (p. 33). The editor has included three of Nishimoto's reports to JERS in this compilation: "Labor: Nishimoto's Report on the Firebreak Gang"; "Leisure: Nishimoto's Report on Gambling at Poston"; "Demands: Nishimoto's Study of the All Center Conference."

452. Northrup, Solomon (b. 1808). *Twelve Years a Slave*. Mineola, New York: Dover Publications, 2000. ISBN: 0486411435.

> **Notes:** Originally published Auburn, New York: Derby and Miller, 1853.

453. O'Neil, Buck (1911-). *I Was Right on Time: My Journey from the Negro Leagues to the Majors*. Written with Steve Wulf and David Conrads. Foreword by Ken Burns. New York, New York: Simon & Schuster, 1996. 254 pages; photographs; index. ISBN: 0684803054 : 068483247x.

> **Notes:** Paperback published as *I Was Right on Time*.

> **Abstract:** Buck O'Neil, a former player with the Kansas City Monarchs in the Negro Leagues, writes about his life, in particular his time in professional baseball. His first years in baseball were spent traveling around in whatever forms of transportation were available, living in boarding houses open to blacks, and getting whatever pay was offered. After several years of near destitution, he returned home. In 1936, he was offered a spot on the Shreveport Acme Giants, and this quickly led to a job with the Kansas City Monarchs. The Monarchs, one of the foremost teams in the Negro Leagues, was owned by James Leslie Wilkinson, a white man, who earned the respect of his players because of his fair treatment of and respect for them. From this point on, O'Neil had a secure living. He writes about many of his teammates, especially the great Satchel Paige. O'Neil recounts stories about Paige and includes Paige's legendary "Six Rules on How to Stay Young." During World War II, O'Neil was drafted into the Navy. While serving in the Philippines, he and his shipmates got the word that Jackie Robinson had been signed as the first black player in the major leagues, an event that caused more rejoicing than D Day. After retiring as a player, O'Neil was hired by the Chicago Cubs as the first black coach in the Major Leagues. He also scouted for the Cubs and the Kansas City Royals and was responsible for signing Ernie Banks and many other modern-day baseball legends. O'Neil

came to public attention when he was featured prominently in
Baseball, a documentary of the history of the sport by Ken Burns.
The publicity led to many honors, including the naming of a stadium after him: The Buck O'Neil Baseball Complex in Sarasota,
Florida. In 1996, he was given a diploma from Sarasota High
School, a school that had refused to admit him seventy years
before. To this day, O'Neil serves on the Veterans Committee of
the Baseball Hall of Fame, where he and Negro League veteran
Monte Irvin are instrumental in nominating black players of
legendary status who were barred from playing in the major
leagues.

454. Obama, Barack. *Dreams from My Father: A Story of Race and
Inheritance.* New York, New York: Times Books, 1995. 403
pages. ISBN: 081292343x.

Notes: Also published New York: Kodansha International, 1996.
ISBN: 1568361629.

Abstract: In 1959, the father of activist and politician Barak
Obama left Kenya for the University of Hawai'i (UH), the first
African student to enroll there. That same year, Obama's mother
and her family (the Dunhams) moved from previous homes in
Wichita, Kansas and Texas to Hawai'i. White, and with little exposure to African Americans, the Dunhams were nonetheless tired of
Texas-style Jim Crow culture and were looking for a different
experience in Hawai'i. Both of Obama's parents were students at
UH when they met. When they decided to marry, there was little
resistance from his mother's parents, but strong objections from
his father's family. Despite this, his parents married and gave
birth to a little boy, Barack Obama. Obama's father eventually
went back to Africa, leaving his wife and son in Hawai'i. Obama's
mother married again to an Indonesian man, and she and Obama
lived with him in Indonesia for a number of years, until the marriage ended and they returned to Hawai'i. After graduation from
Columbia University, Obama found work in Chicago organizing
conferences on drugs, housing, and unemployment. In the book,
he describes the frustration he had with the people he was trying
to assist as well as those he wanted to enlist to provide help. He
realized that most of the problem stemmed from trying to understand the positions and needs of people from different backgrounds. With perseverance, however, he developed close relationships with the local leadership, and after a long year, their
efforts began to show some results. In the midst of this, Obama
met his half-brother and half-sister from his father's second mar-

riage, who were in the United States. Although his father had died several years before, Obama finally made a trip to Nairobi to meet his extended family there. Through his visit, spending time with his cousins, brothers, sisters, uncles and aunts in Kenya, Obama came to an understanding of who he is and what kind of person his father was.

455. Offley, G. W. (b. 1808). *A Narrative of the Life and Labors of the Rev. G. W. Offley: A Colored Man, Local Preacher and Missionary, Who Lived Twenty-Seven Years at the South and Twenty-Three at the North: Who Never Went to School a Day in His Life, and Only Commenced to Learn His Letters When Nineteen Years and Eight Months Old: The Emancipation of His Mother and Her Three Children: How He Learned to Read While Living in a Slave State, and Supported Himself from the Time He Was Nine Years Old Until He Was Twenty-One.* Chapel Hill, North Carolina: Academic Affairs Library, University of North Carolina at Chapel Hill, 2000.

> http://docsouth.unc.edu/neh/offley/offley.sgml
> http://docsouth.unc.edu/neh/offley/offley.html

> **Notes:** Documenting the American South (Project).

456. Okihiro, Gary Y. (1945-). *Whispered Silences: Japanese Americans and World War II.* Photographs by Joan Myers. Seattle, Washington: University of Washington Press, 1996. 249 pages; photographs. ISBN: 0295974974 : 0295974982.

> **Abstract:** A native of Hawai'i and a third-generation Japanese American (Sansei), Gary Okihiro was born two months after the surrender of Japan to the Allies in World War II. "My Japanese American past, thus, was buried by the shapers of the national identity and my parents and me insofar as we had bought into the notion . . . to 'speak, dress, and think American'" (p. 95). Returning from two years in Botswana with the Peace Corps, Okihiro made his first visit to Japan in 1970. When he arrived in Osaka, he was overwhelmed with the feeling of being in his country with his people. By the end of the day, however, he realized that "Japanese American is not Japanese" (p. 97). In 1972, he visited the Manzanar Relocation Center and decided to write this book. In it he weaves elements of his own life story with the stories he has collected from first and second-generation Japanese Americans of their immigration to the United States and their mass incarceration during World War II. Okihiro also outlines the history of Japanese immigrants to Hawai'i and the mainland United States.

457. Okwu, Julian C. R. *As I Am: Young African American Women in a Critical Age.* San Francisco, California: Chronicle Books, 1999. 149 pages; photographs. ISBN: 0811820734.

> **Notes:** *See* abstract for following entry (458).

458. —. *Facing Forward: Young African American Men in a Critical Age.* San Francisco, California: Chronicle Books, 1997. 149 pages; photographs. ISBN: 0811816311 : 0811812154.

> **Abstract:** Photographer, film producer, and writer Okwu was born to Nigerian parents in London, England, in 1966. His family moved to Connecticut while he was still a young child. Okwu attended Dartmouth College and graduated with degrees in comparative literature and psychology. He was moved to write these two books because of "one racist and unforgettable experience on the corner of a San Francisco street" (p. 4). Okwu felt that presenting the stories of African-American men might help counteract the low opinion the general public has of them as well as the negative images so often portrayed in the media. *Facing Forward* presents the stories of forty men between the ages of eighteen and thirty-two from a variety of backgrounds and careers, including a former gang member, dancer, medical student, political activist, and entrepreneur. The interviews focus on their careers, education, sexual orientation, and aspirations. *As I Am* presents the stories of thirty-six women under the age of thirty-five. Okwu's aim was to "create a forum for the erudition, complexity, diversity, pain, and passion of young African women" (p. 3). His subjects are of varied ethnic and socio-economic backgrounds and have careers in writing, religion, music, and construction. Some are cancer survivors, and all have been subjected to racial and gender discrimination. Okwu conducted the interviews and photographed each subject. For his work on these two books, Okwu won awards from the New York Public Library and the Boston University School of Social Work. He was also named the San Francisco Public Library's Literary Laureate for the year 2000.

459. Olajuwon, Hakeem. *Living the Dream: My Life and Basketball.* Written with Peter Knobler. Boston, Massachusetts: Little, Brown and Company, 1996. 300 pages; photographs. ISBN: 0316094277.

> **Abstract:** Hakeem Olajuwon was born and raised in Lagos, Nigeria. His family is Yoruba, one of three prominent population groups in Nigeria. Olajuwon's parents were cement mixers and

fairly successful. He attended boarding school beginning at age twelve and then later, the Muslim Teachers College. While at the teachers college, Olajuwon played handball. When the handball team was excluded from participation in a sports tournament, Olajuwon got a quick introduction to basketball and joined the basketball team for the tournament. From the high school team, he was recommended to the Lagos State teams for both basketball and handball. Olajuwon's fate was set when he was recognized first by the National Basketball Team coach, an American, and then by a U.S. basketball ambassador, Christopher Pond, who had coached the Central African team in a game against Lagos State. Pond arranged interviews for Olajuwon at several U.S. universities. Olajuwon's first stop was the University of Houston, and that was where he decided to stay. From there he was drafted by the Houston Rockets. While with the team, the Rockets won four NBA championships. Olajuwon also reconfirmed his Islamic faith and made two pilgrimages to Mecca.

460. Olds, Mark C. *Not without Scars—: The Inspiring Life Journey of Mark C. Olds*. As told to Christopher Broussard. University Heights, Ohio: MCO Media Group, 2000. 220 pages; photographs. ISBN: 0970133707.

Abstract: Christian activist Mark Olds was born in Farmville, North Carolina, into a family of sharecroppers. Olds was an avid student, but when, at age sixteen, he saw that his college prospects were bleak, he quit school and left for New York, where several brothers and cousins were living, and from there moved to New Haven. He tried to work and go to college, but ended up hustling and gambling. This escalated into drug dealing and armed robbery, and he was eventually arrested and imprisoned. He escaped from prison in 1978, but was once again arrested in 1979. This time Olds was given a thirty-year sentence. Early on in his incarceration, Olds began studying the Bible and underwent a religious conversion that turned his life around. He describes his work in the prison, his efforts to preach to other prisoners, and his determination to maintain contact with the world outside. Olds developed a fortuitous relationship with Dr. Harold Carter of New Shiloh Baptist Church, who helped him study for ordination and then aided him in establishing a prison church. Olds eventually became the unofficial Protestant chaplain at the prison. He describes the difficulties and dangers of prison life, the low probability of prisoners giving up criminal lifestyles when released, the division between Muslims and Christians in prison, and the intense racism among inmates and guards. Olds was released in

1989, and he set about pursuing his desire to preach and to fulfill all the conditions of his parole. Olds was sympathetic when people had a difficult time forgiving and forgetting his past, but he found that he also had sufficient support to make personal progress and threw himself into preaching and community activism. This eventually led him to Cleveland, Ohio, where he founded the Redirection of Young Minds program, which he began first for young black men and later expanded to include black women. He earned a master's degree from Case Western Reserve University, and entered the Ph.D. program. Olds preaches an Afrocentric theology, but, to his surprise, has found that he can reach white congregations as well.

461. Ortiz Cofer, Judith (1952-). *Woman in Front of the Sun: On Becoming a Writer.* Athens, Georgia: University of Georgia Press, 2000. 127 pages. ISBN: 082032261x : 0820322229.

Abstract: This book by writer Judith Ortiz Cofer is a collection of previously published essays. Ortiz Cofer grew up in Paterson, New Jersey. Her parents were Puerto Rican and her father worked for the U.S. Navy. While neither parent satisfactorily assimilated to life in the United States, they stayed for the sake of the opportunities that their children would have, both in terms of education and career. The first essay in the book is about a modern-minded Catholic nun, a teacher at her school, who introduced her to literature by recommending classics that contained a great deal of sex. Another describes how Ortiz Cofer got needed attention from a favorite uncle who had many problems, including alcohol abuse. In other essays, Ortiz Cofer identifies the major influences on her writing. One is a little-known legend of how Christopher Columbus discovered a women's village inhabited by what Ortiz Cofer calls "macho women," women who made men deal with them on their own terms. Ortiz Cofer explains how this legend has motivated her as a creative artist. She feels that Latinas face forces that seek to destroy their creativity. The "macho" writer must take control of her life and bear certain scars so that the art inside her is not destroyed. She discusses the writers who have inspired her, specifically Flannery O'Connor and Alice Walker, who taught her that human nature and, thus, writing are more complex than race. Finally, Ortiz Cofer considers the notion that she remains a Latina writer even while living and teaching in the state of Georgia, separated from Latin culture.

462. Oshley, Navajo Ak'é Nídzin. *The Journey of Navajo Oshley: An Autobiography and Life History.* Edited by Robert S. McPherson. Foreword by Barre Toelken. Logan, Utah: Utah State University Press, 2000. 226 pages; photographs; index. ISBN: 0874212901 : 087421291x.

Abstract: Oshley's autobiography is the result of a taped interview. Although some changes were made to make logical connections from one segment to the other, the printed page gives a fair representation of the oral narrative. To accompany Oshley's life story, editor Robert S. McPherson includes essays which provide a social and historical context. He describes the final decades of Oshley's life in Blanding, Utah, the changes taking place within the Navajo culture as the Navajo people interact more frequently with the white communities, ceremonies and practices, and living conditions, and the state of white-Navajo relations. Oshley was probably born toward the end of the nineteenth century and died in 1988. He lived most of his life herding sheep and chopping wood to make a living. He worked for white sheep farmers and had his own family herd as well. Oshley was married three times. His first wife and three children all died of tuberculosis. He describes the cultivation of corn, sheep-herding practices, the dangers of gambling, and relationships between and among families and clans. He discusses the increasing presence of white ranchers and the accompanying land grabs and theft of Navajo sheep and horses. Oshley was a hand trembler, a person who receives visions and messages and heals the sick. He describes his own experiences with a variety of ceremonies, including the Evil Way, Blessing Way, Enemy Way, and Wind Way ceremonies. He notes that as the younger generations attend schools, they distance themselves from these practices. He believes this is why there is so much less rain and snow. Oshley describes the livestock reduction program of the 1930s and his increasing dependence on white farmers and townspeople for goods and employment. He moved with his third wife and family into the town of Blanding in the 1950s and remained in the vicinity with his growing family until his death.

463. Parker, Allen (b. ca. 1835). *Recollections of Slavery Times.* Chapel Hill, North Carolina: Academic Affairs Library, University of North Carolina at Chapel Hill, 2000.

> http://docsouth.unc.edu/neh/parker/parker.sgml
> http://docsouth.unc.edu/neh/parker/parker.html

> **Notes:** Documenting the American South (Project).

464. Parker, Gwendolyn M. *Trespassing: My Sojourn in the Halls of Privilege.* Boston, Massachusetts: Houghton Mifflin, 1997. 209 pages. ISBN: 0395822971.

> **Notes:** Also published Boston: Hi Marketing, 1999. ISBN: 0395926203.

> **Abstract:** Lawyer, former businesswoman, and writer Gwendolyn Parker writes about her childhood, education, and various careers. She was born and spent her early childhood in Durham, North Carolina, "a small segregated Southern town, extolled by virtue of its thriving black community as the black Wall Street and the home of the black middle class" (p. 8). Her grandfather was the town's first citizen, Aaron Mcduffie Moore, cofounder of the North Carolina Mutual Life Insurance Company, and she was a pampered child. When the family moved to Mount Vernon, New York, she had her first taste of racial discrimination in the school system and was sent to a private boarding school for high school. In 1968, she was accepted at Radcliffe College, where she found black companionship as well as more conflict, both inter- and intraracial. After law school, Parker was hired by "an old white-shoe firm," where she was one of only a few blacks and the only black woman. During her time at this firm, she found being a woman among men the more exhausting of her battles. After a few years at a more progressive company, American Express, where she was named Black Achiever in Industry in a program sponsored by the Harlem YMCA, she decided to give up the corporate life and become a writer. Six years later, she published her first novel, *These Same Long Bones* (Houghton Mifflin, 1994), and began her book tour back home in Durham.

465. Parker, Henry (b. 1835). *Autobiography of Henry Parker.* Chapel Hill, North Carolina: Academic Affairs Library, University of North Carolina at Chapel Hill, 2000.

> http://docsouth.unc.edu/neh/parkerh/parkerh.sgml
> http://docsouth.unc.edu/neh/parkerh/parkerh.html

> **Notes:** Documenting the American South (Project).

466. Parker, Idella. *Idella: Marjorie Rawlings' "Perfect Maid."* Written with Mary Keating. Gainesville, Florida: University Press of Florida, 1992. 135 pages; photographs; maps. ISBN: 0813011434 : 0813011442.

467. —. *Idella Parker: From Reddick to Cross Creek.* Written with Bud Crussell and Liz Crussell. Tallahassee, Florida: University Press of Florida, 1999. 240 pages; photographs; maps; illustrations. ISBN: 0813017068.

Abstract: Parker was born in Reddick, Florida in 1914. Although her parents had little formal education, they insisted that the children go to school. Parker and her siblings attended every day, except during the winter months when the entire family worked in Palmetto. Because of the limited public school opportunities for black children, the Parker children had to attend private high schools. Parker attended Bethune-Cook in Daytona Beach, Florida, and was taught by Mrs. Bethune. Parker began teaching in 1929 while she was still a student. The work load and social code for teachers was strict, and she decided to quit teaching to work full time as a housekeeper. It was this decision that led Parker to her employment with Marjorie Kinnan Rawlings, author of *The Yearling.* Off and on from 1940 to 1950, Parker cooked and cleaned and kept her employer company. She describes her relationship with Mrs. Rawlings and her unpredictable behavior and drinking problems. Parker had very little freedom to come and go or to socialize with anyone not connected with Mrs. Rawlings and her work. She viewed the conditions of her employment as not dissimilar to those of slavery except that she received a salary. Parker writes more extensively about this period of her life in *Idella: Marjorie Rawlings' "Perfect Maid"* (1992). After her second marriage, Parker worked as a beautician. Following her husband's death she became more active in politics, working for the NAACP and the voter registration drive. Parker was proud to see the "Whites Only" signs start coming down. In her later years, Parker returned to teaching. She taught home economics skills to unemployed mothers and to mentally-handicapped teenagers. She took part in the Marjorie Kinnan Rawlings (MKR) Society meetings, and began speaking publicly in schools and at gatherings. Parker is concerned about the future of children today and, in her speaking and writing, seeks to present them with positive role models and advice for moving forward.

468. Parker, John P. *His Promised Land: The Autobiography of John P. Parker, Former Slave and Conductor on the Underground Railroad.* Edited by Stuart Seely Sprague. New York, New York: W. W. Norton & Company, 1996. 165 pages. ISBN: 0393039412 : 0393317188.

Abstract: The interviews for John P. Parker's autobiography were originally made in the 1880s. They were then placed in the archives of Duke University. This is the first time they have appeared in a published format. Editor Sprague provides in-depth historical background, as well as a textual interpretation. He has prepared the present narrative to ensure Parker's own words are accurately represented. Parker, born in 1827, was sold away from his mother at the age of eight. He walked from Norfolk to Richmond, Virginia chained to an old man. The old man was later beaten to death in front of him. He writes that this and similar experiences filled him with hatred. Later that year, Parker was chained together with four hundred slaves, men and women, old people and children, and marched to Mobile, Alabama. "Some of the slaves were sullen, others gay and happy, others were mere animals. As for me, I was designing, hateful, and determined. Ragged and barefooted, I was resentful of the freedom of nature" (p. 27). In Mobile, Parker was sold to a doctor who had him trained in iron work. During this time, Parker came up with several useful inventions which he was able to patent after he was freed. He made numerous attempts to escape, and was imprisoned several times. When his owner decided to sell him for a field slave, Parker, at age fourteen, convinced a widow to purchase him so that he could buy his freedom from her. Parker describes his owners, the doctor and the widow, as generally kind and considerate toward him, "[b]ut I hated the injustices and restraints against my own initiative more than it is possible for words to express. To me that was the great curse of slavery" (p. 70). He concluded his financial obligations to the widow at age eighteen, and left the South for Indiana and then Ohio where he set up his own iron foundry business. In 1845, Parker was asked to assist several escaping slaves in crossing the Ohio River on their way to Canada. He subsequently decided to pack up his shop and moved to Ripley, Ohio where white families operated safe houses. From there he helped more than 400 slaves find their way to freedom over a period of fifteen years. Since aiding slaves in this way was a federal offense, Parker was a wanted man and had a bounty on his head. Parker describes what some of the escaping slaves had to overcome to make it to the Ohio River.

469. Parker, Star. *Pimps, Whores, and Welfare Brats: The Stunning Conservative Transformation of a Former Welfare Queen*. Written with Lorenzo Benet. Introduction by Rush Limbaugh. New York, New York: Pocket Books, 1997. 205 pages. ISBN: 0671534653.

Abstract: Star Parker was a rebellious teenager who took out her anger and sense of persecution on the white people around her. She bombed the cars of two of her teachers and was involved in many robberies, break-ins, and other violent crimes. After high school, she went to Los Angeles and began living on welfare. She had a number of abortions that were paid for by welfare, and she managed to live in relative comfort by selling her Medi-Cal stickers to others to use for abortions, check-ups, dental work, etc. Parker began to change her way of thinking when she became involved with a church. The next time she got pregnant, she carried the baby to term and decided to raise her herself. She completed her college education, and began making a living by starting a magazine that listed the social calendars of a number of black churches in Los Angeles. To fund the magazine, Parker solicited advertising from small businesses, many of them in the South Central Los Angeles area. During the ten years that the magazine was in operation, Parker married a white man and the two had a daughter together. Just when the magazine had started earning money, the 1992 Los Angeles riots, ignited by the initial verdict in the Rodney King police brutality case, destroyed most of the businesses in the South Central area, thus wiping out the advertising revenue that had kept her magazine going. During and after the violence, Parker called in reports to a Christian call-in show on KKLA. After that, she became known as a black conservative. She was invited to speak at presidential-candidate Pat Buchanan's conference on New Conservatism in 1993 and has participated in other media activities in which she spoke from a black conservative viewpoint. After one program, she was contacted by Rush Limbaugh, a popular conservative radio personality. The two spoke at length, and Limbaugh wrote an article about her in his monthly newsletter and mentioned her in his radio program. At present, Parker is involved in the Coalition on Urban Affairs and speaks at colleges and universities. She was also hired as a correspondent for GOP television during the 1996 Republican National Convention in San Diego, where she gave a speech on the convention floor. The second half of the book is devoted to her ideas and opinions on the breakdown of the black family, the black urban crisis, moral restraint, liberalism, and using capitalism and independent efforts to end dependence on welfare.

470. Patel, Kusum (1919-1999). *A Passage From India: Notes to My Grandchildren*. Plattsburgh, New York: Pennysaver Press, 1998. 168 pages; photographs. ISBN: none.

Abstract: Kusum Patel writes her story at the request of one of her grandsons, and as a means of "utilizing my time fruitfully without being bored in a foreign country" (p. 163). Patel is the mother of four sons, one of whom died in infancy, and grandmother to seven grandchildren, all of whom were born in the United States. She moved to the United States when she was sixty-four. She was born in Madras to a wealthy family. The family moved to Bombay, where Patel was raised and educated. Unlike most young women of that time, she was allowed and even encouraged to get an education. She attended Bombay University College and Elphinstone College. Her father helped to establish schools in the Bombay area and sponsored many students who could not afford to attend college. Her husband was one of those students, a poor young man in poor health, and Patel married him despite her parents' objections. After she received an M. Ed. from the University of Baroda in 1951 and worked as a lecturer there, Patel sent out applications to universities in the United States. She received a Fulbright Travel Grant and a Ford Foundation Fellowship to pursue graduate studies at Yale University, where she earned an M.S. in Education in 1955. Patel returned to India to be with her husband and three children and served in many positions, including the principal of the Government Female Teachers' Training College, Assistant Educational Inspector, and Deputy Director of Education for the State of Gujarat. She retired in 1977. In the meantime, all three of her sons settled in the United States. Patel's husband died in 1973. She remained in India until 1983, when she moved to Plattsburgh, New York, to live with her oldest son until her death in 1999. She respected the changes she observed in the lifestyles of her sons and their wives and the different ways that her grandchildren were raised, recognizing that she herself had broken away from traditional expectations. In her book, Patel encourages her grandchildren to live according to the Hindu culture by respecting their mothers, ancestors, and teachers: "You, my children and grandchildren, should remember this and believe and behave accordingly—never do any harm to anyone. Be kind and helpful. Try to go up the ladder but be satisfied with what you have. . . . Human life is very precious" (p. 163).

471. Patience, Alice Patterson. *Bittersweet Memories of Home.* Wilkes-Barre, Pennsylvania: Wilkes University Press, 1999. 71 pages; photographs. ISBN: 0966113020.

Abstract: Alice Patterson Patience, aged eighty-two at the writing of her autobiography, lives in the house that has been in her mother's family since at least 1850. Through the years, the house has been improved and added to. Patience and her husband made their contribution to the house by adding indoor bathrooms, hot and cold running water, and other amenities. As a child, she and her family lived on one side of the house and her maternal aunt and family lived on the other. Patience describes the times of her childhood, particularly conditions for African Americans in Pennsylvania. Although circumstances were not as desperate as in southern states, she and her family witnessed cross burnings, experienced ridicule, and had limited opportunities for employment. Patience was part of a large, closely knit family that came together for regular meals, activities, and all special occasions. She and her cousin Blanche were two of just a few African Americans attending the public schools. They attended their senior prom with cousins as their escorts, and were the first of the family to attend college. Patience attended Bennett College, an all-African-American women's college in Greensboro, North Carolina: "I remember the first time I walked into the auditorium and saw people who looked like me—all looked like me. And for the first time a great weight fell off my shoulders. I no longer had to struggle; I could just be myself" (p. 29). In 1937, she and her classmates initiated a boycott when movie theater managers decided to cut portions out of films that showed African Americans in "uncharacteristic" roles. The boycott lasted for months and was ultimately successful in halting the practice. During World War II, Patience joined the WACs and served in the medical corps. She married Edgar Patience, a sculptor who became world-famous for his work with anthracite coal. Patience earned a master's degree from the University of Scranton, and worked for forty years with Blue Cross. She credits the top management of Blue Cross for hiring her, having her work in the front office with customers, and promoting her to a position in which she supervised white managing supervisors, all during a time when most corporations would not hire blacks to do anything but menial labor.

472. Payne, Lucille Mable Walthall. *The Seventeenth Child.* Written with Dorothy Marie Rice. North Haven, Connecticut: Linnet Books, 1998. 101 pages; photographs. ISBN: 020802414x : 0208024158.

Abstract: Payne was born the seventeenth child in her family on a small farm in Glenland, Virginia, in 1929. In her book she describes growing up during the Great Depression. She notes that black farmers were among the poorest class of people in the United States during that time and that her family was no exception. Payne and her family lived in a segregated society. They didn't know why, but they accepted it. Nonetheless, her parents were not afraid of white people; the family was continuously moving because her father, born in 1865, did not hesitate to speak his mind. At one point the family packed up and moved to be near siblings in Montclair, New Jersey, but her parents found it impossible to find work there, and they returned to Virginia. Both of her parents insisted that the children attend school, and chores were left until they returned home in the evening. Still, Payne was only able to receive a seventh grade education. She describes her family, the houses in which they lived, their various forms of entertainment and occupation, food, and clothing. She also discusses methods of planting, maintaining, harvesting, and preserving tobacco, their primary crop. At fourteen, Payne moved to New Jersey on her own, but was called back home by her mother, who wanted her to finish her schooling. After she married, Payne moved with her husband to Danbury, Connecticut, where they raised and educated their children. In 1971, she returned to Virginia to live.

473. Payton, Walter. *Never Die Easy: The Autobiography of Walter Payton*. Written with Don Yaeger. New York, New York: Villard Books, 2000. 268 pages; photographs. ISBN: 0679463313.

> **Notes:** Large print edition published Thorndike, Maine: Thorndike Press, 2001. ISBN: 0786231262 (456 pages); Paperback edition published New York: Random House Trade Paperbacks, 2000. ISBN: 0375758216.

> **Abstract:** This work was completed posthumously and is a combination of the reflections of those close to football player Walter Payton as well as of Payton himself. Born in 1954, Payton was raised in the small Mississippi town of Columbia. During his childhood, he spent as much time as possible playing sports. Because black athletes were not recruited by the schools in the Southeastern Conference (SEC) during the early 1960s, Payton chose to attend college at Jackson State, a small school in the Southwestern Athletic Conference (SWAC). Payton writes that SEC athletes received a lot of attention and were treated as celebrities. In SWAC, students used football as a way to attend college where they trained to be preachers and teachers. The athletes at Jackson State worked hard and were treated equally no matter how well they performed. There was no time to bask in one's glory, and drawing attention to oneself was strongly discouraged. Payton believed that it was the attitude of coach Bob Hill to "keep it real" that kept players focused on their work with the team.

Despite being overlooked for the Heisman Trophy, Payton was the number-one pick for the Chicago Bears, and after he began to adjust to cold weather and big-city life, Chicago became his home. Payton looks back over his career and the details of individual games. He remembers his close friends from the team, especially Roland Harper and Matt Suhey. Important milestones for Payton were breaking Jim Brown's rushing record in 1984 and winning the Super Bowl in 1985. Payton retired in 1987 at the age of thirty-three after thirteen years with the Bears. After several post-retirement options fell through, Payton found his niche with racing cars, first as a driver and then as an owner. His Walter Payton Foundation developed and runs the Wishes to Santa program, which provides gifts to poor children at Christmas time, and has also taken responsibility for various inner-city school programs. Payton was inducted into the Pro Football Hall of Fame shortly before he was diagnosed with primary sclerosis cholangitis and cancer of the liver. He died from the disease in November 1999.

474. Peltier, Leonard. United States Prisoner #89637-132. *Prison Writings: My Life Is My Sun Dance.* Edited by Harvey Arden. Introduction by Arvol Looking Horse. Preface by Ramsey Clark. New York, New York: St. Martin's Press, 1999. 243 pages; photographs. ISBN: 0312203543.

Notes: Published in paperback New York: St. Martin's Press, 2000. ISBN: 0312263805.

Abstract: The general tragedy of the U.S. government's treatment of Native Americans over the history of this country and the personal tragedy of the wrongful imprisonment of Leonard Peltier are the subject of the essays and reflections in this work. Peltier became involved with the activities of AIM (the American Indian Movement) following the occupation by Indians of Alcatraz Island in the San Francisco Bay in 1969. He participated in the successful occupation of Fort Lawton near Seattle in 1970, which is now an Indian cultural center; the occupation of the Bureau of Indian Affairs Building in Washington, D.C.; and many other Indian rights activities. During what is called the "reign of terror" on the Pine Ridge Reservation in South Dakota, members of AIM were called in to protect tribal elders who seemed to be targeted by a combination of local "nontraditional" residents organized into a group called GOON, and FBI and BIA personnel. During a firefight possibly started by one of these groups, two FBI agents were killed, and Peltier and three other AIM members were accused of this murder. Two of the defendants were found innocent and one had his case dismissed. Only Peltier was found guilty and sentenced to two consecutive life sentences. Peltier describes the fabrication of evidence and the false witnesses who were used to convict him, much of which has been admitted to by government personnel involved in prosecuting the case. He describes his treatment in prison and his concern for the well being of Native Americans and for justice and opportunity for all people. While in prison, Peltier has remained active as an advocate for Native Americans. He writes,

> Prison hasn't prevented me from helping people. I organize clothing, food, and toy drives year round. I support women's shelters and Head Start programs. I have established a scholarship for Native law students at New York University and also helped to fund a newspaper by and for Indian children. I'm a foster parent to two young boys in Guatemala and El Salvador. I've been working on ways to improve the health care system on the Rosebud Reservation, and recently have become involved in economic reform for Pine Ridge. (p. 37)

Peltier ultimately decided that his only crime is being an Indian. At the time this book was published, he had been in prison nearly twenty-five years, and despite the fact that the government prosecutor and one of the trial judges involved in the case have stated that there is no true evidence to support Peltier's conviction, he remains there, with no presidential pardon forthcoming.

475. Pendergrass, Teddy. *Truly Blessed.* Written with Patricia Romanowski. New York, New York: G. P. Putnam's Sons, 1998. 319 pages; photographs; discography. ISBN: 039914420x.

Notes: Also published New York: Berkeley Boulevard, 1999. ISBN: 0425171108.

Abstract: Singer Teddy Pendergrass was born after his father left his mother, and was raised by her in Philadelphia. He spent his early years living over a church, surrounded by religion and enveloped in the dedicated love and attention of his mother. He sang his first solo in church at the age of three. Pendergrass's musical career began when he was hired as a drummer for Little Royal, and then as a singer for Harold Melvin and the Blue Notes. He quickly became the most prominent member of the group, which subsequently changed its name to Harold Melvin and the Blue Notes Featuring Theodore Pendergrass. The group was phenomenally successful, but Harold Melvin appeared to be the only member making any profits. After falling out with Melvin, Pendergrass became a solo act. He was able to work large crowds of women into a frenzy with his voice and sexiness. In 1982, at the age of thirty-two, Pendergrass was in a car accident that left him permanently paralyzed from the chest down. He describes the hopelessness of the first years after the accident, the dedication of his mother and Karen Still, a woman whom he later married. He eventually was able to sing well enough to continue recording successful albums and he has received numerous awards for his contribution to the field of rhythm and blues. The book ends with a description of a tour he made in 1996, fourteen years after his accident. Pendergrass voices his appreciation to the wonderful reception he received from his fans.

476. Perez Firmat, Gustavo (1949-). *Next Year in Cuba: A Cubano's Coming-of-Age in America.* New York, New York: Anchor Books, 1995. 275 pages. ISBN: 038547296x.

Notes: New York: Anchor Books, 1996. ISBN: 0385472978; Houston: Scrivenery Press, 2000. ISBN: 1893818144 (296 pages, revised edition).

Abstract: Poet, writer, and professor Gustavo Perez Firmat was born in Cuba in 1949. He came to the United States with his family at the age of eleven. Perez Firmat and his family considered themselves to be in exile as opposed to having emigrated. Looking back on the family's thirty-five years in Miami, Perez Firmat sees that his parents expected to be able to go back to their lives in Cuba. His father, who had been a successful merchant in Havana, held cabinet posts in several Cuban governments-in-exile. During his childhood, Perez Firmat's parents neglected their children and failed to direct them in their education and professional careers because they considered themselves to be in a temporary state. Perez Firmat talks about the hatred of the exiles for Castro. He finds it impossible to ever forgive the dictator for what he did to Cuba, and as time passes, he hates him even more for what the exiles have lost in terms of culture, home, and family life. Perez Firmat describes some of the culture the Cubans brought to the United States and how the culture has changed as the original immigrants age and their children and grandchildren become more Americanized. He describes himself as being a member of the "one-and-a-half generation," Cubans who came to the United States as children or adolescents. At this point in his life, Perez Firmat doesn't think he would be able to go back to Cuba and live, but he feels the day is drawing near when this decision will have to be made.

477. Perez, Luis (1904-). *El Coyote, The Rebel.* Introduction by Lauro Flores. Houston, Texas: Arte Público Press, 2000. 164 pages. ISBN: 1558852964.

> **Notes:** Originally published by Henry Holt and Company, 1947.

478. Perry, Cynthia Shepard. *All Things Being Equal: One Woman's Journey.* Houston, Texas: Stonecrest International Publishers, 1998. 255 pages; photographs; facsimiles; maps. ISBN: 0967557100.

> **Abstract:** Perry tells the story of setting and accomplishing her long-term goal of becoming an ambassador to an African country. In 1956, at the age of twenty-six and mother to three children, Perry was ready to accomplish something beyond child rearing and housekeeping. After a discussion with her high school principal and mentor, Perry worked out a plan to earn a B.A. in political science and eventually her Ph.D. and then enter government service. Her mentor advised her to think in terms of twenty-five to thirty years for reaching her goal. By 1969, Perry was at the University of Massachusetts as a doctoral fellow in the Center for International Studies, the only woman and only African American in the program. It was suggested to Perry that she might be more comfortable in the Center for Urban Studies with the "others." Perry, however, was intent on her career path and refused to be diverted. She earned a doctorate in international education and went on to work with the Peace Corps and with A.I.D. (Agency for International Development). She developed graduate programs for Peace Corps volunteers, assisted A.I.D. by developing policies and programs for Africa, and worked to secure public and private funding for African human-resource development. Perry also lived in Africa while working for the United Nations to develop training and educational programs for African professionals. In 1986 (thirty years after first setting out her plan), Perry, who was Chief of Human Resources Development for A.I.D., received a phone call inquiring about her interest in serving as ambassador to Sierra Leone for the Reagan Administration. She was in South Africa on business when President Reagan called and asked her to take the position. It was not long before Perry was packing up her family and preparing for a move to Sierra Leone. She writes in detail about her work there, the trials and successes and the personal and familial demands and hardships. Perry writes about the

politics of rice and diamonds, the continual threat of terrorism, and the difficulties of being female in a male-dominated career and culture. She approached her work with single mindedness and a desire to do what was best for her country and for the people of Sierra Leone. During her tenure as ambassador, ongoing research into slave ancestry and roots uncovered the clear connection between the Gullah and Geechee people of the Sea Islands off the coast of South Carolina and Georgia and the people of Sierra Leone. Perry worked with other officials to arrange a visit by President Momah to the South Carolina Sea Islands, and a reciprocal visit by a group of Gullahs was planned for 1990-1991. At the end of her term in Sierra Leone, Perry was appointed by the Bush administration to be ambassador to the small central African country of Burundi.

479. Peters, James Sedalia (1917-). *Family Generations: Stories of My Father, My Son and My Daughters*. Storrs, Connecticut: Peters & Associates Publishers, 1999. 48 pages; photographs. ISBN: none.

480. Petersen, Lt. General Frank E. *Into the Tiger's Jaw: America's First Black Marine Aviator*. Written with J. Alfred Phelps. Novato, California: Presidio Press, 1998. 334 pages; photographs. ISBN: 0891416757.

> **Abstract:** Frank E. Petersen was born and raised in Topeka, Kansas, but he has no fond memories of his boyhood there. He writes that his experiences in high school reflected the climate of Topeka in general. He went to school under conditions of "quasi-integration, which highlighted, even celebrated, the segregated way of living" (p. 18). Petersen was anxious to leave home and see the ocean, which meant to him joining the Navy. Receiving the reluctant good wishes of his parents, he set out to accomplish this goal. Racism began with the Navy recruiter, who asked Petersen to retake the test, assuming from his high score that he must have cheated. The recruiter then offered Petersen a "good job" as a steward, which Peterson turned down. Petersen had a very successful military career. He was the only black cadet in his cadet training course in Pensacola. In 1952, he was the first African American to be commissioned as a Marine Corps aviator, the second to be promoted to second lieutenant, and the first black fighter squadron commander. He was often the only African-American officer on a base or with a troop. He was arrested for impersonating an officer, continuously asked to show his ID, and

constantly challenged by superiors and subordinates alike. As he neared promotion to full colonel, charges of falsifying his flight records were leveled against him. No merit was found in the charges, and all evidence of the case was expunged from his record. Despite the opposition he faced, Petersen always had someone who believed in his abilities and others who were his comrades and friends. This was enough to keep him from giving up. After tours in Korea and Vietnam, Petersen served in Japan and Okinawa. He was later made the first Special Assistant for Minority Matters to the Commandant of the Marine Corps. He worked at minority officer recruitment and toured bases in Europe to observe and report on conditions. Petersen noted abysmal morale and disaffection among minority troops and a complete lack of awareness of this situation on the part of the highest ranking officers associated with them. His work in this area made him a controversial figure across all branches of the military. Petersen offers a thorough discussion of issues of race, integration, and cultural differences as manifested in the Marine Corps and in the armed services in general. He achieved the rank of lieutenant general before retiring in 1988. Petersen became vice president for aviation at the Dupont Corporation and, after retiring at age sixty-five, began his own business addressing aviation safety.

481. Pham, Andrew X (1967-). *Catfish and Mandala: A Two-Wheeled Voyage through the Landscape and Memory of Vietnam.* New York, New York: Farrar, Straus, and Giroux, 1999. 344 pages. ISBN: 0374119783 : 0374119740.

   Notes: Also published New York: Picador USA, 2000. ISBN: 0312267177.

   Abstract: Andrew Pham's book is a travelogue interwoven with memories from various points in his life as a child of war, a refugee, and an immigrant. He begins and ends his story with the suicide of his thirty-two-year-old sister, the oldest child in the family. After the death of his sister, Pham takes off on a bicycle ride through the deserts of Mexico. He returns to his family home in San Jose, California, long enough to plan his next escape: a bicycle ride up the Pacific Coast and then on to Vietnam with a stopover in Japan. Pham is returning to Vietnam twenty years after escaping in 1977. Once there, Pham reunites with family, visits his old neighborhood and home, travels by bicycle to his native village, and then goes to Hanoi and back again to Saigon. On the road to Hanoi, Pham is reviled and scorned repeatedly for being a Viet-kieu or foreign Vietnamese, a Korean, or a Japanese. He recalls being similarly attacked when bicycling up the California coast. Pham suffers from fevers and dysentery and is repulsed by the deterioration of the countryside and the poverty and squalor of his accommodations. He is also embraced by his family and treated kindly by strangers when he no longer expects any such consideration. As he records his travel experiences, Pham recounts memories of his childhood before the fall of Saigon. He remembers the family's harrowing escape by fishing boat and the last-minute rescue by an Indonesian freighter. He examines the legacy of violence his family has brought with them to America and the wrenching transition to life in the United States. Pham also looks back on the life of his oldest sister, Chi, who, once in America, lived her life as a boy, ran away from home, and later underwent a sex change. Chi returned home as Minh after an absence of over fourteen years and killed himself within the year. Pham contemplates the meaning and necessity of forgiveness, whether for parents who have made mistakes, for veterans of the Vietnam Conflict, for himself as a Vietnamese who left the country, or for the Vietnamese and Americans who fail to accept him as a countryman. As Pham nears the end of his journey, he considers staying on in Vietnam, but finds that he is more than ready to return to the United States, although unsure of whether he is an American.

482. Pham, David Lan. *Two Hamlets in Nam Bo: Memoirs of Life in Vietnam through Japanese Occupation, the French and American Wars, and Communist Rule, 1940-1986.* Jefferson, North Carolina: McFarland & Company, 2000. 299 pages. ISBN: 0786406461.

Abstract: Pham was born in 1940 during the Japanese occupation of Vietnam. He was born in Tuy An, his father's village, but spent his earliest childhood years with his mother's family in Binh Chuan. Pham writes that life was peaceful during the years of the Second World War, but following the war and the escalation of fighting between the Viet Minh and the French, the town of Tuy An, where he was sent for schooling, was completely destroyed. Pham's father was suspected by both the French and the Viet Minh, and was eventually arrested by both. His family moved to a town near Saigon. At ten, Pham was disillusioned by the French influence on Vietnam and he left home to join the Viet Minh only to be sent back home because he was too young to fight. He continued his education and became a teacher and a librarian. Pham describes the brief period of Vietnamese independence beginning in 1954, the growing cultural and military influence of the United

States, and the rise of the Viet Cong. He discusses the many political parties, the individuals who aspired to leadership, and the state of affairs between North and South Vietnam. In 1973, following the takeover of Saigon by the Communists, Pham lost his job, his family suffered from malnutrition, and his belongings and property were confiscated. He sought to farm in his father's village but was not recognized as a resident by the local government. Local villagers would sabotage his crops while they grew and raid whatever was available for harvest. Pham began to practice traditional Vietnamese medicine and acupuncture to treat his own health problems. Soon people, friends and enemies alike, came from throughout the surrounding area in hopes of a cure. Along with his other hardships, Pham was watched closely by the local government and police and questioned on a regular basis. He found that despite his dire situation, he could not decide whether or not to leave Vietnam: "Staying meant accepting the status quo. Leaving meant missing and renouncing everything for good" (p. 203). In 1986, Pham finally decided to escape with two brothers and his oldest son. They made it safely to the Philippines, where they stayed in two different refugee camps before being sent to Toledo, Ohio. Pham's story ends as he is learning to adjust to life in the United States. He faces his first cold winter in Ohio suffering with intense loneliness and homesickness for his native country.

483. Pierce, Chester. *See* Griffith, Ezra E. H. (1942-).

484. Poitier, Sidney. *The Measure of a Man: A Spiritual Autobiography.* San Francisco, California: HarperSanFrancisco, 2000. 255 pages; photographs. ISBN: 0062516078 : 0062516086.

> **Abstract:** This is Sidney Poitier's second autobiography. According to the introduction, the Academy Award winning actor wrote his first one about his life in Hollywood, and decided to write this one about "life itself." He describes his poor but idyllic childhood on Cat Island in the Bahamas, a place where bartering was more frequently used than money and where he was free, even as a very young child, to wander all over the island and enjoy the beaches, woods, and fruit that grew wild. Poitier's parents were poor their entire lives. Despite this, they retained a philosophy that helped to steer them through the loss of their livelihood as tomato farmers on Cat Island and the menial work they were subsequently reduced to in Nassau. Poitier writes, "I didn't think about the color of my skin. Not any more than I would have bothered to wonder why the sand was white or the sky was blue" (p.

29). Growing up not seeing or believing race to be an issue prepared him to make his way in the white world of Hollywood. "[H]aving arrived in America with a foundation that had had time to set, the Jim Crow way of life had trouble overwhelming me" (p. 42). Poitier never became outwardly outraged at racial slights, but he refused to give in to inferior images others may have had of him. He did not accept roles that he felt were beneath his dignity. He writes about the difficulty of his divorce from his first wife, his effort to maintain his relationship with his children, and his ideas on life following the peak of his career in movies and theater.

485. Portwood, Shirley Motley. *Tell Us a Story: An African American Family in the Heartland.* Carbondale, Illinois: Southern Illinois University Press, 2000.   242 pages; photographs.   ISBN: 0809323133 : 0809323141.

Abstract: Shirley Motley Portwood traveled through Arkansas, Mississippi, and Tennessee looking through library, church, and county records to trace her family history back seven generations. Portwood opens her book with the story of how she and her siblings proudly watched as their father chased a white man, who was attempting to cheat him, off their farm. This was a proud moment for the children and is part of the repertoire of stories that her family has shared over the years. Portwood tells this and many other stories of her childhood, of her parents' lives growing up in rural southern Illinois, and of the children and grandchildren. Portwood and all six of her siblings attended college, instructed by their mother to wait to get married until after they had graduated and begun careers. Portwood's father earned both a bachelor's and master's degree after he was a grandfather, and eventually moved from farming to being a vocational rehabilitation counselor for the state of Illinois. Portwood tells a favorite story about how her grandfather and two of his friends walked more than 300 miles to Jefferson, Missouri, to present themselves to the president of Lincoln University, at that time a college for African-American students, who had visited their school and encouraged the students to come to Lincoln. Portwood's grandfather and his friends took the president at his word and, upon arrival, went straight to the president's office to tell him that they were ready to attend. They asked him for his help in enrolling, finding jobs and housing, all of which he gave. Portwood concludes her book by describing her travels through the South to establish her family's history. She reflects on her family's slave ancestry and the emotional impact of finding concrete evidence that her great great grandparents had the legal status of inheritable household property. Portwood also makes peace with the apparent truth that her great great grandparents were not heroic rebels in the style of Harriet Tubman or Nat Turner and comes to appreciate them for having managed, under nearly impossible circumstances, to hold together a family of six children who brought forth the proud Motley family of Portwood's childhood.

486. Potts, Willie Frank, Jr. *Journey to God's House.* Starkville, Mississippi: American Voices, 1999. 198 pages. ISBN: 1928959008.

> **Abstract:** Willie Frank Potts, Jr. served as a soldier in the Vietnam Conflict. He was involved in fierce fighting and returned home after being seriously wounded. Back in civilian life, Potts participated in many robberies for which he served several years in jail. Out of jail, he began buying property in the Bronx with an eye towards renovating buildings and thus improving the neighborhood. He also became involved in politics, starting a group called the New Breed Republicans and working to register voters. Potts and his group were honored by President Ronald Reagan at the White House. Potts also worked as a Christian evangelist. When he realized he was unable to support himself working on civic projects, he returned to illegal methods of making money. After more time in jail, he moved to Mississippi, where he started another branch of the New Breed Republicans, opened a sewing factory, and got married. The book ends with Potts involved in producing Christian programming on a local cable television station.

487. Powell, Colin L. *In His Own Words: Colin Powell.* Edited and collected by Lisa Rogak. A Perigee Book. New York, New York: Berkeley Publishing Group, 1995. 150 pages. ISBN: 0399522247.

> **Abstract:** This book is a collection of short published statements by Colin Powell. It can be used to get an idea of his views on politics, government, and social issues, such as affirmative action, abortion, education, and his own upbringing.

488. —. *My American Journey.* Written with Joseph E. Persico. New York, New York: Random House, 1995. 643 pages; photographs. 0679765115.

> **Notes:** Published as a large print edition New York: Random House, 1995. ISBN: 0679765115 (987 pages). Published in paperback New York: Ballentine, 1996. ISBN: 0345407288.

Abstract: Colin Powell's parents were born in Jamaica and met in Harlem. Powell fell in love with the army while a member of the ROTC and the Pershing Rifles at City College of New York. An oddity in a family which seemed to churn out professionals, Powell was an indifferent student and exhibited no particular drive. In the ROTC, however, he was motivated to work hard. He became a regular in the army after graduation from college. Powell rose steadily through the ranks. He served in Germany and completed two tours of duty in Vietnam. Powell describes the problems encountered by the United States during its military involvement in Vietnam and the many tragedies of that conflict. Upon his return to the United States, now married and with a family, Powell pursued graduate studies and became a White House Fellow. His work as a fellow was viewed favorably by the government, and Powell found it difficult to fulfill his dream of commanding troops as a uniformed soldier because he was continually called back to serve as a military assistant in Washington, D.C. Powell served in the Carter administration, he was an assistant to Secretary of Defense Caspar Weinberger, and he was National Security Advisor during the Reagan administration. He was appointed chairman of the Joint Chiefs of Staff during the Bush administration, and continued to serve under Clinton in this capacity. Powell dealt with the Iran hostage crisis (1979-81), the Lebanon truck bombing (1983), the Iranian arms deal and the covert siphoning of money to the Nicaraguan Contras (1985), the invasions of Grenada (1983) and Panama (1989), and the Gulf War (1990-91). During a brief respite from duty in Washington, D.C., Powell returned to the field to command the 75,000 troops of V Corp in Frankfurt, Germany. Powell recognizes the work of those African Americans who broke barriers and suffered from and resisted discriminatory policies and treatment, making it possible for his generation to accomplish their goals. Powell wished to memorialize the early contributions of African Americans in the army by providing a memorial to the Buffalo Soldiers, all-black troops formed after the Civil War: "I believed I had a duty to those black troops who had eased my way. Building a memorial to the Buffalo Soldiers became my personal crusade" (p. 278).

489. Powell Family. *See* Benton, Corrine.

490. Powell, Henry W. (1924-2000). *Witness to Civil Rights History: The Essays and Autobiography of Henry W. Powell.* Compiled and with an introduction by Patrick Louis Cooney. Hasting, New York: Patrick Cooney, 2000. 171 pages; photographs. ISBN: none.

Abstract: This compilation includes autobiographical writings and essays on African-American history. Powell was born in Pittsburgh, raised in Philadelphia, and attended Virginia Seminary and Virginia Union College, where he majored in English. He describes himself as a chronic mischief maker, a condition from which he did not recover until after graduating from college. His father bought a farm about the time Powell and his brother were finishing school, and they both ended up working there. Powell remained at the farm for nine years, 1948-1957. He describes the work as difficult and monotonous and life as very quiet and lonely. A high point of his life was his growing acquaintance with his father's friend and colleague, Dr. Vernon Johns. Powell writes at great length about Dr. Johns's qualities as a pastor and his personal attributes, his many accomplishments, and his contributions to the Civil Rights Movement. Powell left the farm to pursue a teaching career, and it was while teaching that he met his wife. They moved briefly to Philadelphia, but then returned to Virginia, finally settling in Lynchburg. Powell writes extensively about his father's career as pastor at Shiloh Baptist Church in Philadelphia and two terms as president of Virginia Seminary. He describes his father's task of righting the seminary's economic woes and his sudden dismissal after seeing the institution to solvency. Powell also writes about the seminary's current condition and prospects for the future. Compiler Cooney published this work after the death of Henry Powell.

491. Powell, William J. *Clearview: America's Course: The Autobiography of William J. Powell.* As told to Ellen Susanna Nösner. Haslett, Michigan: Foxsong Publishing, 2000. 147 pages; photographs. ISBN: 0967700027 : 0967700019.

Abstract: Powell was born in Greenville, Alabama, in 1916. The family moved north to Minerva, Ohio, when the economic climate of World War I forced his father's general store out of business. It was in Minerva that Powell was first exposed to golf. He caddied for a local doctor who gave him lessons and thus access to courses where he might otherwise not have been welcome. Powell writes his life story in terms of defining moments. One was when his school principal took him aside and told him that it would not

do for him to do as well as the white boys, but that he would have
to do better to succeed. Powell accepted this honesty and took the
message to heart. He played golf while attending Wilberforce
College in Xenia, Ohio. He would have liked to join the professional tour, but "opportunity was not part of the equation. What I
do know is I never had the chance to find out [whether or not I
would have succeeded]" (p. 21). Marriage, fatherhood, and golf
were all interrupted by induction into the army. Powell spent his
war years in England, playing on courses in England and Scotland
whenever he got the chance: "In Great Britain I was seen as a golfer
who happened to be black. Back home I was a black man trying
to play a white man's game" (p. 55). His return to the States meant
the return to Jim Crow conditions and the reality that the German
POWs lived in better conditions with better treatment than the
African-American soldiers returning from combat. Powell found
that there were only two golf courses that welcomed him, and it
was this scarcity of opportunity that led him to decide to build his
own. In 1946, Powell, with the support of his wife and family,
bought seventy-eight acres of land in Stark County, Ohio, to
design, construct, and operate a nine-hole golf course. Ten years
later he bought another fifty-two acres to expand his course to
eighteen holes. In 1978, his golf course was finally completed.
Powell describes the task of making a business out of his course
once it was completed. His daughter Renee was an LPGA/PGA
professional and became the course's head pro. His son Larry
became the course supervisor. In 1988, Powell was inducted into
the Canton Negro Old Timers Hall of Fame. This honor was the
first of a steady stream of awards and honors. The PGA recognized the historic importance of Powell's Clearview course and
sponsored renovations and improvements. Clearview was to celebrate its grand reopening in 2000.

492. Powers, Georgia Davis. *I Shared the Dream: The Pride, Passion,
and Politics of the First Black Woman Senator from Kentucky*. Far
Hills, New Jersey: New Horizon Press, 1995. 321 pages; photographs. ISBN: 088282127x.

Abstract: Politician Georgia Powers was born in Jimtown (formerly Jim Crow Town), Kentucky, and grew up in Louisville. She
was always a rebellious child and chafed at the idea that she
would grow up to marry and have a house full of children. She
attended local segregated schools and started undergraduate
work at Louisville Municipal College, but did not finish. After a
brief first marriage, Powers worked at a number of jobs, including
riveting, sewing, and insurance. She was invited to work on the

campaign of Wilson Wyatt for U.S. Senate and the gubernatorial campaign of Ned Breathett, but was discouraged following the Breathett campaign when she was the only member of the staff not offered work in his administration. Frustrated, Powers channeled her political energy into the Civil Rights Movement, and began working for Allied Organizations for Civil Rights. She was instrumental in planning the march on Frankfort in 1964, and she participated in the march to Selma in 1965. During this time, Powers was in close contact with many of the important civil rights leaders, and she describes her close friendship with Martin Luther King, Jr. and his brother, A. D. King. She reflects on the hard work of many women and their second class status within the movement. Powers went on to learn the ropes of the Democratic Party when she ran for Democratic Chairman of the 40th legislative district and the party executive committee. She then set her sights on the state senate. Although there were several African Americans serving as representatives, Powers was the first black senator in Kentucky. During her twenty years in office, she worked for an open public accommodations law, an end to housing and school desegregation, and a stronger Kentucky Civil Rights Act covering age and sex discrimination. In 1984 and 1988, Powers worked for Jesse Jackson's presidential campaign. She resigned from the Kentucky Senate in 1988. Since then she has founded the Friends of Nursing Home Residents, Incorporated (FONHRI) and has worked with Quality Education for All Students (QUEST), which was formed to fight the attempts of the superintendent of schools of Jefferson County to undo the desegregation of its public schools.

493. Powers, Tyrone. *Eyes to My Soul: The Rise or Decline of a Black FBI Agent.* Dover, Maryland: Majority Press, 1996. 487 pages; photographs; index. ISBN: 0912469331.

Abstract: Tyrone Powers, currently a criminal justice and law enforcement college instructor, was born into a family of six in Baltimore, Maryland. His parents were divorced. His father abused both Powers's mother and sister. Living in the Baltimore inner city, Powers and all of his siblings were either drug dealers or drug users. One brother was killed because of a deal gone wrong. Despite his unstable home life, Powers managed to stay in school, married early, and was hired by the Maryland State Police. During his time on the police force and subsequent employment with the Federal Bureau of Investigation, Powers was constantly at the mercy of the racist attitudes and actions of his colleagues, as well as under pressure from his brothers to leave the field of law

enforcement altogether. Powers asserts that racism is institutionalized in police departments and at the FBI and that there is an
unending struggle to break the will of black employees. In one
typical situation, Powers complained to a superior about the constant racist goading of a supervisor:

> He informed me that he, too, had noted the
> insensitivity of the supervisor. He stated that the
> issue had also been brought to his attention by a
> female Special Agent. He stated that he had
> rated the supervisor low in this area on his per-
> formance appraisal. Within four years of this
> incident, the supervisor was promoted twice.
> Further, I was informed by a supervisor in
> Detroit that [the superior] in Cincinnati had
> labeled me a "racist" and a "troublemaker" and
> had passed these comments on to the ASAC in
> the Detroit division prior to my being trans-
> ferred there. In the weeks, months, and years
> that followed, the supervisor, with the assistance
> of the Bureau tried to "break" me. . . .   (p. 311)

Powers, who has worked extensively in drug-related matters, feels
strongly that all efforts at fighting drugs in the United States are
no more than cosmetic and that there are people in power who
refuse to take effective action to change the status quo because it
would not be to their economic benefit to do so.

494. Primus, Rebecca and Addie Brown. *Beloved Sisters and Loving
Friends: Letters from Rebecca Primus of Royal Oak, Maryland and
Addie Brown of Hartford, Connecticut, 1854-1868.* Edited by
Farah Jasmine Griffin. New York, New York: Knopf, 1999. 303
pages; photographs; illustrations. ISBN: 0679451285.

Notes: Also published New York : Ballantine Books, 2001. ISBN:
0345408543.

Abstract: Editor Griffin presents the letters of Rebecca Primus and
Addie Brown as one step toward filling in the gaps in the history
of nineteenth-century African-American women. Both women
were from Hartford, Connecticut, but from different educational
and economic backgrounds. Included are the 150 letters of Addie
Brown to her friend Rebecca Primus, written between 1859 and
1868, and sixty letters written by Primus to her family. Brown
worked as a domestic in various cities in Connecticut and New
York. Her letters shed light on the lives of African-American

working women in New England and New York at the time. They also give a detailed picture of an intense friendship between two young women. Primus's letters were written following her departure for the South after the Civil War. She was sent to Royal Oak, Maryland, by the Hartford Freedman's Aid Society to teach newly freed African-American children. Her letters describe southern prejudices, her experiences teaching the children, her view of Reconstruction politics, and her life as part of an Africa-American community. Both women openly discuss their feelings about racism and white people. They write about the books they are reading, the politics of the time, the details of family and work life, and their surrounding environments. Griffin provides historical context and commentary to accompany the letters.

495. Prince, Nancy (b. 1799). *A Narrative of the Life and Travels of Mrs. Nancy Prince.* New York Public Library Digital Library Collections. Digital Schomburg. New York, New York: New York Public Library, 1997.

> http://digilib.nypl.org:80/dynaweb/digs/wwm97263/@Generic%5F%5FBookView

> **Notes:** Also University of North Carolina, Chapel Hill. Documenting the South (Project).
> http://docsouth.unc.edu/neh/prince/prince.html
> http://docsouth.unc.edu/neh/prince/prince.sgml

> Also published as *A Black Woman's Odyssey through Russia and Jamaica: The Narrative of Nancy Prince.* New York, New York: M. Wiener Publishing, 1989. ISBN: 1558760199 (93 pages).

496. Proctor, Samuel DeWitt (1921-1997). *The Substance of Things Hoped For: A Memoir of African-American Faith.* New York, New York: G. P. Putnam's Sons, 1995. 243 pages; photographs. ISBN: 0399140891.

> **Notes:** Also published Valley Forge, Pennsylvania: Judson Press, 1999. ISBN: 0817013253.

> **Abstract:** Proctor tells his story in the context of his education and his work to make education available to as many young African Americans as possible. He writes about his early years in school, highlighted by African American teachers suing for equal pay from the state of Virginia. He attended Virginia Union University, supported by an anonymous donor, and then Crozer Seminary, his sights set on becoming a minister. Proctor earned a Ph.D. from

Boston University and began his ministerial career at a small church in Providence, Rhode Island. By 1955, he was president of Virginia Union and went on to become president of North Carolina A&T University. Proctor was appointed by President Kennedy to direct the first full-scale Peace Corps Unit in Nigeria. He continued to work with the administrations of Kennedy and Johnson and with the Humphrey presidential campaign, writing many of Humphrey's speeches. Proctor left Washington, D.C., as the Nixon administration took charge. Following his governmental work, Proctor continued his efforts in education. He worked first for the University of Wisconsin to recruit black Ph.D. candidates and then went to Rutgers University as Martin Luther King Memorial Professor. There he developed a number of successful programs, including the Career Opportunity Program (COP), which brought African Americans who were without bachelor degrees but who were active in their communities into the masters of education program. Through COP, 120 new teachers were certified within three years, and Proctor traces the successful career paths of many of these individuals. He also describes the difficulties, frustrations, and culture shock of African Americans with poor educational backgrounds recruited into higher education at predominantly white schools. Looking at the state of education today, Proctor observes that segregation in many school systems is still common, and that programs such as school vouchers only spell the continued deterioration of public education. A man with a strong Christian faith, and a firm believer in the necessity of education as a means to personal and social improvement, Proctor writes,

> Crisis comes with hopelessness. The crisis grows as frustrated blacks fall behind in school and become comfortable with failure and nihilism. . . . Next, the crisis breeds half truths, spurious anthropology, historical hearsay, and propaganda. Finally, the crisis spirals ever upward as racists grab each opportunity to amplify all the bad news. (p. 171)

But, Proctor also notes that "[b]lack people have a long history of standing up to the impossible and making the possible real" (p. 213).

497. Pryor, Richard. *Pryor Convictions: And Other Life Sentences.* Written with Todd Gold. New York, New York: Pantheon Books, 1995. 257 pages; photographs; index. ISBN: 0679432507 : 037570048x.

Abstract: Comedian and actor Richard Pryor was born and raised in Peoria, Illinois. His parents had a volatile on-again off-again relationship, and he was raised by his grandmother, who ran a brothel. Pryor initially did well in school, but became discouraged by instances of racism and a lack of parental attention. He stopped trying to succeed and became a troublemaker. He enjoyed performing, however, and did comedy routines to keep his family entertained. A drama teacher did her best to encourage him. When, at age fourteen, he used his talents to disrupt class, he was thrown out of school. By the time he was eighteen, he was spending most of his time drinking and womanizing, so he volunteered for the Army to try to keep himself out of trouble. He spent some time in Germany, but was kicked out of the Army after almost killing a man in a disagreement. Back in Peoria, he began getting jobs doing stand-up comedy routines and emceeing. In short order, his career in comedy took off. Pryor appeared in forty movies and made twenty-five stand-up comedy albums. He had a short-run television variety series and his own film production company. Over the entire thirty-year span of his career, Pryor suffered from drug and alcohol addiction. He married six times, carrying on affairs with other women throughout each of his short-lived marriages. He confesses to beating his wives and doing little for the six children he fathered. In 1980, during a three-day cocaine binge, he set himself on fire and almost died of the burns. At the age of forty-nine, Pryor was diagnosed with multiple sclerosis, a disease that debilitated him to the point where he could no longer perform comedy. He had several heart attacks, the last one resulting in quadruple-bypass heart surgery. As the book ends, Pryor is fifty-four years old, unrepentant, but amazed that he has lived as long as he has.

498. Qi, Shouhua. *Bridging the Pacific: Searching for Cross-Cultural Understanding between the United States and China.* San Francisco, California: China Books and Periodicals, 2000. 204 pages. ISBN: 0835126757.

Abstract: In 1988, Qi came to the United States as a graduate student and English writing instructor at Illinois State University. In the first part of the book, he writes about the difficulty of leaving China, the task of making his way from the airport to his school in

Illinois, and his first months in Chicago. It was difficult, as a Chinese immigrant, to stand up to American students as an English teacher, and he writes about several particularly awkward situations. Although he always rode a bicycle in China, he learns the importance of owning a car in the United States and discusses the cars he has owned since coming to this country. Other essays are about his father who was "re-educated" by the Communists after the Chinese revolution, and about a lengthy visit by Qi's wife's father and new stepmother. Following the section on personal matters, Qi's essays turn to politics, particularly the relationship between China and the United States. Other subjects are the Taiwan Strait crises, the influence of Deng Xiaoping on China, fallacies about China that pass for truth in the West, and some brief notes about a trip Qi made back to China. The final section is entitled "A Happy Mean," and in it he recalls some of his impressions of the United States as a newcomer. He touches on topics such as the Monica Lewinsky scandal, election-year politics and his own desire to be able to cast a vote, the difficulty of pronouncing names in the United States, the Olympic games, and differences in the way Americans and Chinese give out praise.

499. Queen Latifah. *See* Latifah, Queen.

500. Ramirez, Juan (1949-). *A Patriot after All: The Story of a Chicano Vietnam Vet.* Albuquerque, New Mexico: University of New Mexico Press, 1999. 179 pages. ISBN: 0826319580 : 0826319599.

Abstract: Juan Ramirez was a third-generation Californian raised in a protective family atmosphere. He took pride in his Mexican heritage, but also felt that it was something to hide. Following high school, Ramirez joined the Marine Corps. This was in 1968 during the Vietnam Conflict and after the escalation of U.S. involvement began. Ramirez describes the psychological and physical abuse he and others endured in basic training and then the horrors of his experiences in Vietnam. He served two tours of duty and was rebellious and disillusioned through them both. He attempted suicide during his second tour, went AWOL on several occasions, and finally received an undesirable discharge. After leaving the army, Ramirez made a living delivering newspapers and began taking drugs. He worked for two-and-a-half years with the United Farm Workers, but his dependence on alcohol and drugs, combined with his violent temper, made it difficult for him to interact positively with others. It was years before he was able to confront the trauma of his experiences in Vietnam and deal with his anger and addictions. Eventually he appealed his undesirable discharge and was awarded an honorable discharge. The panel of Marine officers at the hearing was shocked that someone with his record of honors and accomplishments in battle had been discharged as undesirable. Through therapy and group sessions, Ramirez came to a better understanding of himself and of his veteran colleagues: "I, and all the other young Americans like me, were victimized by the U.S. war machine, which played on our honest patriotic desire by lying to us about the nature of the war. At the same time, we are morally responsible for our own actions in the war" (p. 162). Ramirez began working for Veterans' Services and speaks in schools about the Vietnam Conflict and his experiences as a soldier and a veteran.

501. Ramón, Dorothy (b. 1909). *Wayta' Yawa' Always Believe!* Written with Eric Elliot. Banning, California: The Malki Museum Press, 2000. 894 pages; tables. ISBN: none.

Abstract: Born in 1909, Dorothy Ramón never learned English. She attended the Sherman Indian School for a very brief period and remembers learning nothing. Elliott met with Ramón over a period of eight years, learning the Serano language and recording her stories. In his introduction, he provides an extensive analysis of this language. The book is divided into 721 brief segments, presented bilingually, in which Ramón recalls her personal experiences and history and tells stories of her tribe and neighboring tribes, such as the Pass Cahuilla and Mountain Cahuilla. She describes religious rites, medicinal practices, and food preparation and talks about traditional dances and songs. Ramón's memories include the destruction of the Indian tribes of Southern California. She gives accounts of massacres, lynchings, the theft of Indian water and land by whites, and the wholesale drafting of Serrano young men during World War I, most of whom never returned. Serrano tells of white ranchers allowing their cattle to wander freely over Indian lands and of the Indians who stole and killed the cattle because they were starving. She doesn't remember going hungry as a child, but most of her siblings died in childhood.

502. Randolph, Rev. Peter (1825-1897). *From Slave Cabin to the Pulpit: The Autobiography of Rev. Peter Randolph: The Southern Question Illustrated; and, Sketches of Slave Life.* Chapel Hill, North Carolina: Academic Affairs Library, University of North Carolina at Chapel Hill, 2000.

> http://docsouth.unc.edu/neh/randolph/randolph.sgml
> http://docsouth.unc.edu/neh/randolph/randolph.html

> **Notes:** Documenting the American South (Project).

503. Raybon, Patricia. *My First White Friend: Confessions of Race, Love, and Forgiveness.* New York, New York: Viking, 1996. 236 pages. ISBN: 0670859567.

> **Notes:** Also published New York: Penguin Books, 1996. ISBN: 0140244360.

> **Abstract:** Raybon describes the process of self-healing she undertook to rid herself of a lifelong hatred for whites after realizing that her hatred had shaped and controlled her, essentially causing more damage to herself than to the object of her hatred. To understand the root of her hatred, Raybon looks to her parents' childhoods and her own upbringing and childhood experiences. Despite a clear sense of justification, based on historical evidence of white oppression of blacks, Raybon seeks to forgive rather than to continue to hate. She provides the details of her path to forgiveness: the friends and family members who inspired her, the books that have influenced her and have helped her understand the nature of forgiveness, and the changes she has made to accomplish her goal. Specifically, she writes about her journalism career and the shift in the tone of her articles from anger to hope and the accompanying shift in the tone of the letters she receives—from predominantly hate mail, to letters expressing a renewed hope, inspiration to change, and a thankfulness to hear some optimism. Raybon also describes her experience teaching at the University of Colorado at Boulder, a university with a predominantly white student body. She explains that she chose to teach at such an institution because she not only provided these students with the opportunity to work with an African American woman professional, but provided herself with the opportunity to get to know some of the white students as individuals rather than as whites. She writes

>> So I am naive enough, perhaps, to believe that my presence in the classroom if nothing else, is a direct challenge to the stereotypical attitudes some of them still hold. But it turns out that they

> challenge my own stereotypical attitudes. So, in
> the end, all of us learn something from each
> other. My being here forces us each to cross a
> bridge and stretch.   (p. 208)

Perhaps Raybon reveals the most about her struggle when she
writes about her second husband who is biracial, white and
African American, and very light skinned, and their daughter who
was born white and blue-eyed. "She looked like everything I had
learned so long ago to fear. She was that racial presumption—
light is good; dark is bad—that had shaped all my early days" (p.
173). Later, as Raybon further examines her feelings, she continues, "[b]ut color was not synonymous with her essence. . . . Call
this a breakthrough. I was learning. From this baby I was finally
understanding that our outside covering simply cannot matter"
(p. 175).

504. Raymundo, Angeles Monrayo (1912-). *Tomorrow's Memories:
From the Diaries of Angeles Monrayo Raymundo, January 10, 1924-
November 17, 1928.*   Compiled and edited by Rizaline R.
Raymundo. San Jose, California: R. R. Raymundo, 1998. 226
pages; photographs.

505. Red Shirt, Delphine. *Bead on an Anthill: A Lakota Childhood.*
Lincoln, Nebraska: University of Nebraska Press, 1998. 146
pages. ISBN: 0803239084 : 0803289766.

> **Abstract:** In this collection of essays, Delphine Red Shirt writes
> about the important aspects of her childhood. Red Shirt grew up
> with stories told to her in the Lakota Language by her mother and
> aunts. The stories served to pass on elements of Lakota culture,
> helped her to learn the intricacies of the language, and guided her
> in her behavior. Her oldest brother then took the responsibility of
> explaining to Red Shirt how to behave in a manner consistent with
> traditional Lakota practices. She explains how speaking and liv-
> ing as a Lakota Indian have helped her to live a focused and
> directed life. Red Shirt writes about her oldest sister, the oldest of
> her mother's eleven children. This sister cared for Red Shirt and
> raised her as her own child because she was unable to have chil-
> dren herself. She died from complications of alcoholism. Red
> Shirt describes her education at the government school and at a
> small Catholic school where she learned to speak and write
> English fluently. Despite some of the school's shortcomings, the
> teachers were hard-working and cared about the progress of the
> students. Red Shirt includes essays about her experience as a tra-

ditional dancer and as a drummer and singer, about the Lakota coming-of-age ceremony for young women, and about the gathering, preparation and use of certain foods, including chokecherries, wild plum, and wild turnip.

506. Redford, Dorothy Spruill. *Somerset Homecoming: Recovering a Lost Heritage*. Written with Michael D'Orso. Chapel Hill, North Carolina: University of North Carolina Press, 2000. 166 pages; photographs; family trees; illustrations. ISBN: 0807848433.

> **Notes:** Originally published New York: Doubleday, 1988 (266 pages). ISBN: 038524245x; Anchor Books, 1989 (266 pages). ISBN: 0385242468.

> **Abstract:** Genealogist Dorothy Spruill Redford grew up during the period of the Civil Rights Movement. In college, while she was working with the Congress of Racial Equality (CORE), she first began to think about her own ancestry. In 1977, when she was thirty-three, she was newly inspired after reading *Roots* by Alex Haley. Thus, began the long and laborious process of learning the family stories. Redford had hoped to discover her family's roots in Africa, but this was not possible. She did, however, manage to go back seven generations to the Somerset Place Plantation, which was situated quite near her hometown of Columbia, North Carolina. It was the often-referred to "over the river" that many in her family mentioned as a place where other family members had lived. Redford spent the next ten years studying all that could be learned about slave history on the Somerset Place Plantation. She was able to distinguish twenty-one family lines, the descendents of which were spread across the country. She relates much of the history, the daily life of the Somerset slaves, the disruption of families, and the changes that came with the Civil War. She describes the slave owners, their families, and their manner of interacting with their slaves. In 1986, Redford decided to arrange a homecoming for as many of the descendents as she could reach and convince to come. She traveled all over the surrounding area, made contacts, and sent fliers out wherever there was interest. Stories about her work appeared on the front pages of the *Washington Post, USA Today*, and the *New York Times*. Major magazines also picked it up, and news of Redford's homecoming spread throughout the world. Eventually, the state of North Carolina became officially involved, taking responsibility for renovating the dilapidated tourist site the plantation had become. When the big day arrived, festivities were attended by more than two thousand people, including the governor, Alex Haley, and the

descendants, black and white, of families from the plantation. When the state decided to re-create the environment of Somerset Place, Redford was placed in charge of reproducing the conditions and community of the slaves, the slave quarters, and the areas in which they worked and farmed. She would also be able to document, through pictures and text, their everyday lives and accomplishments. It is clear from the responses of participants in the homecoming how important it was to their personal identity and self-esteem to learn of their family origins and their many and varied achievements in the most unpromising of circumstances.

507. Rekdal, Paisley. *The Night My Mother Met Bruce Lee: Observations on Not Fitting In.* New York, New York: Pantheon Books, 2000. 211 pages. ISBN: 0375409378.

Abstract: Rekdal's mother is a second-generation Chinese American, and her father is of Norwegian descent. In this collection of essays, Rekdal writes about her Chinese heritage. Most of the essays focus on her experiences while traveling. Topics include her visit to Taipei with her mother, her experiences as a high-school exchange student in Japan, teaching on a Fulbright grant in South Korea, trips to mainland China and to the Philippines, and a visit to Natchez, Mississippi, where her great aunt lived for a period of time. The common theme in all of these essays is Rekdal's awareness of being an outsider. In South Korea, Rekdal spoke the language fluently, but she never felt accepted and never quite understood what was going on. Her experiences mirrored her personal struggle to come to terms with her identity as a person with two ethnic backgrounds. In one essay she writes that "at heart I have come to believe I am and always was fully Chinese" (p. 142). But in another, she states: "For me to choose to become one ethnicity so that I can define myself for strangers is to fall victim to a monolithic, constructed idea of race that nothing in my personal history would support as true. . . . I cannot choose one identity without losing half of myself" (p. 208). While in Japan as an exchange student, Rekdal found herself denying that she was an American and insisting that she was Chinese. She became more confused, however, after asking her mother what she found during her first trip to China. Her mother answered, "I found out that I was American" (p. 155). One essay recalls Rekdal's friendship with Agatha, the only African-American girl at the Catholic high school they both attended. Rekdal was intrigued by Agatha, who seemed to be different in every way from the other girls she knew. She was adopted, her mother and siblings were white, she seemed not to care whether her clothes fit into the peer-approved style, and she had impeccable behavior. Agatha proved to be a loyal friend to Rekdal until she underwent her own identity crisis.

508. Relova, Lia. *Sacred Places.* Palos Verdes, California: Cyrus Lam, Pumpkin Enterprises, 1997. 92 pages; photographs; illustrations; index. ISBN: none.

Abstract: Like many Filipinos, Lia Relova's ancestry is a mixture of Filipino, Chinese, and Spanish. Relova's mother was Filipino and her father was American. They separated when she was seven, and during the week she lived with her father and stepmother with whom she was forbidden to speak Tagalog. Her stepmother abhorred anything Filipino, and both she and her father encouraged Relova to think of herself as white. With her mother and her extended family on the weekends in Pila Laguna, Relova was immersed in the Filipino culture. But even at her mother's home there was a strict sense of hierarchy, status, and class consciousness; both sides of her mother's family were considered to be upper class in Filipino society. When her father relocated to the United States, Relova went with him. There she was left to her own devices because her father spent most of his time with his wife who did not want to live with Relova. Relova gravitated to the Filipino youth in high school, but found that despite her own immigrant status, she did not fit in well. She was too Americanized to be easily accepted. Relova struggled with her own desire to be more Filipino and her own parents' prejudices against certain classes and skin shades. She suffered from a severe identity crisis and allowed herself to become alienated from her family. She began developing her own prejudices, which in turn became self-hatred. Relova had always felt a connection with the spirit world, and she began having dreams in which she was visited by deceased grandparents and long-dead ancestors. Her understanding of dreams and research and exploration into her family history helped her to start understanding herself, the Filipino people, and her own unique heritage.

509. Revard, Carter. *Family Matters, Tribal Affairs.* Tucson, Arizona: University of Arizona Press, 1998. 202 pages. ISBN: 0816518424 : 0816518432.

Abstract: Carter Revard was born in Pawhuska, Oklahoma, in Osage County on the Osage reservation. He had one older brother and a twin sister. Their father was a mixed-blood Osage and his mother was of Irish and Scotch-Irish descent. She later remarried another Osage man with whom she had four more children.

Revard grew up in a large extended family, Indian and non-Indian. His Irish grandfather, shortly before his death, urged Revard, then in sixth grade, to go to college, and Revard set it as his goal. He graduated from eighth grade as the covaledictorian in Osage County. He and his sister were then thrust from their thirteen-student one-room schoolhouse into the local high school with twelve hundred students. The transition was difficult, but Revard graduated and won a scholarship to the University of Tulsa by placing third in a college quiz event. In 1952, just after being named a Rhodes Scholar, Revard was given a naming ceremony by his Osage grandmother. A professional scholar and writer, Revard received his Ph.D. from Yale. In this collection of essays, Revard also writes about his travels in England, France, Spain, and Greece; he explores the theme of identity in Osage and other Indian cultures; he compares a variety of creation stories; and he writes about the American values that surface in American Indian literature.

510. Reverend Run. *See* Simmons, Joseph.

511. Reyes, Norman (1922-). *Child of Two Worlds: An Autobiography of a Filipino-American, or Vice-Versa.* Boulder, Colorado: Lynne Rienner Publishers, 1995. 289 pages; photographs; drawings. ISBN: 0894107771 : 089410778x.

> **Notes:** Originally published Colorado Springs: Three Continents Press, 1995.

> **Abstract:** Norman Reyes's mother was an American woman from Brooklyn, New York. His father, a Filipino, met her while working for the Philippine government in the United States. They married and moved to the Philippines, where they lived with the family of Reyes's father. His father, who was the first novelist to write in Tagalog, grew up in the middle of the transition from a Spanish-dominated culture to an American-dominated one. Reyes writes that in his American-influenced schools he developed a picture of immigrants as Europeans,

>> . . . white people who came from continental Europe to America. Never mind that many other nationalities around the earth had, for untold centuries, trekked across each other's borders. . . . The most numerous immigrants on this west wind are Filipinos, who are simply transplanted Malays with chromosomes that bear 2,000 years of Chinese infusion, 400 years of Spanish, and nearly a century of American.

>> (p. 5)

Attending English language schools and speaking English at home, Reyes learned Tagalog by roaming his neighborhood and through visits with his relatives. As he grew, Reyes developed a sense of what was Filipino and what was American. The most noteworthy difference seemed to him to be the independent individualism of Americans versus the interdependence, spiritually and materially, of Filipinos. As an adult, Reyes began working as a radio broadcaster, going from announcing local basketball games to preparing reports of the war in Europe and Asia. Reyes tells of his family's evacuation from Manila as the Japanese invasion drew closer and of his own escape. He joined the U.S. military to work as a broadcaster for the Voice of Freedom and was at Corregidor when it was taken by the Japanese. Following the war, the family left for the United States rather than return to live in what remained of Manila. Reyes joined his family there and went to school at Vanderbilt University. He married an American woman and they moved back to the Philippines, but soon chose to return to the United States. While attending Vanderbilt, Reyes experienced the difference between privileged and democratic and between elitist and bourgeois. He found that he could not live the privileged, elitist life expected of him as a Mestizo in the Philippines, and so he chose a democratic and bourgeois life in the United States.

512. Reynolds, Barbara A. *No, I Won't Shut Up: Thirty Years of Telling It Like It Is*. Nashville, Tennessee: J. C. Winston Publishing Company, 1998. 332 pages; photographs. ISBN: 1555238661.

Notes: Also published Temple Hills, Maryland: JFJ Publishing, 1998. ISBN: 0966507304.

Abstract: This book is a collection of Barbara Reynolds's columns and reports published over a thirty-year period. Reynolds has been a columnist for *USA Today*, a news commentator for CNN, founder and director of the Reynolds News Service, and a Pentecostal minister. She writes in her introduction, "What I hope this book will do is encourage the unheard, the invisible, the unlistened to, the misdefined, the unnoticed, the misinterpreted to find their voice and be heard." Reynolds's writings and outspoken opinions have resulted in her being ostracized, rebuked, and threatened, but she has only felt shame "when I did shut up, when I did look the other way when people were hurting" (p. xx). She sees her voice as one of the few being heard in the media that can counteract the voice of the privileged white male and the corporate board room. Her collected writings include commentary on current national and global events, media politics, her calling to the ministry, and other personal experiences. She includes special reports on the deaths of Dr. Martin Luther King, Jr. and U.S. Secretary of Commerce Ron Brown, and two of her sermons.

513. Rhee, Chi Sun (1933-). *Letters to Hyun A: Bridging Two Cultures.* Chapel Hill, North Carolina: Professional Press, 1999. 193 pages. ISBN: 1570874808.

514. Richards, Roosevelt. *Growing Up in the Bittersweet South.* Chicago, Illinois: Bhards Publishing Company, 1997. 204 pages; discussion guide. ISBN: 0965533107.

Notes: Separate twenty-seven page discussion guide. ISBN: 0965533115.

Abstract: Richards writes in his introduction, "When I grew up, African-Americans in the South were 'free,' but they were living under bitterly harsh Jim Crow laws, which were second only to slavery in their cruelty and inhumanity. At the same time, however, they were enjoying sweet family ties and community bonds" (pp. iii-iv). Richards describes his own experience with "sweet family ties and community bonds." His family owned their own land and worked hard planting, growing, and harvesting cotton and vegetables. All of the children worked in the fields, their father worked at a sawmill as well as the farm, and their mother worked in the house, but suffered from serious heart problems and high blood pressure. The Richards children, as in most families with which they were acquainted, lived by rigid rules, the breaking of which resulted in harsh punishment. Though they had loyalty to the family and fondness for each other, the children were each anxious to move on as opportunities arose. Richards describes life on the farm: cotton picking, hog butchering, the foods eaten, and how any free time was spent. All the children looked forward to the few months they were able to attend school. Among other things, it meant a respite from fieldwork. Richards writes that, even when attending school, it was difficult to combine studying with the heavy chores for which he and his siblings had responsibility. Richards and his family lived in the shadow of extreme racism. The children were lectured by their parents to keep their place because if they were mistreated, their father would surely kill the person who mistreated them and then he would likely be killed as well. Richards describes several threatening events during his childhood and adult years. He also writes about the impact that World War II and the drafting of

African-American men had on his parents' circle. It seemed a
monstrous contradiction to them that they were denied the right
to vote, a proper education, and freedom of movement, but were
expected to die for the country that supported such laws and conditions.

> To young people today, African Americans and
> whites as well, it may be hard to believe that this
> was the way it was in the recent past in the "land
> of the free," not centuries ago. But many, many
> Negroes living today struggled under these
> unfair and demoralizing standards.   (p. 114)

515. Richburg, Keith. *Out of America: A Black Man Confronts Africa.*
New York, New York: BasicBooks, 1997.   257 pages; maps.
ISBN: 0465001874.

Notes: Also published San Diego: Harcourt Brace, 1998. ISBN:
0156005832 (266 pages).

Abstract: Keith Richburg, an African-American journalist for the
Washington Post, spent three years on assignment in Africa, stationed in Nairobi, Kenya. He arrived on the continent in 1991, full
of hope and enthusiasm about covering "the land of my roots,"
and left in 1994, completely disillusioned and feeling no connection with Africa. Richburg covered the United Nations forces in
Somalia, the wholesale slaughter of Tutsis and Hutus in Rwanda,
and civil war in Liberia. In Somalia, he watched as the UN troops
came into the country and achieved some degree of order, and
then watched that order disintegrate until the troops finally pulled
out. He found it impossible to understand how the Somalis themselves could let the country deteriorate into an anarchy. Richburg
comments: "No one ever calculated what you do next if the people
you come to help have no interest in being saved" (p. 78). He came
into contact with many African leaders and describes the corruption and shortsightedness he encountered. He talks about the
dangers of being a black reporter, always having to prove that he
was not a member of an enemy tribe or country when crossing
borders between countries, and the difficulty of living up to expectations that Africans had for American blacks. Another source of
dismay was the way black American leaders dealt with Africa. An
opposition leader in Gabon is quoted:

> "The Americans come here to create a dialogue,"
> he told me. "They need to understand our prob-
> lems of education, in health care. . . . But they are
> not going around enough, to be able to see the

true problems of the country, to talk to members
of the opposition."   (p. 140)

Richburg observes,

> when the subject turns to the lack of democracy
> and human rights elsewhere in Africa, those
> same black Americans . . . offer tortured expla-
> nations as to why America shouldn't criticize
> Africa, why America shouldn't impose its stan-
> dards, and why reform must not be immediate
> but gradual. . . .   (p. 141)

Richburg feels that Zimbabwe and South Africa have managed a
fairly efficient transition to black rule because they did not run the
white population out of the country. Whites had the know-how
and assets for running a society, and the black majority needed to
draw on these. Richburg concludes his book, aware that his point
of view will most likely be unpopular in the United States, especially among African Americans. But now home in the United
States, when he hears about turmoil in Africa,

> I will understand . . . the complexities behind the
> conflicts. I will also know that the problems are
> too intractable, that the outside world can do
> nothing, until Africa is ready to save itself. I'll
> also know that none of it affects me, because I
> feel no attachment to the place or the people.
>   (p. 247)

516. Ríos, Alberto Alvaro.   *Capirotada: A Nogales Memoir.*
Albuquerque, New Mexico: University of New Mexico Press,
1999. 145 pages; photographs. ISBN: 0826320937 : 0826320945.

Abstract: Ríos's autobiographical work is a collection of essays in
which he depicts childhood memories and reflects on the nature of
the border towns of Nogales, Mexico, and Nogales, Arizona. Ríos
focuses on vivid recollections of childhood accidents, celebrations
and food, the local Catholic church and its Irish priests, and his
activities as an altar boy and leader of the Vikings of America gang
with its impromptu parades and Friday night lemon juice initia-
tions. Ríos's father was born in Mexico, and his mother was born
and raised in England. His father ran away from home at the age
of fourteen and moved to Nogales, Arizona, where he had aunts
and grandparents. He joined the army and was kicked out after
basic training because of his illegal status. Dropped off at the border, he returned and enlisted, carefully reversing the order of his

first and last names on enlistment documents. This time the paperwork didn't catch up to him until after he had been all over Europe and North Africa and promoted to sergeant, at which point the army was no longer interested in kicking him out. His fourth year in the army was spent in England, where he met his future wife. The couple became engaged, and Ríos believes that the commander of the post sent his father home just before his wedding as a means of preventing the marriage. Despite this abrupt separation, his mother, who had never been more than two train stops from her home, took a ship to New York and a train to Salt Lake City, where she joined Ríos's father. They traveled to Nogales together to be married, and there they remained until Ríos's father's death in 1995.

517. Robinson, Clarence (1919-). *The Impossible Dream: One Man's Drive to End Racial Oppression: An Autobiography.* Written with Kenneth Brooks. Vallejo, California: Amper Publishing Company, 1998. 198 pages; photographs. ISBN: 0963904299.

Abstract: Clarence Robinson was born in Arkansas, but moved with his family to St. Louis while he was still very small. He quit high school to get married and moved to Vallejo, California, to work in the shipyards during World War II. Following the war, Robinson was laid off and found work as a janitor with the Vallejo School District. He was promoted to a supervisory position and began to take an active interest in employment conditions for African Americans. He started his protests by picketing businesses that did not hire African Americans, and he formed the Citizens Advancement Committee. Robinson's first real success was convincing a Safeway supermarket with a primarily black customer base to hire African-American employees. Over time, he also challenged the Vallejo School District to hire black teachers and the City of Vallejo to hire black police officers, black firefighters, and black city hall employees. He fought the city on its civil service test-scoring practices and protested local housing segregation. Robinson was active in politics. He formed a Democratic club, but he eventually switched to the Republican party because he was dissatisfied with the lack of fulfillment of Democratic promises. This alliance, as well as his lack of education and occupation as a janitor, isolated him from the black community. Robinson ran for city council, but received very little support. When black leaders were trying to get an African American on the Vallejo Redevelopment Agency board, the mayor offered the seat to Robinson. Although he was not the choice of the black leadership, he served on the board for nineteen years and as chair in 1963,

1966, and 1973. Robinson describes his work with prominent national politicians, his wife and children, and his many other challenges to the systematic exclusion of African Americans from housing and work opportunities in the Vallejo area.

518. Robinson, Eddie. *Never Before, Never Again: The Stirring Autobiography of Eddie Robinson, the Winningest Coach in the History of College Football.* Written with Richard Edward Lapchick. New York, New York: St. Martin's Press, 1999. 268 pages; photographs. ISBN: 0312242247.

Abstract: College Football Hall of Famer Eddie Robinson was born in 1919 in Jackson, Louisiana. He was in third grade when he first fell in love with football. Inspired by the local high school football coach, Robinson was organizing street teams when he was in ninth grade and playing quarterback for the high-school team by his junior year. He attended Leland College and upon graduation hoped to find a job coaching. In 1941, he was offered the coaching position at Grambling State University, where he stayed until his retirement in 1997. In his book, Robinson describes his work and training as a coach and his goal to win, thereby opening opportunities for African Americans. He realized that he needed to assist his students with their academic planning as well as with their athletic activities to assure their success. He also felt it was important to set a good example for his players, and he made sure that they saw him, not only as a coach, but also as a dedicated and involved husband and father. During his years at Grambling, Robinson was witness to many changes. His players were the first black athletes to be served at a local Holiday Inn, a breakthrough which he credits to the students who participated in lunch counter sit-ins during the early days of the Civil Rights Movement. He discusses the integration of his own football team and the effect on athletic programs at historically black colleges when the big southern universities began to recruit black athletes. Robinson has received four honorary degrees, including one from Yale University in 1997, and he was inducted into the College Football Hall of Fame in 1998. Grambling dedicated its Eddie Robinson Stadium in 1983.

519. Robinson, Frazier. *Catching Dreams: My Life in the Negro Baseball Leagues.* Written with Paul Bauer. Foreword by John "Buck" O'Neil. Introduction by Gerald Early. Sports and Entertainment. Syracuse, New York: Syracuse University Press, 1999. 230 pages; photographs. ISBN: 0815605633 : 0815606583.

Abstract: Robinson grew up playing baseball with his brother Norman and joined a professional team at the age of seventeen. At nineteen, he moved to Cleveland to live with an older brother and worked at Goodyear, where he joined the Goodyear Wingfoot Tigers baseball team. From there, he was drafted back into professional baseball. A catcher, he played with, among other teams, the Abilene Eagles, the Kansas City Monarchs, the Baltimore Elite Giants, and the Winnipeg Buffaloes. On many of these teams, Robinson played with his brother Norman. He writes about many notable players, especially Satchell Paige, a close friend and teammate. Robinson was forty when Jackie Robinson broke the color line in major league baseball. This event signaled not only a major change for sports in the United States and for professional African-American athletes, but the end of the Negro Leagues. Robinson, along with many other great Negro League players, was just past his prime as the teams in the Negro League began to lose their top players and their audience to the major leagues. Although never bitter about not having this opportunity, he notes that the pay and working conditions did not compare with what would have been offered to African-American players had the major leagues been open to them.

> Looking back on Jim Crow and baseball's color line, I'd have to say that segregation was just something I'd gotten used to. . . . As long as I could get along, it didn't bother me. . . . I knew it wasn't fair, but you had to accept it. When Jackie Robinson signed with the [sic] Branch Rickey, I just said, "So well and so good."
>
> (p. 103)

Frazier Robinson's last years in professional baseball were in Canada, playing with the Winnipeg Buffaloes, which he found a paradise. No hotels or restaurants were closed to him, nobody looked at him twice. Segregation seemed not to exist. After two years there, Robinson retired and finished more than twenty years in professional baseball. He returned to Ohio, and met his second wife in Cleveland. They eventually moved to California and then retired to North Carolina. Frazier Robinson died in 1997, the day after the Antioch Missionary Church of Kings Mountain, North Carolina, dedicated the newly constructed Frazier "Slow" Robinson Gymnasium.

520. Robinson, Granville H. *Inside Ajar Cottage: Bermuda.* Pittsburgh, Pennsylvania: Dorrance Publishing Company, 2000. 259 pages; photographs. ISBN: 0805945865.

Abstract: Granville Robinson was born and raised in Bermuda. He emigrated to the United States as a young man, joined the United States Army, and married. He recounts many anecdotes of his family and experiences growing up in Bermuda. He includes descriptions of attending school, learning the carpentry trade, working with his father on the family farm and in the family-owned grocery store, his romantic attachments with several young women, and the fortunes and fates of his brothers and sisters. Robinson first visited the United States on tour with his church. At that time he attempted to stay, having met a young woman in Akron, Ohio, who would later become his wife, but he was unable to extend his visa, and returned to Bermuda for another two years. Robinson writes about his experiences in the U.S. Army. He was stationed in the deep South while undergoing basic training and was shocked by the virulent racism which confronted him there. He was later stationed in Germany, but he ran into difficulty because of his alien status and found himself under investigation by the military and the FBI. Robinson concludes his book with the story of his efforts to find and meet members of his father's family on the islands of St. Kitts and Nevis.

521. Robinson, Jackie. *I Never Had It Made: An Autobiography.* Written with Alfred Duckett. Introduction by Hank Aaron. Hopewell, New Jersey: Ecco Press, 1995. 275 pages. ISBN: 0880014199.

Notes: Originally Published Greenwich, Connecticut: Fawcett Publications, 1972 (256 pages); New York: Putnam, 1972. ISBN: 0399110100 (287 pages).

522. Robinson, Randall (1941-). *Defending the Spirit: A Black Life in America.* New York, New York: Dutton, 1998. 304 pages; index. ISBN: 0525944028.

Notes: Published in paperback New York, New York: Penguin, 1999. ISBN: 0452279682.

Abstract: African-American activist Randall Robinson was raised in Richmond, Virginia. He was not an enthusiastic student and was quickly drafted into the U.S. Army after quitting college. Robinson was saved from going to Vietnam by a special exemption for students planning to register for college, and successfully went back and completed his course work at Virginia Union University. He then went to Harvard Law School. He did well, but chose not to become a lawyer. In 1970, Robinson made his first trip to Africa, to Dar es Salaam, Tanzania. After this, he became deeply involved in matters relating to African and Caribbean nations, working through the organization TransAfrica. Robinson was one of the people who forced the United States to come to terms with the reality of apartheid in South Africa after decades of ignoring it and continuing to invest in that country. He and several black leaders were arrested when they refused to leave the South African embassy in the United States until their demands were met. This act initiated continuous picketing of that embassy that lasted for almost a year. Robinson has also spoken out and worked against cruel dictatorships in Africa, such as in Nigeria. In 1994, he supported president-elect Aristide of Haiti, who was forced to flee his country. Robinson was influential in the effort to help Aristide return to the country as president. Robinson also seeks a way to end the monopolization of the banana market by Chiquita. The multinational corporation is trying to prohibit subsidized sales of bananas to European markets, which have been a lifeline for tiny Caribbean nations not affiliated with Chiquita. Robinson predicts that when legal livelihoods are cut off, democracies will fail and people will be forced to grow drug crops. Robinson discusses the general lack of U.S. interest in African and Caribbean countries, citing a tepid response to the genocide in Rwanda as an example. He also talks about the pervasive and almost-casual racism in U.S. society and the insidious effect it has on the African-American population.

523. Rock. *See* The Rock.

524. Rodman, Dennis. *Bad As I Wanna Be.* Written with Tim Keown. New York, New York: Delacorte Publishing, 1996. 259 pages; photographs. ISBN: 0385316399.

    Notes: Also published New York: Dell Press, 1997. ISBN: 0440222664.

    Abstract: Before becoming involved with professional sports, Rodman was homeless and working odd jobs. One such job was as a janitor at the Dallas-Fort Worth Airport. After a night in jail for stealing watches at an airport gift shop, he decided to turn himself around and returned home. Rodman played for some community basketball teams and was noticed and recruited by Cooke County Junior College. At the age of twenty-one, he was recruited by Southeastern Oklahoma State University. In 1988, Rodman was a second-round draft pick for the Detroit Pistons. He loved his coach, Chuck Daly, and enjoyed playing with the Pistons as they worked their way to a streak of championships. When Daly was fired, however, Rodman lost his interest in the team. He had a difficult year, which ended with him contemplating suicide. Rodman decided to change his life rather than end it. This meant acknowledging his bisexual nature, wearing the clothes he want-ed to wear, and acting on his own instincts. Rodman was traded to the San Antonio Spurs. There he was unhappy with his pay, the coaching, and the team. He alienated himself from the Spurs to the extent that they traded him to the Chicago Bulls. Rodman gives his opinions of the qualities and salaries of other players, speaks out on behalf of AIDS victims and talks about racism in and out of sports, about his relationship with singer and enter-tainer Madonna, and about his appreciation for Bulls coach, Phil Jackson.

525. —. *Walk on the Wild Side*. Written with Michael Silver. New York, New York: Delacorte Press, 1997. 261 pages; photo-graphs. ISBN: 0385318979.

Abstract: In this book Dennis Rodman talks about his flamboyant lifestyle and how it is important for him to live his life just the way he feels it. Close to suicide in 1993, Rodman decided that it would be better to be himself than to end his life. Partying, sex, and showy clothes as well as playing a hard game of basketball are important aspects of his lifestyle. "When the vibes are good, I'm in the zone of love" (p. 40), he says. He mentions his fallout with singer and entertainer Madonna, posing nude for *Playboy*, getting married to his fans in a symbolic wedding, and his guest spots on MTV. Favorite singers and performers are Pearl Jam, Elvis, Frank Sinatra, and Jimi Hendrix. Amidst his fast-paced life, Rodman makes time for his daughter Alexis.

526. Rodriguez de Rochín, Juanita. *Juanita: My Life with Refugio.* East Lansing, Michigan: Julian Samora Research Institute, Michigan State University, 1998.   56 pages; photographs. ISBN: none.

Abstract: Juanita Rodriguez de Rochín was born in Colton, California in 1913. She writes, "My goal is to leave a lasting set of memories of the way things were and the way my life turned out to be" (p. 3). She was raised on O Street in Colton in the house that her father built shortly after arriving in California from Mexico. Rodriguez de Rochín met Refugio, her future husband, when she was just fifteen. Her parents liked him, but they were unhappy with the growing seriousness of their relationship. Rodriguez de Rochín convinced Refugio to run away with her, and at the ages of fifteen and twenty, they left for Mexicali in Mexico. Rodriguez de Rochín's father had Refugio arrested, and he spent a month in jail in Colton. Not long after his release, the couple married. Angered that they married without consent, Rodriguez de Rochín's parents did not speak to the newlyweds for one year. The years of Refugio's and Juanita's marriage were devoted to their various businesses. Refugio ran a wholesale food business until he decided to move the growing family, eventually numbering five children, to Carlsbad. There they opened a small grocery store and diner and eventually, in succession, two large restaurants. The first restaurant was an expansion of the original diner. They had to close it during World War II because they were not allowed to operate after dark. The second restaurant closed after fifteen successful years. Refugio opened one more restaurant in San Diego that he and Juanita operated together until his retirement. Throughout the years, Rodriguez de Rochín raised five children, suffered from health problems, and worked at their restaurants seven days a week, all year round. She remembers some difficult and unhappy times, but she remembers most of all her love for her husband and her desire to be with him and involved in the family businesses.

527. Rolling Thunder. *Rolling Thunder Speaks: A Message for Turtle Island.* Transcribed and edited by Carmen Sun Rising Pope. Santa Fe, New Mexico: Clear Light Publishers, 1999.   249 pages; photographs. ISBN: 1574160265.

Abstract: In this book, Rolling Thunder describes his life and work as a medicine man. He talks about the proper way of living, spirituality, reincarnation, and death.   Editor Pope tells how Rolling Thunder began recording tapes for his autobiography in

1996 and continued until shortly before his death in 1997. After he
died, Pope decided to put the book together. She writes that
Rolling Thunder was born into the Paint Clan of the Cherokee
Indians. The Paint Clan was a medicine society, and Rolling
Thunder's father was a traditional chief and medicine man.
Rolling Thunder was chosen to follow in his father's footsteps, but
he chose to learn his calling from many different tribes. He tells
how, after leaving his hometown of Big Cedar, Oklahoma, he traveled from reservation to reservation, looking for a wife and learning medicine ways. Rolling Thunder talks about what it means to
be a medicine man, his own vision, and the rules for following the
medicine trail. He gives his view of Indian history and ancient
civilization, in particular, the origin of the Cherokees. He talks
about the role of women and children in Indian society; the
destructive relationship Indians have had with white people,
including the cultural annihilation, genocide, and Indian resistance; his contact with extraterrestials, and his many prophecies for
the future of the earth. Around 1979, Rolling Thunder built Meta
Tantay, a traditional Indian camp. He describes the work that went
into making this a self-sufficient community, its guidelines for living, and suggestions for diet. Rolling Thunder's work concludes,

> All I'm asking is that you make a good prayer.
> Don't forget to pray for the animals, the birds,
> the plant life, the rocks, and the mountains so
> that you may walk a long beauty trail and into
> the land of the Great Mystery. And don't forget
> me. . . . [T]he best way not to forget me is to learn
> to live with each other.   (pp. 248-249)

528. Ruiz, Mona. *Two Badges: The Lives of Mona Ruiz*. Written with
Geoff Boucher. Houston, Texas: Arte Público Press, 1997. 288
pages. ISBN: 1558851658 : 1558852026.

Abstract: Mona Ruiz was born and raised in Santa Ana,
California. Her father kept his daughters sheltered, sending them
to private schools to keep them out of trouble. After her father suffered a serious injury and could no longer work, Ruiz and her sisters had to transfer to the public school. Through their cousins,
the girls began to associate with local gang members and seek
their acceptance. This led to a growing distance between the girls
and their parents. Ruiz describes how her perspective on life
changed as she became more involved with gang members and
gang life. When, as part of a school career program, Ruiz was
assigned to work as a filing clerk at the Santa Ana Police

Department, she came into conflict with the interests of her friends, but it was a step toward fulfilling the wish of her father that she become a police officer. To everyone's surprise, Ruiz excelled and began to advance at the police department. The two officers with whom she worked became her friends and mentors. They helped her complete her high school education and get started on college courses that she would need to become a police officer. Ruiz, however, was involved romantically with a young gang member who resented both her working at the police department and her college courses. When Ruiz became pregnant, they married. She quit work and school, and found herself at the mercy of her husband's drug-induced temper tantrums. Ruiz made many attempts to leave him, but the couple had three children together before she ended the marriage. She describes the difficulty of breaking her emotional attachment to her husband, raising her children alone, and finally, after hard work and overcoming prejudice based on stereotypes, fulfilling her dream of becoming a police officer.

529. Run, Reverend. *See* Simmons, Joseph.

530. Sababu, Akida K.   *Evolution of a Revolution.*   Nashville, Tennessee: James C. Winston Publishing Company, 1995.   141 pages.   ISBN: 1555236413.

Abstract: Akida Sababu was born in 1959 in Canton, Ohio. In this autobiography, Sababu writes about various episodes in his life, and the different directions his career as a community activist has taken him. Just out of high school, Sababu became involved in black militant youth movements. He developed a reputation as an individual with commitment and a willingness to act, but remained unemployed during this period of his life. As his network disintegrated, his father insisted that he find work, and he got a job with the Coca-Cola Company. He got involved with the labor union, but there were no major issues to contend with. When the plant he worked in was significantly damaged by fire, Sababu was accused of arson. A grand jury failed to indict him due to lack of evidence, and Sababu was rehired by the company. Sababu later worked as a youth director for the Indian River School for Boys in Ohio. Conditions for inmates and staff were intolerable, and Sababu, once again involved with the union, found himself in the midst of a bitter controversy within the school and between the state and the school. Some of the issues were gradually resolved, and Sababu left to find new employment challenges. He remained active in labor issues, became involved with AIDS advocacy, and worked in city government. Sababu attended the 1980 World Parliament of the Peoples for Peace in Sophia, Bulgaria, and spoke before 1,500 delegates on unionization and African Americans. Sababu founded Executive Management Consultants, Inc., through which he sought to manage performing artists, especially emerging black artists and performers. This enterprise continued for two years before having to close, but by that time Sababu had formed a new corporation, The International Labor and Management Resource Center.

531. Said, Edward. *Out of Place: A Memoir*. New York, New York: Knopf, 1999. 295 pages; photographs. ISBN: 0394587391.

Notes: Also published in paperback New York: Vintage Books, 2000. ISBN: 0679730672.

Abstract: Writer and intellectual Edward Said recounts his childhood and early adult years. He was the child of a Palestinian mother and a father who was born a Palestinian but who became a naturalized U.S. citizen during a decade in the United States, which included military service in World War I. Thus, Said and his siblings had U.S. citizenship, but they were raised in Cairo, summered in Dhour, Lebanon, and attended British schools. For all of these reasons, Said often felt out of place. For example, he comments on the languages he and his family used:

> Our families shopped for food at Groppi's, talking with the plainly Greek or Egyptian employees . . . in jaw-shattering French, when it was perfectly clear that we all could have done better in Arabic. . . . I had picked up spoken French early but never felt confident enough to use it as an everyday language. . . . So although English had become my main language . . . I found myself in the odd situation of not having any natural, or national, position to use it. The three languages became a pointedly sensitive issue for me at the age of about fourteen. Arabic was forbidden and "wog"; French was always "theirs," not mine; English was authorized, but unacceptable as the language of the hated British.
>
> (p. 197)

Another important difficulty was the personalities of his parents, whose manipulative practices tended to keep their children feeling insecure and hostile toward each other. Said was a youth at the time Palestine became Israel, but these events had little impact on him. He went to a boarding school in the United States for his final years of high school and then to college at Princeton and graduate school at Harvard. After he finished, he returned to Cairo and worked for his father's office equipment business. When his father named Said the principal in a contract which involved illegal business practices and Egyptian authorities discovered the transactions, he was banned from re-entering Egypt, the only place he felt comfortable, for the next fifteen years. Said wrote this memoir during the five years that he was being treated for leukemia, using the project as an attempt to sort out his own identity and his relationship to his parents and sisters.

532. Sakamoto, Mitsuo. *My Best World War II Souvenir: Chronicles of One Man's Experiences in the United States Army.* [Hawai'i]: The Author, 1995. 64 pages; photographs. ISBN: none.

Abstract: Sakamoto was born in Honolulu and raised in Kona, Hawai'i. His father died when he was two and his mother when he was nine years old. In this work, Sakamoto writes about his positive experiences in the army as a member of the 442nd Regimental Combat Team, beginning with the end of World War II, when his regiment was stationed in Donauwörth, Germany. It was there that he met fifteen-year-old Anneliese. He describes their seven-year courtship and the various maneuvers he executed to be stationed close enough to visit her regularly. The couple married in 1952, and had three daughters. Following their marriage, they returned to Hawai'i, but Sakamoto re-enlisted for another tour, and the family went back to Germany. After three years, they returned to Hawai'i, where Sakamoto attended NCO school. He was then sent to Pusan, Korea, without his family. After nearly two years away, in 1963, he retired and returned to Hawai'i. While in the army, Sakamoto worked in Quartermaster, Class I Supply. Besides describing his work and family, Sakamoto describes many of his friends and comrades in the 442nd.

533. Sanchez, Reymundo (1963-). *My Bloody Life: The Making of a Latin King.* Chicago, Illinois: Chicago Review Press, 2000. 299 pages. ISBN: 1556524013 : 1556524277.

Abstract: Sanchez was born in Puerto Rico in 1963. His mother was sixteen and his father, whom he has no memories of, was seventy-four. After his father's death his mother remarried twice, and the family moved to Chicago with her second husband. Both stepfathers were abusive. Driven out of his home, Sanchez became a full-fledged gang member at thirteen. He writes that he believed he was behaving like a man, although he was just a child, a child who never had the chance to experience childhood. He took and sold drugs and was initiated into the cycle of killing and revenge. Sanchez tells of the many different gangs active in his area, his addictions to drugs and sex, his homelessness, and his eventual decision to leave his gang just before a former girlfriend and her small child were attacked. The child died, and Sanchez cooperated with police, but never personally took action against the killers. In this way, he managed to break his pattern of revenge. Sanchez wrote this book under a pseudonym to provide some insight into the reasons young children join gangs and to make it clear that adults, not peers, often provide the motivating factor.

534. Sanders, Deion. *Power, Money & Sex: How Success Almost Ruined My Life*. Written with Jim Nelson Black. Foreword by T. D. Jakes. Nashville, Tennessee: Word Publications, 1998. 194 pages; photographs. ISBN: 084991499x : 0849937760.

Abstract: Deion Sanders, National Football League player, writes about his life and his football career. Lessons learned early in life have kept him away from many vices. His mother once let him sit for several hours alone in a jail cell when he and some other boys were picked up by the police for vandalism. He vowed he would never do anything that would send him back. Life with a drug-abusing father and alcoholic stepfather have kept him away from substance abuse. As a young man, he was a talented athlete and a diligent student and was aggressively recruited by many colleges. He chose Florida State University and quickly became a star on the football team. As a senior, Sanders played both college football and professional baseball. He was employed by a New York Yankees farm team and already had money and fame by the time he graduated and was drafted by the Atlanta Falcons football team. In Atlanta, he played for both the Falcons and for the Atlanta Braves baseball team during the football off-season. Later he moved to the San Francisco 49ers and played baseball with the San Francisco Giants. Then he joined the Dallas Cowboys. Despite his popularity and success, Sanders felt empty and unfulfilled. The low point in his personal life came when his wife left him and took their two children with her. He drove his car off a cliff in a suicide attempt, but walked away without a scratch. At this point, he recognized his problems and turned to Christianity. In the second half of the book, Sanders talks about how he turned his life around and keeps it on an even keel. Sanders includes many of the teachings of his spiritual leader, Bishop T. D. Jakes.

535. Sanematsu, Ben. *Inward Light: An Asian American Journey*. San Mateo, California: Asian American Curriculum Project, Inc., 1998. 191 pages; photographs. ISBN: 0934609047.

Abstract: Sanematsu was born in Riverside, California. His parents, who had emigrated from Japan, lived on a three-acre farm. By his early teens, Sanematsu had begun to lose his vision and was diagnosed with retinitis pigmentosa. His parents encouraged their six children to pursue education, and following high school graduation, Sanematsu enrolled at the University of California at Berkeley. As he was preparing for his finals in December of 1941, the Japanese attacked Pearl Harbor. Sanematsu's father was arrested by the FBI and Sanematsu had to withdraw from school to return to work on the farm. In May of 1942, the whole family was sent to Poston, Arizona. Sanematsu describes the conditions of the camp. He writes that, in retrospect, there were some advantages to internment. He had the opportunity to teach and make friends, women were given a respite from farm labor, and after the war Japanese began to settle in states other than California and found new opportunities. In 1945, Sanematsu returned to U.C. Berkeley and earned a secondary teaching credential. His advisors discouraged him from pursuing a teaching career because he was becoming increasingly blind, and there were, in fact, no Asian Americans teaching in the California public schools in the late 1940s. Sanematsu decided to earn a certification for special education to work with blind students, and in 1958 he received his first full-time position at Camden High School in Campbell, California. As part of his training, Sanematsu learned Braille and how to use a cane for independent travel. To test himself, he went alone to New York City. He traveled throughout the city and to neighboring states, taking buses, trains, and taxis. He visited many schools for the blind in the region as well. Sanematsu retired from a successful teaching career in 1982. He discusses the condition of blindness and the importance of developing a sense of independence.

> The blind are not *deprived of* experience; they are *separated from* experience. The way to master blindness is to use this powerful inner light to find your way back to—not away from—the outside world. . . . The handicap of blindness is not sensory deprivation but the deprivation of exile to a separated world.   (p. 176)

536. Sano, Iwao Peter (1924-). *One Thousand Days in Siberia: The Odyssey of a Japanese-American POW*. Lincoln, Nebraska: University of Nebraska Press, 1997. 210 pages; photographs; illustrations; map. ISBN: 080324262x.

> **Notes:** Paperback published Lincoln: University of Nebraska Press Bison Books, 1999. ISBN: 0803292600.

> **Abstract:** Sano writes of his experiences as a Japanese POW of the Soviet Union after World War II. He was born in 1924, the son of Japanese immigrants running a farm in Imperial Valley, California. He was raised as an American citizen whose first language was English. At the age of fifteen, he was sent back to Japan to be adopted by a childless aunt and uncle. He was finishing his high school education and planning to go to college when he was drafted by the Japanese army and sent to officer's training in Manchuria. Several months later, the war ended, and his commanding officer marched his troop of trainees into a Soviet prison camp. They were soon sent to Siberia and imprisoned for the next three years. Sano describes his life as a POW. He worked in a factory, a coal mine, and on a farm. He suffered frostbite, near death from malnutrition, and malaria. When he was finally shipped home in 1948, he went to work for the U.S. Occupation Army as a translator and interpreter. In 1952, he cut his ties with his adoptive parents and went back to the United States to live with his parents and brothers and sisters, only to find that, during the war, U.S. authorities had obtained a picture of him in his Japanese high school uniform and mistook it for an army uniform. His father had been subsequently arrested and sent to a camp in Bismarck, North Dakota. By the time Sano returned to California, the family had been reunited and was living in Palo Alto, California. Sano had lost his U.S. citizenship because he served in the Japanese army, but he and his wife, also Japanese, were eventually naturalized.

537. Santiago, Esmeralda. *Almost a Woman*. Reading, Massachusetts: Perseus Books, 1998. 313 pages. ISBN: 0738200433.

> **Notes:** Published in paperback New York: Vintage Books, 1999. ISBN: 037570521x.

> **Abstract:** Esmeralda Santiago was born in Puerto Rico and came to New York with her mother and six brothers and sisters in 1961. Her parents had never been married and her father did not come with them. He eventually settled down with another woman in Puerto Rico. Santiago's mother had two more lovers and four

more children. She never married and never went to church, but insisted that her daughters be properly married in a Catholic cathedral when the time came. Santiago, the eldest of the children, excelled academically. She was accepted into the Performing Arts High School and prepared to go on to college. Following gradua- tion, she got a small part in *Up the Down Staircase*, a film directed by Robert Mulligan. She then decided that instead of going to col- lege, she would look for acting and modeling jobs. When she found none, she began to work at clerical jobs and to take classes on a part-time basis at Manhattan Community College. One of her professors brought her attention to a production that was holding auditions, and she got the part of Sonia in *Babu*, a play being per- formed by Children's Theater International. The company played in the New York area and toured throughout New England. It was not until after high school that Santiago had her first relationships with men. Although she was strongly attracted to many, she was held back either mentally or physically by her mother. The book ends when her current lover, an older man to whom she is devot- ed, asks her to go with him to Florida, where he will seek medical help. Santiago, now aged twenty-one, refuses because she knows her mother would never agree to let her go off with a man to whom she is not married.

538. Santos, Bienvenido N. *Memory's Fictions: A Personal History*. Quezon City, Philippines: New Day Publishers, 1993. 268 pages. ISBN: 9711005360.

Abstract: Noted English-language Filipino writer Bienvenido Santos was born in Lubao in the Philippines. He was writing poetry at the age of ten and was eighty-one when he finished his autobiography in 1992. In 1941, at the age of thirty, married and with three children, Santos left the Philippines on a government scholarship to study at the University of Illinois, Urbana- Champagne. He arrived in San Francisco in October, shortly before the Japanese attack on Pearl Harbor and was unable to return home until 1946 when the war and Japanese occupation of the Philippines had both come to an end. While in the United States, Santos also attended Columbia and Harvard Universities and was sent by the Philippine government-in-exile on a tour of twenty-two colleges and universities throughout the United States to speak on Filipino life and customs. When Santos finally returned to Albay and his family, he taught in the schools and was appointed vice-president and then president of Legazpi College. When he accepted a Rockefeller Foundation grant to study at the University of Iowa Writers Workshop, the family moved back to the United States. He subsequently received a Guggenheim Fellowship and was made a member of the University of Iowa faculty. The Santos family remained in Iowa City off and on until 1972, when they decided to return to the Philippines. However, because of the declaration of martial law by President Marcos and the Philippine government's confiscation of their property, they decided to stay in the United States. Santos was offered the Distinguished Writer in Residence position and a professorship at Wichita State University, and the couple remained in Kansas until Santos's wife's death ten years later, in 1981. After his retirement, Santos returned to the Philippines, spending six months of each year there. He is grateful to have had the opportunity to "write about the Filipino away from home, a rich and satisfying source of material that had to be written, and about which not many . . . have written" (p. 227).

539. Santos, John Phillip. *Places Left Unfinished at the Time of Creation.* New York, New York: Viking, 1999. 284 pages; photographs. ISBN: 0670868086.

Notes: Published in paperback New York: Penguin, 2000. ISBN: 0140292020.

Abstract: John Phillip Santos, a writer and television producer, tells the story of his family. The apparent suicide of his paternal grandfather, an event that takes many years and much prodding of reluctant elderly relatives to uncover, is its focal point. In an effort to explain and find meaning in this suicide, Santos goes back in history to the pre-Columbian civilizations in Mexico and the Spanish explorers. He studies Mexican mythology and religious beliefs; the many characters that peopled both sides of his family and their influence while they lived and after they died; the Mexican culture that was preserved long after it was clear that the family would not be returning to the mother country; and the tendency to depression and withdrawal that has plagued many generations of his family. The newspaper article that reported finding the body of his grandfather was entitled "All in Vain." Santos explains his work and final conclusions, which he discovers are anything but conclusive, as follows:

> Since learning of the mystery of Juan Jose's death . . . now twenty-five years ago in journals, letters, poems, and stories, in conversations with family, journeys in Texas and throughout Mexico, I have sought to defy those three words, with little success. I wanted to tell a single story, bound

together like an old *amate* codex, to carry the
saga of Mexico into the story of Texas, and into
the story of our family, walking like a tribe of pil-
grims out of a tattered past of conquests,
upheavals, revolutions, and migrations.

(pp. 259-260)

540. Saralegui, Cristina. *Cristina! My Life As a Blonde*. Translated
from the Spanish by Margaret Sayers Peden. New York, New
York: Warner Books, 1998. 273 pages; photographs. ISBN:
044652008x.

Notes: Also published in the original Spanish. New York: Warner
Books, 1998. ISBN: 0446522589 : 0446674389 (293 pages).

Abstract: Television personality Cristina Saralegui describes an
idyllic childhood growing up in pre-Castro Cuba. All four of her
grandparents were Basque. The Saralegui family had begun a
magazine empire in Cuba, and after the family moved to Miami in
1960, Saralegui's father published *Bohemia Libre* to counter
Bohemia, which had been taken over by Castro. He later restarted
another Cuban magazine, *Vanidades*, and it was with *Vanidades*
that Saralegui began her journalism career. Energetic and ambitious, she moved on to the new Spanish language edition of
Cosmopolitan, Cosmopolitan en Español. She later became editor,
changing the image of the "Cosmo girl" from one preoccupied
with sexual matters to one intent on self-improvement. From
journalism, Saralegui went into television. She became host of *El
Show de Cristina*, a Spanish talk show on Univision Network, the
leading Spanish-language television network in the United States.
While she had been labeled by American schoolmates as an outsider because of her accent and upbringing, she found that her
Hispanic audience was unhappy with her because she was too
white, and it took about six months to gain their acceptance. She
describes the topics, routine, challenges, triumphs, and trials of
work in television. Saralegui views her program as a public service. She confronts issues such as AIDS, gay marriage, domestic
abuse, as well as more sensational topics such as multiple personality disorder. Entertainment is also important, and her guests
have included many prominent Hispanic entertainers. Saralegui
started the Up With Life! foundation to raise money to fight AIDS.
She writes about her second husband, Marcos, their three children,
and the importance to her of family.

541. Scales-Trent, Judy. *Notes of a White Black Woman: Race, Color, Community.* University Park, Pennsylvania: Pennsylvania State University Press, 1995. 198 pages. ISBN: 027101430x.

   Notes: Published in paperback University Park: Pennsylvania State University Press, 2001. ISBN: 0271021241.

   Abstract: Scales-Trent's work is a collection of essays on a number of topics. She began writing after sharing with her friends her thoughts, written in the form of a diary, on her condition as a black woman with white skin. She writes of the pain of an unclear racial identity, of her feeling of not belonging anywhere, and of the healing that took place as she wrote about and shared her experiences. Although many of Scales-Trent's family members are light-skinned, Scales-Trent is aware of only one white ancestor, her great-grandfather. The family history records that he married her great-grandmother and together they had ten children. The evidence is that he loved his family and took good care of them. Therefore, to reject her connection to the white race would be to reject her great-grandfather, whom she has no reason to despise. Scales-Trent also writes about her careers as a school teacher, a civil rights attorney, and an academic. As a school teacher, one principal felt he should make a public announcement that Scales-Trent was black to prevent any misunderstanding about her race. As an academic, Scales-Trent confronted the double-edged sword of affirmative action: the misapprehension that you didn't have to work to earn your position and no matter how hard you work, it is never enough to prove yourself. On the matter of racial understanding, Scales-Trent proposes that African-American culture be taught in the schools in the same way that Spanish, French, and German are often taught, that is by discussing language, customs, practices, food, and clothing and by field trips. She imagines a country where everyone is bicultural and bilingual. She writes, "And why is it that we look so hard for sameness when we are, each and every one of us, so different from each other? And why is it that we find it so hard to find sameness, when we are, in so many ways, so much the same" (p. 32).

542. See, Lisa. *On Gold Mountain.* New York, New York: St. Martin's Press, 1995. 394 pages; photographs; maps. ISBN: 0312119976.

   Notes: Published in paperback, New York: Vintage, 1996 as *On Gold Mountain: The One Hundred Year Odyssey of My Chinese-American Family.* ISBN: 0679768521.

Abstract: Lisa See, who is only one-eighth Chinese, considers herself to be first and foremost of Chinese descent. She writes the history of her family, beginning with her great-great grandfather, who came to California in 1866 to tend to the Chinese workers on the railroad using herbal medicine. He eventually went back to China, but his fourth son, Fong See, came to California, the Gold Mountain. He started a business in Sacramento selling herbs to his Chinese customers and handmade underwear to prostitutes. He married a Caucasian women via legal contract, as interracial marriages were against the law. Together, he and his wife made their way to Chinatown in Los Angeles, where the family left the underwear business and became antique and curio dealers. The couple had five children, the fourth of which was Lisa See's grandfather. Fong See was the most prominent merchant in Chinatown for many decades, and throughout the century, he and his family owned and operated various branches of the F. Suie On Company in Southern California. The company was supplied with goods acquired during numerous trips to China before the country became inaccessible under Communism. The See family was unique in that they were interracial from the start, and increasingly so with each passing generation. Yet they adhered strongly to their Chinese background, remaining mostly in Chinatown and New China City in Los Angeles. Their way of surviving in a decidedly non-interracial society was to always put the family first, thus managing to avoid estrangement, despite years of geographical separation or severely clashing viewpoints. They also maintained surprisingly close ties with family both in China and the United States. See herself comes in only towards the end of the book, but she uses the stories of her grandparents, parents, aunts, uncles, and countless cousins to tell her own. She explains herself in the passage in which she introduces her fiancé to her family:

> But he also needed to pass another "test": to step into those dark, murky musty rooms [of the family store] and touch and *feel* . . . and finally to fall in love in his own way with this *stuff*. A few weeks later, Dick proposed. Very soon after that, his father asked my mother something along the lines of "Is Lisa stable? Does she understand about family?" And my mother could answer, without a hint of irony or falsehood, "Family means everything to Lisa."   (p. 347)

543. Shabazz, Bakari. *Coming Clean: A Tale Told from the Heart.* [Missouri]: Bird in Paradise Publishing, 1999. 306 pages. ISBN: 0967351804.

Abstract: Bakari Shabazz writes about his teenage years from fourteen to seventeen, during the years 1968 to 1971. He was a student at Martin Luther King, Jr. Junior High School and Central High School in Kansas City. In junior high, Shabazz had begun earning good grades and taking an interest in his studies, but as he turned fourteen and was transferred to King, he started skipping school, spending time in the streets, committing crimes, and taking and selling drugs and alcohol. He witnessed rapes and participated in shootings, fights, purse snatching, and other crimes. He describes his growing numbness to violence and cruelty, writing that he was "losing sensitivity for people and situations that I should have shown more care and concern, [sic] for and about" (p. 138). Shabazz's mother was a school teacher and his relationship with her was distant. His father worked as a janitor. He was loving and concerned when he was sober, but became angry and violent when he was drunk. Shabazz remembers many times that he tried to stand between his mother and father, taking on the role of her protector. He felt bitter because his mother never offered him any protection or support in return. Shabazz believed that he was the unwanted child in the family. Shabazz ends his story when, at the age of seventeen, he awaits the arrival of his father to pick him up, once again, from juvenile detention. The narrative ends with the promise that in the future Shabazz will convert to Islam and stay away from drugs, alcohol, and crime.

544. Shakoor, Jordana Y. *Civil Rights Childhood.* Jackson, Mississippi: University of Mississippi Press, 1999. 216 pages; photographs. ISBN: 157806192x.

Abstract: Jordana Shakoor's childhood was shaped by her father's involvement in the Civil Rights Movement. She tells his story as part of her own. Her father, Andrew Jordan, and mother, Arella Love, both grew up on plantations in Mississippi. Although both families were sharecroppers, Arella's family worked on a plantation owned by people who were fair and treated the tenant farmers with relative respect. Andrew Jordan's family, on the other hand, worked for landlords who kept as much of the profits as they could, leaving very little to the tenant farmers who did the work. Jordan was determined to get off the farm and had plans to be a teacher. At the age of twenty-one, however, he had not yet graduated from high school and was drafted into the army to fight in the "colored unit" in Korea. Jordan completed his tour of duty, returned to Mississippi, passed his G.E.D., and attended Mississippi Vocational College on funds from the GI Bill. While at college, Jordan was introduced to the Student Nonviolent Coordinating Committee and became involved in the Civil Rights Movement. By the time he graduated, he had married and started a family, and he also accomplished his goal of becoming a teacher by getting a job in Greenwood, which was about fifty miles from home. Jordan stayed active in civil rights and helped to form a local chapter of the NAACP. The family livelihood, however, was lost when Jordan was fired because he and his wife had attempted to register to vote. In 1964, no longer able to make a living, Jordan moved his family to Toledo, Ohio. They found life there, while not free from racism, much easier. Registering to vote was simple and without repercussions, the children played with white children for the first time in their lives, and Mr. Jordan was able to resume his teaching career. Three of the five Jordan sisters graduated from college. Shakoor graduated from Ohio State University and owns a consulting and management training firm.

545. Sharpton, Al (1954-). *Go and Tell Pharaoh: The Autobiography of the Reverend Al Sharpton*. Written with Anthony Walton. New York, New York: Doubleday, 1996. 276 pages; photographs. ISBN: 0385475837.

Abstract: Al Sharpton writes that he hopes his book will

> . . . shed at least a little light on one man's experience at the front lines of racial and ethnic conflict in our society, and in so doing contribute to the sort of understanding that will allow all of us to forgive each other what has happened here and begin the real work of providing a just and prosperous society for all our citizens . . . and securing the as-of-now-uncertain future of our children and grandchildren and beyond.   (p. 7)

Born in 1954, Sharpton began preaching at the age of four. In first grade he was signing his school assignments as Reverend Alfred Sharpton, and at ten he was an ordained and licensed minister of the Pentecostal Church. His early heroes were Adam Clayton Powell and Malcolm X. Later he would look to Jesse Jackson as a mentor and guide. Early on, Sharpton became involved with the Civil Rights Movement. He worked with Operation Bread Basket run by the Southern Christian Leadership Council. He later broke from that organization and began his own National Youth

Movement. Singer James Brown became interested in Sharpton's work, and together they organized a concert in Brooklyn to raise money for Sharpton's organization. Brown took a fatherly interest in Sharpton and took him on tour. While traveling with Brown, Sharpton organized new National Youth Movement chapters, raised money, and continued to preach at churches across the country. Sharpton's high media visibility and his direct-action tactics have placed him in the middle of many controversies. In his book, Sharpton describes a number of events from his point of view and refutes the accusations that have been brought against him. Some of his most prominent work has been, as he describes it, to place a value on the lives of African Americans, most notably young black men. In describing events that took place in the New York City neighborhoods of Bensonhurst, Howard Beach, and Crown Heights, Sharpton writes that "young black men . . . lived in a society where, by all appearance, their lives were not worth a dime" (p. 166). By insuring that individuals receive due process within the judicial process, Sharpton shows that their lives are valuable. Sharpton describes his campaigns for public office in 1992 and 1994 and discusses black nationalism and the growing division between blacks and Jews. Sharpton writes that he is "only interested in justice," and that he wants

> every little kid to have a chance to become whatever he or she can imagine, I want to help get my people out from under the grip of Pharaoh—the blind and arrogant indifference to their lives and hopes by individuals and institutions in the country of their births that has maimed, for no reason, so many for so long. (p. 270)

546. Short, Bobby. *Bobby Short: The Life and Times of a Saloon Singer*. Written with Robert Mackintosh. New York, New York: Clarkson Potter/Publishers, 1995. 265 pages; photographs. ISBN: 0517595648.

Abstract: Bobby Short began entertaining at the piano while still a child. At eleven, he went to Chicago, where he performed as a singer and pianist for nearly two years. He returned home to Danville, Illinois, to finish high school and to rest. At seventeen, he was back in Chicago singing and playing at the Dome. Short describes his long musical career in Los Angeles, New York, Paris, and London. He discusses the artists he admired and worked with, the club owners and promoters, his audience, and his style. His first New York engagement was an unsuccessful four-week opening act at the Blue Angel. He subsequently left New York to work in Los Angeles, where he was well received at the Haig. He polished his skills and developed his personal style during a long stay in Paris and then returned to New York, where he stayed for the rest of his career. About Paris, Short writes, "For a black entertainer, Paris was a symbol of hope. The race problem was minimal, and performers were judged—glory be—on performance" (p. 134). Toward the end of the 1960s, the audiences in nightclubs and supper clubs began to dwindle. It was at this seemingly bleak point that Short's career took off with performances at Lincoln Center, Town Hall and Carnegie Hall and on Broadway. In 1968, he began his longest engagement, performing nightly at the Café Carlyle. He celebrated his twenty-fifth anniversary at the café in 1993.

547. Shuffer, George Macon, Jr. (1923-). *My Journey to Betterment: An Autobiography*. New York, New York: Vantage Press, 1999. 190 pages; photographs. ISBN: 0533126541.

Abstract: Shuffer begins his life story by describing his colorful family history. The paternal grandfathers of both his mother and father were white slave owners, and both his mother and father's families ended up in Vistula, Texas, following emancipation. After some years, for reasons related to their successful farming and ranching enterprises, they were targeted by the Ku Klux Klan. Told that the local police establishment would not protect the families, they left everything behind and scattered. Shuffer's mother and father, already married, moved to Palestine, Texas, where Shuffer was born. Convinced that, because of poverty, racism and segregation, he had no hopes of attending college and bettering himself, Shuffer left home at the age of seventeen to join the army. His military career spanned thirty-five years, and he achieved the rank of brigadier general. Racist America was accurately reflected in the army during his earliest years. Shuffer recalls donning his "tailor-cut officer's uniform" and thinking, "At last, I am an officer and gentleman of the United States." But upon attending his first officers' call he found that the seating was segregated. The colonel addressing the group began his remarks, "Gentlemen and Colored second lieutenants!" Shuffer writes, "Disappointment, frustration and disgust so crowded my mind that I heard only scattered fragments of his thirty-minute speech" (p. 49). After serving as a much-decorated officer during World War II, the Korean War, and the Vietnam Conflict, Shuffer was sent to Panama, where he introduced his Equal Opportunity and Race Harmony program. This successful program directed that all barracks, activities, and platoons be integrated. In the early 1970s he also introduced the program in Germany. It was so successful that he expanded it to include business establishments surrounding the army base. Establishments were told that no business operating under a policy of segregation would be patronized by any member of the armed forces. Shuffer was in line for a promotion to full general, but his career was cut short by a degenerative bone condition. He retired from the army in 1975. A devout Catholic, Shuffer then began to study and train to become a permanent deacon in the Roman Catholic Church. He was ordained in 1977 in El Paso, Texas. Shuffer is the father of eleven children. He and Cecilia, his wife of over forty years, whose family history he also provides, met while he was stationed in Arizona.

548. Simmons, George W. *A Determined Man: An Autobiography*. Frankfort, Kentucky: Kentucky Color Publishing, 1997. 160 pages; photographs. ISBN: 0965165310.

Abstract: George Simmons's mother and father bought two houses and forty acres of land at Squirrel Lake in Mississippi when he was about two years old. Simmons describes his childhood growing up on this land. He recalls various activities, including baseball, dating, school, and hunting. Simmons attended school away from home in Tennessee and Mississippi, but had to quit when his father became ill. Besides farming, Simmons took any other jobs he could find. He describes working on the railroad with men that acted like "lower animals" (p. 32) and were treated like lower animals. Despite his unhappiness with his work and frustration at not being able to continue his education, he continued to help his family and did not graduate from high school until he was twenty-five. Simmons then taught school for a few years before enrolling at Kentucky State College in 1937. He worked hard at his studies, but found that he was not well-enough prepared for college to succeed. In 1942, Simmons was drafted and spent the next three-and-a-half years in the army. He was sent to North Africa, where he worked with the medical corps as a clerk typist. After his discharge, Simmons was determined to make something of himself professionally and to work for social change. He returned to college in 1948 and graduated two years later at the age of thirty-eight. He became a teacher of vocational agriculture, not only teaching classes, but visiting with farmers and advising them on methods and procedures. He also worked in state government as a child welfare worker, an employment counselor, and an employment advisor to prisoners on parole. Simmons retired from his government position in 1973, frustrated with the corruption and lack of opportunities for advancement. He began to volunteer at a local hospital, with the Senior Citizen Agency, and he participated in many other community activities. Simmons writes about his years of work, his views on the community, his marriage, building a house, and his ordeal with colon cancer.

549. Simmons, Joseph. *It's Like That: A Spiritual Memoir*. Written with Curtis L. Taylor. New York, New York: St. Martin's Press, 2000. 158 pages; photographs. ISBN: 0312204671.

Abstract: Joseph Simmons, better known as Run of the rap group Run D.M.C., was barely a teenager when the group rapped its way to the top of the charts with platinum albums and sold-out concert tours. After the release of Run D.M.C.'s wildly-successful third album, *Raising Hell*, Simmons began to experience depression. He was addicted to drugs, alcohol, women, and money and he wanted more of everything. He reached his lowest point when Run D.M.C.'s fourth album failed to produce the anticipated popular acclaim. A fifth album did worse, concerts stopped selling out, a movie project failed, Simmons was accused of rape, and his first wife took their children and left him. He decided to visit Zoe Ministries and started attending regularly. By 1994, he had become a minister. Simmons describes his spiritual renewal, provides his rules for life, gives examples of his faith and enthusiasm and his new way of living. He has remarried, started a new family, regained his wealth, and continues a successful performing career with Run D.M.C.

550. Simms, Lois Averetta. *A Chalk and Chalkboard Career in Carolina*. New York, New York: Vantage Press, 1995. 268 pages; photographs. ISBN: 0533113903.

Abstract: Lois Simms devoted her life to teaching in the public school system of Charleston County, South Carolina. She begins her narrative with her earliest experiences as a teacher. She provides background on the various schools in which she taught, most notably the historic Avery Normal Institute and Laing Industrial High School. Simms took summer college sessions each year and completed her M.A. at Howard University the same year that Thurgood Marshall received an honorary degree for his work on *Brown v. Board of Education*. Simms notes that she learned from her students as well as they from her. It was through their influence that she developed a black literature component for her English classes, creating a reading list with the names of authors provided by her pupils. She writes, "Many times since my career has ended, I have wondered about the word *teach*. I think now that the student-teacher relationship is a shared learning experience in terms of knowledge (subject matter) and human behavior" (p. 47). She recalls with fondness many of the students she taught and describes the ways in which they have succeeded in life, hoping to convince the reader of the value of the public school system. Along with her personal experiences, Simms comments on the significant social progress she has witnessed, including the improvement in conditions for African-American teachers.

551. Singh, Surjit (1921-1995). *From Punjab to New York: A Reflective Journey*. New Delhi: A.P.H. Publishing Corp., 1999. 303 pages. ISBN: 817024966x.

Abstract: Surjit Singh was born in the village of Jamki in Punjab. He moved to New Delhi in 1946, just before the British division of India, Nehru's declaration of independence from Britain, and the terrible riots that took place in India and Pakistan following both of those events. A Jat Sikh, Singh attended Khalsa College, a Sikh religious school. He first began work in libraries at the Punjab Public Library, associated with Punjab University, and later moved to the Central Secretariat Library in New Delhi. Singh left India in 1948 to attend library school at the University of Michigan. Following graduation he took a four-month internship at the United Nation's Library and ended up working there until his retirement in 1981. Singh returned to India in 1958 to marry Dr. Narindar Singh. He spent six years in Addis Ababa, Ethiopia setting up a new U.N. library. He returned to New York in 1964, where he resumed his duties at the newly constructed Dag Hammerskjold Library, a gift to the U.N. from the Ford Foundation. Singh retired from the U.N. in 1981 to take on the responsibilities of a full-time house husband. As he narrates the details of his life, Singh also discusses the history of Punjab, as well as the political, religious, and social upheavals of India and Pakistan. He writes about the development of the United Nations, those who have led that body, and the organization's goals and accomplishments. Singh reviews the events of world history, wars within nations, between nations, and the often-harmful interference of powerful countries in the matters of weaker and poorer countries. Singh describes his vision for world peace and analyzes the role of the various religions in maintaining or hindering that peace.

552. Singleton, William Henry (1835-1938). *Recollections of My Slavery Days*. Introduction and annotations by Katherine Mellen Charron and David S. Cecelski. Chapel Hill, North Carolina: Academic Affairs Library, University of North Carolina at Chapel Hill, 2000.

> http://docsouth.unc.edu/neh/singleton/singleton.sgml
> http://docsouth.unc.edu/neh/singleton/singleton.html
>
> **Notes:** Documenting the American South (Project).

553. Sings-Alone, Grandfather Duncan. *See* Duncan, C. W.

554. Skinner, Daniel T. *Ustaz Aswad = Black Professor: A Literary Memoir*. [Baltimore, Maryland]: D. T. Skinner, 1996. 173 pages; photographs. ISBN: none.

> **Abstract:** Daniel Skinner was born in Boston, Massachusetts, in 1916. He attended integrated schools and graduated first in his high-school class of 680 students. His father was a Jehovah's Witness, and his mother was a Methodist. Skinner and all of the other children in the family converted to Roman Catholicism under the influence of their eldest sister. Skinner attended Harvard University and received a master's degree from Boston College. An expert in eight languages, he began his teaching career at Virginia State College in the French department. He later taught Spanish at Dillard University in New Orleans. During World War II, Skinner was drafted into the army. He attended Officers Candidate School and Military Intelligence School and was sent to Europe in 1945. Once, while on active duty in the United States, Skinner was issued a first class train ticket by the army to get to his next assignment, but was ordered by the train company to move to the Jim Crow coach. When he refused, he was imprisoned overnight. "Good Lord! What a War to spread Democracy abroad while practicing Racism at home!" (p. 61). Following the war, Skinner spent the next thirty-five-and-a-half years teaching at Morgan State College in Baltimore, Maryland. While at Morgan State, Skinner took a leave to return to Harvard and earn his Ph.D. He also spent a year with his wife and two sons serving the U.S. State Department in Europe. He writes that because he could not act as an apologist for racial conditions in the United States, he was not given a permanent appointment. Skinner retired from Morgan State in 1981. He held post-retirement teaching positions at Sojourner-Douglass College and Coppin State College. During his years of teaching, Skinner devel-

oped an appreciation for black studies and Négritude. He believes that African-American students should have the opportunity for an Afrocentric education rather than the more typical Eurocentric education. Although he remains a faithful Catholic, Skinner gave his memoir an Arabic title and quotes generously from *al Quran* because he wishes to "ally Black Americans with Muslims of the third World since many of our African forebears knew Arabic and *al Quran*" (p. 129). Skinner's wife died in 1995. As he concludes his book, he looks to his own final years and death.

555. Skolnick, Sharon Okee-Chee and Manny Skolnick. *Where Courage Is like a Wild Horse: The World of an Indian Orphanage*. Lincoln, Nebraska: University of Nebraska Press, 1997. 148 pages. ISBN: 0803242638.

Abstract: Skolnick, a visual artist, describes the twenty-six chapters of her book as photographs resurrecting memories of the year she and her younger sister Jackie spent at the Murrow Indian Orphanage near Muskogee, Oklahoma. They were the only Apache children. Most of the others were from Oklahoma tribes: Cherokee, Osage, Delaware, and Kiowa. Because her year at Murrow was painful, Skolnick preferred to keep her memories at bay: "To complete the ritual of forgetting, I'd send memories of those long, stifling afternoons right up in smoke. But that is something you want to be careful about, killing memories. . . . I've just turned a corner and found some of mine. The Murrow memories" (p. 1). Skolnick, who suffered from a severe disfiguring skin condition, describes her sense of isolation and her eagerness to fight in defense of her honor and to protect her sister. She writes about becoming lifelong friends with a girl she had mistakenly singled out as one of her enemies. When this friend told her a story from Kiowa tradition, Skolnick was inspired to interpret it into a picture which won a contest. This event, along with meeting the famous Native American artist Richard West, empowered Skolnick to view herself as an artist. At Murrow, prospective parents would often come by to visit children. One day, Skolnick and her sister were visited by Lynette Reeves, who took a special interest in Skolnick because of her artistic abilities. Reeves, who was half Delaware, also seemed to appreciate Skolnick's fighting nature. Unlike many of the adults with whom the girls were in contact, Reeves was proud of her Indian heritage and was full of information about Native accomplishments and traditions. On her second visit with the girls, Reeves gave Skolnick her Indian name from the Delaware language, Okee-Chee, which means Blue Bird, after the blue bird that Skolnick had drawn for her. Reeves and her husband did adopt the girls, and in an afterword, Skolnick gives a brief synopsis of their life with them. Following high school, Skolnick was accepted with a full scholarship into the Institute of American Indian Arts in Santa Fe. She writes, "I found myself at the heart of a cultural and intellectual ferment unlike anything I'd experienced before. I learned that being Indian was a prideful thing" (p. 148).

556. Sloan, John Steward (1918-). *Survival! A Purple Heart Tuskegee Airman*. Danbury, Connecticut: Rutledge Books, 2000. 414 pages; photographs. ISBN: 1582440824.

Abstract: John S. Sloan grew up in South Louisville, Kentucky. He attended George C. Moore School, "the sole colored school in South Louisville" (p. 44). Sloan describes himself as a reclusive adolescent, happy to be spending his time with books. He graduated from high school in 1935 and attended Kentucky State Industrial College with plans to be a lawyer. As the U.S. entered World War II, however, Sloan began keeping close track of the NAACP fight to open up flight training to African-American soldiers. He volunteered for the Air Corps as soon as the opportunity presented itself. Although he had a number of hurdles to overcome, he was at last accepted into the Air Corps and received orders to report to Tuskegee Air Base in October of 1942. When his training was complete and Sloan had graduated as a second lieutenant, he and his wife moved to his next assignment at Selfridge Field, near Detroit, Michigan. While there, Sloan was unfairly charged with buzzing and low-altitude acrobatics and was confined to his quarters for nearly two months. He never knew who reported him or any of the details of the charge. He describes the period leading up to and including the court martial as a kind of nightmare of which he remembers little. Shortly after he was cleared of charges, he and his company were sent to Taranto Bay, along the coast of Italy. On his seventh mission, in March 1944, Sloan was hit by gunfire and made a crash landing. The remainder of his autobiography deals with his hospitalization, treatment, and recovery. He returned to the United States in June of 1944, but was not released from the hospital until the spring of 1945. While convalescing, Sloan enrolled in classes at Fisk University and was executive secretary for the Nashville NAACP. After his discharge, he and his wife moved to Chicago, where he worked for the Urban League. Sloan's other career activities included founding and editing a newspaper, working as a counselor, and being involved in politics. Sloan is a poet and he has included a number of his poems in this work.

557. Smith, Amanda (1837-1915). *An Autobiography: The Story of the Lord's Dealings with Mrs. Amanda Smith, the Colored Evangelist, Containing an Account of Her Life Work of Faith, and Her Travels in America, England, Ireland, Scotland, India, and Africa, As an Independent Missionary.* Written with J. M. Thoburn (1836-1922). New York Public Library Digital Library Collections. Digital Schomburg. New York, New York: New York Public Library, 1997.

> http://digilib.nypl.org:80/dynaweb/digs/wwm97264/@Generic%5F%5FBookView

> **Notes:** Also available Chapel Hill: Academic Affairs Library, University of North Carolina at Chapel Hill, 1999. Documenting the American South (Project). http://metalab.unc.edu/docsouth/smitham/smith.html.

> Available in paper as *An Autobiography: The Story of the Lord's Dealings with Mrs. Amanda Smith, the Colored Evangelist.* New York: Oxford University Press, 1988. ISBN: 0195052617.

558. Smith, David (b. 1784). *Biography of Rev. David Smith of the A.M.E. Church Being a Complete History, Embracing over Sixty Years' Labor in the Advancement of the Redeemer's Kindgom on Earth: Including "The History of the Origin and Development of Wilberforce University."* Chapel Hill, North Carolina: Academic Affairs Library, University of North Carolina at Chapel Hill, 1999.

> http://metalab.unc.edu/docsouth/neh/dsmith/dsmith.html

> **Notes:** Documenting the American South (Project).

559. Smith, James L. *Autobiography of James L. Smith Including Also, Reminiscences of Slave Life, Recollections of the War, Education of Freedmen, Causes of the Exodus, Etc.* Chapel Hill, North Carolina: Academic Affairs Library, University of North Carolina at Chapel Hill, 2000.

> http://docsouth.unc.edu/neh/smithj/smithj.sgml
> http://docsouth.unc.edu/neh/smithj/smithj.html

> **Notes:** Documenting the American South (Project).

560. Smith, Margaret Charles (b. 1906) and Linda Janet Holmes. *Listen To Me Good: The Life Story of an Alabama Midwife*. Women and Health Series. Columbus, Ohio: Ohio State University Press, 1996. 178 pages. ISBN: 0814207006 : 0814207014.

Abstract: Margaret Charles Smith, born in 1906, was a midwife. Smith started out by assisting relatives and friends with births. She often worked with midwife Ella Anderson, whom she credits with teaching her everything she knows about delivering babies. When the state of Alabama started a certification program for lay (with no formal medical training) midwives, Smith was encouraged by a local doctor to take up this calling. Her formal training consisted of three Saturday morning workshops and a two-week course at the Tuskegee Institute. The midwives were given strict guidelines to follow, and their traditional methods, which included uses of particular teas and roots, were forbidden. Smith remembers the extreme poverty in which many women lived in Alabama's Greene County. She describes one household as having a pig in one corner, a goat in another, the mother and father sleeping in one bed, and a young woman trying to deliver her eighth child in another. Smith would see her mothers through labor and delivery, staying until mother and child were both stable. The work was exhausting. Racism was always part of the system: black midwives were not allowed to deliver white babies and pay was sporadic and always ridiculously low. The Alabama Lay Licensing Program lasted into the late seventies, when it was abruptly terminated. Smith was able to work until 1981. Janet Holmes provides historical material, including the history of the practice of midwifery in Alabama. Despite the low status of the midwife within the medical profession, Smith writes, "I'm worth millions of dollars for what I've done. I thought I was doing a big thing. I was proud of it. The lives that I've saved, going to deliver all these babies, still I got something to be thankful for. The children have grown so. . . . I am thankful, yeah" (p. 156).

561. Smith, Otis Milton. *Looking beyond Race: The Life of Otis Milton Smith*. Written with Mary M. Stolberg. Foreword by Vernon E. Jordan, Jr. Detroit, Michigan: Wayne State University Press, 2000. 257 pages; photographs; index. ISBN: 081432939x.

Abstract: Otis Smith was born in 1922 in Memphis, Tennessee. He and his older brother Hamilton lived with their mother. A half-hearted student, Smith dropped out of high school to work full time and supplement the meager family income. He later graduated from high school and received a full scholarship to

Morehouse College, but delayed his enrollment until he had earned money for living expenses. Smith was selected for a patronage job by the Democratic Party machine and given a position at the Game and Fish Division of the State Department of Conservation in Nashville. Although Smith was thankful for the work, he was not fooled by the party's motives. He, like many other African Americans working at the largesse of the party, chose to join the NAACP as a way of taking an independent stand. After World War II and time in the military, Smith attended Syracuse University, where he studied journalism. He then attended Catholic University Law School and passed both the Washington, D.C., and Michigan bar exams. Smith traces his legal career, from work in criminal law to an appointment as chairman of the State of Michigan Public Service Commission. From this position he was nominated and elected to state auditor general, and then to the Michigan Supreme Court, where he served two terms. Following this, Smith joined the legal staff at General Motors, where he was general counsel until his retirement in 1983. Smith was active in the NAACP and Urban League. He writes about the progress made by African Americans during the 1960s and 1970s. He notes that this progress has since slowed down and in some cases gone backwards, and he criticizes those who, with short sightedness, claim that all is well: "[M]any whites have dealt with the nation's racial problems by simply denying that they exist . . ." (p. 205). He rejects the notion, however, that there have been no advances at all. To claim this, he says, is to deny the hard work and sacrifices of so many. He maintains that it is important to acknowledge the tremendous gains of the Civil Rights Movement, but to admit that more needs to be done.

562. Smyers, David D. *The Hustler's Handbook: Reflections of the Insane, Known As the Mack Game, and an Escape from the Wrath.* Point Richmond, California: Sur-Mount Publishers, 1999. 149 pages. ISBN: 0967351707.

Abstract: David Smyers was thirteen when he went to the store to buy dog food. After he accused the salesclerk of overcharging him, the clerk hit him in the head. Smyers hit back with his can and then left, throwing an empty bottle at the store as he retreated. When this incident was reported to his school, the administration decided to put him in the troubled-student class. Smyers's parents took him out of the school, but no other school would accept him. Smyers describes a life haunted by this incident, and he seemed doomed to repeat it over and over. Smyers would have a violent outburst or slip into illegal activity, negating any progress he had made in getting his life together. In verse, he describes his experiences as a criminal and as a prisoner. Each time he was released from prison, he was determined to lead a different life. His family would welcome him home, he would find work, remain happy for a time, and then slip back into his old habits. Smyers discusses various religions. He had contact with African Americans of the Islam faith in prison, he was exposed to a branch of East Indian Spirituality, and his father was a Christian minister. He tried to draw on these, and even went as far as organizing his own church, but pride, money, and women interfered with Smyers's sincerity and spirituality. Smyers writes about his mystically obtained ability to play piano, his period as a clothing salesman, wandering into the world of prostitution, providing transportation for the elderly, operating a catering truck, selling Persian rugs, dancing, operating a limousine service, and his several marriages. The book ends with Smyers struggling with his conscience, but believing that his Christian faith will win out over his weakness in the face of temptation.

563. Snell, Alma Hogan (1923-). *Grandmother's Grandchild: My Crow Indian Life*. Edited by Becky Matthews. Lincoln, Nebraska: University of Nebraska Press, 2000. 213 pages; photographs; index. ISBN: 0803242778.

Abstract: Alma Hogan Snell was born and raised at the Crow Agency along the Little Bighorn River in Montana. She was raised by her grandmother, Pretty Shield, who was a traditionalist. She tried to raise her children and grandchildren in the same way she had been raised. Snell's grandfather had scouted for the United States Government and had been with the Union Army with General Custer. A convert to Christianity, he did not want Pretty Shield to practice medicine or magic in the way of her Crow ancestors. Pretty Shield persisted, however, as she thought necessary for the wellbeing of her children and grandchildren. Snell loved and respected her grandmother, and she also loved the church. She attended the Burgess Memorial Baptist Church, which she considered a home away from home and the pastor and his wife her surrogate parents. When Snell went away to South Dakota to attend the Indian School, Pretty Shield felt that her usefulness was over. She believed the schools were teaching her grandchildren to "live in the white man's way" (p. 107), and that this spelled the end of the tribal customs she found so important. Snell writes about her school days and her homesickness. She met her future husband, Bill Snell, while at Flandreau Indian School, but it would be some time before they were able to marry. He was a member of

the Assiniboine Tribe, and her family was opposed to her marrying outside of the Crow Tribe. The two separated for a while, and
during that time Snell was raped and bore a child. They were,
however, eventually reunited, and lived both at his family farm in
Fort Bell Knap and at the Crow Agency. Snell describes the work
she did at both the Assiniboine and Crow agencies, including senior activities. One of the Crow traditions Snell continues is col-
lecting and using roots and other plants for medicinal purposes.
People come from around the world to consult with her. Snell
writes about the progress of her own children and expresses her
hope for the future of all Crow Indians. She writes, "I want Crow
children to know they have a place under the sun. That place is
that they are a Crow tribe of Indians. The material in their roots is
as good or better than what's happening today. I think we are
beginning to blossom from our roots. A blossom is growing, and
I'm glad" (182).

564. Sneve, Virginia Driving Hawk. *Completing the Circle.* Lincoln,
Nebraska: University of Nebraska Press, 1995. 119 pages; photographs; map. ISBN: 0803242263.

> **Notes:** Paperback published Lincoln: University of Nebraska
> Press Bison Books, 1998. ISBN: 0803292546.

> **Abstract:** Virginia Driving Hawk has written several children's
> books about Native Americans and has published her research on
> Native-American history. In this book, she looks into the history
> of her grandmothers, noting that much Native-American history
> has little to say about the women: "To the Dakotas and Lakotas
> . . . and other American Indians, the circle is a sacred symbol of all
> life. A great deal is known of that circle, yet, just as within my
> family's circle, there are great gaps because so little is known about
> the women" (p. xii). She is particularly drawn to the stories of her
> grandmothers because, traditionally in Indian society, mothers
> have to devote themselves to their husbands, and grandmothers
> are in charge of the education and care of their grandchildren.
> This meant that her grandmothers were the most important
> people to her while she was growing up. Sneve uses material she
> has researched to fill in the details of the daily lives of several gen-
> erations of women on both her mother's and father's sides and to
> learn about the historical events that would have influenced their
> lives. Her family has been Christian for several generations, and
> she learned that when the first forefathers were converted, they
> had to choose one of their several wives to live with. This means
> that some of the women in her family were "put away" when their

husbands chose another wife to live with. Other female ancestors were married to white men, and their status varied throughout the generations. Many times, joining white society meant isolation and giving up other women to share housework and child-rearing duties with. Toward the end of the book, Sneve writes about her own childhood. She was born to a full-blooded Indian father and mixed-race mother. Her father was an Episcopalian priest, and she and her brother had a happy but poor childhood on a reservation during the Great Depression. As an adult, she and her husband and children brought her paternal grandmother to live with them during the cold winters. During these times, her grandmother Flora passed the lonely time making quilt tops for Sneve's children, just as she had for her own children.

565. Snipes, Bill (1956-). *Against the Odds: The Story of a Modern American Mulatto Living in Asia.* New York, New York: Vantage Press, 1996. 141 pages. ISBN: 0533117496.

Abstract: Bill Snipes's parents met and married in England during World War II. Snipes's father, an African American, was a medical sergeant in an all-Negro regiment of the United States Army. His mother was a white British nurse. They moved to Harlem after the war, where Snipes was born in 1956. His father suffered from alcoholism and his mother supported the family both spiritually and economically. Snipes attended Bronx High School of Science, graduating at the age of sixteen. He went to college at St. Lawrence University in Canton, New York, and then to Stanford Law School. He has practiced law in California and Virginia and throughout Asia. In his memoir, Snipes focuses on his experience growing up as a person of mixed race. Snipes describes himself as light skinned, with light-colored hair and dark features, which usually make his race a mystery to people. When asked about his background, he may or may not choose to explain the mystery for the questioner.

> We should remind ourselves that, as a nation and as a people, we have always drawn strength and creativity from our diversity. But at the end of the day, we are and remain first and foremost *American.* Any "balkanization" due to race, language or economics is not only unfortunate but dangerous. We do not all have to agree on every issue, or physically look alike, as long as we share that one common, inviolable bond.
>
> (p. 92)

In his book, Snipes also writes of his marriage and difficult divorce and about fatherhood. He concludes with an account of his travels and work throughout Asia. Snipes includes a bibliography of readings on various countries in Asia, "Eurasians," "marginality," and a brief selection of autobiographies that have inspired his own writing, including Arthur Ashe, Michael Crichton, Sarah and Elizabeth Delany, and Kirk Douglas.

566. Snoop Dogg. *Tha Doggfather: The Times, Trials, and Hardcore Truths of Snoop Dogg.* Written with Davin Seay. New York, New York: William Morrow & Company, 1999. 229 pages; photographs. ISBN: 0688171583 : 0061076074.

Abstract: Snoop Dogg describes his childhood growing up in East Long Beach, California as a happy one. His father left the family when Snoop was a toddler, but his mother was very loving, making up in part for his father's absence. One of Snoop Dogg's most positive childhood experiences was playing football in the Pop Warner Football League under a coach whom he credits with teaching him self-respect and instilling the confidence that he could accomplish what he set out to do. By the time he was in his teens, Snoop Dogg became involved in gang life, joining the Crips and eventually selling crack cocaine. In the midst of this lifestyle, Snoop Dogg and two friends began writing rap pieces and performing at parties. As he became more involved in performing, his motivation to sell drugs diminished. He had decided to sell off the last of his cocaine and pay off his debts when he was caught in a sting and arrested. Snoop Dogg spent one year in jail. Through the inspiration of his mother and his own religious faith, he decided to change the course of his life. After he was released from prison, Snoop Dogg connected with rap impresario Dr. Dre, and began recording. His first successful album was *The Chronic*. He describes the transition to fame and notoriety. As he became a prominent figure, he also became a target for rival gangs. While working on his second album Snoop Dogg was accused of murder. He describes the incident that led to his arrest and the arrest of two others, their court trial, and their acquittal. Snoop Dogg writes about his relationship with Shanté Taylor, his wife and the mother of his three children. He also writes about his friendship with the late Tupac Shakur. Snoop Dogg recalls that after the murder of Tupac, he and other rap artists realized that their image and culture should change. It was no longer enough to tell it "like it is"; they needed to tell it "like it could be" (p. 201). Snoop Dogg's goal is: "To increase the peace. To spread the music. To elevate and educate. . . . [I]f you remember those words you'll know all you need to about Snoop Dogg" (p. 1).

567. Song, Shuimei. *A Rough Lifetime for Fifty Years: An Autobiography of a Lady Fighting against Misfortunes.* Brooklyn, New York: S. Song, 1995. 98 pages; photographs. ISBN: none.

Abstract: Shuimei Song was born in Guangdong Province in China near the Vietnamese border. Her father died days after she was born and her mother left her with her paternal grandparents when Shuimei was three. Shuimei describes her education and early teaching career, her coming of age during the Japanese invasion and occupation, and her work with resistance youth movements. She married at the end of the occupation when the country was in a period of upheaval and confusion. She believed that she had no other options. Her husband had had previous marriages and she found out too late about his and his family's true natures. She and her husband went to live in Vietnam, where she set up her own sewing business. She writes of enduring the abuse and beatings from her husband and his family while managing to run her business. After the Communists took over South Vietnam in 1973, Song spent all of her money trying to escape with her children. There were several failed attempts and her children ended up in prison more than once. The family finally succeeded in leaving the country in 1980. They went first to a refugee camp in Malaysia and then immigrated to the United States, settling in Brooklyn, New York. Shuimei's children graduated from high school and several graduated from college. They found husbands and wives and moved away. Shuimei has been ill most of the time since arriving in the United States and unable to work. She has felt abandoned as, one by one, her children have left to lead their own lives, rarely visiting her even when she has been sick in the hospital. She is proud of what she has accomplished for them, but wonders what her reward will be for all of her sacrifices.

568. Sosa, Sammy. *Sosa: An Autobiography.* Written with Marcos Bretón. Warner Books, 2000. 209 pages. ISBN: 0446527351 : 0446676985.

Abstract: Sammy Sosa charts the path of his baseball career, from the age of thirteen, when he first owned a baseball glove to his 1999 season with the Chicago Cubs. Sosa was born in Consuelo, Dominican Republic. His father died when Sosa was six, leaving his mother to raise six children on her own. Sosa describes the hardships of his childhood, noting that his own conditions of poverty and hunger were shared by many of the children growing up in his country. When he was thirteen, he and his family moved to San Pedro. There Sosa went to work at a shoe factory owned by

Bill Chase. Sosa writes that he and his brothers looked to Chase as a father figure and would ask him for help when they needed it. Most Dominican boys grew up playing baseball, but Sosa had no real interest in it until Chase gave him his first glove. Sosa's older brother, Luis, played semipro ball and got Sammy onto his team. At the age of fifteen, Sosa was signed by the Philadelphia Phillies and began training at their Dominican camp. He was dropped from the roster the next year, but picked up by the Texas Rangers. He spent his first year on one of the Rangers' minor league teams, eventually making his way through the ranks to the major leagues. Over the next several seasons, Sosa was traded to the Chicago White Sox and then to the Chicago Cubs, where he stayed. Sosa's career was not without its bumps, but he went on to have a series of successful years and became the Cub's team leader. In 1998, Sosa was engaged in a homerun race with Mark McGwire of the St. Louis Cardinals. Both broke the record held by Roger Maris, but McGwire finished the year four homeruns ahead of Sosa.

569. Souljah, Sister. *No Disrespect*. New York, New York: Times Books, 1994. 360 pages. ISBN: 0812924835.

Notes: Paperback published New York: Vintage Books, 1996. ISBN: 0679767088.

Abstract: Singer Sister Souljah (born Lisa Williamson) was born in the Bronx and lived with her mother and father and three siblings. They were a happy and stable family until Souljah's father was diagnosed with epilepsy and lost his truck driving job. At that point, the family began to disintegrate. Her mother took the children and moved to the projects. Life was difficult there, but Souljah paid attention to her mother's warnings about drugs and pregnancy and did her best to keep to her books despite the social damage this did to her reputation. She received many academic awards and found opportunities to take part in extended educational activities. In her book, Souljah tells about her relationships with men, all of which ended unhappily. She provides these as examples of how difficult relationships are between men and women in general, but particularly for couples living in conditions of poverty, few economic options, and little to look forward to. Souljah graduated from Rutgers University and worked with Rev. Benjamin F. Chavis at the Commission for Racial Justice. She set up a summer camp for homeless children in concert with the United Church of Christ. In 1992 she released a successful rap recording: *360 Degrees of Power*.

570. Sowell, Thomas. *A Personal Odyssey.* New York, New York: Free Press, 2000. 308 pages; photographs. ISBN: 0684864649.

Notes: Published in paperback New York: Simon & Schuster Touchstone Edition, 2002. ISBN: 0684864657.

Abstract: Scholar and academician Thomas Sowell was adopted by his aunt as an infant. He enjoyed his childhood in New York until his adopted parents separated. His broken family was united in their intent that Sowell should have better opportunities than they had had, but his home life became too disruptive. Sowell did well academically, but he dropped out of school as soon as possible after he turned sixteen. After a long struggle with his adopted mother and the court system, he also left home. Sowell periodically patched things up with his New York family, but they were never close again. In the meantime he was able to contact his birth siblings, all of whom were in Washington, D.C. Sowell joined the Marine Corps during the Korean War, but he was not one to conform nor to follow arbitrarily applied rules, and he frequently found himself in trouble with military authorities. He took his first chance to get out of the military and begin college. Sowell attended Howard University and then Harvard, from which he graduated magna cum laude. Sowell was interested in economics and did graduate work at Columbia University and the University of Chicago, studying with Milton Friedman, Arthur F. Burns, and George J. Stigler. He pursued an academic career, but found that his teaching methods, which tended to reach the brightest students and leave behind those less prepared, were unappreciated by both students and faculty. He was also at odds with affirmative action policies as it affected student admissions and faculty hiring. Sowell was most happy teaching at UCLA and at Brandeis University. He conducted research for the Urban Institute and was appointed a Senior Fellow at the Hoover Institute. Sowell has written prolifically on economics and race and ethnicity.

571. Sperling, Vatsala and Ehud Sperling. *A Marriage Made in Heaven: A Love Story in Letters.* Berkeley, California: Ten Speed Press, 2000. 276 pages; photographs. ISBN: 1580081827.

Abstract: Vatsala Sperling, the youngest child in a Tamil Brahmin family, was born in 1961 in Jamshedpur, Bihar, in North India. A clinical biologist at Childs Trust Hospital, she had a B.A. and masters degree in microbiology from Nagpur University and a Ph.D. from the University of Delhi. In 1995, she was actively investigating the matrimonial advertisements in search of the perfect husband, when she read one sent in by Ehud Sperling, a Jewish-American man and the head of the Vermont publishing company, Inner Traditions. She wrote first to his Indian go-between and then corresponded directly with him. This was the beginning of a letter-writing courtship that lasted nearly six months. Both parties were clear about what kind of person they were looking for and what they wanted from marriage, and by the time they finally met face-to-face, both fully intended to marry the other. Vatsala Sperling charts the course of their correspondence, their first meeting, how they planned the wedding, and their marriage in February 1996. Vatsala's last letter is to her mother, describing her first days in a wintry, rural Vermont and her belief that she and her husband are completely compatible.

572. Starr, Robert E. *If I Could, You Can Too.* Fort Worth, Texas: Total Security, 2000. 116 pages; photographs. ISBN: none.

Abstract: Starr's mother and father moved to Fort Worth, Texas, from rural Texas to take advantage of jobs in the meat-packing industry. Most African Americans moving to Fort Worth lived in the neighborhood known as Quality Grove. Starr describes the community, its churches, recreational activities, local schools, and businesses. During World War II, Starr was a member of the medical corps in Europe. Although this was not a happy time for him, he benefited later from the G.I. Bill, which helped him to earn two academic degrees, and from the Veteran Loan Program, which helped him get started as a businessman. Starr graduated from Texas College in Tyler and earned a master's degree in elementary education from Texas Southern University. He earned an additional certificate from the University of Southern California and attended seminars related to civil rights law and business at the University of Oklahoma and Harvard University. Starr and his brother-in-law started the Expert Cleaners, a major African-American-owned business in the Fort Worth area. Starr was involved in the NAACP for over thirty years. Active at the local and national levels, he served for twelve years on the national board of directors. He volunteered as a fund raiser for Texas College and made it a member of the United Negro College Fund. He was a board member of the Sickle Cell Anemia Association of Texas and the Minority Leadership Luncheon, a youth director for the McDonald YMCA, an equal opportunity specialist for the Federal Aviation Administration, director of affirmative action for the City of Fort Worth, and the executive director of the City of Fort Worth's Human Relations Commission. He has been employed by the Equal Opportunity Commission, and in retirement has been a legal aid volunteer and a member of the board of the Texas Commission on Human Rights. He believes success is possible if you try to make something good out of every bad situation. Throughout his life, he has relied on what he calls the four P's: prayer, preparation, persistence, and patience.

573. Stepto, Robert B. *Blue As the Lake: A Personal Geography.* Boston, Massachusetts: Beacon Press, 1998. 209 pages. ISBN: 080700944x : 0807009458.

Abstract: Writer and professor Robert B. Stepto writes about his family, dividing the book into three sections. The first describes the three places where he spent most of his life as a child. One was Idlewild, a resort area in Michigan populated in the summer by many middle-class black families. The second was the Washington Park area of Chicago, where he and his family lived with his grandparents. The third place was the Woodlawn neighborhood of Chicago, where his family moved as they became more well-to-do. The second section of the book is a history of both sides of his family. It includes some of the events that have always been of interest to the author, such as how his grandfather met his grandmother, and how an aunt married a white man. The final section is about Stepto's own upbringing, his relationship to his mother, and his feelings about the city of Chicago after her death. He also writes about how he has accepted Martha's Vineyard as a latter-day Idlewild and about the changes in the types of people who frequent the island.

574. Stevenson, Lemmon. *Three Mountaintops: An Educators Adventure through Destiny.* Edgewood, Maryland: Duncan & Duncan, 1997. 178 pages; photographs. ISBN: 1878647431.

Abstract: Lemmon Stevenson was born on May 27, 1928, in Fairfield County, South Carolina. His mother died when he was only five months old, and he was adopted by his mother's best friend, Miss Ella Stewart, while his four siblings stayed with Stevenson's father. Stevenson's adoptive mother lived with her mother, seven siblings, and six nieces and nephews on a 269-acre cotton farm. The family was impoverished and had had no formal education. However, Stevenson writes that Miss Stewart was brilliant and had taught herself to read. The family possessed "many noneconomic virtues" (p. 17), including self-sufficiency, generosity, respect, tolerance, and support for all. His adoptive family encouraged Stevenson to go to school. They allowed him to work off the farm and keep the money he earned. It was difficult for

African-American children to attend school in South Carolina. School was available to them only through the sixth grade, and most were only able to attend six months out of the year because of fieldwork. Although the teachers were often poorly educated themselves, Stevenson writes that "the teachers helped us feel worthy, as human beings, and made us work hard on the difficult tasks of learning to read, count, write, and think" (p. 22). After finishing sixth grade, Stevenson attended the Fairfield County Training School and, after major setbacks, was able to find work that allowed him to attend South Carolina State College, and eventually earn a master's degree. Although Stevenson had felt unprepared for his advanced studies, his instructors encouraged him, saying, "You are at South Carolina State College now, and we have nothing in the world more important to do than to see to it that you get all the help, assistance, and assurance you will ever need for success. Helping students is our job and we are good at it" (pp. 43-44). Stevenson's years of education were followed by military service, working as a barber, teaching, and finally, a nationally recognized career as a principal. He pioneered experimental non-graded education programs in South Carolina and Pennsylvania, and administered desegregation programs in Pennsylvania. He worked tirelessly and was even criticized for doing more than he was paid to do. Stevenson's response was that his only goal was to educate children, and he would do what he had to to accomplish that goal.

575. Stimpson, Eddie (1929-). *My Remembers: A Black Sharecropper's Recollections of the Depression*. Introduction by James W. Byrd. Foreword by Frances Wells. Illustrated by Burnice Breckenridge. Denton, Texas: University of North Texas Press, 1996. 167 pages; illustrations; photographs; index. ISBN: 092939898x.

Notes: Published in paperback in 1999. ISBN: 1574410679.

Abstract: Eddie Stimpson was born in 1929, a fifteen-and-a-half pound baby, to his fifteen-year-old mother, Millie, and nineteen-year-old father, Eddie Sr. He was the first of their three children born in Collin County, Texas, near the city of Plano, where his father farmed twelve acres in a sharecropping arrangement. Stimpson describes his parents as loving, hardworking, and good providers. His childhood years during the Depression were the best years of his life. Stimpson describes his daily responsibilities, which included the household chores of cleaning, washing clothes, and cooking and fieldwork and caring for the animals.

The entire family worked out in the cotton fields. He describes play time, church activities, the local Juneteenth celebration, and the dust storms that plagued the area during the spring and early winter months. Stimpson recalls that although they were poor, they never wanted for food while they lived on the farm. During the Depression many people suffered from "missed meal cramps," but they could always find a meal at the Stimpson household. Stimpson recalls that the many travelers passing through would be welcomed to stop in for a cool drink or a meal or to spend the night. Once fifteen white people arrived at their house after their bus had tipped over. All were accommodated. Stimpson spent twenty-one years in the army, joining as soon as he graduated from high school. He writes that he entered the army as a farm-hand and, twenty-one years later, he left the army as a sergeant and returned to working as a farmhand. Stimpson believes it is important for people to know their family history, to know what their parents and grandparents did to survive and prosper:

> Even my kid don't believe I had to wash and iron
> for house rent while growing up, or chop cotton
> with blister in hand or pick cotton until you can't
> stand up and knees so sore you could not crawl
> on them. I don't want to go back, but I don't
> want to forget where I come from. . . . I would
> like to think that some day some body would
> ask Where is that book that a no body wrote?
> And some body will say Look on the book shelf
> and find *My Remembers*.   (pp. 153-154)

576. Strawberry, Charisse and Darryl Strawberry. *Recovering Life.* Foreword by Derek Jeter. North Farmington, Pennsylvania: Plough Publishing House, 1999.   141 pages; photographs. ISBN: 0874869889.

Abstract: Darryl and Charisse Strawberry write about Darryl's fight with drug and alcohol addiction and his diagnosis and recovery from colon cancer. Shortly after the birth of their first child, Darryl acknowledged his drug and alcohol addiction and checked into the Betty Ford Clinic. Charisse writes that the clinic was important in teaching her what her role and responsibilities were in the recovery process. Strawberry left the Giants for the Yankees and after one year was released. He was then offered a position on the St. Paul Saints, an independent team with the Northern League. At first, Daryl refused to go to such an unknown team, but resigned himself to it when no other offers surfaced. Charisse and Darryl enjoyed their time in St. Paul and received strong support from the Saints' fans. They were, however, excited to return to the Yankees when the chance came. It was during Darryl's successful 1998 comeback that he was diagnosed with colon cancer. The Strawberrys describe the surgery, recovery, and setbacks. Back playing with the team, Darryl once again had to fight insecurity and uncertainty about his future and returned to his addictions. Through the support of friends and their Christian faith, Darryl and Charisse face the future with optimism.

577. Sullivan, Leon Howard (1922-2001). *Moving Mountains: The Principles and Purposes of Leon Sullivan.* Valley Forge, Pennsylvania: Judson Press, 1998. 300 pages; photographs; index. ISBN: 0817012893.

Abstract: Born and raised in a coal-mining town in West Virginia, Leon Sullivan was discovered as a teenager by Adam Clayton Powell, Jr. He spent two years with Powell at the Abyssinian Baptist Church in Harlem before accepting a call to a church in South Orange, New Jersey. While in New Jersey, he attended Union Theological Seminary and Columbia University. It was also in New Jersey that Sullivan began his experimentation with community projects. From New Jersey, Sullivan moved to Zion Baptist Church in Philadelphia. There he began a "selective patronage" movement in which visitation committees would call on targeted companies to let them know about needs in the black community. If, after a certain amount of time, the company still refused to offer equal employment opportunities, a boycott would be called. Sullivan was aware of the economic power African Americans wielded as consumers, and used this system with great success. Sullivan also started the Opportunities Industrialization Centers (OIC), a project which provided extensive job training. To date, over one million youth have been trained, and OICs are located throughout the United States and around the world. Next, Sullivan began the 10-36 program, which encouraged church members to invest ten dollars a month for three years to support the development of African-American enterprises and businesses. Over four thousand individuals participated, and the end results were apartment complexes, shopping malls, and employment training centers. Sullivan's high profile in the business community led to his appointment to the General Motors Board of Directors in 1971, a position that gave him the opportunity to use his influence to even greater advantage both domestically and internationally. In 1975, Sullivan visited South Africa and left determined to help end apartheid. He developed the Sullivan Principles, which had among their goals improved conditions of employment, the right to vote, the dismantling of apartheid, and the freeing of Nelson Mandela. Sullivan provides excerpts from and transcripts of his speeches and sermons promoting these principles, he outlines the history of U.S. corporate participation, and he describes the ultimate triumph of the principles in reaching their goals. Following the crumbling of the apartheid system in South Africa and the election of Nelson Mandela as its first black president, Sullivan shifted his ideas to address global issues and adapted his principles accordingly. Specifically interested in the condition of Sub-Saharan Africa, Sullivan has attacked the issue of debt relief, investment, education, health, and job training in this part of the world. To this end he founded the International Foundation for Education and Self-Help (IFESH), and has organized the African African-American Conferences, at least five of which have been held. While working globally, Sullivan continued to develop programs to empower African Americans economically. One such domestic program is the Self-Help Investment Program (SHIP), which encourages individuals to buy stock in corporate America and also to invest in the development of African-American-owned businesses. Sullivan focused on self-help, self-esteem, and self-sufficiency. He believed in working constructively with the business world: "Today, corporations have an opportunity to be forces for peace. More than any other institutions, businesses have the power to influence economic realities" (p. 111).

578. Sweeting, Ora Mobley (1927-). *Nobody Gave Me Permission: Memoirs of a Harlem Activist.* Written with Ezekial C. Mobley, Jr. Introduction by Ruby Reeves. Philadelphia, Pennsylvania: Xlibris, 2000. 76 pages; photographs. ISBN: 0738808849 : 0738808857.

Abstract: Ora Sweeting was born in 1927 in Greensboro, North Carolina. She remembers being puzzled by the segregation and Jim Crow laws that separated the African Americans from the white members of her community. In seventh grade, when she asked why they were not taught anything about black people in history, her embarrassed teacher called her a "smart aleck" (p. 21) and kept Sweeting from competing in the seventh grade academic contests. Sweeting's family could afford to send only her twin brother to college, but one of her teachers arranged for her to receive a scholarship to Barber-Scotia College. After completing two years there, Sweeting transferred to Johnson C. Smith University in North Carolina. After graduating, she married Ezekial Mobley. Sweeting moved to New York after her marriage and worked for the Department of Welfare as a social investigator. She became politically active in her community when she found out her son would be attending first grade in a dilapidated and dangerous school building. Sweeting worked through various channels to have a new building constructed. She joined the New Era Democratic Club of Harlem and formed the Central Harlem Mothers Association through which she lobbied to rename the streets, buildings, and schools of Harlem after notable African Americans. As an elected member of the school board for District 5, she began the Duke Ellington-Rafael Hernandez Music Festival and was responsible for many other programs and events that helped to motivate and encourage Harlem children to succeed in school. Besides Sweeting's narrative, an appendix includes a brief narrative by her first husband which records his experience as an African-American soldier in France during World War II.

579. Tagle, Lillian Lorca de. *Honorable Exiles: A Chilean Woman in the Twentieth Century.* Edited by Joy Billington and Chris Lucas. Austin, Texas: University of Texas Press, 2000. 214 pages; photographs; drawings. ISBN: 0292716060 : 0292716095.

Abstract: Lillian Lorca de Tagle was born in 1914 into two aristocratic families in Chile: the Lorcas and the Bunsters. The Lorcas arrived in Chile from Spain in the seventeenth century and the Bunsters from England in the nineteenth century. Tagle's earliest years were spent in San Francisco, and her father's work as an ambassador also took them to London, Belgium, and Germany. She returned periodically to Chile to live and to visit. As an adult, she became a reporter and correspondent in her home country and married there. In 1952, a widow with two young children, Tagle was ordered by her mercurial mother to leave the country. No questions were asked, and Tagle vowed never to return. She left for the United States, where her career has included an editorship at *Americas* magazine and twenty-five years at Voice of America. Tagle describes the high and low points of her career and her friendships and relationships. About her exile to the United States, Tagle writes,

And as a cast out, what did I do with my life? I focused on my children and myself. I knew, yet I refused to dwell on the fact, that banishment had a traumatic effect on both my daughters. Their solutions of choice were quite opposite. While Ximena never has overcome her nostalgia for Chile, Rosa cut the ties and created her own

American self. And I hover between the two,
knowing what I left behind with small regrets
and loving what I have found in my American
life.   (p. 211)

580. Tahira, Chieko. *Lotus.* Pleasant Hill, California: Gerald Tahira,
     1996. 392 pages; photographs. ISBN: none.

Abstract: Tahira begins her story with the emigration of her father
from Japan during the first years of the twentieth century. By 1912
he had saved enough money to arrange for Tahira's mother to
come to the United States to be his wife. Together they farmed and
ran a boarding house for Japanese "blanket rollers," or migrant
workers. During the Depression, Tahira's parents and four of her
siblings returned to Japan. She married and remained in
California, raising tomatoes and strawberries with her husband.
They had two small children by the time Japan bombed Pearl
Harbor and the orders arrived to evacuate all Japanese, both resident aliens and U.S. citizens, from the West Coast. Tahira
describes in detail her feelings of disbelief and horror as the U.S.
government and her white neighbors all assumed that she, her
family, and all Japanese Americans in the community were guilty
of disloyalty. She writes about the evacuation and the many
details involved in closing up their house and leaving their farm.
When they arrived at the Turlock Assembly Center, they were
relieved to find that families were kept together, and all of the
inmates quickly worked to create a livable environment from the
dirt and desolation. Just as their gardens were beginning to
bloom, most of the Turlock inmates were sent to the Gila River
Relocation Center in Rivers, Arizona. Forced to begin again, the
Gila River inmates made gardens, established classes, and created
and ran a productive farming operation. Tahira mentions some of
the positive aspects of camp life. The many homeless migrant
workers who lived hand to mouth in the outside world could, for
the first time in their lives, count on regular meals and a place to
call home, and trained professionals who had no outlet for their
skills in society, were now in demand among camp inmates and
administrators. A unified and harmonious camp life was disrupted when camp inmates were forced to answer the infamous questions No. 27 (willingness to serve in combat) and No. 28 (swearing
allegiance to the United States). Tahira answered "yes, yes,"
although she resented being asked. Her husband answered "no,
no," and the family was consequently sent to the Tule Lake
Segregation Center for "disloyal" Japanese Americans. Life at Tule
Lake was much more like a prison camp, with riots and martial

law. As the war ended, the Tahiras were faced with losing their U.S. citizenship, but were rescued by a defense committee which operated on behalf of those who were coerced or forcefully persuaded into making the decision. Tahira ends her story as the family relocates back to Contra Costa County, California. They could not return to their home or their farm, but had to start afresh with only their sugar ration tickets and twenty-five dollars given to them by the U.S. government as they left Tule Lake.

581. Takabuki, Matsuo (1923-). *An Unlikely Revolutionary: Matsuo Takabuki and the Making of Modern Hawaii: A Memoir.* Assisted by Dennis M. Ogawa with Glen Grant and Wilma Sur. Extraordinary Lives. Honolulu, Hawai'i: University of Hawai'i Press, 1998. 237 pages; index; photographs. ISBN: 0824820835 : 0824820231.

Abstract: Nisei Takabuki grew up on a sugar plantation. His mother valued education and prevailed over Takabuki's father, who wanted the children to quit school as soon as they were old enough to work. Working during the summers of his high school years, Takabuki earned seventeen cents from his first full day's work and seventeen dollars for his first fifteen days. After he graduated from high school in 1940, Takabuki went on to the University of Hawai'i Teachers College. Teaching was the chosen profession of many Nisei because it was an affordable educational program and other professions were open only to whites. Takabuki quit school and volunteered for military service after the bombing of Pearl Harbor. He and his fellow Nisei were anxious to show their loyalty to Hawai'i and to the United States. He credits Japanese values and the Japanese language school for the commitment and valor of Japanese-American units fighting in Europe. He and his fellow Nisei returned to Hawai'i after the war realizing that they could no longer accept their second-class citizen status, and they were ready to initiate change within Hawai'ian society. Takabuki worked with land investment and promoted the tourist industry. In all of his business dealings, his decisions were based on a philosophy of fairness and equitable treatment. Despite this, Takabuki was a controversial figure, both because of his Japanese background and because he was a successful entrepreneur. His appointment as a trustee to the all-white and Chinese board of the Bishop Estate, which managed the vast land holdings that funded the Kamehameha private schools for Native Hawai'ian children, was very unpopular, and he and his family received death threats. During his term of service, it became evident, however, that he did indeed act in the best interest of the schools and of the children that the schools were established to benefit. Working within the system, Takabuki was ever aware of the continuing division between white and nonwhite in Hawai'i. He writes that he was "driven by a sense of insecurity and gnawing anger" (p. 191) derived from the conditions of poverty and the discriminatory nature of the Hawai'ian society of his youth. He believes, however, that Hawai'i can make an important contribution to the mainland and the world by "enhancing an awareness of, and appreciation for cultural pluralism" (p. 172). Takabuki closes his memoir with his assessment of the problems of and prospects for Hawai'i's economic future.

582. Tallchief, Maria. *Maria Tallchief: America's Prima Ballerina.* Written with Larry Kaplan. New York, New York: Henry Holt and Company, 1997. 351 pages; photographs; index. ISBN: 0805033025.

Abstract: Ballerina Maria Tallchief was born on the Osage reservation in Fairfax, Oklahoma in 1925. Her father was a full Osage Indian and her mother was Scotch Irish. The family was wealthy thanks to the discovery of oil on Osage land. Tallchief provides a brief history of the Osage Indians in Oklahoma and of her family life during childhood. The family spent their summers in the cooler climate of Colorado Springs, and it was there, at the Broadmoor Hotel, that Maria and her sister Marjorie began dance lessons. When the family moved to California, their futures in dance began to take shape as they studied at the school of Bronislava Nijinska, where Tallchief was a favorite of the famous teacher. Following graduation from high school, Tallchief left for New York, where she immediately was taken on as an apprentice with the Ballet Russe. Her apprenticeship quickly turned into a regular position in the corps de ballet. Soon Tallchief became a soloist. In 1946 she married choreographer George Balanchine, and for the next six years, she danced for and studied under him. She credits her husband with her development into the premier American ballerina. Tallchief describes the many dances choreographed by Balanchine, her roles in those dances, and touring with the New York City Ballet, Ballet Russe, and Ballet Theatre. Tallchief danced for television productions, starred in the film *The Million Dollar Mermaid* with Esther Williams, and received numerous awards and recognitions, including the Washington Press Club's Woman of the Year plaque for 1953. Her professional connections with Balanchine remained close following their divorce, and he continued to choreograph ballets for her. Tallchief talks about her second and third marriages, her attachment to dancer Rudolf

Nureyev, her various partners, her work with the Chicago Lyric Opera, and her final years of dancing.

583. Tamizin, Zena M. *Zenidah of Many Colors*. [S.l.]: Xlibris, 2000. 344 pages; photographs. ISBN: 0738831808.

Abstract: Zena Tamizin is a clothing designer by profession and a spiritualist by avocation. She believes in multiple lives and Karma. In her book she focuses on her relationships with the three great loves of her life, baseball player Bo Belinsky, Man (Manuel), and L. B. She describes the volatile nature of her relationships, as well as her first marriage. Tamizin left the Philippines with her first husband, who was in the U.S. Army. She and her family spent two years in Spain, and then moved to the United States, where she got a divorce. Her ex-husband subsequently ran off with their two daughters, and it was years before the girls were reunited with their mother. Tamizin lived and worked throughout the South, but settled in the Los Angeles area. She describes her spiritual life and beliefs and her motivation for writing her life story.

584. Tate, Kimberly Cash. *More Christian Than African-American: One Woman's Journey to Her True Spiritual Self*. Emmaus, Pennsylvania: Daybreak Books, 1999. 197 pages. ISBN: 0875965482.

Abstract: Kimberly Tate describes her interests and priorities as a high school student, as a college student at the University of Maryland, and as a law student at George Washington University. While in her second year of law school, Tate developed a close relationship with Bill, a Ph.D. student. When Bill was offered a position at the University of Wisconsin at Madison, Kim had to decide whether to go with him to the predominantly white area or stay in Washington, D.C., which was more familiar to her. Tate found work in Madison and moved there, but was anxious to leave. Her life changed when she and Bill became involved at St. Paul A.M.E. Church. Besides providing them with an African-American community, they found the pastor to be sincere, straightforward, and honest. Their Christian faith became a priority for them. Tate writes of her changing sense of how to live her life and what it means for her to trust in God's will. She provides examples of making major life decisions according to her newly revived faith. Tate describes her fascination with the music business, her ties with rhythm and blues artists Popeye and Stokley, and her own gospel-oriented singing and song writing.

585. Tate, Sonsyrea. *Little X: Growing Up in the Nation of Islam.* San Francisco, California: HarperSanFrancisco, 1997. 230 pages. ISBN: 0062511343 : 0062511351.

Abstract: Sonsyrea Tate's paternal grandparents converted from Christianity to the Nation of Islam because of its empowering message to black Americans. They appreciated the clearly defined gender roles and delineated rules for living, and they raised their children in strict accord with the rules as taught and enforced by their temple. Tate's father eventually moved away from the faith, but her mother converted so that the children could attend the Muslim schools. Tate describes her experiences at the University of Islam in Washington, D.C. from the time she was three until she completed the sixth grade at age ten. The students were expected to work hard and excel. They learned about Islam and the teachings of Elijah Muhammed as well as regular school subjects. They also followed a strict dress code. Through her education at the University of Islam, Tate developed strong self-esteem as a young African-American woman. She writes that children in the Nation of Islam were taught to believe that they were little gods and goddesses. The school closed during Tate's sixth grade year, but even as she struggled with being a Muslim child in a secular public school system, her strong academic background and her sense of pride stayed with her. As Tate grew dissatisfied with the limited expectations for women within the Nation of Islam, her mother began to chafe against the rigid rules and discipline, shifting from the Nation of Islam to Orthodox Islam. The children were expected to convert as well and were told that much of what they had originally been taught was incorrect. Tate was dissatisfied with both manifestations of Islam and tired of standing out among her school peers. She also had a growing disillusionment with her adult role models and what she viewed as their hypocrisy. She saw her own family begin to splinter despite the enforcement of Islamic customs and rituals. Tate writes about the death of Elijah Muhammed and the changes to the Nation of Islam brought about by his son. She welcomed his move away from separatism and the encouragement of interfaith dialog. Tate attended the University of the District of Columbia to study journalism, and she has written for the *Washington Post*, the *Chicago Tribune*, and the *Virginian-Pilot*.

586. Tateishi, John (1939-). *And Justice for All: An Oral History of the Japanese American Detention Camps.* Foreword by Roger Daniels. Seattle, Washington: University of Washington Press, 1999. 262 pages; photographs. ISBN: 029597785x.

Notes: Originally published New York: Random House, 1984. ISBN: 0394539826.

Abstract: Tateishi's aim in compiling these oral histories was not to produce a definitive history of the evacuation and internment of Japanese Americans from the West Coast during World War II, but to present in "human and personal terms the experience of the only group of American citizens ever to be confined in concentration camps in the United States" (p. vii). Individuals interviewed spent time in one or more of the ten camps spread throughout the United States: Manzanar and Tule Lake in California; Poston and Gila River in Arizona; Minidoka in Idaho; Topaz in Utah; Heart Mountain in Wyoming; Amache in Colorado; and Jerome and Rohwer in Arkansas. Over half of the 120,000 Americans of Japanese ancestry were United States citizens. The rest were first-generation resident aliens who by U.S. law were prohibited from becoming naturalized citizens. Almost all of the Japanese Americans lost everything they owned, including property, belongings, businesses, careers, not to mention interrupted educations. Each of the thirty internees presented here believed that the United States was their country and that their rights would be protected by "Uncle Sam." Many had family in Japan and were confused by the Japanese attack and uncertain as to what it might mean for them. Bitterness and outrage were common feelings when confronted by the notorious "loyalty questions" 27 and 28 which demanded that internees declare their loyalty to the United States and renounce Japan. Families were divided, faced with forced repatriation, and decisions as to whether they should renounce their U.S. citizenship. Most of the individuals interviewed here have come to terms with the event of evacuation, although bitterness, anger, and feelings of betrayal remain a part of their memories. Many also believe that they and their children should remain vigilant in case the same thing should happen again, if not to them, then to some other ethnic group. Contributors are

> Mary Tsukamoto, Eddie Sakamoto, William Hosokawa, Yuri Tateishi, Haruko Niwa, Donald Nakahata, Helen Murao, Paul Shinoda, Mitsuye Endo, Minoru Yasui, Tom Watanabe, Mio Senzaki, Mabel Ota, Morgan Yamanaka, John Kanda, Violet de Cristoforo, Iwato Itow, Emi Somekawa, Raymond Katagi,

Shig Doi, Jack Tono, Tom Kawaguchi, Henry Ueno, Fred Fujikawa, Theresa Takayoshi, Yoshiye Togasaki, Frank Chuman, Chiye Tomihiro, Ben Takeshita, Wilson Makabe.

587. Taulbert, Clifton L. *Eight Habits of the Heart: The Timeless Values That Build Strong Communities—Within Our Homes and Our Lives*. New York, New York: Viking/Dial Books, 1997. 123 pages. ISBN: 0670875457.

> **Notes:** Also published New York: Penguin, 1999. ISBN: 0140266763.

> **Abstract:** Taulbert looks back on his childhood and youth growing up in a loving family in the closely knit black community of Glen Allan, Mississippi, where everyone looked out for the well-being of one another. Taulbert provides examples to demonstrate the nurturing and guidance provided to him by the people he knew there. The titles of the seven chapters indicate the values Taulbert wishes to illustrate: "Nurturing Attitude," "Dependability and Responsibility," "Friendship," "Brotherhood," "High Expectations," "Courage," and "Hope." Taulbert speaks professionally on these concepts, calling them the eight habits of the heart. He writes that "human rights have a prominent place where the Habits are practiced." Taulbert grew up "shadowed by the menace called racism, but this menace was unable to keep my elders from exercising their responsibility to build a world for me. Had they not valued the Habits of the Heart and nurtured the tiny sapling of hope in me, I would not be here lecturing today" (p. 99). Taulbert concludes his book with an explanation of a series of activities designed to help groups practice the eight habits, and to work toward the building of community.

588. —. *Watching Our Crops Come In*. New York, New York: Viking, 1997. 157 pages; photographs. ISBN: 0670859524.

> **Notes:** Also published New York: Penguin Books, 1998. ISBN: 0140244344.

> **Abstract:** Taulbert's first two books, *Once upon a Time When We Were Colored* (1989) and *The Last Train North* (1992), document his childhood and his move to St. Louis. *Crops* covers his service in the United States Air Force as a member of the 89th Presidential Wing at Andrews Air Force Base. Taulbert joined the air force in 1964 hoping to avoid serving in Vietnam. His wish was granted when he was assigned to the special division in Washington, D.C. Taulbert arrived at his new post as riots were breaking out in the

nation's capital and in other parts of the country. He writes that
he was glued to the media and any information that he could
glean of events in the South and the progress of the Civil Rights
Movement. On leave, Taulbert returned to his childhood home of
Glen Allan, Mississippi. When he left the town at the age of seventeen, Glen Allan was a legally segregated community. Upon his
return, he found that many things had changed, not the least of
which was the involvement of the African-American community
in the Civil Rights Movement. Taulbert was also surprised to note
the visible presence of outside volunteers, both white and black,
working with the local black citizens. Taulbert's mother was one
of those who had found a new calling and new opportunities. She
had quit domestic work to attend the University of Alabama to
train to teach in the new Head Start program and had become
director of the Yates Head Start Center. Under her leadership, the
center was flourishing and had received a visit from Marian
Wright Edelman and Robert Kennedy. Taulbert left Mississippi
anxious to contribute to the movement as well. He found himself
drawn to the politics of Robert Kennedy and volunteered to work
on his presidential campaign. Taulbert describes his intense grief
at the assassination of Martin Luther King, Jr. and then at that of
Robert Kennedy. As the end of Taulbert's tour of duty drew near,
he struggled with whether to re-enlist or choose some other occupation that would fulfill the expectations of his family and neighborhood. Taulbert ends his story with his decision to attend Oral
Roberts University in Oklahoma.

589. TeCube, Leroy. *Year in Nam: A Native American Soldier's Story*.
Lincoln, Nebraska: University of Nebraska Press, 1999. 261
pages; photographs. ISBN: 0803244347.

> **Notes:** Published in paperback Lincoln: University of Nebraska
> Press Bison Books, 2000. ISBN: 0803294433.

> **Abstract:** In this book, for which he won the 1996 North American
> Indian Prose Award, TeCube documents his year in Vietnam as an
> infantryman assigned to the Americal Division from January 1968
> to January 1969. TeCube, who was orphaned at a young age and
> raised by his extended family and tribe on a reservation, spent
> most of his youth out-of-doors. This upbringing was invaluable
> during the time he spent in "the field" in Vietnam, where he often
> volunteered to walk ahead of his company as point man. One
> advantage he felt he had when dealing with the Vietnamese was
> that he looked like them; he found it easier to strike up friendships
> in the villages his company passed through. TeCube describes in

detail the life of infantrymen, their daily routine, sleeping and eating in the field, and dealing with the heat, bees and wasps, and rain. He also chronicles the many patrols, guard duties, and nighttime ambushes that his company was involved in, and he tells about the casualties they suffered and those they inflicted. Early on in his tour, TeCube realized that the United States was fighting for a country that did not want its help. Discussing the aftermath of the massacres at My Lai in 1968, he says,

> The finger is pointed at the grunts, but we were merely pawns of the grand scheme of things. The local villagers, top U.S. military brass, and politicians back home had a major responsibility. The grunts were dying in an effort to free the country from Communist domination. We wanted the local villagers' assistance in destroying the VC for them. Early on in the war we realized this was never going to happen, but we couldn't convince the top military brass and politicians of this. During the first stages of the war, during the critical time, no one listened to the grunts. As a result the war escalated.
> (p. 99)

Despite his personal feelings, TeCube served with distinction, finishing his tour as platoon leader with the rank of sergeant. He concludes:

> So, from the infantry standpoint, we all died. None of us came back the same person he was beforehand. We had gone through too much for that to be possible. It was bad enough to see fellow soldiers get killed, but the hardships we went through and the violent world we lived in would forever change us.   (p. 260)

590. Terrell, Mary Church (1863-1954). *A Colored Woman in a White World*. African American Women Writers, 1910-1940. New York, New York: G. K. Hall and Company, 1996. 436 pages. ISBN: 0783814216.

   Notes: Originally published Washington, D.C.: Ransdell, Inc., 1940.

591. Tham, Hilary. *Lane with No Name: Memoirs and Poems of a Malaysian-Chinese Girlhood.* Boulder, Colorado: Lynne Rienner Publishers, 1997. 211 pages; photographs. ISBN: 0894108301 : 089410831x.

> **Abstract:** Poet Hilary Tham recounts her parents' story and recalls her own childhood in Malaysia. In so doing she examines the customs and practices of her family and the Chinese community, her Indian and Malaysian neighbors, and Eurasian friends. Tham describes the environment of her youth, including lifestyles, treatment of elders and children, wedding and burial customs, food, and housing. Tham's mother was fourteen and her father was twenty-two when they were married. In typical fashion, they lived with the husband's family. The mother-in-law was unkind, making many demands and putting restrictions on Tham's mother. She also made it clear as the children were born that the boys were to be favored. At one point the grandmother tried to persuade Tham's father to give away the next child if it was a girl. Her father was too taken with the new baby to give it away, but Tham's mother underwent surgery so that there would be no more risk of conceiving and therefore losing any future children. Tham was appalled at her grandmother's distaste for her and was painfully aware of her desire to give away girl babies. Attitudes of the culture towards women kept Tham in a continuous state of rebellion that was nurtured by the Western-style education she received from the nuns at her Catholic school and her participation in the Joyful Vanguard, a version of the Girl Scouts. When she was baptized, she changed her name to Hilary, one that could be considered either male or female. Tham writes about laws that were passed forbidding the discussion of politics or religion and encouraging various ethnic groups to remain separate. She recalls the novel experience of visiting the home of a Eurasian girlfriend in which the family would discuss events over the dinner table and ask Tham for her opinion. Tham writes that she had to practice speaking up and to carefully think over what her opinion might be, having never been encouraged to have one before. Tham married an American Peace Corps worker and moved to the United States. She has published several books of poetry, including *Men and Other Strange Myths: Poems & Art* (1994), *Tigerbone Wine: Poems* (1992), and *Paper Boats: Poems of Hilary Tham* (1987).

592. Thanh, Trg. *Mosaics of Mind.* Olympia, Washington: South Puget Sound Community College, 1998. 120 pages. ISBN: none.

593. The Rock (Dwayne Johnson). *The Rock Says . . .: The Most Electrifying Man in Sports Entertainment.* Written with Joe Layden. New York, New York: Regan Books, 2000. 292 pages; photographs. ISBN: 0060392983 : 0060392991.

Notes: Also published New York: Regan Books, 2000. ISBN: 006103116x (417 pages).

Abstract: The Rock (born Dwayne Johnson) was born into a wrestling family. His maternal grandfather, Peter Maivia, was a well-known Samoan-American wrestler whose only daughter married Rocky Johnson, an African-American wrestler. The Rock was their only child, and he grew up in the world of wrestling. He attended the University of Miami to play football and had hopes of being drafted into the National Football League. He was not drafted by any NFL teams, and consequently had a short and impoverished stint in the Canadian Football League before going back to his father and asking him to let him train as a professional wrestler. After about a year in training, he debuted on center stage for the World Wrestling Federation (WWF). The Rock writes candidly about the entertainment aspect of professional wrestling: how the bouts are predetermined by the WWF, how the wrestlers themselves carefully choreograph their moves, and the importance of "promos," the statements which the wrestlers give before bouts to get the audience excited and which The Rock enjoys writing almost as much as he likes to wrestle. He is also certain that fans have no illusions about what is actually going on:

> Wrestling fans are not stupid, especially in the 1990s. They're in on the con, and that's part of the reason the business has become so popular. Our fans love the serpentine story lines, the wild soap-opera element, the comic-book violence . . . as well as the extraordinarily high level of athleticism.   (p. 206)

He writes about the development of his persona, how the WWF management decided to turn him into a "heel," or villain figure. This let him be himself, but "with the volume . . . turned . . . WAY . . . UP!" This new persona led to his outstanding popularity as a professional wrestler. The book contains descriptions of his most famous bouts, an outline of the sort of life he leads, his attitude toward his fans, and how he and his wife Dany deal with his fame.

594. Thompson, John (b. 1812). *The Life of John Thompson, a Fugitive Slave Containing His History of 25 Years in Bondage, and His Providential Escape.* Chapel Hill, North Carolina: Academic Affairs Library, University of North Carolina at Chapel Hill, 2000.

> http://docsouth.unc.edu/neh/thompson/thompson.sgml
> http://docsouth.unc.edu/neh/thompson/thompson.html
>
> **Notes:** Documenting the American South (Project).

595. Thornton, Jeanette F. and Rita L. Thornton. *A Suitcase Full of Dreams: The Untold True Story of a Woman Who Dared to Dream!* Atlantic Highlands, New Jersey: Thornton Sisters Publishing House, 1996. 219 pages; photographs. ISBN: 1889469009.

> **Abstract:** Jeanette and Rita Thornton have written this book about their mother in part as a rebuttal to their sister Yvonne's book *The Ditchdigger's Daughters.* They felt that Yvonne ignored the role their mother played in the success of the six Thornton Sisters and gave all of the credit to their father, Donald. Although essentially a biography, the sisters have written in the first person as though it is their mother, Itasker Edmonds Thornton, telling her own story. Itasker's childhood is described and insight into the family tendency to develop Lupus is given, as well as the early signs that Itasker herself suffered from this disease. Jeanette and Rita document Itasker's mock marriage to a professor at Blufield State Teacher's College in West Virginia, by whom she became pregnant and was abandoned. The birth of her first daughter and her false marriage were secrets, along with her age, that Itasker kept from all but her two oldest daughters. Itasker was unable to finish college and left for New York City to try to make a living in the entertainment business, hoping to earn enough money to return to college. Before that could happen, however, she met Donald Thornton and they married. She soon gave birth to Donna and then one daughter after another, until there were five in all. Later, she and her husband adopted one more girl. Donald Thornton was determined to have all of his daughters become doctors. He also decided that he would finance their education by forming them into a band. Itasker describes how her husband devised impossible plans and then somehow managed to carry them out. He worked three to four jobs to support his family and raised the money for their house, music lessons, and all of their college educations. In their book the sisters describe the personalities of each of the girls and how they either did just as their father demanded

or rebelled against him. They track the college and career paths of each daughter as they entered the fields of psychiatry, medicine, law, court reporting, dentistry, and nursing. Rita and Jeanette describe the disintegration of their mother's mental state as her children began to leave home and her belief that they dismissed her as a mere domestic. They portray her as feeling intense guilt at not having raised her first daughter and sinking ever more deeply into depression. It was not until after her death and an autopsy that doctors discovered that Itasker had suffered from Graves Disease, which is related to Lupus. Donna, the oldest Thornton sister, would also die of Lupus in 1991.

596. Thornton, Yvonne S. *The Ditchdigger's Daughters: A Black Family's Astonishing Success Story*. As told to Jo Coudert. Secaucus, New Jersey: Carol Publishing Group, 1995. 261 pages; photographs. ISBN: 1559722827.

Notes: Also published New York: Plume, 1995. ISBN: 0452276195; New York: Kensington, 2002. ISBN: 0758201168.

Abstract: Yvonne Thornton, a prominent obstetrician, writes about her childhood from the 1950s through 1970s. She was the third of five daughters in a poor, black family. Her parents, and especially her father, Donald Thornton, raised the girls with unrelenting strictness, focused completely on their becoming doctors. His philosophy was referred to by his daughters as "the gospel according to Donald." They committed to memory the lines he regularly used to keep them in line, in particular, "You're black and you're ugly and you're girls, and the world's already written you off. You can grow up and be a bag lady. You can be on the streets and the world won't give a damn whether you live or die. But if you listen to me, we can get out of this." His choice of occupation for them was based on the notion that "[a] man can be a Ku Klux Klan member who hates blacks . . . but if he's layin' in the road hurt and bleedin' and you tell him you're a doctor, he's gonna beg you to help him" (p. 257). A man who worked two jobs a day for twenty-five years and a genius at convincing people of his ability to make good on debts, Donald Thornton made sure his family had every advantage he and his wife could provide. All of the girls learned how to play musical instruments, and they formed the Thornton Sisters, a group that appeared on *Ted Mack and the Original Amateur Hour*, won a week of appearances at the Apollo Theater, and eventually specialized in performances on college campuses, work that allowed them to stay safely in school on the weekdays and work all weekend. The band earned enough money to send the five girls through college. Loathe to let his daughters leave home, Donald sent them all to Monmouth College, a small school in their home town that had never sent a graduate to medical school. Of the five sisters, Yvonne was the first to become a doctor. She was accepted at Columbia University of Physicians and Surgeons, was a resident in New York City, went on to the Bethesda Naval Hospital, and subsequently to other prominent positions. Of the five sisters, two became medical doctors, one became a dentist, another a science teacher, and the eldest became a court stenographer. All lived up to their father's declaration that "women can do anything."

597. Thunder, Mary Elizabeth. *Thunder's Grace: Walking the Road of Visions with My Lakota Grandmother*. Edited by Augusta Ogden. Barrytown, New York: Station Hill Press, 1995. 259 pages; photographs. ISBN: 0882681664.

Abstract: Mary Elizabeth Thunder describes the difficult years that led to her life as a spiritual teacher and healer. Abandoned by her mother three weeks after birth, while her father was serving in the Navy during World War II, Thunder lived with her grandparents, her father and stepmother, and in a variety of foster homes. At one of her lowest points as an adult, with a failing marriage and three children to raise, Thunder began to explore her Indian heritage. Her father was a descendent of Mohawk and Cheyenne Indians, and her mother was probably of Native-American descent as well. Thunder's genealogical exploration introduced her to many Native elders, including Grace Spotted Elk, Wallace Black Elk, Leonard Crow Dog, and Rolling Thunder. Following her recovery from a near-fatal heart attack, Thunder was convinced by her tribal elders to take part in a Sun Dance Ceremony. Since then she has become a teacher and "pipe carrier." She tours and teaches at Thunder Horse Ranch, a spiritual university in Texas.

598. Tijerina, Reies López. *They Called Me "King Tiger": My Struggle for the Land and Our Rights*. Translated and edited by José Angel Gutiérrez. Foreword by Henry A. J. Ramos. Houston, Texas: Arte Público Press, 2000. 236 pages; photographs. ISBN: 1558853022.

Abstract: Tijerina writes of his twenty years of political activism on behalf of "Indohispanos," or Mexican Americans, and their claim to land holdings under the Treaty of Guadalupe Hidalgo. Tijerina went to Mexico and Spain to research land laws, to uncover details surrounding the initiation and implementation of the treaty, and to look for documents supporting local claims to Tierra Amarilla in New Mexico. Founder of *Alianza Federal de Mercedes* (Federal Land Grant Alliance) and the *Alianza de los Pueblos y Pobladores* (Alliance of Towns and Settlers), Tijerina was a target for local white landowners, white and Mexican-American politicians, local law enforcement agencies, and the FBI. In this book, he documents his five court trials, two imprisonments, the harassment of his children and wife, and the bombings of his home, the homes of others involved in the movement, and his organization's offices. He notes that there were no police investigations into these attacks. Tijerina persistently sought a response to his land-claim work from Presidents Eisenhower through Ford, but never received any response to his letters or memoranda. He writes, "It must be that the Anglo sees in me his criminal history, and that's why he cannot tolerate my claims for the rights of the Indohispanos and the Indians" (p. 156). Although the fight for recognition of land claims continues, Tijerina saw some progress before the end of the 1970s in terms of sympathy for his cause and some recognition of his claims from the political establishment. He also writes of his attempts to form a self-sufficient community in Arizona during the early 1950s. He and his fellow community members bought 160 acres of land and named it Valley of Peace. They wanted to live away from the "Anglo" cities and the "Anglo" education system. Tijerina prefers the use of the term *Indohispanos* over the term *Chicano* because it unites Mexican Americans with the Mexican people. He feels that the term *Chicano* separated the Mexicans in the United States from Mexicans in Mexico. Translator of this book and founder of *La Raza Unida* party, José Angel Gutiérrez notes that as the Chicano movement has faded, the use of the term has gone out of vogue, and that *Hispanic* and *Latino/Latina* are now more frequently used. This work was originally published in Spanish in 1978 by *Fondo de Cultura Económica*. It was not until 1994 that Tijerina sought to have it translated into English.

599. Tillage, Leon Walter (1936-). *Leon's Story.* Collage art by Susan Roth. New York, New York: Farrar, Straus, and Giroux, 1997. 107 pages; illustrations. ISBN: 0374343799.

   Notes: Also published in 2000. ISBN: 0374443300.

   Abstract: At the time Tillage wrote his book, which is aimed at younger readers, he had been the custodian at Park School in Baltimore, Maryland, for thirty years. Each year he talks to the seventh grade class, telling them about his childhood as a share-cropper in North Carolina and his participation in the nonviolent protests that eventually led to voting rights, desegregated schools, and the dismantling of Jim Crow. In his book, Tillage, who was born in 1936, describes the system of sharecropping under which he and his family worked. He explains how his family became indebted to the landowner for supplies, food, and clothing and rarely broke even when accounts were settled after harvest. Tillage writes about the segregated conditions in Fuquay, North Carolina, which he calls a "Jim Crow town," the lack of opportuni-ties for black children growing up, the difficulty of attending school when you were needed to work in the fields, and the poor condition of schools for black children. On Tillage's fifteenth birthday, he and his siblings watched as their parents set off on foot to go into town to buy a birthday present. As the two entered the road, a car driven by white teenagers hit and ran over Tillage's father, killing him. His mother escaped into a ditch. Although the children identified the murderers, the Tillage family received no more than an apology. Mrs. Tillage went to court to press charges, but nothing resulted from this effort. Tillage was not raised to question Jim Crow, but it was plain to him that the way he and his family were treated was wrong. He began to take part in march-es and other forms of nonviolent protest. Although he did not have the support of family or friends, he writes,

> [O]ur friends and relatives and also the white man didn't understand the way we felt and the way we thought about the situation, which was we didn't care who we sat beside. We didn't care who we lived beside. We didn't care so much about walking in the front door. What we cared about was who are you to tell us what we can and can't do in America, the land of freedom, the land of democracy. That is what we got beat up for. It was as simple as that. (p. 97)

600. Tillis, James Quick. *Thinkin Big: The Story of James "Quick" Tillis the Fightin Cowboy.* As told to J. Engleman Price. Toronto, Ontario: ECW Press, 2000. 177 pages; photographs. ISBN: 1550224301.

Abstract: Tillis was born in 1957 in Tulsa, Oklahoma. He was inspired to pursue his boxing career after watching a fight featur-ing a young Cassius Clay. Tillis was a wild teenager and believes that boxing channeled his natural athleticism, attitude, and meanness in a constructive direction. By 1975 Tillis had won the regional Golden Gloves. He then went to work as a garbage collector before heading with his manager to Chicago to train. He arrived with enough money for one week's rent and no money for food. In 1976, he took part in the Olympic trials. Tillis describes his pivotal fights and his battle with fatigue. Before winning his fight with Mike Tyson, Tillis visited a health-food advisor and went on a strict health-food diet. Tillis describes the downside of boxing, including dishonest promoters and managers. He himself was cheated out of most of the money he earned. Tillis describes his love of Oklahoma and the cowboy life and writes about his hero, his mother Rose Tillis.

601. Tilmon, Levin (1807-1863). *A Brief Miscellaneous Narrative of the More Early Part of the Life of L. Tilmon, Pastor of a Colored Methodist Congregational Church in the City of New York.* Chapel Hill, North Carolina: Academic Affairs Library, University of North Carolina at Chapel Hill, 1999.

> http://metalab.unc.edu/docsouth/tilmon/tilmon.sgml
> http://metalab.unc.edu/docsouth/tilmon/tilmon.html

> **Notes:** Documenting the American South (Project).

602. Tomita, Mary Kimoto. *Dear Miye: Letters Home from Japan 1939-1946.* Edited with introduction and notes by Robert G. Lee. Asian America. Stanford, California: Stanford University Press, 1995. 400 pages; photographs; index. ISBN: 0804724199 : 0804729670.

> **Abstract:** Mary Kimoto Tomita was born in 1918 on the family farm in Ceres, California. The family owned their property only because her father had immigrated to the United States around the turn of the century and bought property three years before California passed its Alien Land Law, which prohibited Japanese and Chinese nationals from buying property. Following graduation from Modesto Junior College, Tomita realized that her employment opportunities were limited to domestic work, a job in a Japanese-owned shop, or the family farm. She decided to work as a domestic for one year to earn money for passage to Japan. She left in 1939 and enrolled in Waseda International University (for non-Japanese students) in Tokyo. Tomita's letters to her friend Miye Yamasaki Nishita back home in Modesto describe her adjustment to life in a foreign country where her rebellious nature, not to mention her U.S. citizenship, made it difficult for her relatives

and Japanese hosts to accept her. Because of the poor relations between the U.S. and Japan, Tomita had trouble receiving reading material from the United States. Her news was filtered through the Japanese media and this contributed to her ongoing confusion as to where she belonged and with which country her loyalties should lie. After the attack by Japan on Pearl Harbor, Tomita was stranded in Japan and was unable to repatriate until 1947. She endured homelessness, hunger, and poverty. Encouraged to add her name to her family's register so that she could receive a rice ration, Tomita found out later that this meant she had effectively given up her American citizenship. She finally made her way to Osaka, where she reunited with her Nisei friend Kay Oka. Following the war they worked for the occupation forces, and Tomita was able to reinstate her U.S. citizenship and return to the United States, where she was reunited with her family. During the war, Tomita had been unable to correspond outside of Japan, and all of her letters sent from Japan were lost. The letters in the book for that period were recreated as part of a writing assignment for an English course at Boston University shortly after she returned from Japan. In her introduction, Tomita writes,

> It is my hope that the letters presented here will strike some universal chord with those who have had to adjust to different cultures, and specifically, with those who, like me and my fellow Nisei in Japan, had no choice but to do so. I will feel rewarded if they bring some understanding to those who have never been in similar situations. Perhaps these letters will show also that people are fundamentally the same, regardless of culture and place, that everyone deserves to be treated with dignity and respect, and that tragedies and adversities strengthen a person as long as they are met with a positive attitude. (p. ix)

603. Toussaint, Rose-Marie. *Never Question the Miracle: A Surgeon's Story*. Written with Anthony E. Santaniello. New York, New York: One World, 1998. 377 pages. ISBN: 0345407237.

Abstract: Toussaint is a surgeon specializing in liver and kidney transplants. In this book she describes the path from her childhood in Haiti to her graduation from medical school in Washington, D.C., and finally to her career in her chosen area of specialization. Toussaint was born in Haiti into a farming family.

Her parents had left the children in Haiti while they searched for work in the United States and sent for them when they settled in Miami. Toussaint came to the United States ready to begin ninth grade. Her transition was difficult because of cultural differences, racial prejudice, and difficulties with language, but she worked hard to fulfill her dream to become a doctor. Toussaint attended a small Catholic college in New Orleans. She graduated as a premed student, but received no letter of acceptance into medical school. Toussaint describes the years between her initial rejection and her eventual acceptance into a medical school in Washington, D.C. She discusses the difficulties in medical education facing women, especially African-American women, and the problem of balancing school and medical residencies with any kind of normal life. Toussaint includes episodes of success and failure and encouragement and the lack of it leading to her becoming a surgeon. She also gives a glimpse into the life-and-death decisions made by organ transplant specialists.

604. Townsend, Henry. *A Blues Life*. As told to Bill Greensmith. Urbana, Illinois: University of Illinois Press, 1999. 145 pages; photographs. ISBN: 0252025261.

Abstract: Musician Henry Townsend was born in 1909. His family moved repeatedly between city and farm, and so he never had much of an opportunity to attend school. His grandfather, who had a prosperous farm in Cairo, Illinois, set an example for Townsend as a self-taught man, and Townsend looked to him as a model of what he might accomplish. Townsend ran away from home when he was about nine, going to St. Louis and supporting himself with a variety of odd jobs. While working, he heard conversations about the local musicians. When he was old enough, he began going to hear them perform whenever possible. He was inspired by guitarists Son Ryan, Dave Pearchfield, and especially Lonnie Johnson, and he learned to play the instrument using other people's guitars. After he convinced a girl friend to buy him one of his own, he began to join in with other musicians. Townsend became a figurehead in the St. Louis blues scene, spending most of his time traveling between St. Louis, Chicago, and Cairo and Future City, Illinois. He made his first recording in 1929 and went on to record for more than sixty years. In his autobiography he recalls the many musicians he played with. He describes their styles and talks about the venues in which they performed. Townsend made a number of European tours and was performing at folk festivals into the 1990s.

605. Tripathy, Ghana Shyam. *Best of Two Worlds*. Dover, Ohio: G. S. Tripathy, 1997. 123 pages; photographs; documents. ISBN: none.

Abstract: Ghana Tripathy grew up in the state of Orissa in India. His family was of the Brahmin caste, and he lived with his entire extended family in what was known as a "joint family." Tripathy was adopted by his aunt and uncle but was always near his birth parents as well. He notes his good fortune at being born a boy. With two sets of parents and his status as a male, Tripathy lived a spoiled and charmed life. He graduated from high school at the age of twenty-one, and then entered medical college. In 1952, he participated in an exchange program with the United States and was sent to Peoria, Illinois, for a pathology residency. He soon transferred to surgery, working at Aultman Hospital in Canton, Ohio. Tripathy describes his work at Aultman and then at a series of veterans hospitals before setting up his own practice in Dover, Ohio. He married Rita Landers, the head recovery room nurse at Aultman, and they had five children. Although Tripathy had planned to return to India following the completion of his residency, he and Rita chose to stay in the United States. Rita did not travel to India with Tripathy until they had been married twelve years. By then, Tripathy's family had learned to accept his marriage to a Christian American, and she received a warm welcome. Tripathy discusses his childhood and youth within the context of history, customs, and traditions of his home region in India. He writes about the conditions of World War II and the fear of Japanese occupation, the events surrounding India's declaration of independence from Great Britain, and his personal experience with caste restrictions and marriage practices.

606. Trujillo, Marie Oralia Durán. *Autumn Memories: My New Mexican Roots and Traditions*. Pueblo, Colorado: El Escritorio, 1999. 120 pages. ISBN: 0962897477.

607. Tuan, Yi-fu. *Who Am I? An Autobiography of Emotion, Mind, and Spirit*. Wisconsin Studies in American Autobiography. Madison, Wisconsin: University of Wisconsin Press, 1999. 139 pages; photographs. ISBN: 0299166600.

Abstract: Prominent geographer Tuan notes the popularity of autobiography during the closing years of the twentieth century as a manifestation of a search for identity and roots. "Everyone seems to be asking it. Not only individuals but groups and even nations 'who am I?' or 'who are we?'" (p. 4). He writes, that because of his own rootlessness, he is a "natural for self-examination" (p. 4). Not only has he lived in sixteen cities on three different continents, but he has spent most of his life as a single person because of his discomfort with his gay sexual orientation. He feels that this, more than his ethnicity, has been a shaping feature in his life. "The one portable soil—family—in which an individual is given natural grounding is not available to me" (p. 4). He attributes his passion for geography to having an "inordinate fear of losing my way. . . . I concluded that I had to be a geographer so as to ensure that I should never be disoriented" (p. 93). Indeed Tuan's desire for a clear orientation is expressed in his many publications which explore the variety of meanings that can be attributed to the word or concept of "place." A prolific writer, Tuan's works include *Segmented World and Self* (1982), *Cosmos and Hearth: A Cosmopolites Viewpoint* (1996), *Dominance and Affection: The Making of Pets* (1984), *Passing Strange and Wonderful: Aesthetics, Nature, and Culture* (1993), and *Space and Time: The Perspective of Experience* (1977), as well as many articles and contributed chapters.

608. Turner, Janet Driskell (1920-). *Through the Back Door: Memoirs of a Sharecropper's Daughter Who Learned to Read as a Great-Grandmother.* Boulder, Colorado: Creativa Press, 2000. 87 pages; photographs. ISBN: 0967374480.

Abstract: Janet Driskell Turner grew up the eldest of twelve children on a small farm in rural Georgia where her parents sharecropped. Turner describes the farm owners, her father's bosses, as deeply racist and controlling. They tried to keep the children out of school and busy on the farm and gave her parents no opportunity to better their situation. Turner believes that the bosses were jealous and wanted to keep down the black families that worked for them because they had so little themselves. The twelve Driskell children attended school sporadically. All of the children worked in the fields and the girls had to work in the house as well. As the eldest, Turner had the responsibility of caring for the younger children, sewing, and doing laundry and other household chores. Although she managed to complete the ninth grade, her reading skills were never adequate. Many years later, Turner, a sixty-six-year-old widow, moved from Atlanta, Georgia, to Boulder, Colorado, to live with her son and his family. There she learned about a literacy program at the Boulder Public Library called BoulderReads! Having grown up under Jim Crow and the carefully enforced rules for blacks and whites, Turner was initially fearful about approaching the librarians about the program, but she soon found that they were warm and encouraging. Turner thrived under the program, and her life changed once she was able to read and understand what she was reading. The short vignettes presented in this book were written as a result of her participation in the literacy program, in which she was encouraged to write and give speeches. In 1991, Turner was diagnosed with Parkinson's Disease. She describes the effects of this disease, her fear, and her determination to fight it.

609. Turner, Tony. *All That Glittered: My Life with the Supremes.* Written with Barbara Aria. New York, New York: Dutton Books, 1990. 308 pages; photographs. ISBN: 0525249109.

> **Notes:** Also published New York: Penguin Books, 1990. ISBN: 0451402758 (334 pages); Lincoln: toExcel, 2000. ISBN: 0595010903.
>
> **Abstract:** Tony Turner was twelve years old when he met Florence Ballard, a member of the Supremes, at a Manhattan department store in 1964. The famous trio were in New York and making their first appearance on the *Ed Sullivan Show*. Turner was taken on as a sort of mascot and assistant, and Ballard would call him whenever they were in New York. He soon became a permanent fixture with the group. Turner stayed with the Supremes even after Ballard left the group. He managed Mary Wilson in the late 1980s when she was touring as Mary Wilson of the Supremes. In his book, Turner describes the fiery relationship between Ballard and Diana Ross and the change that took place within the Supremes as Ross became the star and Ballard and Wilson were relegated to the background. He writes about the tempestuous dismissal of Ballard by producer Barry Gordy and her replacement by Cindy Birdsong. He relates Ballard's descent into poverty, sickness, and early death. He writes about the post-Ballard Supremes and their attempt to survive following Ross's departure for a solo career and his own brief interlude working with the Three Degrees. Turner speaks on behalf of Florence Ballard and describes the obstacles that were placed in the way of her success as a solo artist by Barry Gordy and Motown. Finally, he writes about his years touring with Mary Wilson and how he managed to put the Supremes behind him as his working relationship with Wilson came to an unhappy end.

610. TwoTrees, Kaylynn Sullivan. *Somebody Always Singing You.* Jackson, Mississippi: University of Mississippi Press, 1997. 166 pages; photographs. ISBN: 0878059814.

> **Abstract:** Kaylynn TwoTrees was born to an African-American mother and a Lakota Indian father. Their marriage was plagued

by cultural differences and the objections of TwoTrees's maternal grandparents, and her parents soon divorced. Up until she was six, TwoTrees lived with her mother in Iowa and spent the summers with her paternal grandmother on the Pine Ridge Reservation in South Dakota. After TwoTrees's stepfather murdered her mother, her grandparents cut off all contact with the Lakota side of TwoTrees's family. They sent TwoTrees away to a Catholic boarding school in Illinois. She describes the misery of her years there: the severe punishment, the agony of being the only black child, and the trauma of the weekly shampooings. Expelled during her last semester, TwoTrees went back to Iowa to live with her grandparents. She finished high school, but was pregnant before graduation. Later TwoTrees reluctantly agreed to her grandparents' wish to have an aunt and uncle adopt her daughter, who was almost two years old at the time. She then left home and moved to Chicago, where she met her future husband. The two went to Europe to study dance in Germany and England, and they both had successful careers in the dance world, he as a choreographer and she as a dancer and costume and set designer. The marriage, however, disintegrated as their careers diverged and her husband became an alcoholic. TwoTrees has spent the subsequent years trying to put together her identity by reconnecting with her daughter and her Native-American heritage. She has been able to express the tragedies in her life through her art, using inspiration from native cultures in Africa, New Zealand, and the United States.

611. Tyson, Neil De Grasse. *The Sky Is Not the Limit: Adventures of an Urban Astrophysicist.* New York, New York: Doubleday, 2000. 191 pages. ISBN: 0385488386.

Abstract: Astrophysicist Tyson was born in 1958 and raised in the Bronx. He first became enamored of the night sky in sixth grade. In seventh grade he received his first telescope and at fifteen gave his first public lecture. He credits a childhood friend who introduced him to games, brain teasers, and binoculars for getting him started along the path he was to follow steadily from such an early age. Tyson had invaluable travel and scholarship opportunities while still in high school through his participation in the New York Explorer's Club. He took courses as a youth at the Haydn Observatory. As a high-school junior, Tyson visited Cornell University and interviewed with Carl Sagan. Tyson writes that Sagan was "warm, compassionate, and demonstrated what appeared to be a genuine interest in my life's path. . . . [A]t every stage of my scientific career that followed, I have modeled my encounters with students after my first encounter with Carl" (pp. 28-29). Tyson earned his Ph.D. in astrophysics at Columbia University. Besides discussing his education and experiences as a practicing astrophysicist, Tyson writes about scientific method and accuracy, science and religion, the laws of physics and every-day life, space exploration versus conquest of space, and gives an explanation of some of the more fascinating celestial events in recent history. As a scientist, and with the advantage (or "keys to the candy store") of being the director of the Haydn Planetarium, Tyson has sought to "bring the universe down to Earth for every-body who wanted to see it. Along the way, I have also tried to raise public literacy in science a notch or two" (preface).

612. Tywoniak, Frances Esquibel (1931-). *Migrant Daughter: Coming of Age As a Mexican American Woman*. Written with Mario T. Garcia. Berkeley, California: University of California Press, 2000. 237 pages; photographs. ISBN: 0520219147 : 0520219155.

Abstract: Frances Tywoniak was born in New Mexico. Her moth-er was a native of the state and her father had emigrated from Mexico. Until 1937, she and her family lived on her grandmoth-er's ranch. She was part of a Spanish-speaking community, and her father insisted on Spanish being spoken in the house. Tywoniak writes that her New Mexican background "gave me a sense of belonging, a sense that I could count on family acceptance and total support" (p. 24). During the Depression, her family moved to California to find work as farm laborers, living in work camps until they moved to Visalia. This was Tywoniak's first introduction to urban life and the barrio. As she grew older, she became more "Americanized," and began to distance herself from Mexican students, feeling more comfortable in English than in Spanish. Along with this loss of Spanish fluency, Tywoniak felt herself separating from her family. She had been raised to be a good wife and mother, but she wanted to go to college. Tywoniak was a good student, but eventually she realized that there was limited support for Mexican students and that she had been tracked into vocational courses. Tywoniak was lucky to find teachers who recognized her abilities and supported her college aspirations. She was awarded an alumni scholarship to attend the University of California at Berkeley. Tywoniak immersed herself in life as a student, experiencing the diversity of the Berkeley cam-pus, adjusting herself to its immensity, and absorbing new ideas and ways of looking at the world. She describes Berkeley as a "sanctuary for differences" (p. 192). Halfway through her college career, Tywoniak met her future husband, Ed. He was seventeen years her senior and a veteran of World War II. She found that he was interested in her life as a student, supported her career goals, and, after their marriage, shared household, child-rearing, and bread-winning responsibilities with her. Tywoniak never considered giving up her studies or her aspirations to teach. In 1953, she graduated from Berkeley, already a year into her marriage and a new mother. She received her teaching certification in 1954 and began teaching in 1955. In 1991, she retired from the San Francisco school district after a career as a teacher, counselor, principal, and administrator.

613. Ung, Loung. *First They Killed My Father: A Daughter of Cambodia Remembers*. New York, New York: HarperCollins, 1999. 241 pages; photographs; map. ISBN: 0060193328.

Notes: Published in paperback, New York: Harper Perennial, 2001. ISBN: 0060931388 (238 pages).

Abstract: Loung Ung was born into a comfortably middle-class Cambodian family of seven children. Her father was a member of the military police in the Lon Nol government, so when the Khmer Rouge took over Phnom Penh, when Ung was just five, the family was in great danger. With the aid of about one hundred pages of family history and recollections provided by her second eldest brother who was sixteen in 1975, Ung tells the story of her family during the reign of Pol Pot and the Khmer Rouge in one of the areas of the country where treatment was the most brutal. The family managed to escape Phnom Penh and pass as peasants for quite a while. The older children were sent to youth camps, and Ung's eldest sister succumbed to dysentery. Finally, Ung's father was led away by soldiers, never to return. After a while, her mother sent away three of the children still with her, including Ung, certain that the Khmer Rouge would come for her next. The three went to separate camps. The family had a brief reunion when almost all of the surviving members, suffering from malnutrition, were reunited at a hospital. However, they were once again split up, and Ung never saw her mother or youngest sister again. When the Vietnamese Army invaded Cambodia, all of the youth camps dissolved in the confusion, and Ung escaped with her brother and sister. After months in a refugee camp, they finally found their two older brothers. The family returned to their mother's birthplace and were taken in by aunts and uncles. Eventually, Ung and her eldest brother and sister-in-law escaped to Thailand by way of Vietnam and were able to immigrate to Vermont in 1980. Despite the subsequent efforts of her brother and his wife, the entire family has still not been reunited because the number of refugees accepted into the United States has been reduced. Ung, who is the spokesperson for Campaign for a Landmine-Free World, lives in Washington, D.C. and recently made her first trip back to Cambodia in fifteen years.

614. Upchurch, Carl. *Convicted in the Womb: One Man's Journey from Prisoner to Peacemaker*. New York, New York: Bantam Books, 1996. 236 pages. ISBN: 0553097261 : 0553375202.

Abstract: Upchurch grew up in South Philadelphia. Neglected from earliest childhood, he essentially raised himself on the street. Whenever he was caught at a crime, he was sent to a youth facility where he would get food, shelter, and human warmth, but he would eventually be released and be back on his own. As an adult, except for a brief period in the army, Upchurch was in prison until he was thirty-six. During this time he earned a GED and began reading anything he could find. His exposure to literature began to change his life and way of thinking. It taught him emotions he had never been exposed to and gave him motivation to plan a new direction for his life. Given the opportunity to take university courses, Upchurch became acquainted with Professor Martha Connamacher, who became his mentor. After his release from prison, he worked on her farm and she introduced him to the Friends Church. He considered careers in the ministry and social work, but found that university programs did not address what he saw as the important issues. He was certain that he wanted to serve youth. Upchurch started a program called the Progressive Prisoners' Movement through which he provided legal and emotional assistance to prisoners. He spoke in schools with both white and black children. With the help of his Baptist church, Upchurch started the Council for Urban Peace and Justice in 1992. In 1993, through this organization, he organized a gang summit, bringing together gang leaders from twenty-six cities for a week of religious services, discussions, goal-setting, and planning. One of the outcomes of this event was a lasting truce between two Los Angeles gangs, the Bloods and the Crips. Success in Kansas City led to similar summits in other areas, including Minneapolis, Chicago, and San Antonio, Texas. Upchurch discusses the importance of education, economics, and politics as tools for justice: "Education is power. *That* is what we have to give to ourselves and our children" (p. 201). He also examines the current state and future of black leadership in the United States. He sees an important role for black churches to provide and nurture new leaders, and he considers his own most important role to be working with youth to convince them that they can achieve something meaningful with their lives. Upchurch sees that his responsibility is to be a role model and that, therefore, his life must exemplify moral behavior, integrity, and forthrightness.

615. Urrea, Luis Alberto. *Nobody's Son: Notes from an American Life*. Camino Del Sol. Tucson, Arizona: University of Arizona Press, 1998. 188 pages. ISBN: 0816518653.

Abstract: This book, the third in Urrea's border trilogy, won the American Book Award in 1999. Urrea's childhood was marred by the unhappy marriage of his mother, a white woman from Staten Island, and his father, an officer in the army with close connections to the President of Mexico. The two met in San Francisco and eventually moved to Tijuana, where Urrea was born. Urrea's mother claimed heritage to family that ran a Virginia Plantation and owned slaves. He describes her as virulently conservative, with racist attitudes toward Hispanics and African Americans. His father came out of what Urrea calls the Mexican melting pot. He was blonde and blue-eyed, with Irish, Apache, German, Chinese, and Basque relatives in his family tree. Despite his varied background, Urrea's father mistrusted white Americans and was also very conservative. When Urrea was three, his father lost or gave up his position of importance, and the family left Mexico. In the U.S., his father went from one menial position to the other, and his mother became depressed and reclusive. Urrea has no memories of love or warmth with his parents. He eventually found a nurturing family environment when his father began taking him to a Mexican woman who practiced herbal healing. The woman's family took him in and cared for him, both medically and spiritually, and Urrea spent as much time as possible with them. Urrea talks about his Anglo-Mexican heritage and his confused sense of identity. He was pulled in opposite directions by his parents and taunted with racial epithets by both children and adults. Urrea writes of his initial admiration for the writer Edward Abbey, who "with his championing of lizards and watersheds, seemed to be championing us, too. Ed made some of us hope" (p. 102). The disappointment came with Abbey's book *One Life at a Time, Please* (Holt, 1988), in which he wrote of the dangers to the United States of uncontrolled migration from Latin-American countries, describing the immigrants (as quoted by Urrea) as, "hungry, ignorant, unskilled, and culturally-morally-genetically impoverished people" (p. 103). Urrea concludes the book with an essay describing his journey along the highways of the United States, going from truck stop to truck stop to see the country in an attempt to discover and define home.

616. Uyeda, Clifford I. *Suspended: Growing Up Asian in America*. San Francisco, California: National Japanese American Historical Society, 2000. 247 pages. ISBN: 188150610x.

617. Veciana-Suarez, Ana. *Birthday Parties in Heaven: Thoughts on Love, Life, Grief, and Other Matters of the Heart*. New York, New York: Plume, 2000. 177 pages. ISBN: 0452282004.

> **Abstract:** Ana Veciana-Suarez's book is a collection of stories about her past, her parents, who emmigrated from Spain to Cuba to the United States, and the small and momentous events that have shaped her life. Veciana-Suarez describes her father's anti-Communist, anti-Castro activities in Cuba, Bolivia, and elsewhere. She writes about her mother's quieter contributions to the family, and her escape from Cuba with three children to settle in Miami. Veciana-Suarez married and had five children before her husband died at age thirty-seven. She writes about raising the children as a single parent and helping them through the death of their father. Veciana-Suarez also presents issues of sibling rivalry, childhood rebelliousness, her second marriage, making marriage work, caring for her mother-in-law who suffered from Alzheimer's disease, and facing her mother-in-law's death.

618. Vilar, Irene (1969-). *The Ladies' Gallery: A Memoir of Family Secrets*. Translated by Gregory Rabassa. New York, New York: Vintage Books, 1998. 324 pages; photographs. ISBN: 0679745467.

> **Notes:** Originally published *A Message from God in the Atomic Age: A Memoir*. New York: Pantheon Books, 1996. ISBN: 0679422811.

> **Abstract:** In 1954, Irene Vilar's grandmother, Lolita Lebrón, stormed the U.S. House of Representatives with three other Puerto Rican nationalists, firing guns and wounding five congressmen. Lebrón was sentenced to fifty-seven years in prison. This proved to be the defining event in the life of Vilar's mother, who committed suicide in 1977 after waiting for twenty-three years for her mother to return to her. When her mother died, Vilar was only eight years old and this set in motion the many tragic events in her life. In 1988, she was admitted to a psychiatric hospital after an attempted suicide, not her first. In this book, Vilar chronicles her short history, alternating memories of her time in the psychiatric hospital with memories of her childhood leading up to her hospitalization, in an attempt to find some peace of mind. Following her mother's death, Vilar lived with a variety of aunts and uncles

and then with her father and his long-term girlfriend. In 1977, she moved to New Hampshire with cousins to attend a private school, spent one year in Spain when she was thirteen, and then returned to Puerto Rico for her father's wedding to a seventeen-year-old girl. Vilar describes a time when, at the age of fifteen, she had a sexual relationship with an older man, and her lengthy relationship with a young man while attending college at Syracuse University. She tells the story of her grandmother as she knows it, explores her mother's feelings about losing her mother, and Vilar's ongoing grief at her mother's death.

619. Voget, Fred. *They Call Me Agnes: A Crow Narrative Based on the Life of Agnes Yellowtail Deernose.* Assisted by Mary K. Mee. Norman, Oklahoma: University of Oklahoma Press, 1995. 220 pages; photographs; maps. ISBN: 0806126957.

Abstract: Agnes Yellowtail Deernose was born in 1908, in a time of transition for most American Indian cultures. She was raised in a traditional setting on a reservation, but was sent to a Baptist school where she learned English and received a white American education. She and her second husband, Donnie, worked to pass their language and tribal practices on to their children. While seeking to continue tribal ways, they also adapted to the many inevitable changes that come with living in close proximity to another culture. In this narrative, Yellowtail Deernose describes traditional Indian customs such as give-aways, family ties, the clan system, interaction between boys and girls, brothers and sisters, marriage practices, and ceremonies. Yellowtail Deernose describes the various celebrations of the year, including the holidays of American culture that the Crows adopted. Yellowtail Deernose devotes a significant portion of her narrative to describing adoption among the Crow people and how this family practice has touched her life and the lives of her children. An adoption means that a Crow child has many adults who take a significant interest in his or her life, thus strengthening family ties, and ensuring that a child has many opportunities to learn and to take on important roles in the tribal community. Yellowtail Deernose speaks with extreme fondness of the annual Crow Fair, the event during which she was born. "Early in July . . . people get their tipi poles ready for our grand tribal camp, the Crow Fair. We all look ahead to that time with great joy. . . . We can relax with our relatives, friends and visiting tribal members. We can be ourselves— be Indians" (p. 201).

620. Wade-Gayles, Gloria Jean. *Rooted against the Wind: Personal Essays*. Boston, Massachusetts: Beacon Press, 1996. 197 pages. ISBN: 0807009385.

Abstract: Wade-Gayles is a professor of English at Spelman College in Atlanta, Georgia. The author of a number of books, she has one other autobiographical work, *Pushed Back to Strength: A Black Woman's Journey Home* (Beacon Press, 1993). In *Rooted against the Wind*, Wade-Gayles discusses several topics from the point of view of her own experiences. One is social attitudes towards aging. Approaching her sixth decade, Wade-Gayles examines society's definition of age and the commonly held expectations for, and stereotypes of, women as they get older. In another essay, Wade-Gayles reveals her fear and distrust caused by being the victim of a robbery and attempted rape. She continues to fear for herself, her daughters, and all women. Wade-Gayles discusses her teaching style and the expectations she has for her students at Spelman College. She writes about examining her teaching priorities following confrontations with several students who insisted that she had silenced them by ignoring lesbians in her assigned readings, topics, and discussions. In other essays, Wade-Gayles addresses the pain experienced by African-American women when African-American men marry white women. She takes us on her own journey through this issue and describes how she was able to resolve her feelings of anger. Wade-Gayles discusses the importance of Historically Black Colleges and Universities, which offer both a high-quality education and a freer, and more supportive atmosphere. Wade-Gayles writes that they are generally overlooked by the media and are mistakenly considered by the general public to offer a lower quality of education. Finally, she celebrates the black community, her identity as a black woman, and her resolve to work for the betterment of black lives. Wade-Gayles writes,

> Memory tells me that blackness is in my essence as surely as blood is in my veins. It is an antenna I do not always know I am wearing, but which is surely there, identifying me as a woman who belongs to a group different in particularities from women who are Asian, Latina, Chicana, Native American, or Jewish. . . .
>
> (p. 195)

621. Wakamatsu, Jack K. (1918-). *Silent Warriors: A Memoir of America's 442nd Regimental Combat Team.* New York, New York: Vantage Press, 1995. 279 pages. ISBN: 0533114306.

> **Notes:** Originally published Los Angeles: JKW Press, 1992. ISBN: 0941369447 (212 pages).

> **Abstract:**   Jack Wakamatsu was a sergeant with the 442nd Regimental Combat Team, an all Japanese-American regiment, throughout World War II. Drafted in 1940, Wakamatsu had already been promoted to the rank of sergeant at the time of the Japanese attack on Pearl Harbor. Although many soldiers of Japanese descent were discharged at this time, Wakamatsu always had the support of his officers. Many of the men in his regiment were volunteers who were fierce in their dedication because they were fighting on behalf of their families and friends who were incarcerated in internment camps. Wakamatsu writes of his regiment's formation and training and their service in North Africa, Italy, and France. He writes with admiration and warmth for all of his comrades, the many who were killed in action and the few who survived. He made a pledge to one of his comrades who died in battle that he would record the story of the 442nd in book form, a painful process he began forty years later. Wakamatsu was raised in Southern California. His parents were both Japanese nationals whose ideas did not fit in with their more traditional parents.   His mother married Wakamatsu's father, who was already established in the United States, and left Japan without asking permission or even telling her parents. Wakamatsu writes of the limited opportunities for Japanese Americans in California before the war. Many of the young people attended college, but the only employment opportunities they had were in farming, selling produce, or running restaurants. Drafted before completing college, Wakamatsu was not interned with the rest of his family. However, he recounts many painful events surrounding the evacuation of the Japanese Americans from the West Coast, especially the betrayal of friends by neighbors who destroyed or used for personal gain the homes, property, and land with which they had been entrusted. Wakamatsu, however, does not forget the few white Americans who remained true friends and did what they could to help and to alleviate the suffering, indignity, and pain of evacuation and incarceration. Following the war, the veterans and their families continued to face hatred and discrimination as they returned to the cities and towns they had been forced to leave by Executive Order 9066. Wakamatsu writes that even in post-war years there were still many wrongs to right, including undoing the Japanese nationals' inability to become naturalized citizens and the Pacific States Alien Land Law.

We fought for the rights of free expression and
opportunity for all. What else could we do to
make this nation great? We went to court to
obtain these basic rights, as other people in this
land took them for granted. The lesson we
learned is that human rights must never be taken
for granted. We went to war to defeat an enemy
of freedom, but now our foe was our own government. Does this make any sense at all?

(p. 257)

622. Walker, Alice (1944-). *The Same River Twice: Honoring the
Difficult: A Meditation on Life, Spirit, Art, and the Making of the
Film, The Color Purple, Ten Years Later.* New York, New York:
Scribner, 1996. 302 pages; photographs; index. ISBN:
0684814196.

Notes: Published in paperback, New York: Washington Square
Press, 1997 as *The Same River Twice: Honoring the Difficult.* ISBN:
0671003771 (307 pages).

Abstract: Well-known author Alice Walker writes about the
process of making her Pulitzer-prize winning novel *The Color
Purple* into a motion picture. She tells of her struggle to decide
whether she should sell the film rights to the book and how she
was won over by the director Steven Spielberg and Quincy Jones,
who wrote and produced the music. The book itself was controversial. Many critics accused Walker of liberating her black female
characters at the expense of the masculinity of her black male
characters. This controversy followed her throughout the making
of the film and long afterwards. Although Walker was asked to
write the screenplay for the film and spent several months doing
so, the version used was written by Menno Myges, a Dutch immigrant to the United States. Walker served as a consultant, advising both Spielberg and Myges. She also worked to ensure that a
large percentage of the technical staff were African American. The
book contains the screenplay written by Walker, entries from her
journal prior to the making of the film and long past its premier,
many reviews of the film, correspondence Walker had with people
connected with the film, and some fan letters. In her correspondence and journal entries, Walker discusses her impressions of the
work of Spielberg, makes detailed comments on music written by
Jones, and writes about her growing appreciation for the actresses
and actors, including Whoopi Goldberg in her first major film, and
film veteran Danny Glover. She discusses her misgivings about

changes in the story and shifts in the plot and their influence on the overall spirit of the film. Because the book meant so much to so many readers, Walker felt responsible for assuring that the movie would not let them down. In the end, however, she decided that the film version was necessary. "So much of my constituency just doesn't read," she says. "People in other countries, in Africa, who can't read English. I know that people in my own hometown [Eatonton, Georgia] might not read the book. But I knew they would see the film. . . . I wanted it to be there, to appear in the villages" (p. 175 as quoted in an article by Susan Dworkin published in *Ms.* magazine, December 1985).

623. Walton, Anthony. *Mississippi: An American Journey.* New York, New York: Knopf, 1996. 279 pages; photographs. ISBN: 0679446001.

Notes: Also published New York: Vintage Books, 1997. ISBN: 0679777415.

Abstract: Anthony Walton was born and raised in Aurora, Illinois. After graduating from Notre Dame University and earning a graduate degree from Brown University, he decided to explore the past and present state of race relations in the United States, in particular in Mississippi, his ancestral home. To do so he made a number of trips to Mississippi with his mother, with his father, and on his own. Walton met relatives and spoke with strangers, both African Americans and whites and with people at both ends of the socioeconomic spectrum. He considers the history of the state of Mississippi and some of its more famous residents, including Richard Wright, Medgar Evers, and William Faulkner. Walton asks about race relations, social interactions, and work conditions both past and present. Walton visits Civil War sites, explores the history of school desegregation, and analyzes the blues. When Walton looks back at his father's life and compares it with his own relatively comfortable childhood and the range of opportunities open to him, he realizes that his father "created my privilege when he himself had none" (p. 212). Walton's mother, in talking about her childhood in Mississippi and her unfulfilled desire to attend the formerly all-white University of Mississippi, expresses regret that so many of the present generation of African-American youth seem to have neither knowledge of nor interest in the changes, through struggle and sacrifice, that her generation and those before her brought about. Walton believes that the history of Mississippi casts "a large shadow" over the American past and present: "To me, American amnesia about the past was perhaps worse than the many crimes that had been committed, because that willful refusal to confront history made impossible any meaningful action now" (p. 272). He concludes that it is important for both whites and blacks to acknowledge the past of slavery, Jim Crow, and the institutionalized debasement of one group of human beings and American citizens.

> White Americans might understand and show more compassion toward the problems of blacks in New York, Chicago, Miami and Los Angeles were they to admit that many of those situations are best understood as continuations of the tragedy of the South. Black Americans, in turn, might reassess the true nature of their predicament, and reassess their goals and possibilities.
>
> (p. 273)

624. Wamba, Philippe E. (1971-). *Kinship: A Family's Journey in Africa and America*. New York, New York: Dutton, 1999. 383 pages; index. ISBN: 0525943870.

Notes: Published in paperback New York: Plume, 2000. ISBN: 0452278929.

Abstract: The son of an African-American mother and a Congolese father, historian Philippe Wamba uses his own family as a backdrop for a detailed study of Afro-American relations since slavery. Wamba was raised near Boston, Massachusetts. He moved with his family to Dar es Salaam, Tanzania, when his father was offered a job at the national university and in the wake of the death of his elder brother from leukemia. During the family's time in Tanzania, Wamba's father attempted a trip to his native Zaire (now the Congo) and was arrested and imprisoned for a year for subversive activities. Wamba went to high school in the United States and was accepted at Harvard, where he studied African and African-American subjects. He discusses in detail the difficult and complex relationship that African Americans as a whole have had with Africa and Africans. For example, in the interest of solidarity, U.S. civil rights activists have publicly praised and supported dictatorships in Africa, much to the confusion of the general populace in those countries. Wamba also noticed that on U.S. campuses, African-American students had little enthusiasm for the political activities of African students and vice versa. He describes the era when freed American slaves went back to Africa, themselves becoming colonists who manipulated and abused the indigenous population. On a lighter side, he discusses the assimilation of popular culture by both sides. Wamba provides historic fact and his own theories of how the situations evolved and how relations might be improved. At the end of the book, Wamba's father is again involved in political activities in the Congo, and Wamba expresses his own hopes for the desperate situation:

> Perhaps this war will do what no other war in the Congo's history has: silence the guns once and for all by returning power to the Congolese people, allowing them to take control of their own destiny. If the much-touted "African renaissance" is to become reality, if the twenty-first century is to be the moment of Africa's triumph, perhaps it begins here.   (p. 350)

625. Ward-Royster, Willa. *How I Got Over: Clara Ward and the World-Famous Ward Singers*. As told to Toni Rose. Foreword by Horace Clarence Boyer. Philadelphia, Pennsylvania: Temple University Press, 1997. 263 pages; photographs. ISBN: 1566394899 : 1566394902.

Abstract: Gospel singers Willa and Clara Ward were the daughters of the indomitable Gertrude and George Ward. Gertrude felt called to sing gospel music and, with her daughters, formed the Ward Singers. Willa describes a childhood that included church, singing, and surviving the controlling wrath of their mother. The Ward Singers eventually became Clara Ward and the Famous Ward Singers. They toured the world, held long engagements in Las Vegas and played the Apollo Theater, Carnegie Hall, and jazz festivals. Willa broke away at the age of nineteen, getting married, having a baby, and living independently of her mother. Clara attempted to break away, but her mother always managed to convince her to come back. She had a brief marriage at the age of eighteen and then an attachment with Reverend C. L. Franklin, the father of Aretha Franklin. Her mother wrested her from both of these relationships. Willa tried to establish an independent career, but was never free of the interference of her mother, who would take over engagements, coax away her singers, and otherwise disrupt her professional activities. Clara always worked with her mother, and while she was beloved by music lovers around the world, she literally worked herself to death. Tired and depressed most of the time, Clara was dependent on alcohol and died at the age of fifty-one after suffering several strokes. Ward-Royster writes about the difficulties of fame, rising and falling fortunes, and the struggle to maintain a home life and career. She ends her story with messages to her late sister, mother, and father, and to her two daughters.

626. Ward, Samuel Ringgold (b. 1817). *Autobiography of a Fugitive Negro, His Anti-Slavery Labours in the United States, Canada, and England.* Chapel Hill, North Carolina: Academic Affairs Library, University of North Carolina at Chapel Hill, 1999.

http://metalab.unc.edu/docsouth/wards/ward.sgml
http://metalab.unc.edu/docsouth/wards/ward.html

Notes: Documenting the American South (Project).

627. Watkins, Mel. *Dancing with Strangers: A Memoir.* New York, New York: Simon & Schuster, 1998. 320 pages. ISBN: 0684808641.

Abstract: Watkins presents his life story through his graduation from college. When still an infant, his family moved north from Memphis to Youngstown, Ohio, during the great northern migration. In Youngstown, Watkins's father worked in the steel mills, and the family's fortunes followed those of the industry. The family moved into a section of the city that had rapidly shifted from an integrated to a primarily black neighborhood. The schools that Watkins's attended, however, were integrated. His experience with racism was muted.

> . . . I never faced direct or overt segregation in Youngstown. In part it was luck, of course, but primarily it was because as a child, I had usually followed the lead of others without question—complied with the unwritten rules, and without even knowing it, effectively stayed in my place. Later, when I became aware of the restrictions, I simply refused to put myself in a position of asking or insisting on being accepted anyplace where I was clearly unwanted.
>
> (p. 145)

In junior high and high school, Watkins turned to athletics as a way to belong and excel. After scoring in the top one percent of his high school class on a college aptitude test (and being asked to take the test over again because school administrators could not believe it), Watkins decided to take academics seriously and was courted by colleges from all over the country. He accepted Colgate College's offer of an academic award that allowed him to play basketball, as opposed to an athletic scholarship which required him to participate in sports. While at mostly-white and exclusive Colgate, Watkins found himself struggling with the geographic and social isolation. By his second year, he had resolved many of these issues and had begun to think more about being black in a white community and what his role might be in the growing Civil Rights Movement. Watkins spent one summer in Harlem while working for the *New York Daily News*, and it was there he discovered the multifaceted nature of African-American culture

> It seemed evident to me that the bond that united me and all these multicolored folks was not some primal racial identity that defined character and behavior but the externally imposed experience of repression. I was convinced of it. What was truly amazing to me was the richness of the folk culture that had emerged despite the oppression.   (p. 302)

Watkins graduated from Colgate and set off again for New York City, "determined to study and celebrate the cultural riches that had flowered from the so-called Negro's resilient spirit and bizarre American experiences" (p. 320).

628. Watson, Bernard C. *Colored, Negro, Black: Chasing the American Dream*. Philadelphia, Pennsylvania: JDC Books, 1997. 265 pages; photographs. ISBN: none.

Abstract: Bernard Watson was born in Gary, Indiana. His mother graduated magna cum laude from Talladega College in Alabama at the age of fifteen and became a teacher. His father joined the army at nineteen and served in France during World War I. Seventy years after the Armistice, Watson wrote to Washington, D.C., to see why his father had received no medals despite his accomplishments in the army. Without any fanfare, Watson received three medals that his father had earned but had never been awarded. Watson juxtaposes his own story and activities against the backdrop of the history of African Americans in this country, in Indiana and Philadelphia, within the armed services, and in the field of education. Watson settled on teaching as a career after graduating from the University of Indiana in 1951, but was unable to find employment. After working in the steel mills of Gary and military service, Watson went to graduate school at the University of Illinois and the University of Chicago. He earned his Ph.D. in two years while a fellow of the Midwest Administration Center and then went with his wife to

Philadelphia to serve in the administration of Mark Shedd and Richardson Dilworth of the Philadelphia Public School System in 1967. Watson describes his three years of service, which included racial strife, civil rights protests, near riots, and student takeovers. During this time, Watson was able to help improve the conditions for minority educators and students in Philadelphia. He later joined the administration at Temple University as Vice President for Academic Administration, where he brought more minorities into all levels of the school. His own office was ethnically diverse, and he pushed his secretaries and other staff to earn their degrees while they worked for him. Watson left Temple to become president of the William Penn Foundation, a grant-making institution which supports community building, culture, environment, and human development. Watson describes the politics of Gary and Philadelphia, the details of his work and contributions to education and to the fabric of the city of Philadelphia. He writes about his family and gives his views on child raising and his philosophy of education. He stresses the importance of caring for our children and the irony of the existence of malnutrition, poverty, and the lack of opportunity in a country such as the United States.

> [H]ere in the United States, I see malnourished children and homeless adults. I see schools no child should have to attend. I see parents struggling mightily day after day to create a sense of order for their families, trying to make their lives better. In this, the richest country on earth, more of us should be not only angry but ashamed.
>
> (pp. 257-258)

629. Watson, Bob (1946-). *Survive to Win*. Written with Russ Pate. Nashville, Tennessee: T. Nelson Publishers, 1997. 240 pages; photographs. ISBN: 0785271937.

Abstract: Baseball player Bob Watson was born in 1946 in South Central Los Angeles. He was introduced to baseball when he was eight years old. By the time he was in high school he was well known for his home runs and had earned the nickname "Bull." He attended Harbor Junior College in Wilmington, California, where he was noticed by a scout for the Houston Astros. In 1965, he was on his way to Cocoa, Florida, for the Astros training camp. Following spring training, Watson was sent to one of the team's class A affiliates in South Carolina. He was stunned by the virulent racism and segregation, not only in town, but on the team. As late as 1969, Watson and his fellow African-American ball players found it impossible to find hotels or restaurants in the South in which they could stay. He recalls being forced to sleep in the team clubhouse while working as a catcher for a minor league team in Savannah, Georgia. After moving up through the minor leagues, Watson was in and out of the Astros major league starting line-up until 1970, when he was suddenly required at first base. He proved himself to be a powerful hitter, and he was chosen twice to play on the All-Star team. Watson also played for the Boston Red Sox, the New York Yankees, and the Atlanta Braves. After retiring in 1985, he was encouraged by his wife Carol to stay with baseball, and his first post-retirement job was as a part-time batting coach for the Oakland A's minor league teams. He was then offered a position as assistant general manager with the Houston Astros, and then, in 1993, he was promoted to general manager, the first African American to be named to this position in major league baseball. In 1995, he went to the New York Yankees and succeeded in taking the team to the World Series. He gives a full account of the Yankee 1995-96 winning season and their subsequent World Series victory. In the midst of his success as a general manager, however, Watson was diagnosed with prostate cancer. He was lucky to have been diagnosed while in the early stages of the disease and had a successful operation and recovery. Watson writes about the inroads made by minority players at all levels of professional baseball, including treatment, compensation, and equal access to accommodations throughout the United States.

630. Watson, Henry (b. 1813). *The Narrative of Henry Watson.* Chapel Hill, North Carolina: Academic Affairs Library, University of North Carolina at Chapel Hill, 2000.

> http://docsouth.unc.edu/neh/watson/watson.sgml
> http://docsouth.unc.edu/neh/watson/watson.html

> **Notes:** Documenting the American South (Project).

631. Watson, Vernice. *You Can't Get There from Here: The Story of Music Industry Promoter Vernice Watson's Rise—From the Radio Kings of the 60s to the Gospel Explosion of the 90s.* Written with Milton B. Allen. Baltimore, Maryland: Verlen Publishing Company, 2000. 208 pages; photographs. ISBN: 1892970007.

632. Wattleton, Faye. *Life on the Line.* New York, New York: Ballantine, 1996. 489 pages; photographs. ISBN: 0345392655 : 0345416570.

Abstract: Faye Wattleton became the president of Planned Parenthood in 1978 at the age of thirty-four. She was the first woman to head the organization since its founder, Margaret Sanger, and the first African American ever to take the position. In her book, Wattleton provides her perspective on the volatile history of family planning and the abortion rights campaign in the United States. As a child, Wattleton lived in both the North and South, in white communities and black, as she and her father followed her mother, a minister in the Church of God, from one church to the next. Wattleton was outspoken and precocious; she started school early and was quickly promoted two grades. She earned her degree in nursing from Ohio State University, and through her work as an obstetric and gynecological nurse, developed her views on women's rights to choose, to obtain safe and effective birth control, and to have access to safe medical treatment. As president of Planned Parenthood, Wattleton kept the organization in the public eye. Her work focused on defending *Roe v. Wade*, promoting international family planning services, preventing teen pregnancy, lobbying in Congress, and monitoring the Supreme Court. She also maintained a heavy speaking schedule. For the fourteen years she was in office, her leadership often caused controversy within the organization. To add to the turmoil, the anti-abortion movement became increasingly aggressive in its opposition to Planned Parenthood, and emotions ran high on both sides of the debate. Wattleton resigned in 1991, completely exhausted from her work and the struggles within and outside the organization.

633. Webb, William (b. 1836). *The History of William Webb*. Chapel Hill, North Carolina: Academic Affairs Library, University of North Carolina at Chapel Hill, 2000.

    http://docsouth.unc.edu/neh/webb/menu.html

    Notes: Documenting the American South (Project).

634. Weems, Renita J. (1954-). *Listening for God: A Minister's Journey through Silence and Doubt*. New York, New York: Simon & Schuster, 1999. 204 pages. ISBN: 0684833239 : 0684863138.

    Abstract: Renita Weems is a Methodist minister and professor of Old Testament Theology at Vanderbilt University. In this book she writes about what she calls her "seasons of faith," a phrase that helps her to describe her shifting relationship with God. Weems grew up in the Pentecostal Church but began attending a Methodist Church while in college. After a brief career on Wall

Street, she attended seminary and became a Methodist minister. Twelve years later she married a Baptist minister and began attending the Baptist Church with her husband: "Let's face it: there's nothing exotic about being a Methodist minister and ex-Pentecostal who is now married to a Baptist preacher. Nothing exotic about it at all" (p. 102). In this book, Weems describes her life of prayer and meditation and her personal struggle with her faith. She writes about her marriage and the challenge posed to two people who attempt to combine their fears, moods, insecurities, and the ebb and flow of love in a sustained, positive relationship. Weems also discusses the importance of the experience of care-giving, whether for children, the sick, or the elderly, in order to develop a love of and sense of stewardship toward all of humanity. She explores the hectic life of motherhood, marriage, and career, which leaves little time to concentrate on prayer or meditation or professional activities such as writing. Weems is the author of several books including *Just a Sister Away* (1988), and *I asked for Intimacy* (1993).

635. Weglyn, Michi (1926-). *Years of Infamy: The Untold Story of America's Concentration Camps.* Updated edition. Seattle, Washington: University of Washington Press, 1996. 351 pages; photographs. ISBN: 0295974842.

   Notes: Originally published New York, New York: William Morrow & Company, 1976. ISBN: 0688029965 : 0688079962.

636. Wells, Alethea A. *Lady in the Moon.* Wallingford, Kentucky: Unole Publishing Company, 1996. 247 pages. ISBN: 0964578719.

   Abstract: Alethea Wells, a former fashion model and member of the United States Air Force, describes her years living alone in the mountains following the death of her mother. Wells had been planning to travel the length of the Trail of Tears from the Cherokee reservation in North Carolina to Tahlequa, Oklahoma, when she received a telephone call from a sister informing her that their mother had died. After a four-month-long drinking spree, Wells decided to go to the mountains to deal with her alcohol abuse. She found a cabin, cleaned it up, acquired a kitten and a horse, and began her solitary life. She tells of the different friends who joined her in her retreat and how she made a living growing beans and making and selling moonshine. Despite periods of bad health and insobriety, Wells managed to develop a reputation for her ability to handle horses and guns. In the end, she was run off of her property and forced to part with many of her animals, including her beloved horses. Wells intersperses her story with songs she has written for her friends. She now lives happily with her husband, writing books and songs and designing book covers.

637. Wells-Barnett, Ida B. (1862-1931). *The Memphis Diary of Ida B. Wells.* Edited by Miriam DeCosta-Willis. Foreword by Mary Helen Washington. Afterword by Dorothy Sterling. Black Women Writers Series. Boston, Massachusetts: Beacon Press, 1995. 214 pages; photographs. ISBN: 0807070645.

Abstract: African-American journalist and civil rights activist Ida B. Wells-Barnett grew up during the years of Reconstruction following the Civil War and experienced the great political and social advancements made by African Americans during that brief period. Her diary, which she began at the age of twenty-four and kept between the years 1885 and 1887, is in manuscript form at the University of Chicago's Regenstein Library. Editor DeCosta-Willis has made it available in published form for the first time. In her diary, Wells-Barnett writes about her shaky confidence in her ability to succeed in her chosen field of journalism. She was just beginning to earn a living as a teacher living away from her family. Wells-Barnett struggled with the confines of societal restrictions on female behavior, both in the realm of courtship and within her profession. She describes her recreational activities, work, travels, illnesses, and expenses. She also documents her suit against the railroads in which she challenges the "separate but equal accommodations" law, a case which went, albeit unsuccessfully, to the Tennessee Supreme Court. Wells-Barnett chronicles her work with various civic organizations formed to protect African Americans from white violence. Included with this edition of Wells-Barnett's diary are her 1893 travel diary recording her trip through England and Scotland to solicit support for her anti-lynching campaign, her 1930 Chicago diary, and a selection of her published articles.

638. West Dorothy. *The Richer, the Poorer: Stories, Sketches, and Reminiscences.* Preface by Mary Helen Washington. New York, New York: Doubleday, 1995. 254 pages. ISBN: 0385471459.

Notes: Published in paperback, New York: Anchor Books, 1996. ISBN: 0385471647.

Abstract: Born at the turn of the twentieth century, Dorothy West began writing and selling her short stories as a teenager and has continued to do so throughout her life. She wrote her first novel, *The Living Is Easy*, in 1948 and her second, *The Wedding*, which became a bestseller, in 1995. West was raised in a middle class family in Boston and in her twenties was in New York as part of the Harlem Renaissance. Her stories recall elements of her childhood and youth. In one of the essays, "Fond Memories of a Black Childhood," she describes a train trip her family took to their summer home, and the puzzlement of white passengers at the existence of a prosperous black family:

> We were black Bostonians on a train full of white ones. Because we were obviously going the same way, laden as we were with all the equipment of a long holiday, children, luggage, last-minute things stuffed in paper bags, a protesting cat in a carton, in addition to the usual battery of disbelieving eyes, we were being subjected to intense speculation as to what people with our unimpressive ancestry were doing on a train that was carrying people with real credentials to a summer sojourn that was theirs by right of birth.
> (p. 172)

In the 1930s, West worked as a welfare investigator, and her stories began to reflect the contact with poverty she had then. After 1945, West moved to Martha's Vineyard, where she had spent all of her childhood summers, and she lived there on a year-round basis until her death in 1998. The stories and essays in this collection have all been published previously in magazines and newspapers, such as the *New York Daily News* and the *Vineyard Gazette*.

639. White, Barry. *Love Unlimited: Insights on Life and Love.* Written with Marc Eliot. New York, New York: Broadway Books, 1999. 246 pages; photographs; discography. ISBN: 0767903641.

Abstract: Barry White grew up in South Central Los Angeles. He was involved with gangs by the age of ten and in jail at fifteen. He was motivated to change his life by two desires: one to stay out of prison and the other to make his mother happy. In this pursuit, White quit school during his last semester of high school and walked to Hollywood to find a career in music. There he did a little of everything in the music industry, from helping out with recording sessions to writing and arranging songs to singing and touring. He eventually decided to produce his own group and began working with the female trio that would become Love Unlimited. At about the same time, White was contacted by his old friend Larry Nunes, who asked him to go into partnership with him in his production company Mo' Soul Production. This project gave White the cash he needed to rehearse and put together a first-rate debut album for Love Unlimited. It was a huge success. White thought that he would also like to work with a male singer and began writing songs and looking for possible talent. The "talent" turned out to be himself. His first album, like that of Love Unlimited, was a chart topper. White describes the intricacies of the music business and the ups and downs. He also writes about his family life, his marriage to Glodean of Love Unlimited, and their work together. He describes the problems he has had with the labels with which he has been affiliated, his long career, and the changing nature of his music as a soloist and with the Love Unlimited Orchestra. After forty years in the music business, White continues to seek to "open the door for you. The door to experience, knowledge, romance and soul" (p. 177).

640. White, Link Suh. *Chesi's Story: One Boy's Long Journey from War to Peace.* Tallahassee, Florida: Father and Son Publishing, 1995. 304 pages; photographs. ISBN: 0942407318.

Abstract: White begins his story in 1950 in North Korea. He was working in a G.I. mess hall in the town of Hamhung, when he was invited to move with the U.S. troops when they evacuated. White (called Chesi, or "shorty" by the G.I.s) writes that politics had nothing to do with his decision, but rather his stomach. "Stomach first, 'isms' second" (p. 49). With his father's permission, he left Hamhung and headed for Pusan in South Korea. He then worked at various jobs for the army until the war ended, at which time he was faced with the dilemma of no home and no family. A journalist, A. T. White, Jr. noticed White (then Chesi) and offered to adopt him. In 1955, Chesi, now officially Link S. White, flew to La Guardia airport, where he was met by his new parents, A. T. and Helen White. They lived in Paramus, New Jersey, where White went to junior and senior high. He began college at Muhlenberg in Pennsylvania, but unsure of what he wanted to do with his life, he took a leave of absence after his sophomore year and joined the U.S. Army. The military sent him to Korea and Germany and to Officers' Candidate School in Georgia. White went as a lieutenant to Okinawa and then to Vietnam. Following his tour of duty in Vietnam, he returned to Muhlenberg College and majored in humanities. He worked in an embassy position for the U.S. government and then for an aviation company for which he made a number of business trips to South Korea. Amazed by the progress and changes made there, he looks forward to the unification of north and south, "[f]or, no one in this world is the greater loser from the continued division than the Korean people themselves" (p. 304).

641. White, Walter Francis (1893-1955). *A Man Called White: The Autobiography of Walter White*. Athens, Georgia: University of Georgia Press, 1995.   382   pages.   ISBN: 0820317160 : 0820316989.

   Notes: Originally published New York: Viking, 1948.

642. Whitmore, Terry. *Memphis, Nam, Sweden*. As told to Richard Weber. Jackson, Mississippi: University of Mississippi Press, 1997. 202 pages. ISBN: 0878059830 : 0878059849.

   Notes: Originally published Garden City: Doubleday, 1971.

643. Wickham, DeWayne. *Woodholme: A Black Man's Story of Growing Up Alone*. New York, New York: Farrar, Straus, and Giroux, 1995. 275 pages. ISBN: 0374292833.

   Notes: Also published Baltimore: Johns Hopkins University Press, 1996. ISBN: 0801854024.

   Abstract: Journalist DeWayne Wickham was in third grade when his father murdered his mother and then killed himself. The five children in the family were split up and sent to live with various relatives. Wickham went to live with an aunt and uncle in Baltimore, Maryland, but his aunt's family of seven barely had enough money to meet their own needs. After a brush with crime and jail, he began to look for a legal way to make money. On the advice of a friend, he went to the Woodholme Golf Course, a Jewish country club, to get a job as a caddy. Wickham spent four years working there. He describes his first summer during which he earned enough money to buy a full wardrobe of clothing, much of which was later stolen by a cousin. Wickham writes about his work and relationships with other caddies and the white golfers who treated the caddies with a strange mixture of respect and paternalism. Woodholme kept Wickham clothed and fed through- out his adolescent years. It also gave him a place to go away from home and away from school. Learning was a struggle for him, and he was kicked out of three high schools. Wickham finally had the good fortune to come under the wing of the vice-principal of Douglass High School, who continually encouraged him and made sure he had a second chance. During this time, his girlfriend got pregnant. Wanting to be a good father and to care for his girlfriend, Wickham decided not to finish high school and joined the United States Air Force instead. In this work, Wickham acknowledges the individuals who cared about him and helped him to make positive decisions that kept him alive and heading, if by an indirect route, to a purposeful future. Wickham went on to become a journalist and a syndicated columnist for *USA Today*.

644. Wiley, Ralph. *Serenity: A Boxing Memoir*. New York, New York: Henry Holt and Company, 1989. 230 pages. ISBN: 0805006702.

> **Notes:** Also published Lincoln: University of Nebraska Press, 2000. Includes new afterword by the author. ISBN: 0803298161 (242 pages).

> **Abstract:** Ralph Wiley was raised in Memphis, but one of his earliest influences was his Uncle Charles in California. Uncle Charles had been a boxer in his youth, and Wiley looked to him to teach him how to fight off bullies. Wiley describes his friends and their various temperaments and tendencies toward fighting. After college, Wiley was employed by the *Oakland Tribune* in Oakland, California. After a year as a copyboy, Wiley grabbed a chance to do a story on basketball great Julius Irving and was eventually moved into the sports section. His first beat was boxing, and he began to frequent the New Oakland Boxing Club, where many promising boxers were training. Wiley writes about the careers of boxers from the area, such as George Cooper, Erwin Williams, and Bashiru, a Nigerian student at UC Berkeley who wanted to box to earn money. He also writes about boxers he came across in Las Vegas, most notably Muhammad Ali as a young man and Joe Lewis just before his death. Along with boxers, Wiley comments on other boxing-related personalities, such as announcer Howard Cosell and promoter Don King. He describes the times and careers of the two "Sugar Rays," Robinson and Leonard, and his experiences with them. Another boxer featured is the young Mike Tyson. Wiley gives sympathetic opinions of some of Tyson's difficulties, notably his relationship with his former wife Robin Givens and the fight in which Tyson bit off the ear of Evander Holyfield.

645. Wilkens, Lenny. *Unguarded: My 40 Years Surviving in the NBA*. Written with Terry Pluto. New York, New York: Simon & Schuster, 2000. 302 pages. ISBN: 0684873745.

> **Abstract:** Wilkens grew up in Brooklyn, New York. His Irish-American mother and African-American father were married in 1935, and when Wilkins was five years old, his father died. Although his mother worked hard, there was never enough

money to make ends meet. Because Wilkens was a serious student and held a job to assist with the household finances, he didn't have much time for basketball. The Wilkens family was Catholic, and Wilkens and his siblings attended Catholic schools. Wilkens always felt encouraged and supported by the church and the priests connected with the school. One priest, a long-time mentor to Wilkens, recommended him for a basketball scholarship to Providence College, knowing that it was the only way Wilkens would be able to continue his education. Wilkens was accepted, and he joined one other African-American student in a freshman class of three hundred. In 1960, as he neared graduation from Providence, Wilkens, a defense specialist, was the number one draft of the St. Louis Hawks. Wilkens remarks on the changes that have taken place within college basketball and with the NBA draft in the forty years since he began his professional career. Basketball was a good job when he was starting out, but players had no promise of fame or fortune. Wilkens played with the Hawks for eight years before moving to the Seattle Supersonics. In 1969, after one year as a player, he was asked to be their "player/coach." Bill Russell was the only other African-American coach, also a player/coach, in professional basketball at the time. Wilkens has played for and coached the Cleveland Cavaliers, coached the Atlanta Hawks and the Portland Blazers, was general manager to the Seattle Supersonics, and, as he wrote this book, he was coaching the Toronto Raptors. He discusses racism in professional sports, the current state of professional basketball, and his thoughts on coaching and playing.

646. Williams, Barney (1929-). *I Remember to Forget*. New York, New York: Tom-Pat Publishing, 1998. 496 pages; photographs. ISBN: none.

Abstract: Barney Williams grew up in Jacksonville, Florida. His father left home, but Williams was fortunate to have a caring and responsible stepfather. The family moved with him to New York City, where Williams spent most of his life. As an adult, he started working for music distributors promoting new songs to the New York City radio stations. He was assigned to white as well as black radio stations, and then sent out on the road to do promotions throughout the country. During this time he worked for a variety of companies, including Capitol and Dementia. Willliams decided to set up his own business and began Bar-Wil Record Company and Tom-Pat Publishing (ASCAP). Despite his success, Williams developed a drinking habit which took over his life. He left the music business and drank until he was completely destitute. He entered a Salvation Army Shelter and was so impressed by the humane way in which he was treated and the sincere support and respect that he received that he entered Salvation Army counseling, therapy and AA programs. Williams never returned to drinking, although he had many psychological and emotional traumas to work through over a lengthy period of time. He worked successfully in the Salvation Army programs and eventually went on its regular payroll, managing the organization's stores. After he was assigned to Booth House II in the Bowery of New York, Williams reentered the music world. He also reconnected with his family, a wife and seven children, but never told them about his period of homelessness. Williams worked at Booth House II until his retirement. He describes the services offered by the Salvation Army and the people connected to the organization, his work with the residents of Booth House II, his road back to self-esteem and self-respect, and his renewed ability to trust himself and others enough to form friendships.

647. Williams, Edward C. *My Life*. Chapel Hill, North Carolina: Professional Press, 1998. 81 pages; photographs. ISBN: 1570874182.

Notes: Originally published as *Triumph of Another Black Man*. New York, New York: Carlton Press, 1996, photographs. ISBN 0805252006 (62 pages).

Abstract: Edward Williams suffered a severe head wound when he was quite young. Because of his family's rural isolation and the second-class treatment given to blacks in Louisiana by the medical profession, Williams never received a thorough examination, and he was never sure if he suffered permanent damage from the wound. He was slow in school, and between having to help on the family farm and his apparent learning disabilities, Williams was still in sixth grade at age sixteen. In 1945, when Williams was seventeen, he quit school and joined the navy. After basic training, he was assigned to Steward Mates School. The work, catering and bed making, was not to his liking, but it was better than farm work. After touring Asia on two carriers, Williams received an honorable discharge because of severe seasickness. Armed with the G.I. Bill, he set out to receive his high school education. The rest of Williams's story describes his efforts to get his diploma, his training as a medical laboratory technician, and his career in the United States Air Force in the medical field. During his air force career, Williams was promoted to staff sergeant. He served in Madison, Wisconsin, Mississippi, Ankara, Turkey, and elsewhere, before retiring after a final tour of duty in Denver, Colorado. During his air force career, Williams married, and he and his wife had four children. The marriage failed because his work kept him away from home so much. Following his retirement from the military, Williams worked as a private investigator and a Colorado peace officer. He returned to Louisiana and, after the failure of his second marriage, found work as a psychiatric aid. After retiring from this position, Williams married a woman whom he met through an "international companion" company. They had one son together before Williams was diagnosed with prostate cancer. He describes his full recovery from cancer, but not without chronic complications due to his substandard treatment in the hospital. Williams does not look back with satisfaction on the course of his life, and he hopes that his new son will have a more rewarding one.

648. Williams, Gregory Howard. *Life on the Color Line: The True Story of a White Boy Who Discovered He Was Black.* New York, New York: Dutton, 1995. 285 pages; photographs. ISBN: 0525938508.

  Notes: Also published New York: Penguin Books, 1996. ISBN: 0452275338 : 0452275334.

  Abstract: Williams describes his early years in Virginia with his white mother, black father, and three siblings living above the family-owned-and-operated Open House Café, which, in defiance of local law, served both black and white patrons. Most summers, Williams and his younger brother Mike visited his maternal grandparents in Muncie, Indiana. After one visit, the boys returned home to find that their mother had left with the younger children. As business deteriorated and their father began drinking more, they were left hungry and dirty. Williams's father finally packed up their things and moved the two boys to Muncie to live with a great aunt. On their trip to Muncie, Williams's father explained to the boys that they were black, that they would not be visiting their white grandparents, but living with their black relatives, and that from now on they would have to get used to the fact that they "were colored." Williams's paternal relatives in Muncie had barely enough money to feed themselves, let alone two growing boys. The boys' father left them in the care of their great aunt, but they were soon sent to their grandmother, who, like their father, was an alcoholic. The boys had little to eat and no clean clothes. They were eventually rescued by a friend of the family, Miss Dora, who raised them on her income of twenty-five dollars a week until they left home. Williams describes the difficulty of looking white and being black and of being embraced grudgingly by his black family and rejected completely by his white family. Williams was determined to lead a different life from his father. He worked hard at school and participated in sports. Determined to be a lawyer, Williams attended Ball State University while working full time as a sheriff's deputy. He went on to earn a master's degree, a law degree, and a doctorate. He has been a history teacher, a lawyer, and a law professor. At about age twenty, Williams and his brother were reunited with their mother. His mother was eager to have the boys rejoin her family, but Williams realized that this meant rejecting his black family, especially Miss Dora. Because he was not prepared to turn his back on his life in Muncie, he rejected his mother's offer. He writes, "I realize now that I am bound to live out my life in the middle of our society and hope that I can be a bridge between races, shouldering the heavy burden that almost destroyed my youth" (p. 284).

649. Williams, Hallie E. *The Living Legacy.* [Virginia]: H. E. Williams, 1996. 100 pages; photographs. ISBN: none.

> **Abstract:** Hallie Williams has written a brief history of her life to leave to her three children, Eddie, Gregory, and Kelli Lynne. Born in 1941, Williams grew up in Newport News, Virginia. She provides brief histories of her mother and father. Williams's father was her mother's second husband. Williams's siblings were from her mother's first marriage and were grown by the time Williams was born. Williams writes about her activities growing up, her schools and teachers, the neighbors, and the families at her church. She met her husband while in high school, and although she had planned to attend Hampton Institute, she became pregnant and stayed home to raise her child. She left Newport News to live with her husband while he was stationed in Abilene, Texas. From there they spent three years in Hawai'i. It was while living in Hawai'i that Williams became a civilian employee with the military. She worked at the base at Pearl Harbor, and when she and her husband returned to Virginia, she began working at Fort Monroe. She worked in a variety of divisions before retiring in 1995. Williams and her husband divorced in 1977. She concludes her life story by writing about her post-marriage loves, providing short narratives about her children, and presenting photographic collages of her grandchildren.

650. Williams, James (b. 1825). *Life and Adventures of James Williams, a Fugitive Slave with a Full Description of the Underground Railroad.* Chapel Hill, North Carolina: Academic Affairs Library, University of North Carolina at Chapel Hill, 2000.

    http://docsouth.unc.edu/neh/williams/menu.html

    Notes: Documenting the American South (Project).

651. Williams, Jayson. *Loose Balls: Easy Money, Hard Fouls, Cheap Laughs & True Love in the NBA.* Written with Steve Friedman. New York, New York: Doubleday, 2000. 276 pages; photographs; index. ISBN: 038549226x.

    Notes: Also published in paperback New York: Broadway Books, 2001. ISBN: 0767905695.

    Abstract: Jayson Williams tells about his basketball career from the time he was a reluctant first-draft pick for the Phoenix Suns, through his years under the wing of Charles Barkley with the Philadelphia 76ers, to his best years with the New Jersey Nets. Williams describes the traps of fame and money, including sex, alcohol, and drugs, and the personalities, foibles, and virtues of his team mates and competitors. He also talks about race relations in the NBA and friendships, rivalries, losing teams, and unhappy players. Williams writes about his development as a player. His first years were tarnished by his drinking and lack of self-control, and most of his time with the Suns and the 76ers was spent on the bench. With the Nets, he developed his skills as a rebound player and became an All-Star player. Despite the Nets lengthy losing streak, Williams found the motivation to excel that he had previously lacked. In the book, he also talks about his family. Williams grew up in South Carolina and New York City. In the former, especially, his white mother and black father made him somewhat of an anomaly, not only in town, but with family both black and white. Now the adoptive father of the children of his two half-sisters who died of AIDS, Williams maintains that, while he enjoys the fame and fortune of being an NBA All-Star, he looks forward to the day he retires, marries, and has more children: "All I want to do when I retire is love my family, my wife and my kids and my parents" (p. 263).

652. Williams, Montel. *Life, Lessons, and Reflections.* Written with Daniel Paisner. Carlsbad, California: Mountain Movers Press, 2000. 73 pages. ISBN: 1588250016.

Abstract: Williams, the author of *Mountain Get out of My Way*, writes an inspirational work about maintaining a positive attitude after he was diagnosed with multiple sclerosis in 1999. Williams is donating all proceeds from the book, which was published by his own publishing company, to the Montel Williams MS Foundation.

653. —. *Mountain, Get out of My Way: Life Lessons and Learned Truths.* Written with Daniel Paiser. New York, New York: Warner Books, 1996. 207 pages. ISBN: 0446519073 : 0446604178.

Notes: Also published in a large print edition Thorndike, Maine: Thorndike Press, 1996. ISBN: 0786208228.

Abstract: Talk show host Montel Williams talks about his life and philosophy. Williams was raised with three siblings in a family headed by a hardworking father who was also a strict disciplinarian. After high school, Williams enlisted in the U.S. Marines and was recommended for a prep school that eventually led to his acceptance by the Naval Academy in Annapolis, Maryland. Of forty marines who entered the prep school, he was one of just four who graduated from the academy. After graduation he became a cryptologic officer in the Navy. He excelled at his work and enjoyed it, but his life changed when he was asked by a friend to give a talk at a MORE (Minority Officer Recruiting Effort) leadership seminar aimed at getting high school students to enlist in the armed forces. His talk was an enormous success, and he realized that this, more than code breaking, was what he was meant to do. Schools all over the East eagerly agreed to have him speak to students, but the Navy only reluctantly allowed him to schedule talks and refused to sponsor him in any way. Williams left the Navy to be able to spend more time speaking and spent the next two years traveling throughout the country. He writes about his message: "What I had to say was basic: stay in school, stay off drugs, set realistic goals and work to accomplish them. I expanded on my themes of restraint, responsibility, and respect to include the hot-button issues facing each community" (p. 170). As he became known, local television stations occasionally broadcast his talks. This led to several television specials and eventually to *The Montel Williams Show*. Despite the pressure for talk shows to cover sensational topics, Williams has worked hard to keep his program focused on topics pertinent to and helpful for young people.

654. Williams, Neil Allen O'Rourke. *Let Your Spirit Shine: A Poetic Memoir.* New York, New York: Vantage Press, 1998. 97 pages. ISBN: 0533116406.

> **Abstract:** This book is primarily a collection of poetry inspired by his family and the events of Williams's childhood and youth. He also writes a brief autobiography describing his childhood. Williams's mother was the daughter of Irish immigrants, and his father's background was African American and Seminole Indian. His parents sent him for financial reasons to live with his grandparents in Florida when he was ten months old. He remained with his grandparents for ten years. During that time, Williams had the benefit of many role models, both male and female, including teachers, pastors, and the many friends of his grandparents. He believes that African-American children had to study much harder than their white counterparts because they were learning African-American history along with the standard history lessons. "I would not trade this experience because I would learn later that white kids did not learn as much as we did about our resilience as a people" (p. 9). He did not move back with his parents until he was ten, by which time there were eight children in the family. Williams writes,
>
> > I remain convinced that we must continue to progress on this journey up the road apiece, despite exceptions to progress often seen in the state of American race relations, and America's internal period of redefining what it means to be an American in this vast global society.   (p. 23)

655. Williams, Thomas Edgar. *Gold Street: A 56 Year Odyssey Which Ends Where It Begins, on Gold Street in Baltimore.* Baltimore, Maryland: Gateway Press, 1997. 272 pages; photographs; maps. ISBN: none.

656. Willis, Rudolph E. *To Walk in My Shoes: Saving Grace on a Less Traveled Road.* Fort Bragg, California: Lost Coast Press, 2000. 179 pages; photographs. ISBN: 188289734x.

> **Abstract:** Willis moved to the Cabrini-Green housing projects in Chicago in 1962, when he was twelve. For his family, this was a move upward, but they found a mere continuation of their grinding poverty, a growing violent and criminal element, spiritual and physical hunger, and hopelessness. Willis's father, a decorated World War II veteran, was chronically unemployed, and the fami-

ly was on and off of General Relief. Willis was exceptionally bright. He taught himself to read before he could talk fluently. He excelled in school and was accepted at Lane Technical High School, a selective school for gifted students. Willis blocked out the reality of Cabrini-Green by surrounding himself with books and spending most of his time in his room reading and studying. He attended Northwestern University in Evanston, Illinois, where he blossomed under the mentorship of such professors as Dr. Welks in the sciences, Rabbi Vogel in religious studies, and South African poet-in-exile, Dennis Brutus. A premed student, Willis was accepted into the medical school at Washington University during his junior year at Northwestern. He writes about his professors, internships, rotations in various medical departments, and residency. He writes about professors who sought to develop and nurture great doctors and those who actively discouraged and blocked the success of students. Finally, Willis writes about his fellowship at the National Cancer Institute, the controversy surrounding Dr. Robert Gallo and the discovery of the AIDS virus, and his own professional work as an oncologist. Willis emphasizes treating patients with dignity and recognizing each patient's individual worth. He writes of the importance of helping them to maintain or develop an attitude of hope and possibilities: "[M]any of us do a remarkable job repairing broken bodies. But this is too often done with a cold heart. Human beings are much more than the flesh we attempt to revive. And more often than not, it is a broken spirit that causes us to lose the battle" (p. 179).

657. Wilson, Sunnie. *Toast of the Town: The Life and Times of Sunnie Wilson*. Written with John F. Cohassey. Great Lakes Books. Detroit, Michigan: Wayne State University Press, 1998. 200 pages; photographs. ISBN: 0814326951.

Abstract: Sunnie Wilson was born in 1908 in Columbia, South Carolina. His mother was a maid who traveled with the people she worked for. Wilson never knew his father, and so he was raised by his grandmother and aunts. Wilson dropped out of high school for a time to work in New York, but returned to South Carolina to finish high school and to attend Allen University, where he was an art and theater major. Wilson then made his way to Detroit, where he began managing bands and producing shows. Although he often cooperated with police and counted many of them among his friends, Wilson and his club patrons were often subjected to arbitrary harassment. He challenged this treatment, filing complaints and testifying at hearings. Wilson also promoted boxing matches. He sometimes ordered his boxers to use strong-arm tactics: to convince white restaurant owners to deseg-regate their businesses and to prevent landlords from evicting tenants in the dead of winter. Wilson owned or co-owned many establishments, including the Brown Bomber's Chicken Shack (an enterprise he shared with Joe Louis), the Forest Club, the Mark Twain Hotel, and Sunnie's Celebrity Room. He also ran business-es in the black-owned Idlewild Resort. In addition, Wilson was active in politics and ran for mayor of his community, Paradise Valley. Wilson describes the devastation of the 1943 Detroit race riots, during which his apartment and all of his belongings were destroyed by members of the Detroit police, and the riots of 1967. Wilson describes the urban renewal of the early 1960s that destroyed much of the community of Paradise Valley and many landmarks of Detroit black history.

658. Winans, CeCe. *On a Positive Note: Her Joyous Faith, Her Life in Music, and Her Everyday Blessings.* Written with Renita Weems. New York, New York: Pocket Books, 1999. 218 pages; photo-graphs. ISBN: 0671020005 : 0671020013.

Abstract: Singer CeCe Winans was the first girl to be born into a family with seven boys. She was followed by two more girls for a total of ten children. The children were raised by their parents within the strict guidelines of the Church of God in Christ. She was not allowed to participate in most outside activities of other girls, didn't wear makeup or jewelry, wore longer dresses, and never wore pants. The children did not go to movies, join clubs, dance, or even play cards, so CeCe was most comfortable being with her family and at church. The entire Winans family enjoyed singing together, both at home and in church. Each year during the Christmas season, her parents organized a Winans Family con-cert at Detroit's Mercy College. After graduating from high school, Winans and her older brother BeBe received an invitation to audition for Jim and Tammy Bakker's PTL Singers in North Carolina. Both of them were accepted, and they stayed with the group for three years. It was during this time that BeBe and CeCe began their career as a duo. Following their PTL years, the two signed a contract with Sparrow Records. They specialized in a cross between gospel and rhythm-and-blues and had several chart-topping hits. In 1995, CeCe recorded her first solo album and gave her first solo concerts. In 1996, she won a Grammy and two Dove Awards (the annual awards for Christian and Gospel music), including best female vocalist. She views her singing as a ministry to God, and this remains her foremost motivation in per-forming and recording. She writes,

My whole life is good, despite all the ups and downs. It always has been. I've grown up. I'm both the shy, quiet girl from Detroit who had to be forced into the limelight to sing her first solo, and I am a performer making decisions about her career, negotiating with industry heads who is unafraid to say no. (p. 217)

659. Winfrey, Oprah (1954-). *The Uncommon Wisdom of Oprah Winfrey: A Portrait in Her Own Words.* Edited by Bill Adler. New York, New York: William Morrow & Company, 1996. 290 pages. ISBN: 0688143822.

Notes: Also published by New York: Carol Publishing Group, 1997. ISBN: 1559724196 : 0806518944.

Abstract: Adler has compiled a collection of Oprah's quotations and interview excerpts and grouped them into categories to make this "autobiography." Oprah discusses her childhood, her entry into a career in television, the creation and evolution of her talk show, and the founding of her media enterprise, Harpo Studios. Winfrey's views on love, men, and marriage are also included here, as well as her views on politics, her humanitarian interests, and other causes that are important to her. Winfrey was born in Kosciusko, Mississippi, and had an early childhood of rural poverty. She began learning to read at the age of three, so that by the time she finally started school she was skipped several grades. After her parents separated, she found that she preferred life with her father and stepmother, who encouraged her to learn and demanded that she work hard. Before entering her career in television, Winfrey won several beauty pageants and was crowned Miss Fire Prevention, Miss Black Nashville, and Miss Black Tennessee. Despite this, she has never thought of herself as beautiful and feels that she won the titles because of her talent and poise. Winfrey's first professional television work was in Baltimore, Maryland, where she worked for four years before heading to Chicago to begin her own show. Winfrey describes what she has sought to accomplish through her widely acclaimed talk show and how her programming has changed as she has grown as a professional. She also talks about her acting career, her relationship with Stedman Graham, her struggle with weight, and her goals for the future.

660. Wing, Kathleen Kong. *Inside the Oy Quong Laundry.* Written with Carolyn Wing Greenlee. 3rd Edition. Kelseyville, California: Earthen Vessel Productions, 1998. 175 pages; photographs; letters. ISBN: 1887400133.

Notes: First edition published in 1995. ISBN: 1887400087 (88 pages). Revised edition published in 1996.

Abstract: Kathleen Kong Wing, a first generation Chinese American, was born in Merced, California. She was one of six children, three boys and three girls. Her parents emigrated to the United States from China. Her father entered the country as a "paper son," using false documents which identified him as having been born in the United States. He returned to China to marry and returned to the United States nine years later, followed by his wife and child, Wing's mother and brother. The Kong family business was the Oy Quong laundry. Wing describes how hard her parents worked, especially her mother. In China, the women worked very hard all day, but because they lived in close-knit villages, they socialized regularly with friends and family. In Merced, Wing's parents worked, took care of the children and the house and the cooking, but had no friends to relax with. Her mother, who had lived in China much longer than her father and never gave up traditional Chinese ideas and practices, was distant and very strict. She made it very clear that boys were more valuable than girls. Wing grew up feeling that she was useless to the family. She remembers an argument between her parents late at night during which she believes her father was telling her mother that she could not kill their youngest daughter, a practice which was fairly common in China. Wing has many memories of overt racism and discrimination in Merced. It was a tradition that honor students graduating from the local high school were automatically given employment in town, but Wing, one of four graduating honor students, did not benefit from this practice. "The way we always lived, we were never superior to anybody and we were never inferior to anybody. It infuriated us to be treated as if we were inferior just because we walked by and we looked a little different" (p. 105). Wing worked for her parents in their new Lincoln Market and married Tom Wing, an herbalist and chiropractor. She concludes her story with the death of her father, who was hit by a car. The family spent the entire day in the hospital with him until he died, and during that time, not one doctor or nurse came in to monitor his progress or to treat him.

661. Wing, Thomas W. (1915-). *Son of South Mountain and Dust.* Written with Carolyn Wing Greenlee. Illustrated by Thomas W. Wing and Duncan Chin. Kelseyville, California: Earthen Vessel Productions, 1999. 149 pages; illustrations. ISBN: 1887400273.

662. Wingo, Dorothy Maria. *The Imperfect Dream.* New York, New York: Vantage Press, 1998. 95 pages. ISBN: 053312302x.

663. Witt, Edwin T. *Witt's End.* Victorville, California: E&C Publishers, 1996. 361 pages. ISBN: 0966370007.

  Abstract: Witt writes both about his childhood in a segregated neighborhood of Birmingham, Alabama, and the conditions of African Americans in general during that time. Born in 1920, Witt experienced the deprivation of the Great Depression. His family, however, raised vegetables, chickens, and hogs, and so benefited from a balanced diet. Witt remembers the malnourished look of the children who subsisted on little more than biscuits and syrup. His home life was chaotic. His parents made a tenuous living selling moonshine and participating in the numbers racket. His father, an alcoholic, abused both Witt and his mother. Witt was kicked out of the house when he was fourteen, and his mother was later murdered. No charges, however, were ever brought against his father or anyone else. Witt recalls the conditions of segregation and the reign of terror carried out by Eugene H. (Bull) Connor who was elected Commissioner of Public Safety in Birmingham in 1932. Black men were frequently accused of rape and murder. Most of the time these accusations were false, and "justice" was often dispatched by a lynch mob. Witt had the benefit of many fine teachers and doctors who inspired him to pursue an education. Unable to save the money necessary to attend the Tuskegee Institute, Witt attended nearby Miles College. Following graduation, he was accepted at Meharry Medical College in Nashville, Tennessee. He became a pediatrician and practiced in Harlem, Los Angeles, and Las Vegas. Witt also had affiliations with several public institutions, including as an assistant clinical professor at the Martin Luther King, Jr. Hospital in Willowbrook, California.

664. Woods, Victor Martin. *A Breed Apart: One Man's Journey to Redemption, Through Friendship, Humiliation and Spiritual Evolution.* Written with Earl N. Caldwell. Chicago, Illinois: A.B.A. Publishing, 1998. 578 pages. ISBN: 0966490401.

665. Wright, Mary Herring (1924-). *Sounds like Home: Growing Up Black and Deaf in the South.* Washington, D.C.: Gallaudet University Press, 1999. 282 pages; photographs. ISBN: 1563680807.

Abstract: Mary Herring Wright was born into a large family in 1924. She lived in the community of Iron Mine, North Carolina, and attended a two-room school. She describes the community as strictly segregated, with most white businesses on Front Street and the black businesses on Back Street. She was nine years old when she began to suffer from an inflammation in her left eye which seemed to be connected with her growing inability to hear. By the time the inflammation left her left eye and traveled to her right, she was almost completely deaf. Her condition was never diagnosed and her hearing did not return. Although she felt left out and lonely, Wright was very attached to her family and especially her mother. When her parents decided to send her to the state school for the deaf and blind, where children were boarded the entire school year, the transition was difficult for her. Despite her homesickness, however, Wright thrived at the school, developing friendships and maturing to adulthood. When it came time to leave, Wright was unsure as to her readiness to face life away from the school and people who understood and accepted her. She moved to Washington, D.C., to live with a cousin, and got a job with the Department of the Navy. Wright eventually returned home to North Carolina to care for her sick mother. Later, she married James Wright and raised a family of four children.

666. Wyman, Nona Mock. *Chopstick Childhood in a Town of Silver Spoons: Orphaned at the Ming Quong Home, Los Gatos, California.* Walnut Creek, California: MQ Press, 1999. 280 pages; photographs. ISBN: 0835126455.

Notes: Previously published in 1997. ISBN: none (320 pages).

Abstract: Wyman lived alone with her mother in San Francisco's Chinatown until she was two-and-a-half years old. One day her mother and a stranger took a drive with her and left her in Los Gatos, California, at the Ming Quong Home, an orphanage for Chinese girls begun through the good works of Donaldina Cameron in the early part of the century. Although traumatized by her sudden and inexplicable abandonment, Wyman learned to love the home. The teachers were not demonstratively affectionate, but they were caring and nurturing. All the girls were well cared for, attended the local public school, and made life-long friends. As the youngest and the only one not in school, Wyman received ample attention from both the teachers and the older girls. The home gave instruction in Chinese, fed the girls Chinese food, and taught them respect for themselves and their culture. Wyman was not to learn anything about her mother or the reasons for their separation until she was much older and reunited with the remnants of her family, including a brother and sister who had also been sent to orphanages. Wyman looks back over the events of her childhood and adolescence at Ming Quong, describes the history of the home and its mission, and reports on its current state and role. Wyman currently owns a clothing and gift shop in Walnut Creek, California, which she calls Ming Quong. Her son operates the MQ jewelry store next door.

667. X, Marvin. *Somethin' Proper: The Life and Times of a North American African Poet.* Castro Valley, California: Black Bird Press, 1998. 277 pages; photographs. ISBN: 0964967219.

Abstract: Activist, poet, and playwright Marvin X, born Marvin K. Jackmon, grew up in Oakland and attended Oakland City College and San Francisco State University. He got his first introduction to black nationalism when he met Richard Thorne and Black Panther Huey Newton. He dropped out of San Francisco State to start the Black Arts West Theater, but continued to participate in the Black Student Union. X's contacts grew to include African-American activists LeRoi Jones (Amiri Baraka), Ed Bullins, Ethna Wyant, Eldridge Cleaver, and Bobby Seale, and his activities broadened to include work in the black theater movement in New York, Chicago, Philadelphia, and San Francisco. During the Vietnam Conflict, X evaded the draft and sought asylum in Canada, where he renounced his U.S. citizenship. He returned to the United States to teach drama and English in the Ethnic Studies Department at Fresno State University, but his appointment was controversial. Students and faculty alike were divided in their opinions of him, and Governor Ronald Reagan worked to have his position terminated. From Fresno, X went to Mexico. He was arrested there and deported to the United States, where he stood trial for draft evasion and served five months in a minimum security prison. In his book, X writes of his conversion to the Nation of Islam and his continuing fight against cocaine addiction and alcoholism. Marvin X has written numerous books of poetry, including *Fly to Allah: Poems* (1969), *Liberation Poems for North American Africans* (1983), and *Love and War: Poems* (1995). His plays include *Take Care of Business* (1967), *The Black Bird: A One Act Play* (1969), and *One Day in the Life* (1996). He is the founder of the Recovery Theater, Black Bird Press, and the newsletter *Poetletter* (http:/www.marvinx.com).

668. Young, Al. *Drowning in the Sea of Love: Musical Memoirs.* Hopewell, New Jersey: Ecco Press, 1995. 273 pages. ISBN: 0880013885.

Abstract: Poet Al Young is a native of Mississippi and was raised in Detroit, Michigan. He has written a series of vignettes that pair a memory of a particular event, place or emotion with a particular performer and song. Young describes his travel by ocean liner to Portugal during which he met and bonded with the African-Portuguese cook; the inner confusion he felt and the outward hostility he provoked by driving an old used Mercedes which cost him $600.00 and which he finally sold for a Datsun 510 wagon; and working at the docks for the U.S. Postal Service hauling sacks of mail to the trucks under a criminally insane supervisor. He recalls hearing Billie Holiday's rendition of "What a Little Moonlight Can Do" on a particularly beautiful evening in Australia and a life-changing ride that he hitched with a snowy-haired man who charged him with studying and thinking until he felt he could explain God to an eight year old. Young imagines a Robert Leroy Johnson Memorial Museum complete with tour guide, Luther Washington, in Greenwood, Mississippi, and he considers the music and influence of this famous blues man. Music connects him to the tragedy of his brother's suicide, the sadness of his wife's illness, and the death of his mother after a long life. Young's love and knowledge of music covers rock, pop, jazz, zydeco, gospel, and soul.

669. Young, Andrea (1955-). *Life Lessons My Mother Taught Me.* New York, New York: Jeremy P. Tarcher/Putman, 2000. 255 pages; photographs. ISBN: 1585420077.

Abstract: Although this work is primarily a biography of Young's mother, Jean Childs, Young writes about how her mother's words and behavior have influenced her own life. Young, who is an attorney and has worked as a policy analyst, activist, and writer, is, like her mother, an independent woman who balances career, family, and a busy husband. Besides influencing Young's roles as a mother and wife, Childs passed on a commitment to community service, and caring for others as well as a strong belief in the importance of education and the importance of knowing your history. Young's father is civil rights activist Andrew Young.

670. Young, Andrew (1932-). *An Easy Burden: The Civil Rights Movement and the Transformation of America*. New York, New York: HarperCollins, 1996. 550 pages; photographs; index. ISBN: 0060173629 : 0060928905.

Abstract: Andrew Young describes his family, his childhood, his education, and the ideas and organizations that led him to his work in the Civil Rights Movement. He writes about the movement and its successes, trials, and tragedies, his own contributions, and the contributions of those with whom he worked. Young was born in New Orleans to parents who were successful professionals. His father was a dentist, and his mother taught school. They viewed education as the highest possible attainment and hoped that Young would follow in his father's footsteps by becoming a dentist. Young started school at the third grade level and was nineteen when he graduated from Howard University. While working with the youth programs of the United Church of Christ, in Hartford, Connecticut, Young was introduced to nonviolent theory and the writings of Ghandi. He decided to enroll in Hartford Seminary despite the disappointment this would mean to his parents. He met his wife, Jean Childs, while filling in as pastor at a small church in Alabama. She was independent-minded and determined to maintain her own identity. She earned a master's degree while raising their three daughters. After graduation from seminary, Young's first full-time call was to Bethany Congregational Church in Georgia. While serving the church, the Youngs became active in the black voter registration drive, and Young's belief in nonviolent confrontation was put to the test when the activities of the black community attracted the attention of the Ku Klux Klan. From Georgia, Young and his family moved to New York City, where he worked for the National Council of Churches (NCC). He became involved with the Southern Christian Leadership Conference (SCLC) and Martin Luther King, Jr. when he left the NCC to administer a grant to develop literacy and leadership programs through the Citizenship School Programs. This work gave him the opportunity to work with such courageous women as Fannie Lou Hamer, Septima Clark, Dorothy Cotton, and Bernice Robinson. Young's history of the Civil Rights Movement provides an account of the many contributions made by women and their successful refusal to be sheltered by their male counterparts from the many risks of their involvement. Young takes the reader through the events in Birmingham, Alabama, the march to Selma, the less successful movements in Albany and Savannah, Georgia, and the growing disarray within the SCLC during the Poor Peoples' Campaign. He writes about the FBI surveillance of and attempt to discredit Martin Luther King, Jr., describes events leading up to King's acceptance of the Nobel Peace Prize in Oslo, Norway, his assassination, and the subsequent disintegration of the SCLC. Young describes the careful strategy and methods employed by Martin Luther King and discusses why these methods worked and why they can still be effective:

> The nonviolent approach is not emotional, although it is deeply spiritual. It is a rational process that seeks to transform, rather than defeat, the oppressor and the oppressive situation. Any kind of emotional outburst—violence, arrogance, intentional martyrdom—endangers the process of transformation. Emotionalism confirms the prejudices of those that nonviolence aims to transform. The oppressed must be transformed, too. They must learn to value and respect themselves, to understand the ways they support an oppressive system, and they must learn to forgive those who have hurt them.
>
> (p. 252)

Young was elected to Congress in 1972, he served as the mayor of Atlanta, and he was ambassador to the United Nations during the Carter administration.

671. Young, Penny (1952-). *Survival: The Will and the Way.* New York, New York: Vantage Press, 1999. 173 pages; photographs. ISBN: 0533127599.

Abstract: Penny Young was the twelfth child in a family that operated a large farm in the small town of Perote, Alabama. Although a number of the older children had left home for college and families of their own, Young and her remaining siblings did their share of work in the fields. They also worked in other people's fields and, during breaks in the agricultural season, they found other odd jobs. Young describes her siblings as stubborn and strong willed. Most of the children put themselves through college, even though the local schools for African-American children only went through the ninth grade, and the children usually left home having to borrow the $1.35 they needed to take the bus to Montgomery. Despite their close family and community, neither the children nor the parents were untouched by issues of race and discrimination; the many rules that separated the races were quite clear. Most troubling to the children was that white children had

schoolbooks and took the bus to school. Black children walked
and had to leave their books at school. Eventually, Young's father
was so fed up with the situation that he demanded and succeeded
in arranging busing for the black children. Never one to take
things quietly, her father also joined the local chapter of the
NAACP. This act angered his white landlord, who then gave the
family one week to pay up their debt on the farm or to get off the
property. Young's sister Ruth, who was working in another state,
was able to provide the money necessary to pay off the stunned
landlord. Ruth eventually went on to college at Alabama State,
where she became active in the Civil Rights Movement and was a
founding member of the Student Nonviolent Coordinating
Committee. After graduation, she was blacklisted from teaching
in Alabama because of her activism, and she moved to San
Francisco to pursue her teaching career. Her family followed her
to California, but Young never got over leaving Alabama. She
writes,

> We had good times and bad times. . . . We did
> not have all that much from the start. But we
> had some. Mainly we had each other. And like
> most black folks where we lived, we built the rest
> from determination and hard work. Staying
> alive was a mighty big job. But we were up to it.
> (p. 173)

672. Youssef, Sitamon Mubaraka and Adam Youssef. *Mail from Jail:
A Glimpse into a Mother's Nightmare*. Tallahassee, Florida:
Tillman Sims Communications, 2000. 86 pages. ISBN:
0967822408.

673. Zhu, Xiao Di. *Thirty Years in a Red House: A Memoir of Childhood
and Youth in Communist China*. Foreword by Ross Terrill.
Amherst, Massachusetts: University of Massachusetts Press,
1998. 255 pages; photographs; index. ISBN: 1558491120 :
155849216x.

   Abstract: Xiao Di Zhu, a research associate in the United States,
   was born in China after the Communist takeover and lived there
   until 1987. In this book, he describes his childhood in the midst of
   constant turmoil that enveloped China beginning in the 1960s. He
   interweaves his personal story with that of the history of the entire
   country during this period. Zhu's parents had both been
   Communists since before the takeover, and his father had become
   an official in the party. He was eligible for the privileges accorded

government officials, but he usually turned them down because he did not feel that such privileges were in accordance with the spirit of Communism. As policy changed within the party, Zhu's father went from being a man with authority to an enemy of the people, and both he and Zhu's mother spent years in labor camps because of their early work. Even his elder sister was sent to the countryside. Zhu lived with his grandparents and his nanny, visiting his parents whenever he had a chance. As time went by, he realized that his position at school appeared to be determined by how favorably his parents were officially viewed at any particular time. As a method of self-defense, Zhu memorized the teachings of Mao and learned to use them when it was most convenient. He also became an expert in the type of behavior approved of by the party. In 1977, Zhu was in the first group of students since 1966 allowed to sit for entrance exams for a full four-year course of college study. He was admitted to the Department of Foreign Languages at Nanjing Teacher's University and earned his B.A., the first class to do so since the Communist takeover in 1949. By this time the country had such a dearth of people with college educations that all of the graduates were promptly hired. Zhu got a job teaching English at a college in Nanjing in 1982. Although the country had become more open, cronyism still existed, and Zhu lost an opportunity to study in Australia to a woman with better connections. Instead of going overseas, he was sent to teach at a college on the Siberian border. He then decided to apply to graduate schools in the United States on his own. He was accepted and received grants sufficient for him and his wife to live on. They left China in 1987.

674. Zia, Helen. *Asian American Dreams: The Emergence of an American People*. New York, New York: Farrar, Straus, and Giroux, 2000. 356 pages; photographs; index. ISBN: 0374147744 : 0374527369.

Abstract: Helen Zia intends her book to be primarily a history of the growing politicization of Asian Americans in the United States. Zia, a community activist, also provides brief snapshots depicting the defining moments in her life. The daughter of immigrants from Suzho and Shanghai in China, Zia was raised in a strongly Confucian household in which parents and teachers were given unquestioned authority. Daughters answered to their parents and were second in all things to their brothers. She received several scholarship offers, but her father refused to sign her college registration papers because he believed an unmarried daughter belonged at home with her parents. Zia took her first rebellious stand by insisting that she would go to college no matter what her father had to say. At Princeton, she became involved in the "Third World" student group, and learned to speak out as she joined in the antiwar movement. It was when confronted with the patriarchal nature of the student groups that Zia became interested in the women's movement. She also came out as a lesbian. Her family supported her as she made her sexual identity known, but she discovered that she was rejected by some of her fellow activists. Zia later joined a comfortable community in Detroit. She writes about movements and organizations and recounts episodes of community violence and racism excused by the justice system. She writes about legislative change and progress in labor, housing, and marriage laws. Zia stresses the importance of knowing your history. She says that claiming her Asian-American identity rescued her from a sense of self-hate that had been growing since early childhood:

> I eventually discovered a community intent on asserting its Asian-American identity and reclaiming its history and contributions to building American heritage that every American should know. This knowledge helped me to meld my Asian and American identities and to see that they were never really separate.
>
> (p. 313)

Index

www.ingramcontent.com/pod-product-compliance
Lightning Source LLC
Chambersburg PA
CBHW030532100426
42813CB00001B/233